SCRIBAL CORRECTION AND LITERARY CRAFT

This extensive study of scribal correction in English manuscripts explores what correcting reveals about attitudes to books, language and literature in late medieval England. Daniel Wakelin surveys a range of manuscripts and genres, but focuses especially on poems by Chaucer, Hoccleve and Lydgate, and on prose works such as chronicles, religious instruction and practical lore. His materials are the variants and corrections found in manuscripts, phenomena usually studied only by editors or palaeographers, but his method is the close reading and interpretation typical of literary criticism. From the corrections emerge often overlooked aspects of English literary thinking in the late Middle Ages: scribes, readers and authors seek, though often fail to achieve, invariant copying, orderly spelling, precise diction, regular verse and textual completeness. Correcting reveals their impressive attention to scribal and literary craft – its rigour, subtlety, formalism and imaginativeness – in an age with little other literary criticism in English.

DANIEL WAKELIN is Jeremy Griffiths Professor of Medieval English Palaeography in the Faculty of English Language and Literature, University of Oxford, and a fellow of St Hilda's College. He is the author of *Humanism, Reading and English Literature 1430–1530* (2007) and co-editor with Alexandra Gillespie of *The Production of Books in England 1350–1500* (Cambridge, 2011).

CAMBRIDGE STUDIES IN MEDIEVAL LITERATURE

This series of critical books seeks to cover the whole area of literature written in the major medieval languages – the main European vernaculars, and medieval Latin and Greek – during the period *c.* 1100–1500. Its chief aim is to publish and stimulate fresh scholarship and criticism on medieval literature, special emphasis being placed on understanding major works of poetry, prose and drama in relation to the contemporary culture and learning which fostered them.

RECENT TITLES IN THE SERIES

Lisa H. Cooper *Artisans and Narrative Craft in Late-Medieval England*
Alison Cornish *Vernacular Translation in Dante's Italy: Illiterate Literature*
Jane Gilbert *Living Death in Medieval French and English Literature*
Jessica Rosenfeld *Ethics and Enjoyment in Late Medieval Poetry: Love After Aristotle*
Michael Van Dussen *From England to Bohemia: Heresy and Communication in the Later Middle Ages*
Martin Eisner *Boccaccio and the Invention of Italian Literary Culture: Dante, Petrarch, Cavalcanti, and the Authority of the Vernacular*
Emily V. Thornbury *Becoming a Poet in Anglo-Saxon England*
Lawrence Warner *The Myth of 'Piers Plowman'*
Lee Manion *Narrating the Crusades: Loss and Recovery in Medieval and Early Modern English Literature*
Daniel Wakelin *Scribal Correction and Literary Craft: English Manuscripts 1375–1510*

A complete list of titles in the series can be found at the end of the volume.

SCRIBAL CORRECTION AND LITERARY CRAFT

English Manuscripts 1375–1510

DANIEL WAKELIN

CAMBRIDGE
UNIVERSITY PRESS

University Printing House, Cambridge CB2 8BS, United Kingdom

One Liberty Plaza, 20th Floor, New York, NY 10006, USA

477 Williamstown Road, Port Melbourne, VIC 3207, Australia

4843/24, 2nd Floor, Ansari Road, Daryaganj, Delhi - 110002, India

79 Anson Road, #06-04/06, Singapore 079906

Cambridge University Press is part of the University of Cambridge.

It furthers the University's mission by disseminating knowledge in the pursuit of education, learning and research at the highest international levels of excellence.

www.cambridge.org
Information on this title: www.cambridge.org/9781107431683

First published 2014
First paperback edition 2017

A catalogue record for this publication is available from the British Library

Library of Congress Cataloging in Publication data
Wakelin, Daniel.
Scribal correction and literary craft : English manuscripts 1375–1510 / Daniel Wakelin.
pages cm. – (Cambridge studies in medieval literature ; 91)
Includes bibliographical references and index.
ISBN 978-1-107-07622-8 (hardback)
1. English literature – Middle English, 1100–1500 – History and criticism.
2. Manuscripts, Medieval – England – History. 3. Transmission of texts.
4. Literature, Medieval – Criticism, Textual. 5. England – Intellectual life – 1066–1485.
I. Title.
Z106.5.G7W35 2014
091′.0942 – dc23 2014010611

ISBN 978-1-107-07622-8 Hardback
ISBN 978-1-107-43168-3 Paperback

Contents

Illustrations

Tables

Acknowledgements

I received some generous grants for travel to study manuscripts in various places. The most important were two scholarships from the Huntington Library, San Marino, at which I was a Francis Bacon Foundation Fellow in 2006 and a Mayer Fellow in 2009. I was also able to visit libraries in the eastern USA when I was kindly invited to be the Charles A. Owen Jr Visiting Professor of Medieval Studies at the University of Connecticut in September 2009, and in Illinois thanks to the Newberry Library, Chicago, and to the Faculty of English in the University of Oxford. Grants from the Master and Fellows of Christ's College in Cambridge and from the University of Cambridge's Research Travel Fund allowed me to commute over several months to the British Library and to visit the Huntington Library once more. Toshiyuki Takamiya generously invited me to see his manuscripts in Tokyo, and he and his Round Table welcomed me there very warmly. The research was also expedited when I was granted a term of sabbatical as an Early Career Fellow at CRASSH, and when the Isaac Newton Trust in Cambridge and the Faculty of English in Oxford paid for Sara Harris and Daniel Sawyer each to spend a week gathering and checking some transcriptions and bibliography for Chapter 3. Lately, I have benefited a great deal from the opportunities provided by my new post in Oxford, which has been generously created by John and Jeanne Griffiths. I am extremely grateful to all these people and institutions.

I am grateful, too, to the librarians who have facilitated this research, at Corpus Christi College, St John's College, Trinity College and the University Library, Cambridge; the University of Illinois, Urbana–Champaign; the Newberry Library and the University Library, Chicago; the University Library, Durham (especially A.I. Doyle); the University Library, Glasgow; the Cathedral Library, Lincoln; the British Library, London; the John Rylands Library, Manchester; Columbia University Library (especially Consuelo Dutschke) and the Pierpont Morgan Library, New York;

Corpus Christi College and the Bodleian Library, Oxford; the Rosenbach Museum and Library, Philadelphia; the University Library, Princeton; Longleat House, Wiltshire; and most of all the Huntington Library, San Marino.

People at conferences of the New Chaucer Society, the Early Book Society, the Early English Text Society, the Material Text Network and the Medieval Song Network and at seminars at the Universities of Cambridge, Connecticut, Glasgow, Harvard, Illinois, London, Oxford and UCLA all put me right on many useful points. Among many who offered advice, Richard Beadle, Orietta Da Rold, Catherine Nall, Derek Pearsall and Kathleen Tonry time and again not only tolerated my obsession with correcting but encouraged it. For Cambridge University Press, Anna Bond, Linda Bree, Damian Love and Alastair Minnis were encouraging and patient, and two anonymous readers offered some extremely constructive criticism.

Most importantly I must thank Joel Harvey who, when I long ago mentioned a manuscript with 'unusually many corrections', asked 'How do you know what's usual?' and 'So what?' This book began as an attempt to answer these two questions – especially the second, which people who are not palaeographers quite reasonably ask.

Note on transcriptions

In transcribing corrections from manuscripts, I use the following conventions:

cats ⌐and dogs¬	*and dogs* added level in a blank space or adjacent to the end of the line
cats dogs ⌐and¬	*and* added in the margin
cats ^and dogs	*and dogs* interlineated above the line, in this case with a *caret* mark of some sort
cats and [cats]dogs	*cats* crossed out, subpuncted or erased
cats and [cats]^dogs	*cats* crossed out, subpuncted or erased; *dogs* interlineated above the line
cats and [cats]{dogs}	*cats* erased; *dogs* written over the erasure (overwritten)
cats [–d] dogs	a word between *cats* and *dogs* crossed out, subpuncted or erased and impossible to read, but likely having three letters, two of them indeterminable, the last likely *d*
[->]{cats and dogs}	*cats and dogs* written over erasure; the erasure now illegible but of the same length as the writing above it
[->]{cats and dogs }	*cats and dogs* written over erasure; the erasure now illegible and slightly longer than the writing above it, with space left blank
cats <and> dogs	*and* difficult to read for whatever reason

The terms *cross out*, *subpunct*, *erase* and *interlineate* or *interline* are explained in Chapter 5.

I have used italics to mark all expansions of abbreviations, which is ugly but necessary here, as the argument often concerns points of spelling. I have not usually noted my policy for deciding which possible marks of abbreviation to treat as 'otiose' strokes, unless relevant to the argument. As most of the manuscripts date from the fifteenth century, I have tended to ignore flourishes and horizontal marks as otiose when they would add <e> to word-final <ch>, <gh>, <ght>, <m>, <n> and <th> (for instance, ignoring an otiose stroke on **ll** in 'will' in the epigraph to Chapter 1), but tended to expand them when they would add <e> to <r> or would add <i>, <n> or <u> to <on>, <iou> or <ion>. I have reproduced the punctuation in manuscripts as best I could in typescript. The *punctus elevatus* is reproduced thus: .' with a full-stop followed by an apostrophe. For clarity about what is a scribal *punctus*, my ellipses of quotations are in square brackets thus [. . .].

I place letters discussed for their spelling in angle brackets, such as <ght>, phonetic symbols in virgules, such as /xt/, and graphs discussed as visual phenomena in bold, such as **ȝ**.

I provide line numbers from manuscripts only when the feature discussed seems difficult to spot. Such line numbers follow the folio and a virgule / and, where relevant, 'a' or 'b' to specify which column: f. 1^{r}/a7 is the seventh line on the first column of the first page.

If modern editions have line numbers, I use them rather than page numbers. I place 'book' numbers in roman numerals before a point: *Fall*, 1.1421 is book 1, line 1421 of Lydgate's *The Fall of Princes*. If the line numbers restart on each page, as in some editions of prose, the page number is given followed by the line number after a point: *Brut*, 243.6 is line 6 on page 243 of the Middle English prose *Brut* as edited by Friedrich W.D. Brie.

Abbreviations

BL	London, British Library
BodL	Oxford, Bodleian Library
Brut	Friedrich W.D. Brie (ed.), *The Brut or The Chronicles of England*, EETS os 131, 136, 2 vols. (London: Kegan Paul, Trench, Trübner, 1906–8)
CCCC	Cambridge, Corpus Christi College Library
ChRev.	*Chaucer Review*
CUL	Cambridge, University Library
EETS	Early English Text Society os original series es extra series ss supplementary series
EMS	*English Manuscript Studies*
Fall	John Lydgate, *Fall of Princes*, ed. Henry Bergen, EETS es 121–4, 4 vols. (London: Oxford University Press, 1924–7), with book numbers and line numbers thus: VIII.426
Gamelyn	*Gamelyn*, in Donald B. Sands (ed.), *Middle English Verse Romances* (1966; University of Exeter Press, 1986), 154–81
GUL	Glasgow, University Library
HEHL	San Marino, CA, Henry E. Huntington Library
HLQ	*Huntington Library Quarterly*
Hoccleve, *MP*	Thomas Hoccleve, *Minor Poems*, ed. Frederick J. Furnivall, EETS es 61 (London: Kegan Paul, Trench, Trübner, 1892)

Hudson (ed.), '*Omnis plantacio*'	'The Egerton sermon', in Anne Hudson (ed.), *The Works of a Lollard Preacher*, EETS os 317 (London: Oxford University Press, 2001), 2–143, with line numbers
JEBS	*Journal of the Early Book Society*
JRL	Manchester, John Rylands Library
LALME	Angus McIntosh, M.L. Samuels and Michael Benskin, with the assistance of Margaret Laing and Keith Williamson, *A Linguistic Atlas of Late Mediaeval English*, 4 vols. (Aberdeen University Press, 1986)
LMES	Linne R. Mooney, Simon Horobin and Estelle Stubbs, *Late Medieval English Scribes*, www.medievalscribes.com, ISBN 978-0-9557876-6-9
Lydgate, *LOL*	John Lydgate, *Life of Our Lady*, ed. Joseph A. Lauritis, Ralph A. Klinefelter and Vernon F. Gallagher, Duquesne Studies: Philological Series 2 (Pittsburgh, PA: Duquesne University Press, 1961)
Lydgate, *MP-I*	John Lydgate, *Minor Poems*, ed. Henry Noble MacCracken, EETS es 107 (London: Oxford University Press, 1911)
Lydgate, *MP-II*	John Lydgate, *Minor Poems*, ed. Henry Noble MacCracken, EETS os 192 (London: Oxford University Press, 1934)
MÆ	*Medium Ævum*
MED	Hans Kurath and others (eds.), *The Middle English Dictionary* (Ann Arbor: University of Michigan Press, 1952–2001); http://ets.umdl.umich.edu/m/med
Mirror	Nicholas Love, *The Mirror of the Blessed Life of Jesus Christ*, ed. Michael G. Sargent (University of Exeter Press, 2005)
N&Q	*Notes and Queries*
NHC	Anne B. Thompson (ed.), *The Northern Homily Cycle* (Kalamazoo, MI: Medieval Institute Publications, 2008)
NM	*Neuphilologische Mitteilungen*
OED	*The Oxford English Dictionary*, ed. John A. Simpson and E.S.C. Weiner, 2nd edn, 20 vols. (Oxford: Clarendon Press, 1989); www.oed.com

OTC	Oxford, Trinity College
Piers A	William Langland, *Piers Plowman: The A Version: Will's Visions of Piers Plowman and Do-Well*, ed. George Kane, rev. edn (1960; London: Athlone, 1988), with passus-and-line numbers for the poem ('xx.1'), or followed by 'ed. Kane' and page numbers for the introduction
Piers B	William Langland, *Piers Plowman: The B Version: Will's Visions of Piers Plowman, Do-Well, Do-Better and Do-Best*, ed. George Kane and E. Talbot Donaldson, rev. edn (1975; London: Athlone, 1988), with references as for *Piers A*
Piers C	William Langland, *Piers Plowman: The C Version: Will's Visions of Piers Plowman, Do-Well, Do-Better, and Do-Best*, ed. George Russell and George Kane (London: Athlone, 1997), with references as for *Piers A*
PML	New York, NY, Pierpont Morgan Library
Polychronicon	Ranulph Higden, *Polychronicon*, trans. John Trevisa, ed. Churchill Babington and J. Rawson Lumby, RS 41, 9 vols. (London: HMSO, 1865–86), with book, chapter, and page numbers thus: III.33.57
Prick	Richard Morris (ed.), *The Pricke of Conscience (Stimulus conscientiae)* (Berlin: Asher, 1863)
PUL	Princeton, NJ, Princeton University Library
Regiment	Thomas Hoccleve, *The Regiment of Princes*, ed. Charles R. Blyth (Kalamazoo, MI: Medieval Institute Publications, 1999)
RS	Rolls Series
SAC	*Studies in the Age of Chaucer*
SB	*Studies in Bibliography*
Scale	Walter Hilton, *The Scale of Perfection*, ed. Evelyn Underhill (London: Watkins, 1923)
STC	A. W. Pollard and G. R. Redgrave, *A Short Title Catalogue of Books Printed in England, Scotland, and Ireland, and of English Books Printed Abroad, 1475–1640*, ed. W.A. Jackson, F.S. Ferguson and Katherine F. Pantzer, 2nd edn, 3 vols. (London: Bibliographical Society, 1976–91)

Tales	Geoffrey Chaucer, *The Canterbury Tales*, in *The Riverside Chaucer*, ed. Larry D. Benson (Oxford University Press, 1988), with fragment-numbers and line numbers
TCC	Cambridge, Trinity College Library
Troilus	Geoffrey Chaucer, *Troilus and Criseyde*, ed. B.A. Windeatt (London: Longman, 1984), with reference to book and line numbers (1.515), or followed by 'ed. Windeatt' and page numbers for the introduction
UL	University Library
Walton (trans.), *Boethius*	John Walton (trans.), *Boethius: De consolatione philosophiae*, ed. Mark Science, EETS os 170 (London: Oxford University Press, 1927)
Wycliffite Bible	Josiah Forshall and Frederic Madden (eds.), *The Holy Bible, Containing the Old and New Testaments, with the Apocryphal Books, in the Earliest English Versions Made from the Latin Vulgate by John Wycliffe and His Followers*, 4 vols. (Oxford University Press, 1850), with book, chapter and verse thus: Galatians 5.16
YLS	*Yearbook of Langland Studies*
Yorkshire Writers	C. Horstmann (ed.), *Yorkshire Writers: Richard Rolle of Hampole, an English Father of the Church, and His Followers*, 2 vols. (London: Sonnenschein, 1895–6)

Some chapters cite certain MSS frequently by the following sigla, repeated here for ready reference:

Ar	BL, MS Arundel 38
Bm	BL, MS Add. 10574
Bo	BodL, MS Bodley 814
Cot	BL, MS Cotton Caligula A.xi
D	BodL, MS Douce 372
Ds	Tokyo, Takamiya collection, MS 24, *olim* 'The Devonshire Chaucer'
Du	Durham, UL, MS Cosin V.iii.9
Ee	CUL, MS Ee.1.12
En^1	BL, MS Egerton 2726

Gl	GUL, MS Hunter 197 (U.1.1)
Gw	GUL, MS Hunter 83 (T.3.21)
H2	BL, MS Harley 4775
Ha^4	BL, MS Harley 4866
HM 58	HEHL, MS HM 58
HM 111	HEHL, MS HM 111
HM 744	HEHL, MS HM 744 (Part II)
Hy	BL, MS Harley 3730
Mc	Chicago, UL, MS 564
Mm	CUL, MS Mm.2.5
Pet	Cambridge, Peterhouse, MS 190
Ra^1	BodL, MS Rawl. poet. 141
Ry^3	BL, MS Royal 17.D.xviii
SR 9	BL, MS Harley 2281
SR 18	HEHL, MS HM 130

CHAPTER I

Introduction

Ther will I first ^ be gynne .   ⌐^ amende *and*¬

London, British Library, MS Harley 1758, f. 32v
Geoffrey Chaucer, *The Canterbury Tales*, I.3074

A late fourteenth-century scribe of a priest's Manual seems proud of his craft, for at the end he records his name 'Hankok' in red, and he seems proud of correcting that book, for he writes in red adjacent to that 'co*rrigitur*', a common mark of noting that a book *is corrected.* The book has been checked well: for example, Hankok makes twenty-one corrections, most by erasing and writing on top, in the marriage service alone.[1] Two of those corrections, to English vows of marriage, suggest what the people who correct are worried about:

> Ich .N. take þe N. to my wedded wyf .^ for bettere for wors . for richere for porere in synesse *and* in hethe til det vs departe ȝif holychirch it wole ordeyne *and* þe*r*to y plyth þe my truthe .
>
> Ich .N. take þe .N. to my wedded hosebound ^ for bettere for wors for richere for porere in syknesse *and* in helthe to be boneyre and bouxsum in bedde *and* at borde til deth us departe ȝif holycherch it wole ordeyne and þerto y plyȝt þe my treuth*e*.

Hankok adds here two *caret* marks, marks like upward arrows signalling that something *is lacking*, and he then writes at the foot of the page in paler, greyer ink something to be inserted at each *caret*:

> ^ to hauin *and* to holden from þis day forthward[2]

How needful is correcting here, or elsewhere? Accurate transmission is not needed for the informational content of these vows. One might quibble

[1] HEHL, MS HM 30986, ff. 12r–19v, with 21 corrections, of which 2 differ from the text printed by Jefferies Collins (ed.), *Manuale*, 45–56. See Chapter 5, pp. 123–5 below, on 'co*rrigitur*'.

[2] HEHL, MS HM 30986, f. 12v; Jefferies Collins (ed.), *Manuale*, 47–8. This scribe dots **þ** and y inconsistently; the transcription instead follows grammatical sense.

that the words restored, *to have and to hold from this day forward*, add nothing to the sense: *have* is implied by *take* and *this day* and *forward* are implied by the present moment of speaking and by the pledge *till death*. Anyway, an experienced priest might not need the vows written in full; a cue might suffice to jog the memory, as is found in some other liturgical books.[3] And fourteenth-century people recognized that there could be some error in the words of the sacraments, given the poor Latin of many priests, and that such error would not matter: as John Mirk put it, one need not worry about the exact 'wordes' as long as just one 'sylabul' is right; when the 'entent' is clear, the sacrament will be 'gode'.[4] So if the spirit is what matters, why correct the letter? The reverence due to holy books might explain this correction: with Latin, music, handwriting in textura and red ink nearby, this is language in its best attire for the happy occasion. These vows also need correcting as part of the Church's discipline of the laity: they will speak with 'the priest teaching' ('docente sacerdote') and the priest will follow a book which is well ordered too. And they need correcting given the customariness, legal force and ecclesiastical sanction of these vows.[5] Correcting seems designed less to preserve the content than the conventional form of words and to pay respect to them.

An interest in verbal form emerges in another correction which might at first seem to preserve the content. In an extract from a poem listing Macer's herbal cures, a late fifteenth-century scribe muddles what is needed to cure deafness. As an ingredient that would mix well with the juice of leeks and would improve his hearing, he lists goats' milk. He is wrong: it is goats' gall. So he crosses out 'mylk' and adds 'galle':

> Iuce of lek*ys* w*ith* got*ys* [mylk] galle
> For euyl heryng help it shall
> Too p*artys* of þe Iuce þe third of gall
> m[a]^{e}llyd smal *and* warme w*ith* all
> In noise or eyn wheþ*er* it be do
> for g*ra*te hede wark wel it slo[6]

[3] E.g., Exeter, Cathedral Library, MS 3513, f. 94^{v} (fifteenth-century Pontifical); however, a late fifteenth-century user then wrote the rest of the vows in full in the margin.

[4] Discussed by Breen, *Imagining an English Reading Public*, 37–8.

[5] The text for speaking, rather than the rubrics, in HEHL, MS HM 30986, ff. 12^{r}–19^{v}, is identical to that printed by Jefferies Collins (ed.), *Manuale*, 45–56, except in 14 closed-class words or word-order. The only two bigger divergences are written over erasure in HEHL, MS HM 30986, ff. 13^{r} (Collins, 48), 19^{r} (Collins, 56).

[6] HEHL, MS HU 1051, f. 85^{r}; Robbins (ed.), *Secular Lyrics*, no. 80, lines 1–6. I treat word-final flourishes as otiose strokes, whereas Robbins expands them.

With the error 'mylk', the scribe might have been assuming that the text would be simple and familiar: milk is more commonly drunk and easier to get from a goat than gall is. The goats' milk might also be eyeskip to a reference to 'womans mylke' which appears six lines earlier in the full poem from which this extract comes, so it might betray that this scribe is excerpting for himself from a fuller exemplar.[7] Whatever thoughtlessness caused the error, though, there is attention to correcting: he too writes 'co*rrigitur*' at the foot of over half his pages and in only twelve lines of this excerpt makes four corrections. Some reflect the general practices of scribes as they seek to write clearly: for example, he mends an ambiguous spelling of *ought* meaning *anything* ('or þ*o*u tak [out]^{ought} þ*er*of').[8] But in turning *milk* to *gall* he attends not only to his own craft of writing; he is attending also to the poem's craft, to its verse-form. *Milk* does not rhyme with *shall*. Of course, turning *milk* to *gall* might seem like a correction to the essential ingredients of the cure. But (to be honest) the cure would be equally useless either way, and the scribe is not rethinking, like a doctor, how to improve a patient's hearing; what he is trying to improve is the rhyme – the verbal form of the text – for that verbal artefact is the focus of the scribe's attention in correcting.

The argument of this book: making and thinking

These moments exemplify the correcting which this book traces in manuscripts in English from the late fourteenth century to the early sixteenth. The scribes of English are craftsmen of words and it is to words that, when correcting, they attend. They seek to reproduce wording exactly, to spell conventionally, communicate unambiguously, be precise in every syllable. Moreover, in the craftsmanship of correcting, these scribes think. The corrections made by scribes, their colleagues and their readers – most being by the scribes – suggest the intelligence developed and exercised in stopping to reflect on one's own errors, and exercised even in the process of copying accurately in the first place. This intelligence is manifested in a generalized quality of attention or concentration that, extended over long works, is no mean feat. These scribes of course often err, nor do they always catch those errors; but they do recognize that copying is prone to error and think about correcting it. They are invested in the processes of correcting entailed in their craft and its procedures of writing (as is traced especially in

[7] Cf. BL, MS Sloane 140, ff. 52^{r}–53^{r}, the only other extant copy, which lacks two lines from an eyeskip on 'gall' (f. 52^{v}) so cannot be the exemplar for HEHL, MS HU 1051.

[8] HEHL, MS HU 1051, f. 88^{r}.

Chapters 5 to 7). Then, their meticulous craftsmanship manifests itself, from time to time, in specific sorts of thinking with considerable intelligence (traced in Chapters 8 to 10). The scribes seem to think that one word is preferable to another, because it is a more accurate transcription – a thought we do not always credit them with; they ponder language and the problems of rendering its sounds; they show respect for the words chosen by writers and their power; they reflect on verse-form and its workings; they imagine the complete form of a work when they have not seen it; and finally, when the scribes are also the composers or deliberate revisers of works, they pursue the creative activity we call authorship by means of correcting. Correcting, then, although it reflects external pressures – cultural expectations; institutional habits of work – is not an automatic or unreflective thing to do; it witnesses processes of thinking consciously about language and texts. That is the argument of this book: that the scribes, and sometimes readers, of English in the late fourteenth and fifteenth centuries often exercised intelligence in correcting it; and that thereby they contribute to the long history of critical attention to English literature. The craft of correcting is analogous to things we call philology or literary criticism.

Where does this drive to close textual attention come from? Whether some interest in the text's words prompts the practical process of correcting or is prompted by it is difficult to say: there is some sort of feedback loop. On the one hand, it looks as though the practical craft makes possible the insights, like those of the critic, into language and form; on the other hand, literary language sometimes influences the scribe's craftsmanship. The craftsman's insights as a reader develop in the material process of writing, while his material process of writing reflects his ideas about literature. Moreover, it might be suggested that by bothering over every nuance of a vow or over rhyme in a medical book, a scribe might betray his inherited sense of the prestige of religious language or of poetry by correcting and being seen to correct the words. Or, indeed, he might conjure that prestige into being, for this is *only* vernacular religion and only doggerel, practical verse.

After all, that somebody should correct the words he copies is not to be taken for granted. Although speakers do 'repair' misunderstanding in conversation, as linguists call it, they do not always do so. Most of us speak sloppily, and careless vagueness can be appropriate when precision would be socially odd. Descriptive linguists observe the regular use of constructions which prescriptive grammars would say are wrong. Moreover, most people speak a variety of English linked to their country, region and class which has been dismissed as incorrect by dictionaries and grammars but which works just fine; correcting such speech constitutes snobbery, 'talking proper' or hypercorrection. So even modern standardized English only deserves correction when certain conditions apply. Writing might be one such condition: people who speak some non-standard variety switch to standard English – in effect correcting their dialect – when they write; mispronunciations are not committed in English's fixed spelling; and we are trained by school to write in sentences, whereas we do not always speak in them. Yet we do not always correct our writing either. It is common to write e-mails without capitals or with typos and to find errors of grammar or puntcuation in internet journalism or printed ephemera. Contemporary novelists worry about the decline of proofreading: Jonathan Franzen, author of a novel called *The Corrections*, withdrew another novel because there were uncorrected typographical errors.[9] But mostly we put up with these slips in print and online without confusion. (Were you confused by the misspelling of *punctuation*?) Printed and digital media are not always, nor always need to be, corrected.[10]

That makes it all the more striking that correcting has long been part of the making of books. The methods and inspirations for correcting printed books are well known. Proofreading and press-correcting became more professionalized over the sixteenth and seventeenth centuries. There were many distinctive procedures for correcting print, such as the provision of errata sheets or humanist textual criticism; annotations of early printed books often include corrections, such as those which schoolboys entered into their textbooks before studying them. Of course, early printed books were still riddled with errors, and attempts to remove them often failed or even compounded the mess. Nonetheless, the early makers and users of printed books sometimes seem to have dreamed that they could make them creditable, accurate and stable.[11] Though early printed books were incorrect, people sought to correct them.

What happens in manuscripts, before and just as printing is introduced in England? This book argues that correcting is ubiquitous in manuscripts in English from the late fourteenth century to the very early sixteenth. The frequent correcting in manuscripts is worth noting because it has been less studied than correcting in print. This is despite the fact that correcting

[9] Davis and Flood, 'Jonathan Franzen's Book'.

[10] Though Horobin, *Does Spelling Matter?*, 4–5, reports evidence of intolerance for error online.

[11] For these processes and their problems, see Grafton, *Culture of Correction*, 23, 212–13; Simpson, *Proof-Reading*; Blair, 'Errata Lists', 36; [Alcorn Baron, Lindquist and Shevlin], 'A Conversation with Elizabeth L. Eisenstein', 414–16; Chartier, *Inscription and Erasure*, 29–33, 37–40; McKitterick, *Print, Manuscript and the Search for Order*, 97–144; Lerer, *Error and the Academic Self*, 17–29.

might be more visible – to us and to the earliest readers – in manuscripts than in print: in printed books many corrections are invisible, unless a rare proof-sheet survives; by contrast, most corrections made in manuscripts can be seen by the naked eye. Nonetheless, most handbooks of palaeography mention it only briefly, and most editors say little about corrections in the manuscripts they study.[12] Two of the greatest palaeographers remark that we tend not to believe 'that medievals had either the desire or the capacity to engage in such wholesale, disciplined pursuit of textual accuracy'.[13] But the presence of correcting has been recognized in manuscripts of English before.[14] Several shorter studies have identified how individual scribes and readers tried their best to correct the errors they made or met. They included Wycliffite scribes, who had a devout deference to certain texts, and members of holy orders copying religious poetry; they included authors such as John Capgrave or people working close to authors such as John Trevisa; London clerks copying books for money, or other professional scribes; and even provincial laymen copying books as amateurs for their own delight.[15] This book places those individual stories within a widespread habit of correcting English from the late fourteenth to the early sixteenth century.

That widespread habit complicates the argument that scribes did not consider English to have qualities which would merit correction or accurate transcription. That is often now assumed to be the case. The argument for it is most thoroughly and powerfully made by Tim William Machan in his wide and deep study *Textual Criticism and Middle English Texts*. In this view, there were linguistic disincentives to correcting: the English language did not yet have standardized rules for spelling, grammar or metre, or even one dialect as its preferred standard; nor were there institutions, people or books which would disseminate standard versions of texts. Therefore, it 'lacked the grammatical and rhetorical regularity that was used to assess the quality and correctness of any piece of writing'; and nor, 'without a sense of linguistic correctness and incorrectness', could people 'evaluate' the style of a piece of writing. While people recognized in Latin 'the possibility of textual correctness or incorrectness', for they studied it from

12 Exceptions are Petti, *English Literary Hands*, 28–31; Clemens and Graham, *Introduction to Manuscript Studies*, 35–8, 76; Kerby-Fulton, Hilmo and Olson, *Opening Up Middle English Manuscripts*, xxv, 28, 32, 37, 93–4, 209, 214, 235–6, 329, 339.

13 Rouse and Rouse, 'Correction and Emendation', 334.

14 Pearsall, 'Editing Medieval Texts', 93–5.

15 E.g., Hudson (ed.), *English Wycliffite Sermons*, 138–51, 189–95; Lucas, *From Author to Audience*, 75–89; Briggs, 'MS Digby 233'; Hanna, 'Scribe of Huntington HM 114'; Da Rold, 'Significance of Scribal Corrections'; Kato, 'Corrected Mistakes'; Turville-Petre, 'Putting It Right'. Most thorough will be the forthcoming study of the 'Winchester' manuscript of Malory's works by Takako Kato, previewed in Kato, 'Corrected Mistakes in the Winchester Manuscript'.

books in schools, by contrast there were 'no medieval linguistic contexts that would have fostered similar expectations for Middle English'.[16] That is, there was little sense of correct grammar, spelling or style, nor any authoritative literary institutions, which could motivate correcting literary works in English for textual fixity or stylistic distinction.[17] Machan argues that it was only the Italian humanists and later textual critics who fetishized 'the *correct* form of the text' in a way quite unlike users' attitudes to 'the vernacular during the *medium aevum*' or Middle Ages.[18]

Machan's brilliant history offers the fullest explanation of the textual variation which is very common in English books of the fourteenth and fifteenth century. That variation must not be forgotten, yet I have two qualms about defining English manuscripts by it. The first is the risk of 'periodization', of seeing the textual attitudes of these years as somehow incorrigibly different from those of others. If we seek to discover 'the textual and cultural factors that characterize Middle English works as Middle English', as Machan searchingly does, there is a risk that we isolate and reify a period as being distinct in some way. Machan worries that if nothing were characteristic of this period, then a 'label like *Middle English*' would be 'problematic'.[19] But this label is as problematic as *medieval* is; both were developed with hindsight and historical condescension; it seems dangerous to presume that a culture and its attitudes to texts are completely unified in themselves, and that they are completely distinct from those of other ages. We might instead wonder whether the late fourteenth and fifteenth centuries in particular, when the making of books in English altered in scale, kind and motive, might have different textual practices from earlier centuries of 'Middle English', or whether the scribes of these years might share attitudes with people of later centuries. Then, my second qualm is that alongside all the variance – *alongside* it and not *instead of* it – there is indeed some 'recognition and expectation of the possibility of textual correctness or incorrectness' in English in the late fourteenth and fifteenth centuries. There are frequent corrections in English manuscripts, and behind those processes it is possible to infer some interest in correctness. This interest did not eclipse or eliminate variance – by no means – but it did complement it. That makes correcting not more important than variance necessarily

[16] Machan, *Textual Criticism*, 153, 149. I argue with it here because it is extensive and thoughtful enough to merit argument – to merit correction.

[17] *Ibid.*, 145.

[18] *Ibid.*, 14, 39. Machan (42–4) rightly links humanist textual scholarship and Caxton's editions. My own article 'Scholarly Scribes', 42, suggests that humanism might have influenced some fifteenth-century manuscripts with many corrections and overlooks longstanding traditions of correcting.

[19] Machan, *Textual Criticism*, 3–4.

and not even more common (for this book has not measured variance enough to argue that point quantitatively) but makes it intriguing: if the scribes could choose to write 'incorrectly' or to tolerate changes during textual transmission, just as people in speech and e-mail do, why did they sometimes choose to correct?

Their corrections seem to reflect their attitudes to two things: to their own craft as copyists and to 'textuality' and literature. The first half of this book suggests that scribes strove to do a good job. As well as meeting the patrons' demands or cultural expectations, craftsmanship has its own internal logic and autotelic reward of doing something well. (The terms *craft* and *craftsmanship* are used in this sense throughout this book to refer simply to the process of copying; they make no claim that this activity is pursued as employment in a craft guild after an apprenticeship, though sometimes it might be.) Yet the second half of this book suggests that care for the craft of copying exists in synergy with the scribes' attitudes to the works they copy. Correcting manuscripts nurtures intelligent responses to literary works and, in a knot that cannot be untied, is also nurtured by these responses. Thereby, the craft of correcting becomes a little like literary criticism. That is of course a loose analogy: the scribes and earliest readers did not follow our definitions of literature nor conceive of our practice of criticism. Yet correcting requires the scribes to attend closely to what they copy, as though every word matters, and to think about style, form and structure. They do not explain their close reading or general thinking in works of their own; we can, though, infer their attitudes from their corrections. The study of manuscripts has before been recognized as offering evidence for these 'interpretative possibilities' open to early scribes and readers.[20] In particular, Barry Windeatt recognized the scribes of *Troilus and Criseyde* as Chaucer's 'early critics', who revealed their responses to poetry in the things they varied and got wrong.[21] This book suggests, in complementary fashion, that the things they put right might also involve critical insight. Indeed, the consciousness needed for correcting, as opposed to unwittingly erring, perhaps makes the craft of correcting even more akin to literary criticism. For this reason the corrections are important not only for palaeography but for the history of English literature.

Yet identifying critical thinking does not require us to assume what the category of *literature* is for these scribes. The word had a quite different meaning for them.[22] The scribes exercise their skilled writing and reading

[20] Meyer-Lee, 'Manuscript Studies', 13–14; Brantley, 'Prehistory of the Book', 637.

[21] Windeatt, 'Scribes as Chaucer's Early Critics'.

[22] Revealed by *MED*, *lettrure* (*n.*), and *litterature* (*n.*); *OED*, *literature* (*n.*).

on works of quite varied quality or prestige, beyond the obviously literary. As Ralph Hanna has explained, studying manuscripts often upsets our sense of a literary canon or of a distinct sphere of literary interest in the fourteenth and fifteenth centuries.[23] Studying correcting debunks any reverence for literature not by finding it nowhere but by uncovering it everywhere (so to speak), as the scribes attentively and intelligently correct things from *The Canterbury Tales* to practical texts such as the versified list of cures, in ways which make no distinction between 'literary' and 'ordinary' language but treat all sorts of writing as extraordinary. As Robert Meyer-Lee argues, an important element of the history of literature is the history of the 'articulation' of the 'possibility of literature': points where people strive to define what would be valuable, what would be worth attention, what would be literary among the writing they see.[24] The history of the book can show us how cultures come to treat some sorts of writing differently as 'literature'.[25] Some such points are the corrections: people's attention to certain works or elements of works reflects their sense of the possibility that they were worth such attention – the 'possibility of literature'. Their craftsmanship forges not a fixed canon of good writing but a practice of responding to writing with care and skill as if it were good; and literature looks like something in the eye of these beholders, emerging from the practice of artisans and not only of authors.

Even somebody sceptical of literary distinction still needs to explain how literature first came to earn the attention and distinction which people give it.[26] What made the scribes pay attention to this writing? The corrections in the end reveal that some works invite the scribes' attention and correction, implicitly by their various properties and explicitly by what they say. While literature depends on the hard work of artisans and on material conditions – on shaping letter-forms, scraping parchment, finding exemplars – conversely the labour of artisans is shaped by literature's qualities of style, form and structure, and by the scribes' thinking about those qualities. In this conclusion, the book diverges slightly from some studies of the 'material text' which have urged us to consider the life of books as material things 'far beyond the literary or even the linguistic', as Leah Price has put it.[27] Instead, this book stresses the power of the text and of ideas

23 Hanna, *Pursuing History*, 8–9, 12–13. Meyer-Lee, 'Manuscript Studies', 2–3, is sceptical of this avoidance of literature.

24 Meyer-Lee, 'Emergence of the Literary', 323, 'Conception is a Blessing', 133–4.

25 Chartier, *On the Edge of the Cliff*, 22.

26 Noted by Greenblatt, 'What is the History of Literature?', 470.

27 E.g., Price, 'From *The History of a Book*', 120.

about it – 'the literary or even the linguistic' – to direct the physical work of scribes and their handling of materials.

Incidentally, the book might thereby avoid technological determinism, which could in theory be a problem in studies of material culture.[28] Palaeographers sometimes risk such determinism, when they make the production and use of books seem influenced by materials and physical processes – the arduousness of manual labour, the supply of red ink, the amount of space on pages – almost unthinkingly, or with thinking only of reductive economic sorts about supply, profit or efficiency. This book can avoid that reductiveness because of two distinct qualities in corrections. First, the corrections are produced not only by users of books but more often by their makers, and while many users of artefacts do not understand them – how many people who can word-process know how a laptop works? – far more makers of them *do*.[29] Scribes understand the books they correct especially well. Secondly, corrections are not, or not only, made from materials with physical properties which challenge human comprehension, such as metal for scraping-knives or galls for ink; they are 'made' from man-made words which scribes and readers can comprehend. In corrections, then, we see not only the importance of material things for shaping human thought but also the importance of literary thinking for shaping the material text.[30]

The methods of this book: counting and close reading

This argument, though, is the conclusion rather than the origin of this study (and is summarized here in rather abstract terms). This study began with the simple recording of material phenomena – scraped pages, ink splodges, extra leaves – and reconstructing how they were produced. It began with a wide survey of manuscripts, in order to see which techniques and which concerns were common in correcting. The models for this larger survey were the 'bibliometry' associated with studies of printed books and the 'quantitative codicology' of Continental Europe; but this survey was pursued with less scientific rigour and statistical nous than those traditions, and with scepticism about the value of numbers and with methodological eclecticism.

First, I surveyed a variety of manuscripts which are direct copies or cognate copies of other surviving manuscripts, in order to understand scribes' ordinary copying which would throw their correcting into relief.

[28] Boivin, *Material Cultures*, 148–53, 165–6, traces this danger.

[29] An example from *ibid.*, 160.

[30] For a similar feedback loop, see *ibid.*, 23, 47–50.

(This shorter survey is only discussed in Chapter 3 and so can be introduced there.) Second, more importantly, I surveyed a cross-section of copying in all the manuscripts in English in one collection, the Henry E. Huntington Library in San Marino, California. This library's holdings are large enough to be useful but small enough to be manageable; it has what have been catalogued as fifty-two once separate books which contained primarily English, as well as fragments of English in twenty-eight books largely in Latin or French.[31] There was already a state-of-the-art catalogue and a thorough handlist of the English prose, so that it was possible to study the corrections without starting from scratch deducing what the texts were, or what the collation, provenance and distribution of hands might be.[32] In the fifty-two books and twenty-eight snippets of English, the survey counted the corrections exhaustively, with one exception for a manuscript which had been corrected so heavily that covering it all would have skewed the figures for the whole sample.[33] As it happens, the Huntington Library's holdings are reasonably representative in contents, origins and qualities: they range from practical and domestic books, such as medical recipes or devotional prose, to works of literary ambition in diverse genres and modes: couplets, rime royal and alliterative verse; moralistic, pseudo-historical and comic poems; the prose of biblical paraphrase, mysticism and medicine. The main omission is of romance, which general impressions suggest might well have been very different.

All the manuscripts surveyed date from a period of about one hundred and fifty years from the second half of the fourteenth century to the turn of the sixteenth century. There are no earlier manuscripts in English in the Huntington Library, although a few texts are earlier in composition than the date of the copies here.[34] Nor did the survey include manuscripts by

[31] Some 6 of the 52 are now bound into 3 pairs, making 49 volumes; but where Dutschke, *Guide*, treats items as once separate parts, with roman numerals, so do I. I also consider HEHL, MS HM 744, as having two separate parts (for reasons which emerge in Chapter 7). They are listed in Table 5.1.

[32] Dutschke, *Guide*, supplemented for acquisitions since 1989 by Kidd, 'Supplement', and Hanna, *Index of Middle English Prose: Handlist I.*

[33] The copies in HEHL, MS HM 128 of *The Prick of Conscience* and Langland's *Piers Plowman*, contained more corrections in one quarter than did the whole of the next most heavily corrected MS; so, to avoid skewing the figures with this 'outlier', the survey took in the shorter works in this MS, *The Siege of Jerusalem* and *How the Goodwife Taught her Daughter* (ff. 205^{r}–219^{r}), with 47 corrections, and only the first 3 quires of each of *The Prick of Conscience* (ff. 1^{r}–16^{v}, 25^{r}–32^{v}, misbound late; *Prick*, 1–2266), with at least 304 corrections, and *Piers Plowman* (ff. 113^{r}–136^{v}; *Piers B*, Prol. 1–VI.35), with at least 436 corrections. The corrections in *Piers* have also been the subject of an excellent case-study by Turville-Petre, 'Putting it Right', and are visible in Calabrese, Duggan and Turville-Petre (eds.), *Piers Plowman Electronic Archive: 6.*

[34] There are four copies of *The Prick of Conscience* (HEHL, MSS HM 125, HM 128, HM 130, HM 139), most recently dated to the second quarter of the fourteenth century, and one of *The Northern Homily*

authors engaged in the Reformation, such as John Bale or Miles Hogarde, or later than them.[35] This makes the survey focused enough in chronology to allow comparisons but sets limits to its significance. The survey cannot prove that corrections were new, more frequent, or better quality in this period relative to any earlier period. It has been suggested that correcting 'blossomed in the fifteenth century as never before' among various religious groups with an interest in written works for devotion, including the Wycliffites;[36] but this survey does not cover the earlier books which would prove or disprove such comparisons across time. Indeed, there was some continuity from the techniques of correcting used in the monasteries and bureaucracies of previous centuries (as Chapters 2, 4 and 5 note), and some earlier authors such as Ælfric and Orrm were concerned with rectifying errors.[37] In earlier centuries, though, there were different sorts of text produced in different sorts of institution with different notions of what copying might entail. In the twelfth and thirteenth centuries the English language faced different challenges in its written form, which fostered corrective activity such as modifying orthography or morphology to establish new conventions for them.[38] For example, Orrm used correcting to establish his spelling conventions such as the doubling of consonants or to halt linguistic change such as the shift from 'wifmann' to 'wimmann'.[39] Fussiness over spelling continues in the late fourteenth and fifteenth centuries (as Chapter 7 observes), but there might be differences in motive. One hypothesis would be that Orrm corrects the vernacular because he and others are still trying to shape habits of writing and reading it; scribes of English by the fifteenth century are striving to participate in established conventions.[40] But the Huntington Library's sample does not allow such hypothetical histories of correcting over many centuries.

Likewise, this book does not pretend to offer a comprehensive history of correcting even within its century and a half. Obviously, the holdings

Cycle, which predates that (MS HM 129), on which dates see Hanna and Wood (eds.), *Richard Morris's 'Prick of Conscience'*, xxxvi–xxxvii. The earliest text is Robert of Gloucester's *Chronicle*, composed in the very late thirteenth or early fourteenth century, and present in HEHL, MS HM 126, dated palaeographically to the very late fourteenth century.

35 The latest datable book included is HEHL, MS HM 745, records of the funeral of Henry VII in 1509. The survey of HEHL, MS HM 140 ignored the additions made in the 1520s, on which see Boffey, *Manuscript and Print in London*, 17–19, 33–5, 41–3.

36 Rouse and Rouse, 'Correction and Emendation', 335.

37 Bryan, *Collaborative Meaning*, 8–15.

38 E.g., Liuzza, 'Scribal Habit', 155–64; Dobson (ed.), *English Text of the Ancrene Riwle*, xcix–cvii, cxxvi–cxl.

39 Holm, *Corrections and Additions*, 1–34, lists examples (here quoting 19). Some other 'correction' is meticulous rewriting of the style and content that is better considered as revision (34–55).

40 For subtler contrasts, which this simplifies, see Breen, *Imagining an English Reading Public*, 109–15, 223–7; and Cannon, *Grounds of English Literature*, 82–107.

of one modern library do not offer a truly 'random' sample but only an 'opportunistic' one, shaped by whatever biases a modern collector had.[41] Moreover, the survey was limited to books, rather than documents, and to English, rather than Latin and French. In the books I surveyed containing English, I ignored the corrections to separate works which were wholly in Latin, although I did include any macaronic Latin elements in works otherwise in English. I studied the corrections to short fragments of English in manuscripts primarily in Latin and French, but I did not count the corrections in the rest of those books. It would be essential to survey all three languages and documentary writing too if one sought to reconstruct a full history of correcting and of the institutions and working conditions which made it possible, from schooling in literacy to different sorts of bureaucracy. The purpose was not, though, to study correcting in general but correcting in English and its relationship to English literature; and the purpose was not an historical narrative about book production but an interpretation of what scribes do and think about their craft and about the texts they work on.

Why, then, bother to count and categorize large numbers of things? After all, there are limits to such a broad survey: it is not possible to study fifty-two books in the same depth as it would be to study one.[42] Quick judgements of various phenomena are needed, as often is an admission of defeat when things are 'unknown' (as Chapter 4 in particular records). But counting is useful, first, for practical reasons: the corrections are numerous, tiny and individually unique, so that it is difficult to spy patterns in them unless one takes them in aggregate. It is telling that a few prior studies of corrections in English have also tried counting them.[43] Second, a full survey of one library's holdings stops us from preselecting the juiciest examples and ignoring or assuming patterns in the past.[44] Of course, the categories used to sort the data do impose presumptions, but the indiscriminate process of counting might allow other things to emerge. Finally, as Franco Moretti puts it, counting lets us turn 'from the extraordinary to the everyday' and to explore the 'meaning in small changes and slow processes'.[45] Anglo-American palaeography tends to prefer the case-study; yet case-studies might lead to a focus on the quirky or exceptional – perhaps including the more outlandish examples of variance. By contrast, counting what is

41 Contrast the sample of Bozzolo and Ornato, *Pour une histoire du livre manuscrit*, 15.

42 Derolez, 'Codicology of Italian Renaissance Manuscripts', 223, 228.

43 E.g., Hamel, 'Scribal Self-Corrections'; Kato, 'Corrected Mistakes'.

44 Derolez, 'Codicology of Italian Renaissance Manuscripts', 223.

45 Moretti, *Graphs, Maps, Trees*, 3, and 'Style, Inc.', 143, 145. See also St Clair, *Reading Nation*, 1–3, 17.

common helps to reveal the unexceptional things in books – in this case, their run-of-the-mill corrections.

However, this book offers its counting sceptically, tentatively. First, the numbers are almost certainly wrong – and almost certainly too low. When a previous editor had enumerated a manuscript's corrections, I always found more, likely due to consulting the real books and not microfilms. And were you to recount the corrections in the manuscripts you would probably find more again. In the full Huntington sample, I counted most manuscripts' corrections completely just the once; when I recounted some manuscripts' fully as a check, I had always undercounted the first time by three or four corrections. I would expect a further count to find more and certainly to dispute some details, especially the identifications of the people correcting, which was the hardest thing to judge. The numbers, then, are to be taken not as definitive facts but, in the words of opinion polls, 'indicative' patterns. Palaeographers sometimes generalize from experience but cite in their footnotes only a few exemplary instances. Rather than assume that authority, this book uses counting to license its generalizations and to gloss its terms such as *sometimes*, *often* or *always*, so that the numbers are more like a rhetorical device than a claim to certainty.

Moreover, generalizations are not enough and this book is more qualitative than quantitative in its argument. To decide that one might be able to generalize and count things is not to assert that one must always or only do so. This would be just as impoverishing. Instead, Katie Trumpener has argued for the continued usefulness of more subjective and haphazard 'Browsing in addition to quantification', which, she proposes, 'will show us new ways to think'.[46] So, having identified patterns in a survey, I moved beyond it to study further and particular books. Some were connected to the books from the Huntington Library in some way; these helped to contextualize things seen in the survey. The majority were copies of works of English poetry popular in the fourteenth and fifteenth centuries. I turned to them because, having seen scribal acumen applied to all sorts of texts, I wondered how well scribes exercised their craftsmanship on works of evident poetic ambition, especially Chaucer's *The Canterbury Tales* and John Lydgate's *The Fall of Princes*. Finally, I looked at other interesting case-studies for things missed by these surveys. This stage of the research was extensive rather than exhaustive, and I did not include these further books in any tallies or percentages; the purpose was to interpret attitudes to English literature and not to quantify the history of book production.

[46] Trumpener, 'Critical Response I', 171.

Here the study also moves beyond counting to close reading, and though the argument often begins with comments on patterns, it often ends by interpreting single examples. Even its keenest advocate, Franco Moretti, has noted that counting eschews the fine-grained analysis of individual works which is the proper concern of literary critics. He intends his quantitative surveys, which he calls 'distant reading', to lead back to close reading. Identifying patterns on the surface of pages might make us look afresh at that surface and see things we previously missed.[47] In that spirit, this book combines palaeography and codicology with something more like literary criticism. It is just that this is the close reading not of an edition, nor even of a text as it appears in any one manuscript, but of processes – processes of writing. That is not criticism as it is usually pursued: Christopher Cannon has noted that studying a scattering of words across many texts rather than the words which make up one text might be 'antithetical . . . to the kind of textual attention we call "reading"'.[48] This is instead an exercise in the practical criticism of actions, and actions which are usually studied as part of book history.

Nonetheless, attention to the textual surface is at the heart of palaeography too: the art of reading old words closely. Such attention is a slight divergence from the best recent palaeographical study of English books, which has usually focused less on texts than on context, and notably on the external conditions of book production and ownership. Much exciting research has rightly sorted out, first, the settings of scribes' work: the organization of their labour, their identities, their speech communities, their networks. With the exception of their dialect, which has been brilliantly studied, the scribes' handling of texts has been less discussed. But as Arthur Bahr and Alexandra Gillespie have argued, there are opportunities for scholars to explore the forms and aesthetics of books in a literary critical vein, as well as their placement in an historical milieu: all kinds of 'codicological data . . . can be the occasion for literary interpretation – for close reading'.[49] Besides learning who scribes were, and where and when they worked, it is possible to study more closely their working practices and to infer some of their thinking about those practices and about the texts they copy. That is what this book does: not draw deductions about the external conditions – the training, milieux, dates or places – of correcting, but interpret the internal processes of reading and writing.

[47] Moretti, 'Critical Response II', 173–4, 'Style, Inc.', 152–3, 'Slaughterhouse of Literature', 287, 288, and *Graphs, Maps, Trees*, 92.

[48] Cannon, *Making of Chaucer's English*, 2.

[49] Bahr and Gillespie, 'Medieval English Manuscripts', 358 and also 348–9.

Is there a risk of overinterpreting or 'squeezing the last drop of implication from the merest hint'?[50] There is, yet as D.F. McKenzie notes – undoing a famous argument against the intentional fallacy – the details of any one book reveal the intentions and agency, the 'human presence', of the craftsmen who made it.[51] And the things being counted in this book are imbued with such agency: moments of individual thought, skill, even creativity. While not all the things scribes did need be understood as consciously 'meant', for some were surely habits, it is pusillanimous not to credit their agency even in what is habitual. As Matthew Fisher puts it, 'writing is always intended' and 'Whether that writing is composition or copying, medieval manuscripts did not come into being by accident.'[52] So we might well explore the human presence or intention in correcting. While others focus on the scribes' agency in changing what they transmit, a kind of composing, it is intriguing to focus too on their engagement in correcting their copies and in keeping things the same. The practicalities of correcting involve making a choice about one's copy, so in the moment of correcting scribes think consciously (this book argues) about the details of the text. It is not, therefore, inappropriate to interpret their intentions and speculate about what their thoughts were. It is also important to counterbalance counting – which might suggest that scribes were the unwitting carriers of wider cultural trends – with attention to individual people's efforts and their agency.

It might also not be anachronistic to offer a close reading of either the English literature or the scribal practices of this period, because that parallels the scribes' own activity: they too read details closely, when they corrected. They checked their errors successfully; respelled words needlessly; added tiny words such as *full* and *so*; adjusted the layout of verse on the page; filled in the gaps of single lines in long poems; revised the metre of carols. This could seem a pedantic blindness to the big picture. Yet it is this frequent, ubiquitous close reading which constitutes the big picture. The corrections reveal that the scribes care for things which individually seem trifling or even baffling but which, in the accumulated details, attest to their intelligent attention to English writing.

[50] Tanselle, *Bibliographical Analysis*, 25–6.

[51] McKenzie, *Bibliography*, 19, 26–7. This approach is well explained by McDonald and Suarez, 'Introduction', 6.

[52] Fisher, *Scribal Authorship*, 13.

PART I

Contexts

CHAPTER 2

Inviting correction

> owt of þe roote of jesse schulde the [roote] ^ȝerde of correccyon come
>
> Durham, University Library, MS Cosin V.iii.24, f. 48r
>
> *The Doctrine of the Hert*, 58.419–20

Where does the impulse to correct things come from? Political zeal, self-improvement books and exercise regimes suggest our will to correct things we see amiss in ourselves, and there is some impulse to correct errant bodies and souls in medicine, psychology and law. These corrective institutions have a long history, back to and beyond the fourteenth and fifteenth centuries. The most powerful institution in that culture, the Church, was built around correcting. The doctrines of penance, purgatory and redemption and the Church's pastoral care might all be considered forms of correction: the errant Christian could confess his sins and 'make amends' for them or he could be 'corrected' by his neighbours or could even correct his elders and betters in 'fraternal' correction. It was 'adede of charite for to vnder nymen men of þ*er* defautes'.[1]

In such a culture, it is no surprise to find that scribes and readers emended books too, and it is possible to wonder whether religious ideas shaped people's interest in textual correcting. In the Huntington Library's manuscripts, the scribes and their collaborators encountered discussions of making amends in William Langland's *Piers Plowman*, *The Prick of Conscience*, religious lyrics and instructive prose. With accidental but delightful self-reflexiveness, they often emend the texts of those discussions. Some of these scribes were professional religious, worrying about doctrine: for instance, in a copy of *The Prick of Conscience* likely from a religious house in the West Midlands, one scribe adds in the margin only two of the many lines he omits; these two are lines about the arcane theological point that in the afterlife God 'schal amende in no paartyes | þe defautes of lemys

[1] HEHL, MS HM 112, f. 13r (*Scale*, 36). Fraternal correction has been thoroughly traced by Craun, *Ethics and Power*, esp. 13–14, 24–6, 34.

of synful bodyes'; the doctrine about what God will put right in bodies needs getting right on the page.[2] Professional scribes, working for money rather than for salvation, could also worry over these things: for example, a probably Netherlandish scribe in a deluxe collection of devotional poems writes for his patron a prayer that Christ will 'My fautes with his mercy redre[---]{sse}' and he must complete that last word over erasure, redressing some slip of the pen.[3] Scribes and readers lived in a culture which dreamed of correction.

But these theological notions could only indirectly prompt the practical business of correcting books; more direct influences would be a parallel set of ideas and some powerful institutions which policed textual practice. While craftsmanship and the techniques of book production might have an in-built aspiration to do a good job (which the rest of this book traces), there were external encouragements too. Several of the milieux and communities where books were produced between the late fourteenth and early sixteenth centuries had procedures or beliefs which might foster correcting (as Chapter 4 traces). There were also specific encouragements to correct books in two literary traditions (which are traced in this chapter, to set the scene for what follows). The first tradition is written by members of the religious orders who, for a millennium, had directly encouraged scribes to correct books. These works were mostly not written in England and were written in some cases long before the late fourteenth century; but they suggest the textual attitudes which English scribes inherited from Christian culture. The second set of injunctions to correct might have been more familiar to the scribes of English, for English poets from the late fourteenth century on frequently ask people to correct their books. It would be easy to read these requests as empty conventions; but might there be some relationship between what poets say and the real and frequent correcting of their poems? The sort of correcting requested does not describe exactly what scribes do – indeed, the poems describe it less well than do earlier monastic instructions; but the poets do suggest some of the spirit behind correcting which makes it of interest for the history of responses to English literature.

Minutiae matter

The religion which scribes inherited depended on written texts of Scripture, liturgy, the Fathers, commentators and others, and its interest in correct

[2] HEHL, MS HM 128, f. 54^{v} (*Prick*, 5021–2).

[3] HEHL, MS HM 142, f. 15^{r} (Dyboski (ed.), *Songs and Carols*, no. 68, line 54). Of course, other lines on the same theme do not need correcting: e.g., 'Alle my defautes lord redresse' (HEHL, MS HM 142, f. 32^{r}; Maidstone, *Penitential Psalms*, 483).

texts licensed a concern for minute details in copying over centuries. Of course, the Christian quest for the spirit sometimes brought wariness about the letter of the text. St Augustine in *De doctrina Christiana* belittles the grammarians who correct barbarisms, solecisms and errors; they pursue a 'knowledge of signs' instead of a 'knowledge of things, by which we are edified' ('non rerum scientia qua aedificamur, sed signorum').[4] But as well as opposing secular learning, St Augustine puts another point starkly: 'the attention of those who wish to know the divine Scripture must first focus on the task of correcting the manuscripts' ('nam codicibus emendandis primitus debet invigilare sollertia eorum qui scripturas divinas nosse desiderant').[5] Such calls for attention to textual error are repeated across a millennium: since its first circulation, people had been aware that the Vulgate needed correcting, due to errors in the original translation and slips over centuries of copying. Various people, including intellectual powers such as Peter Abelard and Nicholas of Lyra, had warned of 'error on the part of the scribes' and warned that a 'lack of skill on the part of correctors' means that 'the meaning of the text (*sententia literae*) is inconstant'.[6] Studying the literal sense especially required getting right the letter of the text.

This led to the first striking element of Patristic, scholastic and monastic comments on correcting: the intense pernicketiness and smallness of the corrections prescribed and pursued. This attention to tiny and seemingly superficial details also foreshadows the correcting of English (as will emerge). Exhortations to correct holy books seldom seek to correct interpretation, theological error or pastoral errancy, although they do seek regularity in liturgical observance. Rather, the myopic focus is on the words on the page, as in philology, palaeography and textual criticism. St Augustine himself gives a few practical procedures for this.[7] But the stress on details really begins to thrive with Cassiodorus' *Institutiones* or instructions for monks. Even in the preface, slightly obsessively, he discusses the practicalities of his own collating, correcting and punctuating and he reports that he composed a book on orthography; later he returns to procedures for fixing spelling, punctuation and accuracy.[8] Of course, he does elsewhere judge matters of substance as right or wrong, such as the heresies of

4 St Augustine, *De doctrina Christiana*, II.xiii.19.46. His acceptance of the apparently incorrect constructions in Scripture might reflect secular training in grammar which granted licence to poets.

5 *Ibid.*, II.xiv.21.52.

6 Quoting Minnis and Scott, with Wallace (eds.), *Medieval Literary Theory and Criticism*, 89–90, 268–9. See in general de Hamel, *The Book: A History of the Bible*, 32, 36, 76–8, 122; and Smalley, *Study of the Bible*, 37, 43, 79–80, 221–2, 331–3, 335, 342–4.

7 St Augustine, *De doctrina Christiana*, II.xv.22.53–6.

8 Cassiodorus, *Institutiones*, praef. 8–9, XV.7–11, XXX.1–5 (*Institutions*, 106, 109–10, 142–4, 164).

Origen. But even when he does that, he uses the techniques of copying, correcting, punctuating and annotating: he has revised some glosses on Romans and left them in a papyrus book for others to emend; he has had a translation made of Clement of Alexandria's letters which cleanses them of erroneous ideas; he has fixed symbols in the margins of Tyconius' works on the unacceptable statements.[9] The surviving books from his monastery bear evidence of these systems in use.[10] Yet the censorious comments on content are scattered and short; Cassiodorus writes more concertedly about the need to correct the orthography and pointing and mistranscription, through good grammar and scribal craft.

Such care for verbal detail continued through centuries of textual criticism of the Bible from the Carolingians to the thirteenth-century Parisian efforts.[11] Comments on correcting the Bible reveal an impressive understanding of scribal transmission, its errors and their correction. For example, Nicolò Maniacutia comments palaeographically on slips which occur when scribes 'are deceived by the ambiguity or similarity of syllables or parts of words' ('sillaborum, vel partium similitudine, vel ambiguitate decepti'); his pedantic doublets in phrasing this capture the pedantry of uncovering such things.[12] One of his works consists of close readings of errors in the Psalms: he shows a knowledge of Hebrew words or inflexions; he notes grammatical slips in gender, case or number; he considers scribal slips such as missing syllables or faulty word-division.[13] Near the end he briefly generalizes some causes of error, but he generalizes not about big principles but about minutiae, constantly referring to the power of single letters or the difficulty of distinguishing and counting single syllables ('quandoque litteram quandoque sillabam', 'plures sillabas sine litterarum variatione diminuunt', 'trisillabum in bisillabum redigunt').[14] The care over syllables could serve the important duty of pronouncing the liturgy or reading aloud in monasteries at mealtimes.[15] It also typifies the closeness of the reading offered here and in other works. For instance, the *correctoria* or lists of errors in biblical manuscripts compiled by thirteenth-century Dominicans show some understanding of orthography and of problems in scribal copying, as they

9 *Ibid.*, I, VIII, IX (*Institutions*, 113–14, 127, 128, 131, 132).

10 Traced by Troncarelli, '*Litteras pulcherrimas*', e.g., 104.

11 Wonderfully reconstructed by Linde, *How to Correct*, esp. 39–48, 105–97.

12 Denifle, 'Handschriften', 274.

13 Printed by Peri, 'Correctores', e.g., respectively, 98.20, 100.17–21, 98.12–15, 99.31–3, 100.5–6, 102.16–18, 103.1–5. Linde, *How to Correct*, 118–22, discusses Maniacutia's Hebrew.

14 Peri, 'Correctores', 118.1–119.22.

15 Boyle, 'Friars and Reading in Public', 11, 13–14, reports that a 'corrector mensae' would sometimes guide and correct the pronunciation of the monks at the dinner table, and that treatises on reading taught the minutiae of this.

affect single letters and syllables.[16] There were centuries of attention to the textual surface of the Bible.

Such pernicketiness about textual minutiae is often considered an avoidance of larger theoretical thinking; yet this practical criticism does reflect some theory of what matters. Such close reading is not to be taken for granted. That is evident when people stress that they will not in fact pay such attention. For instance, among the Dominican authors of the *correctoria*, one of them, Gérard de Huy, acknowledges that he might choose whether minutiae matter, for he declares limits on how far he will go. He will not correct such details as names, as he has composed a separate treatise on them; the varying methods of co-ordination by *et*, the enclitic *–que* or asyndeton; the demonstrative pronouns which are often interchangeable; and alternation between *deus* and *dominus* ('God', 'Lord') which might interchangeably refer to the deity – the latter a surprising laxity about religious language.[17] This list imagines limits to correcting and thereby suggests that the detailed attention of correction could seem extreme even to the people doing it. Yet de Huy is only sketching these limits for practical reasons, as he seeks brevity and eschews prolixity ('brevitati', 'prolixitate').[18] And in fact he exceeds these limits in the corrections he does make. He does correct the optional uses of *et*, does correct the pronoun *eos* into *illos* and does even once correct 'time deum' into 'time dominum' ('fear God', 'fear the Lord').[19] He corrects spelling too: rather nicely, five times he corrects the spelling of the word *correctio* into *correpcio* – alternative terms for 'correction', used in Scripture in the moral sense, but here treated as an orthographical problem.[20] Given that de Huy and others profess not to care for such close correcting, it is more striking when they do pay such attention.

There is extended thought about the excess of such attention by the Carthusians, an order which encouraged moral and institutional obedience in the tiniest of details. Carthusian statutes give a few strikingly specific instructions about the spellings to be used, even down to <s> and <ss> or <c> and <t>.[21] Short works which circulated among the

16 E.g., de Huy's comments (Denifle, 'Handschriften', 304–5) on the aspirant letter **h**, single syllables omitted by eyeskip, word-division and the confusion of letters which look alike in handwriting of this period (**i**, **m**, **n** and **u**; **c** and **t**; **b** and **v**).

17 Denifle, 'Handschriften', 308. Dahan, 'La critique textuelle', 368, n. 16, 379, refers to this *correctorium* E as de Huy's work.

18 Denifle, 'Handschriften', 308.

19 *Ibid.*, e.g., 484, 495 twice, 484, 494, 485.

20 *Ibid.*, 484 twice, 518, 521–2, 522.

21 Hogg (ed.), *Evolution of the Carthusian Statutes*, vol. II, 274, 288, mentioned in Oswald de Corda, *Opus pacis*, *22, *54.

Carthusians give rules for further details, such as diphthongs or stress-marking.[22] The correct treatment of textual minutiae is essential, one such work warns, because 'dangerous' ('periculosi') errors of pronunciation destroy the power of speech to express meaning ('virtutem significandi').[23] Yet one widely circulated Carthusian work worries about fussy correcting. This is *Opus pacis*, written by the German Carthusian Oswald de Corda in 1417. Oswald begins with the concern that correcting has made many monks anxious, fretting not only about single words or syllables but even about single letters ('non dico propter orationis siue dictionis nec sillabe quidem, sed et propter unius littere mutacionem aut diminucionem').[24] Oswald urges them to avoid anxiety in close reading by developing a refreshing relativism about textual detail, recognizing and listing the variety of spelling and pronunciation within Latin between ancient times and the present, and from country to country.[25] The respect for national differences could reflect the particular timing of Oswald's work: the papal Schism had divided the Carthusians, and forbearance and toleration would foster harmony within the order as it recovered from that; Oswald further softens his criticism of different local practices in his second draft of *Opus pacis*.[26] But he tolerates diversity not only from place to place but within one manuscript: even when a word varies in spelling within the same text due to 'uncertain changes in the scribes' ('propter uicium scriptorum incertum'), nonetheless if it remains clear in its meaning ('significacione'), then 'it is better to tolerate something than to correct it' ('ibi pocius est tolerandum quam corrigendum').[27] He elsewhere repeats that variation might be tolerated rather than emended ('toleranda quam corrigenda') where meaning survives ('significacio').[28] However, the repeated verb *tolero* or *tolerate* implies that the variety and error are nonetheless unwelcome: we tolerate only what we dislike; consistency and accuracy are preferred. And although Oswald dismisses textual fussiness in his prologue, that prologue precedes his own lengthy work of extremely detailed instructions on orthography and pronunciation, far exceeding those of most other commentators.[29] In his autograph manuscript he and some later reader have picked out tiny details in the margin, making the work into a reference book of finicky details. By contrast, in this copy there are no annotations on the general exhortations to tolerance in the introduction.[30] Even when authors claim

[22] See the excerpt printed by Ouy, '*Valdebonum*', 203, lines 8–16. [23] *Ibid.*, 203 (lines 5–7).

[24] Oswald de Corda, *Opus pacis*, 3.1–12. [25] *Ibid.*, 4.49–52, 5.68–7.112, 26.647–29.740.

[26] Rouse and Rouse, 'Correction and Emendation', 343.

[27] Oswald de Corda, *Opus pacis*, 8.145–53. The Carthusian text *Regula* also tolerates some variety in Latin (printed *ibid.*, 81).

[28] *Ibid.*, 9.176, 12.264–6, 28.691–4. [29] Linde, *How to Correct*, 196.

[30] The autograph MS is now bound with an incunable as HEHL, shelfmark 86299.

not to worry about the letter of the text, then, there is a widespread interest in textual minutiae from the sixth to the fifteenth centuries.

Rules for correcting

Indeed, people describe correction not only as a remedial necessity but also as an activity meritorious in its own right; the process is as important as the outcome. This praise for the work of correcting extends praise for the divine work of copying books, which is evident in many texts, such as Richard de Bury's *Philobiblon* in the fourteenth century.[31] More extended praise of the process of writing comes from Jean Gerson at the start of the fifteenth century and Johann von Tritheim (Johannes Trithemius) at the end, who both wrote works *De laude scriptorum*, with von Tritheim's lifting material from Gerson's. Von Tritheim explains the power of books not only to instruct their readers but also to inflame the mind of the monk who copies them; they have a transformative, almost performative, force in the process of being written out.[32] Both men briefly address the business of correcting: Gerson compares the inspection of cloth, bread and knives in other 'mechanical arts' ('artibus mechanicis') and recommends the inspection of copies too; Gerson was much concerned with regularity and control in disseminating texts and ideas.[33] Von Tritheim devotes a complete, short chapter to correcting.[34] If writing is a religious duty, then so is correcting what one writes.

Such attitudes can be traced as early as Cassiodorus' (aforementioned) *Institutiones*, which some later writers cite.[35] Cassiodorus praises the work of scribes highly, but with the caveat 'if they write correctly' ('si tamen veraciter scribant').[36] Yet we can also trace in Cassiodorus' work some wariness about judging what is correct. In typical Christian fashion, the high praise becomes an injunction to lowliness, when Cassiodorus stresses the need for the person correcting to be submissive to consensual or communal standards:

31 Although Richard de Bury, *Philobiblon*, says relatively little about correcting and worries about false scribes who correct with zeal but end up mangling the text further ('falsis scriptoribus', 'pro zelo corrigere', 48–9, chap. IV). Fisher, *Scribal Authorship*, 25–6, discusses his ambivalence about correcting.

32 Trithemius, *De laude scriptorum*, 52, 60.

33 Gerson, *De laude scriptorum*, 428. Hobbins, *Authorship and Publicity*, 41–9, 166–7, traces Gerson's wishes to regulate texts in general and scribes in particular.

34 Trithemius, *De laude scriptorum*, 66.

35 E.g., Richard de Bury, *Philobiblon*, 148–9 (chap. XVI); and Oswald de Corda, *Opus pacis*, 20.520, which is one of many points picked out by a reader of the autograph manuscript (HEHL, shelfmark 86299, f. 10v).

36 Cassiodorus, *Institutiones*, XXX.1 (*Institutions*, 163).

> Vos igitur, qui divinarum et saecularium litterarum cognitione polletis, et scientia vobis est ab usu communi reperire quod dissonat, tali modo sacras percurrite lectiones [. . .]. quapropter prius introite diligenter, et sic scriptorum delicta corrigite, ne iuste arguamini si praecipitanter alios emendara temptetis; istud enim genus emendationis, ut arbitror, valde pulcherrimum est et doctissimorum hominum negotium gloriosum.
>
> You who have a good knowledge of divine and secular letters and the understanding to discover what is not in harmony with common usage, read through sacred literature in the following manner [. . .]. Therefore, first read carefully and correct the errors of the scribes in such a way that you do not deserve criticism for trying to correct others without due deliberation; this kind of correction is, in my opinion, the most beautiful and glorious task of learned men.[37]

There are clear ethical imperatives on the person correcting, to avoid doing so 'precipitanter' and to do so with 'nulla praesumptione'. There should be slow method, not speedy genius, and this pursuit of humility rather than genius is yoked to service of the community or common opinion: although Cassiodorus does warn against judging the difficult language of Scripture by the lowest common understanding ('intellectum communem'),[38] he also states that the standard against which a text will be measured will be 'common usage' ('usu communi') in order to avoid discord ('quod dissonat'). In his own advice on spelling he has hunted for 'as many of the earlier writers on orthography as I could find', relying on authorities beyond himself ('paravi quoque quantos potui priscos orthographos invenire'). He stresses repeatedly the dangers of treating books with 'presumption' or 'hastily' ('praesumptio', 'praecipitanter').[39] The ethos of the correcting which he encourages is consensual, even submissive.

This humility is the first of two important dimensions stressed by commentators on correcting from the sixth century to the fifteenth. Before Cassiodorus, St Augustine warned Christians not to presume to correct the Septuagint, for 'it would not be right or proper for any one person, however expert, to think of correcting a version agreed by so many experienced scholars' ('ne sic quidem quemquam unum hominem qualibet peritia ad emendandum tot seniorum doctorumque consensum aspirare oportet aut decet').[40] In Cassiodorus' own work this stress on consensus might reflect the ethos of the cenobitic or communal monasticism, which was developing in the fourth, fifth and sixth centuries, and in which Cassiodorus was a

[37] *Ibid.*, xv.1 (*Institutions*, 139). [38] *Ibid.*, xv.2 (*Institutions*, 139).

[39] *Ibid.*, praef. 8–9 (*Institutions*, 109–10). [40] St Augustine, *De doctrina Christiana*, II.xv.22.54.

pioneer. Later writers in religious orders often addressed textual correcting as a sort of subjection to communal discipline. In the twelfth century, Stephen Harding corrected his Bible amidst the zeal of early Cistercian monasticism in order to achieve the authentic observance of St Benedict's rule and St Ambrose's liturgical practice.[41] In the 1140s another Cistercian, Nicolò Maniacutia, offers his work on correcting the Psalms as an act of obedience within his order: he writes at the request of Abbot Domenico and will 'emend' the Psalter following 'our exemplar' – that of the Cistercians – in a revealing plural ('emendare', 'ad exemplar nostrum').[42] The people who make corrections in this vein often refuse to finalize their work, by writing alternatives in the margins rather than deciding firmly which textual version is right. This could be pusillanimity, as Christopher de Hamel proposes, or a delight in multiple readings, as Beryl Smalley suggests.[43] It could also be explained by contemporary comments on the consensus and humility needed in correcting. Maniacutia offers the fullest defence of these qualities. He allows conjecture as one method of correcting but prefers collation of the Hebrew sources.[44] Yet even in deferring to the Hebrew he 'would not presume to touch' the Latin if all the copies he has collected agree with each other anyway ('tangere non praesumerem').[45] His pledge to self-restraint uses the verb *praesumo* which recurs with negative connotations throughout his discussion of variation by scribes and meddling by correctors: the Bible is muddled 'by the carelessness of scribe or the presumption of whatever other people' ('vel scriptorum incuria vel quorumlibet aliorum praesumptione'); people 'presume' to remove things ('presumimus'), and some who try to fix errors show 'praesumptio', but Maniacutia will not follow his 'own judgement' ('proprium arbitrium'). He has not 'presumed' to correct too much ('presumpi'), noting 'what great presumptuousness it would be if we judged canonical books to need correcting now according to the conjecture of our own judgement' ('magne presumpcionis sit si ad nostri arbitrii coniecturam libros presertim canonicos estimaverimus corrigendos'). And that reliance on one's own judgement or *arbitrium* – evoking the risky quality of free will – is another flaw in correcting: men add to

41 Stercal, *Stephen Harding*, 24. Harding's account of the errors (52–3) sounds naively astonished that a text with one source could err.

42 Peri, 'Correctores', 88.12–18.

43 De Hamel, *The Book: A History of the Bible*, 122; Smalley, *Study of the Bible*, 220, 335; Munk Olsen, *La réception de la littérature classique*, 14–15. E.g., the corrections in Harding's Bible, discussed by Załuska, *L'Enluminure et le scriptorium de Cîteaux*, 73.

44 Peri, 'Correctores', 92.27–35, 96.32–97.4.

45 *Ibid.*, 106.29–13. But he adds that when the Latin copies diverge but some agree with the Hebrew, he will follow the Hebrew. Munk Olsen, *La réception de la littérature classique*, 19–20, discusses Maniacutia's humble rejection of conjecture.

the text following 'the whim of their judgement' ('arbitrii nostri libitum'); lines are inserted or removed by people who follow 'their own judgement' ('sui [. . .] arbitrii').[46] Maniacutia's work was not necessarily known in fourteenth- and fifteenth-century England, but his dislike of presumptuousness in correcting was shared later. For instance, Richard de Bury linked overzealous correctors of books to the 'presumption' ('praesumptio') of the builders of Babel.[47] The Carthusians too emphasized the need for submission to communal, often institutional, authority in correcting (as is noted in Chapter 4). In such accounts, the final correctness of the text is not the only thing that matters – or else initiative would be good, as in the heroic classical editing of Housman; rather the process of correcting is itself fraught with moral significance and must be pursued consensually and conservatively. There was always a tension between concern with grammatical truth and tradition or custom, but, as Cornelia Linde has shown, custom often won out and correction was reined in.[48] Although there was in Christian traditions an exhortation to correct textual minutiae, this was tempered by an admonition to correct with humility and in quest of consensus. This balance of close attention with self-restraint will throw light on the mixture of meticulousness with non-intervention which typifies correcting in English in the fourteenth and fifteenth centuries (traced in later chapters).

Describing scribes

This illumination from the monastic tradition is useful, because direct comments by and about the scribes of fourteenth- and fifteenth-century England are hard to find and, once found, hard to mine for explanations of their correcting. Scribes seldom comment on correcting books, and when they do they often under-report their own involvement in ways which harm their reputation. Perhaps that is a measure of their humility, for the scribes spend their time recording other men's words, not their own. Just as social history is written by elites, the history of the book is written more fully by the authors whom the book producers humbly serve. Nonetheless, a very few colophons by scribes do suggest some rationale for the efforts in correcting which the manuscripts reveal. These colophons need wary interpreting because they are deeply conventional – although that might make them a better index of the ordinary assumptions of

46 See variously Peri, 'Correctores', 88.12–13, 97.5–11, 121.5; Denifle, 'Handschriften', 271.

47 Richard de Bury, *Philobiblon*, 48 (chap. IV).

48 Linde, *How to Correct*, 246.

the age, as Lucien Reynhout suggests.[49] But scribes scattered over many centuries and countries do sometimes report that they have corrected the book, comments which imply the desirability of correcting if it merits mention in their colophons.[50] Such reports of correction done might seem like requests for payment. But many of them come from members of the religious orders who might be driven more by vocation than money, and as well as reporting correction, there is the confession of error and the request for amendment by others. It has been suggested that confessions of one's faults are more common among monastic scribes, which would chime with the humility praised by monastic writers.[51] Such Christian humility would also explain one conventional colophon, a prayer that the scribe be free from *crimen* (*sin* or *crime*): 'Explicit iste liber sit scriptor crimine liber' ('This book is finished; may the scribe be free from sin').[52]

Yet humility is not the tone of one frequent colophon which does request correction: the colophon 'qui legit emendat, scriptorem non reprehendat' ('the reader emends, and let him not blame the scribe'). This colophon recurs fairly frequently; a number of examples can be found in books from England in the fifteenth century.[53] It is not of course a comment on the scribe's own correcting; it assumes that the scribe will need correcting by others. But it does suggest that scribes could envisage the sort of close reading which correction demands. And the fact that the scribes chose to write such a colophon suggests that they themselves thought such corrective attention would be desirable; they profess not to have corrected but imply that they should have done. There is also a self-consciousness in saying this at all, and in the fact that 'qui legit emendat, scriptorem non reprehendat' is a playful rhyming form. The verse which likely made this line memorable also conveys a slight archness, which suggests the scribes' delight in correcting. That tone belies the more obvious implication of this colophon, that scribes were willing to leave correction to others. Indeed, we might wonder whether any scribe who had *not* checked his work dare offer it to readers' judgement so brazenly as 'qui legit emendat' does?

49 Reynhout, *Formules latines*, 17–18. None of the commonest conventions discovered by Reynhout refers to correcting explicitly.

50 E.g., Les Bénédictins du Bouveret, *Colophons*, nos. 1850, 5851, 5898, 5768, 5796, 6094; Watson, *Catalogue*, nos. 122, 243, 245, 459, 820. A few others report the accuracy of the exemplar or copying: e.g., Watson, *Catalogue*, nos. 55, 92, 210.

51 Derolez, 'Pourquoi les copistes signaient-ils leurs manuscrits?', 49.

52 See, e.g., Reynhout, *Formules latines*, 103–8.

53 Reynhout does not consider it, but see, e.g., Les Bénédictins du Bouveret, *Colophons*, nos. 5792, 9309, 21582, 23076, 23077, 23381, 23471; Watson, *Catalogue*, nos. 93, 785; BL, MS Harley 372, f. 69^{v}; BL, MS Harley 2270, f. 236^{v}; BodL, MS Fairfax 16, f. 201^{r}.

That playfulness and self-consciousness continue in some unusual and interesting colophons which were versified in English. Here, the literary games betray assumptions which glorify the work of scribes rather than rebuke it, whatever they seem to say. For instance, a scribe of ordinances for the Mercers' Company of London in 1442–3 writes a stanza of rime royal pretentiously addressing the book of documents as though it were a tragedy, in echo of Chaucer's *Troilus and Criseyde*: 'Go litel boke go litel tregedie | The lowly submitting to al correcc*i*ou*n*'.[54] Likewise, a poem by the prolific fifteenth-century copyist John Shirley invites correction from readers but, in the process, tells us about his, the scribe's, awareness of standards for correcting:

as for fayllinge of þe scripture
of þe meter or ortagrafyure
wouch saue it to correcte
elles of þe defaute am I suspecte
þ*at* thorugh yo*ur* supportacion
yow list to make correccion
sith to such craffte I am not vsed[55]

The flaws here are all scribal: errors in the 'scripture' or inscription, in the orthography, in 'þe meter', or by 'defaute' or 'fayllinge' or omission.[56] Yet Shirley does not blame scribes in general; instead, he singles out himself for not doing as well as other scribes do. When he says that he is not 'vsed' to the 'craffte' of being a scribe, he implies that this 'craffte' of being a scribe *usually* does not need correcting by others; usually the scribes would have got the copying, spelling, metre and omissions right themselves. Anyway, this is not a factual description of his efforts but a poetic humility topos; he uses a similar one in a verse preface to another miscellany, where he apologizes if his simple wits have hampered him.[57] The assumption behind that pose of humility is not that scribes normally do shoddy work which readers need to emend, but that scribal work should normally include tidying up the orthography, attending to the verse-form and avoiding omissions – as (we will see) it normally does.

[54] Robinson, *Catalogue*, no. 110. For the source, see n. 65 below.

[55] BL, MS Add. 29729, f. 178^{v}, printed by Connolly, *John Shirley*, 210, lines 67–75. Connolly explains (95–6) that this MS is a sixteenth-century transcript by John Stow, likely of leaves since lost from TCC, MS R.3.20.

[56] This is the only citation in English under *MED*, *ortografiure* (*n.*), and precedes those under *ortografie* (*n.*), or *OED*, *orthography* (*n.*).

[57] BL, MS Add. 16165, f. 1^{r}; Connolly, *John Shirley*, 206. Interestingly this MS by Shirley only has 77 corrections in 516 written pages, far lower than the mean frequency in Table 6.1 below.

A more famous poem about scribes offers a similar mismatch between the underlying assumption that correctness matters and the claim that one particular scribe is incorrect. This poem, known by the title in its only manuscript copy as 'Chauciers wordes. a Geffrey vn to Adame his owen scryveyne', seems to refer to a real scribe called Adam Pinkhurst who copied some works by Chaucer, and seems to condemn him for inattention and error.[58] (It is too well known to need reproducing.) All too many accounts of English scribes, even well-informed ones, use this single poem to sum up 'in general terms what the situation was'.[59] Yet who knows if all that Chaucer writ about Adam were true about scribes in general? First, we cannot be sure that this writing is even Chaucer's or describes a very close relationship between him and Pinkhurst. It was preserved and perhaps titled by John Shirley in a miscellany which probably also once included Shirley's versified preface (quoted above), which makes one wonder whether this poem expresses Shirley's self-abasement as a scribe and reverence for authors.[60] But even if it is by Chaucer and about Pinkhurst, then this poem is inaccurate in its particulars and in general. Pinkhurst himself was a reasonably careful copyist and a skilful corrector of the things he and others copied.[61] Nor does it describe the full range of situations in which authors correct their own or others' copies of their work, for a variety of reasons.[62] Nor should this poem be interpreted to imply that the scribes of English never copied accurately or never corrected their copies. It makes that criticism of only one man, and the only general point to be gleaned from this poem lies in its assumption that getting things right should be the purpose of scribes' work. The poet actually hopes that 'þowe wryt*e* more truwe'. He does concede that scribal copies might never be entirely 'truwe'; they might just be a little bit 'more' so. But correct copying is here not unthinkable but assumed to be desirable.[63] Indeed, the

[58] TCC, MS R.3.20, p. 367, edited by Benson in *Riverside Chaucer*, 650, 1083. Mooney and Stubbs, *Scribes and the City*, identifies Adam. It is possible to transcribe 'Chauciers' as 'Chanciers', as the two minims do join at the top like **n**; I transcribe it as **u** tentatively, because in other instances of Shirley's display script for headings **u** looks like **n** in having minims joined at the top (e.g., TCC, MS R.3.20, p. 356, line 9, 'oure laureal poete').

[59] Lucas, *From Author to Audience*, 90–1. See another citation at 78–9, although Lucas also recognizes there that 'Scribes come in all varieties, from the meticulously accurate to the carelessly inaccurate' (78).

[60] For doubts, see Edwards, 'Chaucer and "Adam Scriveyn"', and Gillespie, 'Reading Chaucer's Words'; for Shirley, see Lerer, *Chaucer and His Readers*, 121, 123–4.

[61] As described by Horobin, 'Adam Pinkhurst'; and Wakelin, 'Editing and Correcting', 256–8.

[62] Traced in Chapter 11 below.

[63] As Fisher, *Scribal Authorship*, 31, also notes, though he stresses a latent fear of supplanting the author.

oath which scriveners such as Pinkhurst swore was to be 'true in my office and my craft', writing without 'haste or covetousness'.[64]

There are similar assumptions latent in another notable English lament for poor scribes, also by Chaucer, in the envoy to *Troilus and Criseyde*. Here he bids his work farewell ('Go litel boke go litel myn tregedye'), and urges it to 'kis the steppes' of various classical poets and worries that scribes will miscopy his poem:

And for ther is so grete diuersite
In Englissh and in writyng of oure tonge
So prey I to god that non myswrite the
Ne the this mysmetre for de faute of tonge
And red wher so ȝow be or elles songe
That thow be vnderstonde god biseche [. . .][65]

The envoy contrasts the poet's poetic ambitions with the difficulties of manuscript transmission ('writyng'). The envoy is not only, though, about scribes: there might also be risks of mispronunciation of the metre when reading aloud ('tonge') or of misinterpretation ('vnderstonde').[66] Of course, miscopying would contribute to these things: ironically, the line 'Ne the this mysmetre for de faute of tonge' is itself mismetred in what is often considered the best copy (quoted); the needless 'this' adds a jarring extra syllable. But there is only fleeting comment on scribal error and there is no claim that people will not try to correct those errors. Rather, there is once again the belief that what is wanted is correct reproduction of the poet's words, attention to metrical and linguistic detail and an alert mental response or understanding. Although he fears not receiving it, Chaucer, like Shirley and the authors of colophons, assumes the desirability of close attention to correcting books.

Imagining corrective reading

Yet as in monastic traditions, the interest in textual correcting went with a Christian favour for humility. It is much more common for poets in English to voice not a fear of scribal error but a hope for correction of themselves by others – others who could conceivably include scribes. After his fear of miswriting in *Troilus and Criseyde*, Chaucer goes on a few stanzas later to pray for correction from God and to 'directe' his poem to John Gower

64 Steer (ed.), *Scriveners' Company*, 5–6, quoted by Olson, 'Author, Scribe and Curse', 292.
65 CCCC, MS 61, f. 149r (*Troilus*, v.1786–98).
66 Burrow, 'Scribal Mismetring', 169, suggests a concern with pronunciation.

and Ralph Strode for them 'To vouchen sauf ther nede is to correcte'.[67] This gesture of humility is a sly boast: it implies that the poem is for educated readers and that it is not too bad already – needing correction only 'ther nede is' and so not everywhere. But the pose of humility is typical of Chaucer, for he often worries whether he speaks accurately, with propriety or plainly, or he uses the rhetorical tricks of *correctio*, *metanoeia* or *epanorthosis* as though struggling to get his poem right.[68] When he thus requests correction, it is not because the scribes are deficient but because he professes to be so himself. For example, in *Troilus and Criseyde*, he interrupts a love scene to warn that his 'wordes' are 'alle vnder correccioun' from more experienced lovers who might use their 'discrecioun' to 'encresse or maken dymyncioun | Of my langage', adding or deleting things.[69] These pleas might echo ancient or Italian models,[70] but Chaucer inserts these lines into a scene which he was otherwise closely modelling on his source, which suggests that the gesture of humility is deliberate.[71]

Moreover, the profession to be 'vnder correccioun' evokes the powerful religious and political institutions which pursued moral and textual amendment. The phrase 'vnder correccioun' echoes one used in ecclesiastical life, where it described a person's subjection to the power, and the ability to punish or correct, of superior clergy.[72] In monastic culture, wielding a pen went with yielding to the rod. The piety of this humility is clearer in another use of the phrase by Chaucer in the Parson's Prologue, where it is a cleric, the Parson, who places his tale 'vnder correcciou*n*' from other 'Clerkes':

> I putte it ay / vnder correcciou*n*
> Of Clerkes / for I am nat textueel
> I take but sentence / trusteth weel
> Therfore I make a protestaciou*n*
> That I wol stonde to correcciou*n*[73]

[67] CCCC, MS 61, f. 150ʳ (*Troilus*, v.1856–8).

[68] E.g., *Tales*, I.75, 726–9, 789, V.7–8, 35–41, 72, 105–9.

[69] CCCC, MS 61, f. 85ʳ (*Troilus*, III.1331–6). Ironically, 'dymyncioun' is lacking <u>.

[70] E.g., Tatlock, 'Epilog of Chaucer's "Troilus"', 115–23.

[71] *Troilus*, ed. Windeatt, III.1324, notes that other MSS have these stanzas in a different position, suggesting that Chaucer added them (f. 84ᵛ; III.1329) in a later stage of composition, perhaps on separate leaves.

[72] *MED*, *correccioun* (*n.*) 1b, only lists textual correction for 'under correccioun', although sense 5 lists the sense of 'Authority or jurisdiction for reproof'; *OED*, *correction* (*n.*) 1b, rightly notes the link between institutional and textual senses. See, e.g., *Paston Letters*, ed. Davis, Beadle and Richmond, nos. 180.66, 248.96, but also a literary echo in no. 1046.127–33.

[73] HEHL, MS El. 26.C.9, f. 206ᵛ (*Tales*, X.56–60). I quote the 'Ellesmere Chaucer' simply because it is in the Huntington Library's sample. Also comparable is the Second Nun's Prologue, which asks people who 'reden that I write' to 'my werk amende' (HEHL, MS El. 26.C.9, f. 186ᵛ; VIII.78–84).

There is a game internal to Chaucer's poem going on here, as these lines echo an apologetic passage earlier in *The Canterbury Tales*, where another narrator claims not to be 'textueel' or bookishly learned; for the Parson, a pretence at simplicity is a claim to moral honesty instead.[74] But it is fitting for a parson to be humbly 'vnder correcciou*n*' for the phrase evokes religious obedience. That ecclesiastical subjection is suggested by two very similar lines from the poem *The Prick of Conscience*:

> I make here openly a protestacion
> Þat I wol stonde to alle maner correcc*i*on[75]

It would not be surprising for a parson to know this poem, which offered religious instruction suitable for priests to use when teaching their parishioners. Nor would it be surprising for Chaucer to know this poem.[76] The quotation is from the Southern Recension of the poem; the Main Version lacks the word 'openly' and that makes the lines even more like Chaucer's. Like Chaucer's Parson who claims ignorance of 'rym' and alliterative verse, the poet of *The Prick of Conscience* also makes an extended claim that he does not care ('recche') whether the 'ryme' is rough and requests correction from any 'ylerned' man or 'clerk'.[77] The phrasing suggests not moral correction, which could come from somebody without education,[78] but learned emendation by people within the hierarchy of the Church. It is possible that this epilogue was the direct source for the Parson's Prologue; it is likely that the general ecclesiastical humility they convey were models for the humble requests for correction which are, more than criticism of scribes, ubiquitous in other English poems.

Yet while *The Prick of Conscience* might influence the request for correction in Chaucer's poetry, or might transmit to vernacular literature the ecclesiastical idea that we all require correction, it is Chaucer's poetry which is more audibly echoed in subsequent comments on correcting in the fifteenth century. Many poets borrow the Parson's claim to be 'vnder

74 Cf. HEHL, MS El. 26.C.9, ff. 204^{v}, 205^{v} (*Tales*, IX.235, 316). Scribes often mangle the word 'textueel' (e.g., BodL, MS Laud. misc. 600, ff. 266^{v}, 267^{v}; OTC, MS 49, ff. 260^{r}, 261^{r}), as noted by Manly and Rickert (eds.), *Text of the Canterbury Tales*, vol. VIII, 163, 170, 182, on their H.235, H.316, I.57.

75 HEHL, MS HM 125, f. 99^{v} (*Prick*, 9593–5). For the 'Main Version', see, e.g., HEHL, MS HM 139, f. 44^{r}.

76 Lewis and McIntosh, *Descriptive Guide*, nos. MV8, MV11, MV49, MV56, MV76, MV85, SR3, SR 11, SR12, SR18, record copies circulating in London and adjacent counties by the fifteenth century at least.

77 HEHL, MS HM 125, f. 99^{r-v} (*Prick*, 9581–96). For the Main Version, see, e.g., HEHL, MS HM 139, f. 44^{r}.

78 As demonstrated well by Craun, *Ethics and Power*, e.g., 13–14, 34.

correcciou*n*' or Chaucer's address to Gower and Strode, and with these lines they borrow not the expectation that future scribes will err but the hope that future people will correct. In fifteenth-century poems the request for correction by others is extremely frequent. In particular, John Lydgate – who as a monk might have inherited monastic ideas too – makes requests for correction very frequently, and then the influence of both Chaucer and Lydgate seems to prompt the recurrence of requests for correction in poems of the mid fifteenth century. They recur in poems with factual subject-matter, in which a concern for accuracy would suit the content, such as *On Husbondrie*, *Knyghthode and Bataile* and *The Court of Sapience*, and George Ashby's instructive poems for princes, as well as in other poems of a Lydgatean cast such as *Reson and Sensuallyte* or John Metham's *Amoryus and Cleopes*.

The conventionality is the most striking thing about these requests for correction: they recur at similar points, at the beginnings or ends of poems or sections; they are phrased in similar terms from poem to poem. The poets are often *under correction*, echoing the phrase from the Parson's Tale.[79] What needs correcting is their *rudeness*, *rude enditing* or *rude style*, on which they seek rueful pity.[80] They might hope that people *reform* their work so that it will *conform*.[81] They *direct* readers to *correct* their work, or they *direct* the pen to *correct* it.[82] They do not *presume* or they show no *presumption* but they admit that they need *correction* which they hope will be done with *compassion*.[83] The worry about presumption is an intriguing echo of monastic advice on correcting books, with its repeated warning against *praesumptio* (as noted above). But as the chiming sound of these words suggests, one motive for these requests is often to fill a stanza or find a rhyme. Although they profess that the poet is inept, then, these lines serve to polish his verse. The literary ambition of these lines is evident too in one final echo which they often share of Chaucer's 'Go litel boke' and 'kis the steppes' at the close of *Troilus and Criseyde*.[84] For instance, in *The Fall of Princes* Lydgate once urges 'go litil book tre*m*bli*n*g'

79 Hoccleve, *Regiment*, 756; Lydgate, *MP-I*, 17.i.49, 37.75, 38.401; 51.309; Lydgate, *MP-II*, 4.109, 20.385; Metham, *Amoryus and Cleopes*, 52, 2183.

80 Lydgate, *LOL*, 1.869–70; Lydgate, *MP-II*, 20.382, 24.40; Metham, *Amoryus and Cleopes*, 51, 2182; Harvey (ed.), *The Court of Sapience*, 38; and without a request for correcting, Lydgate, *MP-I*, 4.137, and *MP-II*, 21.905.

81 Lydgate, *MP-I*, 17.ii.664, and *MP-II*, 24.49; Ashby, *Poems*, 1.326, 11.31.

82 Lydgate, *Troy Book*, prol. 29–30, 11.201–2; Lydgate, *MP-I*, 51.314–15, and *MP-II*, 28.69.

83 *Fall*, 1.436–9; Lydgate, *LOL*, 1.879–80; Lydgate, *MP-I*, 17.i.55, 17.ii.660, 31.114, and *MP-II*, 4.107, 22.587; Lydgate, *Lives of Ss Edmund and Fremund*, 3577–8; Ashby, *Poems*, 1.317, 323–9.

84 Ashby, *Poems*, 1.309; Lydgate, *Lives of Ss Edmund and Fremund*, 3572; Lydgate, *MP-I*, 31.113, 38.401, and *MP-II*, 20.379; Metham, *Amoryus and Cleopes*, 2178.

with shaking 'leuys' (*leaves*), wittily comparing the page to the quivering Criseyde like an aspen leaf, and another time urges his book to 'Go kis the steppis' of previous laureate poets.[85] Earlier in his envoys he admits his deficiencies compared to Virgil, Homer, Dares and Ovid, three of them among the five poets in Chaucer's 'kis the steppes' stanza, and compared to Gower with his 'moral mateer' and Strode 'in his philosophye', another echo of *Troilus and Criseyde*. Curiously, Lydgate also defers to the poet who 'Drowh in Ynglyssh the Prykke of Conscience', which might echo the epilogue to that poem where the poet says that 'þis tretice drawe I wald | In Inglise tung þat may be cald | Prik of Conscience' and requests correction.[86] But Chaucer remains the clearer model: indeed, elsewhere Lydgate wishes that Chaucer himself could return to correct his work, for he would not 'gruche at eu*ery* blot', where a 'blot' could be a flaw or could be an ink crossing-out.[87] His deference to Chaucer makes explicit the literary aspiration in these and other repetitious requests for correction. And the repetitiousness of these requests shows the poets' adeptness in literary convention.

Conventional though they are, nonetheless several of these poems also specify the practicalities of textual correcting. In the most vivid scene, the poet of *On Husbondrie* not only requests correction in the future; he imagines his patron, Humfrey, Duke of Gloucester, having already corrected, and a gap on the page seems to represent the pause between request and correction.[88] The poet describes the procedure in technical detail: the duke 'gynnyth crossis make | With a plu*m*met' marking up faults. This is the first record of the English technical term for a lead writing implement ('plu*m*met') which scribes do indeed use to make crosses in the margin as prompts for correction.[89] Other poets employ further technical terms for correcting: they request *inspection* or *examination*, which recall the bureaucratic process of *inspexio*, checking documents and books,

[85] *Fall*, IX.3589, 3605.

[86] Cf. *Fall*, IX.3401–14 and *Prick*, 9549–51. Lydgate ascribes *Prick* to Richard Rolle (IX.3413), as do five MSS, two of them from Lydgate's county of Suffolk and one from the neighbouring Isle of Ely (Lewis and McIntosh, *Descriptive Guide*, nos. MV6, MV30, MV46, MV61 and L6).

[87] Lydgate, *Troy Book*, V.3519–36; Lydgate, *LOL*, II.1646–57. Few others make this odd request, but Ashby, *Poems*, II.1–28, asks them to return to teach him.

[88] Liddell (ed.), *Middle English Translation of Palladius*, I.1200–2, with the spacing in BodL, MS Duke Humfrey d.2, f. 22ᵛ, discussed by Wakelin, *Humanism, Reading*, 52–5. De la Mare, 'Duke Humfrey's English Palladius', 49–50 n.12, suggests that crosses in this MS might be in Humfrey's handwriting.

[89] Liddell (ed.), *Middle English Translation of Palladius*, II.481–2, and in general I.1184, II.1206–12, IV.981. *MED*, *plumet* (*n.*), sense (d), and *OED*, *plummet* (*n.*), 3. *Fall*, I.436, also imagines Humfrey correcting a poet.

which scribes recorded by writing 'ex*aminatus*' on them.[90] For Lydgate, 'inspecciou*n*' will lead the reader

> To race & skrape þoruȝ-oute al my boke,
> Voide & adde wher hem semeth nede

As Matthew Fisher has noted, there might be a literary echo in the phrase 'race & skrape' of Chaucer's worry that he will have to 'rubbe and skrape' the errors of Adam; the fact that the next two rhyming words of Lydgate's poem are 'newe' and 'trewe', as Chaucer's are, might amplify the echo.[91] But there is also reference to the practical techniques of correcting: the use of a scraping-knife to erase things; the term *void*, which might be a technical term otherwise little recorded, for it occurs adjacent to at least one deletion in English manuscripts (known to me).[92] The use of the verb *add* for correcting is confirmed by *The Court of Sapience*, in which people are asked to 'detray or adde' (*remove or add*), or to 'mynysse, and eche' (*diminish and supplement*) corrections to the text.[93] The tools of writing are evoked too when Lydgate seeks guidance for his 'poyntel', a tool which could be used to write things on wax tablets but also to 'plane' them away.[94] The same tool is evoked when several poets hope that the people correcting will 'my stile [. . .] directe'.[95] The 'stile', with the physical verb 'directe', is the stylus, the classical name for the 'poyntel' used to write on and erase wax tablets.[96] The tool calls to mind the way that authorship, when drafting on wax tablets, involved both writing and removing, creating and correcting.

The word *style* does, though, also refer metaphorically to the characteristics of the literary work, for the poets allude not only to tools of correcting but also to the textual details of language, style, verse-form and completeness which correcting might fix. They request correction of *lines*

[90] Lydgate, *MP-I*, 14.332, 17.1.52; Lydgate, *LOL*, 1.877. Lydgate, *MP-II*, 24.47, uses 'inspeccion' to mean something more like *expertise*.

[91] Lydgate, *Troy Book*, v.3536–42; Fisher, *Scribal Authorship*, 34–7. This echo might suggest the circulation of 'Chauciers wordes' beyond the one copy by John Shirley. *MED*, *scrapen* (*v.*), reveals that Robert Mannyng's *Handlyng Synne* also rhymes 'scrape' and 'rape', as 'Chauciers wordes' later do, and in proximity to a reference to a 'Bishop Troyle'.

[92] *MED*, *voiden* (*v.*) 6e, with only one other citation; *OED*, *void* (*v.*) II.6a, does not distinguish this sense. Cf. 'voide' in BL, MS Add. 25718, f. 70^{v} (*Tales*, IV.441, wrongly duplicated on f. 71^{r}). *MED*, *rasen* (*v.*) and *scrapen* (*v.*), are common terms for 'erase'.

[93] Harvey (ed.), *The Court of Sapience*, 35, 64. *MED*, *detraien* (*v.*), and *OED*, *detray* (*v.*), miss this technical sense.

[94] Lydgate, *LOL*, II.1661; see also Lydgate, *Troy Book*, II.1900–2. *MED*, *pointel* (*n.*), and *OED*, *pointel* (*n.*) 1a, record its use to translate Latin *stylus*; *Tales*, III.1742, 1758, mentions pointels used to erase.

[95] Lydgate, *Troy Book*, prol. 29–30, II.201; Lydgate, *MP-II*, 28.69.

[96] On the stylus, see in Chapter 11, p. 279 below.

and *traces* on the physical page.[97] They worry about stylistic propriety or aptness in diction, when poets contrast writing 'Imp*ro*purly' and with 'p*ro*pre speche'.[98] Adding and subtracting, the common terms for methods of correcting, are understood to affect the metre or spelling. This is set out clearly in one poem which asks the scribe or 'writer' to copy correctly the 'cadence and [. . .] Ortographie, | That neither he take of ner multiplye'.[99] Few others refer directly to spelling thus but many refer directly to problems with 'cadence', 'metre', 'balladys', 'rymyng' or 'incorrectid v*er*sis rude' which are 'mys met*ri*fied'; much of the English vocabulary for verse in this period is recorded in requests for its correction.[100] Even when they imagine patrons correcting, they imagine those patrons judging the metre: for instance, Hoccleve's two outright requests for patrons to correct his poems both imagine them improving style and metre: Hoccleve is 'vndir [. . .] correccio*u*n' of Edward, Duke of York, but asks him 'to amende and to correcte' the quite verbal niceties of 'Meetrynge amis' or speaking without 'ordre' or with rhetorical devices or 'colours ^sette ofte sythe awry'. It is a nice irony that Hoccleve set the word 'sette' in its proper order by a correction between the lines.[101] In another poem, he asks one Master Massy to see how badly his book is 'metrid' and 'what is mis ~ rectifie'.[102] Similarly, Lydgate worries about his metre repeatedly and in quite specific terms: he asks people to correct 'any word mis-sit | Causing the metre to be halt or lame', as though he recognizes that every word counts; he worries that his poem is 'Falsly metrid, boþe of short & long', borrowing terms from Latin metrics, for he is ignorant of 'metring' and 'metre' and because 'in ryme ynglysch hath skarsete'. The reference to scarcity of rhyme echoes one of Chaucer's poems which is apologetic about the poet's skill.[103] Because the metre and style are supposed to be so poor, the poets do therefore profess not to worry about 'coryouste | Boþe of makyng and of metre'

97 Lydgate, *LOL*, II.1649–50.

98 Dyboski and Arend (eds.), *Knyghthode and Bataile*, 118–19.

99 Dyboski and Arend (eds.), *Knyghthode and Bataile*, 3026–8, directly paraphrasing *Troilus*, V.1856, 1786, as discussed by Wakelin, 'Scholarly Scribes', 26–7. For *orthography*, see n. 55 above.

100 *Fall*, IX.3390, 3397, 3404; Metham, *Amoryus and Cleopes*, 2184; Liddell (ed.), *Middle English Translation of Palladius*, I.1198–9, II.486. And in general Lydgate, *MP-I*, 51.307, and *MP-II*, 22.583, 22.587; Ashby, *Poems*, II.41; Lydgate, *Pilgrimage of the Life of Man*, 170.

101 HEHL, MS HM 111, f. 33v (Hoccleve, *MP*, IX.46–54). Hoccleve otherwise tends to seek patrons' 'mercy' or 'grace' but not correction, even when he imagines that they have 'ouyr redde' the book: e.g., Hoccleve, *MP*, XXIV, envoy; *Regiment*, 5440–63; Robbins (ed.), *Secular Lyrics*, no. 99, line 1. Hoccleve, *MP*, XXI.793–6, XXII, moral. 5–6, also asks a fictional friend to 'ouersee' in a more general way.

102 HEHL, MS HM 111, f. 37v (Hoccleve, *MP*, XI.13–18).

103 Lydgate, *Troy Book*, respectively V.3484, 3491, II.184, 164–8. Cf. Chaucer, 'The Complaint of Venus', line 80.

and instead to prefer the deeper 'menyng'; but mentioning the verse only draws attention to it.[104] Of course, the comments on verbal and metrical correction are never more detailed than this: reference to metre is a sort of slogan with less substance spelled out. Yet the fact that the slogan had force suggests that the poets and the readers they addressed were interested in the methods and tools of correcting and in niceties of verbal artifice and verse-form, which are the focus of much correcting.

Fact and fiction

But how do these conventional invitations relate to the corrections which actually occurred? Did the poetic fictions mould behaviour? As Seth Lerer asked, when English poets 'appeal to their audiences [. . .] to correct them', as they often do, are they invoking 'a social practice or a literary trope?'[105] Although there is a loose likeness between poems and practice, it is not possible to say much more about these poetic clichés; it is difficult to link too directly what poets say to what scribes do.

First, although they mention some scribal procedures for correcting – adding, voiding, using a 'poyntel' – most of these poets do not explicitly specify the involvement of scribes. Even those poets who were themselves employed copying documents for the government, Thomas Hoccleve and George Ashby, do not mention that scribes do the correcting.[106] So whom do they ask to do it? One poet suggests that he himself will correct his work and invites others to 'wise' or advise 'me tamende it'.[107] More often they invite other people to do it. Lydgate once hopes that 'goodly rederys do correccion'.[108] Sometimes poets address earthly patrons, patron saints or pagan gods, or even abstractions such as the graces.[109] Most of these addressees were obviously unlikely to show up and check the text, and even when human patrons are mentioned there are often plural pronouns ('they', 'hem') making it vaguer who in particular might do the correcting. Poets commonly leave unspecified who will correct, referring

104 Lydgate, *Troy Book*, II.180–91; Lydgate, *Pilgrimage of the Life of Man*, 147–8, 164–5; and also Ashby, *Poems*, I.325, 328.

105 Lerer, *Chaucer and His Readers*, 209, 210.

106 E.g., *Regiment*, 985–1029, and Ashby, *Poems*, I.64–70.

107 Dyboski and Arend (eds.), *Knyghthode and Bataile*, respectively 2240, 315–18.

108 Lydgate, *Lives of Ss Edmund and Fremund*, 3599, where he alters the refrain of this envoy, which is usually 'be soget to al correccion', to mention them.

109 Lydgate, *Troy Book*, prol. 29–37; *Fall*, I.392, 435–6; Metham, *Amoryus and Cleopes*, 2179–84; Lydgate, *Lives of Ss Edmund and Fremund*, 24; Harvey (ed.), *The Court of Sapience*, 35; Lydgate, *Saint Albon*, 1993; Lydgate and Burgh, *Secrees of Old Philisoffres*, 26.

inclusively to *all who read* or *all who see* or some similar phrase.[110] It is possible that the scribes might be included among *all who see* the book, and especially when that seeing sounds like close attention: 'all | That ther of shall haue Inspection'.[111] But it is fair to say that poets almost never directly request scribes to correct their work, which is what most commonly occurred.[112]

Nor could one argue for any simple causal effect, as though people read these poems and went out to put their advice into practice, because the chronology does not fit. Actual examples of correcting English precede these poems by centuries. But one could speculate that the invitations of poets to correct might help people to articulate or alter the attitudes enshrined in the correcting they were already doing or to license the continuing practices of correcting. Techniques and materials – books, pens, knives; interlining, erasing – need ideas and imaginings as prompts for their use (as discussed in Chapter 1). After all, these requests were repeated from poem to poem and in prominent position at the beginnings and ends of works where scribes and readers might notice them. What attitudes might they be? The answer comes in the obvious fact that humility topoi, even in an age of genuine Christian humility, are not very humble; they serve to bolster one's literary reputation. As topoi, they show the poet's literary art, as he pretends to be artless; as rhetorical strategies, they establish the poet's ethos and win good will. Most crucially they suggest the poet's high aspirations to write properly, metrically, stylishly: seeking to be corrected suggests that if not the execution then the underlying intention is good. Hoccleve says as much when he asks various readers to 'weye | What myn entente is' or to note that 'I mene wel'.[113] Lydgate prays to a saint to correct his work for 'my will was good'.[114] Poets seldom spell it out thus, but this seems to be what is going on elsewhere: people protest that their poems are in need of correcting, but the protest implies that their intentions were good, that their poems therefore deserve attention, and that readers are competent to recognize those intentions and to pay

110 *Fall*, IX.3378; Lydgate, *MP-I*, 31.115–19, 38.406, 51.310, and *MP-II*, 28.71–2, 32.69; Lydgate, *Pilgrimage of the Life of Man*, 163; Sieper (ed.), *Lydgate's Reson and Sensuallyte*, 20.

111 Lydgate, *LOL*, 876–7.

112 One prose writer does very clearly: Usk, *Testament of Love*, III.1115, hopes for 'a good booke amender in correction'.

113 BL, MS Royal 17.D.xviii, respectively ff. 100^r (Robbins (ed.), *Secular Lyrics*, no. 98, lines 21–2, unrevised in HEHL, MS HM 111, f. 37^v), 37^r (*Regiment*, 1986).

114 Lydgate, *Saint Albon*, 1983–4.

them the attention they deserve. To correct somebody is, in a strange way, to respect him; the poets invite that respectful attention.

Moreover, in the kind of attention they invite there is an implicit likeness between poetic theory and scribal practice. This seems unlikely for, apart from Chaucer and Shirley, the poets seldom hope that people will transmit their works unchangingly; they envisage them correcting in ways which sound like revising or rewriting. The poets here would seem to diverge from the scribes who indulge in relatively little rewriting while correcting (as Chapter 6 will show). Yet the poets do not in fact give people licence to rewrite wilfully. As in moral correction, so in textual correction there is to be a principle of charity: the corrector will avoid malice and will have the errant person's good interests at heart.[115] For example, Lydgate asks that we do not correct 'of hasty mocyou*n*' but only 'Where ȝe fynde þat I fayle or erre'; he worries that people who do not understand metre tend to stumble into tinkering with it in other men's poems.[116] The poet of *The Court of Sapience* imagines and then limits the processes of rewriting: he asks people to 'modefye' their 'hastyf dome' and then 'not detray' or delete anything; only those with 'Meke herte, good tonge, and spryte pacyent' are permitted to 'detray or adde'.[117] The poet of *Reson and Sensuallyte* enjoins this restraint most fully: like Lydgate he hopes that correcting hands will not be 'hasty' and he frets that people unskilled 'in metre and prose' will modify things. Envious folk, he notes, criticize poems before they can 'any lake espye'. He addresses only those who strive to 'sen and rede' his poem with 'dilligence'. Even this person is licensed to correct only 'Al that ys mys' and only 'Yif hee therin kan fynde offence'; he must not, it is implied, emend what is not actually amiss.[118] This limit to correcting only *if* there is something wrong is mentioned in passing in other poems: people are told they should correct 'Yif ought be wrong' or 'where I erre' or in some synonym like *if there is need* or *where need is*.[119] The reservations, with *if* or *where*, might be a cliché but they might well have force. After all, a millennium of monastic writers had urged that correcting proceed with restraint and humility and only where there is genuinely an error. In this caveat there is the first element of the motives which animate the actual correcting of books in English.

115 Cf. Craun, *Ethics and Power*, 24–5. 116 Lydgate, *Troy Book*, I.4429–35.

117 Harvey (ed.), *The Court of Sapience*, 58–64.

118 Sieper (ed.), *Lydgate's Reson and Sensuallyte*, 22–40. This poem has in the past been ascribed to Lydgate but is not now generally believed to be his.

119 Lydgate, *MP-II*, 22.583, 24.43, 32.70; Lydgate, *LOL*, I.882; Lydgate, *Troy Book*, II.202; Lydgate, *MP-I*, 17.ii.664.

While a few people were willing to correct in ways which involved dramatic rewriting, it was more common for corrections to reproduce accurately or at least sensibly what people found in their exemplars (as later chapters will show). There is respect for the inherited text in correcting English, like that enjoined explicitly by monastic writers and implicitly by English poets.

The second thing that the poets request explicitly and which then does occur in English manuscripts is close reading. The ways in which poets and monastic writers enjoined close attention might well have justified the attentiveness exercised in correcting. By conceding their own need for correcting, the poets invite readers to pay the close attention their work deserves. Like monastic authors, the poets fantasize about readers who might study precisely the textual surface – details of language, style and form – and who will think their works merit such engagement. From a millennium's reflection on textual transmission and from the comments of contemporary poets, the scribes and readers of English in the fourteenth and fifteenth centuries could have inherited or encountered this encouragement to correct their books as though every word mattered.

CHAPTER 3

Copying, varying and correcting

To euery chaunge redy to decline
⌐lakketh a *verse*¬
Which of nature be diuers of corage

London, British Library, MS Add. 21410, f. 114v
Lydgate, *The Fall of Princes*, VI.502, 504

Correcting is not important in numerical proportion to other things that scribes do but is interesting itself and for what it tells us about scribes' thinking about their work and about the works they copy. Nevertheless, it is useful to consider other elements of scribes' work, in order to see what it is that correcting corrects. Copying is the immediate context – the space on the page, the preceding task – for the process of correcting. How, then, might it prompt correcting? After all, one common impression is that these manuscripts are essentially characterized by variation – both unwitting errors and deliberate changes – which preclude any interest in a correct text. In fact, this impression is not complete. Often – not always, merely often – scribes copy with little variation; this suggests that they do sometimes have some notion of correct reproduction. And when they do vary, the motive seems sometimes to be corrective in some way. If we can see the scribes' intelligence and corrective spirit even in copying, do we need to turn to correcting for evidence of that? Might not copying alone reveal scribal thinking? As it turns out, the difficulties of studying the process of copying also suggest the methodological value of turning to correcting for more insight into scribes' work. It is not that correcting is relatively more important than other elements of their work; obviously, scribes spent far more time copying the bulk of texts uncorrected, unemended, than they did correcting a few discrete words. But there is a limit to our evidence of the scribes' thought in their copying, and correcting therefore offers useful further evidence. Equally, though, copying is the essential context for correcting and must be considered first.

It often looks as though copyists did not seek exact reproduction and were willing to alter texts from one copy to the next. This willingness is suggested by the results of their work: the manuscripts of English copied in this period tend to vary one from another. Sometimes they vary in tiny details, such as dialectal spellings or what look like automatic slips of the pen, but other times they vary in what looks like conscious editorial rewriting, even on a major scale. This variation has fascinated many scholars, who have characterized it as *mouvance* or *variance*, the French terms used by Paul Zumthor and Bernard Cerquiglini.[1] These phenomena are not exactly synonymous: Zumthor's *mouvance* is an awareness of the deliberate openness of the literary work to refashioning for new functions. Cerquiglini's concept of variance is more relevant and offers a subtle account, subtler than is sometimes recalled, of the experience of writing. While he emphasizes the empowerment of scribes of the vernacular as they appropriated the skill of literacy, he recognizes the full run of scribal processes from 'deliberate revision' to 'careless' or even unwitting error ('Du remaniement délibéré à l'inattention fautive').[2] This praise of variation has inspired numerous studies of English manuscripts, so that people now take for granted the ubiquity of variation.[3]

It might, though, be worth refining our sense that variation is ubiquitous by considering precisely where, when, how and why it occurs, and where sometimes it does not. As Matthew Fisher has warned, we might have 'privilege[d] difference and the variant over what manuscripts *do* have in common'; he suggests that when scribes sought to copy accurately they were good at it.[4] First, we might want to differentiate scribes' working processes in diverse genres, discourses and milieux. Even within one language in one short span, English between the late fourteenth century and the early sixteenth, scribes treat different texts or traditions or authors differently, in their different places and institutions, with their different motives, training or wit. For instance, there is huge variation in the texts of the English romances whereas the textual tradition of Thomas Hoccleve's *The Regiment of Princes* is 'remarkable for its conservatism' in not varying from copy to copy; causes for the differences are easily deduced.[5] Variance is not always present to the same degree or for the same reasons.

Yet as well as explaining the variousness of variance, one might question the importance of variance overall for the people who first made and used

1 Well explicated by Millett, '*Mouvance* and the Medieval Author', 12–13.

2 Cerquiglini, *In Praise*, 2–3, *Éloge*, 19.

3 As Pearsall, 'Variants vs. Variance', 202, notes.

4 Fisher, *Scribal Authorship*, 19, 27. Of course, Fisher's focus is on moments when they deliberately rewrite.

5 Cf., e.g., Allen, 'Some Sceptical Observations', 15–16, 18–19; and Greetham, 'Challenges of Theory and Practice', 61–2. See also Pearsall, 'Variants vs. Variance', *passim*; and Fisher, *Scribal Authorship*, 40, 43–4, 57.

these manuscripts. Questions emerge from reconsidering the evidence. Although variation emerges when we compare manuscripts, it is difficult to be sure how readers would have responded: as is often noted, many readers would have encountered only one manuscript and not have collated it with others. There were some fanatics who did seek out multiple copies, but the dearth of exemplars and the haphazard systems for circulating them make it difficult to be sure how much people intended or noticed variance in any one instance.[6] Which scribes knew, and which did not, when they copied variant texts? Even if a copy differs from another extant copy, it is often difficult to say whether or not it was the scribe of this particular copy who made the choice to do so.[7] The scribe could be reproducing perfectly what he does not know is variation generated in one or more earlier exemplars. For instance if a manuscript contains a consistent pattern of adding element X, that might be the result of this scribe's consistent preference for X but equally it might be the result of lots of previous scribes of now lost exemplars each adding X just the once, and this scribe reproducing those Xs with fidelity. We might have an accidental cumulative effect which looks like deliberate rewriting. It is difficult, then, to see how many scribes are truly introducing variation and how many, conversely, are inheriting and reproducing it unvaryingly. One option is to study one scribe's handling of numerous different works for any consistent oddities across his career.[8] Other useful evidence comes from those copies for which the exemplar survives: direct copies. Supporting evidence comes from manuscripts which are not copied directly one from another but which seem to be both copied from a shared exemplar: cognate copies.[9] Direct and cognate copies are 'a palaeographer's paradise', the best evidence for what a scribe was varying or, perhaps, striving not to vary.[10]

To assess their evidence of scribes' variance, or lack thereof, this chapter surveys some direct and cognate copies (listed in Tables 3.1 and 3.2). The survey includes a copy of *The Canterbury Tales* and a continuation to

6 For different situations – importantly understood as complementary – see Hanna, 'Problems of "Best Text" Editing', 88–9, and *Pursuing History*, 8–9.

7 A conundrum raised by Carlson, 'Scribal Intentions', 50; and Hudson, 'Tradition and Innovation', 371.

8 Carlson, 'Scribal Intentions', 51.

9 Another term is 'genetic group', explained by *Piers B*, ed. Kane and Donaldson, 40. Seymour, *Catalogue*, vol. II, 75, 184, describes one such pair as 'closely affiliated'.

10 Ker, *Books, Collectors and Libraries*, 96, and also 77. Reeve, *Manuscripts and Methods*, 145–74, discusses how to identify them. Also informative are direct copies made from early printed books, but as this book is focused solely on manuscripts, it omits them. For discussion, see Reeve, 175–84; Wakelin, 'Writing the Words', 51–3; Blake, 'Manuscript to Print', 419–29; Moore, *Primary Materials*, 11–18.

Table 3.1 *Divergences in some direct copies of still surviving exemplars, and the number of corrections in the direct copies*

	the sampled passage	*words in the passage*	*words diverging*	*total % diverging*	*corrections which remove divergence*	*corrections which preserve or increase divergence*
a) i	Mm, ff. 35^{r}/40–37^{v}/47; Gl, ff. 17^{r}/a40–18^{v}/a12 *Tales*, I.3208–444	1,856	65	4%	7	0
ii	Mm, ff. 64^{r}/5–64^{v}/21, and ff. 65^{r}/1–66^{r}/47; Gl, ff. 27^{v}/b4–28^{r}/a15, and f. 28^{r}/a37–28^{v}/b39 *Tales*, VII.435–87, 509–643	1,488	39	3%	3	0
b) i	En^{1}, ff. 40^{v}/25–43^{r}/39; Ds, ff. 39^{r}/32–41^{v}/38 *Tales*, I.3187–398	1,644	27	2%	0	0
ii	En^{1}, f. 122^{v}/27–126^{v}/37; Ds, ff. 114^{v}/32–117^{v}/1 *Tales*, IV.1177–448	2,190	50	2%	2	2
c)	D, ff. 37^{r}/b32–39^{v}/a11; H2, ff. 162^{v}/b42–165^{r}/a42 Hamer and Russell (ed.), *The Gilte Legende*, no. 124	3,365	15	0%[1]	0	0
d) i	Gw, ff. 15^{r}/1–16^{r}/35; Hy, ff. 2^{r}/1–3^{v}/21 *Brut*, an unprinted prologue and then 1.1–3.30	1,342	21	2%	12	0
ii	Gw, ff. 121^{r}/1–122^{r}/30; Hy, ff. 96^{r}/33–97^{v}/34 *Brut*, 368.18–372.33	1,343	11	1%	5	1
e) i	Hy, ff. 106^{r}/1–107^{r}/30; Pet, ff. 197^{v}/8–198^{v}/31 a continuation of the prose *Brut*	1,288	39	3%	0	0
ii	Hy, ff. 113^{r}/1–114^{r}/34; Pet, ff. 203^{r}/24–204^{r}/34 a continuation of the prose *Brut*	1,063	10	1%	7	0
iii	Hy, ff. 118^{r}/1–119^{v}/31; Pet, ff. 207^{r}/10–208^{r}/21 a continuation of the prose *Brut*	1,102	11	1%	2	0
f) i	Gw, f. 141^{r}/1–141^{v}/41; Pet, ff. 215^{v}/21–216^{v}/37 Matheson (ed.), *Death and Dissent*, 95.8–99.8	1,211	27	2%	0	2

Table 3.1 *cont.*

	the sampled passage	words in the passage	words diverging	total % diverging	corrections which remove divergence	corrections which preserve or increase divergence
ii	Gw, f. 144r/1–144v/41; Pet 219r/16–220v/2 Matheson (ed.), *Death and Dissent*, 106.10–110.13	1,348	39	3%	1	1
iii	Gw, f. 148r/1–148v/34; Pet ff. 223v/39–225r/6 Matheson (ed.), *Death and Dissent*, 121.5–124.7	1,042	22	2%	0	0
total		20,282	376	2%	39[2]	6

Samples (a.i) and (a.ii) are adjacent to Beadle, 'Geoffrey Spirleng', 142–5 (*Tales*, I.3187–207, VII.488–508). Samples (e.i) to (e.iii) are adjacent to samples in Wakelin, 'Writing the Words', 50–3.

[1] Rounded down from 0.45 per cent.

[2] This ignores two more corrections in Gl and six more in Hy in later handwriting.

Table 3.2 *Divergences between cognate copies, and the number of corrections in all two (a) or three (b) of the cognate copies*

		the sample passage	words in the passage	words diverging	total % diverging	corrections which remove divergence	corrections which preserve or increase divergence
a)	i	Mc, ff. 1r/1–4v/30; RaI, ff. 21r/15–24v/31 *Tales*, I.3859–4097	2,002 × 2	66 × 2	3%	11	2
	ii	Mc, ff. 68v/21–71v/17; RaI, ff. 84r/6–86v/20 *Tales*, VII.435–606	1,351 × 2	49 × 2	4%	1	0
b)	i	Bo, ff. 53v/28–55r/34; Bm, ff. 53v/28–55r/34; Cot, ff. 235r/1–337r/1 *Piers B*, XIII.225–354	1,276 × 3	43 × 3	3%	11	6
	ii	Bo, ff. 76r/5–77r/38; Bm, ff. 76r/5–77r/38; Cot, ff. 262v/18–264v/2 *Piers B*, XVIII.1–109	1,100 × 3	29 × 3	2%	17	1
	iii	Bo, ff. 84r/10–85v/18; Bm, ff. 84r/10–85v/18; Cot, ff. 272v/25–277v/25[1] *Piers B*, XIX.200–336	1,187 × 3	24 × 3	2%	14	4
total			17,395	518	3%	54	13

[1] Cot, ff. 274r–276v are blank.

the prose *Brut* which have been previously studied; the sample here supplements those earlier studies by sampling further sections and, with the continuation of the prose *Brut*, studying other passages of direct copying in the same and related manuscripts.[11] The survey also includes a copy of *The Gilte Legende*, which has been analysed for its evidence of changes in orthography but not for its variation,[12] and a second direct copy of *The Canterbury Tales* which was noted by earlier editors but not examined extensively.[13] These are the four sets of direct copies. There is then a sample of cognate copies: two cognate copies of *The Tales* and three cognate copies of Langland's *Piers Plowman*, all spotted by editors but here examined more extensively.[14] The sampled sections of direct copies amount to 20,282 words (Table 3.1), which were studied in comparison with their direct exemplars. For the cognate copies, the passages amount to 6,934 words but those passages were studied in both or all three of the cognate copies, for each copy could act as a check on the other, and so the passages of 6,934 words, when studied in duplicate or triplicate, amounted to 17,395 words (Table 3.2). The sum total of words was established by counting the words in the direct copy or one of the cognate copies, and adding the number of words omitted from that copy; the word-division for counting was that of the copy, not of current spelling.[15] The sampling involved noting every divergence between the related manuscripts in the choice, inclusion or order of words.

[11] Beadle, 'Geoffrey Spirleng', discusses the copying of two sections of GUL, MS Hunter 197 (U.1.1) (hereafter = siglum Gl) directly from CUL, MS Mm.2.5 (= Mm); Matheson (ed.), *Death and Dissent*, 77–80, deduces that GUL, MS Hunter 83 (T.3.21) (= Gw), served as the exemplar for part of BL, MS Harley 3730 (= Hy) and part of Cambridge, Peterhouse, MS 190 (= Pet); then a different part of Hy served as the exemplar for a different part of Pet.

[12] Hamer, 'Spellings of the Fifteenth-Century Scribe Ricardus Franciscus', and Hamer with Russell (eds.), *Gilte Legende*, vol. III, 7–9, 12–13, 26–7, explains the relationship between BodL, MS Douce 372 (hereafter = D) and BL, MS Harley 4775 (= H2).

[13] Manly and Rickert (eds.), *Text of the Canterbury Tales*, vol. I, 118–19, 131–2, identify Tokyo, Takamiya collection, MS 24, *olim* 'The Devonshire Chaucer' (hereafter = Ds), as copied directly from BL, MS Egerton 2726 (= En^{1}). Seymour, *Catalogue*, vol. II, 106, 240, more cautiously calls them 'closely affiliated'.

[14] Owen, *Manuscripts*, 50, and Manly and Rickert (eds.), *Text of the Canterbury Tales*, vol. II, 75 (but cf. inconsistent comment at vol. I, 451) note the cognate relationship between Chicago, UL, MS 564 (hereafter = Mc) and BodL, MS Rawl. poet. 141 (= Ra^{1}); *Piers B*, ed. Kane and Donaldson, 1–2, 5, 40–2, notes that one or two shared exemplars lie behind BodL, MS Bodley 814 (= Bo), BL, MS Add. 10574 (= Bm) and BL, MS Cotton Caligula A.xi (= Cot). Grindley, 'A-Version Ancestor of BmBoCot', 66–9, concludes that Bm and Bo are twins descended from one lost exemplar but that Cot is descended not from that exemplar but from its twin, also lost.

[15] Some compounds which we spell as one word were counted as two, but others which we separate were combined: e.g., 'after*e* none', 'with oute', 'Newyersday', 'Baynardyscastell' (Pet, f. 203^{r}/37–8, 40).

Copying and varying

When we consider those substantives, most copying involves close reproduction. From the samples of direct copies, about 98 per cent of the words were reproduced verbatim or word-for-word – the same words in the same order (Table 3.1). That closeness is confirmed by previous studies of some of these direct copies, which consistently find that under 3 per cent of the words change in substance.[16] And other assessments of the accuracy of English scribes, notably from their passages of double copying, have similarly found the scribes to be accurate.[17] There is some variety in this sample: the direct copy of *The Gilte Legende* diverges from its exemplar in well under 1 per cent of words (c), whereas a copy of *The Canterbury Tales* (a) diverges in 3 per cent of words (combining a.i and a.ii).[18] It might be possible to offer historical explanations from the training of the scribes: the more accurate copy of *The Gilte Legende* is by Ricardus Franciscus, who copied lots of literary works and whose professionalism is evident in his highly calligraphic handwriting modelled on bastard secretary; the less accurate copy of *The Tales* is by an estate manager more used to utilitarian copying, here writing for his own use. But these historical patterns are not yet proven by this small sample and by so small a difference. In fact, across these different milieux, there is rough consistency. Even when two scribes copy from one exemplar or one of those scribes copies from two exemplars, in (d), (e) and (f), there is a consistently low frequency of variation. This counting of what is common thus reminds us of something which we must not forget as we focus on variant texts: that invariance is also an option for scribes. Even George Kane, who formulated a brilliant account of scribes' errors, noted that most scribes did 'copy a very large number of words in a great many lines faithfully', and Bernard Cerquiglini, who praised variance, noted that scribes also had the 'old dream' of the 'faithful copy' ('le rêve de la copie fidèle').[19] The extreme variance between manuscripts – so striking to us – must not blinker us to invariant copying.

It is not, though, possible to claim from this sample that around 98 per cent of copying in English is 'exact textual reproduction'. First, the comparison in Table 3.1 of substantive differences does not count differences in

16 Beadle, 'Geoffrey Spirleng', 145; Wakelin, 'Writing the Words', 53. Ker, *Books, Collectors and Libraries*, 83, finds an even greater closeness in a twelfth-century MS in Latin.

17 E.g., Wakelin, 'Writing the Words', 49–55; and Beadle, 'Some Measures of Scribal Accuracy'.

18 The biggest divergence is a single omission of 17 words or 2 lines (b.ii), by eyeskip between lines ending with <ence>: En^{1}, f. 123^{r} (*Tales*, IV.1196–7), and Ds, f. 115^{r}. I ignored different paratexts such as titles; they had been systematically changed in some of the MSS.

19 *Piers A*, ed. Kane, 126; Cerquiglini, *In Praise*, 2, and *Éloge*, 18.

the spellings, abbreviations, punctuation or layout. For example, spellings which were both acceptable variants in English in this period were ignored: to take extreme examples, 'þis Iwys' and 'these Iewys' (*these Jews*) were not considered to vary.[20] Second, more importantly, the sample presents a conundrum. The conundrum is that I chose to sample these direct or cognate copies because they were already known to be similar. If the scribe had changed what he copied a lot, we would be unlikely to know that these were direct or cognate copies close enough to be worth comparing; therefore, to find them alike is to some extent tautologous: to prove that things we knew were alike are alike. There is no solution to this conundrum. However, sometimes the relationship of these copies was identified from physical clues or from broader similarities of contents and not from close comparison of their texts.[21] Even if two copies contain broadly the same works, the textual detail could, in theory, vary a lot. Copies of the prose *Brut*, *The Canterbury Tales* and *Piers Plowman* often have different 'continuations', tale-orders or blends of the A, B and C versions, so in these cases what first signalled the connections was the recurrence of larger configurations, which textual closeness serves to confirm.[22] The likenesses of layout offered further confirmation; two of the copies of *Piers Plowman* share the same number of lines on each page; two copies of the prose *Brut* have the same lineation for a few short passages, something unlikely to occur by accident in writing out prose by hand.[23] Dialect is often close too: two of three cognate copies of *Piers Plowman* have almost identical spelling, letter for letter, even down to the choice of <i> or <y>. In these cases, then, the relationship was revealed by things bigger than the textual detail, so that identifying their likeness in that detail is not entirely tautologous – though nor is it entirely satisfactory.

Moreover, the point is not to suggest that this close copying is predominant in all forms of copying. Evidently some people did rewrite radically in manuscripts beyond this sample, and even in this sample some 2 per cent of words diverged. The correct copying is, though, interesting because it contrasts with the possibilities for rewriting: close reproduction is not

20 Mm, f. 65ᵛ (*Tales*, VII.573), and Gl, f. 28ᵛ.

21 Reeve, *Manuscripts and Methods*, 152–3, traces the importance of physical clues to identifying related MSS.

22 Matheson (ed.), *Death and Dissent*, 77–80; *Piers B*, ed. Kane and Donaldson, 1–2, 5. The exception is the direct copy of *The Gilte Legende* which was first identified by Butler, *Legenda Aurea*, 74, comparing textual detail.

23 See identical lineation between Gw and Hy on most of Gw, f. 15ᵛ/27–34, and Hy, f. 3ʳ/7–14, Gw, f. 16ʳ/34–5 and Hy, f. 3ᵛ/20–1. Both instances are the last few lines of the page in the exemplar Gw. Reeve, *Manuscripts and Methods*, 156–8, discusses the infrequency of such shared lineation.

to be taken for granted from the scribes' perspective. For instance, as the prose *Brut* observes, it was 'compilid *and* writen' not by one man but by 'many diu*er*se good men' who wrote, revised and extended the chronicle variously.[24] The copies of the prose *Brut* in the sample (d–f in Table 3.1) contain a continuation to 1460 first devised for, and here copied from, Caxton's edition of *The Chronicles of England*, and a further continuation to 1471 known now as 'Warkworth's *Chronicle*'.[25] In this chain of exemplars and copies, new scribes often take over just before new continuations added to the prose *Brut* begin. But before they add this additional text, they do complete the original text copied by the previous scribe: that suggests fidelity to a colleague's project and might suggest that the additional texts were presented seamlessly in a prior exemplar.[26] As one copyist put it in a note, he wants readers to see all the text in 'my copey in whyche is wretyn a remanente', as though the continuations of the *Brut* seemed like remaining parts of it and not new additions; the act of compiling new texts feels like restoring one whole text.[27] So even in this fluid textual tradition, we find influidity and exactitude in attitude if not in achievement. Moreover (as was noted), although the text of the prose *Brut* cobbles together continuations from different places, in the details of the individual words there is often word-for-word reproduction. Unless composing actual large-scale revisions – a new continuation for the prose *Brut* or spurious links between Chaucer's tales: things better called authorship rather than scribal copying – scribes seem not to vary as they copy.

How do we reconcile this invariance with the striking variation in umpteen other manuscripts? To make sense of this, we need to remember that the surviving manuscripts comprise only a small portion of those formerly in existence, and then to think of the divergences in our lost copies. Direct copies suggest that each scribe alters on average about 2 per cent of the words he copies, but if two surviving manuscripts are not direct copies but are separated by a chain of intervening copies, then we might

[24] Gw, f. 15^r^, repeated verbatim in Hy, f. 2^r^.

[25] Matheson (ed.), *Death and Dissent*, 80–9, debates the authorship, once wrongly linked to John Warkworth, Master of Peterhouse, the College in Cambridge where (d), (e) and (f) were likely made.

[26] Only once does adding a new continuation look disruptive: in the earliest exemplar in the chain, Gw, scribe B takes over 9 lines before the end of the common text ending at 'rewell and gou*er*naunce' at the start of a new quire (f. 128^r^), as though cancelling the last leaves of scribe A's final quire (ff. 110^r^–127^v^, which seems to collate as VII^{24}, with 19–24 cancelled after f. 127^r^).

[27] Pet, f. 214^v^. This scribe seems to copy these words from Hy, the scribe of which copied Caxton's continuation but then directed his readers to 'Warkworth's *Chronicle*' in Gw; the scribe of Pet then dutifully copies this direction but, inconsistently, also copies 'Warkworth's *Chronicle*' himself from Gw (Matheson (ed.), *Death and Dissent*, 77–80).

expect some multiplication of this divergence, as indeed we find in the cognate copies. The closely cognate copies corroborate the predominance of invariant copying but they also diverge from each other more than do direct copies from their exemplars, namely in about 3 per cent of words (Table 3.2). This further divergence is likely because these cognate copies are connected through one or more intermediate manuscripts. While a scribe who copies directly varies about 2 per cent of words, two scribes copying might each vary 2 per cent of words from their shared exemplar but, varying different ones, might diverge more than that from each other. That might suggest how the apparently great variance among English manuscripts emerges. If a surviving manuscript A is copied from a lost manuscript B which in turn is copied from surviving manuscript C, then we might expect manuscripts A and C to diverge in about 4 per cent of the words; or if a surviving manuscript A is copied through a chain of lost manuscripts B–E and we have the ultimate source F, then we might expect manuscripts A and F to diverge in about 10 per cent of words. Incidentally, such rates of divergence might suggest the number of lost manuscripts which produced the variant copies which survive.[28] In fact, although the cognate copies show increased divergence, they do not show quite as much divergence as they might, perhaps because of convergent variation, where multiple scribes make the same mistake, or because of correction.[29] Even when three copies stem from one or two sources (b) there is only divergence in under 3 per cent of the words in the passages.[30] Yet the multiplication of small amounts of divergence across multiple lost copies could generate much of the variance in the surviving manuscripts.

Then such variance in extant *manuscripts* would be explicable alongside a will to *in*variance on the part of any one *scribe*. A large amount of variation between two surviving books could occur even if each scribe, of the surviving books and the lost ones between them, only varied a little. This raises questions about the significance of variance for the scribes themselves. Was it as easily perceived by them as it is by us? And most importantly, did they accept it or even really intend it? If we are not evaluating texts but are attending closely to the scribes' working processes, then we might see that each single scribe is less invested in variance than its prevalence in the surviving manuscripts would suggest. This is partly a perceptual problem: while we can easily see the variance between manuscripts, we can

[28] As proposed by McIntosh, 'Two Unnoticed Interpolations', 73–4; Dain, *Les manuscrits*, 46.

[29] *Piers A*, ed. Kane, 55, 60–2, explains convergent variation.

[30] To be exact, 2.69 per cent in total in Table 3.2, (b.i, b.ii, b.iii). But copies of *Tales* again diverge most (3.43 per cent in total) in Table 3.2 (a.i, a.ii).

seldom catch any single scribe in the act of varying things as conveniently as we can see him reproducing things closely; to identify a scribe varying, we would need to see what was in his direct exemplar, but identifying his exemplar is difficult when he has varied what he found in it. But that limit to our perception might not be too misleading: for even if he is compiling his exemplar from more than one source like the scribes gathering continuations for the prose *Brut*, what seems to matter to many scribes is correct reproduction of the text or texts. It is of course not what was always sought: it was permissible to work not as a scribe but as a compiler, translator, commentator, reviser or author for oneself. But these were different tasks. And, given the permissibility of them, the decision to reproduce some texts so closely might well be as significant a choice for the scribe as varying texts would have been.

Intention in variance

Could, though, mere correctness in copying be a choice? Were scribes thinking about their work this consciously? Common sense invites the suspicious question whether copying closely requires much intention, attention or intelligence. It might seem that varying requires thought but that copying closely requires the scribe *not* to think too hard but to reproduce things unreflectingly. Especially if correct copying was common (as the evidence in Table 3.1 suggests), then it might be done automatically and without recognition. One measure of that thoughtlessness might be the fact that close copying does sometimes lead scribes to reproduce foolish things. For example, two scribes of cognate copies of *Piers Plowman* reproduce the line 'Þre gree ȝit haþ he genten .' for al his grete wounbe', which obscures the words *gotten* as 'genten' and *wound* as 'wounbe'.[31] One copyist of *The Canterbury Tales* reproduces from his exemplar a nonsense word 'awther' as 'awthere' for a *wether*, a kind of sheep; the verb 'thenke' as 'thynke' with a final <k> that is good English but a bad rhyme for 'wenche'; and the obviously wrong repetition 'briȝht briȝhter' as 'bryght / bryghter'.[32] The reproduction of such nonsense might make the other passages of accurate reproduction look more bovine than intelligent. Yet copying such nonsense is rare: there are very few obvious errors repeated.

31 Bo, f. 77^{r} (*Piers B*, XVIII.98); Bm, f. 77^{r}, only altering the spelling of 'his' to 'is', a form found in both MSS. Cot, f. 264^{r}, has the more legible 'geten' and the even odder 'wombe'.

32 Mm, f. 35^{v} (*Tales*, I.3249, 3253, 3255), and Gl, f. 17^{r}. *MED*, *thinken* (*v.*) 2, does record this verb spelled sometimes with final <ch>, as Chaucer here requires. All three oddities in Mm were corrected in an early modern hand, after the copy in Gl was made.

And we might not want to dispraise the thoroughness which records such things; indeed, older textual critics used to praise as a purer witness to textual traditions the perfect copyist who even reproduced the flaws in his exemplar.[33] The scribes themselves lived in a culture with some inherited ideas about copying books (seen in Chapter 2) which preferred obedience and conventionality in scribes. And we should not assume, with intellectual snobbery, that meticulous work with the hands is witless nor privilege one kind of thinking over another: not all thinking need involve creativity and originality; thinking can be meticulous and admirably unimaginative. Non-variant copying might involve immense concentration and attention and be just as effortful and thoughtful as variation.

This suggestion is perhaps counterintuitive, for it might seem as though varying requires more thought. Modern editors have, over the decades, often wondered what scribes were thinking when they varied texts. How deliberate were their divergences? And, if deliberate, what was the quality of their thought? There have been many excellent studies of variants for their insights into scribal thinking: first and foremost, B.A. Windeatt brilliantly showed how variants in Chaucer's *Troilus and Criseyde* record the scribes' responses to the poem: what they change reflects what they find surprising or perplexing, he suggests.[34] Others have followed up this discovery fruitfully, finding meaning and intention in variant texts.[35] Curiously, though, the sample of direct and cognate copies suggests that variance is sometimes witless, while correct reproduction might be witting, the product of conscious effort. In one respect, this confirms the dismissal of scribes' thinking by George Kane, who stresses that much variance came from unconscious slips of the eye, hand or brain, like those recognized by many classical philologists.[36] Kane does distinguish 'between mechanical and conscious variation' and grant that some variation had to be knowing: if the scribes' default was 'an obligation to follow the exemplar', then some textual divergence must have been 'deliberate' in ignoring that obligation.[37] However, Kane dismisses the quality of thinking in such deliberate fault. When they deliberately diverge, the scribes produce 'drabness', make things 'easier' or offer 'sophistications'; the author's genius is 'quite beyond [the scribe's] conception'.[38] Scribes' responses are 'jejune' and if they might be

33 Dain, *Les manuscrits*, 17, traces this notion.

34 Windeatt, 'Scribes as Chaucer's Early Critics', 120–1.

35 E.g., Lerer, *Chaucer and His Readers*, esp. 8–9, 211–12; Reiter, 'Reader as Author', 167.

36 *Piers A*, ed. Kane, 116–24.

37 *Ibid.*, 125–7, an approach discussed by Brewer, *Editing Piers Plowman*, 363–6.

38 Chaucer, *Legend of Good Women*, ed. Cowen and Kane, respectively viii, 128, 96, 43, 133. For a critique, see Dane, *Abstractions of Evidence*, 34–7, 39.

considered commentary on the text then 'the essence of such commentary fits easily into half a dozen sentences and is banal'.[39] Kane cites and objects here to Windeatt's interest in scribal variance, in ways that are not fair.[40] Nonetheless, Kane's dispraise of variance does show what is at stake: whether variance is evidence of scribes' thinking. If there is an absence of attention and intelligence in the errors, that might suggest, by contrast, the presence of conscious thought required to avoid such errors through correct copying or through corrections of errors (the subject of later chapters).

Sure enough, most of the variation in direct and cognate copies looks like unthinking error prompted by the physical processes of copying. In copying, the scribe looks at an exemplar, must look away from it at the page on which he is writing, must remember the text of the exemplar by visual recall or by an act of 'internal dictation' of it back to himself, and must put marks on the new page.[41] Sometimes, the scribe does not look at the exemplar carefully and so picks from it the wrong piece of text, causing a jump or repetition in his copy. This results in the largest errors in sample. For example, a scribe of *The Canterbury Tales* skips two whole lines of his exemplar when he finishes writing a line ending with 'defence', glances at his exemplar to see where he's got to but glances instead at the similar looking 'offence' two lines further on and resumes from there.[42] Sometimes the scribe seems attracted while copying to similar words nearby: this can result in nonsense so that 'to done' in one copy becomes 'do done' in another, repeating the nearby **d** instead of **t**, or so that a saint's 'hous' goes to heaven rather than her 'soule', when the word 'hous' nearby has distracted the scribe.[43] Some slips could be interpreted as interesting revisions. It might be powerfully insistent to describe 'dede' men emerging from 'dede graues', as one manuscript puts it, rather than 'depe graues', as others put it; or the repetition of *find* might form a nice parallel in the lines 'He can wel fynden in myn eye a stalke | But in his owne he connot fynde a balke', whereas cognate copy has 'he can not see': but in each case the repetition is likely caused by the proximity of the letter or word nearby.[44] It is possible

39 Kane, *Chaucer and Langland*, 208.

40 *Ibid.*, citing *Troilus*, ed. Windeatt, 33. Windeatt, 'Scribes as Chaucer's Early Critics', 121, 140, does distinguish scribal error from deliberate rewriting and warns us not to give the scribes' responses more credit than they're due.

41 Parkes, *Their Hands Before Our Eyes*, 63–7, reviews these processes and errors.

42 En^{1}, f. 123^{r} (spelled 'diffence'); Ds, f. 115^{r} (*Tales*, IV.1195–8). In the other eyeskip, a scribe in prose skips 24 words between two instances of 'delyd': Hy, f. 107^{r}/8–9, and Pet, f. 198^{v}/13.

43 Bo, f. 54^{v} (*Piers B*, XIII.290), and cf. Bm, f. 54^{v}, and Cot, f. 236^{r}; H2, f. 165^{r} (*Gilte*, 124.275), miscopied from D, f. 39^{v}.

44 Cot, f. 263^{v} (*Piers B*, XVIII.62), and cf. Bo, f. 54^{v}, and Bm, f. 54^{v} (and another MS has 'dede', according to the apparatus of *Piers B*, XVIII.62); Ra^{1}, f. 22^{r} (*Tales*, I.3919–20), and cf. Mc, f. 2^{r}.

that these errors are deliberate revisions but more probable that they are visual confusions. The divergences seem unwitting, then – which suggests, by contrast, that accurate copying requires the scribe to keep his wits about him.

Other visual errors occur when the scribe misreads the letters in the exemplar, especially the looped shapes of **b**, **d**, **h**, **l** and **w** used in fifteenth-century handwriting. For example, one scribe of the prose *Brut* writes 'albion' or 'albyn' (*Albina*, the woman after whom Albion is named) with pronounced loops on the letters **lb**, and, as a result, those letters together look like his looped **w**; the person copying his work then writes 'Awion' and 'awyn'.[45] One scribe confuses the tall letters **b**, **h** and **l** and so turns 'nolle' into 'noble'; another turns the 'brewehous' into a 'bredhous', which could perhaps be a misreading of the looped **w** in his exemplar as **dd**.[46] When nonsense occurs from the scribe following what the exemplar looks like, he seems to intend to reproduce it closely: its visual features are guiding his efforts; but he is merely unable to see it clearly enough. Fewer errors seem to be auditory, but some do occur when the scribe remembers the text of the exemplar and internally dictates it back to himself. The internal sound leads some scribes to mishear their copy and produce sound-alike words, so that they start a speech beginning 'Now syres' as the echo 'Now certes'.[47] Finally, some errors seem prompted when the physical properties of books distract scribes from the intellectual process of reading, remembering and writing. For example, one copyist of a continuation to the prose *Brut* five times skips or adds *and*, *the* or *with* where he reaches a line-break on his own page.[48] A copyist of the prose *Brut* itself omits *by* where he turns his page from one side of the leaf to the next and he thereby shortens 'by herbes and by rotes' into 'by herbes and | [page-break] Rotes'.[49] These slips in little words look likely to have resulted from a break in concentration when scribes moved their eyes about the book. Problems at line-breaks have been noted in another direct copy by a scribe employed by John Capgrave.[50] In all these instances, inattentiveness seems to prompt most of the divergences, rather than clever rewriting, and the effort of attention which inerrant copying would require is evident.

45 Gw, f. 15^{r}/23–4; Hy, f. 2^{r}/27–8. These errors were corrected by a later reader of Hy, who writes **lb** over **w** and interlineates **o** into 'a[w]{lb}y^{o}n', but as this was a later intervention, these words are counted as divergences in Table 3.1.

46 Mc, f. 2^{r} (*Tales*, 1.3942), and Ra^{I}, f. 22^{v}; En^{I}, f. 42^{v} (*Tales*, 1.3334), and Ds, f. 41^{r}.

47 Mc, f. 1^{v} (*Tales*, 1.3909), and Ra^{I}, f. 22^{r}.

48 Hy, f. 106^{v}/7–8, 9, and Pet, ff. 198^{r}/14–15, 198^{r}/16–17, twice cutting 'wyt*h*'; Hy, f. 107^{r}/7, and Pet, f. 198^{v}/10–11, adding 'and'; Hy, f. 119^{r}/16, 20, and Pet, f. 208^{r}/6–7, 10–11, twice adding 'the'.

49 Gw, f. 15^{r}/28; Hy, f. 2^{r}/2.

50 Lucas, *From Author to Audience*, 106.

A little inattentiveness does seem tolerated. Many of the divergences affect short words of just two or three letters, usually prepositions, articles or determiners, the use of which tends to reflect idiom more than grammar, and which are often interchangeable. For instance, the copyist of the prose *Brut* interchanges the words *that*, *the*, *their*, *there* and *this*, which often consist of just **þ** and an abbreviation or superscript: 'þat' becomes 'þ*er*', 'þe' becomes 'þ*a*t' and 'þis'.[51] Similarly, another copyist from this same exemplar, transcribing 'Warkworth's *Chronicle*', varies in whether to omit or include the definite article *the*. Four times the exemplar omits *the* in haste or careless error, but the copy includes it, so that, for instance, 'þ^{e} comons off cite' becomes 'the Comons of the Cite', or 'reule of Cite' becomes 'reule of the Cyte'.[52] Conversely, three times it is the copy which omits it clumsily, as when 'in the evenyng' becomes 'in evenynge'.[53] Too few patterns emerge consistently to suggest deliberate divergences; rather, it is easy to suggest physiological or linguistic pressures which would cause these changes: these closed-class words might be less memorable than open-class ones; *the* might be more vulnerable to elision when it occurs after prepositions; a copyist might misread the abbreviated forms with just **þ**; the speedy reading of an exemplar might make it easy to omit things this brief. The mechanics of writing, then, would let the scribe alter these words unwittingly.

Do any of the divergences, though, look witting and considered? Across other English manuscripts, many definitely do, of course; but in the sample of close copying, very few do. Sometimes the occasion invites witting changes: one copyist adds 'amen' to the end of a chapter of a chronicle likely because he ends his stint of copying there, whereas in his exemplar the same scribe continues for further chapters.[54] Otherwise, it is easiest to suggest a rationale for those changes that are recurrent, but the sample only includes two such patterns. A scribe of *The Canterbury Tales* repeatedly modifies the words which introduce speech, *quod* and *quoth*: four times where his exemplar has 'koth' he writes 'quod', each time restoring the form which modern editors think is Chaucer's; yet his motive does not seem to be authorial reconstruction, for twice more he turns the verb 'seith', which editors think is Chaucer's here, into 'quod' as well. The repetition

51 Gw, f. 15^{r}/6, 23; Hy, f. 2^{r}/6–7, 28.

52 Gw, f. 144^{r}/38, and Pet, f. 219^{v}/22; Gw, f. 144^{v}/24, and Pet, f. 220^{r}/19; and also Gw, f. 141^{v}/21, Pet, f. 216^{v}/13; Gw, f. 144^{r}/10, Pet, f. 219^{r}/27.

53 Gw, f. 141^{v}/14, and Pet, f. 216^{v}/5–6; and also Gw, f. 148^{r}/35, Pet, ff. 224^{r}/40–224^{v}/1; Gw, f. 148^{r}/40, Pet, f. 224^{v}/6.

54 Gw, f. 122^{r}/30, and Hy, f. 97^{v}/34. *Brut*, 372.33, also recounts Henry IV's death here, so 'amen' is appropriate for the narrative as well as for the scribal stint.

of this shift to 'quod' regardless of its authority suggests some conscious concern with this word.[55] Likewise, the copyist of 'Warkworth's *Chronicle*' some eight times removes the phrase '*et cetera*', which the exemplar often has at the end of chapterlets. The copyist seems to be tidying up these final words which sound a little rough and unfinished. Yet he does not do so thoroughly for he also preserves just as many uses of '*et cetera*' as he removes.[56] Other one-off changes might sometimes be interpreted as meaningful and meant: twelve open-class words diverge between two cognate copies of *The Canterbury Tales* in ways which it is difficult to explain as mechanical (Table 3.3). For instance, 'carie' varies with 'brynge' or 'corn' with 'flour', and there can be no visual or sonic confusion; they look like refinements of meaning (vi, viii). Yet even in these words where no mechanical explanation is forthcoming, interpreting the scribe's intention is difficult: why would the scribe reword the time from 'half wey p*r*ime' to 'almost pryme' (i)? Few of the divergences look like meaningful decisions.

Of those few divergences which might be interpreted as meaningful, many are most plausibly interpreted as meant for one purpose: to correct perceived errors in the exemplar by diverging from it. The sample of direct and cognate copies suggests that when scribes do alter things wittingly, they do so, ironically, in order to correct them as they copy. This tendency for scribes to correct what they copy, during the process of putting pen to paper (rather than in the later corrections which are the subject of the rest of this book), has long been recognized; it is often called 'conjecture' or interpolation in textual criticism.[57] George Kane says that the scribes offset a tendency to 'copy word for word' with a willingness 'to alter the substance of their copy' in order to produce 'a more correct' text, whether in its basic intelligibility or its style.[58] The desire for intelligibility seems to drive some of the divergences in the direct and cognate copies from what

55 En^{I}, ff. 123^{r} (*Tales*, IV.1215), 123^{v} (IV.1243), 124^{v} (IV.1296), 125^{r} (IV.1346 twice), 126^{r} (IV.1419), and Ds, ff. 115^{v}, 116^{v}, 117^{r}, 118^{r}. By contrast, one copyist of *Piers Plowman* writes 'Coth' where the cognate copies have 'Quod': Cot, f. 273^{r} (*Piers B*, XIX.207), and cf. Bo, f .84^{r}, and Bm, f. 84^{r}. Phillips, 'Seeing Red', 450, notes another scribe of *Piers* modifying 'quod' to 'seide'.

56 For cuts, see Gw, f. 141^{r}/5, and Pet, f. 215^{v}/27; Gw, f. 141^{r}/7, Pet, f. 215^{v}/29; Gw, f. 141^{v}/12, Pet f. 216^{v}/3; Gw, f. 141^{v}/20, Pet, f. 216^{v}/12; Gw, f. 144^{r}/19, Pet, f. 219^{r}/39; Gw, f. 144^{r}/43, in the addition in the foot margin, and Pet, f. 219^{v}/25; Gw, f. 144^{v}/5, Pet, f. 219^{v}/35; Gw, f. 144^{v}/14, Pet, f. 220^{r}/7; Gw, f. 148^{v}/29, Pet, f. 225^{r}/1. Table 3.1 counts '*et cetera*' as two words of divergence, because of the word-division in the MSS. One third possible recurrent pattern is 'manly' becoming 'manfully' twice (Gw, f. 121^{r}/28, 31, and Hy, f. 96^{v}/25, 28), but the copyist also preserves his exemplar's 'manly' on the next four occasions (Gw, f. 121^{r}/33, 35, f. 121^{v}/1, 3, and Hy, ff. 96^{v}/30, 32, 35, and 97^{r}/1).

57 For discussion, see Reeve, *Manuscripts and Methods*, 147.

58 *Piers A*, ed. Kane, 128; see also 136, with illustrations 128–36.

Table 3.3 *Variants in open-class words which are difficult to explain 'mechanically' in sampled passages of Mc and Ra*^{I}

	Tales	Chicago, UL, MS 564		BodL, MS Rawl. poet. 141	
i)	I.3906	Lo depford *and* hit is half wey p*r*ime	1^{v}	Lo depford *and* hit is almost pryme	21^{v}
ii)	I.3921	Aat Trumpyngton not fer fro caunterbrugge	2^{r}	AT trompyngton not fer fro Ca[<unt*er*>]{m~}brigge	22^{r}
iii)	I.3989	And namely þ*er* was a grete colage	3^{r}	And namely ther was a gret colage *and* an huge	23^{r}
iv)	I.4002	þ*er*e were þan ȝonge pore scoleres to	3^{r}	Ther were then yonge scoleres two.	23^{r}
v)	I.4009	And hardely þei durste ley here nek	3^{v}	And hardely thei durst yeue hur necke	23^{v}
vi)	I.4032	To grynde oure corn *and* carie hit home ageyn	3^{v}	To grynde oure corn *and* brynge hit hom a yeyne.	23^{v}
vii)	I.4061	Byhynde þe mylle vnd*ur* a lefsell	4^{r}	Bi hynde the dore vnder a lesell	24^{r}
viii)	I.4093	He half a busshell of her flour hath take	4^{v}	He half a busshel of hure corn hath take	24^{v}
ix)	VII.436	Nowe longe mote þ*o*u s*ir* ryde by þe cost	68^{v}	Longe mot thou sir*e* ryde bi cost.	84^{r}
x)	VII.453	A lord lord ih*esu*s þy name how m*er*ueylous	69^{r}	A lord Ih*esus* in heuene how meruelows	84^{r}
xi)	VII.508	his aue maria as he goth by þe wey	70^{r}	His aue maria as he wente bi the way	85^{r}
xii)	VII.509	Þus hath þe wydewe her lyttell chyld ytauht	70^{r}	¶ Thus hath the wydewe hur lytel sone taught	85^{r}

are evidently errors in the exemplar. For example, one exemplar garbled the verb *were* as 'warne' when his ear got caught by the next word, 'sworne', so that he wrote 'warne sworne'; but the person copying this wrote 'wer*e* sworne' instead, correctly.[59] All the scribes of direct or cognate copies seem capable of such divergences which serve to correct things. One of the most divergent scribes, of a cognate copy of *Piers Plowman*, nonetheless manages to notice when the inherited text which two other copies give as 'he lerid to be lee' should be 'he lerid to be leel' for *loyal*, and he converts 'astromye' into 'ast*ro*nomye', which suggests that he saw the shorter form as an error. His infidelity results in a more correct sense of what Langland seemingly said here.[60] At the other end of the scale of accuracy, in the astonishingly

[59] Mm, f. 36^{r} (*Tales*, I.3301); Gl, f. 17^{v}.

[60] Cot, f. 273^{v} (*Piers B*, XIX.244, 250); cf. Bo, f. 84^{v}, and Bm, f. 84^{v}. Cf. Blake, 'Astromye', who doubts that 'astromye' could be a malapropism in 'The Miller's Tale'.

meticulous copy of *The Gilte Legende*, there are only fifteen divergences and three of them correct evident errors in the exemplar: for instance, the exemplar describes early Christians hiding 'for drede of grete persecion', but the copyist rightly says that they hid 'for drede of grete persecucion'.[61] The scribe copying, the experienced Ricardus Franciscus, seems to recognize, like a palaeographer or editor, that two adjacent syllables ending with c could cause elision; so he corrects while he copies, with alertness and with reflection on scribal craft and its hiccups.[62]

A corrective spirit also inspires some of the variants which are less successful: that is, even erroneous variation often seems to be intended as correction during the process of copying. For example, scribes in the fifteenth century have problems with some of the slightly archaic vocabulary of the fourteenth-century poets Chaucer and Langland; they modify it – mistakenly, according to modern editors, but likely in a spirit of correcting what seemed incomprehensible. One direct copy of *The Canterbury Tales* replaces 'rodde' for *rood* (*face, complexion*) with 'hed'. This could be an auditory slip, caused by the presence of the word 'red' further along the line; or it could be deliberate in removing what seemed odd: the odd spelling of *rood* with single <o> and double <dd> might be puzzling and 'hed', a proximate body-part, might be the solution.[63] One scribe of a copy of *Piers Plowman* three times removes fairly rare forms of words which the scribes of two cognate copies preserve: their 'p*r*isoun' (*prisoner*) becomes his 'prysoune*r*'; tellingly, lots of other scribes make this change, as the language finally did, perhaps because of the confusing polysemy of *prison* as both a place and a person.[64] There is a question in such cases whether the scribe intends assimilation to what he considers good English or emendation of what he judges to be a poor exemplar – a change of *langue* or *parole*; but what is evident is the generally corrective attitude behind such conjecture. Conjecture is rarer than mechanical error; as Housman noted, mechanical error might occur everywhere, conjecture only when there is something troubling in the exemplar.[65] But when variation does not seem merely mechanical, then the likeliest intention is often to conjecture a correction.

61 D, f. 37v (*Gilte*, 124.41), and H2, f. 163r. See also D, f. 38v (*Gilte*, 124.197: 'belue' for *believe*), and H2, f. 164v; D, f. 39r ('tha' for *that*, where *Gilte*, 124.270 has 'tho that'), and H2, f. 164r.

62 Driver, 'Me fault faire', 442–3, lists MSS by Ricardus Franciscus, scribe of H2.

63 En1, f. 42r (*Tales*, I.3317: 'His rodde was rede'), and Ds, f. 40v ('His hed was red').

64 Cf. Cot, f. 263v, with Bo, f. 76r, and Bm, f. 76r, and the textual apparatus to *Piers B*, XVIII.58; *MED*, *prisoun* (*n*.) 7.

65 Housman, 'Application of Thought to Textual Criticism', 12. He calls this conjectural rewriting 'interpolation'.

That intention to get things right is visible most strikingly in one final set of divergences: points where the scribe does not in fact copy anything but leaves a gap. This is a relatively rare phenomenon. For example, among the fifty-two once separate manuscripts in the Huntington Library, it occurs in only ten of them and in most only once or a few times.[66] Among the sample of direct and cognate copies, it is only found in a direct copy of *The Canterbury Tales* which was finished by Geoffrey Spirleng in 1476. He leaves gaps in total at twenty points for which the exemplar survives for comparison (listed in Table 3.4) and at another twenty points (not discussed here). In (x) and (xi) he is baffled by words quite legible in his exemplar but seemingly incomprehensible to him: the word 'rood' (*face, complexion*), which bothered another scribe, and the verb 'clippe' (*to shave or cut*). Neither word is extremely rare, so it is not clear what upsets him; it is possible that he is worried that these are the homographs *rood* meaning *the cross* or perhaps *rod*, a sexual euphemism, and *clip* meaning *embrace*, none of which would fit the context and some of which would be scandalous. It is possible that the handwriting of the exemplar confused him with 'clippe', as the exemplar has a ligature joining the letters **cli** so that they look like **c** and a large two-compartment **a** to give 'cappe' which would again not make sense.[67] Once he leaves a gap where the text in the exemplar is written over erasure which might make him nervous of copying it (vii). Otherwise, it just seems that the vocabulary is unusual, such as 'opie' and 'sparth' (v, viii), or is a name which cannot be guessed (xv–xvi, xviii). Other scribes have problems with the same sorts of thing.[68] Sometimes the exemplar has mangled this unusual vocabulary, as it does the rare scientific words *ceruse* and *narcotic* (ii, v), and Spirleng chooses not to reproduce this nonsense. Twice he writes the word from the exemplar in the margin, rather than using it to fill the gap. He evidently can read his exemplar but does not want to copy something which seems to him incorrect; he leaves these words for future consideration and debate (xvii–xviii). This reticence is typical. These gaps seem to reflect the impulse to get things right which influences the process of correcting as one copies too. These gaps for words which scribes cannot read are not common in English manuscripts, except when scribes leave gaps where the exemplar is missing a whole line or more of verse (as

[66] I shall discuss this phenomenon in 'When Scribes Won't Write'.

[67] Mm, f. 36v (*Tales*, I.3326). Elsewhere, Spirleng copies 'clyppe or shere' without trouble: Gl, f. 30r (VII.2067).

[68] E.g., cf. (xvi) with BodL, MS Arch. Selden B.14, f. 145v, which leaves a gap for 'atazir' (*Tales*, II.305). Manly and Rickert (eds.), *Text of the Canterbury Tales*, vol. V, 468, records numerous scribes mangling this word.

Table 3.4 *Gaps left in part of Gl, for which the exemplar survives in Mm*

Tales	CUL, MS Mm.2.5	folio	GUL, MS Hunter 197 (U.1.1)	folio
i) I.357	An anclas ande a gisperal of silke	4^{v}	An <gap> and a gysperall of sylk	1^{r}
ii) I.630	Boras orsur*e* ne oylle of tartr*e* noone	7^{v}	Boras <gap> ne oyle of tartre non	2^{v}
iii) I.1376	Beforne his celle fantastyke	15^{v}	By forne hise <gap> fantastyke	5^{v}
iv) I.1385	Hym thouȝht howe þat þe wenched godde M*er*curye	15^{v}	Hym thought how þat þe <gap> god Mercurie	5^{v}
v) I.1472	With nertok*es* and opie of thebes fyne	16^{v}	With <gap> and <gap> of thebes fyne	6^{r}
vi) I.1941	Ne narciscus of fair*e* of ȝor*e* a gone	21^{v}	Ne Narciscus of Fayrye of <gap> a gone	9^{r}
vii) I.1962	A boue hir*e* heuede [->]{hire dowues flat}erynge	22^{r}	Above hir hed <gap>	9^{r}
viii) I.2520	He hath a sparth of xx. li~ of weȝhte	28^{r}	He hath a <gap> of xxli of wyght	12^{r}
ix) I.3076	With all thanes her*e* of my pa*r*leme*n*te	34^{r}	With alle <gap> of this my parlemente	16^{r}
x) I.3317	His rood was reede his eyen gray as goose	36^{v}	His <gap> was reed his eyen gray as goos	17^{v}
xi) I.3326	Wele coude he lete blode clippe and schaue	36^{v}	Weel coude he lete blode <gap> and shaue	17^{v}
xii) I.3480	Ther with ye myȝht spell he seith onon riȝhtes	38^{r}	Ther*e* w*ith* ye myght s<gap> a non rightes	18^{v}
xiii) I. 3485	For þe nyȝhtes verye þe white pat*er* nost*er*	38^{r}	For þe nyghtes verye <gap> white p*at*er nost*er*	18^{v}
xiv) I.4004	Testyff þei wer*e* and lustiff for to pleye	44^{r}	<gap> they were and lusty for to pleye	21^{v}
xv) *Gam.*3	Sir Iohn of koundes was his name	48^{v}	Sir Iohn of <gap> was his name	24^{r}
xvi) II.305	O mars o ataȝir as in this caase	81^{v}	O mars o <gap> as in this caas	35^{v}
xvii) II.782	Fy manyssh. fy. o nay be god I lye	86^{v}	Fy <gap> fy o nay by god I lye	36^{r}[1]
xviii) IV.1373	The peple of god and made hym Marche	101^{r}	The peple of god and made hym <gap>	40^{v}[2]
xix) IV.87–90	To assur*e* enchaunted for to be And carie in a Cofr*e* or in a lappe But opon peyn of his hede of f[y]{o}r to swappe Þat no man schuld knowe of his entente ¶ But at Boleyn to his suster der*e* [. . .]	146^{v}	To assure enchaunced for to be And cary in a cofre or in a lappe And vpon peyne of his hed of for to swappe That no man shuld knowe of his entente <gap for a whole line> ¶ But at Boleyn to his suster dere [. . .]	106^{v}
xx) IV.599	Eu*er* full of clappyng der*e* ynowe a Iane	151^{r}	Eu*er* full of clappyng <gap>	108^{v}

1 Here the scribe of Gl writes 'manyssh' in the adjacent gutter.

2 Here the scribe of Gl writes '+ marche' in the adjacent gutter.

in xix in Table 3.4 and as in Chapter 10). But the fact that these gaps exist at all shows that the scribes were, at least intermittently, thinking about what they were copying, and choosing not to copy things they thought they could not render correctly. It is ironic that the gaps show that the scribes are unable to think *enough* about the solution to what puzzles them, so that they create further variance: a little cognition is a dangerous thing in textual traditions. But the gaps suggest that they are at least thinking while copying, and what they think about is how to reproduce things carefully.

These moments of divergence in corrective rewriting and in gaps throw light on two things. First, they illuminate the process of accurate copying itself. Because the scribe sometimes makes a thoughtful choice to vary his text, or not to copy a word in it, then the longer tranche of time when he does not vary or interrupt the text might itself be thoughtful. The ability to switch from exact reproduction to varying in this sensible way seems to suggest that the scribe is thinking about what he copies. If the word *thinking* seems to overstate what might lie behind reproduction, then at least *attention* or *attentiveness* might describe the craftsmanship of scribes. As the sociologist Richard Sennett puts it, we must not belittle the 'manual skill' of craftsmen; craftsmanship involves 'the special human condition of being engaged', and engagement is what is evident in the effort to copy accurately.[69] Especially given that rewriting was an option, this lack of rewriting looks like a choice that scribes made knowingly and effortfully. Some words of course do vary, often evidently from brief lapses in concentration, say, overlooking small words, hindered by the physiology of language or the materials of writing. But when scribes deliberately change what they copy, many of their changes are corrective in spirit. Even if the divergences result in versions of the text which modern editors reject, those versions can plausibly be explained as corrections of what was in the exemplar or cognate copies. Behind accurate copying, which is more common than we sometimes think, and behind variant copying, there is often a conscious effort to be correct.

In praise of correcting

However, this effort to be correct is most evident when it goes awry, as the scribe conjectures some changes or leaves gaps. And studying these changes or gaps made while copying is difficult because (as was noted) it is seldom

[69] Sennett, *Craftsman*, 20.

possible to be sure whether a scribe is introducing these modifications or is unchangingly copying a text that includes them. Direct and cognate copies are seldom identified and, when they are, they contain few such visible divergences. It is not, then, often possible to demonstrate a scribe's will to be correct, nor other elements of his thinking, from his copying alone. There is, though, one sort of change which is visible in almost every manuscript in English from these centuries: not change between exemplar and direct copy or between cognate copies but change visibly within each copy itself where the scribe writes one thing and then changes it to another thing. These changes are what palaeographers usually call corrections: changes made after the scribe has already copied something, by techniques such as erasing, interlining and so on. These changes occur (as the rest of this book shows) in almost every manuscript, whether we have its parents or siblings to consult or not, and they offer excellent evidence of scribes' thinking – and of their thinking, obviously, about correctness of various sorts.

It is a surer claim that these corrections involve conscious thought than it is that divergences during copying do. In reading a faulty line in the exemplar and then writing it out as a much more sensible line in the copy, it is just possible that the scribe effects the corrective divergence without recognizing it. If he were reading and writing quickly, he might almost slip into something more grammatical. But in reading a faulty line which he has already written out and then changing it to something different a second time, he needs to recognize what he is doing. Correcting involves visible techniques which disturb the surface of the page and thereby render the error and its remedy noticeable (as Chapter 5 argues). And correcting involves a special class of thought: retrospection. This retrospection is obvious, of course, when correcting is done by another scribe or done later. Yet any correction, even just interrupting the run of the pen over the page (*currente calamo*), is a correction of at least some tiny piece of a text, even of just a premature letter, *after* the piece has been written. That retrospection might occur only a split second later, but the delay involves conscious recognition of, and reflection on, one's own copying. In such moments, the scribe's work is not automatic: he looks backwards and reflects on it. As Richard Sennett proposed, correcting is at the heart of the craftsman's acts of attention.[70]

It could therefore be suggested that correcting is more interesting than variant copying because it more surely involves conscious thought. That would in some ways support the warnings of editors against rating

[70] *Ibid.*, 134, 159–60.

intelligence in variance too highly, even corrective conjecture. George Kane observes scribes' conjectures in their copies but warns that such activity was not 'systematic' nor the result of 'reflection'.[71] Jill Mann warns that we cannot consider the scribe of the earliest two copies of *The Canterbury Tales* to be knowingly correcting the metre where one of his copies is better; we should consider him rather to be unknowingly bungling it in the other.[72] The mistakenness of finding intention in all variation or error was wittily argued by Sebastiano Timpanaro, when he criticized the concept of 'Freudian slips' and insisted that we could explain muddled words by palaeographical, linguistic and physiological causes.[73] We might well thus explain lots of the variance which arose in English texts *during* the process of copying. Yet while it is difficult to prove that a divergence in copying was even created by the scribe, let alone that it was intended, let alone that the intention was corrective, it is equally difficult to describe any correction, which is made visibly on the surface of the previously copied page and is made retrospectively, as completely mechanical. So divergences in the copying of manuscripts might be the more boring, often accidental phenomenon, whereas correcting after copying is more interesting as it is more likely to be intended and thought about.

This difference emerges if we consider some of the things which the scribes of direct and cognate copies fix in what they have already written. They effected these corrections by a variety of methods, some of which, such as marginal additions, might have been done at a much later stage, while others give no evidence of when they were made. Many, though, show some attention to the process of copying and a reflective understanding of it. The errors which prompt the corrections betray the sort of lapses in consciousness or concentration typical of divergences between copies. For example, in a direct copy of *The Canterbury Tales*: the copyist writes, 'This knave wente hym vp full [fir] sturdely', apparently conflating the two adjacent words 'full' and 'sturdely' into something beginning 'fir', perhaps because the crossbar in **t** of **stu** makes the long **s** and **u** look like the preceding **fu**; but he realizes after only three letters and starts again.[74] Likewise, the scribes of William Langland's *Piers Plowman* sometimes slip by jumping ahead or back to the alliterating words, which presumably

71 *Piers A*, ed. Kane, contrasting 128, 145–6. This paragraph is repeated from Wakelin, 'Editing and Correcting', 254–5.

72 Mann, 'Chaucer's Meter'.

73 Timpanaro, *Freudian Slip*, 21–2, and on such slips 30–1, 35–7, 63–4, 97–100; Timpanaro, *Il lapsus freudiano*, 11–12, and 20–1, 25–6, 51–2, 81–4.

74 Gl, f. 18^{v} (*Tales*, 1.3434); cf. Mm, f. 37^{v}.

stuck in a scribe's mind given their prominence of sound and sense; but the scribes also spot their attraction to these alliterating words and stop themselves from jumping to them.[75] Copying was prone to unconscious slips of sight and sound, but some consciousness of those risks emerges through correcting.

What is most striking in the sample of direct or cognate copies is the attempt to keep the text the same. The corrections tend not to make the copy less like its exemplar or cognates; they tend, instead, to bring the copies in line. This can be seen from the tally of the effect of the corrections. The sample of direct copies includes some forty-five corrections, which we can compare with what was in the exemplars (the final two columns in Table 3.1); the sample of cognate copies includes some sixty-seven corrections, here counted in all the cognate copies, as each can be measured against the others (the final two columns in Table 3.2).[76] This gives 112 corrections for which we can fairly guess what the scribe was reproducing, and of them 83 per cent (93 of 112) achieve a 'centripetal' effect of restoring the text found in the direct exemplar or converging with that found in cognate copies. The corrections remove divergence. This is close to the typical rate of 'centripetal' correcting found in a larger sample of corrections from the Huntington Library, where 84 per cent are centripetal (in Table 6.4 below).

It should also be noted of the direct copies, that their exemplars also contained corrections, affecting a total of 168 words (not counted in Table 3.1).[77] By chance, the direct exemplars include more corrections than the direct copies do, half as many again; perhaps the evident carefulness of the scribes of the copies meant that they made fewer errors which needed fixing. Yet the corrections in the exemplars are also signs of careful work as the scribes stop and fix their faults: these corrections likely prevent some sort of divergence from the exemplars' exemplars in turn – though that can only be speculation without finding those lost manuscripts. They certainly prevent problems in these exemplars which the scribes of the direct copies would have had to solve, diverging in some other way. And the direct copyists almost always follow the corrections they find in their exemplars except in eight of the 168 words.[78] For example, the later copy of 'Warkworth's *Chronicle*' includes almost all of the frequent corrections in its

75 Bo, f. 85^{v} (*Piers B*, XIX.325); Bm, f. 53^{v} (XIII.268), 76^{r} (XVIII.7); possibly Cot, f. 264^{r} (XVIII.99).

76 The sample also included an unusually large number of corrections made by much later, sixteenth-century readers, which are ignored for present purposes.

77 En^{1} = 16 corrections; Mm = 15; D = 3 (debatable: 3 words on D, f. 37^{v}/a7 over erasure?); Gw (section d) = 32; Hy = 38; Gw (section f) = 64.

78 The exceptions: En^{1}, f. 41^{v}, where 'as' is over erasure, but Ds, f. 40^{r} (*Tales*, I.3257) diverges with 'so'; Hy, f. 113^{r}, where 'so *n*¯nes' has a macron for abbreviated **n** added, but Pet, f. 203^{v}, leaves a

exemplar, including an addition two lines long in the bottom margin of the exemplar which is seamlessly incorporated into the copy; the correct*ed* text is assumed to be the *correct* text.[79] There is just one exception, when the copyist omits one interlineation of the words 'þ^e day a for*e*' in the exemplar, perhaps because they are difficult to see squashed between the lines.[80]

What is the effect of the corrections in the copies alongside the divergences which remain? There was not, of course, that much divergence to remove: in the direct copies correcting reduces the rate of divergence by only a fraction of a percent and in the cognate copies only from 4 per cent to 3 per cent. Moreover, divergences do remain in each of these copies: there are roughly ten times as many words diverging as there are words corrected to remove divergence: in direct copies 376 with 39 (Table 3.1), in cognate copies 518 with 54 (Table 3.2). This must be stressed: there are still numerous divergences in the direct and cognate copies after correcting. Nonetheless, the direction of correction is clear: it does lessen the amount of divergence. For example, in one direct copy of *The Canterbury Tales*, there are 104 divergent words (Tables 3.1, a.i, a.ii); eight of them look like conjectural improvements of things that the exemplar had got wrong, so perhaps there are ninety-six new errors; but ten more errors are then corrected after copying in ways which bring exemplar and copy in line. Similarly, in the three cognate copies of *Piers Plowman* (Table 3.2, b.i–b.iii) there are ninety-six divergences between the copies, but a further forty-two divergences are prevented by corrections which result in a text identical to that of the other two cognate copies. Without having a soundly established authorial text to collate, scribes might best judge what constitutes a good correction by seeing whether it accords with their exemplars; on forty-two occasions, this is what these three scribes of *Piers Plowman* seem to do, bringing the copies closer together, even down to the minutiae of spelling sometimes.[81]

Closer but not always identical: the corrections are not, it must be stressed, always successful in preventing divergences. The correcting only

gap for the whole word; Hy, f. 114^r, where 'þe' is added at a line-break, but Pet, f. 204^r, skips two words when copying this line-break; Hy, f. 114^r, where 'w[-]{e} rayned' has one letter over erasure, but Pet, f. 204^r, rightly diverges with 'war*e* rayned'.

79 For the long addition, see Gw, f. 144^r, included into Pet, f. 219^v/23–5. Matheson (ed.), *Death and Dissent*, 78, suggests that this correction in Gw reveals that the scribe is composing the text as he goes along in this MS, but I think that other slips of the pen suggest that he is copying.

80 Gw, f. 148^r/3, and Pet, f. 223^v/4.

81 E.g., Bm, ff. 55^r, 'mon^^eþ' (*Piers B*, XIII.336), 84^r, 'gr^^eate' (XIX.208), bringing it in line with Bo, ff. 55^r, 84^r ('moneþ', 'grete'), but not Cot, ff. 236^v, 273^r ('monthe', 'gret').

removes divergence in 83 per cent of cases: a sixth of the corrections (17 per cent) let the copy continue to diverge or in a few cases even create new divergence. Yet these erroneous corrections are often explicable if we turn from the aggregate to the particulars. Two corrections in the copies of *Piers Plowman* leave the three manuscripts diverging, but it is an uncorrected manuscript which is the odd one out of the three.[82] Otherwise, all the corrections to these copies of *Piers Plowman* which still diverge from the shared text occur in the slightly later copy, whose scribe seems to be correcting by guesswork, at some time after his copying, to judge by the different colour of his ink, rather than by consulting his exemplar.[83] It is just one person whose efforts go wrong here because he did not have the exemplar to hand. The situation sometimes limits what corrections can achieve.

Even with these corrections which not only preserve but introduce divergence, though, it is often plausible to suggest a corrective intention. This scribe of *Piers Plowman* did not have the right solutions but he did identify problems and try to fix them. Another telling example emerges in one cognate copy of *The Canterbury Tales*, where the scribe corrects what looks like it was the older form of the place-name 'Caunt*er*brigge' to the newer form 'Ca[unt*er*]{m~}brigge'. He turns the two minims of **u** into the first two minims of **m**, adds a third minim and adds a line to fill the space (represented by ~ in the transcription) over a longer erasure, likely of **nt** and an abbreviation for ***er***.[84] Later one copy rhymes 'Cambrugge' with 'a grete colage' (*college*) but the other copy expands the phrase – this time before or during copying, not through correcting – to 'a gret colage *and* an huge' as though it would rhyme better with 'Cambrigge'.[85] Because we have these cognate copies, we can guess that the latter corrective addition of '*and* an huge' for the sake of rhyme was most likely this scribe's conscious choice but we cannot be sure. But we can be sure that the change of 'Caunt*er*brigge' to 'Ca[unt*er*]{m~}brigge' was done by this scribe and done knowingly, because he did it visibly later by correcting, stopping to go back and put right an obsolescent place-name. Unlike other conjectures while copying, in his correcting we have evidence on the page

[82] Bm, f. 84ʳ corrected (*Piers B*, xix.207), Bo, f. 84ʳ, and cf. Cot, f. 273ʳ (diverging); Bm, f. 76ʳ corrected (*Piers B*, xviii.70), Bo, f. 76ʳ, and cf. Cot, f. 263ᵛ diverging.

[83] Cot, ff. 235ᵛ (*Piers B*, xiii.265, 273), 236ʳ (xiii.300), 236ᵛ (xiii.325, 340), 273ʳ (xix.246 twice), 277ᵛ (xix.312). *Piers B*, xix.312 is also corrected the same way in Bm, f. 85ʳ, but this counts as divergence, because Bo, f. 85ʳ, still differs.

[84] Ra¹, f. 22ʳ (*Tales*, i.3921); cf. Mc, f. 2ʳ.

[85] Mc, f. 3ʳ (*Tales*, i.3989–90), and Ra¹, f. 23ʳ.

of him thinking – or rather rethinking. And although he is wrong this time, what he seems to be thinking about is getting things right. Thorlac Turville-Petre noted two scribes who correct *Piers Plowman* with 'pedantic unease' and insufficient understanding, but who nonetheless are impressive for their 'very considerable trouble . . . to get their text right, if possible even righter than their exemplar'.[86] The description could apply here: correcting sometimes included a willingness to rewrite what one finds in an exemplar to restore what seems the better text – a different sort of corrective motive.

We find, then, not correct*ness* in the text but the pursuit of correct*ing* in the experience of the scribes. Most of their correcting, however, proves centripetal, consensual, faithful to the exemplar, as is their dutiful copying: the goal seems to be to reproduce the textual tradition which the scribe found in his exemplar. This characteristic of much scribal copying – *much* but not *all* – is important as part of the context for correcting. If we considered variance the predominant goal of scribes, then correcting would seem almost inexplicable, even unthinkable; but neither accurate copying nor the decision to correct are outlandish. Through such efforts we see the attentiveness and intelligence with which scribes could work. The visible attention in conjectures and corrections suggests the attention latent when copying proceeds without such a struggle. There might be fluctuations in the kind of attention scribes exercise in such wholesale copying, fleeting conjectures or retrospective corrections. Roy Michael Liuzza describes some scribes of Old English usefully as shifting not in and out of consciousness but between different kinds of thinking 'from moment to moment'. Sometimes, the scribe is an artist of visual reproduction, at other times an 'editor' of a text he interprets in linguistic and literary ways; but the shifts between these roles are 'to a great extent under his conscious control'.[87] A fuller study of copying would attend to this temporal flux in that process; palaeography is often best understood as a sort of biography or narrative of a scribe's activities changing over time.[88] There is, though, a problem of evidence for some stretches of the story of the scribe's work: we only have sure evidence of a scribe's thoughts intermittently, in his conjectures and his corrections; the seamless stretches of close copying are difficult to peer through for glimpses of the scribe's consciousness. It is helpful, then,

86 Turville-Petre, 'Putting It Right', 41, 51.
87 Liuzza, 'Scribal Habit', 146, 164. See also Parkes, *Their Hands Before Our Eyes*, 67.
88 See also Wakelin, 'Writing the Words', 34–8.

to focus primarily on correcting for evidence of scribes' experiences and intentions (as the rest of this book will). The corrections reveal that the craftsman's work is not always, if ever, mechanical or effortless; in correcting we see the craftsman thinking.

CHAPTER 4

People and institutions

For [þei] correctours claweþ her on. *and* correcteþ first ȝoure silue
⌐þi ye⌐
London, British Library, MS Add. 10574, f. 39v
William Langland, *The Vision of Piers Plowman*, the B-text, x.289

Whose attention and intelligence were being exercised in correcting? As far as can be gauged, the majority of correcting in books in English was done by the scribe whose work is being corrected at the point in question. These scribes did also inherit centuries-old procedures for getting their work checked and corrected by others, and such interventions by other people occur in a large minority of cases. But the making of books in English, dispersed among varied agents, was only occasionally organized to allow consistent collaboration, so unsurprisingly much correcting was done by the scribe himself. There were many people working as scribes for themselves or in freelance employment alongside other duties – a growing number of people thanks to increasing literacy, faster styles of script and cheaper materials in the fourteenth and fifteenth centuries. The dispersal of writing among more but independent scribes sets the scene for scribes to correct their own copies – exercising and fostering careful thought about their craft and about the works they passed on.

This tendency for corrections to be done by the person whose copying is being corrected has been proposed before.[1] It might be confirmed by the sample of English manuscripts from the Huntington Library. Confirmation is not easy: corrections are often difficult to apportion with surety, especially in a broad survey with only a short amount of time to get to know each scribe. Also, single or few letters are riskily small samples to

[1] Petti, *English Literary Hands*, 28. By contrast, Kerby-Fulton, Hilmo and Olson, *Opening Up Middle English Manuscripts*, 208, 214, suggest that correction was 'often the annotator's job' and refer to the 'annotator-corrector' as a common combined role distinct from the 'rubricators'. The HEHL sample suggests different patterns, although correction is sometimes combined with rubrication, as they propose elsewhere (235–6).

identify securely: a scribe correcting himself often writes less fluently and much smaller than he usually does, and sometimes with different pens or ink, so that his writing might look different. Conversely, somebody else correcting another scribe's work might try to imitate its look and conceal the interference.[2] Often the correction consists only of subpuncting with dots or of crossing out which defy easy identification. Yet sometimes distinctive combinations of dots or lines or the colours of ink strongly suggest that a mark is by somebody identifiable elsewhere. The principle of Ockham's razor can be applied to recurring patterns without evidence to the contrary to group similar contributions. The same principle, though, must not prejudice us to expect fewer rather than more hands correcting. So, in surveying the Huntington Library's books, it was important to balance the need to offer a judgement, however tentative, with the need not to oversimplify. Discounting complete puzzles, then, four-fifths of the corrections could be linked to the scribe or to somebody else; almost a fifth (18 per cent or 1,640 of 9,220) had to be classified as 'uncertain'.

With those deducted, the overall results show a clear tendency for correcting to be done by the people who do the copying itself. Nearly 62 per cent of corrections (5,733 of 9,220) are recognizably the work of the scribe who is copying the passage being corrected (Table 4.1). Or removing those corrections which could not be apportioned, the sample shrinks, and of the remainder nearly 76 per cent (5,733 of 7,580) are apportionable to the scribe in question. Moreover, that proportion almost certainly under-records self-correction, for many of the fifth which were impossible to apportion with certainty are likely by the scribe as well, especially if the scribe is involved in other changes nearby. So the commonest scenario is for scribes to correct their own work.

Calling that person the *scribe* requires some definition. By *scribe* this book means simply *the person currently wielding a pen* and makes no claim about whether that was a full-time job or a temporary activity, vocational, paid or unpaid. Identifying the occupation of these people is not the primary focus of this book; this book does not use the corrections as evidence for the wider conditions of book production such as training or working habits. It is, though, useful to consider what the occupations or situations are within which scribes might correct their work. Who were these people and which milieux or institutions might encourage this self-correction? (The first section of this chapter considers two important milieux for such self-correction.)

[2] Lemaire, *Introduction*, 180, and Hudson (ed.), *English Wycliffite Sermons*, 142, offer warnings.

Table 4.1 *The person responsible for corrections for manuscripts in English in the HEHL*

shelfmark	contents	corrections	unclear	the scribe	scribe and collaborator	collaborator alone	later user
El. 26.A.13: I	Hoccleve, *The Regiment of Princes*	587	7 1%	565 96%	13 2%	2 0%[1]	–
El. 26.A.13: II	*Joseph and Asenath*	16	1 6%	14 88%	1 6%	–	–
El. 26.A.17	Gower, *Confessio amantis*	52	–	46 87%	–	–	6 12%
El. 26.C.9	Chaucer, *The Canterbury Tales*	143	16 11%	117 82%	–	–	10 7%
El. 35.B.63	Edward of York, *Master of Game*	134	25 19%	65 49%	–	8 6%	36 27%
HM 1	Towneley plays	170	16 9%	110 65%	4 2%	23 14%	17 10%
HM 55	Capgrave, *St Norbert*	111	25 23%	82 74%	–	–	4 4%
HM 58	*Agnus castus*; recipes	154	7 5%	146 95%	–	–	1 1%
HM 64	medicine	138	21 15%	114 83%	–	–	3 2%
HM 111	Hoccleve, short poems	51	–	51 100%	–	–	–
HM 112	Hilton, *The Scale of Perfection*	489	125 26%	103 21%	–	261 53%	–
HM 113	prose *Brut*	44	1 2%	41 93%	–	–	2 5%
HM 114	Langland, *Piers*; Chaucer, *Troilus, etc.*	373	44 12%	329 88%	–	–	–
HM 115	Lydgate, *Life of Our Lady*	73	7 10%	66 90%	–	–	–
HM 124	*Speculum Christiani*	68	13 19%	52 76%	–	–	3 4%
HM 125	*Prick of Conscience*	64	7 11%	52 81%	–	–	5 8%
HM 126	Rob. of Gloucester, *Chronicle*	128	23 18%	99 77%	–	6 5%	–
HM 127	religious miscellany	63	10 16%	37 59%	3 5%	13 21%	–
HM 128	*Prick of Conscience*; Langland, *Piers*	787	439 56%	208 26%	–	140 18%	–

(*cont.*)

Table 4.1 *cont.*

shelfmark	contents	corrections	unclear	the scribe	scribe and collaborator	collaborator alone	later user
HM 129	*Northern Homily Cycle*	500	87 17%	407 81%	–	–	6 1%
HM 130	*Prick of Conscience*	442	19 4%	7 2%	–	416 94%	–
HM 131	prose *Brut*	8	1 13%	7 88%	–	–	–
HM 133	prose *Brut*	343	51 15%	208 61%	–	84 24%	–
HM 134	Wycliffite New Testament	428	57 13%	191 45%	25 6%	155 36%	–
HM 135	Hoccleve, *The Regiment of Princes*	22	7 32%	15 68%	–	–	–
HM 136	prose *Brut*	57	2 4%	43 75%	–	–	12 21%
HM 137	Langland, *Piers*	75	29 39%	40 53%	–	–	6 8%
HM 139	*Prick of Conscience*	54	21 39%	32 59%	–	–	1 2%
HM 140	miscellany	74	34 46%	39 53%	–	1 1%	–
HM 142	religious miscellany	25	5 20%	14 56%	5 20%	1 4%	–
HM 143	Langland, *Piers*	416	161 39%	208 50%	–	–	47 11%
HM 144	miscellany	318	–	318 100%	–	–	–
HM 147	*Vices and Virtues*	110	4 4%	99 90%	–	–	7 6%
HM 148: I	religious miscellany	75	24 32%	51 68%	–	–	–
HM 148: II	Rolle, *Psalter*	685	122 18%	563 82%	–	–	–
HM 149	Love, *Mirror*	81	11 14%	22 27%	–	48 59%	–
HM 266	Hilton, *The Scale of Perfection*	172	19 11%	108 63%	–	39 23%	6 3%
HM 268	Lydgate, *Fall of Princes*	219	32 15%	108 49%	25 11%	51 23%	3 1%
HM 501	Wycliffite Psalter	71	8 11%	9 13%	–	50 70%	4 6%
HM 502	religious miscellany	132	19 14%	102 77%	–	–	11 8%
HM 503	Wycliffite sermon	184	7 4%	110 60%	21 11%	46 25%	–

Table 4.1 *cont.*

shelfmark	contents	corrections	unclear	the scribe	scribe and collaborator	collaborator alone	later user
HM 505	Daniel, *Dome of Urynes*	186	53 28%	100 54%	–	–	33 18%
HM 744: I	religious miscellany	154	3 2%	34 22%	–	117 76%	–
HM 744: II	Hoccleve, short poems	51	2 4%	49 96%	–	–	–
HM 745	Tudor royal accounts	25		25 100%	–	–	–
HM 1336	medicine and prognostica- tions	12	1 8%	9 75%	–	–	2 17%
HM 1339	Love, *Mirror*	228	32 14%	192 84%	–	–	4 2%
HM 19079	medicine	52	5 10%	16 31%	–	–	31 60%
HM 26054	*arma Christi* roll	1		1 100%	–	–	–
HM 28561	Trevisa, trans. of *Polychronicon*	248	29 12%	197 79%	–	8 3%	14 6%
HM 39872	trans. of *Livre de bonnes meurs*	31	5 16%	26 84%	–	–	–
HM 60320	astrology	11		10 91%	–	–	1 9%
fragments in other MSS	various	85	3 4%	76 89%	–	–	6 7%
total		9,220	1,640 18%	5,733 62%	97 1%	1,469 16%	281 3%

[1] Rounded down from 0.34 per cent.

Yet it is also important to ask in which situations copies were corrected by somebody else. After all, about a fifth of the corrections are by somebody else who collaborates in the book's production in some way: some 17 per cent of them all or 21 per cent of the apportionable ones are by these 'collaborators', who either assist the scribe to correct or correct him on their own (combining penultimate and antepenultimate columns in Table 4.1). The term 'collaborators' is designedly vague, for it encompasses different sorts of involvement. Surprisingly few of these collaborations are by somebody who writes part of the manuscript but then corrects the scribes of other parts: only 17 or 1 per cent are made by another copyist. For instance, one miscellany is made of two booklets, the first by perhaps six scribes, two of them finishing off each other's pages; yet only one correction is made by one scribe on another's copying.[3] But beyond fellow copyists, the 'collaborators' include people who otherwise rubricate or finish off the book. In one copy of *The Prick of Conscience* and *Piers Plowman* roughly one in ten corrections might be by the rubricator.[4] Some other people labelled 'collaborators' only correct the book, and then it is difficult to be sure whether their work was envisaged by the main scribe himself. But the people thus classified correct the book so extensively and often methodically that they might be considered among the personnel who produced the book from the outset and not among the later users.[5] The final group of collaborators do not write full corrections but they are evidently working with the scribe because they write prompts for corrections which he then enters. This sort of supervision by others is sometimes assumed to be the mainstay of correcting but in the Huntington Library's sample it occurs rarely and in two specific situations (surveyed at the end of this chapter). And even these occasions when the scribe is prompted to correct by somebody else need not diminish our sense of the alertness of the scribe to correcting; they might heighten our sense of the consciousness of what he is doing.

This engagement in correcting is what allows the scribes to become skilful readers of what they copy. It is worth noting, though, how seldom corrections are made by readers in the usual sense of the word – people who use rather than create books. This is a surprise: most English manuscripts of these centuries bear traces of their readers, in marginalia, doodles on blank space, notes of ownership, recipes on the flyleaves and so on. Sure enough, almost all manuscripts have a few corrections by these users, but most have only a few: about 3 per cent of the corrections or 4 per cent of the apportionable ones. Only in two medical books do users emend the text a lot, and what is correcting and what rewriting for new purposes is difficult to distinguish, for they also add further details to the text.[6] The corrections by readers are usually in visibly different and much

3 HEHL, MS HM 140, f. 54r (Lydgate, *Saint Albon*, II.1680). On this MS, see Chapter 1, n. 35 above. There are also eight corrections by one scribe on another's work in HEHL, MS El.35.B.63, and eight in HEHL, MS HM 28561.

4 HEHL, MS HM 128: 79 of 787 corrections on my selectively sampled folios (Chapter 1, n. 33) seem to be by the rubricator, identified by Calabrese, Duggan and Turville-Petre (eds.), *Piers Plowman Electronic Archive: 6*, 'Introduction', II.1.3.2.

5 The debatable 'collaborators' are in HEHL, MS HM 130 and MS HM 149 (discussed below); both could be later 'users'.

6 In HEHL, MS HM 505, a reader with very late fifteenth-century handwriting adds 18 per cent of corrections and also foliates the MS. In HEHL, MS HM 19079, a reader adds 60 per cent of

later handwriting; they are often in different colours of ink; unlike the methodical work of collaborators, these corrections are often sporadic or clustered, as marginalia by readers tend to be, especially in the earlier folios of a book; they also often seem to be guesses, quite unlike the version of the text found in other manuscripts. Otherwise, correction is seldom by users, is sometimes by collaborators with the scribes, and most often by the scribes themselves, which suggests their agency and engagement in this aspect of their craftsmanship.

Scribes in holy orders

Many institutions would seem to have encouraged the correction of books by other people with some authority over the scribes or texts. For example, in the thirteenth and early fourteenth centuries several universities developed systems for subdividing the exemplars of set texts into pieces or *peciae* so that students could make their own copies independently; in some universities these *peciae* were supposed to be checked by officials or stationers.[7] This particular organizational system is, though, unlikely often to be pertinent to manuscripts in English. What were the systems or institutions in which people did copy English in the late fourteenth and fifteenth centuries, and were their scribes licensed to correct themselves or were they supervised by others?

As well as universities, the religious orders had ideas about the importance of correcting. From Cassiodorus to Johann von Tritheim, members of various orders had issued injunctions to correct books (as Chapter 2 traced), and these ideas were paralleled in well-organized procedures. When English houses made a large effort to expand their book collections in the eleventh and twelfth centuries, the monks routinely undertook checking and correcting of each other's work, as is evident in books from many houses.[8] Some houses or cathedrals appointed a precentor, whose duties included getting new books copied and 'old ones repaired and corrected' ('antiquorum reparacione et emendatione'). In some, a chancellor or other official had the duty of correcting the books made by other monks or, as occurred increasingly, made by scribes hired from outside.[9] Some had

corrections, but some of them look like cross-references, and he also adds marginalia (ff. 50^{r}, 83^{r}, 94^{r}, 96^{r}, 129^{v} twice, 115^{r}, 152^{v}, 167^{v}, 181^{v}, 182^{r}), extra recipes (ff. 18^{v}, 50^{v}, 96^{r}) and an interlinear gloss (f. 152^{v}).

7 Rouse and Rouse, 'Dissemination of Texts in Pecia', 72; Parkes, 'Provision of Books', 465 n. 281.

8 E.g., Ker, *English Manuscripts*, 50–2; Webber, *Scribes and Scholars*, 12, 19–21; Coates, *English Medieval Books*, 50, 53 and fig. 8.

9 Gullick, 'Professional Scribes', 2–4; Parkes, *Their Hands Before Our Eyes*, 50; Webber, *Scribes and Scholars*, 20–1.

systems whereby the senior monks trained the junior ones in writing and checked their work.[10]

But the busiest period for restocking English monastic libraries fell in the twelfth century; by the late fourteenth and fifteenth centuries, religious houses were no longer responsible for as great a proportion of the books produced overall in England. Some of the bigger monasteries and cathedral priories such as Durham and St Albans did, though, continue to copy manuscripts, as did new establishments such as Syon.[11] There were in force statutes such as those of the Benedictines of 1277, 1343 and 1444 which recommended writing and correcting books, and they were echoed in local injunctions, such as some from St Albans, which exhorted the monks not only to copying, illuminating and binding but also to correcting ('in scribendo, corrigendo, illuminando, et ligando').[12] There is some evidence in this period for correcting by senior monks and friars of the work of other scribes, whether their brethren or outsiders hired for the purpose. For instance, John Dygon, a Birgittine recluse of Sheen, corrected a Bible and a volume of spiritual prose, the latter for the use of scholars in Oxford.[13] There is evidence too of supervised copying and correcting of both Latin and English in the Augustinian priory of John Capgrave in the mid fifteenth century (as discussed in Chapter 11). The religious of fifteenth-century England, then, could exercise the communal discipline of correcting other people's copies.

An interesting case-study comes from one order, the Carthusians. From its foundation, this order issued firm demands for uniformity in its liturgical and other texts, from their wording to their pronunciation. The correction enjoined on the largely solitary monks was to be communal in spirit: statutes of 1258 required that copies be corrected only by the common agreement of the general chapter, the prior or some 'prudent monks' ('monachorum discretorum'), and that copies be 'corrected according to books corrected by' or 'emended by the Order' ('ad libros qui correcti sunt in ordine corrigantur', 'exemplariis in ordine nostro emendatis').[14] The idea recurs in statutes recorded in English manuscripts and dated to 1432.[15] Several works circulated among the Carthusians which warned the corrector to 'take care not to emend books incautiously and on his own initiative'

10 E.g., Cohen-Mushlin, *Medieval Scriptorium*, vol. 1, 53–82, and 'Division of Labour', 52–3.
11 Doyle, 'Book Production', 1. See e.g., Clark, *Monastic Renaissance*, 97–123.
12 Doyle, 'Book Production', 3; Clark, *Monastic Renaissance*, 99, 116.
13 Hanna, 'John Dygon', 127–8, and 'Two British Library Biblical MSS', 190.
14 Hogg (ed.), *Evolution of the Carthusian Statutes*, vol. 1, 61.
15 BL, MS Cotton Caligula A.ii, f. 180^{v}.

but to follow 'the ancient and correct books of the Order' ('Caueat corrector ne incaute libros emendet ex proprio capite, sed ad libros antiquos ordinis et correctos').[16] These statutes and instructions were followed in the late fifteenth and early sixteenth centuries, when the members of the Charterhouse in London wrote to the prior of La Grande Chartreuse with questions about the liturgy. Most concerned pronunciation and procedure, but some extended to the accuracy, spelling and punctuation of liturgical books, down to such fine points as grammatical cases after prepositions, spelling with a silent <h>, double consonants or confusions over lookalike letters such as **cl** and **d**.[17] It is suggestive that these questions and answers were themselves copied and so, presumably, further disseminated, in books which have their own corrections: people took care that these rulings were circulated communally in authoritative form.[18] As the statutes preached, so these English monks obeyed, even to the extreme extent of writing to the Alps for advice. Rather than stress the scribe's intelligence and initiative, these writings from the Carthusian order stress consensus.

Yet even the Carthusians admitted some latitude. The Carthusian questions on correct practice were themselves altered and updated in dissemination.[19] Despite their zeal for uniformity, the Carthusians actually achieved little uniformity in their books at this period, perhaps because they worked so much alone.[20] Indeed, some of the most thorough Carthusian efforts at correcting look more like quirky obsessions than the orderly communal control of textual transmission: James Grenehalgh and others undertook advanced emendation of devotional works, some of them already printed, and William Darker undertook meticulous changes to Stephen Dodesham's work, seemingly of personal preferences in spelling.[21] This eccentricity in correcting seems typical of the wider conditions of book production in religious houses in the late fourteenth and fifteenth centuries: the arrangements were often ad hoc; the monks or canons were often acting under local initiatives, rather than orderly programmes, or acting of their own volition.[22] In this period, the enclosed religious learned more casual forms of cursive handwriting for use in record-keeping, and

16 From the 'Introduction' to Oswald de Corda, *Opus pacis*, *27, *81.

17 Gribbin (ed.), *Liturgical and Miscellaneous Questions*, 7, 8, 18.

18 BL, MS Cotton Caligula A.ii, ff. 144^{r}–148^{r}: for corrections, see, e.g., ff. 144^{r}/3, 144^{r}/19, 146^{v}/7, 147^{r}/19.

19 Gribbin, *Aspects of Carthusian Liturgical Practice*, 12–16.

20 As repeatedly stressed by Doyle, 'William Darker', 206, 'English Carthusian Books', 122, and 'Book Production', 13–15.

21 Sargent, *James Grenehalgh*; Kerby-Fulton, Hilmo and Olson, *Opening Up Middle English Manuscripts*, 329–32; Doyle, 'William Darker', 202.

22 Pouzet, 'Book Production', 217–24.

so equipped they were able to make books for their own use without the organization of the whole house behind the project.[23]

Works in English might especially fall outside organized systems of book production, as they were less essential to monastic reading or liturgy. A rough indication of this might be the fact that very few of the Huntington Library's fifty-two manuscripts with English seem to be corrected in religious houses by people other than the scribe; even when they are so corrected, the organization is not thorough or orderly. This is seen in a book produced by a Carthusian, John Clerk of Hinton Priory. Nearly a quarter of the corrections (39 of 172) are in a different ink and even use a few different graphs, and these differences might suggest that there is a second hand correcting Clerk's work. This is not completely sure: it is always more difficult to prove that dissimilar specimens of handwriting could definitely not be one person than to argue that similar specimens possibly could.[24] But there is only one correction which looks like a marginal prompt by somebody telling Clerk what to fix.[25] And far more of the corrections (108 of 172) are definitely by Clerk himself and look as though they were made in the same ink as that in which he first copied the text, as moments of instant recognition of his errors. Clerk uses protocols or techniques which were common to monastic scribes for centuries; the same techniques are used in the fewer corrections by the second hand in this book too; and they are used in another book copied by Clerk.[26] This all reveals that Clerk's correcting was not idiosyncratic; it was informed by common practice. Similarly, at least one of the passages restored at the foot of the page is missing in some manuscripts and so might here be found by orderly collation of different exemplars, as could other missing passages too long to

[23] Doyle, 'Book Production', 3.

[24] The later corrections in HEHL, MS HM 266, use a paler brown ink; one-compartment **a** formed with two curving strokes, rather than the usual one with broken strokes or rather than two-compartment **a**; an abbreviation for *and* with a crossbar mid-height, rather than the usual one with a macron over it; loopless **d**; and word-final **e** without a right-pointing spur. But the repertoire of other graphs is the same as Clerk's, and there is a sporadic occurrence in these corrections of Clerk's forms of **a**. Dutschke, *Guide*, vol. 1, 230, notes corrections 'in another contemporary hand' but wonders whether one, the added leaf f. 1r–v, is by Clerk.

[25] HEHL, MS HM 266, f. 18r, restoring 'etyn' to *Scale*, 177, in a pale red.

[26] For monastic erasures and for *signes de renvoie* in similar style and phrasing, see Chapter 5, pp. 104–8 and 118–20 below. For the second scribe's additions at the foot of pages, see HEHL, MS HM 266, ff. 20v (restoring *Scale*, 185), 79r (364), 39r (391), 6r (mostly restoring 453), 9v (mostly restoring 457), 10r (458). (The leaves are now bound in the wrong order.) For Clerk's reuse of similar *signes de renvoie*, compare the style of the cross in Cambridge, St John's College, MS E.22, f. 62v, and HEHL, MS HM 266, f. 1r, and the virgule and pairs of dots on Cambridge, St John's College, MS E.22, f. 78r, and HEHL, MS HM 266, f. 39r.

restore by guesswork without checking.[27] This suggests the submission to common exemplars exhorted in Carthusian statutes. But the key point is that Clerk uses these shared procedures and makes these checks of other books for himself. That is even more evident in a second book made by him, a set of excerpts of Latin theological works seemingly arranged for his private use; it has very few corrections which could be by somebody else but it does again witness Clerk's careful craftsmanship.[28] There he records that his activity as scribe is important to him personally, indeed for his personal salvation, on a flyleaf beseeching us to pray for the soul of him as scribe of this little work ('Orate supplico pro a*nim*a *frat*ris Ioh*ann*is Clerk [. . .] scriptoris hui*us* opusculi').[29] Overall, then, his books offer evidence of shared procedures and sometimes of organized supervision, but also evidence of personal effort and piety in copying and correcting.

Among the Huntington Library's other books with numerous corrections by a second person, some could conceivably come, like John Clerk's, from the clergy, whether enclosed or secular. One is a collection of short pieces of pastoral and catechetical prose commissioned by John Pery, an Augustinian canon at Holy Trinity Priory in Aldgate, London; one is a copy of the instructive poem *The Prick of Conscience* likely produced by brethren in a religious house; one is a copy of Nicholas Love's *Mirror of the Blessed Life of Jesus Christ* which has been interpreted as a book designed for instructing the laity; others include other copies of the same sorts or similar works.[30] The presence of other people correcting these books could be ongoing signs of supervisory correction within the Church. Yet it is always riskily simplistic to judge contexts from contents. And while the process of correcting by a second person suggests orderly supervision, the things corrected in some cases are less orderly, even eccentric. All bar one of these second hands make numerous changes to the other scribes' spelling and even calligraphy, relatively rare things to emend (as Chapter 7 discusses).[31] One of the sets of corrections by a second hand, in a copy of *The Prick of Conscience*, also seems to be a curious attempt to conflate

[27] HEHL, MS HM 266, ff. 28^v (*Scale*, 218, which is missing from three MSS), 20^v (*Scale*, 185), 79^r (364), 39^r (391).

[28] For comparison, the first 4 quires of Cambridge, St John's College, MS E.22, ff. 5^r–37^v, have only 5 of 69 corrections in a different ink and debatably not in Clerk's hand (though 13 are decorated in rubric, usually over the top of Clerk's prior crossing out). Doyle, 'Book Production',13–14, links this MS to Hinton Priory but notes the uncertain provenance of HEHL, MS HM 266, after Clerk's copying.

[29] Cambridge, St John's College, MS E.22, f. 3^r.

[30] Respectively, HEHL, MS HM 112, MS HM 128, MS HM 149 (discussed by Furnish, '*Ordinatio* of Huntington Library', 65), MS HM 744 (Part I) and MS HM 130.

[31] The exception is HEHL, MS HM 149.

different recensions of the poem (as Chapter 6 discusses). Whether these should indeed be considered the work of a colleague or just of some fussy later reader is arguable. What argues for these people being 'collaborators' is their frequency, for such consistent effort is only seldom made by a reader, and their orderliness. Such meticulous work might seem to reflect ecclesiastical concerns with textual authority. But even in the heavily corrected copy of *The Prick of Conscience* there is evidence that this was not at all a regular pattern of supervision for this scribe: this manuscript is in the same handwriting as a second copy of the same poem which is not so supervised but is mostly corrected by the scribe himself.[32] Any careful supervision arranged for one of his copies was not arranged for his other; it was sporadic, even eccentric in its focus on dialect and collating different recensions.

The Huntington Library's sample does not include all possible working arrangements, of course; in manuscripts now in other libraries there is more evidence of organized checking in religious houses. For instance, an anthology of English devotional prose from a nunnery in East Anglia was produced by several scribes working together, one of whom checked and corrected the copying of the others more zealously than they did themselves.[33] Yet even in this instance the system of collaborating was not organized successfully: somebody divided up the exemplars for *The Doctrine of the Hert* among the different scribes, but the person who was checking their work did not understand this arrangement. When the first scribe finished his stint, a few lines down a page, the person who checked it mistakenly thought the first scribe had finished too soon and so added twenty-one lines more on the rest of the page; but a second scribe had already copied these lines in the next quire, for they were at the start of his stint. As a result, it was the seeming supervisor whose work then needed crossing out.[34] This person seems unused to dividing up copies and to correcting, which suggests that it was not his or her frequent established duty. Indeed, when that person's handwriting recurs in another devotional miscellany, she or he is only one scribe among the team.[35] That other book

[32] HEHL, MS HM 130, and BL, MS Harley 2281, discussed in Chapters 6 and 7. Methods and frequencies of correction differ between two other copies of *Prick* by one scribe, JRL, MS Eng. 50, and BL, MS Harley 1205.

[33] Durham, UL, MS Cosin V.iii.24: e.g., in scribe A's stint (ff. 1^{r}–43^{v}) scribe A made 59 corrections, but the overseer made 89 (and 37 were impossible to apportion).

[34] *Ibid.*, f. 43^{v}, with scribe A finishing in the middle of line 5 at 'al þo' and the overseer continuing from '*þat* suffre' down to line 26; the next scribe repeats that passage on f. 44^{r}. Beadle, 'Some Measures of Scribal Accuracy', 236–8, discusses this accident. Chapter 7 below discusses the spelling.

[35] CUL, MS Hh.I.II, ff. 45^{r}–53^{v}, 55^{r}–60^{r} (quires VII and VIII, but leaving blank the last leaf of quire VII, f. 54^{r-v}, which another hand filled). On this MS, see Connolly, *Index of Middle English Prose:*

has no corrections by somebody overseeing the other scribes: the scribes correct their own work.[36] So while there is some supervisory correcting of English in religious houses, instances are often balanced or outnumbered by the scribes' self-corrections; it is not consistent from book to book, even within one milieu; it is often unusual in its focus on dialect or in its manic zeal; and its procedures can fail. This story could be one of a sad decline in older monastic procedures, or it could be a triumphant proliferation of people who intelligently and attentively correct themselves.

Wycliffite books

There is, though, one coherent group of corrections supplied by people other than the scribe in the Huntington Library's manuscripts: they occur in three manuscripts of works connected to the Wycliffites or Lollards. Corrections are supplied by a second hand in a Wycliffite New Testament in the Later Version, extracts of the Wycliffite Old Testament with some supporting materials and a Lollard sermon known by its Latin opening words *Omnis plantacio*.[37] Whether such books were truly made or owned by Wycliffites is unsure; nor is it sure whether people recognized them as distinctively Wycliffite, especially the Bible.[38] But these books have various visual likenesses between themselves and with other Wycliffite books, and they also share the distinctive characteristic of being copiously corrected by one person or more other than the scribe, and with similar techniques, often in rubric and often with marginal additions and *caret* marks to position them.

These manuscripts remind us how difficult it is to distinguish second hands with surety.[39] On the one hand, when corrections do look different

Handlist XIX, 186–90; and O'Mara (ed.), *Study*, 141–6, 154–7, 161–2. A.I. Doyle's draft catalogue-entry on Durham, UL, MS Cosin V.iii.24, available in the Special Collections Reading Room at Durham, UL, identifies the same handwriting in CUL, MS Hh.1.11.

36 In CUL, MS Hh.1.11, 95 of 118 corrections were by scribes on their own stints; 13 were impossible to attribute; 8 were by a user restoring damage on ff. 129^r–132^r.

37 See in Table 4.1 respectively, HEHL, MS HM 134; MS HM 501, on which see Dove, *First English Bible*, 52, 120, 129; and MS HM 503, on which see Hudson (ed.), '*Omnis plantacio*', xx–xxi. Further fragments from HEHL, MS HM 501 are now Tokyo, Keio UL, MS 170X@9/6, but I identified only one correction in them where the scribe adds 'gra*uen*' in the margin at the end of a line. The leaves of HEHL, MS HM 501 and Tokyo, Keio UL, MS 170X@9/6 are badly damaged and covered with gauze which makes corrections difficult to see.

38 Dove, *First English Bible*, 53–5, 67.

39 Especially in a large-scale survey: e.g., in HEHL, MS HM 503, I can only identify 36 of 184 corrections as by another hand and maybe one by a third hand (f. 94^v; Hudson (ed.), '*Omnis plantacio*', 2313), whereas the text's editor after her much fuller study identifies 'more than one other hand' (Hudson (ed.), '*Omnis plantacio*', xx).

from the main scribe's handwriting, this may be because they are written in small spaces, in later inks or with different nibs. Writing which looks thinner, darker and smaller – like the words '*and* cr*is*t is truþe *and* auctor of sc*ri*pture' added at the foot of one page – might turn out to be the main scribe when we look carefully.[40] On the other hand, likeness can be deceptive too: these Wycliffite books, like many, are in handwriting modelled on textura, albeit of a rounded ductus, and the demands of this set script might make the handwriting more regular, so that it is tricky to tell one scribe from another. That likeness might even be a deliberate house style. For example, in another Wycliffite book, a copy of the New Testament, the scribe correcting has handwriting very similar to the main scribe's, which might suggest that they were trained or worked in similar times and places, or that the second was imitating the observable repertoire of the first. On close inspection, the two scribes can be distinguished: whereas the main scribe intermittently forms his letters with a little more of the roundness typical of this variety of textura, the person correcting uses more broken strokes and more pronounced serifs. It is tempting to suggest that the pains taken in imitating the shapes of another scribe are betrayed by this overly fussy execution – though such a complex explanation could not easily be proved.[41] We can, though, suggest that even the script followed, by both scribes, is subordinated to standardization, so corrections might well be too.

Differences in rubrication help to distinguish the second, correcting scribe from the main scribe in this New Testament. The main scribe has some of his additions in the margins adorned with *caret* marks in red, but the second person's are all in regular black, or are occasionally not marked with a *caret* but with two virgules.[42] (Chapter 5 below explains these symbols.) The occasional use of red is typical of these three Wycliffite books: 21 per cent of corrections in the New Testament, 30 per cent in the excerpts of the Old Testament and 21 per cent in the sermon are adorned or are solely

40 HEHL, MS HM 503, f. 77^{v} (Hudson (ed.), '*Omnis plantacio*', 1822–3): compare the cross for insertion with the scribe's on f. 78^{r} and compare other graphs typical of the main scribe: the trailing approach-stroke on tironian *and*, the foot on the stem of **r** and the thickening and slight left-pointing horn where the shaft of **f** joins the top horizontal.

41 The second person correcting in HEHL, MS HM 134 also has a tongue protruding further to the right on **e** and a tail slanting more to the right on **þ**.

42 HEHL, MS HM 134, contrasting a red *caret* on, e.g., ff. 4^{r} (*Wycliffite Bible*, Matthew 5.21) and 8^{r} (Matthew 10.35), with virgules on, e.g., ff. 93^{r} (2 Corinthians 10.1), 98^{r} (Ephesians 2.12). However, on ff. 96^{v} (Galatians 4.14), 102^{v} (Colossians 1.20), 107^{v} (1 Timothy 4.7), somebody draws around the second hand's marginal additions a box in blue ink.

in red.[43] Rubric used for crossing out, *caret* marks or boxes is impossible to apportion securely to anyone, of course, but it is conceivable here that the rubric is applied by somebody else, given the care taken by more than one person in making corrections in black alongside. (And as the argument of this chapter is that scribes mostly correct themselves, it is important to test as many counter-instances as possible, like this rubricating, where someone else might be responsible.) Indeed, some are only in red and some are adornments in red of the earlier corrections by the scribe, say, by drawing a red box around a word the scribe added in the margin.

Such needless additional colouring, alongside the involvement of more than one person, suggests some great concern for correcting behind these Wycliffite books. The conditions and attitudes for making Wycliffite books might foster this submission to careful correction by others on the part of scribes. Wycliffite writing was a team project. Many Wycliffite texts were composed by teams of 'diuerse felawis', as the General Prologue to the Wycliffite Bible twice notes.[44] Their copying was also a shared endeavour. The books in the Huntington Library's sample, like many manuscripts of the Wycliffite Bible, are evidently made by scribes who are well trained and well organized somehow.[45] Likewise, Anne Hudson has noted that the correcting of the Wycliffite sermon cycle was 'done systematically and under supervision', collating other exemplars, and without the 'disorganization' of correcting found in copies of poetry produced by London scribes.[46] Some similar if less outstanding organization and expertise are evident in these three books.

That might reflect Wycliffite ideas about texts, for Wycliffite writers show a notable interest in accurate writing, especially of the Bible, for they put their faith in Scripture. Echoing Wyclif's own sense of its special authority, Wycliffite writers argued that Scripture should be treated with reverence and taken whole, not excerpted or altered: 'we schal not put to ne take fro' God's word, one wrote, almost imagining and forbidding additions and deletions to a manuscript.[47] Yet like many earlier scholars they were also concerned about the reliability of manuscripts as witnesses to the

[43] Respectively, HEHL, MS HM 134 (with 88 of 428 in red), MS HM 501 (21 of 71), and MS HM 503 (36 of 184).

[44] Hudson, 'Five Problems', 303, 308–9; Dove, *First English Bible*, 79; Hudson (ed.), *Selections*, 14.27, 14.35.

[45] Hudson, *Premature Reformation*, 197, 203. Hudson does, however, warn about variability in the quality of other texts (204).

[46] Hudson (ed.), *English Wycliffite Sermons*, 139, 190, 193.

[47] Somerset (ed.), *Four Wycliffite Dialogues*, 12.335. In general, see Dove, *First English Bible*, 50–1.

Word. The Wycliffite translators emended the text of the Vulgate carefully before translating it, by collating copies and commentaries for alternative readings; they were concerned to make the text 'sumdeel trewe'.[48] These ideas were put into practice in composing other Wycliffite texts: authors often checked and emended their sources;[49] their works show the ongoing revision, even of minute linguistic details;[50] and some of the revision is corrective in spirit, bringing works closer to their biblical sources, for instance.[51] Some of these works invite correction by readers too. The end of the sermon *Omnis plantacio* invites people to 'ouerse' the text, *oversee* being a common term for checking a text for correction, used for example by Thomas Hoccleve.[52] The General Prologue to the Wycliffite Bible invites people to emend the text if they find 'ony defaute of þe truþe of translacioun', although it also warns that such a reader should 'examyne truli his Latyn bible' and be cautious for he will find many of them to be 'ful false' with 'more nede to be correctid [. . .] þan haþ þe English bible late translatid'.[53] The Wycliffites were well aware of the dangers of independent and haphazard correcting: one Wycliffite work warned that the text of Scripture had been marred by 'writeris' or scribes or 'vnwise amenderis'.[54] As Anne Hudson has noted, this professed interest in verbal accuracy might well have encouraged painstaking correction by scribes too.[55] That could explain why the three Wycliffite books in the Huntington Library's sample are corrected, with a consistency not found elsewhere, by someone other than the scribe, and often in red in ways which seem to draw attention to the corrections.

These Wycliffite ideas could also, though, license careful correcting by the scribes of their own work. The bulk of the corrections in these books is nonetheless in the main scribe's handwriting – unless it has been so brilliantly imitated that we cannot tell – and the corrections in red, too, are in many cases adornments to the corrections already entered by the scribe. For example, the scribe of the New Testament in this sample corrects himself meticulously hundreds of times, and often for tiny details of spelling which seem of little consequence, given the flexible spelling

48 Hudson, 'Five Problems', 302–3; Dove, *First English Bible*, 79, 173–4, 180–8; Hudson (ed.), *Selections*, 14.26–35, 14.75–90.

49 Hudson, 'Five Problems', 302–3; e.g., Hudson (ed.), *Two Revisions*, vol. 1, xc.

50 Hudson, 'Five Problems', 302, 305–8; Dove, *First English Bible*, 139–43, 150–2; Hudson (ed.), *English Wycliffite Sermons*, 194–5.

51 Dove, *First English Bible*, 166–7, 175–7, 180–1; Hudson (ed.), *Two Revisions*, vol. 1, ci, civ.

52 Hudson (ed.), '*Omnis plantacio*', 2940–8, on which see Hudson, *Premature Reformation*, 184. Cf. n. 80 below.

53 Hudson (ed.), *Selections*, 14.69–75. It also asks for charitableness in correcting (14.120–2).

54 Dove, *First English Bible*, 183.

55 Hudson (ed.), *English Wycliffite Sermons*, 192, also 139.

in English then, adding <e> in 'que$^{\wedge e}$ne', an extra <o> in 'so$^{\wedge o}$ne' and word-final <e> on 'sitti*ng*$^{\wedge e}$'. In such minutiae, the main scribes share the concerns with textual accuracy, conventionality and clarity of the wider Wycliffite community.[56] Indeed, the main scribe of the New Testament and the second person correcting his work make similar changes. For instance, each just a few times emends the preposition *into*: the main scribe writes 'in' or 'to' and somebody adds between the lines or in the margins the extra 'to' or 'in' to give *into*; some such additions seem to be by the second scribe, others by the main scribe correcting himself – as far as one can judge such tiny marks.[57] Overall this book has thirty-one corrections to grammatical constructions or closed-class words such as prepositions which seem to be needless, as the copy was grammatical beforehand. But the change to *into* was a common one: when the Wycliffites revised another work, an adaptation of Richard Rolle's rendering of the Psalter, they often changed Rolle's *in* into *into* when it translates Latin *in* followed by the accusative case.[58] This concern with translating Latin *in* is, then, shared both by the main scribe and by his collaborator and by a wider community of like minds. Self-correction and correction by others are both subject to communal textual practices and intellectual concerns.[59]

Urban clerks

These orthodox and heretical religious groups are not the only makers of books from the late fourteenth to the late fifteenth century; there is also in this period a proliferation of copying in English by professional scribes. These were scribes not only in the broad sense that they were *people currently wielding a pen* but in the precise sense of people whose profession, training and activity day-to-day primarily involved writing, in two fields. Their involvement was instrumental in the blossoming of book production in English around and after 1400. By this point larger

[56] HEHL, MS HM 134, e.g., ff. 10^{r} (*Wycliffite Bible*, Matthew 12.42), 21^{r} (Matthew 26.64), 22^{v} (Matthew 28.7). Cf. similar corrections in Chapter 7, nn. 68–71 below.

[57] HEHL, MS HM 134, ff. 3^{r} (*Wycliffite Bible*, Matthew 4.5), 13^{v} (Matthew 18.6; *Wycliffite Bible* here only gives 'in'), 15^{v} (Matthew 21.2), 25^{v} (Mark 4.26; second scribe), 118^{r} (Acts 1.12, second scribe; *Wycliffite Bible* here only gives *to* but the apparatus records *into* in other MSS). Related might be adding *up* to *in* ('put $_{\wedge}$^{up} *in* a sudarie', f. 53^{r}, Luke 19.20).

[58] Hudson (ed.), *Two Revisions*, vol. 1, xcv–xcvi.

[59] It should be noted that the corrections by others do not always go well: the person checking *Omnis plantacio* modifies four biblical quotations and references, diverging from the text preferred by the modern editor: HEHL, MS HM 503, ff. 3^{r} (Hudson (ed.), '*Omnis plantacio*', 44), 22^{v} (518), 28^{v} (665), 56^{r} (1308). He also repeatedly modifies the scribe's spelling of *any* and *many*, needlessly shifting the second syllable from <i> to <ye>.

towns had artisans who made their money producing and selling books, especially the academic books, Books of Hours and other things essential to readers' everyday lives and so lucrative for trade. Then in the fourteenth and fifteenth centuries the making of books for money began to be shared with clerks whose primary occupation was making documents. The cursive scripts favoured for documents became common models for the handwriting in books. Cursive writing sped up the production of any one book, perhaps lowering the cost slightly, and made the production of books more feasible for people who had been trained to keep documents, whether as their profession or in private life. In particular, a number of the scribes of imaginative and intellectual literature in English seem to have been people who were for the most part employed as clerks, scriveners, notaries, even heralds, in the bureaucracy of the guilds, cities and monarchy, in the law or in the larger households. These men made literary books 'on the side', outside their primary employment.[60] Linne Mooney among others has described their work in fine detail, bringing London bureaucratic scribes to life and giving them names. She argues that they were most closely linked to the London Guildhall in particular, although the wealth and complexity of her and others' evidence might turn out to suggest that the Guildhall was only one among many bureaucratic milieux from which came scribes who copied books.[61] The exact numbers and identities of these moonlighting clerks are in some few cases disputed.[62] But thanks to the groundbreaking research of Mooney and others, what is clear is the general influence of bureaucratic scribes and practice on copying books in English. How might documentary practice shape their correcting?

These clerks and part-time litterateurs have been characterized as 'professional readers' who transmitted their interpretations to others in the way they copied and presented English literature. Kathryn Kerby-Fulton has described their '*conscious* decisions', based on their reading, about how to present a poem on the page, without merely following the diktats of some mythical 'supervisor'.[63] Such a scribe might be expected to be interventionist, then, rewriting works with which he was keenly engaged. But professional practices in bureaucracy, law and government might predispose these clerkly men not always to intervene in what they copy but

[60] Mooney and Stubbs, *Scribes and the City*, e.g., 2, 16; and Mooney, 'Locating Scribal Activity', 184. Christianson, *Directory*, 22, distinguishes these groups of professional scribes.

[61] For the argument for the Guildhall in particular, see Mooney and Stubbs, *Scribes and the City*; for the wider landscape, see Mooney, 'Vernacular Literary Manuscripts', 200–6, and 'Locating Scribal Activity', 183–90, 194, 198, 201–3.

[62] E.g., Roberts, 'On Giving Scribe B a Name', esp. 247, 254–7.

[63] Kerby-Fulton, 'Professional Readers of Langland', 103–4.

sometimes to seek correct transmission. Notaries and scribes learnt to create new documents, but they also learnt to imitate old ones.[64] Civic and royal authorities sought to record past documents with cartularies and to guide future ones with formularies.[65] Past documents needed to be recorded correctly, for they specified people's legal entitlements, and future ones needed an authoritative form. Accuracy mattered. The scriveners of London, when they joined the guild, swore an oath not to issue documents unless they had been 'well examined word by word' and had to master proper grammar lest 'thei erre' in drafting.[66] Some sense of the wider community's interest in correct documents emerges in the letters of Sir John Fastolf and his circle, a litigious bunch with a passion for paperwork. They obsess about documents as proof of their legal and other claims and often send or receive a 'copé' of things to support their claims.[67] Their care for correct copies is evident in their precise demands for 'a copy woord for woord as it is regestred' or their requests to check 'þ*a*t non errou*r* be founden'.[68] They ask people to send documents back 'wyth your correcc*i*ons' or to get other people 'to see and correct hem' or 'to corrige' a document or have it 'greetly examyned or it be shewed' to anybody else.[69] Such correspondence begins to suggest the interest in correcting and correct copying in this culture awash with documents.

One scribe of documents who also made literary manuscripts has left an evocative record of some of the procedures and concerns of these scribes. This is Thomas Hoccleve, the most accomplished poet from early fifteenth-century England, scribe of his own work and of brief stints in copies of Chaucer's and Gower's works, and clerk in the Privy Seal office. In his poem *The Regiment of Princes* he sets out his understanding of the responsibilities of the professional scribe or 'wrytter':

> ¶ A wrytter moot three thynges to him knytte
> And in tho / may be no disseuerance
> Mynde / ye / and hand / non may from othir flitte
> But in hem moot be ioynt contynuance.
> The mynd al hool / withowten varyance
> On ye and hand / awayte moot alway

[64] Illustrated by Richardson, *Middle-Class Writing*, 56, 61–72. But Dodd, 'Writing Wrongs', 218–19, 230, 238–9, notes a mixture of convention and invention.

[65] Richardson, *Middle-Class Writing*, 73–95.

[66] Steer (ed.), *Scriveners' Company*, 6, 49, 51.

[67] *Paston Letters*, ed. Davis, Beadle and Richmond, 943.19, 964.4, 964.9, 964.14, 981.14, 985.5, 989.108, 989.127, 992.12, 999.44. Sometimes *copy* refers to a book (969.27); sometimes *double* is used as a synonym for *copy* (956.14).

[68] *Ibid.*, 961.17–18, 985.34.

[69] *Ibid.*, 983.25, 986.2, 986.42, 988.6, 989.10, 989.42, 989.45, 989.115, 1005.62, 1009.43.

And they two eek on him / it is no nay.
¶ Who so shal write / may nat telle a tale
With him and him / ne synge this ne þ*a*t
But al his wittes hoole grete and smale
Theer*e* muste appeere / and holden hem ther*e* at[70]

This passage is highlighted in another copy made close to the poet with 'No*ta*' written by the scribe and adorned in gold.[71] This passage is not a comment on the process of correcting but it does imply that scribes sought correctness: there must be no 'varyance' of attention, presumably to avoid error. Hoccleve emphasizes the completeness of focus in repeated unequivocal terms ('no', 'non', 'moot', 'al hool', 'al [. . .] hoole', 'muste'). In some ways this is a description of scribal labour as solitary, for the scribe cannot talk to his fellows; yet the reason for it is the demand for correctness from others – from readers, patrons, users.

Who knows how fictional this description is? But Hoccleve did not only imagine the conditions for clerks; he prescribed them. He was a figure of authority in the Privy Seal office from early in the reign of Henry IV: he seems often to have ordered its supplies, which suggests a supervisory role, and he compiled a formulary of model documents, setting standards for others.[72] The need for correctness in copying is evident in some instructions on a small slip of parchment bound into his formulary, on composing a writ of *procedendo*. The instructions stress the accuracy required: 'In a p*ro*cedendo write word by word / and lett*er* by l*ett*re titel by titel / as þe copie is'; in the first section you should 'chaunge noþ*er* modd ne temps / of verbe noþ*er* of noun'.[73] There needs to be careful copying in administration, then. That his aim is to foster correctness in others' work is evident not only in the mere decision to compile a formulary for them to follow but also in Hoccleve's little notes which accompany the documents in it and direct

70 BL, MS Royal 17.D.xviii, f. 19^{v} (*Regiment*, 994–1005). On this MS, see Mooney, 'Holograph Copy', and Chapter 11, n. 33 below. BL, MS Arundel 38, f. 18^{v}, an earlier MS made close to the scribe, has 'holde a tale' where the later revision in BL, MS Royal 17.D.xviii has 'telle a tale', removing repetition with 'holden' later in the stanza and adding alliteration.

71 BL, MS Arundel 38, f. 18^{v}. Ironically, the line 'Mynde [–]{ye} and hande / non may fro other flytte' is corrected over erasure in this MS, perhaps because of problems spelling *eye*, a word which bothered other scribes (Chapter 9, n. 54 below).

72 Mooney, 'Some New Light', esp. 298.

73 BL, MS Add. 24062, f. 35^{r}. The handwriting could be somebody trained by Hoccleve, and adopting noticeable and imitable graphs such as his **y** with an elaborate descender. But the personal ductus recalls Hoccleve's, e.g., on word-final **e** and **s**. For a 'l*itte*ra de p*ro*cedendo', see f. 67^{v}. The term 'copie' in French recurs elsewhere in this formulary to refer to its model documents: 'Cy ensuyte la copie de la cedule ensy enuoiee' (f. 40^{r}).

the reader where to 'look' ('Respice', 'Regardez'), what 'should be inserted' ('deberet inseri') and what is in a 'previous place' ('loco p*re*cedente').[74] The teacherly tone is clear at a note in the middle of one document, where Hoccleve accidentally leaves the bottom fifth of the page blank and continues on the next page; in case users of the formulary mistakenly think that the interrupted document is complete, he writes a note:

> Heer*e* made y lepe þeer ------- ex negligencia *etcetera* ~ Witnesse on Petebat *etcetera* in the nexte syde folwynge which sholde haue stonden on this syde / but how so it stonde / it is a membre of the mat*ere* p*re*cedent[75]

It is ironic that Hoccleve's own error and 'negligencia' occasioned this note, and the need for a note might betray the expectation that the scribes who will use the formulary are worryingly independent, errant or quibbling. But the purpose is to prevent such error by the other scribes here addressed, by drawing attention to it with this corrective comment.

When these scribes copied literary manuscripts, did they pursue checking and correcting in the ways required in documents? It seems not. The key point about the making of literary books by these bureaucratic clerks is that they seem to have been working freelance and independently. Even those who worked on books commercially and frequently seem to have worked casually and independently, with little supervision.[76] Other professional scribes in London seldom worked in large co-ordinated groups; they mostly worked in small independent premises.[77] The seminal study of their work, by A.I. Doyle and M.B. Parkes, first uncovered the ways that, when these men copied English literature, they did so not in orderly workshops but in some disorder, unsure of the supply of exemplars and the progress of the other scribes who were contributing to the same book. The lack of organized scriptoria for English literary manuscripts is corroborated by, and illuminates, the little evidence of organized oversight of correction in them and the only sporadic evidence of their correction by others. As Doyle and Parkes noted, even when the exemplars were divided up to let different people copy different quires, 'Evidence for supervision is sporadic . . . Each scribe seems to have "proofread" and corrected his own transcription.'[78]

74 BL, MS Add. 24062, ff. 4v (referring to 198r), 14r, 34r, 36r. Knapp, *Bureaucratic Muse*, 31–2, notes the careful organization.

75 BL, MS Add. 24062, f. 194v. The last paragraph on f. 194v is labelled 'xiiij', the first on f. 195r 'xv'; the text on f. 195r refers back to 'prefato' matters ('aforesaid').

76 Parkes, *Their Hands Before Our Eyes*, 47–8, 49–50, 51.

77 Christianson, *Directory*, 29–32.

78 Doyle and Parkes, 'Production of Copies', 165–7, 187.

This is an important point, undoing some past assumptions that copies of Chaucer's verse were checked by a 'supervisor' in a workshop; there is little evidence for that.[79]

There is, of course, some evidence of supervision. Hoccleve imagines scenes in his 'Series' in which a friend offers to 'ouersee' the 'book', which might evoke the 'bureaucratic collaboration' which would have been part of Hoccleve's day-job as a clerk.[80] The scribe known now as Adam Pinkhurst corrects another scribe's copy of *Piers Plowman*.[81] But as in books from religious houses, collaboration in correcting is not consistent enough to suggest an orderly system of subordinate scribes and supervisors. There is a telling example in a copy of Chaucer's *Troilus and Criseyde* from the second quarter of the fifteenth century which was made by four scribes. One of the scribes was Richard Osbarn, who worked as Chamber Clerk at the Guildhall in London from 1400–37, where he contributed to gathering and sorting documents.[82] Another of the scribes is well known from other literary books later in the century.[83] It has been suggested that one more of the four scribes on this book was overseeing the project: this other person copies less than his colleagues but he writes the outer bifolium of the first quire, as though setting a model for Richard Osbarn who wrote the rest of it.[84] Also, it looks as though it is this other person's handwriting which adds foliation in roman numerals in the very top right corner of each folio, so he might be the person gathering the leaves and quires together.[85] Finally, he adds corrections to Osbarn's stint: he writes over three erasures in one

79 For supervisors, see Manly and Rickert (eds.), *Text of the Canterbury Tales*, vol. I, 72–3, 131, 133, 200, 203, 511, 513, rebutted by Edwards and Pearsall, 'Manuscripts of the Major English Poetic Texts', 261, 274–5 n. 40; Kerby-Fulton, 'Professional Readers of Langland', 104. Sánchez-Martí, 'Adam Pynkhurst's "Necglygence and Rape" Reassessed', 369, argues for collaborative correction among London scribes but from only a few examples.

80 Hoccleve, *MP*, XXI.793–6, and XXII, moral, 5–6, on which see Knapp, *Bureaucratic Muse*, 183.

81 Horobin, 'Adam Pinkhurst', 80–2. See also Doyle and Parkes, 'Production of Copies', 166, 187.

82 BL, MS Harley 3943, ff. 2^{r}–7^{v}, 9^{r}–56^{v}, 63^{r}–67^{v}, namely quires I (except outer bifolium), II–VII, and first five leaves of IX (*Troilus*, I.71–497, I.568–III.1078, III.1639–IV.196). On Osbarn, see Mooney and Stubbs, *Scribes and the City*, 17–37, esp. 32, 35–6; and Hanna, *London Literature*, 28–9 (where he is still called the 'HM 114' scribe).

83 BL, MS Harley 3943, ff. 71^{r}–116^{v}, namely quires X–XV (*Troilus*, IV.407–V.1869). Mooney and Mosser, 'Hooked-g Scribes', 189 n. 17. They suggest that he collaborates with the 'upright hooked-g scribe', here mentioned in Chapter 9, n. 87 below.

84 BL, MS Harley 3943, ff. 1^{r-v}, 8^{r-v}, 68^{r}–70^{v}, namely the outer bifolium of quire I and last three leaves of quire IX, quires otherwise written by Osbarn (*Troilus*, I.1–70, 498–567, IV.197–406). Seymour, *Catalogue*, vol. I, 72–3, suggests that this scribe, his scribe C, or scribe A here and on *LMES*, was 'the stationer in control of production'.

85 The foliation has often been trimmed off but, when visible (BL, MS Harley 3943, e.g., ff. 51^{r}, 52^{r}), the loop on the ascender of l resembles that in the handwriting of ff. 1^{r-v}, 8^{r-v}. Also, in quires VI (ff. 41^{r}–44^{v}) and VIII (ff. 57^{r}–59^{r}) people add different quire signatures and leaf-signatures.

line and at four points fills gaps which Osbarn left blank.[86] There is some oversight in copying, then, by one scribe of Osbarn's work.

But as with the oversight in books from the Carthusian order or a nunnery, this supervision among London clerks is not sustained nor entirely successful. First, who is supervising whom is unclear, for Osbarn in turn enters some corrections into the work of a fourth scribe in the collaborative copy of *Troilus and Criseyde*, and he corrects his own work.[87] The supervised scribe becomes the supervisor. Secondly, Osbarn makes a second copy of the same poem and in this one there are no corrections by anybody supervising him. Osbarn corrects his single-handed copy with great effort, if not always success, checking his text against more than one exemplar.[88] His intelligence or meticulousness might emerge in a contrast between the way that gaps left by Osbarn were filled by the overseer of his work in the collaborative copy and by Osbarn himself in his single-handed copy. The person who checks his stint in the collaborative copy does not fill all the gaps Osbarn left and fills two of them with words which the modern editor of *Troilus and Criseyde* thinks are wrong. By contrast, in his own copy Osbarn left a blank space for each of these words or lines and filled them later – as is betrayed by the different colour of ink and the excessive space around the added words – and managed to fill them largely as the editor thinks they should be filled.[89] Osbarn's meticulousness could reflect 'archival instincts' developed at the Guildhall, gathering up and collating records as a 'professional reader'.[90] Yet how professional was his second single-handed copy of *Troilus and Criseyde*? This copy is in fairly current writing, in a casual layout and largely on paper, and bound with an odd assortment of other works.[91] It contrasts with the set aspect of his handwriting in the

86 BL, MS Harley 3943, ff. 17r (II.64, filled wrongly), 20r (II.250), 31v (II.1083, filled wrongly), 45v (III.292). Scribe A does not fill Osbarn's gap on f. 23v (II.509).

87 This other scribe copies BL, MS Harley 3943, ff. 57r–62v, namely quire VIII, now lacking 4–5 after f. 59v (*Troilus*, III.1079–288, 1429–1638). Osbarn's corrections are on ff. 59v (*Troilus*, III.1267), 61v (III.1546–7, with a mistake in the correction), 62r (III.1603). The corrections to III.1267 and III.1603 reproduce the text found in Osbarn's other copy of *Troilus* in HEHL, MS HM 114, ff. 254r, 259r, with only one letter different.

88 HEHL, MS HM 114, ff. 193r–318v, with 194 of 215 corrections in Osbarn's handwriting, and 21 unclear. Hanna, 'Scribe of Huntington HM 114', notes Osbarn's skill, as does Chapter 12, n. 2 below.

89 Contrast n. 86 above with HEHL, MS HM 114, ff. 210r (*Troilus*, II.55), 210r (II.64), 212v (II.250), 225r (II.1083), 239v (III.292). Wakelin, 'When Scribes Won't Write', discusses this episode in making this MS.

90 Bowers, 'Two Professional Readers', 113, 142.

91 When he uses parchment for the outermost and innermost bifolia, the parchment is sometimes poor quality, as in a bifolium formed from the irregular edge of the sheet (HEHL, MS HM 114, ff. 248r–249v).

collaborative copy, which is in a neater symmetrical layout of five stanzas per page, and on parchment with more decoration. So even if he copied *Troilus and Criseyde* for money in the collaborative copy, his self-made copy looks like private property, perhaps copied out voluntarily for passion, given the effort it involved. And might the correction of that copy, then, be interpreted not as obligation or obedience but as enthusiasm? That can only be speculation, but there are puzzles remaining about the motives of the scribes who took up the arduous copying of literary works alongside other, surely more useful work copying documents.

Prompts by others

In various of the settings and scenarios of book production, then, in late fourteenth- and fifteenth-century England scribes most often correct their own work. And while in some religious houses or professional settings other people do contribute, they might well themselves be merely other scribes, serving temporarily as supervisor, and the scribes corrected can also correct themselves. There is, however, in the Huntington Library's sample, one final set of corrections which suggest some organized supervision. These markings are not, though, corrections of the scribe's work but invitations to the scribe himself to correct further. These prompts (as they are here called) are instructions by people to their colleagues, and perhaps sometimes to themselves later, how and what to do.

These prompts were of long-standing use: they are found in Anglo-Saxon books and in Latin books of the eleventh and twelfth centuries.[92] Some consist merely of crosses or other signs, by which somebody gives notice that something needs fixing. Others, more explicit, consist of the text of the addition or replacement which is needed written in the margin as a cue. These prompts can be written in dry-point, that is, an un-inked nib, in grey lead plummet, in an orangey or pale red mineral, or in ink. In the late fourteenth and fifteenth centuries, they are normally written in a current handwriting modelled on anglicana, often baggy with relatively large loops and splay, even when written small. The same conventional sort of rough handwriting is used for some prompts to limners and rubricators.[93] Because they are written in this rougher handwriting, the prompts can usually be distinguished from additions entered more formally into the margins and

[92] O'Neill, 'Further Old English Glosses', 83–5; Ker, *English Manuscripts*, 50–1; Ker, 'Correction of Mistakes', 32.

[93] As in 16 instructions for headings in HEHL, MS HM 268, ff. 10ʳ, 10ᵛ, 111ᵛ, 113ᵛ, 115ᵛ, 119ᵛ twice, 134ʳ, 142ʳ, 146ʳ twice, 148ᵛ, 149ʳ, 150ʳ. Scott, 'Limning', describes such prompts.

intended to be left and seen by the reader. Unlike them, the prompts were meant to be followed by the scribe or his colleagues and then erased. As a result, most books only have a few such prompts surviving. But sometimes some roughness in the parchment and the shadows of a few letters survive to suggest that prompts were present once.[94] At other times the scribe only erased them incompletely. Some of those visible ones are counted in the column of Table 4.1 in which the main scribe and a second collaborator work together, because the main scribe came along later and followed the prompt; some of them, though, are counted only as the work of collaborators because the main scribe never did as he was told and the correction is only entered by the prompter.

In the Huntington Library, these prompts come from a limited range of books with identifiable qualities. Beyond those in Wycliffite manuscripts, they otherwise occur only in a few notably lavish books and seem to be a mark of high quality production. Some occur in a copy of aureate religious verse in handwriting modelled on textura and with decorations more befitting a liturgical book than English poetry; others occur in a copy of Thomas Hoccleve's *The Regiment of Princes*, again in handwriting modelled on textura; the final set occurs in a copy of John Lydgate's *The Fall of Princes* in handwriting modelled on bastard secretary but with many illustrations, which looks likely to have been produced for a wealthy patron whose arms appear in it (Figure 1).[95] The use of prompts seems part of the lavish attention – with different stages of writing, self-checking and emending – needed to make so fine a book. For example in this copy of *The Fall of Princes*, there are twenty-eight crosses which highlight lines which need correcting but only twelve crosses have had corrections supplied; the others were missed.[96] (The tally of corrections in Table 4.1 and elsewhere does not count any non-verbal prompts like crosses if text was nowhere supplied.) Then, as well as these minimal and missable crosses, there are also clearer marginal prompts of words in grey or red. They accompany twenty-one lines where the scribe has then written over erasure the word which

94 E.g., HEHL, MS El. 26.A.13 (Part I), ff. 28^{v}/12 (*Regiment*, 600) 29^{r}/24 (640), 35^{r}/20 (972), 36^{v}/3 (1039), 39^{r}/7 (1183), 39^{r}/19 (1195), 50^{v}/11 (1831), 82^{v}/17 (3629), 86^{v}/21 (3857), 96^{v}/12 (4408), 107^{r}/11 (4995), 112^{r}/28 (5292), 113^{r}/25 (5345). They seem to have been in red-brown colour and baggy handwriting.

95 Respectively HEHL, MS HM 142, MS El. 26.A.13 (Part I), and MS HM 268.

96 HEHL, MS HM 268, ff. 20^{r}/b23 (*Fall*, II.254), 45^{r}/a9 (III.289), 65^{v}/a19 (III.3267), 66^{v}/b13 (III.3422), 99^{v}/b14 (IV.2886), 100^{r}/b15 (IV.2948), 106^{v}/b2 (V.1052), 111^{v}/a20 (V.1830), 116^{v}/b23 (V.2727), 118^{r}/a12 (V.2891), 118^{r}/a23 (V.2902), 118^{v}/b5 (V.2989), 123^{v}/b13 (VI.650), 123^{v}/b22 (VI.659), 132^{r}/b7 (VI.2576), 136^{v}/b10 (VI.3188). Other crosses accompany verbal prompts listed in nn. 97–99 below.

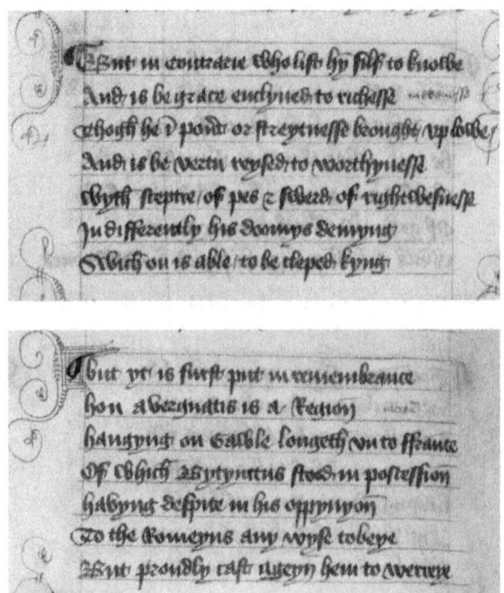

Figure 1 HEHL, MS HM 268, f. 117v: two marginal prompts in John Lydgate's *The Fall of Princes*

recurs in the prompt.[97] But most prompts survive where the scribe has not yet made the change they propose: eight propose replacements for words which are erased but not written over, and forty accompany lines which have not been touched, though they clearly could include the word in the prompt and do in the modern edition of this poem (Figure 1).[98] Despite that oversight, there is sharp-eyed attention and meticulous care by the prompter. This book and the other ones with prompts involved exceptional

97 HEHL, MS HM 268, ff. 14v/b24 (*Fall*, I.6632), 20r/b12 (II.243), 55v/a18 (III.1943), 102v/b7 (IV.3276), 107r/a31 (V.1116), 120r/b2 (V.163), 142v/b5 (VII.303), 142v/b11 (VII.309), 142v/b24 (VII.322), 143v/b20 (VII.451), 146v/b10 (VII.826), 148v/b27 (VII.1123), 149r/a21 (VII.1145), 149v/a35 (VII.1229), 150r/b19 (VII.1311), 150v/b27 (VII.1368), 151r/b22 (VII.1434), 151r/b24 (VII.1436), 155r/b4 (VIII.284), 155v/a22 (VIII.337), 157v/a26 (VIII.1370).

98 HEHL, MS HM 268, with only erasures by prompts on ff. 24v/b26 (II.838), 59r/a24 (III.2418), 67r/a7 (III.3447), 67v/a31 (III.3545), 102r/b20 (IV.3219), 104v/a16 (V.485), 123v/b20 (VI.657), 133r/b18 (VI.2727); and with ignored marginal prompts on ff. 19v/a9 (II.149), 25v/b10 (II.962), 57v/b20 (III.2239), 61v/a25 (III.2748), 62v/b13 (III.2911), 64r/a23 (III.3082), 64v/a19 (III.3134), 66r/b5 (III.3344), 68v/b7 (III.3689), 70v/b30 (III.3992), 71r/b20 (III.4045), 75r/a27 (III.4528), 75r/b17 (III.4553), 79r/b6 (III.5102), 83r/b20 (IV.475), 85v/b18 (IV.1047), 86r/b3 (IV.1102), 96r/b11 (IV.2419), 96v/a26 (IV.2469), 101r/a14 (IV.3038), 101r/a19 (IV.3042), 101v/b24 (IV.3153), 102r/a33 (IV.3197), 104v/b24 (V.528), 110v/a2 (V.1679), 111v/a19 (V.1829), 112v/a11 (V.1945), 115r/b11 (V.2421), 117v/a22 (V.2832), 117v/b9 (V.2853), 121v/b16 (VI.387), 127r/b27 (VI.1141), 127v/a25 (VI.1173), 127v/b18 (VI.1201), 127v/b28 (VI.1211), 128r/b33 (VI.1286), 129r/b29 (VI.1408), 136r/a1 (VI.3074), 136r/a34 (VI.3107), 139v/b2 (VI.3614). The scribe ignored a few prompts by lines which are already identical to the edited text: ff. 93v/b8 (IV.2087), 134v/b2 (VI.2914), 140v/b14 (VII.70) and perhaps on f. 123r (VI.581). Five of the unused prompts (ff. 24v, 57v, 101r, 121v, 136r) are written interlineally. For their contents, see Chapter 8 below.

effort by several craftsmen on script and decoration too; that suggests the kind of production process which allowed for stages of collaborative prompting.

Some of these prompts, then, do reveal scribes working with others who could check their work and issue instructions on what they should write. However, these prompts do not suggest that scribes were disengaged and dumbly effecting changes proposed by others. First, because the prompts are written in the baggy handwriting typical for instructions for rubricating or to limners, and not in the neater handwriting used for copying, it is unsure whether these prompts are indeed written by a colleague; some might be written by the scribes as notes to themselves. To repeat, it is harder to be sure that unlike handwriting is not by the same person than it is to be sure that similar handwriting is. The distinction is especially difficult when the prompts are only crosses: for instance, in the copy of *The Fall of Princes* eight of the tiny pale crosses are by lines where the scribe has already corrected, but only roughly, writing one letter over another without erasure. Such ugly overwriting in a book otherwise beautifully made might look like interim changes of things he spotted as he went, and the crosses might look like his notes to himself to come back and tidy up later.[99] Table 4.1 lists all these prompts as involving the work of collaborators (in order not to favour unfairly the argument of this chapter for the predominance of scribes in correcting), but many prompts could be by the scribe himself.

Even if these prompts were instructions from other people, they need not diminish our sense of the engagement of scribes. To understand this co-operation, a useful model is sketched by Richard Sennett: he sees a 'dialectic' between submission to authority and creative autonomy as typical of craftsmanship.[100] Even in this minority of cases when the scribe was prompted by others, correction still required the practical skills of the scribe to do what was prompted. He needed his wits about him for this: a pale lead cross would be tricky to spot and leave the scribe to decide what needed fixing, or a word in the margin would leave the scribe guessing exactly where it should go. Although the scribes sometimes overlooked them, it is arguable that the presence of such prompts would make the scribes self-consciously, critically aware of the craft of correcting and of the works

99 HEHL, MS HM 268, ff. 45^{r}/a8 (*Fall*, III.288), 70^{v}/b23 (III.3985), 103^{v}/b28 (V.392), 107^{r}/b28 (V.1148), 118^{r}/a12 (V.2891), 121^{v}/b5 (VI.376), 124^{v}/b12 (VI.789), 130^{r}/b28 (VI.2338). Also, four crosses accompany corrections made by erasure and/or overwriting: ff. 71^{v}/b16 (III.4097), 109^{r}/b28 (V.1428, though he forgot to write over the erasure), 118^{v}/a19 (V.2968) and 151^{r}/b23 (VII.1434).

100 Sennett, *Craftsman*, 54, 159–60.

thus corrected; the fact that they were not always followed suggests the attention the prompts would require. So although the prompts tell scribes what to think, they did at least make scribes think. The corrections which do or should follow prompts would be the products of retrospection – one person looking back over the copy and then asking the scribe to look back over it too – and would involve future planning. Moreover, as the corrections which result are following explicit instructions, they might be more conscious than the majority of corrections made quickly by the scribe by himself; somebody here is drawing his attention to his work. Anyway (as this chapter began by noting), the majority of correcting is not done *to* scribes but *by* them – by the person whose work is being corrected at the point in question. And (as the following chapter argues) the techniques they use encourage them to awake their senses to their craft.

PART II

Craft

CHAPTER 5

Techniques

So that al errours / [be]^throgh crafte / be circu*m*cided

San Marino, Huntington Library, MS HM 268, f. 24v

John Lydgate, *The Fall of Princes*, II.838

The scribes and their collaborators who correct English books use techniques, like the prompts which call them to attention, which foster their agency and intelligence. That awakening of human capability and consciousness is one of the defining features of craftsmanship. It is a characteristic of the crafts or skills of book production and annotation, regardless of the employment status and social institutions of the person doing these skilled things.[1] As the sociologist Richard Sennett has brought out: wherever it occurs, what distinguishes the craftsman is the way that he develops his intelligence and self-critical thinking as a form of 'material consciousness'. It is the practical activities of the craftsman which foster intelligence, agency and effort – 'the special human condition of being engaged'.[2] Craft is a special instance of the ways in which 'mind and matter . . . continually bring each other into being', so that human thinking develops through human engagement with material objects.[3] While some have argued that the finished artefact is what stirs reflection, and on the part of the consumer, here the argument is that making things can sharpen the craftsman's awareness and understanding of those things.[4] Making is a form of knowing. The practical procedures of correcting foster among scribes and some readers an alert, conscious knowledge of the properties of the objects – both the material book and the words of the text – that they are correcting.

[1] This focus on the internal dynamics of craft contrasts with other studies, which tend to focus on its social context and ideology, as noted by Pappano and Rice, 'Medieval and Early Modern Artisan Culture', 474.

[2] Sennett, *Craftsman*, 20, 119–20. [3] Boivin, *Material Cultures*, 23.

[4] Contrast the focus on finished works of Hannah Arendt, discussed by Brown, 'Objects, Others, and Us', 191, and Sennett, *Craftsman*, 1–2, 6–7.

Yet how conscious were people of correcting? Their methods of correcting were evidently influenced by prior training and shared protocols, as all craft tends to be. Scribes presumably taught each other what to do, but they seldom wrote it down reflectively. (This chapter, therefore, has to reconstruct their techniques and comprehension from the traces left in books.) Also, practical techniques and physical materials can exert their own duress, through what they can or cannot do, so that there might be less consciousness here than coercion.[5] Given such ingrained habits and material constraints, was the craft of correcting an instance of what has been called 'tacit' knowledge, felt – literally – from the handling of tools and materials but not articulated?[6] Much work is done almost mechanically.[7] But, as Sennett notes, there are moments likely to stir consciousness, intelligence and autonomy when craftsmen have 'solved problems in practice' through 'correction and adaptation' and 'learning from one's mistakes', as the common phrase puts it.[8] When things go wrong, thought is required. So (this chapter will argue) putting things right was likely to invite the attention and nurture the intelligence of scribes.

Did corrections visible on the page also catch the attention of readers? That might seem unlikely. The corrections are often difficult to see, the scribes might have wanted them to be invisible and readers might have taken them for granted as ubiquitous and necessary features of books. For comparison, it would be odd for readers of recent printed paperbacks to pay much attention to the barcode on the back cover. To notice these corrections, then, might be an anachronistic, overly close misreading of these books. Yet this deliberate over-attentiveness is typical of all forms of palaeography and bibliography, which sometimes involve seeing things that the makers did not want the *users* of books to see.[9] And the *makers* of the corrections, by contrast, would notice them to some extent as they stopped and chose to rewrite what they had copied. So (it is argued) the craft of correcting was visible to scribes and readers and gave them insight into the making of books and the literary works they contained.

Visible techniques

Even the best technique for correcting invisibly was highly visible in the culture of the time. That technique was erasure: scraping the parchment

[5] Gilissen, *Prolégomènes*, 36, stresses this point. [6] Sennett, *Craftsman*, 94–5, and also 179, 181.
[7] Sennett, *Corrosion of Character*, 68.
[8] Sennett, *Craftsman*, 134, 159–60, and *Corrosion of Character*, 72–4.
[9] Tanselle, *Bibliographical Analysis*, 62.

with a knife to remove the error and, usually, writing over it. Erasure with a knife was part of the common iconography for picturing scribes. In umpteen illustrations from the eleventh century to the fifteenth people who are writing hold a pen in their right hand and in their left hold a knife. It is not a constant image: it is found, for example, in only a quarter of fifteenth-century English pictures of men writing; but it is frequent enough to make erasure a visible part of what scribes do: scribes not only write but remove and rewrite.[10] Of course, many of the people pictured writing were not scribes copying but were the Fathers or evangelists composing.[11] So these pictures might tell us more about inspiration or invention, in which that rewriting would be a sort of revision; yet they made visible the dependency of writing upon erasure.

Erasure can be clearly reconstructed. The English term for it was the verb *rasen*, 'to erase'.[12] The knife was known in English word-lists as 'a scrapyng iron', 'a shavyng knyf', 'a penne knyfe', 'a shapyng knyf', 'a scrapyn knyfe' or similar terms and in Latin by many different names such as *scarpellum*, *cultellus*, *novaculum* and *rasurium* among others.[13] Knives were on hand in making books, for holding down the springy parchment, for sharpening the quill and maybe for cutting open folded sheets, so were readily available for scraping errors.[14] If the scribe were tidy, he could use pumice, powdered bone known as *pounce* or a piece of ivory known as a *boner* to smooth the scraped parchment ready for overwriting.[15] Erasure could thus remove the erroneous text completely, so that it can be difficult to see whether any correction has occurred. That invisibility might have been intended: for example, among manuscripts of the works of John Capgrave, more correcting is done with this nearly invisible method in the copies for patrons than in working copies, as though Capgrave wished the copies which were gifts to look flawless.[16] More of the time, though, the erasure

[10] Whalley, *Writing Implements*, 14, 17, 31, 33; Scott, 'Representations of Scribal Activity', 132.

[11] Scott, 'Representations of Scribal Activity', 142.

[12] *MED*, *rasen* (*n.*) 1(b). One poet coins the verb 'rade' from Latin *rado*: Liddell (ed.), *Middle English Translation of Palladius*, prol. 6–7.

[13] Gould, 'Terms for Book Production', 93; Griffiths, 'Book Production Terms', 68–9; Teeuwen, *Vocabulary of Intellectual Life*, 161–2, 192; Leclercq, 'Pour l'histoire du canif'; Latham, *Revised Medieval Latin Word-List*, *ras/ura*.

[14] Whalley, *Writing Implements*, 14–17; de Hamel, *Scribes and Illuminators*, 36–9; Clemens and Graham, *Introduction to Manuscript Studies*, 18. On cutting folded sheets, see Gilissen, *Prolégomènes*, 39.

[15] Petti, *English Literary Hands*, 29; Whalley, *Writing Implements*, 91; Hector, *Handwriting of English Documents*, 49–50; *OED*, *pumice* (*n.*) B.1b, B.1c, and *pumice* (*v.*); *MED*, *pounce* (*n.*) 2. *Boner* in this sense appears in neither *OED* nor *MED*; however, bone was used similarly to smooth leather: *OED*, *bone* (*n.*) 5e.

[16] Lucas, *From Author to Audience*, 75–89.

is itself visible. In some manuscripts, the knife has torn the page;[17] in some the pumice, pounce or polish leaves the erased parchment whiter or greyer than its surroundings.[18] Almost always, the ink of the new writing over the erasure bleeds into the parchment fuzzily or dries a slightly different colour. Sometimes the scribe in haste erases the ruling too or leaves the error still visible like a shadow. Even this technique, then, could remain if not obvious then visible.

Erasure and overwriting were the pre-eminent technique of correction in monastic books of the eleventh and twelfth centuries.[19] In the fourteenth- and fifteenth-century books in English from the Huntington Library, it is still the most common method: 42 per cent of corrections (3,894 of 9,220) were made by erasure with writing over the top (Table 5.1). It is used in all sorts of books. Some manuscripts use erasure more frequently, perhaps in order to conceal their imperfections, for they are in high-grade handwriting modelled on anglicana formata and have elaborate layouts: these are some finely presented copies of Chaucer's *Canterbury Tales*, Langland's *Piers Plowman* or Gower's *Confessio amantis*.[20] But equally the shared preference in these books for erasure could reflect not visual concerns but training in one time or place, around London in 1400. Or the decision to erase or not might not be an aesthetic one; it might be practical. Sometimes people do not use much erasure and overwriting because they are writing on paper. It is possible to erase from paper but it is difficult, as paper is more frangible than parchment. The growing use of paper in fifteenth-century books is reflected in the Huntington Library's sample, in which ten of the fifty-two books are wholly or mostly on paper; seven of them have no erasures overwritten.[21] Of the three that do, one has only five such;[22] another has parchment leaves at the innermost and outermost parts of quires, on which many of the erasures were made.[23] Erasures on paper are only frequent in a copy of some medical works, where what look like erasures are so white that they might have been made by daubing something

17 E.g., HEHL, MS HM 28561, f. 154^{v} (*Polychronicon*, 3.33.57: 'þe fiȝtin[–]{g}me*n*ne'). Figuet, 'Corrections', 335–6, identifies a technique for correcting tears from erasure.

18 E.g., HEHL, MS El. 26.A.13 (Part I), *passim* for majuscule I written over erasure, discussed in Chapter 7 below.

19 Ker, *English Manuscripts*, 50.

20 Respectively, HEHL, MS El. 26.C.9, MS HM 137 and MS El. 26.A.17, listed in Table 5.1 and described by Dutschke, *Guide*, vol. 1, 39–50, 183–4.

21 HEHL, MS HM 133, MS HM 139, MS HM 140, MS HM 144, MS HM 505, MS HM 745, MS HM 60320.

22 HEHL, MS HM 135: e.g., ff. 21^{v}/18, 'ha[-]{d}' (*Regiment*, 1165), 37^{v}/24, 'langely[–]{th}' (2348).

23 HEHL, MS HM 114: e.g., ff. 203^{v}/10, '[he]{yn}' (*Troilus*, 1.726), 203^{v}/22, '[T]{F}or whi' (1.738), 205^{v}/5, 's[uch]{yþ}' (1.850).

Table 5.1 *Some techniques for correcting in the HEHL sample.*

shelfmark	*contents*	*no. of corrs*	*replacement by erasure overwritten*	*crossing out, subpuncting or erasure*	*interlineation (and addition on the line)*
El. 26.A.13: I	Hoccleve, *The Regiment of Princes*	587	575 98%	5 1%	4 1%
El. 26.A.13: II	*Joseph and Asenath*	16	4 25%	11 69%	–
El. 26.A.17	Gower, *Confessio amantis*	52	50 96%	1 2%	–
El. 26.C.9	Chaucer, *The Canterbury Tales*	143	99 69%	14 10%	28 20%
El. 35.B.63	Edward of York, *The Master of Game*	134	5 4%	51 38%	66 49%
HM 1	the Towneley plays	170	6 4%	113 66%	48 28%
HM 55	Capgrave, *St Norbert*	111	30 27%	13 12%	65 59%
HM 58	*Agnus castus*; recipes	154	25 16%	35 23%	80 52%
HM 64	medicine	138	59 43%	24 17%	51 37%
HM 111	Hoccleve, short poems	51	40 78%	–	10 20%
HM 112	Hilton, *The Scale of Perfection*	489	141 29%	60 12%	222 45%
HM 113	prose *Brut*	44	39 89%	1 2%	4 9%
HM 114	Langland, *Piers*; Chaucer, *Troilus*, *etc.*	373	77 21%	32 9%	196 53%
HM 115	Lydgate, *Life of Our Lady*	73	20 27%	15 21%	8 11%
HM 124	*Speculum Christiani*	68	46 68%	5 7%	11 16%
HM 125	*Prick of Conscience*	64	11 17%	39 61%	13 20%
HM 126	Rob. of Gloucester, *Chronicle*	128	63 49%	24 19%	28 22%
HM 127	religious miscellany	63	36 57%	12 19%	17 27%
HM 128	*Prick of Conscience*; Langland, *Piers*	787	394 50%	367 47%	8 1%
HM 129	*Northern Homily Cycle*	500	251 50%	80 16%	57 11%

(*cont.*)

Table 5.1 *cont.*

shelfmark	*contents*	*no. of corrs*	*replacement by erasure overwritten*	*crossing out, subpuncting or erasure*	*interlineation (and addition on the line)*
HM 130	*Prick of Conscience*	442	407 92%	18 4%	6 1%
HM 131	prose *Brut*	8	–	2 25%	5 63%
HM 133	prose *Brut*	343	–	215 63%	190 55%
HM 134	Wycliffite New Testament	428	118 28%	101 24%	111 26%
HM 135	Hoccleve, *The Regiment of Princes*	22	5 23%	8 36%	4 18%
HM 136	prose *Brut*	57	29 51%	3 5%	24 42%
HM 137	Langland, *Piers*	75	55 73%	2 3%	2 3%
HM 139	*Prick of Conscience*	54	–	35 65%	3 6%
HM 140	miscellany	74	–	35 47%	26 35%
HM 142	religious miscellany	25	15 60%	3 12%	6 24%
HM 143	Langland, *Piers*	416	125 30%	124 30%	131 31%
HM 144	miscellany	318	–	234 74%	108 34%
HM 147	*Vices and Virtues*	110	90 82%	6 5%	9 8%
HM 148: I	religious miscellany	75	9 12%	29 39%	40 53%
HM 148: II	Rolle, *Psalter*	685	484 71%	145 21%	61 9%
HM 149	Love, *Mirror*	81	48 59%	5 6%	24 30%
HM 266	Hilton, *The Scale of Perfection*	172	99 58%	10 6%	43 25%
HM 268	Lydgate, *Fall of Princes*	219	130 59%	24 11%	10 5%
HM 501	Wycliffite Psalter	71	–	29 41%	15 21%
HM 502	religious miscellany	132	7 5%	23 17%	57 43%
HM 503	Wycliffite sermon	184	23 13%	42 23%	39 21%

Table 5.1 *cont.*

shelfmark	*contents*	*no. of corrs*	*replacement by erasure overwritten*	*crossing out, subpuncting or erasure*	*interlineation (and addition on the line)*
HM 505	Daniel, *Dome of Urynes*	186	–	134 72%	53 28%
HM 744: I	religious miscellany	154	13 8%	10 6%	9 6%
HM 744: II	Hoccleve, short poems	51	44 86%	–	8 16%
HM 745	Tudor royal accounts	25	–	19 76%	6 24%
HM 1336	medicine and prognostications	12	–	1 8%	11 92%
HM 1339	Love, *Mirror*	228	88 39%	33 14%	102 45%
HM 19079	medicine	52	5 10%	7 13%	33 63%
HM 26054	*arma Christi* roll	1	–	1 100%	–
HM 28561	Trevisa, trans. of *Polychronicon*	248	111 45%	33 13%	95 38%
HM 39872	trans. of *Livre de bonnes meurs*	31	17 55%	5 16%	9 29%
HM 60320	astrology	11	–	7 64%	2 18%
fragments in other MSS	various	85	1 1%	51 60%	41 48%
total		9,220	3,894 42%	2,296 25%	2,199 24%

on the page instead.[24] The decision to use erasure, then, might be affected by one's materials. Or it might reflect the type of change required: the requirement to replace one piece of text with another, rather than simply to add or delete something. There are other ways to replace something: scribes could also cancel or subpunct something then add something else in the margin or interlineate it (techniques discussed below). Yet people combine these other techniques thus in only 3 per cent of the corrections (284 of 9,220); far more frequently, for replacing text, the preferred method is erasure and overwriting.

Erasing and overwriting can also be used not only for replacing the wrong word but for adding words where the scribe has omitted them.

[24] HEHL, MS HM 64.

The preferred method for filling in missing text in monastic copying, centuries earlier, had been erasing some words either side of the omission and writing them again over the top, with the missing words now included.[25] The scribes could catch the error immediately and scrape and rewrite as they went, or they could do so later. Such later checking is likely where the words written over an erasure are too long for the erasure; then, in order to fit the overwriting, people use copious abbreviations or unusual superscript letters, leave barely any space between the words or continue the words beyond an erasure into the margin. All these things occur, for example, in a very well-made copy of Nicholas Love's *Mirror of the Blessed Life*.[26] Erasure and overwriting was not the only possible technique here; this book has slightly more additions between the lines than erasures overwritten. But this is a well-made book, with careful pricking and ruling, coloured decorations and a professional handwriting modelled on anglicana formata. The correcting is carefully done, too: the erasures overwritten sometimes had prompts written in the margin by somebody checking the book.[27] The same techniques, of marginal prompts to erasure and overwriting, are used in another copy of the same work which could be by the same scribe or at least from a similar milieu.[28] This shared practice might come from shared training, perhaps in a religious house, and not from any desire for invisibility – for, indeed, the passages squeezed in are clearly seen and unsightly, and other corrections are done more visibly still.

Some 25 per cent of the corrections (2,296 of 9,220) involved removing something without writing over the top. (Although in 284 of those cases, there was an interlineation or marginal addition alongside.) For merely removing text, erasure was a rare technique; commoner were crossing out and subpuncting. This might be because the scribes dislike blank space on the page, into which other people could put things. Such a dislike emerges on those few occasions when scribes do merely erase things or

[25] Ker, 'Correction of Mistakes', 31.

[26] HEHL, MS HM 1339, e.g., ff. 4^{v}/26–7 (*Mirror*, 15.23), 10^{v}/11–12 (28.9–10), 10^{v}/25–6 (28.27–8). On this MS, see Chapter 8, pp. 208–12 below.

[27] The prompts were then erased, but a few were left: HEHL, MS HM 1339, ff. 43^{v}, 't*ur*ne' (*Mirror*, 102.33), 54^{v}, 'telleþ newe' (127.4), 71^{v}, 'world' (163.24), 103^{v}, 'p*re*ci<–>', (235.26).

[28] CUL, MS Mm.5.15, e.g., f. 20^{v}/28–9 (*Mirror*, 35.28), where a marginal prompt, lightly erased, notes that only the adverb 'gladly' was missing but where, in order to insert it, the words '*con*ceyvi*n*ge *and* she gladly' are written over erasure. Dutschke, *Guide*, vol. II, 565, and *Mirror*, ed. Sargent, 107, 111, suggest that HEHL, MS HM 1339, CUL, MS Mm.5.15 and CUL, MS Oo.7.45 are by the same scribe, but Doyle, 'Reflections', 87–8, doubts that. So do I, although the scribes are so alike that they might have been trained together.

erase a passage which is longer than that which replaces it; then they fill the space left with some lines, squiggles or punctuation marks.[29] These fillers suggest a concern for clarity, preventing confusion at the presence of blank spaces, and that might explain why the scribes far prefer crossing out and subpuncting unwanted words, methods which make the deletion visible and prevent additions by others.

The terms for crossing out in the fifteenth century are *to draw* and *to cancel*. Geoffrey Spirleng, as scribe of *The Canterbury Tales*, explains in English why 'This writyng is drawen' where he has crossed out a colophon, for instance.[30] The Latin comes from *cancelli*, a plural noun meaning 'trellis', like the pattern made by hatched lines of crossing out. But most cancelling in English is simpler than a trellis and is one or more horizontal lines. (Therefore, I prefer the term *crossing out* to *cancelling*.) A rougher version of this technique is complete obliteration or blotting. These terms are common in English of the period,[31] but most crossing out is neater than these terms suggest.

Another technique for marking things as deleted is subpuncting, in which one puts a dot under a letter needing to be ignored or, if more needs removing, a row of dots. This method is common in the fourteenth and fifteenth centuries but dies out in the sixteenth. (Palaeographers also call it *expunctuation*, *expunging* and *underdotting*, but *subpuncting* seems better as it is unlikely to be confused with the general term *expunge*.)[32] Most scribes use both crossing out and subpuncting at some point or other, but it is uncommon for them to use both to an equal extent; most prefer one technique to the other. It has been suggested that subpuncting was preferred in deluxe manuscripts, in which a tidy and regular page was more important than an accurate text.[33] This might be so in finely decorated manuscripts in Latin, but in the sample of English books most scribes prefer crossing out to subpuncting. The mess might not be a bother in

29 E.g., HEHL, MS HM 147, ff. 36^{v}, 'feb[->]{elen. / /.}' (Francis (ed.), *Book of Vices and Virtues*, 93.25), 45^{v}, '[-----]{*and* whan~}' (115.35), 58^{v}, '[->]{~at~}' (148.24).

30 GUL, MS Hunter 197 (U.1.1.), f. 102^{v}, on which MS see Chapter 3 above.

31 Petti, *English Literary Hands*, 29; *OED*, *cancel* (*v.*) 1a, *cancelling* (*vbl. n.*), *blot* (*n.*^{1}) 1a, *blot* (*v.*) 2, *obliterate* (*v.*) 2; *MED*, *cancellen* (*v.*) c, *cancelling* (*ger.*) a. Latham, *Revised Medieval Latin Word-List*, records *cancello*, under *cancell/us*.

32 Clemens and Graham, *Introduction to Manuscript Studies*, 35; Johnson and Jenkinson, *English Court Hands*, vol. 1, 78; Denis Muzerelle's website *Vocabulaire codicologique*, http://vocabulaire.irht.cnrs.fr/pages/vocab1.htm, under item 413.05. I cannot trace an English term before *dot* recorded in the sixteenth century (*OED*, *dot n.*^{1}), although Latin *expungo* and post-classical *expunctor* did refer sometimes to textual obliteration (Lewis and Short, *Latin Dictionary*).

33 De Hamel, *Scribes and Illuminators*, 43.

books less lavish, like the numerous English books copied for practical or private use. Moreover, crossing out hides an error more clearly than subpuncting does, so that the text becomes easier to read correctly.

The choice of crossing out might sometimes be determined by the practicalities of the cursive handwriting which scribes of English often use from the fourteenth century on; the relatively greater speed of such writing might encourage the speedy technique of crossing out, rather than erasing. The speed might be imagined in the manuscript in the Huntington's sample of the mystery plays known as the Towneley cycle. This scribe's corrections remedy very slight slips, spotted immediately. There are perhaps only six erasures, and most of them are by later hands.[34] Over half the corrections (100 of 170) were simple crossing out with a single line, twenty-one of them in red ink, which was also used for punctuation and decoration, and seventy-nine in brown ink which looks identical in colour to the surrounding text; this crossing out was likely done by the scribe as he went along.[35] Why did he not use erasure and overwriting, given that he was copying on parchment and adorned the plays with copious red ink and elaborate initials, as though he meant them to look smart? It could be that he avoided interrupting the flow of his more cursive documentary style of handwriting by pausing to scrape an erasure; using the pen to cross things out would preserve his pace. It could be that he did not have a knife because he had a red pen in his other hand, ready for rubrication, and with which he made some crossing out too.[36]

As that suggests, one determinant for the use of crossing out might be when and by whom correcting occurs. Erasure is often used when things are spotted later; by contrast, when problems are spotted immediately while the scribe has the pen still running (*currente calamo*), then crossing out with that pen is common.[37] This emerges because many of the errors crossed out are incomplete or alternative versions of what follows immediately – duplications, jumps forward or egregious misspellings; many consist of only a letter or two or even just part of a letter, which the scribe realizes

34 HEHL, MS HM 1, ff. 34r (Stevens and Cawley (eds.), *Towneley Plays*, 12.179, speech heading erased), 64v/2 (by the scribe; 18.250), 66r/23 (19.181–2), 123r/12 (30.155), 123r/13 (30.157–8), 128r/21 (30.777). The last three might be later damage and repair.

35 Also, twice crossing out in brown is repeated with red ink: HEHL, MS HM 1, ff. 6r (Stevens and Cawley (eds.), *Towneley Plays*, 2.324), 39v (13.199).

36 HEHL, MS HM 1, ff. 4r (Stevens and Cawley (eds.), *Towneley Plays*, 2.122, 2.136), 7r (2.452), 34r (12.179), 35v (12.381), 42r (13.486), 45v (13.933) and so on. Cawley and Stevens (eds.), *The Towneley Cycle: A Facsimile*, xi–xiv, discusses the rubrication. On stages of rubrication, see pp. 120–2 below, and on the choice of script, see Wakelin, 'Writing the Words', 48.

37 On the different timings, see Hudson (ed.), *English Wycliffite Sermons*, 139–44.

is wrong before he can write anything long enough to make sense.[38] With such egregious errors, obviously similar to what immediately follows, or with incomplete words, not something one would leave uncorrected, it is likely the scribe who does the crossing out before he continues with the proper version further along the line. That speed of response need not, though, suggest any less discernment over the text; it suggests the scribes' ongoing and quick-witted attention, as they realize what they are doing wrong in the midst of copying.

Such crossing out with the pen remained visible to readers; and there are occasions when it is possible that the scribe sought that visibility. This seems possible when they cross out in red (discussed below) or in high-grade books. For example, in a copy of English religious poems in handwriting modelled on a dressy textura quadrata, the scribe usually makes replacements with erasure overwritten; but when he only needs to remove something he crosses out. At one point he is confused by two successive stanzas which have the same opening word and rhyming syllable, and which occur at a page-break. He skips a stanza but then realizes and starts the stanza again:

> [. . .] In flesschly synne as I haue tyght
> + [Ih*esu* that art heuen kynge] +
> [f. 17^{v}] Ih*esu* graunt me myn askynge
> Parfyte paciens my disese
> And neuer I mote do that thinge
> That schude the in any wise displese
> Ih*esu* that art heuen kynge [. . .][39]

The crossing out is in red, framed by two small crosses, thus making a decorative feature of it. Crossing out might be preferable to erasure here, for writing over erasure would involve starting the new stanza – whether the correct one or the wrong one – on the last line of a page, leaving a sort of 'widow' or stray part of the text on the page; erasing alone would leave a confusing blank space at the foot of the page. Although it is messier, then, crossing out might be preferable for its visual clarity in marking what is correct.

[38] HEHL, MS HM 1, ff. 1^{r} (Stevens and Cawley (eds.), *Towneley Plays*, 1.59), 1^{v} (1.99), 8^{r} (3.96), 10^{r} (3.359), 14^{r} (4.106), 14^{v} (4.185), 17^{r} (6.97), 18^{r} (7.60), 19^{v} (7.230), 23^{r} (8.205), 23^{v} (8.287), 25^{v} (8.420), 30^{r} (10.225, 228), 37^{v} (12.671), 39^{r} (13.103), 42^{v} (13.540, 541) and so on.

[39] HEHL, MS HM 142, f. 17^{v}; Brown (ed.), *Religious Lyrics of the XVth Century*, no. 64.12–17. The rubric might be by the scribe, as a tiny correction in rubric on f. 43^{r} (interlining 'be') looks like his handwriting. On this MS, see Wakelin, 'Writing the Words', 39, fig. 2.3.

Other techniques likewise remain clearly visible. One final technique for deleting, rare but noteworthy, lets the error itself remain visible and comments on the need for deletion explicitly. People write the Latin word *vacat* meaning 'it is needless' in the margin, with some small markings to show where the needless text begins and ends, or they write *va* at the start and *cat* at the end of what is unwanted.[40] People do write *vacat* by passages of just one or two lines,[41] but they usually only write it where there is a lengthy passage to remove, which it would be tedious and ugly to cross out in full. As a result, this technique is only seldom required: *vacat* appears only five times in the Huntington Library's English books and seldom with a simple purpose.[42] Three of the five examples occur in a Wycliffite New Testament and seem not to mark duplications, for the text is correct, but to mark passages to skip when reading aloud, for this is a Gospel Lectionary which has been annotated for reading aloud. Both the marks for readings and the marks of *vacat* are in red.[43] The term *vacat* was also used for marking passages to skip when excerpting, so this might be an analogous practice.[44] Yet *vacat* is similar to subpuncting and most crossing out in that it not only provides the correct text; importantly, because the error is still legible, it requires people to notice the process of correcting and, as it were, to effect the correction in their mind.

The process of correcting is visible also in various techniques for adding to the text: squeezing text between the lines, known as interlineation, at the end of the line, or in the margins. Adding things (as Chapter 10 shows) is more frequent than removing things. Nearly one quarter of all corrections (24 per cent or 2,199 of 9,220) involve squeezing something between the lines or in a handful of cases between words on the line itself (Table 5.1). (In 273 cases, it is combined with deleting something.) This technique is described in the fourteenth and fifteenth centuries loosely as *setting in* extra material.[45] But terms *interlineal* and *interlinear* also occur, taken from Latin where they describe the glosses which were common in books for study. The verb *interline* is used to describe emending a text,

40 Rare variations are 'nul' (HEHL, MS HM 135, f. 51^{r} twice, where *Regiment*, 2941–53 is duplicated from f. 48^{v}) and 'voide' (BL, MS Add. 25718, f. 70^{v}, where *Tales*, IV.441 will be duplicated on f. 71^{r}).

41 This is rare enough that there were no examples in the HEHL sample. But see, e.g., OTC, MS 49, ff. 60^{v}, 68^{r}, 85^{v}, 174^{r}. That scribe also puts crosses by 13 lines needing deletion (e.g., ff. 11^{r}, 47^{v}, 108^{v}).

42 E.g., HEHL, MS HM 114, ff. 81^{r-v}, 81^{v}–82^{r}, on which see Russell and Nathan, '*Piers Plowman* Manuscript', 123, and Chapter 12, n. 5 below.

43 HEHL, MS HM 134, ff. 97^{r} (*Wycliffite Bible*, Galatians 5.16 to 6.12), 109^{r-v} (2 Timothy 2.11 to 3.9), 122^{r}–123^{r} (Acts 6.10 to 7.54).

44 Jones, 'Jesus College Oxford, MS 39', 237.

45 Hudson (ed.), *Selections*, 14.71.

often in messy or ugly ways, sometimes alongside the verb *blot* ('enterlynit and blotted').[46]

Interlining recurs across books of all sorts: for instance, it is frequent in both Capgrave's neat presentation copy of *The Life of St Norbert* and a plain copy of the prose *Brut* in hurried handwriting on paper.[47] Sometimes people add text between the lines without any further indication of its purpose; normally, though, they add a *caret* mark at the point where the insertion should be made. The *caret* mark most often resembles an upended *v* thus ^ ('folow^^{e}the'),[48] but sometimes it resembles two short sloping lines thus // which seem to be a more casual form, like a *caret* in which the two strokes do not meet.[49] For example, the person who interlineates a lot in the (aforementioned) copy of the prose *Brut* sometimes uses two virgules ('w//^{h}ere'). He more often uses an otherwise rarer variant of just one line or virgule ('w/^{h}ed*er*', 'w/^{h}ere').[50] And like many scribes he combines interlining the right letters with subpuncting or deleting the wrong ones: 'the tone es [q]w/^{h}yte // And the other es rede', 'Vter hym selffe dwellede a [q]w//^{h}ylle at ȝorke'.[51] Though he copies in very current handwriting on unruled sloping lines, and though he does not worry about the method or neatness of the emendation, he does slow down to care for the text. Here, for instance, he even emends tiny dialectal divergences in spelling by removing the Norfolk and northern spelling <qw> in favour of the more widespread <wh>.[52] Indeed, his care extends to consistent efforts to interline single letters, as when some fifteen times he interlines <h> into words which begin with <wh> in Present Day English – even to the extent of doing so unconventionally, turning the verb *were* into something like the conjunction *where*, for example ('there nestes w//^{h}ere in stakkes').[53]

46 *OED*, *interline* (*v.*), *interlineal* (*a.*) 1, *interlinear* (*a.* and *n.*) A.1, *interlineary* (*a.* and *n.*) B.1a, *interlining* (*vbl. n.*); *MED*, *interlīnen* (*v.*), *interlīniārē* (*adj.*), *interlīnieng* (*ger.*); Latham, *Revised Medieval Latin Word-List*, *interlin/eatio*. And see the Paston letter illustrated in Petti, *English Literary Hands*, 59 and fig. 10.

47 In Table 5.1, respectively HEHL, MS HM 55 and MS HM 133.

48 HEHL, MS HM 133, f. 107^{v} (*Brut*, 163.3).

49 Johnson and Jenkinson, *English Court Hands*, vol. 1, 78, illustrates five variants. *OED*, *caret*, is not recorded until 1710, but Latin *caret* ('it is wanting') is common in fifteenth-century English MSS, as noted in Chapter 10, pp. 258–61 below.

50 HEHL, MS HM 133, respectively ff. 18^{v} (*Brut*, 39.4), 27^{v} twice (50.6, 50.12). The needlessness of this change is suggested by uncorrected spellings without <h> such as 'werfore' nearby (f. 27^{v}, 50.18). *OED*, *where* (*adv.* and *conj.*), and *MED*, *wher* (*adv.* & *conj.*), record forms with only <w>.

51 HEHL, MS HM 133, ff. 34^{r} (*Brut*, 58.8), 39^{r} (65.30).

52 *LALME*, vol. 1, 372–3 (dot-maps 272, 275).

53 HEHL, MS HM 133, f. 63^{v} (misinterpreting *Brut*, 94.26). *MED*, *ben* (*v.*) records no spellings with <wh> for *were*, but *OED*, *be* (*v.*), and *LALME*, vol. 1, 337–8 (dot-maps 131–3), do.

And he uses interlining, hurried and simple though it is, on a grand scale, some 105 times in order to emend this book.[54]

Yet although his text is improved, it is also made confusing to read, for the interlining clutters up the page. On the one hand, unlike a gloss, which is supplementary, the interlined word needs to be read smoothly and continuously, as though it were part of the main line. On the other hand, interlineations prevent a smooth reading, for they disrupt the eye-movement of the reader, requiring glances up and then back down, as he recognizes the correction and works out how to incorporate it. The reader assembles the correct text in his mind, for on the page it is in pieces. Some disruption occurs for the person writing the interlineation too, for most interlineations reflect the process of reading the text later. It could be a second person checking the scribe's work later or it could be the main scribe re-reading his work after the process of copying is complete, with retrospective care. Or even when the scribe himself writes between the lines in the midst of the process of copying, he is reading the text later – even if only a split second later, only a word or two further on. Were he correcting before he continued writing the very next word, then he would have been able to write the correction on the same line, as after crossing out; by contrast, he would need to use interlineation when he had already progressed at least a little further. For the scribe, then, interlineation results from retrospective reflection on what he has copied.

Some similar process of having second thoughts pertains with another technique for adding text: putting it in the margin or at the head or foot of the page. (As the head and the foot of the page are margins of a sort, Table 5.1 classifies all these phenomena as marginal additions.) This is rarer but not rare: about 7 per cent of corrections (693 of 9,220) involve adding something in the margins. The word *margin* is recorded in Latin in its current sense since antiquity and in English from the late fourteenth century. The Latin adjective *marginalis* appears by the thirteenth century but English *marginal* not until the 1570s and *marginalia* centuries later.[55] From the fourteenth century, some works in English had marginal annotations accompanying them, copied by scribes, as did some works in French and Latin. Scribes and readers, then, were used to moving their eyes

[54] And a contemporary makes 76 more interlineations in the same volume: e.g., HEHL, MS HM 133, f. 86^{v}, 'harenstreng' (diverging from *Brut*, 136.5). This handwriting differs from the main scribe's in one-compartment **a**, **e** with broken strokes, rather than hurried 'backwards' **e**, and **g** with a clockwise rather than anti-clockwise descender. Some of these differences could result from slower writing when interlining single words, as opposed to copying long stretches.

[55] Latham, *Revised Medieval Latin Word-List*, *margin/alis*; *MED*, *margin(e* (*n.*) c; *OED*, *margin* (*n.*) I.2a, *marginal* (*a.*) A.1a, *marginalia* (*n.*), *margining* (*n.*).

to the side of the page, and so corrections there might not bother them. For example, a copy of Edward of York's *The Master of Game* includes twenty-three additions at the edge or foot of the page, keyed to the main text by a cross or a *caret*.[56] Some are long, all follow the standard textual tradition precisely, and one continues the style of presentation found in the main text, by writing some words of French in red ('Swef mon amy Swef').[57] These marginal additions are, then, clearly restored by people checking the copy with the exemplar, or with a further exemplar, and are integral to the production of the book. Some could reflect commonsense guesses, when they are short additions essential to the grammar such as inserting the subject of the verb, 'þai', or working out that 'shayll dovne the water' is a garbled version of 'shall seile dovne the water'; most of these little changes are made to the first scribe's work by the second.[58] But others must reflect collation of this copy with its exemplar, especially the longer ones added to the second scribe's work by a third person.[59] The resulting text demands attention from the reader, who must put the pieces back together, and suggests the attentiveness of the scribes, especially scribe B who read carefully both scribe A's stint and his own.

Yet marginal corrections are only the most extreme signs of the second-order reflection which might be revealed by interlining, subpuncting and crossing out. Such reflection is a sort of double vision of the text – a wrong prior version, a right later one, visible together like a hologram. And as well as seeing two versions of the text, scribes and readers can see the material processes of craftsmanship which turn one into the other; at these points the process of textual transmission is visible. Overall, only a few corrections, mostly erasures, are thoroughly hidden from the readers' view; some are even highlighted by their prominence in what are conventionally empty spaces or by their messiness. And none of the corrections were hidden from the scribes who troubled to wield the knife or pen: they too enjoy the second-order reflection on their own craft, which might otherwise seem like the prerogative of readers. Like readers, scribes must look back over the text and think about the work of producing it – even if only seconds later – in order to change it. Corrections make visible both the craft of copying the text, by making part of the process less smooth than elsewhere,

56 See nn. 57–8 and also HEHL, MS El. 35.B.63, ff. 1^{r}, 2^{r}, 3^{r}, 4^{r}, 5^{r}, 5^{v}, 7^{r}, 7^{v}, 8^{r}, 11^{r}, 14^{v}, 15^{r}, 17^{v}, 19^{r} twice, 24^{r}, 25^{r}, 38^{r}.

57 E.g., HEHL, MS El. 35.B.63, ff. 15^{v} (21 words), 23^{r} (39 words, including French in red), 31^{r} (21 words), all by scribe C on scribe B's work.

58 HEHL, MS El. 35.B.63, ff. 4^{v}, 7^{v}.

59 This later person differs from scribe B (of ff. 10^{r}–44^{r}), in that, apart from an occasional long **r**, he models his handwriting on secretary, rather than on anglicana formata.

and the qualities of the text itself, by making clear that the final form of it involved rejecting another form of it as though wrong. Corrections allow both scribes and readers to see and reflect on why the book and the text are one way and not another – an implicit commentary on the scribe's craft and the author's.

Intentional visibility

Yet we might wonder: although people could often *see* the craftsmanship behind the book and the text, did they *notice* it consciously? Given its ubiquity, was correcting not ignored by the habitual makers and users of manuscripts? In fact, on the pages of manuscripts there are several marks which are designed to draw attention to the process of correcting. Some corrections take the form of explicit instructions; they are not always complete words but they are nonetheless firmly communicating something. The instructions are meant for the eyes of readers; but in such marks the scribes themselves remark on that craft, explicitly and consciously.

Some explicit comment is necessary when the earlier incorrect version of the text is still visible on the page, and the reader needs to complete the correction in his or her mind. The briefest sorts of comment are clearly a direction for readers, for they originate in the construe-marks used to help learners of Latin with construing or unravelling syntax. Students whose mother tongues had a more fixed word-order than Latin were taught to mark the 'natural' order of the Latin words with the letters *a*, *b*, *c* and so on above the line.[60] Curiously, such construe-marks seem to have expressed some sense among grammars of Latin that there were conventions for correct word-order which the best Latin stylists deliberately flouted as a feature of style; construing was always to some extent corrective, then.[61] By an explicable conceptual leap, people use these letters *a*, *b*, *c* and so on in correcting, to reorder words, lines or stanzas which are out of sequence. This practice too results from the scribe or someone else reading back the text later and trying to make sense of what is wrong – a sort of scholarly study of what is copied. It is very rare in the Huntington Library's books, occurring in only 53 of the 9,220 corrections, for it can only correct the order and not the absence or choice of words.

Scribes can reorder the words within the line; for that, they most often use not *a*, *b*, *c* but two small virgules thus // written slightly above the line

[60] Budny, 'Assembly Marks', 209–11. Hudson (ed.), *English Wycliffite Sermons*, 140, calls them 'reversing marks'.

[61] Reynolds, *Medieval Reading*, 110–19.

in front of the words to be reversed, as for example in a reference to what a soul will do 'for //knowyng //defaut of//.' of hit self'.[62] Very occasionally the word which is out of order is the last word in the line, and then it is difficult to be sure whether the virgules are used to reorder words or to add a missing word in the margin, with the virgules showing where to insert it. This question arises, for instance, in a copy of *The Prick of Conscience* where eleven lines have virgules before the last word thus.[63] Yet such virgules are frequently used to reorder even insignificant details, such as the position of adverbs: for example, in Robert of Gloucester's *Chronicle* the phrase 'This worde was //vnderstonde //wel' would have been well understood with these two words reversed or not; likewise, whether *thither* comes first in 'he //þuder //furst com' is irrelevant to sense.[64]

It is also feasible to reorder whole lines in poetry, where lines are discrete units.[65] Even if the scribe does use virgules for reordering within the line, he uses letters for reordering whole lines; the scribe of Robert of Gloucester's *Chronicle* makes this distinction for reordering lines.[66] He also uses letters in the margin to reinsert lines which he first skipped by mistake but remembered and then copied further down the page – inserting which looks, in result, like reordering.[67] Such insertion is frequent elsewhere in verse, for instance, in a copy of Chaucer's *Canterbury Tales* which has twenty-five sets of construe-marks on what look like lines skipped: the scribe writes hastily and erringly but he quickly spots and includes the missing lines only a line or so later.[68] At such points the scribe's alertness is at first briefly lacking but is revived a few moments on. Moreover, the scribe directs the reader to wake up and recognize his correction, for the

62 HEHL, MS HM 112, f. 3^{r} (the contents list for chap. 34 of *Scale*).

63 HEHL, MS HM 139, ff. 1^{r} (*Prick*, 61), 3^{r} (424), 7^{r} (1104), 20^{r} (3952), 22^{r} (4374), 28^{v} (5862), 34^{v} (7289), 34^{v} (7335), 37^{v} (8034), 37^{v} (8071), 39^{v} (8586). The first three are by scribe A, the others by scribe C.

64 HEHL, MS HM 126, ff. 42^{r} (Robert of Gloucester, *Chronicle*, 2661), 84^{v} (5716). See similarly ff. 22^{v} (1108), 74^{v} (5067), 103^{r} (7170), 125^{r} (8921), 132^{v} (extra line xx.402). Only the reorderings on ff. 64^{r} (4392) and 82^{r} (5561) seem needful for grammar.

65 The HEHL sample also contains one reordering of lines in prose in HEHL, MS HM 147, f. 19^{r} (Francis (ed.), *Book of Vices and Virtues*, 60.3–7). The scribe of BL, MS Add. 17013, f. 16^{r}, who uses this MS as his exemplar, apparently misses the construe-marks, for he keeps the uncorrected order.

66 HEHL, MS HM 126, ff. 98^{r} (Robert of Gloucester, *Chronicle*, 6793–4), 123^{r} (8755–6), 124^{r} (8855–6).

67 HEHL, MS HM 126, ff. 57^{v} (Robert of Gloucester, *Chronicle*, appendix R.1–2), 87^{r} (5890), 127^{v} (extra lines xx.7–8).

68 BL, MS Egerton 2864, ff. 5^{v}, 7^{r}, 11^{v}, 27^{r} twice, 29^{r}, 35^{r}, 38^{r}, 40^{r}, 51^{r}, 63^{v}, 75^{v}, 88^{v} (used wrongly: *Tales*, III.569–70), 98^{r}, 106^{r}, 106^{v}, 137^{v}, 147^{v}, 166^{r}, 170^{r}, 228^{v} (used wrongly; *Tales*, VII.3061–2), 246^{v}, 249^{r}, 250^{r}, 256^{v}. By contrast, scribe B (ff. 274^{r}–341^{r}), only reorders lines twice with these construe-marks (ff. 325^{v}, 336^{v}). See also BL, MS Sloane 1686, discussed in Chapter 10, pp. 250–4 below.

reader must reorder the lines mentally, whereas they stand still disordered on the page. Correctness is drawn to conscious attention.

Conscious engagement is demanded too by marginal additions, which also ask the reader to put the text, scattered round the page, in order. Therefore, scribes often ensure that readers notice their additions quite pointedly by using *signes de renvoie*: signs which direct the eye to text in unexpected positions. In books in English these symbols get used to do lots of things: to direct us when to read some text which has been inserted in the margins at the side, above or below;[69] to direct us when to read lines of verse which are copied at the bottom of the column or page (Figure 2);[70] or sometimes to direct us to extra leaves on which longer sections are inserted. The eye is used to reading straight down a column – English is really read vertically as much as left to right – and so the presence and position of the correction outside the vertical column needs to be noted. These *signes de renvoie* are like the omission signs which had been used for centuries in monastic copying.[71] In the first millennium the signs had often been the letters 'hs' and 'hd' for *hic sursum* and *hic deorsum* or *above* and *below*. But Irish scribes preferred crosses, asterisks, lines and dots, and later English scribes from the fourteenth century on preferred these and other abstract symbols: the *caret*, also used for interlineations, as well as crosses, crosses in boxes, 'hatch' marks, circles with dots in, collections of dots like the modern shorthand for *therefore*, or single letters and numbers.[72] Like construe-marks, the *signes de renvoie* evoke the arts of reading: several were borrowed from textual criticism, such as the *obelus* used in classical scholarship to mark a corrupt passage, or from glossing practices; the Latin word *obelus* was used in English to refer to marks in textual criticism.[73] It is as though these marks reflect a scholarly response by the scribe and invite such a response from the reader.

Although these marks are abstract and do not describe their function in words, they are nonetheless explicit comments on the process of correcting.

69 E.g., HEHL, MS HM 134, f. 83^{v} (*Wycliffite Bible*, 1 Corinthians 4.20), likely omitted through eyeskip on the repetition of 'v*er*tu'.

70 E.g., HEHL, MS HM 143, ff. 6^{r} twice (*Piers C*, I.131–2, 137), 95^{v} (XXI.84–7), 101^{v} (XXII.23), 102^{r} twice (XXII.45, 49). See also nn. 76–8 below on this MS.

71 Ker, *English Manuscripts*, 50; and, e.g., HEHL, MS HM 19915, ff. 21^{r}, 22^{r}, 23^{v}, 24^{r}, 25^{r}, 26^{r}, 27^{r} twice, 29^{r}, 29^{v}. On these signs, see Parkes, *Pause and Effect*, 307; Lemaire, *Introduction*, 180; *OED*, *renvoy* (*n.*) 2, with one citation only, from 1650.

72 E.g., HEHL, MS HM 114, ff. 262^{r}, 277^{v}, 318^{r}; MS HM 129, ff. 68^{r}, 86^{v}, 215^{v}; MS HM 266, ff. 20^{v}, 28^{v}.

73 Budny, 'Assembly Marks', 206–8; Lowe, 'Omission Signs', 349, 378; Parkes, *Pause and Effect*, 305; *OED*, *obelus* (*n.*); Lewis and Short, *Latin Dictionary*, *obelus*; Latham, *Revised Medieval Latin Word-List*, *obel/us*. Contrast *OED*, *obelisk* (*n.* and *a.*) I.2a, and *dagger* (*n.*^{1}) 8, for later terms.

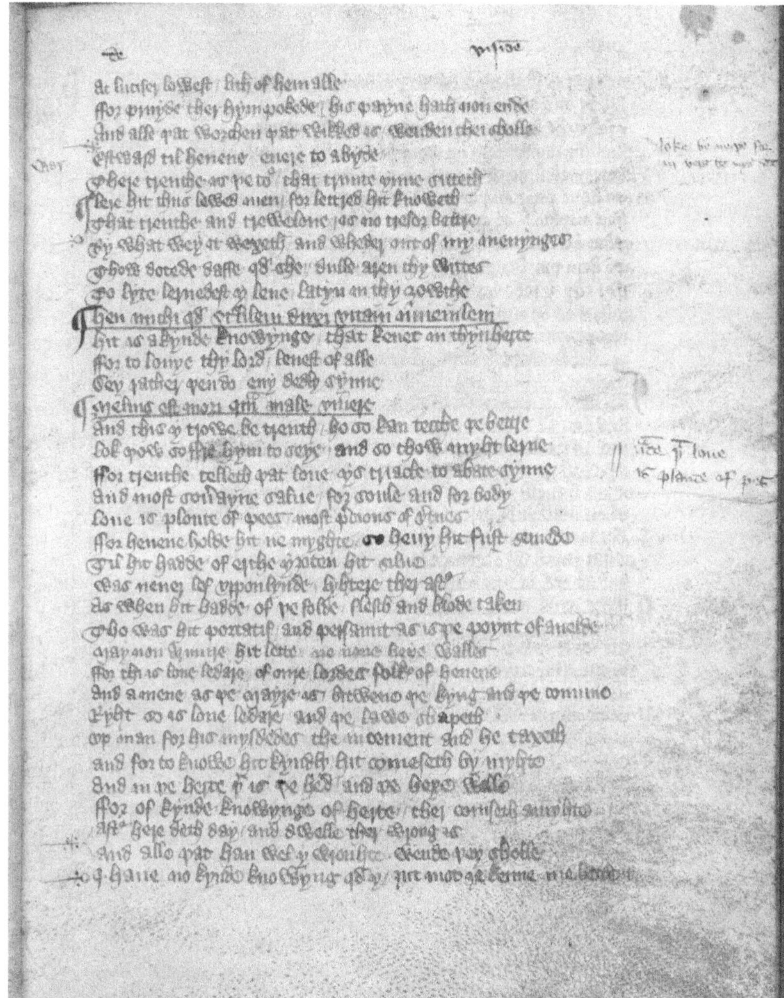

Figure 2 HEHL, MS HM 143, f. 6r: *signes de renvoie* and notes reordering the text in William Langland's *Piers Plowman*

Given the length of their tradition, such symbols could be clearly communicative. The communicative intent is evident also in the usual terms for them – the English word *sign* or the Latin *signum* – and in the use of imperative verbs addressed to onlookers: 'Req*ui*re ad t*a*le*m* sig*nu*m' or 'uide ad tale signu*m*' ('look for a sign like this') or 'looke for the sequell of this storie nyne leves folowynge at the Sygne'.[74] For example, in one copy of *The Prick of Conscience*, the text is reordered with a black cross in a diamond and a pointing hand known now as the manicule; next to these symbols in red ink the scribe writes 'Be : war', 'Turne ouur to þe doþur cros', 'Turne a ȝeyn þer to þe doþur hond' and 'turne ouur to suche a syng'. These instructions throw light on early terms for some particular signs – the 'cros' and the 'hond' – and throw light too on the onus they put on readers to see and beware.[75] Similarly, when a scribe provides missing lines in a copy of Langland's *Piers Plowman*, he not only draws a *signe de renvoie* to show where to insert them but he also writes in black or red 'war', like the previous injunction to 'Be : war'.[76] At one of these points, an early fifteenth-century reader adds further, 'loke be neþe for iij vers be*n* mys set' (Figure 2).[77] This reader writes other annotations instructing readers to see, both literally and metaphorically, as he points out topics of interest in the poem: 'Rede hyer', 'be hold se lo', 'beth war of þis', 'hyer*e* ȝe may se [. . .]'.[78] These annotations both bear witness to this particular user's reading of the poem so far and guide future users of the poem how to read it.[79] Likewise, the *signes de renvoie* both record the scribe's or somebody else's careful reading and enjoin others to notice the state of the text and the craft of correcting which has preserved it.

One final feature also seems to invite us to notice the corrections, although this is not as surely intentional: the use of red ink, known as rubric. Red ink is used for only 7 per cent of corrections (684 of 9,220) in the Huntington Library's books and it is clustered in only a few of them: although many manuscripts have one or two corrections in red, red appears in large quantities in only eight of the fifty-two books largely in English.[80] Was red meant to make the corrections noteworthy or visible? Red was often

74 HEHL, MS HM 114, ff. 277^{v} (*Troilus*, IV.952), 262^{r} (III.1743); HEHL, MS HM 266, f. 16^{r} (*Scale*, 170–2), directing readers to an extra leaf now f. 1^{r-v}; BL, MS Harley 1245, f. 104^{v} (*Fall*). For other uses of *signum*, *ad tale signum* and *require*, see, e.g., CUL, MS Kk.3.20, ff. 142^{v}, 229^{v}; GUL, MS Hunter 215 (U.2.6), ff. 75^{r}, 82^{r}, 118^{r} (cartulary of Holy Trinity Priory, Aldgate); BL, MS Add. 24062, ff. 4^{v}, 138^{v} (Hoccleve's formulary); Oxford, Corpus Christi College, MS 242, ff. 21^{v}–22^{r} (*Fall*, I.1933, 1940). For its use in extracting, see Jones, 'Jesus College Oxford, MS 39', 237.

75 OTC, MS 16A, ff. 19^{r}–20^{v} (*Prick*, 1184–279). Sherman, *Used Books*, 33, finds 15 names for the manicule or 'hond' in the sixteenth and seventeenth centuries.

76 HEHL, MS HM 143, ff. 6^{r} (*Piers C*, I.130–1), 95^{v} (XXI.84–7).

77 *Ibid.*, f. 6^{r} (*Piers C*, I.130–1). 78 *Ibid.*, e.g., ff. 7^{v}, 9^{v}, 41^{v}, 58^{v}, 70^{r}, 72^{v}, 75^{r}, 76^{v}.

79 Wakelin, 'Instructing Readers', discusses the double function of such annotations.

80 HEHL, MS HM 1 (27 of 170 corrections use red), MS HM 58 (44 of 154), MS HM 129 (65 of 500), MS HM 133 (103 of 343), MS HM 134 (88 of 428), MS HM 144 (213 of 318), MS HM 501 (21 of 71), MS HM 503 (31 of 184). The tally excludes corrections of headings or other passages which were already in red, e.g., HEHL, MS HM 128, ff. 4^{v} (*Prick*, 370–1) 10^{v} (932–3), or in one case blue (HEHL, MS El. 34.B.7, f. 23^{r}).

used to highlight things in fourteenth- and fifteenth-century manuscripts, such as numbers, names and quotations which might be thought especially important.[81] Also, the physiology of colour perception suggests that red would catch the eye, and culturally the colour evokes danger, authority or richness. How far was that notability intended for corrections?

Often the use of red reflects not deliberate design but the practicalities of book production, such as cheap work or haste: if the scribe is writing on paper he does not need a knife for erasing, or if he is not planning a second stage of work, he might keep his red pen to hand for punctuation and decoration as he goes and then use it for correction too. Conditions like these seem to encourage corrections in red, for example, in a copy of the prose *Brut* and a religious and moral miscellany in which a lot of the correcting is done in red by crossing out before the scribe continues copying.[82] For example, the scribe of the miscellany misreads the letters f and long s in his exemplar but realizes in time to start the words again: 'For they [softe] fostred the' and 'deceyt [saf] falshede and trecherye'.[83] The way that he can cross out the errors in red while the words are still incomplete suggests that the red pen was at hand during the initial process of writing. These books were rough productions, with quirky textual variation and odd selections of excerpts.[84] Such scribes might not have expected other people to see the book at all, let alone intended the red corrections to be noticeable.

However, red ink was sometimes used designedly. That is so even in the idiosyncratic miscellany, where some of the corrections in red reflect retrospective activity. Some of the crossing out in red is accompanied by interlineations of the right word in the usual brown ink, and the interlining suggests that the changes were made at least a split-second later. As the interlineations are in the ordinary brown ink, the use of red ink for the accompanying deletion looks like a distinct choice to change pens, and might betray the scribe not hurrying forward but pausing or even looking back.[85] This is not unique. Some scribes adorn the corrections they had first made in their usual brown ink with further decoration in red, even in

81 Alcorn Baron, 'Red Ink and Black Letter', 20–1.

82 HEHL, MS HM 133 (with 103 of 343 corrections in red) and MS HM 144 (213 of 318).

83 HEHL, MS HM 144, ff. 129r, 133r; Burgh (trans.), *Paruus Cato Magnus Cato*, 801, 1032. The exemplar was Benedict Burgh (trans.), *Paruus Catho* (Westminster: William Caxton, 1476; *STC* 4851), in which the crossbar on f in 'fostred' is almost invisible (unsigned leaf c8r) and there is a slight gap in 'fal shede' (unsigned leaf D6v).

84 On HEHL, MS HM 133, see Matheson, *Prose Brut*, 202–3; on HEHL, MS HM 144, see Dutschke, *Guide*, vol. 1, 197–203.

85 HEHL, MS HM 133, where 14 of 103 corrections using red have interlineation in brown; HEHL, MS HM 144, where 25 of 213 do.

those manuscripts where red often looks as though it were used in haste. For example, in the (aforementioned) copy of the prose *Brut* the scribe crosses out in red seventy-four words which he has already subpuncted or crossed out in the brown. In the lines 'that he [myght] schuld come' or 'owth off þis [lande] Reame', he fusses over what could be acceptable synonyms and he fusses over what could be already clear crossing out in brown by redoing it in red.[86] The colour is not an accident but an intentional decoration of corrections made earlier in haste. This duplication of effort with red is found widely beyond the Huntington Library's books.[87]

The use of red might be meant to make the corrected text more legible. Red ink was used for clear instructions, the rubrics, on the conduct of service in liturgical books. It was also used to highlight the initials or punctuation marks which clarify the structure of the text.[88] Red ink might, then, have been associated with instructions how to read the right bits of text in the right order and in relation to each other. That association might suggest the reason for using red to tell people not to miss or mistake corrections or their function – to notice which errors to ignore, which interlineations and suchlike to restore. The clearest example of such helpfulness is in a copy of *The Northern Homily Cycle* in which the scribe wrote sixty-seven missing single words in the margins, before he or a colleague drew red boxes round all but six of them.[89] The call to attention is evident in the likeness of these boxed corrections to the scribe's marginal annotations which tell readers what to 'no*ta*' or pick out the odd 'narracio' or 'rel*aci*o' for them (*stories*). The red boxes ensure that the extra words added, many of them very short, are not missed. In most cases somebody had drawn boxes round these words in brown beforehand, so their presence was already highlighted; red adds nothing necessary.[90] Changing pens and doing something twice looks like a conscious effort to direct readers to notice the correcting, and reveals that the scribe or some colleague had reflected on the corrections, their clarity and effectiveness.

More elaborate decoration than this is unusual, but there are a few examples of coloured illumination or gilding on *signes de renvoie* or of

86 HEHL, MS HM 133, ff. 42ᵛ (*Brut*, 70.9), 112ᵛ (195.25). There are also passages subpuncted in brown *after* rubrication, e.g., a proper noun and upper-case A on f. 7ʳ (*Brut*, 23.21–3).

87 E.g., BL, MS Add. 39659, where 38 of 65 corrections on ff. 1ʳ–52ᵛ are subpuncted and crossed out in brown and then further crossed out in red.

88 Alcorn Baron, 'Red Ink and Black Letter', 22; Derolez, *Palaeography*, 40.

89 HEHL, MS HM 129, with brown only on ff. 2ʳ, 33ᵛ, 42ᵛ, 46ʳ, 152ʳ, and no box at all on f. 113ᵛ.

90 The exceptions in HEHL, MS HM 129, with red boxes and no prior brown are on ff. 7ᵛ, 15ʳ, 17ʳ, 17ᵛ, 23ʳ, 24ᵛ, 26ʳ, 34ᵛ, 37ᵛ, 43ᵛ, 47ᵛ, 55ʳ, 71ʳ, 80ᵛ, 83ʳ, 167ᵛ, 219ᵛ and 226ʳ. The lack of prior brown boxes earlier in the MS suggests that his policy of boxing them in brown developed during copying and that he then went back to complete or adorn the boxes in red.

marginal additions written in illusionistic scrolls.[91] People were not averse to highlighting their corrections. But even simpler methods reveal the scribes' reflection on their work and invite readers to pay attention too, sometimes accidentally, by the mess they make, sometimes by the scribe's deliberate adornment. They engender conscious awareness of the craftsmanship behind textual transmission. The processes of correction were not invisible or 'tacit' knowledge but were something on which scribes could comment consciously. As Richard Sennett suggests, 'In the higher stage of skill, there is a constant interplay between tacit knowledge and self-conscious awareness, the tacit knowledge serving as an anchor, the explicit awareness serving as critique and corrective.' It is the exercise of this critical consciousness that improves 'Craft quality'.[92] The corrections are moments where scribes exercise critical judgement on their work; and they leave visible traces of conscious choices about how to transmit texts and about the texts which they transmit.

Their consciousness emerges in one final technique, where they comment on the text explicitly. Their comments fall into three groups. One is the set of prompts by one scribe to another to make corrections (discussed in Chapter 4). Another is a set of comments on things missing, such as 'defectus' or 'fault' (discussed in Chapter 10). The others are comments on the fact that the manuscript has been corrected. People record this by writing the letters **co**, **cor** or **ex** and then a flourish for abbreviation like that for the letters *ur*, shaped like a rounded **u** with a tail to the right. This could abbreviate the Latin passive past participle *correctus* or *examinatus* for *corrected* or *examined*, or it could be the present tense of *corrigitur* or *examinatur* for *it is corrected* or *it is examined*; it might just be the present subjunctive *corrigatur* used jussively for *let it be corrected*. The rare occasions when the word is written in full give conflicting suggestions for expanding these abbreviations. At least one manuscript in Latin has the words 'tot*us* corigit*ur*' ('it is all corrected') with the usual abbreviation here for **ur** at the end of the present tense verb. One book in English has the note 'corrigat*ur* fabul*a*' ('let the story be corrected'), here with the vowel <a> for the jussive subjunctive mood, but again using the same abbreviation on the present tense. However, another Latin manuscript has 'to*tu*m corectu*m*', and one in

[91] E.g., TCC, MS R.3.15, ff. 25ʳ, 33ʳ, 35ʳ, 196ʳ, 218ʳ, 253ʳ, 268ʳ: interlineations repeated in the margins in scrolls; Philadelphia, Rosenbach Museum and Library, MS 439/16, f. 200ʳ (*Fall*, IX.360): a marginal addition in a pink scroll; HEHL, MS HM 1087, f. 29ᵛ (Book of Hours, made in Flanders, with a couplet in English added): wavy lines inside a three-dimensional grisaille drawing of a scroll. See also BL, MS Arundel 38, and BL, MS Harley 4866, discussed in Chapter 11 below.

[92] Sennett, *Craftsman*, 50, 78.

English has 'corect' with a flourish on the crossbar of **t**, suggesting 'corect*us*' or perhaps just 'corect' implying a process already completed and perhaps using a past passive participle instead.[93] (Given the conflicting expansions but the consistent use of the abbreviation for ***ur***, I expand the abbreviation as *corrigitur* in this book but without strong conviction that it is right to do so.) There are a few other rare variants, such as 'le*gitur*' ('it is read').[94] Unusually, in one book a reader writes 'no*n* co*rrigitur*' by some gaps which have not yet been filled but should have been.[95] More usually, these words accompany successful correcting. They are not too common: *corrigitur* or *examinatur* occur in only six of the fifty-two once separate manuscripts in English and one of the twenty-eight manuscripts with snippets of English in the Huntington Library. Yet the word *corrigitur* and its synonyms are found far more commonly than any other book-producing terms.[96] Of course, prompts of words to be inserted and non-verbal marks such as *signes de renvoie* are commoner still but they comment on the process only implicitly. It is intriguing that the commonest thing for scribes to say explicitly about their work is to record the process of correcting.

Sometimes these words are positioned regularly at the end of every quire, as is 'Corr*igitur* i*n* textu' in a copy of Gregory's *Decretalia* with early signs of English provenance.[97] They can even occur on the recto or front of every leaf, as does 'cor' in a copy of Latin sermons from fifteenth-century Exeter.[98] But such frequency and regularity are rare. The manuscript in the Huntington Library with the most such marks, a copy of Langland's *Piers Plowman*, has twenty-five marks of 'co*rrigitur*' but irregularly spaced. If this mark allowed an evidently methodical scribe to keep track of his work, then that work was conducted in fitful bursts; at one point the mark appears twice, once more scruffily, once more neatly, at the foot of one page for some reason.[99] Nor are these marks necessarily written by scribes

93 Respectively, CUL, MS Dd.1.17, f. 12^{v}; BodL, MS Arch. Selden B.14, f. 67^{v}; BodL, MS Auct. F.5.26, p. 219; BodL, MS Bodley 288, f. 24^{v}. In each case, the misspelling with single <r> might suggest that we should not put too much stress on its evidence. Cambridge, Peterhouse, MS 190, ff. 8^{v}, 16^{v}, 24^{v}, 32^{v}, has **cor** with the zed-shaped **r** like the abbreviation for the Latin inflexion **o*rum***, followed by a superscript **t** and the abbreviation for ***ur***.

94 The term 'le*gitur*' does not occur in the HEHL sample but occurs at the end of quires in CUL, MS Mm.5.15, ff. 10^{v}, 18^{v}, 26^{v}, 34^{v}, 50^{v}, 66^{v}, 74^{v}, 98^{v}. See n. 28 above on the scribe.

95 Chicago, UL, MS 565, ff. 75^{v}/10 (*Fall*, 1.4556, almost trimmed in the margin), 92^{v}/9 (1.5552).

96 Scott, 'Limning', 148, 166 n. 31.

97 HEHL, MS HM 19999, at the end of every quire, ff. 10^{v}–251^{v} (with those on ff. 112^{v} and 121^{v} nearly trimmed and rubbed off). This MS has been corrected in both the main text and the gloss (e.g., erasures overwritten on ff. 73^{r}, 92^{v}, 142^{r}), so 'i*n* textu' could mean *in the text (as opposed to the gloss)* or *against what is written (in the exemplar)*.

98 BodL, MS Bodley 865, ff. 2^{r}–88^{v}. On its provenance, see Ker, *Catalogue*, no. 318.

99 HEHL, MS HM 143, ff. 8^{v}, 12^{r}, 16^{v}, 18^{v}, 23^{r}, 29^{v}, 37^{r}, 44^{r}, 49^{r}, 50^{v}, 60^{r}, 62^{v}, 67^{r}, 69^{r}, 70^{r}, 71^{r}, 73^{r}, 74^{r}, 79^{r} twice, 83^{r}, 85^{r}, 95^{v}, 96^{v}, 103^{r}. The MS is in regular quires of eight leaves. See also HEHL, MS HM 147, f. 66^{r}, 'co*rrigitur*', in the middle of quire IX although at the end of a chapter.

with great training or skill. For example, in some Latin alchemical recipes and excerpts seemingly by some scholarly person for his own use, the scribe added the word 'co*rrigitur*' on fifty-seven pages at a later stage in ink that has dried a darker colour.[100] It also appears in a scruffy manuscript of the herbal *Agnus castus* and short cures.[101] Yet the roughness and irregularity might suggest that these notes are the product of reading and thought in stages and are not just automatic procedures or done for show.

There were, however, settings in which 'co*rrigitur*' and its synonyms were well-established procedures, and they suggest some of the motives behind such self-conscious comment if not always the milieux. These words occur in Continental books from monasteries and universities, where textual accuracy would be important.[102] They are used by professional makers of books in France,[103] and in English such notes often occur in books by scribes who look as though they write for a living with some skill and some organization. In some manuscripts 'ex*aminatur*' accompanies prompts to correction in what might be a second hand.[104] The professional skill and pride in craftsmanship emerge in the use of *corrigitur* by 'Hankok', a late fourteenth-century copyist of a Sarum Manual in handwriting modelled on a fine textura (discussed in Chapter 1). His corrections were made in orderly fashion, by checking and entering prompts in pale ink in the margins, then entering the changes with erasure and overwriting, and finally erasing the prompts.[105] He writes 'co*rrigitur*' palely in lead and discreetly close to the gutter at the foot of the final verso of nearly every quire,[106] and finally more boldly in red alongside his own name.[107] This looks like an advertisement of his professionalism and carefulness.

Yet the professionalism of such scribes might have varied origins. Such notes were once considered evidence that copies of *The Canterbury Tales* were produced in orderly workshops under supervision; however

100 HEHL, MS HU 1051, at the foot of ff. 91r–100v, 105r–123r (part of item 61 and items 63–8 in Dutschke, *Guide*, vol. II, 746–7), by the scribe who overall wrote ff. 83r–90r, 90v–125v, 141r–148v, on whom see Chapter 1, pp. 2–3 above.

101 HEHL, MS HM 58, ff. 13v, 42v, 50v, discussed in Chapter 6 below.

102 See, e.g., Pollard, 'Pecia System', 153; Cohen-Mushlin, 'Twelfth-Century Scriptorium', 98.

103 Rouse and Rouse, *Manuscripts and their Makers*, 87, 108, 120; Gehin, *Lire le manuscrit médiévale*, 176.

104 HEHL, MS HM 268, ff. 34v (end of quire V), 42v (quire VI), 146v (XXI), 154v (XXII); HEHL, MS El. 26.A.13 (Part I), ff. 49v (end of quire VI), 73v (quire IX), 91r/8 (mid-quire, mid-page). Prompts in the former MS are listed in Chapter 4, nn. 96–9 above.

105 Though he left a few prompts visible: HEHL, MS HM 30986, ff. 2v/a1, 3r/a12.

106 HEHL, MS HM 30986, ff. 8v, 19v, 26v, 34v, 42v, 49v, 56v, 82v, 97v. On this MS, see Chapter 1, pp. 1–2 above.

107 HEHL, MS HM 30986, f. 89v, ending at Jefferies Collins (ed.), *Manuale*, 162. The next leaf (f. 90r) has a different layout and comes from earlier in the text (Jefferies Collins (ed.), *Manuale*, 5–13), which suggests that f. 89v was originally the last page.

(as Chapter 4 noted), there is little evidence for such arrangements being common. Dan Mosser has noted that in one copy of *The Canterbury Tales*, *examinatur* is usually written by the scribe himself rather than by any supervisor.[108] This note might make sense not only in communal workshops, whatever they would be, but also among scribes working independently and freelance for a stationer, for it would advise others with whom one did not work closely what one had or had not done. Also, marks of *examinatur* have a pedigree in documentary and legal practice, which was the other employment of many scribes of English in the fifteenth century. The verb *examinare* was commonly used to describe the checking of documents. Documents issued by the royal bureaucracy were sometimes checked by an official called the *examinator* and sometimes have notes that they were examined by somebody ('Ex*aminatur* per').[109] For example, Thomas Hoccleve's formulary for the Privy Seal office has one document in a more formal hand than others, with several corrections made by the scribe, and in the top left the scribe has written 'ex*aminatur*'.[110] In the Huntington Library there is an example from a century later: a letter signed by Henry VIII on 4 March 1513, on the reverse of which the scribe has written 'ex*aminatur*'. The letter directs one John Dauncy to pay the Clerks of the Signet forty pounds for their work and their 'papo*ur* p*ar*chement and other stuf'.[111] One inspiration for scribes of books, then, might be training in cursive, documentary handwriting and in bureaucratic concerns with accuracy and veracity.

Yet for whose benefit is the examination recorded? Those notes could be intended for the eyes of readers, especially if they are prominent like Hankok's final one in red. They could work like guarantees to the purchaser or like claims for payment. Yet they most often seem intended for colleagues: after all, *examinatur* occurred in a letter for paying the Clerks of the Signet themselves; Hoccleve used it in a letter meant as a model for other clerks to copy. They could alert one's colleagues to the progress of work: this seems to have been the purpose where these marks accompany prompts for others to correct.[112] But even without collaboration, these marks witness the scribe

108 Manly and Rickert (eds.), *Text of the Canterbury Tales*, vol. I, 72–3, 133, 511, rebutted by Mosser, 'Two Scribes', 119.

109 Guyotjeannin, 'Le vocabulaire de la diplomatique', 130; Chaplais, *English Royal Documents*, 21–2 and plate 25c; Johnson and Jenkinson, *English Court Hands*, vol. II, plate XLIV. Other common verbs were *inspicere* and *intueri*: Teeuwen, *Vocabulary of Intellectual Life*, 268–71.

110 BL, MS Add. 24062, f. 31r.

111 HEHL, MS HM 355. This and other single-sheet documents are not included in the HEHL sample.

112 Briggs, 'MS Digby 233', 253, relates *corrigitur* to prompts for collaborating scribes.

himself recording what he has done; they confirm, then, that correcting has been done consciously, perhaps even self-consciously or proudly. These notes make explicit the alertness implicit in most of the techniques used. Corrections are quite recognisable, with the exception of only the neatest erasures, or they directly invite recognition, like the construe-marks, *signes de renvoie* or red ink which guide the reader. They encourage readers to notice, understand and even to complete the text and they bear witness to the scribes' understanding of their work and of the texts they copy. As Richard Sennett suggests, it is 'dynamic repair' – repair which leaves the process of repairing visible rather than seamless – that helps craftsmen to understand their work.[113] Although some aspects of scribes' work might have been almost automatic, correcting is a process which inherently requires critical thinking: it involves looking back – say, stopping oneself mid-word, or interlining seconds later – and it involves making decisions – which is the right word, or whether to switch to the red pen – and sometimes planning ahead – say, how to prevent confusion by the reader. These techniques of correcting encourage conscious understanding of the craft of copying and of what is copied.

[113] Sennett, *Craftsman*, 200.

CHAPTER 6

Accuracy

it may noȝt ^be wele corrected

San Marino, Huntington Library, MS HM 112, f. 13v
Walter Hilton, *The Scale of Perfection*, I.XVII

The retrospection and the visibility of correcting invite the scribe and others to pause and take note of his craftsmanship. So when scribes stop and make decisions about their work, what do they choose to do? They seem interested first and foremost in not changing things: in accurate transcription or reproduction. This emerged in the sample of direct and cognate copies (in Chapter 3) from the high proportion of correcting which returns the copy to the form found in its exemplar or cognates, with the exception of some by one scribe of Langland's *Piers Plowman* seemingly guessing what to do. Some previous case-studies of correcting have spotted this: so the London bureaucrat, Richard Osbarn, copying Chaucer's *Troilus and Criseyde*, worked 'scrupulously' and with tremendous 'fidelity' in his corrections, collating exemplars, avoiding guesswork and removing rather than exacerbating possible variation.[1] Another copyist of Chaucer's *The Canterbury Tales* seems to have thought that 'a good text was a correct text' and his carefulness belies claims for the prevalence of '*mouvance* in medieval English texts'.[2] Copying involves doing just that: seeking to preserve the text one finds as best one can.

But is this not tautology or common sense? Why would people want inaccurate copies? Why would they *not* correct errors in copying? Yet the texts in English manuscripts from the late fourteenth to the early sixteenth century are often marred with accidental errors which were left unemended. The manuscripts also contain versions of works which differ

[1] Hanna, 'Scribe of Huntington HM 114', 126–7. He is named by Mooney and Stubbs, *Scribes and the City*, 17–37.

[2] Da Rold, 'Significance of Scribal Corrections', 408, 411.

in ways which look deliberate. This openness to error and variance could suggest that there was little need for correcting. As it happens, variation is not always prominent: direct and cognate copies suggest that the majority of words are reproduced accurately in the first place. Yet that success might itself diminish the importance of correcting: with such close copies anyway, correcting can have very little appreciable effect on the text overall, reducing an already low rate of divergence only a little. Moreover, when correcting does occur it does not always remove the error: one sixth of corrections to direct and cognate copies allow divergences to remain or even create them. Most importantly, even more divergences remain uncorrected in those direct copies than are removed by the correcting – perhaps to a ratio of ten to one. (Chapter 3 sets out these tendencies in full.) Therefore, correcting might not actually contribute much to achieving a correct text. This has been noted in previous case-studies: a scribe might work 'conscientiously' at correcting but 'not always consistently', so that his copy remains problematic.[3] In the most rigorous analyses, Hoyt N. Duggan and Takako Kato note that a scribe conscientious in correcting does not necessarily produce an 'accurate' or 'reliable' text.[4] As Kato observes, corrected mistakes might reveal the credibility of a scribe but not 'the textual credibility of the manuscript' or the accuracy which resulted; one would need to study as well the uncorrected mistakes in order to assess those things, say, in order to trust his text for editing from it.[5] These strictures are spot on: not all the errors are corrected, nor indeed are the corrections all correct.

But these concerns with 'textual credibility' are more worrying for the editor or critic whose focus is the text or author. They are less worrisome for the palaeographer whose focus is the experience of the scribes and users of books, especially in two limited respects: what they think about correcting, and what correcting makes them think about the works they copy or read. What is intriguing is not correct*ness*, then, but correct*ing*: the process and the attitudes which provoke it and which it provokes. The mere conscientiousness is interesting, regardless of the text which results from it. No matter what they achieve, when we can observe scribes thinking consciously about their work, as we can in their correcting, what they seek to do is to reproduce the texts they find accurately.

[3] Hamel, 'Scribal Self-Corrections', 121.

[4] Kato, 'Corrected Mistakes', 64; Duggan, 'Scribal Self-Correction', 219, 224.

[5] Kato, 'Corrected Mistakes', 65. See also Duggan, 'Scribal Self-Correction', 217–18; Carlson, 'Scribal Intentions', 50. Wakelin, 'Editing and Correcting', 246, rehearses these points.

The frequency of correcting

Their efforts are evident first in the frequency of the corrections in the sample of English in manuscripts from the Huntington Library (Table 6.1). The sample contains 11,876 pages, roughly calculating half-written pages and suchlike, on which there are 9,220 corrections: so there was on average a correction on just over three out of four pages (78 per cent). Or, to put it differently, somebody made a correction after every page and a third of copying. (There are also gaps left unfilled and prompts for further corrections which were never executed; they are not counted in the 9,220.) This is an artificial figure: the mean frequency, that is, the average made by dividing the total number of pages by the total number of corrections; it does not describe any actual book nor tell us precisely about where correcting actually occurred. Yet the bulk alone does tell us that correction was fairly frequent in English manuscripts. In fact, it was far more frequent than this figure, for the sample ignored much of one outlier: it only included six quires of one copy of *The Prick of Conscience* and William Langland's *Piers Plowman*, for that book had nearly eight corrections on every page and would have skewed the mean frequency by roughly doubling the number of corrections but only adding 131 more pages.[6] Yet even without its contributions, correcting is common in English books.

Of course, the aggregate and the mean frequency hide the variation from book to book. Not least, to describe the number of corrections 'per page' conceals the fact that the pages were different sizes: some had two columns of thirty-five lines, some had one column of only twenty, and so on. For that reason, Table 6.1 lists the manuscripts in an order based not on the simple frequency per pages, but in a ranking moderated by taking into account the size of the book, calculated from number of lines and the width of the written area.[7] What is striking is that the rankings do not follow many obvious patterns. This is important for, in theory, correction could have occurred much more frequently in one genre or sort of material while the aggregate could have misleadingly suggested that it occurred everywhere. In fact, while some single books are more frequently corrected, the varying frequencies are distributed across the full variety of kinds of book and genre. In under half of the manuscripts (twenty-three

[6] HEHL, MS HM 128: the sampled section is described in Chapter 1, n. 33 above.

[7] To get a notional written area, I multiplied the average width and mean number of lines for each MS, given by Dutschke, *Guide*, and Kidd, 'Supplement', with the number of written pages given in Table 6.1. I then divided that notional written area by the number of corrections to moderate any ranking based merely on the number of corrections per page.

Table 6.1 *The frequency of corrections per page for manuscripts in English in the HEHL*

MS	*contents*	*number of corrections*	*number of pages*	*corrections per page*	*% of pages corrected*
HM 128	*Prick*; Langland, *Piers* (sample)	787	124	6	–
HM 112	Hilton, *Scale*	489	156	3	–
HM 744: I	religious miscellany	154	49	3	–
El. 26.A.13: I	Hoccleve, *The Regiment of Princes*	587	228	3	–
HM 130	*Prick*	442	240	2	–
HM 503	Wycliffite sermon	184	259	–	71%
HM 502	religious miscellany	132	179	–	74%
HM 133	*Brut*	343	230	1	–
HM 143	Langland, *Piers*	416	212	2	–
HM 266	Hilton, *Scale*	172	168	1	–
HM 129	*Northern Homily Cycle*	500	461	1	–
HM 134	Wycliffite New Testament	428	320	1	–
HM 148: II	Rolle, *Psalter commentary*	685	398	2	–
HM 55	Capgrave, *St Norbert*	111	118	–	94%
HM 144	miscellany	318	266	1	–
HM 744: II	Hoccleve, short poems	51	88	–	58%
HM 58	*Agnus castus*; recipes	154	190	–	81%
HM 1339	Love, *Mirror*	228	207	1	–
HM 111	Hoccleve, short poems	51	93	–	55%
HM 148: I	religious miscellany	75	44	2	–
El. 35.B.63	Edward of York, *Master of Game*	134	87	2	–
HM 114	Langland, *Piers*; Chaucer, *Troilus, etc.*	373	650	–	57%
HM 127	religious miscellany	63	104	–	61%
El. 26.A.13: II	*Joseph and Asenath*	16	22	–	73%
HM 115	Lydgate, *Life of Our Lady*	73	218	–	33%
HM 501	Wycliffite Psalter	71	301	–	24%
HM 505	Daniel, *Dome of Urynes*	186	262	–	71%
HM 1	Towneley plays	170	263	–	65%
HM 268	Lydgate, *Fall of Princes*	219	316	–	69%
HM 126	Rob. of Gloucester, *Chronicle*	128	269	–	48%
HM 147	*Vices and Virtues*	110	227	–	48%
HM 142	religious miscellany	25	94	–	27%
HM 140	miscellany	74	230	–	32%
HM 149	Love, *Mirror*	81	216	–	38%
HM 19079	medicine	52	486	–	11%
HM 125	*Prick*	64	199	–	32%
HM 137	Langland, *Piers*	75	178	–	42%
HM 139	*Prick*	54	87	–	62%

(*cont.*)

Table 6.1 *cont.*

MS	*contents*	*number of corrections*	*number of pages*	*corrections per page*	*% of pages corrected*
HM 39872	trans. of *Livre de bonnes meurs*	31	244	–	13%
HM 60320	astrology	11	32	–	34%
HM 64	medicine	138	392	–	35%
HM 28561	Trevisa, trans. of *Polychronicon*	248	673	–	37%
HM 1336	medicine and prognostications	12	71	–	17%
El. 26.C.9	Chaucer, *Tales*	143	462	–	31%
HM 136	*Brut*	57	310	–	18%
HM 135	Hoccleve, *The Regiment of Princes*	22	172	–	13%
HM 113	*Brut*	44	332	–	13%
El. 26.A.17	Gower, *Confessio amantis*	52	338	–	15%
HM 131	*Brut*	8	308	–	3%
HM 745	Tudor royal accounts	25	126	–	20%
HM 124	*Speculum Christiani*	68	148	–	46%
HM 26054	*arma Christi* roll	1	1	1	100%
fragments	various	85	28	3	–
total		9,220	11,876	0.78	78%

of the fifty-two once-separate manuscripts) there would be a correction on under half of the pages, if each book's corrections were distributed through it at regular intervals; in just under a third of the manuscripts (fifteen of fifty-two) there would be a correction more frequently than once a page, if, again, they were distributed regularly; and the remainder fall close to the mean frequency. So the mean frequency of correcting, taken from the whole of the sample, only represents what happens in a few books, but is not skewed by just a few zealously or barely corrected books; and the division between heavily corrected and lightly corrected books is not sharp. Contrary to the sort of manuscript uncovered in previous case-studies, and beyond the outlier surveyed only selectively, there were very few extremes: in only two books were the corrections as infrequent as one every ten pages, and in only three were there more than three on every page (Table 6.1). Correction occurred at a variety of frequencies and was just as possible in one book as another; it was unexceptional.

It might be asked whether scribes who model their handwriting on 'set' varieties of script which were more painstaking to execute than others might take greater pains, or might have less time to take pains, over correcting. While in individual cases one could speculate about some connection – say, between the tidy textura of a Wycliffite sermon and the fussy correcting of its text – there is no pattern across the sample. Styles of handwriting seem not to have altered methods of correcting consistently. There is a slight difference between the materials or writing-support of books: on paper correction occurred on average on 63 per cent of pages (1,544 corrections in 2,447 pages) whereas on parchment it occurred on 81 per cent (7,676 corrections on 9,429 pages).[8] The use of paper might explain some differences between otherwise similar books: for example, of two copies of Hoccleve's *The Regiment of Princes*, one on parchment is three times as frequently corrected as one on paper.[9] But these figures might not be fully trustworthy, for the sample of ten paper manuscripts is much smaller than that of forty-two parchment ones. Nor, again, are there extreme numbers which would suggest definite patterns: only one of the eight most frequently corrected books is on paper, but so is only one of the eight least frequently. We cannot, then, make any absolute distinctions between materials: paper might not be a sign of poor-quality book production but might instead suggest that the scribe was used to documentary writing,[10] or was an enthusiastic amateur, both of which could have fostered a care for accuracy. Similarly, while it is more difficult to erase from paper, there were other methods suitable.

Equally, there was no obvious pattern in genre and the commonness of correcting. The ten least frequently corrected books (in the ranking moderated by size in Table 6.1) are heterogeneous in content and include the most intellectually ambitious and courtly poems by Gower, Chaucer and Hoccleve, but also practical 'scientific' books and some prose of religious instruction. They do, though, include three copies of the English prose *Brut*. It is not possible to declare an outright tendency not to correct the prose *Brut*, for a fourth copy of *Brut* is one of the most frequently corrected books. But would something about this work discourage correcting? The content was evidently widely respected – a chronicle of England's mythic past, a sort of secular, national Scripture – yet the specific verbal form of it was not: it received umpteen continuations; it could be speculated that the gist of the history mattered more than its wording. For example, one of the little-corrected copies varies considerably even from the manuscript to

8 The figure for paper includes HEHL, MS HM 114 and MS HM 140, which had parchment for the outer and inner bifolia of quires and so were not completely paper.

9 HEHL, MS El. 26 A.13 (Part I) on parchment; MS HM 135, on paper.

10 Da Rold, 'Materials', 25–6.

which it is most closely related and is one of a group which both abbreviates and interpolates material to restore matter lost.[11] Such a work might well not seem to require correction of textual detail.

The other possible grouping among books which are little corrected is that of books likely copied for money: one of the copies of the prose *Brut* which is little corrected is professional in appearance. It is ruled in two columns in red in a design effortful to execute: there is a thin column, without any ruling across it, between the two ruled columns, which would require precise lifting and replacing of the pen; there are gold initials on blue and pink grounds, with botanical tracery, and chapter headings in red. The handwriting is modelled on anglicana formata, with the minims carefully separated and tricked with feet.[12] This looks like a job by an accomplished scribe and a limner. Other obviously paid-for products with few corrections are a couple of still more lavish productions.[13] For example, Jacques le Grand's *Livre de bonnes meurs* is the least heavily corrected work of religious writing (in Table 6.1) but it is elaborately copied, in handwriting modelled on a calligraphic bastard secretary script, and elaborately decorated, with lovely borders, frequent gold initials, lilac ruling and again expensively generous empty margins.[14] The appearance might suggest that the scribe's engagement was less with the text and more with the provision of the book as a commodity. It could also be that in well-made books the corrections were effected by erasures so skilled that they are invisible and so underreported. But erasures are elsewhere, and sometimes in these books, visible. So until such erasures can be found, a lack of correction could be argued to reflect the disengagement of the scribe from the text when being paid. Disengagement might be suggested by one book for which the quality is poor but which looks like a piece of freelance copying by somebody hard up. It is a scraggy and meagre medical book by a scribe who announces that he is a Cambridge student called Simon Wysbech and that he produced it for one Robert Taylor of Boxford. His carelessness is evident in his very current handwriting, done quickly with many ligatures between letters, varying from moment to moment in spacing and aspect, and with the lines unruled. And he made only four

11 HEHL, MS HM 131, described by Matheson, *Prose Brut*, 213–15.

12 HEHL, MS HM 113.

13 Another example is the so-called 'Stafford' copy of John Gower's *Confessio amantis*: HEHL, MS El. 26.A.17. I have not counted the erasure of a reader's marginalium, originally in a late fifteenth-century handwriting modelled on anglicana, on ff. 6^{r}, 22^{r}. Tokyo, Takamiya collection, unnumbered MS leaf, is a stray from this MS; it contains no further corrections.

14 HEHL, MS HM 39872.

corrections in just over fifty pages, albeit small pages.[15] Yet rough though his copying and correcting are, his colophon nearly fills a page in larger writing and repetitiously records his position as a student of canon law.[16] That colophon could be a clue to the lack of correcting: it could be that Wysbech was a poor student taking on this job merely for money; it could be that as a student of canon law he considered a short English medical text beneath his attention. This can only be speculation, but it may be that only speculation about such quirky and ungeneralizable factors as the interests, intellect and temperament of the scribes can explain why some books are more or less corrected than others.

However, some types of text do tend to get a little more heavily corrected: in particular, works of religious reflection or instruction are more frequently corrected than works with primarily secular themes. Eight of the ten most frequently corrected English books (in Table 6.1) were such works: Langland's *Piers Plowman* in two copies, *The Prick of Conscience* in two copies, Walter Hilton's *The Scale of Perfection*, miscellanies of religious instruction. By contrast, none of the ten books least frequently corrected is a work of religious instruction. The reverence due to religious texts might inspire closer attention to correcting them. Indeed, it might inspire people to copy them more attentively in the first place, producing fewer errors to correct; if so, the higher frequency of correcting in religious books might be even more impressive. Yet, again, it is impossible to be categorical about one category of books: one of the most frequently corrected books was a copy of Hoccleve's *The Regiment of Princes* – although it was corrected in a truly eccentric fashion (noted in Chapter 7).[17] And even ignoring that, it is important not to simplify the category of 'religious writing', for it is so loose that it encompasses many books corrected at average and below-average frequencies too, and includes, even among the most frequently corrected books, works as varied as Langland's *Piers Plowman* and half-a-page-long catechetical extracts in prose. And many of the most heavily corrected religious works were esteemed not only for their piety or pastoral utility but for their capaciousness, authority, learning or vivid style, like those of Langland and Hilton. Even *The Prick of Conscience* has

15 HEHL, MS HM 1336, discussed by Parkes, *Their Hands Before Our Eyes*, 46. Somebody else made two more corrections and ff. 19^{r}–28^{v} are a separate quire by a second hand and contain six corrections.

16 HEHL, MS HM 1336, f. 36^{r}: 'scolar*is* ca*n*tabrigi*ensis* i*n*ceptor canonu*m* *et* legens siue studens i*n* iure canonico Symon Wysbech studens in iure canonico' ('incepting as a student at Cambridge in canon law, and reading or studying canon law, Simon Wysbech, student of canon law').

17 HEHL, MS El. 26.A.13 (Part I), ff. 18^{r}–115^{r}.

vivid, ghastly imagery, versification and learned Latin authorities. So it might be that these works inspire frequent correcting not only for their content but also for their learned, well-crafted form. These patterns do not, then, confirm any one category of book as universally devoid of correction or always pedantically corrected. Correcting was a common occurrence, never a necessity, anywhere, in most kinds of book in English from the late fourteenth to the early sixteenth century.

Ways of correcting

To get a sense of how it was achieved, it is worth breaking up the aggregate of 9,220 corrections and pausing to consider a few examples, one large, one small, one from early in the fifteenth century, one from a century later. One manuscript which shows how heavy correction might emerge from ordinary practice is a copy of Richard Rolle's translation of and commentary on the Psalms and Canticles. On 362 pages copied by the main scribe there are 670 corrections, 554 clearly by the main scribe and 116 which cannot be securely ascribed to him because they are just subpunction or erasure, but which are likely by him: the frequency is almost two corrections on every page, albeit on big pages. Nor does the frequency trail off from quire to quire, after the slightly different first quire (discussed below).[18] This might seem like a special case: this is a commentary on the Psalter by the revered Richard Rolle which includes the psalms themselves in Latin; indeed, 183 of the 670 corrections in Rolle's Psalter are in fact made to the Latin (the highest amount of macaronic correcting in the Huntington Library's sample).[19] A work of such authority might invite strenuous correction. In the prologue Rolle himself speaks of the need for meticulousness in transmitting this text: he professes his aim to 'folow þe lett*er*' of the Latin 'als mykyll as I may'.[20] Verses at the front of another copy urge the scribe to 'wryte on warly lyne be lyne', a concern connected to fears of the Wycliffite revision of this work.[21] And this copy in the Huntington Library has been

[18] HEHL, MS HM 148 (Part II), ff. 23^{r}–203^{v}: quire III^{12} = 75 corrections; IV^{12} = 57; V^{12} = 41; VII^{12} = 42; VIII^{12} = 37 (misbound after the following quire); IX^{12} = 41; X^{12} = 36; XI^{12} = 43; XII^{12} = 44; XIII^{12} = 47; XIV^{12} = 45; XV^{12} = 50; XVI^{12} = 42; XVII^{12} = 50; the first thirteen folios of XVIII^{16} (ff. 191^{r}–203^{v}) = 30. The last 3 leaves of quire XVIII, ff. 204^{r}–206^{v}, and quire XIX, are by another scribe, and there are 15 more corrections in his stint. Part I (ff. 1^{r}–22^{v}) was copied later, as described by Dutschke, *Guide*, vol. 1, 205–7.

[19] Although he leaves uncorrected grammatical errors in the Latin, as Hanna, *Introducing English Medieval Book History*, 182–3, pl. 36, notes.

[20] HEHL, MS HM 148 (Part II), f. 23^{v}; Rolle, *Psalter*, 4–5.

[21] Rolle, *Psalter*, 2; Hudson (ed.), *Two Revisions*, vol. 1, xxi–xxii.

produced with some effort, using coloured initials and paraphs to mark its subdivisions.[22]

Yet, as usual, there is little sign of external supervision of these corrections nor is there anything obsessive or superhuman in the scribe's effort. He can keep up this pace because most of his corrections are tiny and readily made as he goes along. Throughout the book he makes 482 tiny erasures and writes new text over the top of them. Most often, he makes a tiny slip of the pen, often of only one letter, seldom of more than a few, presumably erring in his internal dictation as he transcribes in a hurry; he then erases the slip not daintily but roughly; and he quickly writes over it before continuing. The roughness is evident, because sometimes bits of the erased letters are still visible; at other times the erasure accidentally obscures the adjacent letters or ruling, leaving the parchment grey and untidy.[23] He probably has the knife in his left hand as he writes. For example, when God rescues us from 'synne and pyne' the scribe first writes **p** to start 'synne' but then erases and writes **s** over it to give '[p]{s}ynne and pyne'. The descender and the approach-stroke and spike to the left of his **p** are visible only roughly scraped off under **s**. The scribe presumably jumps ahead to just 'pyne', whether hoping more to flee pain than sin or more likely just skipping between two words featuring the letters <yn> as he glances at his exemplar in a hurry. It is an easy mistake to make but is also easy to mend.[24] Both things are done quickly. This roughness of correction strengthens the impression of the haste of his handwriting which is fairly current; for example, the separate strokes become joined up, such as the vertical minims in **m** which are often just a zigzag. Yet it is not all haste here: he shifts into handwriting modelled on textura for passages from the Latin Psalms, treating the Scripture with respect by slowing down his handwriting; and his layout shows further respectfulness, for he leaves room for red and blue paraphs, which have been supplied, and he rules the book fully in two columns in a laborious way.[25] And while his writing is hasty, it is not heedless, for although he corrects quickly, he nonetheless does correct: he interrupts his flow of cursive writing hundreds of times to do so. He does this even though most of his corrections are minuscule: 368 corrections are shorter than a single word, and only two are longer

[22] Hanna, *English Manuscripts of Richard Rolle*, 196–8, and pl. 6, and *Introducing English Medieval Book History*, 175–7, 184–9, pls. 34, 37–8.

[23] E.g., HEHL, MS HM 148 (Part II), f. 64^{v} (Rolle, *Psalter*, 119): 'o[--]{ft}' (column a, line 1), '[-]{d}redand' (a15), 'of[--]lord' (a17), 'þ*at* [-]{h}is' (a27).

[24] HEHL, MS HM 148 (Part II), f. 177^{v} (Rolle, *Psalter*, 448).

[25] The ruling does not cross the blank space between the columns, except for the top and bottom two rulings; so the scribe labours to lift and reapply the pen 37 times on every one of 362 pages.

than one line of the manuscript's narrow columns.[26] He stops and checks his errors as quickly as he makes them, again and again, as he goes along. Retrospection is built even into speedy writing.

The difference between correcting hurriedly while still writing and later checking is suggested by some further correcting of the first two quires, which do contain slightly more frequent corrections than the others and more examples of a technique other than the erasures overwritten: interlineating letters, sometimes combined with subpuncting erroneous letters.[27] The techniques of interlineation and subpunction might reflect later checking after copying is completed, when the ink is too dry to erase readily or the knife has been put away, as though the first two quires are worked over a second time in order to get a few more details right. The sense of these corrections as unusual extra effort is evident in their content too. The scribe witters over some tiny nuances of grammar, such as adding the superlative suffix to the adjective *perfect* in order to praise further the 'postels and oþ*er* p*er*fit^est men', or adding a different determiner in order to remove any solipsism from a reference to grace working not only in 'þi' or *your* life but in 'þi^s lyff' in general.[28] The greatest sense of the excessiveness of these interlineations is in some fussy changes to spellings which were quite legible beforehand, at least in that they used forms recorded elsewhere in the period. (Table 6.2 lists fifteen from the first two quires.) Pernickety correction to spelling often occurs mainly in the first few quires of a book (as Chapter 7 shows), but otherwise such extra correction in one quire more than another is uncommon. Here it looks as though the scribe might have returned to recheck the start of his book further later, with different concerns and techniques. But that difference in timing can only be speculation, and any second round of interlineations (53) is dwarfed by his commoner habit of correcting as he goes along, in erasures overwritten throughout the book (482). Normally, even in as lengthy and as arduous a task as copying this long work, even in handwriting as current as this book's, correcting was an unexceptional part of ordinary scribal practice page to page.

The ubiquity and ordinariness of correcting might be illustrated by turning from an early fifteenth-century mammoth book of Scripture to something late, short and secular. Correcting can occur on any piece of writing

[26] HEHL, MS HM 148 (Part II): five lines over erasure on f. 36^{r} (varying slightly from Rolle, *Psalter*, 39) and one-and-a-half lines on f. 71^{r} (172).

[27] MS HM 148 (Part II): quire III^{12} (ff. 23^{r}–34^{v}) = 75 corrections; IV^{12} (ff. 35^{r}–46^{v}) = 57. Interlineations are common on ff. 23^{r}–29^{v} and 119^{r}–130^{v}. Of 53 interlineations by the scribe, 20 accompany subpunction.

[28] HEHL, MS HM 148 (Part II), f. 25^{r} (Rolle, *Psalter*, 8), 29^{v} (21).

Table 6.2 *Interlineations which needlessly correct spelling in HEHL, MS HM 148 (Part II)*

	folio	*Rolle,* Psalter	*text*	MED *lemma*	MED *forms or quotations*
i)	23^{r}	3	þ*at* in Ebrew is [cal^^{e}d] called[1]	*callen* (*v.*)	cald(e[2]
ii)	24^{v}	7	þe whilke w[e]^{y}nd þ*at* is p*ride*	*wind* (*n.*)	wend(e
iii)	26^{r}	11	erthli cou[a]^{e}tise	*coveitise* (*n.*)	covatise
iv)	26^{v}	12[3]	open his [h]eghe and lo‸^{u}ke	*loken* (*v.* 2)	lok(e
v)	26^{v}	13	my c^^{o}rou*ne*	*coroune* (*n.*)	croun(e
vi)	27^{r}	14	make me sa^^{u}fe my gode	*sauf* (*adj.*)	saf(e
vii)	27^{r}	14	make me sa‸^{u}fe my god	*sauf* (*adj.*)	saf(e
viii)	27^{v}	15	in p*ro*[ph]^{f}et of my saulle	*prophet(e* (*n.*)	prophete
ix)	32^{v}	29	þe f[y]^{e}lde	*feld* (*n.*)	fild(e
x)	34^{r}	33	tro^^{u}th hope and scharyte	*treuth* (*n.*)	troth(e
xi)	35^{r}	36	god delai‸^{e}s his dome	*delaien* (*v.*)	delayd, delaid
xii)	35^{v}	38	his fautu‸^{o}res	*fautour* (*n.*)	fautour, *but cf. French* fauteur
xiii)	38^{r}	45	erthly go^^{u}ds	*god* (*n.* 2)	godes, godis, *but corr. not recorded*
xiv)	44^{r}	63	in bre^{e}de	*brede* (*n.* 2)	*corr. not recorded*
xv)	44^{r}	63	in gostly bre‸^{e}de	*bred* (*n.* 1)	*corr. not recorded*

[1] The **e** is interlineated, then the whole word is subpuncted.

[2] Cf., e.g., 'incald' for 'inuocaui' on f. 163^{r}.

[3] The words 'and lo‸^{u}ke' are not in the edition of Rolle, *Psalter*.

in English, no matter how trifling. The Huntington Library includes, as well as fifty-two manuscripts largely in English, twenty-eight others with no more than a few pages, and sometimes just a few lines or glosses, in English. These fragments (as they are labelled as a group in Table 6.1) are often written on flyleaves or formerly blank leaves, usually by people other than the main scribes of the rest of the book, and they are usually unrelated to the main Latin or French works in the book. Yet even in this fleeting and fragile writing people attend to the the text. For example, in a copy of Littleton's *Tenures*, somebody who signs himself elsewhere as Richard Brokysby jots two short lyrics, 'hey noyney I wyll loue our s*ir* Iohn *and* I loue eny' and 'I must go walke in þe woed so wyld'. His handwriting looks like it dates from the first half of the sixteenth century, so he is adding something to this manuscript long after it was made; he scrawls very currently on a slope and divides the lines of verse in the wrong place; he is adding amorous lyrics to a French legal text, so nothing essential; and he uses either side of a leaf once left blank by the original scribe. In no

Table 6.3 *Corrections to two lyrics in English in HEHL, MS El. 34.B.60, f. 11$^{r–v}$*

i)	s*ir* Iohn loue me *and* I loue hym the more I [bo] loue hym the more I maye	11^{r}
ii)	he says swett hart cu*m* kys me [brym]$^{\text{[tr] trym}}$ I haue no powre to say hym nay	11^{r}
iii)	he gropith to nyslye a bought my [pape] ^{lape} I haue no pore to sa	11^{r}
iv)	Furres off the [Fyners] Fynest w*it*h <--> thyng*es*	11^{r}
v)	my bed schall be unde^{r} þe ^{grene} // wod tre a tufft off brakes vnder my hed	11^{v}
vi)	as one From Ioye were fled ⌐and all For one¬ thus From my lyff day by. do I Fl<ee>	11^{v}
vii)	The Ronny^^{n}g stremes shall be my drynke	11^{v}

sense, then, was this a careful act of writing; yet even he took trouble to correct his copying of these lyrics (Table 6.3).[29] Twice he crosses out his word before he has finished it, in order to spell more correctly something he seems to have misread in his exemplar (i, iv), just as immediately as the scribe of Rolle's Psalter commentary does. Four or five times, he adds something after he has already finished copying more of the line (ii, iii, v, vii). Also, incidentally, although lyrics scribbled roughly on blank leaves might seem like records of oral circulation, the correction seems to fix problems in reading written exemplars: (i) and (ii) suggest him misreading letters with ascending strokes, **b**/**l** and **b**/**t**; (iv) suggests him misreading long **s** as the long **r** of anglicana script; (vii) suggests him overlooking a macron abbreviating <n>. Even if the almost offhand copying of these lyrics were not premeditated – were, say, jotted on spare pages so that he would not lose or forget them – it was certainly post-meditated (so to speak): Brokysby reflects on what he has done wrong. Why? In this book, such striving might be interpreted as a reflection of some legalistic precision, for Brokysby scrawled these lyrics in a legal manuscript in which even the annotations have corrections on them.[30] The rough handwriting for the lyrics could be a much more casual form of the handwriting of the annotations to Littleton's *Tenures*.[31] Yet such striving might also take

[29] HEHL, MS El. 34.B.60, f. 11$^{r–v}$, with 'Rychard brokysby' on f. 11^{r}. Robbins (ed.), *Secular Lyrics*, 14–15, 20–1 (nos. 20, 26), only records two of these corrections. It is possible that superscript **r** in (v) and **n** in (vii) are not corrections but a needless use of superscript. Snippets of the second lyric recur on ff. 73^{v}, 107^{v}, 108^{v}, 109^{r}, in sixteenth-century hands modelled on legal scripts and on secretary. The second lyric seems a version of a longer lyric otherwise recorded in the 1530s: Muir (ed.), *Unpublished Poems Edited from the Blage Manuscript*, no. XXII.

[30] HEHL, MS El. 34.B.60, has several sets of marginalia. Some late sixteenth-century ones have copious corrections, e.g., ff. 4$^{r–v}$, 8^{r}.

[31] Cf. **g**, **h** and **r** in the lyrics in HEHL, MS El. 34.B.60, f. 11$^{r–v}$, with those in marginalia in French on, e.g., f. 45$^{r–v}$.

inspiration from the poetic pretensions of the lyrics, for Brokysby attends to their style and form: he repairs a literary cliché by inserting the adjective in ‘under þe grene // wod tre’ (v) and mends the stanzaic form or layout by slotting the refrain for one stanza between the lines (vi). Even in as fleeting a textual encounter as this one, correcting registers the scribe’s understanding of the wording, completeness and verse-form of what he copies – something like in kind, if not in quality, to the close reading of such lyrics that a critic might pursue.

The quality of correcting

Yet what is the quality of his correcting? Brokysby might try to preserve the stanzaic structure but he bungles it: he copies the omitted refrain for a stanza into the wrong place (vi). He was hesitant in his correcting, making a false start on the word ‘trym’ before he knew he was right (ii). These glitches and ditherings suggest the intellectual challenges in correcting well. Against these difficulties, what is noteworthy is that most people correcting do not make the sorts of persistent muddle which Brokysby makes; mostly they do better. How could we measure this? It is difficult to measure the quality of all 9,220 corrections in the Huntington Library’s sample without knowing the exemplar or multiple exemplars available to the scribe or without weighing each word corrected singly against the distinct textual, dialectal and metrical traditions which shape it. Given the limits of a broad survey, the simplest expedient was to measure the corrections against information from modern editions. Where possible, the corrected word was collated with the text printed in a modern edition to see whether it agreed with the word at this point in the edition. There were practical limits to this measurement. There were only thirty-eight among the fifty-two manuscripts largely in English for which a comparable edition was available; this reduced the sample to 7,271 corrections which were collated. For a few miscellaneous manuscripts there was an edition only of some works; and of one work, *The Northern Homily Cycle*, there was an accessible edition only of extracts.[32] Furthermore, the editions available varied a lot. Some manuscripts were collated with critical editions which attempt to represent the earliest circulating form of the text; others were of necessity collated with ‘best text’ editions, as of *The Northern Homily Cycle*, say. One edition, of Walter Hilton’s *The Scale of Perfection*, had modernized spelling; but it was based on comparing several manuscripts

[32] HEHL, MS HM 129, collated with *NHC*.

and was therefore preferable for this purpose to an otherwise helpful recent edition in less modernized spelling which is based on just one manuscript.[33] When an edition was based solely or primarily on the Huntington Library's manuscript, as was John Capgrave's *Life of St Norbert* printed from the author's autograph copy, then the corrections were not collated.[34] The 'Ellesmere Chaucer' was collated with *The Riverside Chaucer*, as the text in *The Riverside Chaucer* draws on Hengwrt and other manuscripts for many readings. This seemed the collation of most debatable usefulness, but the manuscript and text were too interesting to leave out. Moreover, the aim was not to count an exact number of places where corrections agree with modern editions but merely to suggest a general tendency.

The tendency is clear: there was an agreement of the corrected wording with that in modern editions in 84 per cent of corrections (Table 6.4). That tendency is consistent with the findings of other case-studies: when two scribes of Chaucer's *The Canterbury Tales* corrected their own work they restored the text preferred in a modern edition in 88 per cent and 85 per cent of cases.[35] In the Huntington Library's books, the figure would be higher were it not lowered by just a few outliers, books which diverge from the text represented in an edition unusually often. Those outliers lower the frequency of agreement more than a few strong ones raise it.[36] Of the full thirty-eight books, the median is 91 per cent and the mode is 93 per cent. So most manuscripts agree with the modern edition most of the time. There are some limits on the measure of this agreement: the collation discounted differences in spelling, punctuation and layout. Given the flexibility of English spelling and punctuation, notably in the predominance of 'dialectal translation', these things were assumed to be irrelevant to what a scribe would consider an exact copy. (Whether that assumption was right is discussed in the next chapter.) Otherwise, 84 per cent of the words corrected – their omission, inclusion, choice and grammar – were the same as those found in modern editions.

What the agreement with modern editions means depends in part on those editions. Comparing the text with editions and not with every other

33 HEHL, MS HM 112 and MS HM 266, collated with Hilton, *The Scale of Perfection*, ed. Underhill, rather than with Hilton, *The Scale of Perfection*, ed. Bestul.

34 HEHL, MS HM 55, not collated with Capgrave, *Life of St Norbert*. However, Lucas, *From Author to Audience*, 82, 86–7, 89, shows that Capgrave, like other authors, could make mistakes in his autograph copies. Chapter 11 below discusses authorial copying.

35 Kato, 'Corrected Mistakes', 66; Crow, 'Corrections', 8. But Crow, 14, finds that further corrections by the MS's owner only agree with the edition in 50 per cent of cases.

36 If we discount the five MSS which least often agree, the overall proportion of agreeing corrections goes up by 5.5 per cent, whereas if we discount the five MSS which most often agree, it only goes down by only 2.5 per cent.

Table 6.4 *The agreement of corrections in some manuscripts in English in the HEHL with modern printed editions of their texts*

MS	*contents*	*corrections collated with editions*	*number that agree with editions*	*percentage that agree with editions*
HM 131	*Brut*	8	3	38%
HM 130	*Prick*	442	214	48%
HM 125	*Prick*	64	34	53%
HM 58	*Agnus castus*	87	49	56%
HM 142	religious miscellany (part)	22	14	64%
HM 502	religious miscellany (part)	116	77	66%
HM 128	*Prick*; Langland, *Piers* (sample)	787	535	68%
HM 114	Langland, *Piers*; Chaucer, *Troilus etc.*	345	241	70%
HM 149	Love, *Mirror*	81	59	73%
HM 136	*Brut*	57	42	74%
HM 133	*Brut*	325	258	80%
HM 126	Rob. of Gloucester, *Chronicle*	128	103	80%
HM 127	religious miscellany (part)	58	48	83%
HM 129	*Northern Homily Cycle* (part)	263	218	83%
HM 115	Lydgate, *Life of Our Lady*	73	61	84%
HM 144	miscellany (part)	220	186	85%
HM 266	Hilton, *Scale*	172	147	85%
HM 503	Wycliffite sermon	184	159	86%
HM 148: I	religious miscellany	75	66	88%
HM 112	Hilton, *Scale*	489	440	90%
El. 35.B.63	Edward of York, *Master of Game*	134	121	90%
HM 268	Lydgate, *Fall of Princes*	219	200	91%
HM 28561	Trevisa, trans. of *Polychronicon*	180	166	92%
HM 139	*Prick*	54	50	93%
HM 1339	Love, *Mirror*	228	212	93%
HM 134	Wycliffite New Testament	428	398	93%
HM 501	Wycliffite Psalter	45	42	93%
HM 137	Langland, *Piers*	75	70	93%
El. 26.C.9	Chaucer, *Canterbury Tales*	143	135	94%
HM 113	*Brut*	44	42	95%
HM 135	Hoccleve, *The Regiment of Princes*	22	21	95%
HM 148: II	Rolle, *Psalter commentary*	670	647	97%
HM 124	*Speculum Christiani*	68	66	97%
HM 140	miscellany (part)	74	72	97%
HM 147	*Vices and Virtues*	110	108	98%
HM 744: I	religious miscellany	151	149	99%
El. 26.A.13: I	Hoccleve, *The Regiment of Princes*	578	573	99%
El. 26.A.17	Gower, *Confessio amantis*	52	52	100%
total		7,271	6,078	84%

possible manuscript is, obviously, a short-cut made for practical reasons.[37] There is a huge risk of circularity in measuring this agreement, as the modern editions are based on manuscripts which might include, or might be descendent from, those in the Huntington Library. Although no edition was collated if it was based solely or primarily on the sampled manuscript, editions were often based on several manuscripts which included the sampled one among others. So is not the agreement of the manuscript's correction and the editor's text circular and obvious? In some ways, yes. Yet the risk of circularity at least applies equally across the sample, rather than suggesting false divisions within it. More importantly, even when the Huntington Library's manuscript was one among many consulted by the editor, then it is interesting that the scribe or reader chose a correction which happens to be that which an editor also would later prefer. That the scribes did not need to do so is evident in the fact that their agreement is not 100 per cent: nearly one in six times (16 per cent) they differ. Yet usually the people correcting, like the modern editors, avoid further errors of copying; they avoid gibberish and ungrammatical phrases; they are not quirkily personal, outlandish or misguided. This is why the scribes usually share, pre-empt or even shape the modern editors' judgements. Comparing modern editions does not suggest that correcting was right but does suggest that it was sensible and consensual.

Good judgement and conventionality are fascinating phenomena and not to be taken for granted – and not only by comparison with twenty-first-century individualism. Scribes could choose to vary the text on occasion, as dialectal translation and variant texts show, but they chose not to do so when they were correcting. Nor can their critical good sense be taken for granted, given the difficulty of stopping to correct oneself or of checking later, of checking one's own exemplar or of checking other exemplars. The fact that the scribes and early users of these books achieved corrections which coincide with the texts established by modern editors, with all their resources, is impressive. If they are checking while they copy, then their copying is not as hasty or thoughtless as the speed of writing might encourage it to be. If they are checking their own or another exemplar later, then they are remarkably meticulous. And even if they are guessing – which seems likely when they guess obvious grammatical slips or misspellings – then they are intelligent in their guesses. Measuring the corrections against modern editions, what emerges most clearly is the scribes' intelligence and care.

37 Cf. a similar procedure tried on copies of the Psalter by Hudson (ed.), *Two Revisions*, vol. 1, lxxxvi.

It is important to stress that this is a quality in the process of correct*ing* alone and not in its outcome: not in resulting correct*ness* of the whole manuscript. The frequency of correcting and the agreement of the corrections with a later established text together tell us only that the scribe was conscientious and conventional at these moments; they tell us nothing about other moments. One might even suggest that frequent correcting shows frequent error in the scribes' first attempts to copy, and the manuscripts sampled still contain numerous silly errors.[38] As other recent case-studies have stressed (noted at the start of this chapter), it is important not to overstate the achievements of scribes and readers as opposed to their aspirations. Nonetheless, although they vary and err in first copying, on second thoughts, on conscious reflection – collating another copy, checking their work later, or just stopping themselves from little slips as they go – they seem to aspire to invariance. In 6,078 places across 38 manuscripts, the text varied before correcting from what modern editors think it should be, but after correcting it accorded. The effect is similar to the 'centripetal' tendency which Anne Hudson identified in manuscripts of the Wycliffite sermon cycle. In centripetal correcting, the scribes remove an error which diverges from the text recorded in other manuscripts by providing a correction which converges with the text recorded in other manuscripts.[39] Most of the time, then, correcting shows scribes to seek, centripetally, to reproduce what they find in their exemplars.

Seeking a better text

Underneath such centripetal correction the person correcting seems to have some sense of the text as an entity which exists despite the accidents of its material transmission. It exists outside the current scribe's new copy and its errors, which he seeks to remove; sometimes it exists outside his particular exemplars too. This interest in the text beyond the materials in hand can be illustrated in two books where the corrections are notably dramatic. In one book, the scribe's interest in reproducing the whole, exact and conventional text is striking because of the contrast with the interests of other users of the book. This is a manuscript of *Agnus castus*, a medical herbal, which lists plants and their uses in alphabetical order. Like other medical works, *Agnus castus* was susceptible to rewriting; herbal lore and medical recipes

[38] Kato, 'Corrected Mistakes', 64; Duggan, 'Scribal Self-Correction', 224.

[39] Hudson (ed.), *English Wycliffite Sermons*, 148–9. There is a big difference, though: Hudson was editing the text and so compared each correction with the text in other manuscripts and not with an edition.

are not only passed on by textual tradition but also modified by custom and use. Sure enough, in this copy of *Agnus castus* the text varies from that printed by the modern editor in several details. Also, some later hands have added further medical and herbal recipes to blank spaces alongside the text, something else which was common in medical books.[40] The people adding this new content do little correcting and show little care over wording; they treat this utilitarian book as something alterable and adaptable in its use.[41] However, it is thus the *book* that they are using – as a material object, a writing surface, an archive – more than its main named *text*. They are like the people studied by William Sherman who use books as places to write rather than as things to read.[42] In this setting, it might seem surprising to find the scribe worrying over the text of *Agnus castus* by correcting it. It might seem merely a body of information to pass on, alter or supplement, rather than a particular textual form which needs reproducing precisely.

However, the scribe's struggle to reproduce the text is visible at several points where he corrects mistakes which would cause his copy to vary from others. The two largest such self-corrections are these. At one point, he jumps from the middle of one entry to another (from 'Edera' to 'Edera terrestris') and then finishes the page with the start of the next herb ('Euforbum') which continues onto the next page. He only notices this omission when it is too late to fix it simply; to fix it, he has to cross out everything from the point where the jump occurs in one recipe down to the foot of that page (Figure 3). Then he slots in an extra leaf of parchment, a singleton, on which he finishes the entry on the interrupted herb ('Edera'), writes separately all of the entry on the herb which had been grafted onto it ('Edera terrestris') and then leaves space so that he only copies enough lines about the next herb ('Euforbum') to reach the point where the text resumes on the next original page.[43] This correction is paralleled elsewhere, where the scribe omits the herb *iasia alba* and jumps straight to *iasia nigra* and continues till the end of the herbs beginning with *I* and begins the herbs with *L*, to judge by what looks like an erased blue *L*. But some time later, after rubricating his initials, he realizes, erases the whole lot apart from initial word 'Iacea' from *iasia nigra* and adds 'alba' in order to start writing

[40] Carroll, 'Middle English Recipes', 183, describes this habit.

[41] The only corrections on the additions in HEHL, MS HM 58 (hereafter HM 58), are on ff. 19^{v} (a line squeezed in), 23^{v} and 33^{r} (wrong words crossed out), all in sixteenth-century handwriting.

[42] Sherman, *Used Books*, 15–16, 59.

[43] HM 58, ff. 18^{v}–20^{r} (Brodin (ed.), *Agnus Castus*, 153). The added leaf has more widely spaced ruling and two top rulings, not one, running through the margin; the loose, early binding makes the quiring visible. He does not leave enough room on it for the added text, so that four words of it needed to be squeezed at the top of the next original page.

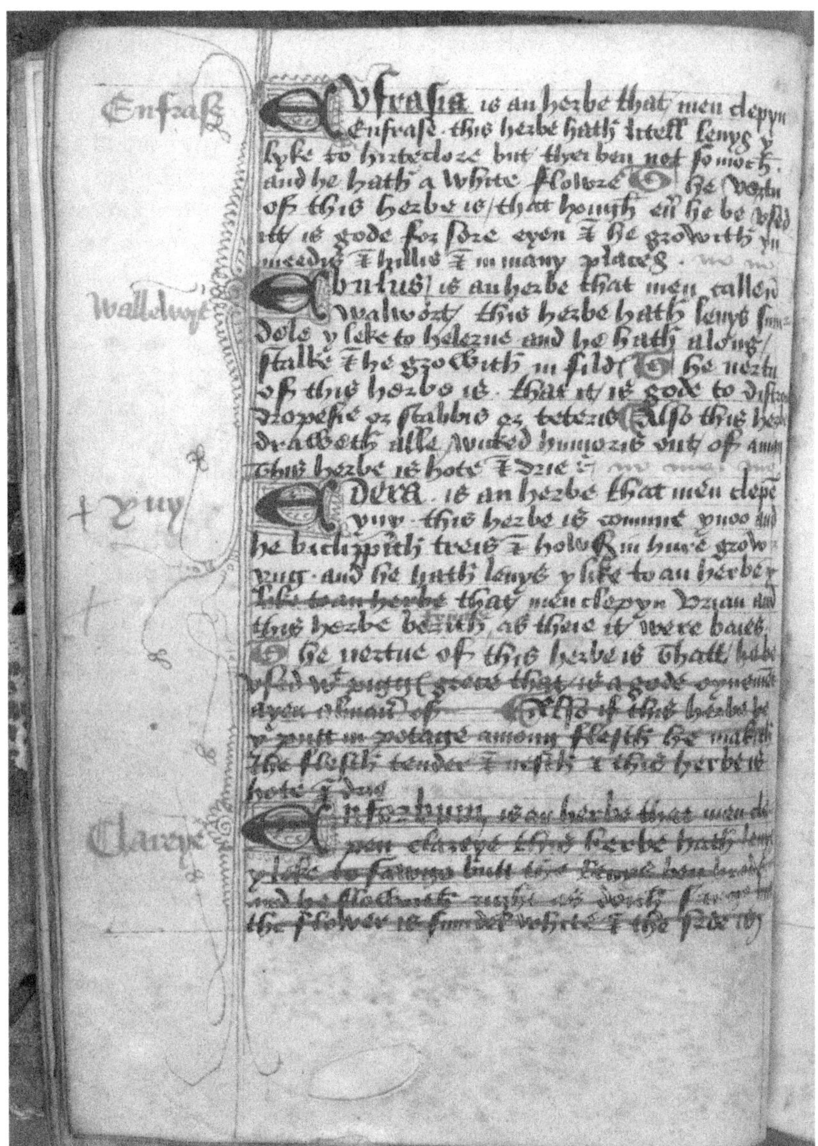

Figure 3 HEHL, MS HM 58, f. 18v: crossing out of a passage copied prematurely in *Agnus castus*

this entry *iasia alba* and all the ensuing ones over the long erasure. Because he has left a space between letters of the alphabet he is here able to squeeze the last of the herbs beginning with *I*, *ipia minor*, in that space before starting *L*.[44] Unlike the recipes added by the later users, who treat the book as a sort of notepad, these additions restore sections which are integral to the text in other copies and which the scribe or his exemplar had skipped in error. The scribe also corrects six shorter passages of eyeskip in red, or in brown but rubricated, with red crosses to mark where to insert them.[45] By such visible disruptions, respect for the tidiness of the book is abandoned; what seems more important is the preservation of the text.

What can we infer about the scribe's actions and attitudes? It looks as though he takes the task of writing seriously: he writes '*christ*o glor*ia*' piously at the top of each folio, blessing or praying for his work.[46] And he takes his checking seriously, for he keeps track of it by writing 'cor', presumably for 'cor*rigitur*' and sometimes with a quire-signature, at the end of some quires in red.[47] This is the sort of thoughtfulness which might well lead somebody to restore large oversights. How and why does he restore the large omissions from *E* and *I*? It might be that he is just checking his first exemplar carefully: when he adds the text about the missing herbs, it is very similar to the text in the manuscript closest to this one – that is, it is centripetal. The small divergences mostly involve pronouns and articles or comprehensible misreading rather than random guessing ('flo*ury*þ' is misread 'flowith', say).[48] Or it might be that he found these added entries by checking a second exemplar: in the additions he uses the letter **þ**, which he does not use much elsewhere, as though he were

44 HM 58, f. 25r–v (Brodin (ed.), *Agnus Castus*, 166). He also uses more abbreviations and superscript letters than normal, perhaps to fit things in the space. 'Ipia minor' ends differently from Brodin (ed.), *Agnus Castus*, 167, and *iacintus ruticus* is missing entirely, perhaps because there was not enough room in the space before entries beginning with *L*. BL, MS Royal 18.A.vi, ff. 78v–79r, and BodL, MS Laud. misc. 553, f. 13r, which Zettersten, 'A Manuscript of "Agnus castus"', identifies as the MSS most closely related to HM 58, do have *iacinctus ruticus*.

45 HM 58, ff. 1r (Brodin (ed.), *Agnus Castus*, 119), 13r (140), 16r (149), 25r (165: just the word 'make'), 33v (189), 40r (200). Of 52 words restored, 47 are identical to the text in BL, MS Royal 18.A.vi, ff. 64r, 70r, 73v, 78v, 85v (and this MS's text is cut short before the final comparable passage). He also corrects four eyeskips in a second collection of recipes in HM 58 (ff. 49v, 53r, 68r twice and 73v), presumably obtaining these recipes too from written sources.

46 HM 58, f. 20r, rectos from ff. 24r–36r, f. 38r, and evidently trimmed off, e.g., ff. 37r, 46r.

47 HM 58, ff. 13v, 42v, 50v.

48 HM 58, f. 19r–v, and BL, MS Royal 18.A.vi, f. 74v, with 169 of 215 added words identical except in dialect. The big difference is that the added leaf in HM 58, f. 19r–v, has an extra sentence of 26 words not in BL, MS Royal 18.A.vi, f. 74v; but this sentence recurs in the crossed-out passage in HM 58, f. 18v, so the scribe seems to be copying it faithfully; it is not his variation but his exemplar's. In the related BodL, MS Laud. misc. 553, the bifolium with most of this passage has been lost between ff. 10v–11r and 18v–19r.

closely following a different scribe's spelling. Whichever source he uses, he compares his copy closely. There is evidence that his copying is closely accurate too. For the lines about 'Edera terrestris' and 'Euforbum' which he copies twice, once prematurely and crossed out, once in due order on an added leaf (as described), he is self-consistent: he reproduces seventy-six of the seventy-seven words verbatim, and fifty-two of them even *literatim* in spelling.[49] He leaves a gap too, twice, where the entry on *hedera terrestris* ends abruptly, as though he thinks that his exemplar is missing something. He seems to have been a scribe, then, who did not change what he copied.

That repeated gap suggests his thinking. He seems to think that somewhere out there is a better text of *Agnus castus*, with a verbal form which is not represented in material form in the exemplars he has, but to which he aspires. There should be words in the gap but there are not. That interest in the work's verbal form, overriding what is possible in the material book, is evident in the fact that the two longest corrections to *Agnus castus*, adding missing recipes in *E* and *I*, are made in ways needless for preserving the work's useful content – which could be passed around any old how, like a recipe – but which preserve its form or structure. What distinguished *Agnus castus* from other herbals in English was its arrangement by alphabetical order, innovative when composed, useful for readers and influential on later works of practical lore.[50] In this copy, the scribe shows an interest in that structure when he takes the trouble to restore these missing entries in their customary position exactly, by writing on an extra singleton or over a long erasure in the midst of entries for *E* and *I*. Restoring the recipes where he does, mid-letter in an exact order, is not necessary: *Agnus castus* is alphabetical but only to the first letter of each word, like most alphabetization at this time. So the scribe could slot in the missing entries in the spaces at the end of *E* and *I* before *F* and *L*, say, and they would still be 'alphabetized' as much as anything is here; there is no need to put the omitted entries in exactly the order in which they appear in other manuscripts. After all, the users of books felt able to interrupt the order of herbs by slotting in extra recipes; the sixteenth-century user even jotted a recipe onto a space on the singleton used for adding the missing herbs in *E*.[51] But the scribe worries over the exact reproduction not only of the work's useful content but of its exact textual form.

His dislike of variance is shared by others. In this manuscript, a sixteenth-century reader annotates and collates the text, noting that this copy still

49 Cf. HM 58, ff. 18^v and 19^r–20^r. The exception is the last word 'is', crossed out (f. 18^v) but not added again (f. 20^r).

50 Keiser, 'Vernacular Herbals', 300–2.

51 HM 58, f. 19^v.

skips over some herbs beginning with *C*, though of fourteen omissions he only spots that 'ther lackyth' seven.[52] And in other copies of practical works which are 'atomized' in structure, fifteenth-century scribes strive to order them conventionally by adding missing recipes on extra leaves slotted in at exactly the conventional point, as in a copy of *The Forme of Cury*.[53] What is odd is that such readers and scribes expend such effort on works with already muddled textual traditions such as these. That means that their corrections do not always meet the stringent criterion (of this chapter) of agreeing with the modern edition: in that copy of *Agnus castus* only 56 per cent of the correcting restores word-for-word the editor's text; the text was too far gone to bring it back. But despite the widespread variation in this book's exemplar, and in this kind of text in general, there seems to be some aspiration to produce the fullest, best ordered and most conventional form of the text.

The difference between the text aspired to and what is permitted by the problems with exemplars emerges most strikingly in the case of another work for which many corrections do not move centripetally towards the text of the modern edition, because there was not one single tradition of manuscripts to restore it to. This is the poem of pastoral theology, *The Prick of Conscience*. The poem survives in various deliberate revisions, divided into what are as good as two different works, one based on the other: a 'Main Version' and a later 'Southern Recension'.[54] The only available edition at the time of research was one produced in 1863 from the Main Version, whereas three of the Huntington Library's four copies are of the Southern Recension. To measure the success of centripetal correcting against that edition is, then, an even more flawed procedure than usual; and, unsurprisingly, much of the correcting of the three copies of the Southern Recension differs from the edition of the Main Version; they are different texts.[55] By contrast, the corrections in the one manuscript of the Main Version in the sample are in agreement with the modern edition nearly all the time (93 per cent). So the lack of a 'centripetal' quality in the

[52] HM 58, f. 16^{r}, which jumps from Brodin (ed.), *Agnus Castus*, 145 to 148; the reader lists numbers 1–4, 6 and 12–13 of the 14, albeit in the order found in Brodin (ed.), *Agnus Castus*, 145–8, which suggests that he was collating another incomplete copy. This reader annotates ff. 17^{r}, 18^{r} and 27^{v}.

[53] JRL, MS Eng. 7, ff. 25^{r-v}, 26^{r}. Cf. the table on ff. 4^{v}–11^{v}.

[54] Lewis and McIntosh, *Descriptive Guide*, 9–10; Beadle, 'Middle English Texts', 78–80; D'Evelyn, 'East Midland Recension' (esp. 182, 187, on BL, MS Harley 2281, hereafter SR 9, which is discussed below), who calls it the 'East Midland recension'.

[55] HEHL, MSS HM 125, HM 128 and HM 130, on which see Lewis and McIntosh, *Descriptive Guide*, nos. MV 94, SR 26, SR 17, SR 18. Since completing this research, as this book went to press, Hanna and Wood (eds.), *Richard Morris's 'Prick of Conscience'*, has published a better text, which might well correct the claims about the text made here.

other three copies in the sample might be a false result from the method of assessment.

Yet even in the manuscript of the Southern Recension in the Huntington Library with the lowest proportion of corrections in agreement with the modern edition (48 per cent), there is some attempt to avoid one kind of variation. Two scribes here reconstruct, from two contradictory exemplars, a form of the text that neither physical exemplar had but which one of them apparently thought preferable to that in either witness.[56] This is a copy of the Southern Recension of *The Prick of Conscience* assigned to Monmouthshire on the basis of its dialect and some decades later owned in London.[57] This copy (HEHL) can be usefully collated with a second copy now in the British Library (BL), close in the textual tradition overall and in dialect.[58] What makes them worth comparing is that they are in the same scribe's handwriting, which can be recognized by several shared letter-forms.[59] Often, when the text is identical in spelling, the scribe even uses the same choice among his repertoire of allographs at the same points.[60] Moreover, besides the likeness of particular graphs, the handling of the pen in their execution is identical, modelled on anglicana formata in design but fairly casual in execution. But though close in origin and in the general textual tradition, these two copies differ in wording in numerous details, and neither seems to be copied from the other. The BL manuscript cannot be copied from the HEHL one, as the BL manuscript includes at least one long passage found in other copies but missing from the HEHL copy.[61] Yet the HEHL manuscript was not copied from the BL one, because the BL

56 HEHL, MS HM 130 (hereafter SR 18). The only lower proportion is in MS HM 131, but it only has eight corrections so is anomalous.

57 Lewis and McIntosh, *Descriptive Guide*, 147–8 (SR 18); *LALME*, vol. III, 680–1 (LP 7271).

58 Lewis and McIntosh, *Descriptive Guide*, nos. SR 9, SR 18; *LALME*, vol. III, 680–1 (LP 7271) and 162 (LP 7280), are almost identical, although *LALME* locates them in adjacent counties.

59 SR 18 and SR 9: e.g., the ascenders of **h**, **k** and **l** have a hook with pronounced splay to the right; the limb of **h** curls far underneath and to the left of the letter; the scribe alternates between **w** in which the first two strokes extend above the *x*-height and have a pronounced splay to the right and **w** in which they do not; the scribe alternates between a frequent **d** formed in one large anti-clockwise loop from the left-hand side of the bowl, and a less frequent **d** formed in a figure-of-eight starting from the same point; he sometimes uses in line-final position **e** in which the upper stroke forming the 'eye' ends in a down-up-down tremolo. The only graph which differs is a rare variant of **h** in SR 9, f. 5^{v}/24, 'shendshepe', and f. 28^{r}/31, 'shal', where the limb instead curves a little left and ticks right at the bottom. The handwriting of BodL, MS Lyell empt. 6, which Lewis and McIntosh, *Descriptive Guide*, no. SR 14, describe as textually close, is different.

60 Comparing SR 18, ff. 4^{v} and 37^{v}, reproduced on the website http://sunsite3.berkeley.edu/hehweb/toc.html, with any identical corresponding words on SR 9, ff. 5^{v}–6^{r}, and 28^{r-v}. The only ones which were not were three uses of **h** in BL, MS Harley 2281 and three line-initial majuscules.

61 SR 9, ff. 17^{v}–18^{r}; SR 18, f. 17^{r}; *Prick*, 1360–7. The likely explanation is an eyeskip between 'For' at the start of *Prick*, 1360 and 1368.

manuscript often diverges from the standard textual tradition – notably by giving different synonyms for nouns and by having extra adjectives – while the HEHL manuscript preserves the standard textual tradition at about three quarters of such points.[62] It is unlikely that somebody rewrote the text consistently in one copy and then that he rewrote it back again, perfectly, in another. Rather, it seems as though the scribe copied the poem on two separate occasions from two different exemplars, one of which had been rewritten prior to his encounter with it, but both of which he himself reproduced accurately. Unless he copied them in quick succession, how would he remember that his exemplars differed in small details of wording? And why would he care? Was his job not merely to copy correctly what he found in front of him?

Curiously, though, somebody did care, for one of this scribe's two copies of *The Prick of Conscience*, that in the Huntington Library, has been corrected by somebody collating a further manuscript. He makes more than four hundred erasures with writing over them in a paler, browner ink. His handwriting differs from the scribe's only slightly: the differences are all differences of execution rather than of the basic repertoire of graphs; they could perhaps be caused by writing over erasure and in discontinuous flow, so this could be the scribe working later; but it is safest not to assume that, given the different handling of the pen.[63] (As a result, this book is classified as having one of the highest proportions in the sample of corrections made by a second hand: 94 per cent in Table 4.1. That might be debatable.) This person corrects all sorts of errors but most strikingly he collates this copy of the Southern Recension against an exemplar of the Main Version, and many of his corrections bring this text of the Southern Recension in line with a modern edition of the Main Version: fully 48 per cent overall. That is not a high proportion. For example, comparing the seventy-eight corrections to book II of *The Prick of Conscience* with the Main Version as printed and the original scribe's other copy of the Southern Recension, reveals that the person correcting had diverse goals and procedures. Thirty-seven, or about

[62] Based on a sample of 230 lines in book II which differ between SR 18, ff. 12^r–21^v, and SR 9, ff. 12^v–21^v (*Prick*, 1017–1663).

[63] The corrections in SR 18 have blunted rather than tapering hooks on the ascenders of **b**, **h**, **k** and **l**; a splay on word-final sigma-shaped **s** that is slightly higher, longer and curlier than the original scribe's; and on **y** a straighter descender, pointing left and ending with a short final tick right, unlike the scribe's more sinuous curl left then right. Less explicable by the change of pace when correcting are the lower position of the ligature from word-initial **g** to **o** (e.g., corrections on ff. 31^v/1 'goode', 31^v/17 'good' twice; original copying, ff. 31^v/2 'god', 31^v/20 'gode') and on the hooked ascenders of **b** and **l** a slight tick or further hook doubling back towards the main body of the letter (e.g., corrections on ff. 31^v/1 'be', 31^v/18 'euel' and 'euele'; original copying, ff. 31^v/3 'beþ', 31^v/21 'cloþ defoulede'). This page can be zoomed into at http://sunsite3.berkeley.edu/hehweb/HM130.html.

half, of his corrections restore the Southern Recension, usually as recorded in the main scribe's other copy of it. But only four of those are larger than a single word, and many emend just a letter or two; they look like guesswork designed to fix slips of the pen or dialectal translation and not collations.[64] Alongside them, there are twenty-two corrections, about a quarter of the seventy-eight in book II, which write over erasure the Main Version, as printed in a modern edition nearly word-for-word.[65] The remainder create something different from either the Main or Southern versions.[66] But the person doing this is not random in his interventions: three-quarters of his corrections in book II are centripetal in that they restore what *some* other copy has; it is just that he has two 'centres' for his centripetal tendency: the text the scribe has actually produced, from the Southern Recension, which he tidies up; and the Main Version, which he tries to turn this text into. He is fairly accurate in his aim, given that he has two different targets to hit.

The first, tidying up the text in front of him, from the Southern Recension, is unexceptional. What is curious is his second project: to turn the Southern Recension into the Main Version. What he erases is not usually visible, but it was most probably the Southern Recension, as is the rest of this copy and the main scribe's other copy; what he writes over erasure is the Main Version. For instance, here a couplet about God's grace is written over fiddly erasures, so that it now gives the Main Version:

ȝett may þe helpe and [----]{the} trauaile
Of asynful man to þe soule availe
yf hit [->]{in biddyng don her*e* be}
Of afrende þat i[->]{s in charite }

The scribe's other copy has instead the Southern Version like this:

And ȝet may þe helpe and grete trauaile
Of þe synful man to þe soule availe
yf so þat hit be þoruȝ gode praier ydo
Of afrende þat in his lif muche he trest to[67]

[64] Of 37 corrections which restore the Southern Recension, 7 restore a text not like SR 9, but like BodL, MS Lyell empt. 6, ff. 12^{v}–22^{r}, which Lewis and McIntosh, *Descriptive Guide*, no. SR 14, describe as also textually close to SR 18.

[65] Excepting tiny slips or dialectal variants such as *much* and *mickle*: SR 18, ff. 17^{r} (*Prick*, 1348), 19^{r} (1479), 21^{r} (1622). On the dialect, see Chapter 7, pp. 165–6 below.

[66] And three corrections occur where the Main Version and the Southern Recension themselves agree: ff. 15^{v} (*Prick*, 1261), 16^{v} (1338), 20^{r} (1556).

[67] Cf. SR 18, f. 47^{v-r} (*Prick*, 3656–9); SR 9, f. 37^{r}.

Such fiddly changes must have been done by collating copies and not by guessing. Often it is plausible to infer some sensitivity to particular words and their use or sense, as in this corrected couplet:

> And wordely richesse hov so hit come
> y. holde nouȝt elles but as [----------]{fantome}

This reconstructs the Main Version whereas the scribe's other copy has the Southern Recension thus:

> And wordly richesse hov so eu*ere* hit come
> y. telle hit nouȝt elles but adreme ynome

The correcting person might dislike the obsolescent verb *nim* (here meaning *to consider*) or might think that *phantom* has more powerful negative connotations for the insubstantiality of worldly things.[68] Yet while it is possible that the scribe is alert to local nuances like this, what seems to be the goal is the general reconciling of two different versions of the poem. It is not the particular differences of wording but the basic fact that the wording differs that irks him and that stirs him to correct; he treats variance – even this careful and wholesale revision of the poem, widely circulated in its own right – as error.

It would seem that he prefers one text to another, but it is not that simple. Often (as was said), he smooths out small details of the Southern Recension rather than removing them; often he does not restore everything he might from the Main Version; and, most oddly, he often conflates the two versions. A quarter of the seventy-eight corrections in book II restore neither the Main Version nor the Southern Recension in full and many combine elements from both. For instance, in one couplet the Southern Recension elsewhere looks like this:

> And þus shulde eu*ery* aman him self biþenche
> yf he wile godes grace to him wrenche.

The collated printed edition of the Main Version looks like this:

> Þus may ilk man do and thynk,
> In whase hert grace of God may synk.

But the heavily corrected manuscript now uses the syntax of one, the rhyme-words of the other, placed over erasure:

68 SR 18, f. 14v (*Prick*, 1196–7); SR 9, f. 15v. See *OED*, *nim* (*v.*), for its retreat from use, and *MED*, *fantom* (*n.*) 1, for collocations.

> And þus shulde eu*ery* man him wel by [-----]{þinke}
> yf he wile godes grace [–]{in} him [-----]{synke}[69]

It could be that the scribe is attentive to rhyming words more than others, because of their prominent sound-patterns or positions at the end of lines.[70] (Chapter 9 shows how alert people are to rhyme.) But the conflation also affects other words: elsewhere he restores a reference to the tide growing 'kene' and to storms from the Main Version but keeps the word 'tempest' from the Southern Recension:

> And þoruȝ stormes [->]{wexiþ kene and blawis}
> And þan [->]{risiþ tempestis and strong wawis}[71]

In such lines, then, the result resembles neither version wholly but seems designed to preserve as much as possible of both. Is there a coherent attitude to the text here?

He is not seeking an authorial original, nor any historical reconstruction of the text at one point in its transmission. He is willing to conflate different versions, so he cannot have considered one more authorial than another, or preferred either as a coherent artefact from the text's history. Nor can he think that a poem exists in only one form, and that his corrections will whittle down the variation in quest of an ideal text, for he has proliferated variation by creating some lines which were present in neither of the exemplars he had to hand. That is the point: his corrections seem to express not a textual idealism necessarily but a rejection of materialism, or to be specific, of the material forms of the text he inherits. It is as though the corrector of *The Prick of Conscience* thinks that neither exemplar is a complete witness to the text; likewise, the scribe of *Agnus castus* is aware that his own copy is liable to be incomplete. In this, they register something distinctive about verbal artefacts: that unlike things such as sculptures, texts can exist without ever being written down; they have if not an ideal form at least a conceptual form which transcends any one material form. As Richard Bucci puts it, 'The verbal work . . . is not a material object, nor is it communicated by purely sensational means.'[72] Sukanta Chaudhuri sees behind the variant copies of works 'a virtual or conceptual text' which exists 'on another plane altogether, before, through and after them'.[73] Although the scribes do not act according to philosophical idealism – not quite –

69 Respectively SR 9, f. 21^{v}; *Prick*, 1646–7; SR 18, f. 21^{r}.

70 E.g., SR 18, ff. 18^{v} (*Prick*, 1457), 20^{r} (1549), and cf. the different rhyme-words in SR 9, ff. 19^{r}, 20^{v} respectively.

71 SR 18, f. 15^{r}. Cf. SR 9, f. 15^{v}, and *Prick*, 1215–17.

72 Bucci, 'Mind and Textual Matter', 33.

73 Chaudhuri, *Metaphysics of Text*, 31.

they do seek the verbal form of the text regardless of what is materially present in their exemplars. This interpretation of their motives can only be speculation and in terms they would not themselves use, but it seems a fair speculation about what lurks in the minds of these people correcting *Agnus castus* and *The Prick of Conscience* (and of others in some later chapters).

Rather than idealism, this is the craftsman's realism: his realization that the products of his craft are not as perfect as the ideas he seeks to transmit; that textual design exceeds and is failed by the practicalities of manuscript transmission. That is a practical realization about book production, which might emerge from the problematic material forms they do encounter and create – finding divergent exemplars of *The Prick of Conscience*; noting an eyeskip in *Agnus castus* – and their efforts to overcome those problems. Correcting as a practical part of craftsmanship has built into it, as do crafts in general, an awareness like that articulated by the sculptor and philosopher David Pye that design – in this craft, the form of the text – is always in some ways unattainable and that the workman has considerable latitude – room for innovation or improvement but also risk of error – in approximating that design.[74] Yet workmanship is, for Pye, nonetheless susceptible to judgement for its approximation to the design.[75] So it seems to be for these people improving their copying. While we must not dismiss the presence or interest of variance, nor must we dismiss the scribes' impulse sometimes *not* to rewrite but to correct the rewriting they unintentionally produce or that they inherit from various exemplars: a pursuit of accurate reproduction.

[74] Pye, *Nature and Art of Workmanship*, 49–50. [75] *Ibid.*, 51.

CHAPTER 7

Writing well

And in hir [----]{term}es / sette hir lust and peyne

San Marino, Huntington Library, MS El. 26.C.9, f. 201r

Geoffrey Chaucer, *The Canterbury Tales*, VIII.1398

An awareness of the limitations of the material forms of texts underpins several corrections of late fourteenth- and fifteenth-century English books. But as well as accuracy in transcription, other problems are addressed, as scribes and their colleagues attempt to record the text as best they can in writing. They seek to make not only an accurate copy but a legible one, and so to improve their methods of book production, and in particular the process of writing. Craftsmanship involves what David Pye calls 'risk', the possibility of variable standards of execution of the design, but craftsmen often seek to reduce that risk through the quest for regularity – internal consistency and closer approximation to the design. Although, Pye notes, 'writing with a pen' is the paradigmatic example of 'the workmanship of risk', even these people seek 'the workmanship of certainty'.[1] Scribes developed methods for regularizing their procedures for making quires or arranging layout; and through correcting they address irregularity in the process of writing: in transcription, in spelling, in dialect and in the style of handwriting. As well as addressing problems in the exemplars and the content of the copy (as in Chapter 6), they also address problems in the orthographic and visual form of the copy. Corrections improve the craftsmanship of capturing words on the page.

This attention to the process of writing well is evident in the myopic smallness of corrections. The lengthy changes to whole lines in *The Prick of Conscience* or missing pages in *Agnus castus* (see Chapter 6) are untypical; in most of the Huntington Library's manuscripts, the majority of corrections are as small as a single word. (I can only say roughly 'the majority',

[1] Pye, *Nature and Art of Workmanship*, 53, 21. Pye prefers the word *workmanship* to *craft*, with its Victorian connotations, but he seems to be talking about what this book calls *craft*.

Table 7.1 *Corrections to single words, spellings and grammar in manuscripts in English in the HEHL*

total corrections	9,220	
• corrections to the choice or inclusion of single lexical words	1,383	15%
• necessary corrections to spelling	1,525	17%
• needless corrections to spelling	1,479	16%
• necessary corrections to a single grammatical word or inflexion	1,749	19%
• needless corrections to a single grammatical word or inflexion	316	3%
• total no longer than one word	6,452	70%

because I did not classify them by size; I only extrapolate figures from other categories used.) The majority of them, some 70 per cent, were corrections of the spelling, grammar, choice or inclusion of a single word or part thereof – changes no bigger than one word (Table 7.1). Even the remainder of corrections which did affect more than one word usually just prevented 'eyeskip' backwards or forwards or fixed the word-order. The smallness of these corrections might suggest that most of the errors which scribes committed were themselves small, although given that correction does not tell us about uncorrected errors, that suggestion cannot be confirmed. Rather, this smallness simply suggests the minuteness of the scribes' attention to tiny verbal details of their copy. Most corrections do not fix major problems in the textual transmission; they fix little slips of the pen. People were just trying to write accurately, legibly and conventionally.

The difficulties of transcription

The effort of simply seeking to write well seems obvious and is so ubiquitous that it is difficult to observe in any one instance. The focus on slips of transcription emerges most strikingly only by contrast with the neglect by scribes of matters of more substance – with a focus on the form over the content of their copies. It has been proposed that scribes were more interested in the underlying 'substance' or meaning of works than in the accidents of their 'words', in 'the core of prelinguistic truth', rather than their language and presentation.[2] That would seem possible, for much writing in English from the fourteenth and fifteenth centuries purports to be factual or to dictate practical behaviour or standards of right and wrong;

[2] Machan, *Textual Criticism*, 141–5, 155–6.

such writing would seem worth correcting for its truth claims rather than mere details of transcription. But just as the people correcting most often refrain from varying the text (as the previous chapter showed), likewise they seldom intervene in the content to improve it. When people visibly attend to the text using the techniques of correction, they seem only to worry about the accuracy and unambiguousness of the written medium.

That emerges in the corrections to religious works. Of course, readers at the Reformation do make numerous changes to outdated doctrine in earlier books. (These fascinating later phenomena are not counted here.) But the earlier makers and users of those books seldom correct their truth claims, heresies or canonicity. This restraint from rewriting might be striking given the importance of right belief, Scripture and liturgy; yet reverence or nervousness might explain it. People were, though, attentive to the process of writing, to mere slips of the pen which could dramatically alter religious statements. One frequent error with obviously dramatic effects was the omission of the word *not* which people then troubled to restore by interlining it. It is wickedly tempting to consider the omission sometimes as a willed heresy or as extremely logical quibbling. There are famous stories of later printers and proofreaders who omitted or added the word *not* with startling effects.[3] Some deliberate modification can sometimes be plausibly imagined for the errors of 'not' in English manuscripts. When the scribes write that one kind of grace 'is gefen vn to ilk synfull creat*ure*' or that 'ȝoure heuenly fader wol forȝeue ȝou', they might be trying to express the mercifulness of God; when they later change these lines to add that grace 'is ^{not} gefen' to all or that the Father 'wol $^{\wedge}$noȝt forȝeue ȝou', they might be changing their mind or balancing mercy with justice.[4] The scribe who writes that the birth of Jesus 'was chargeant' or painful to Mary might reasonably doubt such miracles; when somebody else adds that it 'was $^{\wedge\text{not}}$ chargeant' perhaps he is correcting such doubt. And so on, one can argue about the ten omissions and restorations of *not* from statements of faith in the Huntington Library's manuscripts.[5] But in fact these errors look more likely to be accidents of omitting the short word *not*, easily overlooked in an exemplar, easily skipped in copying it out. For example, it might be significant that one scribe misses out *not* in the line 'he schulde $^{\wedge\text{not}}$ make

[3] Campbell, *Bible: The Story of the King James Version*, fig. 19; Grafton, *Culture of Correction*, 33.

[4] HEHL, MS HM 148 (Part I), f. 2^{v} (Arntz (ed.), *Richard Rolle and Þe Holy Boke Gratia Dei*, 9.3); HEHL, MS HM 502, f. 57^{r} (Moon (ed.), *Þe Lyfe of Soule*, 55.6).

[5] HEHL, MS HM 149, f. 12^{v} (*Mirror*, 30.25). See also HEHL, MS HM 139, f. 2^{v} (*Prick*, 273); HEHL, MS HM 502, f. 84^{r} (John Wyclif, 'Þe Pater Noster', 107); HEHL, MS HM 503, f. 71^{r} (Hudson (ed.), '*Omnis plantacio*', 1644).

þe maist*er* þ*at* is ih*esu* *tra*uayle i*n* veyne', where a closely related copy of the same work has the whole passage over erasure, with *not* at the start of a line where it might be missed.[6] Did some problem in the exemplar cause the omission of *not*, rather than a wish to cause trouble for Jesus? It seems that what the scribes are checking for are these slips of copying, not of theology; and what guides them in correcting is the textual tradition and not debates over doctrine. After all, apart from two corrections which place the *not* too early in the sentence, these changes of *not* are otherwise centripetal.[7] Indeed, one scribe restores *not* in the phrase 'þou forsuke $^{\wedge\text{not}}$ lord sekand þe' which is Rolle's dense translation of the Psalms, and the Latin 'no*n* deliquisti querentes te. d*omi*ne' is there to guide his correction.[8] Although they affect the meaning in the most profound way, shifting statements of belief from positive to negative, the corrections seem merely to reflect care over scribal craft.

Likewise in medical works, where an error could have fatal results, what might look like revisions of the content are more likely improvements of the transcription, when they are made by the scribe.[9] For example, when a scribe corrects 'sawthistille' to 's[a]^{o}wthistille' or '[honI] honysokle', altering his vowels from <a> to <o> or altering the use of the long **I** to **y**, then he is not worrying over medical lore but over confusing letter-forms in his exemplar or conventions of spelling.[10] He was thinking not about medicine but scribal craft. Something similar pertains in corrections to a copy of the English version of Henry Daniel's *The Dome of Urynes*, which has been identified as 'generally accurate' overall.[11] The scribe crosses out the wrong words as he goes along and writes the right ones: so he fixes the words *food* and *flood* in references to the lungs drawing up 'þat mat*er* of the [flode] fode ¶ that is moste answeryng to flewme' or to 'sup*er*fluites of

6 HEHL, MS HM 1339, f. 53^{v} (*Mirror*, 24.21); cf. CUL, MS Mm.5.15, f. 81^{r} (*Mirror*, 124.21). On their relationship, see Chapter 5, n. 28 above.

7 HEHL, MS HM 503, f. 40^{v} (Hudson (ed.), '*Omnis plantacio*', 952); HEHL, MS HM 1339, f. 77^{v} (*Mirror*, 176.33–6).

8 HEHL, MS HM 148 (Part II), f. 33^{r} (Rolle, *Psalter*, 32; Psalms, 9.10).

9 There are, however, comments in a loosely corrective spirit made by readers. They comment on recipes and charms which are 'p*ro*batum', 'aprouyd' and 'approbata' ('approved') or else 'P*ro*hibitu*m* [. . .] ab Eccl*es*ia' ('banned by the Church'): HEHL, MS HM 58, ff. 43^{r}, 43^{v}, 45^{v}, 48^{r}, 50^{r}, 69^{r}, 75^{v}, 84^{r}; HEHL, MS HM 64, ff. 170^{r}, 170^{v}. Some recipes and charms are crossed out disapprovingly: HEHL MS HM 64, ff. 23^{r}, 140^{r}–141^{v}, 158^{r}, 162^{r}, 163^{r-v}, 168^{r}, 170^{r}.

10 HEHL, MS HM 26053, ff. 22^{r}, 13^{r}. Neither *OED*, *sow* (*n.*[1]) or *sow-thistle* (*n.*), nor *MED*, *soue* (*n.*) 2 or, in sense 1d, *soue-thistel*, records spellings with <a>. Hunt, *Plant Names*, 307, *sow-thistle*, only records three spellings with <a> (but see 'fauthystel', 69, under *carduus*, and 153, under *labrum Veneris*).

11 HEHL, MS HM 505, f. 1^{r}, mentioned in 'Henry Daniel's *Liber Uricrisiarum*', ed. Hanna, 191. Keiser, 'Vernacular Herbals', 295, identifies its owner, Richard Dodd.

the [flode] fode' seeping out through the pores.[12] It is possible to imagine unconscious thinking behind these slips, as though, while he copies this tract on urines, in discussions of phlegm and sweating, the scribe jumps to words for liquids rather than solids. But more likely he is just working fast and either looks too quickly at his exemplar and misreads 'fode' as 'flode' or mishears his internal dictation of it as he writes. It is an error in copying, and not an error in medicine, which he amends. Similarly, he corrects an error of transcription when he writes of distinguishing urine which is not 'skyishe *and* cloddyshe' but 'skyishe *and* [cloddyshe] clowdishe'.[13] He might notice the alarming content – if your urine has clods in it, you're really ill; but he might just note an explicable misreading of a looped **w** as double **d** from his exemplar; or he might want to improve the spelling, for this scribe consistently uses <ow> for this diphthong (which bothers other scribes, below).[14] He also emends another diphthong as he goes along in *wises* meaning *ways* ('meving in .2. [weyses] wyses').[15] Later users of the book did engage with the content, adding cross-references, and using *caret* marks and interlineations to do so, so that their annotations look like corrections.[16] But the scribe himself uses correcting to mend the medium, not the message – to ensure that his transcription is accurate and unambiguous.

It is problems of transcription which predominate – though not exclusively – in a final genre which could invite correction for its facts: chronicles. Chronicles in the Huntington Library do receive a few corrections to their factual information; there are roughly thirty in four copies of the prose *Brut.* Yet many of them are the work of later readers, and are more akin to annotation than scribal work. For example, in one copy of the prose *Brut* a few added details seem to be copied from William Caxton's first printed edition of it as *The Chronicles of England*, or perhaps entered while somebody was preparing this manuscript to serve as the exemplar for that edition.[17] In another, heavily corrected prose *Brut*, a second person supplements the scribe's hundred-odd self-corrections with about a hundred more, among them nine to the facts: he identifies people properly, replacing 'harolde' with 'reynolde'; he alters the conventions for names,

12 HEHL, MS HM 505, ff. 5^{r}, 5^{v} (I.iii).

13 HEHL, MS HM 505, f. 87^{r} (II.x).

14 E.g., in HEHL, MS HM 505, f. 87^{r}, 'calefactiown', 'comown', 'wapowrs'.

15 HEHL, MS HM 505, f. 73^{v}.

16 HEHL, MS HM 505, e.g., f. 4^{v}, cross-referring to the '48. leffe' and later 'þe ij leff'; the topics thus marked do occur on ff. 48^{v} and 3^{r}, which he foliates as '47' and '2'. He also writes eight interlineations and two marginal additions that are corrections (ff. 5^{v}, 12^{v}, 14^{r}, 21^{v}, 33^{r}, 35^{r} twice, 58^{v}, 61^{v}, 62^{v}), as well as glosses (ff. 7^{v}, 8^{v}, 11^{v}–12^{r}, 14^{r}–15^{v}, 16^{v}–19^{r}, 48^{v}).

17 HEHL, MS HM 136, discussed by Wakelin, 'Exemplar for Caxton's *Chronicles*?', 68–9.

turning 'Dyodician', like the form *Diodicias* preferred in Anglo-Norman, into 'Dyo[d]$_{//}^{\text{cl}}$ician' (*Diocletian*), preferred in English; and he sorts out people's family trees, replacing 'Doughter' with 'suster'.[18] He sometimes draws on a little knowledge of Normandy, which many fifteenth-century Englishmen would have had from the wars there. His knowledge of Normandy is dangerously little, though, and six of his nine changes are wrong: he does not recognize 'Barflette' or *Barfleur* and corrects it wrongly to the storied *Harfleur* or '[B]$_{//}^{\text{h}}$arflette'; and his interest in Normandy blinkers him to the part which Brittany plays in the events of 1066, so he crosses out 'Bretayn' and inserts 'normandy'.[19] But this mistaken correcting of history is a distinct and circumscribed activity, and even some of the seemingly factual changes could be corrections of copying errors. Glancing at an exemplar, a scribe might muddle 'harolde' and 'reynolde' or 'Dyodician' and 'Dyoclician', for in 'reynolde' the 'backwards' **e** could look like **a** and the **y** like the long **r**, and in 'Dyoclician' the letters **cl** could look like **d**. Likewise, when the scribe emends the spelling of proper nouns several times, this might be rewriting the facts or might be worry over capturing the word in a more felicitous spelling. To turn 'Igerne' into 'Ig$_{/}^{\text{r}}$e[r]ne' might be rejecting the French or Latin *Igerne* or *Igerna* and preferring something more like Malory's *Ygraine*; but it might simply be correcting the common linguistic metathesis where people move the sound /r/ elsewhere in the syllable. Or when the scribe turns 'Tyngagyll' into both 'Tyn[g]$_{/}^{\text{i}}$agyll' and 'Tyn[g]$_{/}^{\text{d}}$agyll' or turns 'Tyntagyll' into 'Tyn[t]$_{/}^{\text{d}}$agyll', he simply seems unsure how to render the consonant cluster /nt/.[20] Although some readers fix errors in the matter of Britain, others fix errors in the manner of writing English.

Correcting the dialect

This quest for legible transcription seems so much like common sense that there might be little more to say. What is curious, though, is that lots of the little corrections tinker with spellings or grammatical forms

[18] HEHL, MS HM 133, ff. 5^{v} (*Brut*, 21.24), 23^{r} (44.31), 91^{v}, where he forgot to complete the crossing out (142.22).

[19] HEHL, MS HM 133, ff. 55^{r} (diverging from *Brut*, 84.2), 85^{r} (*Brut*, 134.20). He also writes 'Bretoun' where he has to correct it to the name 'Bre$_{//}^{\text{cynall}}$[toun]' (f. 67^{r}; *Brut*, 99.6). Further corrections to facts by post-Reformation antiquarians are not here counted.

[20] HEHL, MS HM 133, ff. 39^{v} (*Brut*, 66.21), 39^{v} (66.16), 40^{r} (66.29), 40^{r} (67.6), 40^{v} (67.20), 40^{v} (67.20). He leaves 'Igrene' uncorrected on 40^{r}. For corrected names in another prose *Brut*, see HEHL, MS HM 113, ff. 47^{v} (*Brut*, 116.21), 134^{r} (293.4). For other corrections to Arthurian names, see BL, MS Harley 4203, ff. 164^{v}–165^{v}, where <r> is interlineated into 'Mo^^{r}dred' 11 times.

which already made sense in the English of the fourteenth and fifteenth centuries. That is, the spelling or morphology or grammatical construction which gets corrected is used without correction in some other records of English in the fourteenth and fifteenth centuries.[21] Such is the case with over a third of the corrections to the spelling or grammar (35 per cent or 1,795 of 5,069 combining four rows of Table 7.1) and a fifth of all corrections (19 per cent or 1,795 of 9,220). These changes are not needed for the basic comprehension or grammaticality of the text. But reason not the need, for in some respects most correcting of language is superfluous; basic communication need not be perfect in grammar or pronunciation to be effective. These needless corrections are a minority, then, but they are intriguing because they reveal how far correcting can go, beyond what is merely practical or essential for communication, and beyond right and wrong: they hone the craft of writing.

This correction of written English is surprising because, whereas statements of fact – whether somebody is called 'harolde' or 'reynolde' – can be right or wrong, linguistic usage is often debatable; one man's shibboleth is another's hypercorrection, and what some wince at, others ignore. The changes of spelling and grammar which might be needless, then, test intriguingly the fuzzy border between correcting and rewriting. Yet while we might theoretically recognize that those borders are blurred, if a scribe or reader has used the techniques of correcting, his practice has in some sense implied a difference between wrong and right forms of English. The history of English in this period makes such distinctions possible but also astonishing. For without schools or textbooks teaching English, there was no standardized way of writing English: hence the variant forms from which scribes could choose.[22] Moreover, these variants, largely dialectal, were not as firmly stigmatized as in later centuries. People commented on 'diu*er*se man*er*is of writyng' quite sanguinely: even somebody compiling an alphabetical concordance could comment blithely that sometimes a word 'write*n* of su*m* ma*n* i*n* oo man*ere* is write*n* of a-noþ*ir* ma*n* i*n* a-noþ*ir* manere', say in using <þ> and <ʒ> instead of <th> and <g> or in dropping initial <h>.[23] The alphabetical compiler even urges scribes of his work that if the words are not alphabetized 'in ordre aftir his conseit & his man*ere* of writyng', he can set them in a new order.[24] As a result, scribes felt free to 'translate' texts from the author's or the exemplar's dialect into

[21] I judged difficult cases by seeing whether the 'error' is among the forms recorded in *OED*, *MED*, *LALME* or Mustanoja, *Middle English Syntax*.

[22] Machan, *English in the Middle Ages*, 97, 100–1. [23] Kuhn (ed.), 'Preface', 272. [24] *Ibid.*, 272.

their own.[25] Michael Benskin and Margaret Laing have explained how the mechanics of copying encouraged such translation. By the fourteenth century, many books in English were copied in cursive or 'joined up' varieties of handwriting modelled on the anglicana or secretary scripts. To keep up the speed of cursive writing, which sometimes flowed very currently, scribes were less likely to scrutinize their exemplars letter-for-letter and more likely to read them a few words at a time; they would then turn from the exemplar back to their copy and 'dictate' the text back to themselves internally from memory a split second later. Because they wrote, in effect, from internal dictation in their own voice, scribes were led to 'translate' the text into their own dialect. Indeed, Benskin and Laing argue that cursive writing almost forced dialectal translation, so that it is best not thought of as 'deliberate'; instead, as they say, 'it is close copying that requires deliberate effort for a scribe who writes in cursive script'.[26] As a result, this translation was not always thorough and the scribes tolerated 'mixed and variable usage'.[27] 27

That lack of a standard English makes it curious that people made needless changes to spelling and grammar when there was so much variety tolerated. What is more curious is that they do not concertedly use corrections of spellings and grammar in order to effect dialectal translation. Although dialectal correction has been identified in earlier centuries, when the orthography of English was even less well established, some fourteenth- and fifteenth-century case-studies have noted the fewness of corrections which modify the dialect in any thorough way.[28] The books in the Huntington Library confirm that: the correcting needlessly alters the spelling or grammar only a couple of times in most books; the majority of such changes cluster in just a few books, as though it was an odd thing, done only by a few people.[29] Why is that? Why is there so little dialectal translation in correcting, compared to the ubiquity of it in copying? One reason could be the late date of the manuscripts in the Huntington

[25] McIntosh, 'New Approach to Middle English Dialectology', 27–8, and 'Word Geography', 92–3.

[26] Benskin and Laing, 'Translations and *Mischsprachen*', 90, 94; see also Kato, 'Corrected Mistakes', 77, 87. By contrast, Vinaver, 'Principles of Textual Emendation', 353, 360, stresses the scribe's 'visual' memory of the exemplar, but his account seems to me less convincing than Benskin and Laing's.

[27] Milroy, 'Middle English Dialectology', 190.

[28] Hudson (ed.), *English Wycliffite Sermons*, 146; Duncan, 'Middle English Linguistic Reviser', 162.

[29] The highest proportions are in HEHL, MS El. 26.A.13 (Part I), with 496 or 84 per cent of its corrections being needless changes to grammar and spelling; MS HM 744 (Part I), with 121 or 79 per cent; MS HM 128, with 377 or 48 per cent; MS HM 112 with 194 or 40 per cent. Beyond these 4 MSS, no MS has more than 64 (MS HM 133 with 19 per cent) or more than a third of its corrections (MS HM 149, with 26 or 32 per cent) as such needless changes. Of the 52 MSS in the HEHL sample, 35 have under 10 per cent of their corrections as needless changes of grammar or spelling.

Library: most are fifteenth-century and many are dated palaeographically to the late fifteenth century, by which point dialectal translation becomes less extreme.[30] But another reason lies in the mechanics of copying as opposed to correcting. Cursive copying involves speed and the sound of internal dictation which together make dialectal translation almost automatic (as was noted). But correcting interrupts the flow of that with a pause for retrospection; it interrupts the automatic processing of the exemplar with moments of choice and decision; and it interrupts any reliance on internal dictation with a more visual scrutiny of the exemplar or copy. Correcting is strikingly different from the copying which encouraged dialectal translation.

The temporal delay and the self-conscious scrutiny of dialectal variants occurs in one manuscript where the 'automatic' translation into the scribe's dialect breaks down. This manuscript is the copy of *The Prick of Conscience* in the Southern Recension (mentioned in Chapter 6), in which a second person makes extensive changes to restore the text of the Main Version. That person also alters the spelling of several words. The first scribe's customary dialectal spelling is evident in another copy of the poem that he made; comparing its record of his spellings with the second person's correction of his spelling, it can been seen that the correcting often modifies the first scribe's dialect. The second person makes sixty-one tiny erasures with overwriting to fix the spelling.[31] He corrects *much* and *muchel* twelve times to ensure that the vowel is <o> ('m[-]{o}che'), rather than <u> as in the scribe's other copy.[32] He corrects *here*, *hear* and words rhyming with them, always ending up with a spelling with <e>, such as 'here', whereas the main scribe in his other copy spells these homophones with <u>, such as 'hure'.[33] He also makes three changes to the spelling of *together*, adding a medial vowel <e> instead of <a> which the scribe writes in his other copy.[34] And most extensively he changes *it* from 'hit' to 'yt' some twenty-three times in the first three quires; usually the start of the word

30 *LALME*, vol. I, 3 ('Introduction'); Samuels, 'Spelling and Dialect', 86–7.

31 *LALME*, vol. III, 680–1 (LP 7271), notes differences between the main scribe and the corrector's spellings in HEHL, MS HM 130 (hereafter SR 18). See also Chapter 6, pp. 151–5 above.

32 Cf. e.g., SR 18, ff. 19r (two lines not in *Prick*), 19v (a variant of 1523), 21r (variants of 1620, 1624), with BL, MS Harley 2281 (hereafter SR 9), ff. 19v (two lines not in *Prick*), 20r (a variant of 1523), 21r (a variant of 1620), 21v (a variant of 1624).

33 Cf., e.g., SR 18, ff. 2r (*Prick*, 183), 3r (283), 4r (343, and a variant of 347), with the corresponding lines in SR 9, ff. 3r (183), 4v (283). However, on SR 9, f. 5r (a variant of 347), the main scribe spells 'her*e*' with <e>.

34 Cf., e.g., SR 18, ff. 23v (*Prick*, 1855, 1858), 104r (7937), with SR 9, f. 24r (1855, 1858). SR 9 has lost all text after f. 64v (5764).

without <h> is rewritten over an erasure.[35] Maybe not all of his changes to *it* are dialectal: later in the fourth quire he writes over erasure 'hit' now with <h>, suggesting that he did tolerate the form he erased earlier, but he uses it to replace 'heo' (*she*) where it refers to the 'soule' with the feminine pronoun, as in the Latin word *anima*.[36] He perhaps dislikes 'heo' for the soul and prefers the genderless *it*. Or perhaps his intention is, after all, to remove the regional form of *she* as <heo>, as is found in the main scribe's other copy; he changes 'heo' to 'sche' three times elsewhere.[37] This second person's intervention, then, looks like revision of dialectal spellings. Such fussiness is unsurprising given the meticulousness with which he also collates two recensions of the poem.

The extent of this fussiness is, however, limited mostly to the first three quires of that book.[38] This limit of extent is typical: whenever there is frequent correcting of dialect – otherwise in books outside the Huntington Library – it most often extends only over the first few quires. That reflects a problem with dialectal translation during the process of copying: although dialectal translation often unfolds as good as automatically, scribes spend the opening few pages of a manuscript or of a new text 'working in', while they adjust to a new exemplar and work out which elements of it need translating.[39] It is in this stage of 'working in', where translation is not yet fully accomplished, that there is most correcting of dialect, to regularize it across the copy. This emerges in one other manuscript from the Huntington Library. It is half of a composite volume commissioned by John Pery, a canon of Holy Trinity by Aldgate in London, from two scribes in various discrete stints (illustrated in Figure 4 in Chapter 8).[40] He does not copy it himself: he 'had this book made' ('hu*n*c libru*m* fieri fecit'), he explains in an added colophon; but he does correct it copiously.[41] In the combined

35 SR 18: 'yt' from f. 3^{v} (*Prick*, 296) to f. 35^{r} (*Prick*, 2813, in a variant of the Southern Recension). Cf., e.g., SR 18, ff. 3^{v} (296, 309), 4^{r} (349, 355), with SR 9, ff. 4^{v} (296, 309), 5^{r} (349), 5^{v} (355).

36 Cf. SR 18, ff. 37^{r} (*Prick*, 2960), 38^{r} (3045, 3046, 3047, 3051), 38^{v} (a variant of 3087), with SR 9, ff. 28^{r} (2960), 29^{r} (3045, 3046, 3047, 3051), 29^{v} (a variant of 3087). SR 9, f. 28^{r} (2961), gives the spelling 'hee', but SR 18, f. 37^{r}, has 'h[--]{it}' partly over erasure. Contrast Thomas Hoccleve's revisions to refer to the soul with the feminine pronoun, in Chapter 11, n. 76 below.

37 Cf. SR 18, f. 16^{r} (*Prick*, 1277, 1278), with SR 9, f. 16^{v}.

38 Among 61 needless changes to spelling or grammatical morphemes, there are after f. 35^{v} only 3 of 'here' or its rhyme (ff. 45^{v}, *Prick*, 3538; 45^{v}, 3539; 95^{r}, 6885), 1 of 'tog[-]{e}dre' (f. 104^{r}, 7937) and 8 of 'hit' replacing the feminine 'heo' on ff. 36^{v}–38^{v}.

39 Benskin and Laing, 'Translations and *Mischsprachen*', 56, 66.

40 Patwell, 'Canons and Catechisms', 386–9, discusses BL, MS Add. 10053, ff. 99^{r}–114^{r}, a booklet by a different scribe.

41 BL, MS Add. 10053, f. 83^{r}; HEHL, MS HM 112, f. 78^{v}. Quire signatures of roman numerals starting at 'xviij' in BL, MS Add. 10053, ff. 3^{v}, 11^{v} and so on suggest that the two volumes once formed one book, but blank leaves at the ends of quires and a second set of leaf signatures in BL, MS

volume, Pery's handwriting is recognizable in over half of the corrections (55 per cent or 452 of 819) and might have been responsible for some of the other corrections (23 per cent or 186 of 819) which are impossible to ascribe to anybody with certainty. About a quarter of the corrections in Pery's book emend spelling or syntax in ways which are needless for comprehension but which reflect preferences in dialect, especially in one inflexion. The scribe of most of the book usually spells the third person singular present inflexion with <th> or <þ> ('walketh') but in a few places, and especially in the early parts of each work, he spells it with just <t> ('walket'), a spelling perhaps likeliest to come from Norfolk or the Midlands.[42] Pery then corrects just a few of these inflexions ending in <t> and does not catch all the variety of the scribe's usage.[43] But in the second section of this volume, now in the British Library, Pery corrects the dialect quite consistently during the earlier pages where the scribe is still 'working in' to his dialect. In these earlier pages the scribe often omits <h> from the inflexion <th>, but Pery squeezes it in again, in a slightly different ink and squashed before the next word. He does this to three-quarters of the scribe's uses of <t> alone, all bar one of which fall in the first seventeen folios.[44] The scribe himself uses almost as many examples of <th> or <þ> here, and he later uses these forms almost exclusively.[45] Pery's correcting of these first few folios removes most of the inflexions with the <t> which would upset the dialect of the rest of the book. The initial use of <t> alone suggests just a process of 'working in' to <th>, and Pery's correcting polishes it off.

Nor need the 'working in' always involve changes in dialect; sometimes it involves updating English in the light of diachronic change. There are only a few scattered examples in the Huntington Library's books. A more consistent attempt to do so is found elsewhere in a copy of Walton's verse

Add. 10053, ff. 4^{r}–7^{r} ('aj' to 'aiiij'), ff. 12^{r}–15^{r} ('bj' to 'biiij') and so on suggest that these quires also circulated separately.

42 *LALME* doesn't give a dot-map but traces inflexions with <t> in the North only (vol. 1, 466–7; dot-maps 648–9). *LALME*, vol. 1, 92, describes the dialect of HEHL, MS HM 112, ff. 13^{r}–78^{v}, as 'Surrey' but 'with a strong Nott[inghamshire] underlay', which could reflect Walter Hilton's text.

43 HEHL, MS HM 112, ff. 13^{v} twice (*Scale*, 37), 31^{v} (92), 32^{r} (92), 32^{r} (94), 32^{v} (93; the text is disordered here), 36^{r} (104); two of these seven correct the archaic third-person plural inflexion <th>. This scribe's stint only begins on f. 13^{r}. Pery also corrects, in the 'working in' of this scribe, eight other consonantal clusters representing /θ/ by adding <h> to <t> in nouns such as 't$^{\wedge h}$oght' or 'fait$^{\wedge h}$' which the scribe otherwise spells with <th>: ff. 14^{r} (*Scale*, 37), 15^{v} (44), 16^{v} twice (47), 19^{v} (57), 20^{v} (61), 42^{r} twice (125).

44 BL, MS Add. 10053, ff. 4^{r}–19^{r}, modifying 49 of 63 <t> inflexions to <th>; there are 13 uncorrected <t> inflexions on ff. 3^{r}–12^{v} and 1 stray on f. 27^{r} ('tastyt').

45 BL, MS Add. 10053, ff. 3^{r}–19^{r}, with 61 <th> or <þ> inflexions; in ff. 22^{v}–29^{v} there are 41 <þ> inflexions and 3 <th> ones (ff. 24^{v}, 26^{v}, 27^{r}). The intervening ff. 19^{r}–22^{v} are in the past tense.

translation of Boethius' *De consolatione philosophiae* by a scribe who signs and dates his work as that of 'prior John Clynton' in 1480.[46] After he had written two quires, a colleague interrupted and wrote a page; then, when Clynton resumed, he used a very different orthography and morphology, modernizing Walton's, which was by then seventy years old. After the change in his own practice, Clynton then went back over his first two quires and erased and replaced several spellings and inflexions which were more archaic than those in later quires. For this reason, the opening few pages of the English were corrected about five times more frequently than were later passages. This could be due to fatigue; there is a similar decline in frequency in correcting the Latin.[47] But the Latin is much less frequently corrected in general, for what Clynton attends to is the poem's archaic English. He modifies early in the book the inflexional ending <n>, the word *gan* as an auxiliary marking tense, the initial consonantal cluster <sch>, from which he often removes <c>, and *thilke* and *tho*, which seem to be dying out in the fifteenth century (Table 7.2).[48] He is not perfectly thorough: for example, in one line where he removes the inflexion <n> he does not notice the duplicated 'sche sche' nor its spelling with <c> (xxiv).[49] But some consistency seems to be his purpose: to bring these first two quires of 'working in' in line with the rest of his copy.

In its small way, the correction of 'working in' corroborates the evidence that people did register the differences between dialects; indeed, as Tim William Machan has shrewdly observed, translation only occurs because of such sensitivity.[50] People recognized some conventions for spelling as 'more appropriate, intelligible and desirable', whether because they were right for the locale, institution or author in question.[51] If we are uncertain how witting that linguistic judgement was, we might note that in these cases the change is not automatic, for Pery and Clynton are reflecting

46 Chicago, Newberry Library, MS f36, f. 207^{v}, discussed by Dwyer, 'Newberry's Unknown Revision'.

47 E.g., Chicago, Newberry Library, MS f36, ff. 78^{r}/8–85^{r}/1 (Walton (trans.), *Boethius*, prol. 1–176, I.1–224), have 125 corrections to English, of which 90 change spelling or morphology; ff. 153^{r}/39–161^{v}/26 (IV.1–400), have 25 corrections to English, of which 12 change spelling or morphology. The corresponding Latin passages, in this bilingual copy, have 14 and 3 corrections.

48 Horobin, *Language of the Chaucer Tradition*, 107–8, 111–12, traces scribes' declining use of the inflexional <n>. The longer time-scale of the entries in *OED*, *gin* (*v.*^{2}), and *thilk* (*adj.* and *pron.*), convey their obsolescence better than *MED*, *ginnen* (*v.*), and *thilk(e* (*adj.*). *LALME*, vol. I, 340–2 (dot-maps 142–9), vol. II, 93–110 (item-maps 22–3), reveals no obvious diatopic distribution of spellings <sch> or <sh> in *shall*.

49 Also, on Chicago, Newberry Library, MS f36, f. 82^{r}, as though by hypercorrect analogy, he removes the obsolescent <n> from <abouen> (*above*).

50 Machan, *English in the Middle Ages*, 87–9, 95.

51 Horobin, *Language of the Chaucer Tradition*, 34, 63, but cf. the warning on 76.

Table 7.2 *Some corrections to archaism in Chicago, Newberry Library, MS f36, ff. 78r/8–85r/1, from Walton (trans.),* Boethius, *prol. 1–176, and* 1.*1–224*

	folio	*stanza*	*correction*	*tendency*
i)	78^{r}	prol. 1	The w‸^{h}yle	<w> *to* <wh>
ii)	78^{r}	prol. 1	^{be}gan they for to vsen	*avoid* gan
iii)	78^{v}	prol. 7	th[o]{a*n*}	*avoid* tho *(adv.)*
iv)	78^{v}	prol. 8	hym selue[n]	*avoid final* <n>
v)	79^{r}	prol. 9	And [<ek>e]{also}	*avoid* eke
vi)	79^{r}	prol. 9	[<gan>]{dyde} he sor*e* oppresse	*avoid* gan
vii)	79^{r}	prol. 11	for to take[n] heede	*avoid infinitive* <n>
viii)	79^{r}	prol. 12	he [<gan>]{dyd} pursewe	*avoid* gan
ix)	80^{r}	prol. 18	And soth to sey[ne]	*avoid infinitive* <n>
x)	80^{r}	prol. 19	Atte Ravenne [<eke>]{also}	*avoid* eke
xi)	80^{r}	prol. 21	I sey [y]{ȝ}owe	*avoid initial* <y> *as conson.*
xii)	80^{v}	1.m1.1	w[h]ete[n] they	*avoid 3rd p. pl. pres.* <n>
xiii)	80^{v}	1.m1.2	they solace[n]	*avoid 3rd p. pl. pres.* <n>
xiv)	81^{v}	1.p1.1	I [g<an>]{dide} þe holde	*avoid* gan
xv)	81^{v}	1.p1.1	I cowth her noght dyscre[uen]	*avoid infinitive* <n>
xvi)	82^{r}	1.p1.2	fer a boue[n] ma*nn*es syghte	*avoid final* <n>
xvii)	82^{v}	1.p1.7	[Sche]{Be} gan to loke	*avoid* gan
xviii)	83^{r}	1.p1.12	And sadly [gan]{dyd} þe holde	*avoid* gan
xix)	83^{v}	1.m2.4	And [-]{wh}at	<w> *to* <wh> (?)
xx)	83^{v}	1.m2.4	Off [thilke]{the} fayr*e* fyrste somer seson	*avoid* thilke
xxi)	83^{v}	1.m2.4	he a [sc]{s}hewed	<sch> *to* <sh>
xxii)	84^{r}	1.p2.2	I [y]{g}aue	*avoid initial* <y> *as conson.*
xxiii)	84^{v}	1.p2.2	Thow [sc]{s}hameste nat	<sch> *to* <sh>
xxiv)	84^{v}	1.p2.3	sche sawe me sytt[yn]	*avoid infinitive* <n>
xxv)	84^{v}	1.m3.1	And w[e]{he}n	<w> *to* <wh>
xxvi)	84^{v}	1.m3.1	The sonne þe gynne to s[chewen]{hew}	<sch> *to* <sh> *and avoid infinitive* <n>
xxvii)	84^{v}	1.m3.1	But w[e]{he}n	<w> *to* <wh>

retrospectively while correcting. Their changes are thus not simple reflexes of the sound of speech in their head, for they are not responding to internal dictation as they copy but are examining inconsistencies in the written form as they read the text back. Correcting the 'working in' is a sort of palaeographical recognition of one of the pitfalls of how scribes work. That is why this standardizing is very limited: it is merely a 'focused' rather than 'fixed' standard, concerned with only a few features and not the whole language, and executed only on certain occasions.[52] This is not an effort to standardize the language as a whole nor an unthinking reversion to one's own dialect; it is an effort to finish the writing of a particular book clearly, conventionally and consistently. While the dialectal translation for the most part emerges from echoes of oral language, the tidying up of that translation by correcting emerges from a concern with conventions of written English.

Written conventions

This quest for tidiness, conventionality and fixity is often said to be inherent in writing. Bernard Cerquiglini argues that writing escapes the personal foibles and contextual ties of oral language and 'decontextualizes language and makes it audible to more than one person' ('décontextualise la langue, et la rend audible à plus d'un'). Therefore when a written version of the language comes into 'common usage' it is 'very quickly judged to be "good"' ('l'écriture . . . est toujours un usage commun, et bien vite jugé "bon"').[53] Sociolinguists note that writing 'tends to be more conservative' and to follow 'conventions that are more generally agreed and prescribed'.[54] In these fourteenth- and fifteenth-century books, the worrying over spelling works at the level of the single book rather than across a culture; nor does it even always produce dialectal order or consistency within the one book. Rather, the decontextualization of language seems to prompt not the reformer's concern with standardization but the craftsman's with trying to do a good job.

As they attempt to develop writing as a suitable medium in its own right, what they bear witness to in particular is people's dissatisfaction with writing's echo of sound. That is, it is not so much dissatisfaction with writing's reflection of their dialect as with writing's ability to reflect language at all. There are vivid signs of this in a manuscript of devotional prose made for an East Anglian nunnery in the early fifteenth century. The four scribes spell words in ways which capture sound in unconventional ways. This could be because the scribes are nuns, who as women might not have been trained well, or could be because they copy hastily in very current handwriting.[55] The first scribe, who writes very quickly, with handwriting mostly modelled on anglicana, but with the simple **a** and **w** of secretary,

[52] On this distinction, see Smith, *Historical Study of English*, 63–73, and 'Standard Language in Early Middle English?', 128–9.

[53] Cerquiglini, *In Praise*, 18, and *Éloge*, 38.

[54] Milroy, 'Middle English Dialectology', 165.

[55] O'Mara (ed.), *Study*, 154–6, 162, doubts that the scribes are nuns.

Table 7.3 *Some corrections to spelling in the stint of scribe 1 in Durham, UL, MS Cosin V.iii.24*

	folio	*scribe*	*correction*	*word*
i)	1^{v}	2	the grace of all [mytghy] ^myghty god	*mighty*
ii)	3^{v}	2	thow wilt receyue [wordyli] ^wurthily	*worthily*
iii)	6^{r}	1	Thes smale [thewes] ^theves bringyn In gret theves	*thieves*
iv)	6^{v}	2	wit*h* sekyr kepyng as a [close cardyn] ^cloos gardeyn	*close garden*
v)	7^{v}	1	þat tretowre the qwiche [gryutchid] grutchid	*grouched*
vi)	12^{r}	1	In þ*at* Hows [sculd] chulde be thyn restyng place	*should*
vii)	21^{r}	2 (?)	alle thyn [canell] ^carnell frendys	*carnal*
viii)	27^{r}	unclear	a sc^hort lesson	*short*
ix)	37^{r}	2	we wole noth [weryd] ^were it	*wear it*
x)	42^{v}	1	[chete] ^schette fast þe stabyl dor*e*	*shut*

produces spellings which were fine as rough phonetic transcriptions. But these spellings displease the scribe himself or herself, and displease the second scribe, who checks everybody's work; the two of them then correct the first scribe's spelling seventy-three times in eighty pages (sampled in Table 7.3).[56] The correcting seems not to *reflect* sound automatically but to *reflect upon* sound more self-consciously, and to reflect upon the best method for recording it. The first scribe, for example, does not capture the subtle difference between the voiced and unvoiced sounds in /k/ and /g/ and /d/ and /t/ in 'cardyn' and 'weryd' (iv, ix); he or she spells the sound /v/ as <w> and not <v> and the sound /ʃ/ as <sc> and <ch> and not <sh> (iii, vi, viii, x). These attempts to capture sounds then get refined in correction.

Were these refinements needed? After all, the first scribe was happy to let five of the ten spellings in Table 7.3 stand; of two people working in close proximity, only the second thought some of them wrong. And as representations of speech, the spellings work adequately, if not well: after all, voiced and unvoiced consonants are not always easily distinguished nor need they be, for, spoken quickly, the words *wear it* could just about be deduced from the spelling 'weryd'. The corrections 'sculd' and 'chete' are no better or worse than 'chulde' and 'schette' for *should* and *shut* (vi, x), for

[56] Durham, UL, MS Cosin V.iii.24, described by Whitehead, Renevey and Mouron (eds.), *Doctrine of the Hert*, xlix–li. These two scribes made another 99 other corrections on scribe 1's stint (ff. 1^{r}–43^{v}, apart from passages by scribe 2 on ff. 17^{r-v}, 30^{r}/8–15, 32^{r-v} and 39^{v}/5 to the foot, 43^{v}/5 to the foot). On scribe 2's other copying, see O'Mara (ed.), *Study*, 143, and Chapter 4, n. 35 above.

scribes render the sound /ʃ/ as <sc> or <ch> as well as <ch> and <sch>; nor is there any consistency in these corrections, which turn one <ch> into <sch> but another <sc> back into <ch>.[57] This is not a closer echo of sound, for the sounds are the same though the spellings differ, but is fussiness over the conventions of writing. That is true in other words. For instance, the spelling 'canell' for *carnal* (vii) might work if /r/ was no longer pronounced or rhoticized, as in many present varieties of British English (/kɑ:nəl/). Although /r/ was not fully lost until the eighteenth century, spellings without it such as 'canell' suggest that it was weakening much earlier when it occurred before some other consonants,[58] and restoring the <r> suggests that the change was not universal. Consequently, spelling cannot follow the sound of internal dictation safely.

Of course, orthography in English frequently has its own logic unrelated to sound. It is not perfectly or solely phonographic; orthography also carries historical or etymological information or works by established conventions and has its own graphic logic on occasion.[59] In correcting spelling, then, the purpose might be not merely capturing sound but establishing consistency or visual effect on the page. The <r> could be needed in 'canell' because the first scribe usually spells 'carnell' with <r>.[60] Or there could be an etymological drive to keep the <r> from the Latin word for flesh (*caro, carnis*). Likewise, inserting <h> into consonant clusters such as <sc> for the sound /ʃ/ might reflect not a clear representation of sound but an attempt to apply conventions of its use in fifteenth-century spelling.[61] It seems here that the initial process of writing involves spelling things quickly as they sound, while self-correcting or correcting another involves a second-order, metalinguistic reflection upon the success of that writing process.

So although fifteenth-century English managed without written rules for orthography, some people were thinking about how it worked in practice. In the Huntington Library's sample of books, such thinking is more intermittent than in this book from an East Anglian nunnery but it does nonetheless occur scattered among a wide range of books. One common set of needless corrections to spelling is to diphthongs. Diphthongs are complex vowel sounds which technically include two vowels and a glide

57 The vowel in *shut* was also open to flux: Wright, 'More on the History of *Shit* and *Shut*', 7–8.

58 Lass, 'Phonology and Morphology', 66–7. See also Lutz, 'Vocalisation', 179; and Windross, 'Loss of Postvocalic *r*', 431.

59 Scragg, *History of English Spelling*, 114–15, 116–17; Horobin, *Does Spelling Matter?*, 20.

60 Cf., e.g., Durham, UL, MS Cosin V.iii.24, f. 20^{v}/22 ('carnell').

61 On these broader problems, see Scragg, *History of English Spelling*, 45–7.

from one into the other, but which are heard as some new conflation of the two. Scribes and others worry that these sounds need particular spellings to evoke them: in particular, where a scribe uses one vowel to represent a diphthong, he or another often adds a second vowel, as though in some attempt to capture the doubleness. For example, some scribes worry whether to add <u> or <w> after another vowel. John Pery (mentioned above) emends 'troyng' (*trowing*, 'believing') and 'knoyng' to 'tro^^{w}yng' and 'kno^^{w}yng', despite leaving the verb *know* without <w> elsewhere ('þ*o*u knoest').[62] Comparably, a scribe associated with Syon Abbey, copying John Lydgate's *Life of Our Lady*, four times adds <u> or <w>; for example, once, in the paler ink he uses for marginal prompts to correct, he puts a macron like the abbreviation for **n** over 'bondys', treating the prior <n> as <u>, and thereby expands the diphthong to give 'bou¬*n*¬dys'.[63] Besides <ou> or <ow>, other diphthongs are tinkered with in 'a^^{i}re', 'fe^^{i}nyd', 'poisened' to 'poysowned' and 'pra^^{i}se', for instance.[64] Beyond the Huntington Library's sample, scribes often worry about vowels and diphthongs in words borrowed from French, such as 'du^^{e}te', 'compa^^{i}gnie' and 'seru^^{a}untis'.[65] A few scribes fuss over the derivational morpheme <ous> derived from Latin <osus>; it was on its journey from a pronounced long vowel /u:s/ to a meagre unaccented /əs/ and so it is represented by various letters in the fifteenth century, and people correct that variety between <us>, <ous>, <ose>, <ouse> and <uis>.[66] For instance, in Nicholas Love's *Mirror of the Blessed Life of Jesus Christ* we hear of the Holy Family at the Nativity that 'þei wer*e* not squeymo[s]{*us*} of þe stable', while the second scribe who corrected this book *was* squeamish about the spelling and added the abbreviation for <us> over an erased <s>.[67] These were fussy attempts to establish conventions for writing.

62 HEHL, MS HM 112, ff. 20^{v} (*Scale*, 61), 21^{v} (63), 26^{r} (77); but cf. f. 25^{r}.

63 HEHL, MS HM 115, f. 88^{v} (*LOL*, IV.270).

64 Respectively, HEHL, MS HM 148 (Part I), f. 8^{v} (Arntz (ed.), *Richard Rolle and Þe Holy Boke Gratia Dei*, 44.20); HEHL MS HM 112, f. 15^{r} (*Scale*, 53); HEHL, MS HM 268, f. 96^{v} (*Fall*, IV.2469); HEHL, MS HM 28561, f. 43^{r} (*Polychronicon*, I.1.7).

65 Respectively, PUL, MS Garrett 137, f. 41^{v} (*Regiment*, 2905); BodL, MS Rawl. poet. 163, f. 76^{r} (*Troilus*, IV.707); CUL, MS Ll.4.14, f. 118^{v} (*Richard the Redeless*, IV.46, in Dean (ed.), *Richard the Redeless*).

66 *OED*, *-ous* (*suffix*), and, e.g., HEHL, MS HM 115, f. 80^{v}, 'Fruttuose' with 'fructuouse' in the margin (a variant of *LOL*, III.1616); HEHL, MS HM 144, f. 78^{r}, 'graciously' crossed out and 'graciusly' added (*LOL*, II.987); PUL, MS Garrett 137, f. 53^{r}, replacing 'vertuis' with 'vertuous' (*Regiment*, 3637); CUL, MS Ll.4.14, f. 109^{r}, 'vertu^^{ou}s' (Dean (ed.), *Richard the Redeless*, I.35). HEHL, MS HM 115, f. 80^{v}, also adds <c> as if to echo the etymology in Latin *fructuosus*.

67 HEHL, MS HM 149, f. 17^{r} (*Mirror*, 38.22). *OED*, *squeamous*, notes that the etymology, beyond Anglo-Norman 'escoymous', is obscure; it does not come from Latin <osus>.

Often the concern seems practical, as scribes worry over spellings which could be ambiguous. This concern with ambiguity is prominent in the frequent tinkering with three similar-looking words: the adjective *good*, the plural noun *goods* and the name *God*. These words are worth distinguishing because they are weighty with significance in this culture and frequently appear together both in harmony (*God is good*) or in opposition (*love God, not worldly goods*); scribes might well be concerned that readers do not muddle the name of the deity. But the words look confusingly alike, especially as capitalization is erratic. Unsurprisingly, therefore, the scribes of the Huntington Library's manuscripts trouble to correct the spelling of these words some ten times.[68] So do the scribes of manuscripts beyond the Huntington sample.[69] The result is almost always a double <oo> in *good* and a single <o> sometimes with a double <dd> in *God*; people reduce the variety of spellings. But people correct single or double <o> also in words which are not fraught with ideological importance or rendered ambiguous by this letter, such as 'p*er*so$_{//}$^{o}ne' or 'to^^{o}kyn'.[70] And sometimes people correct other problematic spellings in ways which do not help reduce ambiguity: for instance one scribe turns <e> into <ee> in the homophones *reed* (*a plant*) and *rede* (*advice*), but alters both so that they still look identical ('re$_{\wedge}$^{e}d[e]').[71] Some corrections display this needless attention to spelling in ways which give more or give less information than is needed for legibility.

The importance of conventions for writing emerges from the transmission of the corrected spellings from exemplar to copy. In one case, a scribe of *The Book of Vices and Virtues* changes <o> to <oo> over erasure three times in the words 'good' and 'goods'; his copy then served as the exemplar for another, and that further scribe reproduces the spelling with <oo>

[68] HEHL, MS HM 1, f. 90^{v} (Stevens and Cawley (eds.), *Towneley Plays*, 23.630); MS HM 112, f. 15^{r} (*Scale*, 40); MS HM 126, f. 39^{r} (Robert of Gloucester, *Chronicle*, 2423); MS HM 135, f. 20^{v} (*Regiment*, 1120); MS HM 148 (Part II), f. 87^{v} (Rolle, *Psalter*, 150), the four in n. 72 and (vii) in Table 7.5 below. See the forms recorded in *MED*, *god* (*adj.*), and *God* (*n.*) 1; *OED*, *good* (*adj.*, *adv.* and *n.*), and *God* (*n.*). The confusion was longstanding: see Ker, *Catalogue*, xxxv; and Holm, *Corrections and Additions*, 7–11.

[69] E.g., CUL, MS Gg.4.18, f. 50^{r} (Walton (trans.), *Boethius*, III, pr. 8.9.4); BL, MS Harley 4866, ff. 38^{r} (*Regiment*, 2169), 89^{r} (5050), and relatedly 70^{v} (4050); BodL, MS Rawl. poet. 163, f. 111^{r} (*Troilus*, V.1714, where the edition instead has 'ioie'); Oxford, Corpus Christi College, MS 242, f. 21^{r} (*Fall*, I.1771); Philadelphia, Rosenbach Museum and Library, MS 1083/30, f. 47^{r} (*Regiment*, 3315). The latter is an exception to the tendency to prefer single <o> for *God*: 'Be yeft of go^^{o}d'. See also an eyeskip on these words in BL, MS Egerton 2726, f. 243^{v} (*Tales*, X.154).

[70] HEHL, MS HM 503, f. 52^{r} (Hudson (ed.), '*Omnis plantacio*', 1219); this spelling recurs in a marginal addition by the scribe but in a different ink: 'but i*n* p*er*soone'); PML, MS M.124, f. 21^{r} (*Fall*, I.4029).

[71] Respectively, HEHL, MS HM 114, ff. 229^{v} (*Troilus*, II.1387), 231^{v} (II.1539).

each time.[72] In another case, a scribe who crosses out 'good' to write 'god' copies an exemplar which is extant, for it is a book printed by William Caxton, and the scribe follows it carefully in his correction of 'god' with one <o>. It might not seem necessary to follow an exemplar to spell *God* with a single <o>, which is common, but the likelihood that the scribe is following his exemplar is suggested by the fact that in this 'god' he also breaks his usual habit of capitalizing *God*, as his exemplar does here.[73] Lots of this latter scribe's copying was done from Caxton's printed books of the late 1470s and early 1480s, and so his books offer useful evidence whether corrected spelling reflects people following their exemplars, in an extreme form of fidelity (explored in Chapters 3 and 6), or their own lights. This scribe wrote a religious and moral miscellany with excerpts from Lydgate's *Life of Our Lady* and fables, the Monk's Tale and the Tale of Melibee from *The Canterbury Tales* and Benedict Burgh's translation of Cato's *Disticha*, now in the Huntington Library. In it he makes thirty-one corrections to spelling which are needless, and nine of them can be compared with their exemplars in Caxton's editions (Table 7.4).[74] One of his historical compilations, offering a prose history from Adam to Hannibal, at which it ends incomplete, has sections copied from Caxton's edition of John Trevisa's translation of *Polychronicon*.[75] He makes other needless changes to spelling in this book, fifty-one overall and twenty of them in sections taken from Caxton's print (Table 7.5).

Some correcting might be an attempt to reproduce the sound of words or to reflect changes in pronunciation since Trevisa or Lydgate wrote several decades before. He diverges from his exemplar occasionally, often moving the sound /r/ which was undergoing metathesis in many English words (Table 7.4, i, viii; Table 7.5, iv).[76] But most of his corrections seem not to reflect sound patterns very closely or consistently. For instance, when he emends the symbol for the voiced fricative /v/ in *give* and *wolfess* from

72 HEHL, MS HM 147, ff. 2^{v} (Francis (ed.), *Book of Vices and Virtues*, 6.9), 8^{v} (22.17), 81^{v} (209.33), 96^{v} (249.17), reproduced in BL, MS Add. 17013, respectively ff. 3^{v}, 8^{r}, 63^{r}, 74^{r}. On the fact that this MS is a direct copy of HEHL, MS HM 147, see Francis (ed.), *Book of Vices and Virtues*, lxviii–lxxiii; and Wakelin, 'Editing and Correcting', 243 n. 12.

73 Table 7.4 (vii). Cf. the correction to capitalize 'God' in HEHL, HM 144, f. 54^{v}, in n. 83 below.

74 HEHL, MS HM 144, which Pouzet, 'Southwark Gower', 17, connects with a house of Augustinian canons.

75 OTC, MS 29, and Ranulph Higden, *Prolicionycion* [*sic*] (Westminster: Caxton, 1482; *STC* 13438), identified by Harris, 'Unnoticed Extracts', 168–9. *LMES* identifies the same scribe's handwriting in London, Lambeth Palace, MS 84, which also contains extracts from Caxton's edition of *Polychronicon* interpolated into a copy of the prose *Brut*, on which MS, see Matheson, *Prose Brut*, 309–11, 'Printer and Scribe', 607–9, and 'Arthurian Stories'.

76 Rábade, *Handbook*, 287 (no. 450); Lass, 'Phonology and Morphology', 66.

Table 7.4 *Needless changes to spelling in HEHL, MS HM 144, with extant printed exemplars*

	HEHL, MS HM 144	*printed exemplar*	*word*
i)	[offer] offryd f. 62^{r}; Trevisa (trans.), *Polychronicon*	offryd *STC* 13438, f. 197^{v}	*offered*
ii)	verr//^{e}y f. 115^{r}; Burgh (trans.), *Cato*, 70	verrey *STC* 4851, sig. a4^{r}	*very* ('true')
iii)	se//^{y}th f. 117^{r}; Burgh (trans.), *Cato*, 157	seith *STC* 4851, sig. a6^{v}	*sayeth*
iv)	pouert//^{e}is snare f. 117^{v}; Burgh (trans.), *Cato*, 194	pouertis snare *STC* 4851, sig. a7^{v}	*poverty's* *snare*
v)	bo//^{o}te f. 129^{v}; Burgh (trans.), *Cato*, 880	bote *STC* 4851, sig. c8^{r}	*boat*
vi)	mon//^{e}y f. 130^{r}; Burgh (trans.), *Cato*, 850	money *STC* 4851, sig. c8^{v}	*money*
vii)	[good] god f. 132^{r}; Burgh (trans.), *Cato*, 976	god *STC* 4851, sig. c5^{r}	*God*
viii)	sug/^{e}red f. 136^{v}; Lydgate, *Churl*, 73	sugrid *STC* 17008, sig. a2^{v}	*sugared*
ix)	d[a]^^{o}mage f. 143^{r}; Lydgate, *Horse*, 432	domage *STC* 17018, sig. 11^{r}	*damage*

Table 7.5 *Needless changes to spelling in OTC, MS 29, with an extant printed exemplar*

	OTC, MS 29	Prolicionycion	*word*
i)	b[e]^{i}sege (f. 21^{r})	bisege (f. 15^{v})	*besiege*
ii)	Persid[e]//^{a} (f. 21^{v})	Persida (f. 16^{r})	*Persida*
iii)	Ant//^{h}yochus (f. 31^{r})	Anthyochus (f. 22^{r})	*Antiochus*
iv)	sor^^{o}w (f. 31^{r})	sorow (f. 19^{v})	*sorrow*
v)	Tripolitan[e]^{a} (f. 35^{v})	Tripolitana (f. 23^{v})	*Tripolitana*
vi)	[oth] owther (f. 37^{v})	owther (f. 80^{r})	*either*
vii)	y [heyghte] heythe (f. 41^{v})	y highte (f. 29^{v})	*y-hight* ('adorned')
viii)	re^^{s}ceyued (f. 42^{r})	receyued (f. 32^{v})	*received*
ix)	[yef] yeue (f. 44^{v})	yeue (f. 34^{r})	*gave*
x)	[nyhght] nyght (f. 51^{v})	nyght (f. 52^{v})	*night*
xi)	perpetu[a]el (f. 54^{v})	perpetuel (f. 70^{r})	*perpetual*
xii)	[ledde] ladde (f. 68^{r})	ladde (f. 27^{v})	*led (past ppl.)*
xiii)	Tiburtyn[e]^{a} (f. 134^{v})	tiburtina (f. 97^{v})	*Tibertina*
xiv)	[so^{o}ne] soone (f. 138^{v})	soone (f. 101^{v})	*soon*
xv)	[wolf] woluesse (f. 180^{r})	woluesse (f. 108^{r})	*wolf-ess*
xvi)	so//^{o}ne (f. 186^{r})	sone (f. 114^{r})	*soon*
xvii)	b//^{c}ylde (f. 202^{r})	buylde (f. 119^{v})	*build*
xviii)	[Appollo] Appolyn (f. 216^{r})	appolyn (f. 144^{v})	*Apollo*
xix)	vnes[e]y (f. 218^{v})	vnesy (f. 146^{r})	*uneasy*
xx)	[hous] howse (f. 224^{r})	hows (f. 155^{r})	*house*

<f> to <u> (Table 7.5, ix, xv), he is not updating the sound: the separation of the voiced /v/, spelled <u> until the seventeenth century, from /f/, is long complete by the late 1400s when this scribe is writing; he is following the written convention of using <f>, <v> and <u> in different ways which took centuries to settle.[77] Other changes betray the fact that the English alphabet does not have a simple correspondence of symbol to sound. Several fuss over the unstressed vowel /ə/ which has no one symbol (Table 7.5, i–ii, v, xiii); others fuss over the sound /x/ or /ç/, which English scribes struggle to capture. The sound /x/ did disappear in the fifteenth century sporadically, especially from the cluster /xt/, before its complete disappearance in the sixteenth.[78] For the sound /xt/ this scribe wavers between <ght> and <th> or <ghgt> and <ght>. The fact that he chooses different outcomes on different occasions (Table 7.5, vii, x) suggests that neither <th> or <ght> can have represented the sound exactly. Nor do these corrections create standardization even within the work of this one scribe. Likewise, the correcting of the vowel in *other* ('[oth] owther') is also inconsistent: the word is spelled 'Owther' and 'outher' a line later, in each case reproducing the variety of spellings in Caxton's printed text, and it is spelled 'other' twice a few lines earlier.[79] Rather than seeking standardization in particular, or seeking to capture any one pronunciation or dialect, the scribe seems to be struggling with the basic ability of the alphabet to represent language graphically.

Often his needless corrections restore the orthography of his exemplars, in nineteen of twenty-nine words we can check (Tables 7.4 and 7.5).[80] For example, whether to spell *damage* with <o> is debatable, as hindsight attests; the scribe first, rehearsing his exemplar in his head as he wrote, used <a> for 'damage', which suggests that his pronunciation had the vowel /æ/; the fact that he then emended it to <o> suggests that he sought instead to follow Caxton, who employs this spelling. The scribe is, then, overriding the echo of sound in his internal dictation for visual scrutiny of his sources.[81] As in the switch of 'good' to 'god' and the omission of its capital letter, he tries to write well by copying closely. This closeness is striking, for he

77 Lass, 'Phonology and Morphology', 59. HEHL, MS HM 144, f. 38^{r} makes the same change in a passage without an exemplar to compare: 'ther [lyfe] lyues'.

78 Lass, 'Phonology and Morphology'; Scragg, *History of English Spelling*, 23, 49.

79 Cf. Table 7.5, (vi), with OTC, MS 29, f. 37^{v} ('Owther for lykynge of Reders. outher for to make'), following the spellings in Ranulph Higden, *Prolicionycion* [*sic*] (Westminster: William Caxton, 1482; *STC*, 13438), f. 80^{r}.

80 Or 20 occasions, including (xii) in Table 7.5, where the corrected vowel follows the exemplar, although other letters do not.

81 He may follow the etymology in French *domage* (*OED*, *damage*, *n.* 1).

need not have been so faithful. In each of these manuscripts he copies not only whole works but excerpts of works, especially of *Polychronicon*, and sometimes merely summarizes passages between his excerpts; he rearranges them into new compilations. Such a person might not be expected to seek accurate reproduction of the spelling of his exemplar, for he is not working as a copyist but as the author of a newly compiled work, a task which by definition does not require accuracy. Yet within each excerpt, as he switches from selecting to copying, he copies – and corrects – passages letter-by-letter; his needless changes to spelling continue the general quest for accurate reproduction.

Accuracy is not all he pursues, though. As he collects excerpts, he also packages them in new layouts and punctuation; and sometimes he corrects the visual packaging. He develops a clear system of capitalization for names and keywords and a display script, modelled on a conflation of bastard anglicana and bastard secretary, for headings, names and quotations. When he forgets these visual conventions, he stops himself and starts again with them. For instance, twice he corrects his presentation of the name of 'þe [ch] Childryn of Israell' or 'þe [chil] Childryn of Israel': the ordinary word *children* is here a name.[82] (Underlining represents the display script.) He changes the display script or the capitalization seventeen times in his excerpts from *Polychronicon* and eight times in his religious and moral miscellany.[83] While a few instances might be deletions of repetition when he writes whole words ('how [Iacob] Iacob aftyr'), in ten of these corrections he interrupts incomplete words and recommences with the sole difference being the display script or capital letters ('two [stro] Strompetys'): that suggests that he is not merely removing repetition but is improving the look of his writing. Not accuracy but the visual aspects of his craft are his focus.

This attention is interesting, because it might seem as though it should be the contents rather than the visual form which matter to a person collecting excerpts for himself. It is also interesting, given the seeming lack of rules for these visual elements at the time. Two more manuscripts from the Huntington Library show how noteworthy such efforts at polishing the form of writing could be. The first is a copy of Hoccleve's poem *The Regiment of Princes*, in which the scribe writes the long or majuscule shape I for

82 OTC, MS 29, ff. 144^{v}, 149^{v}.

83 See n. 82, and OTC, MS 29, ff. 7^{r}, 15^{r} (in an annotation), 18^{r}, 34^{v}, 47^{v}, 49^{v}, 51^{v}, 58^{r}, 80^{r}, 81^{v}, 116^{v}, 147^{r} (quoted), 148^{r}, 169^{v} (quoted), 197^{v}, 200^{r}, 212^{v}; and HEHL, MS HM 144, ff. 54^{v}, 68^{r}, 75^{r}, 87^{r}, 95^{r} (twice), 106^{r}.

capital <I> for the first person pronoun or at the start of words.[84] What is curious is that he does this some 495 times over erasure. The parchment is usually rubbed white, and sometimes traces of the letter there beforehand are visible; the original letter was <y>. Sometimes the scribe only erases part of **y**, leaving its near-vertical left-hand stroke, with its tail curling left, to become the curving bottom of long **I**; sometimes the erasure leaves still visible the curl above the dot on **y**.[85] At some earlier stages in the history of English, in the eleventh century, changed spellings with <i> and <y> might have reflected changed pronunciations.[86] But in the fifteenth century, vocalic <y> and <i> or <I> were all suitable and interchangeable for these vowel sounds, so the change is not needed for communication; the scribe can only be concerned about the visual convention, presumably of not using <y> initially or on its own. Such lunacy – replacing <y> with <I> 495 times – is extreme but it reminds us that there might be some awareness of the look of letters behind other unexceptional corrections. That graphic awareness is confirmed in this manuscript by the tightly controlled and finicky handwriting, with calligraphic ascenders on **d** modelled on bastard anglicana and biting between round letters modelled on textura – a high degree of decoration for a secular poem in English and a fussy attentiveness, in calligraphy as in orthography, to the look of the page.

Such fussiness in spelling and script recurs in a less pretentious book: a short collection of prose works of religious guidance copied by four scribes of the mid fifteenth century, one after another, but continuing the same layout and themes. The collection could have belonged once to a priest for it begins with a table for dating Easter, and the ensuing catechetical and penitential works would all be useful for teaching laymen. Some are excerpts from Wycliffite writing, presumably because the scribes are unaware what they are.[87] But though the contents are serious, the correcting is superficial: the scribes' twenty-nine corrections of their own work, all bar one, emend tiny verbal errors such, for example, as spellings which were legible beforehand ('in p^^{e}yne', 'w[el]{ee}l doynge').[88] Moreover, a fourth scribe in an ink that has faded to a pale grey then makes 114 needless corrections to the others' spelling. For instance, when the third scribe rebukes 'an y[u]{v}el word' it is the evil spelling which this fourth scribe modifies, turning the

84 HEHL, MS El. 26.A.13, ff. 18^{r}–115^{r}.

85 E.g., HEHL, MS El. 26.A.13, f. 38^{v}, 'I gat affrik / of that [y]{I} haue renoun' (*Regiment*, 1162). The dot is typical in high-grade scripts when **y** serves as a vowel.

86 Corradini, 'Composite Nature', 8–9.

87 HEHL, MS HM 744 (Part I), ff. 1^{r}–24^{v}, catalogued by Dutschke, *Guide*, vol. I, 247–8.

88 HEHL, MS HM 744 (Part I), respectively, ff. 8^{v} (*Yorkshire Writers*, vol. II, 372), 9^{r} (vol. II, 372).

<u> into <v>. This is not needful for representing sound, because <u> and <v> could both mark the sound /v/ and were simply used in different positions. Rather, this person seems interested instead in visual display, for he gives the grey-inked **v** a pronounced approach-stroke, adding something calligraphic to it.[89] Similarly, when the third scribe tells us not to criticize or backbite people, the fourth scribe implicitly criticizes him by rewriting his spelling, turning <c> into <g> and <i> into <y>: 'Ba[c]{g}b[i]{y}te not þe synner but be sory for hym.'[90] Again the sound and the content were quite clear before, as <i> and <y> are interchangeable for vowel sounds, and <c> is more conventional for the unvoiced velar plosive /k/ than <g>. Indeed, that the spelling was acceptable is suggested by the fact that it is left uncorrected in the verbs 'bacbitist' and 'bacbite' just below.[91] But all this is typical of the grey-ink scribe's pernickety work: he changes <i> to <y> in the words *body, by, thy* and *why* some thirty-nine times; he changes medial <u> for the consonant into <v> ('loued' into 'loved') some nineteen times; and he changes <ou> to <ow> in *thou, though* and *touch* some forty-five times. There is no evidence that his changes reflect changes in geography or period; there is just a dispute over the rules for writing.[92]

Moreover, this meddler also made corrections to calligraphy, when he went through and improved not only the choice of letters but the shape of them, preferring one allograph, or equally valid version of a letter's shape, to another. He worked through the first few pages extending the height of **v** and **w** and adding little hooks to the tops of **w**, **l** and **h**. Whereas many of the ascenders or tall upright strokes of these letters had ended without adornment, this correcting hand went through and added to many of them these hooks typical of handwriting modelled on anglicana formata, merely as decorations.[93] Nor was he alone in this interest in letter-forms, for the third scribe, in his own stint, corrects another. Seven times he replaces the short 'modern' **r** or the short *v*-shaped **r** modelled on secretary with the long **r** protruding below the baseline modelled on anglicana: 'lete

89 HEHL, MS HM 744 (Part I), f. 8^{r} (*Yorkshire Writers*, vol. II, 371).

90 HEHL, MS HM 744 (Part I), f. 7^{v}/14 (*Yorkshire Writers*, vol. II, 371).

91 HEHL, MS HM 744 (Part I), f. 7^{v}/17, 7^{v}/19 (*Yorkshire Writers*, vol. II, 371).

92 Because <v> was preferred over <u> for the voiced labiodental fricative /v/ from the seventeenth century, that might suggest a late date for these grey ink corrections; but they are evidently in fifteenth-century handwriting, very like that of the fourth scribe (ff. 13^{v}–24^{v}) who regularly uses <v> for medial /v/: e.g., HEHL, MS HM 744 (Part I), ff. 19^{r}/2 ('nevyr'), 19^{r}/5 ('yeve'), 19^{v}/22 ('devyll').

93 HEHL, MS HM 744 (Part I), f. 6^{r}/2, on **b** in 'be' three times and **k** in 'meke' and 'kepe'.

þat p*ro*cede of þi lippis þat defouliþ. not þ^e ee[r]{r}en. of þe hee[r]{r}er'.[94] He seems to do so as he goes along, for he uses his normal brown ink. Why does he do this? The problem cannot have been unfamiliarity or lack of consistency, for though he often employs the long **r**,[95] he also uses the short form of **r** elsewhere, as well as the zedmoid 'round' **r**.[96] Other scribes in this book also use the short 'modern' **r** and the third scribe does not go back to correct them. All these forms were well known in England as positional variants.[97] The purpose might be stylistic: the long **r** was one of the most distinctive features of handwriting modelled on anglicana, so perhaps anglicana was a more prestigious model than secretary script, whether for nationalistic reasons or mere fashion.[98] But that is difficult to prove from so few examples. The only thing of which we may be confident is that these scribes worry over the craftsmanship of writing, in calligraphy as well as spelling.

This attention to the shape of letters is striking because it is rare: it occurs only once otherwise in the Huntington Library's manuscripts, although in some other manuscripts readers do modify the allographs of **r**, one to another, once in a while.[99] This particular focus on the written medium is also striking because it is at odds with the ideas being communicated here. For these changes to spelling and lettering occur in works which stress the instrumental 'profite' of books and words in general: 'Redynge truly' will show us how to shun sin; we must avoid 'a vayn word' or 'idil wordis'. They also warn us not to correct others but to discipline ourselves: 'loke not no [*sic*] oþer ma*n*nys defautis but se þin owne' and 'amende þin owne synnes

94 HEHL, MS HM 744 (Part I), f. 7r/24 twice, as well as ff. 7v/5 ('hee[r]{r}ers'), 8v/3 ('tu[r]{r}ne'), 8v/6 ('dese[r]{r}tis'), 9v/19 ('se[r]{r}¯u¯^e'), 9v/20 ('her[r]{r}'). This tiny change is visible because long **r** usually has space between its fat left-hand and thin right-hand strokes, but here there is a horizontal stroke between them at the baseline, where the vertical stroke of a shorter **r** has a rightward tick (as in short **r** on f. 8v/2, 'herte', or 8v/5, 'arette') or the **v**-shaped **r** has two strokes joining (e.g., f. 8v/17, 'vertuis'); on f. 9v/20, the earlier graph is clearly visible beneath.

95 E.g., long **r** formed more simply, not over the top of shorter **r**, HEHL, MS HM 744 (Part I), f. 9v/14 ('heere'), 9v/17 ('her'), 9v/27 ('gretnes').

96 HEHL, MS HM 744 (Part I), f. 9v/16 ('euery', 'merite'), 9v/17 ('after').

97 McIntosh, 'Towards an Inventory', 54.

98 On its history, see Derolez, *Palaeography*, 138, 149–50 (esp. pictures 54–5).

99 HEHL, MS HM 129, f. 172r/34, 'ha[r]{r}d' (*NHC*, 52.655). Elsewhere, in Chicago, UL, MS 565, somebody who may be a reader using a darker ink sometimes converts secretary *v*-shaped **r** to anglicana long **r**: ff. 2r/7 (*Fall*, 1.72), 5r/26 (1.285), 6v/24 (1.377), 6v/27 (1.380), 6v/30 (1.383), 7v/7 (1.422), 7v/12 (1.427), 8r/22 (1.468), 8r/23 (1.469), 11v/22 (1.683), 12v/23 (1.746), and so on. A similar looking ink is sometimes used to write over and clarify minims in **m**, **n** and **u**: Chicago, UL, MS 565, e.g., ff. 11v/20, 'hym' (1.681), 11v/24, 'disobeisaunce' (1.685). See also Durham, UL, MS Cosin V.iii.24, ff.10r/13–16, 18r/12, 36r/25; JRL, MS Eng. 102, f. 54r.

bi how myche þo[u]{w} by holdist oþere mennys'.[100] The very passage in which **r** is rewritten is a warning of the vanity of any language which is not strictly useful:

> lete þe soun of þi voice breke forþ no þing b*ut* þat þat nediþ. lete þat p*ro*cede of þi lippis þat defouliþ. not þ^{e} ee[r]{r}en. of þe hee[r]{r}er. a vayn word is tokene of aveyn consie*n*ce þe tunge of man schewiþ hise maners and [sich ---] sich as þe wordis is sich is þe soule [. . .] lete þi word be w*ith* oute repref lete it be p*ro*fitable to þe help ^of þe heere[r]{r}s Bisie þee not to speke þat þat likiþ but þat þ*a*t neediþ take hede what þu spekist and what þu spekist not and boþe in spekynge and not spekynge be ryȝt ware take good a viseme*n*t what þou seist lest þu maist no calle a ȝen þat þu seidist[101]

The works being corrected, then, urge us to profitable speech and tell us not to quibble with our neighbours. By contrast, the scribes attend to such unprofitable, aesthetic things as the shape of writing. Yet there is not a complete divergence: this exhortation to 'be ryȝt ware' of one's words – a nice overemphasis, by dividing *beware* with an adjective – likely applies to the content of one's words; but it might be interpreted with not too much fancy as an exhortation to verbal hygiene in general, given the mention of the material form of words on the 'tunge' and in the 'ee[r]{r}en'. This might suggest why scribes were not solely concerned with the matter of a text but also its linguistic form – errors of transcription; spelling conventions; even preferences for particular shapes of letters. Meticulousness over language might not be 'vayn' but might be a moral duty.

Moreover, there might also be alongside these pious attitudes the craftsman's interest in the books he makes as artefacts – a secular but praiseworthy labour. An interest in this culture in material artefacts is suggested, loosely, by the fact that this collection of devotional works got bound with an inventory of a household's possessions, copied by somebody whose handwriting resembles that of the fourth scribe, who uses grey ink, but working more scruffily. The inventory shows a similar meticulousness in checking material things, some of them needlessly decorative such as 'An angyng of steyned werk'.[102] And the penpusher signs the inventory with pride as

[100] HEHL, MS HM 744 (Part I), ff. 5^{r-v}, 7^{v} (*Yorkshire Writers*, vol. II, 369, 371, with a variant text which might be under an erasure in this MS under the verb 'loke').

[101] HEHL, MS HM 744 (Part I), f. 7^{r-v} (*Yorkshire Writers*, vol. II, 371).

[102] HEHL, MS HM 744 (Part II), f. 69^{r}. Scribe D (ff. 13^{r}–24^{v}) varies a lot in currency and letter-forms, but some graphs resemble those in the inventory: a less current flat-topped **g** with a nugatory descender (f. 13^{r}/1 'lovyng', 'thyng', 69^{r}/6 'standyng', 69^{r}/7 'angyng'); sometimes a long approach-stroke on **v** (ff. 14^{r}/1 'hevyn', 69^{r}/b10 'coverlett*es*'); **w** formed of two fairly long and fairly straight strokes with a short *ȝ*-shape after them; **y** with a diagonally left-leaning descender. The inventory does not include the words *by*, *thou*, *though* or *through*, but it does show a preference for <w>

being 'wretyn w*ith* <my> own hand', reminding us that good writing might be an important accomplishment even in practical tasks.[103] Then between the religious prose and the inventory was bound a collection of poems of literary ambition, in an autograph copy by their author who was also a professional clerk, Thomas Hoccleve. It is no surprise in such a rich material and poetic culture that a scribe was interested in the craft of writing for its own sake.

over <u> and <y> over <i> in other words (ff. 69^{r}/a10 'peyr', 69^{r}/c3 'cawdron'). The earliness of the binding together is suggested by the fact that the same hand annotates the front and back flyleaves (e.g., ff. ii^{r}, 1^{v}–3^{r}, 69^{r}).

103 HEHL, MS HM 744 (Part II), f. 69^{r}.

PART III

Literary criticism

CHAPTER 8

Diction, tone and style

vn to purpos my [s[--]{ty}le]^stile I will directe
Warminster, Longleat House, MS 254, f. 67v

John Lydgate, *The Fall of Princes*, III.1496

Through correcting, scribes pay attention to copying more accurately and writing more lucidly, conventionally or elegantly. Yet correcting not only allows the scribes to reflect on their own craft; it also encourages insightful or critical appreciation of the works they copy. The 'material consciousness' developed through the practical process of correcting results in an intellectual process of closely reading those works. Their engagement with these works, and not merely their mechanical reproduction and correction of them, is evident in their attention to features of style, verse-form and completeness.

Yet did scribes really have insight into literary works? This has been doubted by editors who have had to tidy up the muddle scribes left. Among the editors of Chaucer's poetry, George Kane, Janet Cowen and Jill Mann have found scribes to garble his metre, simplify his complexity and dull his brilliance: much in the authorial text would be 'quite beyond [the scribe's] conception'. Even Barry Windeatt, who found the mistakes of scribes of Chaucer's *Troilus and Criseyde* to reveal their responses to the poem, found that those responses were often perplexity and warned that we must not give the scribes' responses more credit than they are due.[1] This preference for authorial genius over scribal idiocy, most associated in Middle English editing with George Kane, has a distinguished pedigree.[2] But a palaeographer rather than an editor might want to acknowledge the more successful elements of scribal craft. While the scribes might

[1] Chaucer, *Legend of Good Women*, ed. Cowen and Kane, e.g., 130; Mann, 'Chaucer's Meter', e.g., 96, 98; Windeatt, 'Scribes as Chaucer's Early Critics', 140, and also 121. Chapter 3, pp. 54–5 above, sets out their arguments more fully.

[2] For analysis of Kane's view, see Hanna, 'George Kane', 2; Brewer, *Editing Piers Plowman*, 388, and also 371–2, 378; and Patterson, *Negotiating the Past*, 95–7.

Table 8.1 *Corrections to lexical or open-class words in the manuscripts in English in HEHL*

total corrections	*9,220*	
• all corrections to single lexical words *of which*	1,383	15% of the total
• lexical words replaced	885	10% of the total; 64% of lexical corrections
• lexical words added	498	5% of the total; 36% of lexical corrections
• lexical corrections collatable with an edition	971	
• collatable lexical corrections which agree with an edition	745	77% of those collatable

show little intelligence or understanding when they err, they might show more when they correct those errors. Indeed, it seems more plausible to postulate their intelligence in correcting, which requires them to notice, reflect and make choices. And there are different ways to be intelligent: reading or accurately studying something can be arts just as writing new things can. Their correction might not *create* writing of good quality but it might *identify* some qualities in other people's writing, by bothering to *preserve* them – a more critical or reactive process of thinking, but thinking nonetheless. As Windeatt finds them to be in their errors, so in their corrections they work like 'critics' who can identify elements of style, structure or form (as this and the next two chapters show).

Could the corrections of style just come from the habit of accuracy in general (described in Chapter 6), reflecting the craftsmanship of scribes but not any literary engagement? Of course, it is their general effort to copy precisely and write well which directs their attention to the nuances, tone and style. Yet what distinguishes several of the features of style which the scribes correct is that they did not need to be corrected in order to communicate the meaning of the work or to write grammatically. Among those features (and the few which this chapter has room to discuss) are the choice of synonyms, the use of doublets instead of one word, and the use of adjectives and adverbs. What distinguishes corrections to these features is that they are not usually grammatically necessary. Thinking through examples makes this clear. Nearly 10 per cent of the corrections replace one verb, noun, adjective or adverb with another, as in swapping synonyms (as Table 8.1 records). Replacing one part of speech with another, say, swapping a noun for a verb, is usually essential for grammar; but replacing a word with another of the same part of speech, say, replacing one noun with a different noun, is usually inessential for grammar. Likewise, about 5 per cent of the corrections add a lexical word which was missing, sometimes one which is essential such as the main verb or subject, but often one inessential for grammar as many adjectives and adverbs are. (This chapter later gives examples.) Like the needless changes to spelling (in Chapter 7), these features are the focus of only a small proportion of corrections, but their rarity highlights how curious they are: the scribes pursue centripetal correction to the extent that they even make corrections which are not grammatically necessary. The ability to deduce errors when grammar does not reveal them obviously requires rechecking the exemplar or checking a second exemplar and so is part of the overall meticulousness. That is borne out by the fact that corrections to single lexical words are almost as often centripetal (77 per cent in Table 8.1) as is correcting overall (84 per cent in Table 6.4). The fact that they extend this centripetal quality even to points of diction which do not mar basic grammar or sense is striking: their accuracy did not need to go this far. They act as though every word needs to be accurate, not only in basic content but in the nuances and connotations and tone given by the diction. Indeed, they sometimes attend to these features too fussily, in hypercorrections; those erroneous corrections (noted below) suggest the conscious engagement even within their generally centripetal tendency.[3]

This active and sometimes hyperactive interest in wording, then, tells us something about the work of scribes: does it also tell us something about the works they correct? Observing the few hypercorrections, it might seem not: it might seem as though the scribes not only transmit the verbal niceties of English works but that they imagine them or create them. After all, the corrections might, in their visible fuss, direct further readers or copyists of the manuscripts to notice things as though they are special, whether they are or not. Identifying the role of scribes in forging details of wording could raise doubts whether authors themselves meant their language to be treated as special. After all, like many critics we might not want to identify special qualities if we see the category of 'literary' language as non-existent or pernicious in this period or in general. Indeed, it emerges that the scribes

[3] The fact that the centripetal tendency for needless changes to lexical words is slightly lower (77 per cent instead of 84 per cent) might reflect that over-involvement; but it might also reflect the fact that many grammatically needful corrections can be safely guessed. Most importantly, the sample is neither large enough nor, in its measures of centripetal qualities, sturdy enough to base an argument on little differences in figures.

do *not* attend only to a demarcated set of 'literary' works but also to works in 'ordinary' language too, such as medical cures and religious instruction, with this care. Of course, ordinary language can have 'style' too; stylistics has taught us that. Yet it is also the case that by correcting books, in order to copy accurately and well, scribes act *as if* there were qualities in the texts worth preserving. That allows us not to abandon the category of literary language but to explain it: to suggest some historical origins for this attention to details of diction. The corrections offer specific examples of the things people thought were special enough to correct, even when they were needless. And, more importantly, they suggest how the material production and use of books might help to generate that specialness. By acting *as if* they see special qualities in these texts, the scribes not only reveal the interest of these texts; they exercise their own concentration, intelligence and understanding as readers.

Paraphrase and precision

One measure of the attention which people pay to authors' work is their attempt to prevent the drift into paraphrase. Paraphrase has been called an 'unceasing' element of copying ('incessante'),[4] and editors have long traced how scribes replace words in the text with near synonyms as they go along. This paraphrase could occur unwittingly through the mechanics of copying quickly (described in Chapter 7), as though the scribes were not thinking about every word; often, scribes writing quickly assume that the exemplar says something simpler than it does. Or it could be deliberate as scribes impose their banal preferences on the text.[5] What results is a sort of paraphrase into simpler or more commonplace idioms and wording than those which editors think are authorial.[6]

That need not have been a problem: many works in English in the fourteenth and fifteenth centuries seem to permit paraphrase or banalization; they are designed to do useful things – preaching, worshipping, teaching farming – rather than to cultivate a fine style; these tasks often require a general register rather than a particular choice of words. For instance, *The Prick of Conscience* has a pedestrian and repetitious vocabulary, which might be the poet's ineptitude or might be deliberate simplicity and insistence. Some people felt free to rewrite the poem in a wholesale 'Southern Recension', and in further less thorough revisions and interpolations. But

4 Cerquiglini, 'Paraphrase essentielle', 15.
5 Windeatt, 'Scribes as Chaucer's Early Critics', 127–31; *Piers A*, ed. Kane, 132–4.
6 Jacobs, 'Regression to the Commonplace', 61–3.

that imprecision makes it curious that some corrections interrupt these paraphrases. One scribe of the poem who makes only infrequent corrections nonetheless restores its diction quite precisely at points, even where its sense was still clear. For example, the scribe first writes that Christ took on 'þe kynde of man' which is true but is not what the poet wrote: the scribe trying to read and remember his exemplar reaches for a common idiom over the exact one in the poem. But he recognizes his error, subpuncts 'man' and interlines 'erþe': Christ took on 'þe kynde of [man]^{erþe}'. Thereby he restores a moment of metaphorical language in *The Prick of Conscience*, a powerful evocation of Christ's life *as* earth, a poetic symbol of mortality, and *on* earth, an element which pointedly contrasts in the next line with Christ dwelling 'vp in þe ayer' as Lord.[7] Even bad poetry has good lines, and the scribe eschews paraphrase of them. This reflects the general meticulousness of checking one's copy: presumably to correct a metaphor when the error made literal sense involves not guessing but looking back at the exemplar or collating exemplars. Yet it is striking that their lynxlike gaze encompasses even these details of wording. They did not need to correct everything for utilitarian reasons: *The Prick of Conscience* would still have preached its message with 'man' rather than 'erþe'; but bothering to fix this slip reflects some notion that not only the message but the connotations in and patterns among words deserve accurate transcription; without them, the message would not have been preached as fully or as stylishly.

That notion might be inferred from the corrections to a work in the Huntington Library which professes both to be useful, as *The Prick of Conscience* does, and to seek literary accomplishment. In a copy of John Lydgate's moralizing poem *The Fall of Princes*, nearly a third of the corrections change one lexical word for another, usually in positions where both words make grammatical sense and often, in context, some logical sense. This is surprising, because it can seem as though Lydgate's poem was popular less for its specific wording and textual form than for its larger moral teachings which were excerpted, paraphrased and rewritten.[8] The words of *The Fall of Princes* are themselves a sort of paraphrase, a loose translation of a French version of a Latin work by Boccaccio. Its words are tedious, for it retells hundreds of stories and finds in them all similar lessons – about the ill fortune sequent upon lust, cruelty, presumption and pride – as though

[7] HEHL, MS HM 125, f. 60^{r}. *Prick*, 5172, in the Main Version is very different; but this correction falls in line with, e.g., BodL, MS Laud. misc. 601, f. 66^{r} ('þe kynde of eorþe'), a MS of the Southern Recension which Lewis and McIntosh, *Descriptive Guide*, no. SR 14, identify as textually close.

[8] Mortimer, *John Lydgate's Fall of Princes*, 219, 224–51; Edwards, 'Influence of Lydgate's *Fall of Princes*', 430.

endlessly rephrasing the judgements of God and Fortune. Its structure encourages paraphrase, for many stories end in an 'envoy' which, in each case, reiterates the moral lesson in a brief summary. And its remorseless rime royal squeezes Lydgate into using set phrases in order to rhyme. This repetitiousness is not a problem, for the poem becomes forceful less by the exactitude of words than by the accumulation of them. The material manuscripts also impress as much by their bulk and visual finery as by the details of their text. The copy of *The Fall of Princes* in the Huntington Library looks like a luxury object for showing off: it is copied in a fiddly handwriting modelled on bastard secretary with many coloured and gold adornments of textual divisions; it has some wonderful pictures – another sort of paraphrase which displaces the text. In this book, then, words might be merely padding out a luxurious book or hammering home a general message; specificity of diction might not be valued.[9]

Yet some pictures in this book seem to idolize poets,[10] and respect for the poet's skill in composing words might underpin the corrections, which were made laboriously and carefully. Somebody, using rough handwriting in pale red or grey, all typical of such marks, writes in the margins prompts for the rubricator, attentive to the book's image, and prompts for correction, attentive to the text (Figure 1 above). The main scribe – who may be the same person at a different time – then goes through and enters the corrections and erases the prompts.[11] Happily, in sixty-eight cases he forgets to erase the marginal prompt or to make the correction, so that it is easy to see what change was requested. Most of the prompts correspond to changes in the choice of wording, which constitute a third of the corrections in the book (68 of 219, or 31 per cent, sampled in Table 8.2). Sometimes there is a simple explanation for the error in the mechanical process of copying: the erroneous words repeat words or syllables within the line (v, vii) or from the previous line (ii, x) in the error which editors call 'contamination'.[12] For instance, in (vii) the lion has already abandoned 'felnesse' and so 'fel rage' is repetitive; in (v) both hounds and wolves are described as 'cruel' within the same line.

The person correcting removes this repetition. Yet was it a problem? Structurally (as was said) the poem works by repeating words and ideas, as does much moralizing verse: for example, the word 'cruel' (v) is followed

[9] HEHL, MS HM 268. I extended the Huntington survey to include BL, MS Sloane 2452, a quire which was formerly part of this MS, as noted by Edwards, 'Huntington *Fall*'.

[10] Lerer, *Chaucer and His Readers*, 41–3 (figs. 1–3), 40–4.

[11] See Chapter 4, nn. 96–9, and Chapter 5, n. 104.

[12] Vinaver, 'Principles of Textual Emendation', 358–60.

Table 8.2 *Some marginal prompts changing lexical words in* Fall *in HEHL, MS HM 268*

	text	*prompt*	*folio*	Fall
i)	The sayd Iuges / in myschef did shyne	Fyne	64^{r}	III.3082
ii)	¶ Iustise [. . .]		64^{v}	III.3134
	Punyssheth robbours / for ther gret offence			
	Sluggy truau*n*tes / for ther gret offence	neglig<ence>		
iii)	hou from the sees / shortly to co*m*prehende		68^{v}	III.3689
	Froward princes / doth princes down descende	fortune		
iv)	¶ For tyrannye *and* fals oppressiou*n*		70^{v}	III.3992
	Causeth princes / to stond in gret drede	hatrede +		
	And what is worth ther d*omi*naciou*n*			
	Wythout love / let p*re*ved yt at a nede			
	Men for a tyme may suffre he*m* wel *and* drede			
	but when that drede / constreyned is *and* gone			
	then is a prince / but a man allone			
v)	¶ Thus many tirau*n*tis [. . .]		86^{r}	IV.1102
	[. . .] resembled be			
	To cruel wolves or ellis / to cruel houndes	furious		
	Fret wyth an Etik / of gredy cruelte			
vi)	[. . .] he to his gret fame	diffame	101^{r}	IV.3042
	Compassed hir deth / the story seith the same			
vii)	The lion [. . .]		102^{r}	IV.3197
	Forgate his felnesse / *and* his fel rage	cruel		
viii)	And is be grace enclyned to richesse	mekenesse +	117^{v}	V.2832
	Thogh he i*n* pou*er*t or streytnesse brought vp lowe			
	And is be vertu reysed to worthynesse			
ix)	Scilla [. . .]		127^{v}	VI.1211
	Entryng the town ageyn his oth pardee			
	Thre thousand cytesyns / slow of that contre	cite		
x)	Nothyng atteyneth vn to high noblesse		128^{r}	VI.1286
	But the clere shynyng of v*er*tuous noblesse	cleenesse		

promptly by 'cruelte' and recurs elsewhere in the poem, as it should in (vii) instead of 'fel'.[13] Why should the poem not doggedly repeat 'cruel' or 'fel' within a line as well as between lines, perhaps as part of some rhetorical device such as *epistrophe* or *ploce*? So repetition alone is not the problem here. Rather, these corrections preserve stylistic patterns: substituting 'furious' and 'cruel' (v, vii) not only avoids local repetition but preserves a

[13] And 'cruelte' in (v) recurs in turn too on the previous page: HEHL, MS HM 268, f. 85^{v} (*Fall*, IV.1063).

subtler pattern of variation in synonyms. They also preserve subtleties of thought, often in interesting interplay with rhyme. In (iv) it would have been fine to say that tyrannical princes stand in ‘drede’ of rebellion, and as the poem says a few lines later their subjects ‘drede’ the tyrants in return: that could have been a stylish rime riche, rhyming the noun and the verb ‘drede’ to highlight the mutual terror. But Lydgate’s trick here is a different one and what he specifies is ‘hatrede’, which powerfully conveys the life of the tyrant ‘Wythout love’. Similarly, in (ii) it would make sense to say that tyrants commit ‘offence’ but the correction again avoids rime riche and makes sure that Lydgate’s warning is quite precise: not that truants are guilty of offences, of action, but of ‘negligence’ of their social duty, of inaction. Overall, then, the person correcting pays attention not only to the lovely material artefact that this manuscript is – indeed, the unerased prompts mess up the pretty pages – but to the words and ideas it holds.

He is not alone in that: other scribes of *The Fall of Princes* also trouble themselves with the poem’s diction: they stop themselves to change ‘pollicye’ to ‘power’ or ‘mikil’ to ‘^*ouer*mikil’, all nuances worth preserving.[14] But it is often said that much of Lydgate’s poetry works not by concision and precision but copiousness and fecundity.[15] So were not such corrections of the diction overly careful, a sort of overinterpretation? The suggestion is not that the scribes were right to act as though Lydgate were a genius; the correction which restores the authorial text (as the modern editor has it) is sometimes poorer in thinking or style. For example, in (i) it would be cleverly ironic to describe how wicked judges ‘shyne’ in mischief (meaning *wrongdoing*), the opposite of shining examples; but it is Lydgate’s blunter point that they ‘Fyne’ or end up in mischief (meaning *trouble*). In (vi) ‘fame’ can denote ill fame as well as ‘diffame’ can, but Lydgate’s ‘diffame’ again is blunter. On some critical criteria – say, a New Critical preference for irony – the errors are more fun than the corrections. Yet for the poem’s didactic purpose, the restored dull wording might be more successful – the deliberate dullness of the fifteenth century.[16] The correcting does not necessarily pursue what is now seen as literary flair; it simply pursues reproduction of the text, which sometimes shows flair, sometimes does not.

Moreover, whether Lydgate meant these things – to be dull or sharp – is irrelevant to the present point; the point is that the scribe and his colleague, by bothering to correct these things, act *as if* Lydgate meant them. It is they who intend every word here, intending to avoid paraphrase in copying. This

14 Respectively, PML, MS M.124, f. 7r (*Fall*, I.1391); PUL, MS Garrett 139, p. 146 (III.552).

15 Smith, ‘Afterword: Lydgate’s Refrain’, 189.

16 Lawton, ‘Dullness’.

attitude need not come from any real qualities in Lydgate's poetry nor even from special respect for Lydgate in particular. The opposite is possible: that because the scribes as craftsmen were generally meticulous they therefore treated respectfully and read closely the words of Lydgate – and of Chaucer and *The Prick of Conscience* and other works. Such an explanation of what was going on steps close to a now old idea of Stanley Fish. Fish once proposed that the nuances and excellences of literary language are not inherent in literary works but exist in the eye of the reader: 'the paying of a certain kind of attention results in the emergence of poetic qualities'.[17] Fish argued that a poem does not contain automatic 'directions' for identifying its nuances of meaning or its formal artistry; rather the directions will 'only *be* directions to those who already have the interpretive strategies in the first place' from their training in Augustinian models for allegorizing Scripture, Empsonian practical criticism or whatever.[18] Might this capture what the scribes and readers do when they correct? Their 'strategies' of response – namely, their practical procedures for meticulously correcting – produce the notion that the words they correct are worth such close attention. Without much written literary criticism, we can only speculate whether they articulated that sense of worth explicitly to themselves. But the practice of the craftsman involves close reading.

Tone in literary language

Stanley Fish was deliberately provocative in his point: he suggested that readers '*produce* what can thereafter be said to be there' in a work.[19] Outlandish though it sounds, this is in some senses true of these manuscripts: we can only read these works now and 'thereafter' find nuances in them, because the scribes and other correctors did literally '*produce*' the text in surviving copies. But does their intervention go beyond preserving those details to fabricating them? With some ill-edited authors such as Lydgate, it is not completely clear whether the text which a scribe restores was the poet's. And editors have caught scribes fabricating things, if not when correcting copies then when varying them. George Kane, editing William Langland's *Piers Plowman*, observed that the scribes 'were enthusiastic for the poem, and consciously or unconsciously, if sometimes without intelligence or taste, strained to participate in the experience that it recorded'.[20] They improve the style: they render it more direct and 'increase the

[17] Fish, *Is There a Text*, 326; see also 12, 164. [18] *Ibid.*, 173. [19] *Ibid.*, 327.
[20] *Piers A*, ed. Kane, 138–9. See also Windeatt, 'Scribes as Chaucer's Early Critics', 132–3.

emphasis of statements' by heightening their tone.[21] Kane and other editors note this attention particularly in the scribes' addition of adjectives and adverbs where they are not supposedly authorial. For example, in the 'A' version of *Piers Plowman* Kane catches scribes using *dear*, *deep*, *fair*, *great* (three times), 'lele', *rich* (twice) and *wicked* when Langland supposedly did not; John Ivor Carlson catches Robert Thornton using intensifiers – the subset of adverbs *very*, *really* and *so*, and in fourteenth- and fifteenth-century English *all* and *full* – sixty-seven times when other scribes of the same works do not.[22] But the editorial principle that more emphatic readings should be 'presumed scribal' might not hold.[23] Ralph Hanna finds that the intensifier *full* and the adverb *eke* are often part of Chaucer's writing and that scribes often copy them dutifully.[24] Scribes not only heighten the tone of works by intruding such words when they are not needed; they also restore these words by correction when they are. And whether they are authorial or not, by correcting adjectives and the adverbs known as intensifiers, people thereby act as if they are needful and valued.

Moreover, these adjectives and adverbs are interesting as an extreme sign of scribes' carefulness because they are often needless for basic grammar. When adjectives are used after the predicate *be*, then they are necessary: when Chaucer says of himself, 'My witt is [good] schort ye may wel vnderstonde', some adjective is needed, though which one is open to choice.[25] (It is charming that the scribe at first assumes that Chaucer's wit is good, until he spots the irony.) But when adjectives are used attributively before a noun, they are not needed: the line 'He fonde this holy ^olde vrban a noon' made sense without 'olde'. Nor was any sense of Pope Urban's age missing, in context, for he was called 'good vrban the olde' only eight lines earlier, and all this second 'olde' adds is more reverence or pathos – and a typically Chaucerian use of repetition to highlight keywords.[26] Adverbs too are needless to make a clause grammatical: when we hear that a naughty summoner 'had ^eke wenches at his rettenue' the adverb 'eke' adds no content but heightens the narrator's disapproval of the summoner's dalliance with loose women *as well* as his other sins.[27]

[21] *Piers A*, ed. Kane, 139. Chaucer, *Legend of Good Women*, ed. Cowen and Kane, 84–90, gives clear examples.

[22] *Piers A*, ed. Kane, 138–9; Carlson, 'Scribal Intentions', 60–1, 71. See similar lists in *Piers B*, ed. Kane and Donaldson, 144; *Piers C*, ed. Russell and Kane, 105, 111–12, 142.

[23] Cf. *Piers C*, ed. Russell and Kane, 142.

[24] Hanna, *Pursuing History*, 192–3.

[25] JRL, MS Eng. 113, f. 13r (*Tales*, I.746).

[26] BL, MS Harley 7335, f. 93r (*Tales*, VIII.177, 185). See also the interlineation in 'that ^faire child' (f. 59v, II.1018).

[27] BL, MS Harley 7335, f. 76r (*Tales*, III.1355); see similarly f. 86r, with 'right' interlineated (III.2040).

This otiose quality is especially true of adverbs acting as intensifiers, which modify adjectives and adverbs further: words such as *very* or *so* or *full* can be deleted from most clauses; they reflect the speaker's perspective rather than any factual assessment.[28] Although these words form only a small proportion of the corrections to lexical or open-class words, their needlessness for grammar or basic facts, rather than for conveying attitudes, makes them intriguing clues how correcting helps to preserve the style or tone – those unparaphrasable qualities – of poetry.

Chaucer himself describes the importance of tone or style in *The Canterbury Tales*, when the Host asks the Clerk not to tell a clever or serious tale:

> Telle vs sum ^meri thyng / of auentures
> Ȝoure termes / ȝoure coloures / and figures
> Kepe hem in stoor / til so be ^þ*at* ȝe endite
> Heye stile / as whan þ*at* men / to kynges wryte
> Spekith so pleyn / at this tyme /. we ȝow preye

But the Clerk responds by commending the learned poetry of Petrarch:

> But forth to tellen / of this worthy man
> That taught me this tale / as I began
> I seye / that first / he with h[is]^eye stile enditeth[29]

The scribe of this early copy interlineates words or letters and subpuncts 'is' in 'his', in order to restore two adjectives, *merry* and *high*. Those adjectives are needless for grammar; *merry* even disrupts the common compound *something*, which might be why the scribe first overlooks it. Nor are they needed for sense; mirth is not the obvious opposite of erudition, which is what the Host wants to avoid; and Petrarch could just have written with 'his stile', a physical pen, rather than with 'h[is]^eye stile', a literary quality. The phrase coheres with references to high style a few lines earlier and a few dozen pages later, where the phrase 'stilo [. . .] alto' from Petrarch's Latin is written in the margin beside another reference to 'heye stile'.[30] Corrections by other scribes also suggest that *high style* was a phrase worth preserving.[31]

28 On this use of *so*, see *OED*, *so* (*adv.* and *conj.*) III.14 and some senses under III.13, VIII.35a, VIII.35e, VIII.37, VIII.38, VIII.39a, VIII.39e. But *so* also serves in constructions where it is necessary for grammar, such as *so X that Y*, with *that* or a 'zero' subordinator: *OED*, *so* (*adv.* and *conj.*) V.24a, V.25, V.26.

29 CUL, MS Dd.4.24, f. 92ᵛ (*Tales*, IV.15–19, 39–41). The transcription treats crossbars on 'Spekith', 'taught' and 'with' as otiose. The pronoun *his* is here interchangeable with an adjective because *style* is an abstract non-count noun.

30 CUL, MS Dd.4.24, f. 105ʳ (*Tales*, IV.1148).

31 BL, MS Add. 25718, f. 64ᵛ, 'I say that he "wiþ. "firste "stile "heiȝ stile enditeth' (*Tales*, IV.41); Philadelphia, Rosenbach Museum and Library, MS 1084/1, f. 58ʳ, 'Al be hit thatt y can not sowne

These adjectives *merry* and *high* serve as literary critical terms which help to explain what style or tone are. They also help to characterize the tone of voice of the jolly Host and the snobby Clerk.[32] They are not just *about* the style or tone of a tale but *contribute* to the style or tone. The corrections by this early fifteenth-century scribe, though grammatically unnecessary, are powerful.

Throughout copies of *The Canterbury Tales* adjectives similarly restore specificity, vividness or characterization. The Knight's Tale offers some interesting examples, including the need for things to be again *high*, as when Arcite goes to the temple of Mars 'With petous herte and [hise]^high deuocion'.[33] Like the earlier scribe of the Clerk's Tale, this scribe probably makes a visual slip, perhaps mistaking 'hie' in his exemplar, perhaps skipping to 'his' in the line below.[34] But he overcomes the mechanical error and thereby preserves Arcite's lofty mood and the careful patterning of a doublet with two adjectives and nouns. Numerous local effects are preserved in another copy of *The Canterbury Tales*, in which a scribe frequently attends to adjectives and adverbs, adding fifty-six of them in the margin (Table 8.3). These additions preserve pathos in depicting 'yong' daughters and 'blodie' knives (vii, ix); they preserve irony, as when people praise scoundrels as 'holi' or 'worthi' (xx, xxvi). Many are tautologous, as when the 'terme' of somebody's life is clarified as the 'terme' of 'all' his life, as though life could terminate before it was 'all' finished (lv). A few add a little information such as colour or speed (xl, xliii), but most merely add value-judgements which characterize the tone of voice. Now, these words are only one part of a more widespread campaign of correction: including the 56 adjectives and adverbs, this scribe makes 377 additions in the margins. But the interest of scribes in these words might be gauged by the fact that thirteen of these adjectives and adverbs should not be here, according to modern editors (marked with asterisks in Table 8.3).[35] They might not be this scribe's inventions: he seems to have made his corrections after collating a second exemplar, for some of his other longer additions could only have been made

h[-]{ys sty}le. | Ne can not clymben ouer so hygh a style' (*Tales*, V.105–6). Other scribes also correct references to the *style* or *stylus*: Warminster, Longleat House, MS 254, f. 67^v (*Fall*, III.1496), in the epigraph to this chapter, above; PML, MS M.124, f. 6^r, 'myn. auctoure transported hath [t]his stile' (*Fall*, I.1021). *OED*, *style* (*n.*) II.13a, records *Tales*, IV.18, as one of the first uses of *style* in this sense; but see also II.12. See Chapter 2, p. 37 and Chapter 11, p. 279 on the etymology.

32 Following accounts of these lines by Lerer, *Chaucer and His Readers*, 30, 34; Cannon, *Making of Chaucer's English*, 137, 139, 147–8.

33 GUL, MS Hunter 197 (U.1.1.), f. 11^r (*Tales*, I.2369–72).

34 Copied from CUL, MS Mm.2.5, f. 26^r–v. On this MS, see Chapter 3 above.

35 Also, in Table 8.3, in (xiv) and (xlv) the added adjective is found in editions, but editions omit the adjacent words; in (xxi) it is added one word later than in editions.

Table 8.3 *Marginal additions of adjectives and adverbs to* Tales *in BL, MS Harley 1758*

	text	*addition*	*folio*	Tales
i)	That had . a firy ^ cherubynnes face .	^ reed	7^v	I.624
ii)	Ther sawe I first the ^ ymagynyng .	^ derke	21^r	I.1955
iii)	And spentyn it in venus ^ seruyse	^ high .	26^v	I.2487
iv)	Whan Ector was brought all fresche ^ slayn .	^ newe	30^r	I.2832 *
v)	Yestirday I left seide ^ Gamelyne	^ yong	49^r	*Gam.*, 315
vi)	¶ Parauenture in thilke ^ book .	[¶] large	57^v	II.190
vii)	O Emp*er*ours ^ doughter dere .	[¶] yong	60^r	II.447
viii)	But turne I woll ^ to my matere . /	^ a geyne	61^v	II.581
ix)	And in the bedde the ^ knyf he fonde .	^ blodie	61^v	II.607
x)	And salewith hir / ^ in his [his] langage . /	^ full faire	63^r	II.731
xi)	¶ This messengere dranke ^ ale *and* wyne .	^ sadli	63^r	II.743
xii)	Full ^ he seide allas *and* weylaway .	^ ofte	64^r	II.810
xiii)	[->]{That Alla was} ^ he loked besily .	^ redie	67^r	II.1095 *
xiv)	Vn to my ^ p*ur*pos I woll haue my recours .	^ first	69^r	V.75
xv)	I yaf hym all myn herte *and* ^ my thought .	^ all	73^v	V.533
xvi)	That all thyng repeiryng to his ^ kynde .	[¶] owne	74^v	V.608 *
xvii)	I wole no more as ^ speke of hir Ryng . /	^ now	75^r	V.652
xviii)	To Abigaile by ^ counseile how sche .	[¶] good	77^v	IV.1369
xix)	A boute ^ lordis in full gret estate .	[¶^] worthi	79^r	IV.1495 *
xx)	And mony another ^ man also .	^ holi	89^v	III.58
xxi)	He seide ^ precept had he none .	^ therof	89^v	III.65
xxii)	Of whiche I am expert in ^ myn age .	^ all	90^v	III.174
xxiii)	Ye woot ^ what I mene of this parde .	[¶^] well	91^r	III.200
xxiv)	¶ Ye wyse wyues that can ^ vndirstonde .	[¶^] well	91^r	III.225
xxv)	And all day ^ hid hym as an Owle .	^ aftir	100^r	III.1081
xxvi)	This ^ lymytour this noble Frere .	^ worthi	102^r	III.1265
xxvii)	vp on the Sompno*ur* but ^ for honeste .	^ yet	102^r	III.1267 *
xxviii)	Her p^^{r}aier is ^ of well gret reuerence .	[¶^] full	109^v	III.1932
xxix)	To crist that the sende ^ hele *and* myght .	[¶^] bothe	109^v	III.1946 *
xxx)	And ^ god woot vnnethe the foundement .	[¶^] yet	111^v	III.2103
xxxi)	¶ For that euyr ^ vertuous was sche .	[¶] ^ so	118^r	IV.407 *
xxxii)	So sprad of hir ^ bounte the fame .	[¶^] grete	118^r	IV.418
xxxiii)	Nou it is wers that euyr in ^ our age .	[¶^] all	120^v	IV.627
xxxiv)	She was euyr ^ in hert *and* in visage .	^ oon	121^v	IV.711
xxxv)	And ^ hope I that he will to you sende .	^ so	125^r	IV.1035
xxxvi)	Lord phebus cast ^ thyn merciable ye .	downe	130^v	V.1036 *
xxxvii)	Aurelyus in his lif he sawe ^ non .	^ neuyr	132^v	V.1188
xxxviii)	If this were lyuyng ^ *and* noon other .	[¶^] onli	140^v	VIII.322
xxxix)	Dan Iohn hym maketh feste *and* ^ chere .	[¶] ^mery	162^r	VII.342
xl)	Of the *and* of the ^ lilye flour .	^ white	163^v	VII.461
xli)	Thi v*er*tue *and* thi ^ humylite .	^ gret	163^v	VII.475

(*cont.*)

Table 8.3 *cont.*

	text	*addition*	*folio*	Tales
xlii)	if [. . .] thi cou*n*ceilours a corden ^ or noon	^ ther to	173ʳ	VII.1206
xliii)	take þilke vengeau*n*ce ^° or attemp*er*ally	[¶^°] hasteli	176ʳ	VII.1380
xliv)	as I seide ^ . ¶ Now sir as to þe poynt	[¶] þer	176ʳ	VII.1393 *
xlv)	but if it be þe companye of good ^ folke	[¶] poore	178ʳ	VII.1560
xlvi)	þen seiden þei ^ wit*h* oon vois	^alle	180ᵛ	VII.1764 *
xlvii)	But at the laste he made ^ a fraie	[¶] a foule	185ʳ	VII.2083
xlviii)	Than on her wifes ben thei neuyr ^ faire .	[¶] so	202ʳ	IX.191
xlix)	eu*ery* thyng saf ^ god of heuyn .	^ onli	212ʳ	X.369 *
l)	rebukid in excesse of ^ metis *and* drynkes	[¶] dyuers	213ᵛ	X.445
li)	he ne sparith neither crist ne his ^ modir .	¶ swete	216ᵛ	X.560
lii)	ne traueile with his hondis in no ^ werke	[¶] good	220ᵛ	X.724
liii)	cristendom stant ^ *and* wit*h* outyn fruyt .	^ bare	224ᵛ	X.877 *
liv)	therfore is the brekyng þ*er*of ^ greuous	[¶^] more	225ʳ	X.883
lv)	to terme of ^ his lif .	^ all	227ᵛ	X.967
lvi)	¶ And ^ for as meche as reson of man will not	¶ furþ*er*more	209ᵛ	X.269 *

thus (as Chapter 10 notes). But whoever made that exemplar had intruded more adjectives and adverbs than the poet; the correcting of them, then, feeds off a general interest by scribes in them.

Yet how interesting are these words? Most of the adjectives and adverbs in Table 8.3 are simple and even clichéd, for to be persuasive, value-judgements are best expressed in familiar terms. Abigail's 'counseile' must have 'good' added in the margin (xviii), and the phrase is repeated a few lines later ('By good cou*n*seile').[36] The other words added are simple monosyllables often of absolute qualities: *dark*, *high*, *all*, *worthy*, *holy*, *well*, *great*, *never*, *only*, *merry*, and so on. This is typical of Chaucer's poetry, and of the poetry he influenced, which often describes things as extreme and clear like this: *good*, *great*, *high*, *well* and *worthy*; or else *cruel* or *false*; *only* or *all* or *full* (*fully*) this or that.[37] These terms create a tone of heightened praise or blame – the two tasks, some scholastics said, of any piece of writing.[38] The scribes restore these terms – among others, of course – and thereby restore the tone of clear judgement. This tone is interesting in John Lydgate's *The Fall of Princes*,

[36] BL, MS Harley 1758, f. 77ᵛ (*Tales*, IV.1372).

[37] Tatlock and Kennedy, *Concordance*, 381–7, 394–8, find 996 uses of *good* and 926 uses of *great*.

[38] Minnis and Scott, with Wallace (eds.), *Medieval Literary Theory and Criticism*, 282–5.

where the emotional impact is especially important, so that the heroes and villains become memorable examples. The heroes must be commended for their '^grete fairenesse' rather than mild fairness; they must fall from '^gret prosperitee' rather than middling success, and into '^gret grevaunce' and '^grete outrage' too.[39] When they are wicked then they must be guilty of '^fals presumpcion', '^fals inobedience' and '[---]{fals} dalliau*n*ce', all a little tautologous, as though presumption, disobedience or sexual immorality were not already false.[40] Even the less commonplace adjectives corrected in *The Fall of Princes* sound excessive in tone: for example, in one copy of the poem Joas has not 'His estat' increased but his 'hyȝe' estate, as a marginal addition has it; the skill of writing helps us to see people not only 'seuered from siht' but 'seuered ^fer from siht' as an interlineation insists; Tarquin's crime is 'foule' and Hercules' discipline is 'knyhtli', with the evaluative terms squashed over erasures or interlined.[41] Another scribe interlines 'hyȝe' to stress that Hercules' renown is '^hyȝe renoun'.[42] The brevity of these common adjectives might make them easy to omit, but scribes then take care to restore them and the tone they engender.

Finally, they often preserve the tone by correcting *all*, *full* and *so*. Brevity makes these words also missable, yet in the poetry of Chaucer and others these words are often essential for adding an emphatic tone or filling the number of syllables or allowing the stress to fall in the right place.[43] Scribes' accurate correcting of them preserves these features, knowingly or not. Among the adjectives and adverbs added to the (aforementioned) copy of *The Canterbury Tales* (Table 8.3) the commonest were *all* added five times and *so* added thrice; *full* and *well* were also added twice each. This scribe also restores *all* with other techniques besides marginal additions: he writes that the hot sun has made the Shipman's 'hewe[-]{|al|}brou*n*' with 'al' over a tiny erasure squeezed between two words; an interlineation presents Venus' body swathed with teasing completeness 'fro the nauell doun ^all couerid'.[44] The *all* adds little information and edges into tautology: a suntanned face is usually all suntanned; being covered implies that all of the specified

39 PML, MS M.124, respectively ff. 77r (*Fall*, III.3294), 9v (I.1724); BL, MS Harley 4203, f. 50v (*Fall*, III.724); Champaign, Illinois UL, MS 84, p. 319 (*Fall*, VII.502). PML, MS M.124, f. 105r, does once interlineate 'grete' where the modern editor does not have it (*Fall*, IV.3653).

40 BL, MS Harley 4203, f. 65v (*Fall*, II.3541); Chicago, UL, MS 565, f. 13v (*Fall*, II.3203); PUL, MS Taylor 2, f. 77r (*Fall*, III.914).

41 PUL, MS Taylor 2, ff. 54v (*Fall*, II.1836), 103r (IV.18), 77v (III.995), 32r (I.5143).

42 Champaign, Illinois UL, MS 84, p. 62 (*Fall*, I.5538).

43 Tatlock and Kennedy, *Concordance*, 21–2, 348, 846–7, lists 199 uses of *all*, 105 of *full* and 205 of *so*, even though they list *all* and *full* only selectively (viii). On these words, see Hanna, *Pursuing History*, 192–3; Minkova, 'Forms of Verse', 184.

44 BL, MS Harley 1758, ff. 5r (*Tales*, I.394), 21r (I.1957).

area is covered; rather, the *all* adds mild hyperbole. Similar effects come from restoring *full* and *so* in other copies of *The Canterbury Tales*: there are people in '^so grete astate', waiting '^so many a yere', who '^so wel kan preche', who have pains which '^so soore smoot' or who have considered things not just 'a right' but '[a]^ful right'.[45] And beyond *The Canterbury Tales*, other works have these words restored too.[46] In Lydgate's *The Fall of Princes*, scribes restore *full* to stress the '^ful gret excellence' of people and their '^ful causeless' mistreatment.[47] The scribes trouble to preserve, and perhaps thereby recognize, these words as essential for the emotive tone of much of Chaucer's and Chaucerian poetry.

Ironically, what further suggest their recognition of these words are some mistakes when they intrude them unwarrantedly. One scribe of *The Fall of Princes* turns 'all ther othir Champiouns', as the modern editor has it, into 'all the[------]^worthi Champiouns': he or somebody whose exemplar he copies expects that a word with *o*, *t* and *h* in it should not be the dry *other* but the stirring *worthy*.[48] Others too add these words to sound more emphatic than did the poet.[49] Likewise, one scribe interlineated 'so' rightly in one line but had also, when initially copying, written it wrongly elsewhere in the line: 'he berith him ^so faire / *and* so holyly'. Only the first, corrected *so* is Chaucer's.[50] The error shows how *all*, *full*, *so* and similar short adverbs were easy to omit but also tempting to insert. Editors have long known of the tendency of scribes to add these words as they copy.[51] The incorrect addition of them when copying suggests the scribes' receptiveness to them and the tone which they create. That in turn suggests that when scribes add these words accurately, as in the proper interlining of *so*, they might not merely be following their exemplars blindly, because they are accurate in general; they might also have a witting interest in what they correct; the scribes' general accuracy could be informed by their recognition of these

45 Respectively, BL, MS Royal 18.C.ii, f. 14v (*Tales*, I.956); BL, MS Sloane 1685, f. 32v (*Tales*, I.3086); BodL, MS Hatton donat. 1, f. 114v (*Tales*, III.437); HEHL, MS El. 26.C.9, f. 175r (*Tales*, VII.2599); OTC, MS 49, f. 110r (*Tales*, IV.243). *So* is restored where it is grammatically necessary in the construction *so X that Y*: e.g., BL, MS Egerton 2726, f. 44v (*Tales*, I.3517); BL, MS Lansdowne 851, f. 18v (*Tales*, I.1431); HEHL, MS El. 26.C.9, f. 116r (*Tales*, V.61); Tokyo, Takamiya collection, MS 32, f. 20r (*Tales*, I.229).

46 E.g., *all* and *so* in BodL, MS Rawl. poet. 163, f. 62r (*Troilus*, III.1558, 1560).

47 PUL, MS Taylor 2, f. 105r (*Fall*, IV.252); PML, MS M.124, f. 53v (*Fall*, II.3203).

48 JRL, MS Eng. 2, f. 109r (*Fall*, V.759).

49 E.g., (xix) in Table 8.3 above, mistakenly adding 'worthi'.

50 BodL, MS Arch. Selden B.14, f. 114v (*Tales*, III.2286). He also adds *so* on ff. 55v (I.3715) and 111r (III.2034) where it is an exclamative conjunction.

51 See especially Chaucer, *Legend of Good Women*, ed. Cowen and Kane, 88–90. Their list of variants includes 18 additions of *all*, 11 of *full* and 8 of *so*, though sometimes with several MSS offering the same variant at the same point.

words and their importance. If they did not think these words mattered, they would not intrude them erroneously; equally, if they did not think they mattered, they would have no need to correct them as part of their general accuracy.

Adornment in ordinary language

This might make concrete (as was said) Stanley Fish's old speculation that it is people's techniques for responding to poetry which bring out what is distinctive in poetry. Yet one unsettling entailment of Fish's contention is that 'literature' is therefore defined not by intrinsic qualities but 'is an open category' defined by people's responses.[52] Fish's redefinition of literary language in turn allows us 'to rescue ordinary language' from an 'impoverishing characterization' of it as something lacking the qualities we expect in literature.[53] It is a point often made by linguists who reveal the complexity in everyday speech. It is borne out by the high frequency and centripetal accuracy of correcting, which continues beyond canonical poems across most genres and discourses, from *Piers Plowman* to prose herbals (as Chapter 6 showed). Scribes do not distinguish literary from ordinary language in transmitting its tone and style.

Their breadth of attention can be seen in their corrections which heighten the style of genres with less obvious literary pretensions. They correct adjectives and adverbs not only in manuscripts of poetry but also in religious, medical and practical prose. A few corrected adjectives do add useful information, such as adding the participle *running* in adjectival position to a recipe: 'put in a Saucerfull of fayre //renynge// water'; this could be helpful specificity, as stagnant water would be less beneficial in this recipe for a sort of chicken soup.[54] More often, though, restoring adjectives and adverbs to practical writing does not improve the information delivered but improves the tone of delivery. The tone of recipes matters: emphasis, clarity and energy make them persuasive, and adjectives and adverbs do that. So another scribe twice restores the words *good* and *well* and also *fast* whether by crossing out a noun and going back to include an adjective before it ('of [mede] gode mede wax') or by interlining adjectives and adverbs: 'do he*m* in a panne ou*er* the fyre *and* frie he*m* ^wel w*ith* the foreseid wyne', 'styre he*m* ^fast together *and* boyle he*m* well together', 'I Galon of gode wyne *and* I potell of ^gode welle water', 'Take p*er*celi violett *and* pelitre braie he*m*

[52] Fish, *Is There a Text*, 11.
[53] *Ibid.*, 10, and also 97, 101–2, 106–8.
[54] HEHL, MS HM 64, f. 170r.

^welle togeder'.[55] This is typical: these adjectives and adverbs are ubiquitous in medical books and often corrected by others. For example, a scribe of Henry Daniel's *The Dome of Urynes* makes only six additions or changes of lexical words and five of them are adjectives, as when he inserts between or at the end of lines details of 'the ^gret sictite', the '⌐grete⌐ dist*emper*u*re* of complexiown' and '^all þes spices of Iaundyce' which can afflict us.[56] Such words would be unhelpfully vague in medical practice: identifying good meadow-wax or especially great dryness is difficult, for the adjectives and adverbs are subjective. They are instead words of encouragement, when positive, or urgency, when negative, as if to make the cure sound necessary and successful. The forthright and persuasive style might well be vital to the uptake of a medical recipe rather than to the efficacy of it once taken up, especially when its medicine is (to be honest) of little real benefit. Just as it is reassuring to note that these cures were ones which 'Ladi Beauchamp vsed',[57] as one person adds, so it is galvanizing to note how 'grete' the disease is or that the cures use 'gode' ingredients – just as cookery books today show pretty people doing things with aplomb. Style matters in this practical genre too.

The instrumental force of one of these words is evident in one of the most utilitarian texts: a medical charm. In a charm, language might seem more important for its real-world results than for its style, and charms were not always transmitted with care for their exact wording: they varied from copy to copy, as they were often written on frangible materials worn on the body or were transmitted orally or by memory.[58] Yet of course charms and prayers can gain efficacy from their wording as well as their content. So in two charm-like prayers for good health in a medical anthology, the scribe later interlineates the adjective *worthy*:

> Oure lorde + Ih*esu* *christ*e as sothely as the Iues token a nayle of Iron *and* perisshid thy right hond + As sothely as neu*er* after that tyme was passid hit did not Longe acke ne swell ne Rangkull ne fester ne blede + As sothely lorde + Ih*esu* *christ*e I beseche the *and* hit be thy will that this wond may be hole that neu*er* after this tyme be passid hit acke not longe ne swell ne Rangkull ne fester ne blede thorowe the v*er*tu of that ^worthy wonde + And saye a pat*er* noster and an Aue maria[59]

55 HEHL, MS HM 58, respectively ff. 52ᵛ, 69ʳ, 71ᵛ, 73ʳ, 91ʳ.

56 HEHL, MS HM 505, ff. 50ʳ (Henry Daniel, *Dome*, II.iv), 84ʳ (II.ix), 113ʳ (III.viii). Two other adjectives more precisely distinguish 'gud' from 'mene' or average days of 'cretitaciown' (f. 27ʳ; II.ii).

57 HEHL, MS HM 58, f. 52ᵛ.

58 Skemer, *Binding Words*, notes examples of such variation (102, 106) and of accuracy (119).

59 HEHL, MS HM 64, f. 140ʳ. On this charm, see Jones, 'Discourse Communities', 32.

He makes the same correction ('that ^worthy wond') in a similar charm overleaf.[60] The magical power of the words is evident in the accompanying actions: at each cross, drawn in red, the speaker of the charm should cross himself. And the adjectives contribute to the action of charming. It is evidently important to describe Jesus' wounds as 'worthy', for in this and the other corrected charm *worthy* recurs before *wound* five times; by contrast, the human wound which needs to be healed is only ever called 'this wonde'.[61] The *worthy* shows reverence to Christ, so that being revered He might be pleased to heal. In what seems like ordinary, even utilitarian, language, these grammatically needless words have extraordinary, supernatural force.

The importance of stylistic adornment can be tested by considering a second possible ingredient of it which is inessential for basic communication but contributes to the rhythm and richness of the writing: the doublet. Doublets are syntactically and lexically otiose: two words used and employed where one would do – as in *used and employed*. Half of any doublet might seem needless for communicating the matter and preserving the grammar. Doublets might seem to reflect the loose paraphrase typical of English composition in this period: an inability to choose one word precisely. They might also seem to license scribal variance, by allowing scribes to think that words were interchangeable or expendable. Doublets, though, typify the style of much fourteenth- and fifteenth-century English writing, especially in certain self-conscious modes such as 'curial' prose, where they give a grave pace, adornment or copiousness.[62] And scribes and readers trouble to preserve these otiose doublets, as they do adjectives and adverbs, not only in those literary modes but also in supposedly 'ordinary language'.

The manuscripts from the Huntington Library include several corrections to doublets in the utilitarian and instructive writing. Some could clarify the information or matter of the text. William Rothwell has suggested in passing that their 'otiose repetition' might be useful for ensuring clear communication when a word's sense could 'not be determined unequivocally', in a culture with few dictionaries for the vernacular; pairing a word with others of 'roughly the same sense' served to gloss it.[63] This seems a fair explanation of some corrections in a collection of medical writings where somebody supplies a missing half for five doublets by interlining, and all these doublets loosely gloss things: adding the older,

60 HEHL, MS HM 64, f. 140^{v}.
61 HEHL, MS HM 64, f. 140^{r-v}.
62 Burnley, 'Curial Prose', esp. 596.
63 Rothwell, 'Synonymity and Semantic Variability', 365.

French-derived *mischief* clarifies the Latinate *tribulation* (‘trībulacions ^*and* mischiffis’); adding a reference to a *dog* in ‘a Bicche /or dogge’ might clarify that the text refers to male dogs as well as female ones or might prevent us misreading *bitch* as the French word *biche* (fawn); expanding the name of a herb to ‘lasse ^or lityll dittayne’ perhaps gives a different folk name for it, in case readers know different ones; adding the word ‘crudde’, an odd spelling of the archaic *grede* (‘to crye //or crudde’), perhaps helps to ensure that we recognize ‘crudde’ when it recurs without the helpful ‘crye’ in the following lines.[64] Whether these doublets are copied from exemplars is difficult to say, for these recipes are sometimes unedited and hard to track in other manuscripts. These doublets could, then, be scribal glossing to clarify the matter rather than correcting to preserve the style or manner.

Other corrections, though, suggest that doublets and synonyms can be not only clarificatory but confusing: far from preventing misreading, the use of two words in one position in the clause, in conjunction or grammatical apposition, makes the syntax harder to parse. So people correcting practical genres attend to the syntactical arrangement of doublets by interlining prepositions or articles which make it clear that both halves operate in parallel: ‘Take the Ius of verneyne *and* ^of celidoyne’, ‘kutt w*ith* swerd or ^w*ith* knyfe’, ‘of the stomake or of ^the Raynes’, ‘abstyne he fro*m* muche wakynge *and* muche þoȝt *and* fro*m* co*m*panyyng wyþ wy*m*me*n* *and* ^from muche baþynge’.[65] These seem to clarify the syntax; but they also thereby highlight that syntax: they witness people reflecting not on medicine but on language, with its own rhythms and its own practical problems to cure.

In the most practical uses of language, then, there is attention to style by the people who correct. Sometimes the scribes might correct these features of style – adjectives, adverbs and doublets – without especial interest in them, simply as part of their general meticulousness; but at other times, they might be consciously concerned with these particular features; that seems possible when their corrections turn out to be erroneous inventions on their part, say, by intruding a doublet or adjective where other manuscripts do not have one. Such recognition of the usefulness of certain words might be more likely in practical genres than in poetry. To speculate that scribes registered the nuances of *cruel* and *furious* in Lydgate’s poetry requires the speculation that they registered the specialness of literary language; but with practical writings it is easier to imagine that they recognized that the words they correct do useful things, such as praise the Lord or clarify recipes.

64 HEHL, MS HM 64, respectively ff. 64v, 142v, 178r (Brodin (ed.), *Agnus Castus*, 144, which lacks this addition), 150r (and cf. *OED*, *grede* (*v.*), and *MED*, *greden* (*v.*)).

65 Respectively, HEHL, MS HM 58, ff. 44r, 80r; MS HM 64, f. 183r (Brodin (ed.), *Agnus Castus*, 190, but differing from that edition); MS HM 19079, f. 16v.

Indeed, with practical writing, might it be not that the general process of correcting makes people attend to the text, but that the usefulness of the text invites such craftsmanship?

Correcting religious style

This effect of the text on its transmission might be even easier to imagine for one category of practical writing: religious writing. A millennium of commentators (as Chapter 2 traced) had urged people to handle religious texts with reverence and care. Did such reverent handling of the copy in general engender corrections of the (aforementioned) features of style, adjectives or adverbs and doublets? Or, conversely, did the experience of attending to the details of religious language engender the general meticulousness of scribes?

Attitudes to religious language seem likely to be influential in copies of Scripture in English and parabiblical writing. Among the Huntington Library's books, verbal adornments such as adjectives and doublets are corrected with care in a copy of the Wycliffite New Testament. This has 428 corrections of all manner of words, of which nine restore adjectives, adverbs and doublets, all found in other manuscripts in English and in the Vulgate Latin Bible which was the Wycliffite Bible's source. Three corrections add the word *all*, to heighten the encompassing tone to descriptions of, for instance, things which will last ‘i*n*to $^{\wedge\text{alle}}$ þe generaciou*n*s’, where the Vulgate has the Latin word *omnis*.[66] Five corrections complete doublets, where half the doublet has been omitted; again, the Latin has a doublet.[67] None of the added details adds anything of narrative or theological importance. Indeed, in two final corrections to doublets, both halves of the doublet were already present, but the scribe inserts into the doublets a repetition merely of the preposition: ‘I desire ane*n*tis god boþe i*n* litil *and* $^{\wedge\text{in}}$ greet’, ‘of alle fre me*n* . *and* boonde me*n* *and* of [alle] smale *and* $^{\wedge\text{of}}$ grete’. The repetition of ‘in’ or ‘of’ adds nothing to syntax or sense; it does, however, clarify the grammatical structure and preserve the prose rhythm. Moreover, the preposition is repeated in the Vulgate too.[68] Was this why the corrections were made? What look like elements of style might be preserved not for their own sake but because of their authority,

[66] HEHL, MS HM 134, f. 98^{v} (Ephesians 3.21), and also ff. 18^{r} (Matthew 23.35), 138^{r} (Acts 26.14). See also ff. 86^{r}, interlining ‘now’ (Galatians 3.25, *iam*), and 89^{v}, adding ‘greet’ in the margin (1 Corinthians 6.9, *magnum*).

[67] HEHL, MS HM 134, ff. 15^{v} (Matthew 20.18), 102^{v} (Colossians 1.20), 107^{v} (1 Timothy 4.7), and the two in n. 68 below.

[68] HEHL, MS HM 134, ff. 138^{r} (Acts 26.29: ‘Optarem apud Deum et in modico et in magno’), 159^{r} (Apocalypse 19.18: ‘omnium liberorum ac servorum et pusillorum ac magnorum’).

which the scribes recognize whether from checking an English exemplar or from re-collating the English with the Latin. The accuracy due to religious language looks like the goal; one ingredient of style – words having value for themselves, rather than for what they communicate – seems to emerge here because every word is sacred, even 'in' or 'of'.

The carefulness in preserving the inherited Scriptures transfers to the vernacular a certain patterning of style. Meticulousness is the cause, polish the result. Similar features of style are preserved in other genres of religious writing. For example, a Wycliffite sermon has six adjectives or adverbs restored later in the margins or between the lines: they commend 'good' prayers and 'þe // lord god' who is '//hiȝ' or they condemn the 'feyned' words of priests and 'wickide' Cain.[69] Other copies of the same sermon also restore adjectives in the margins.[70] Adjectives here might convey the heartfelt values of religious writers; adjectives can express judgements. Of course, one imagines that nobody hearing or reading a sermon, perhaps especially within a close Wycliffite circle, needed telling who was 'wickide', who 'hiȝ'; but they add if not information then attitude and tone. The same things might be done by otiose corrections to a religious work from the opposite end of the ideological spectrum: Nicholas Love's *Mirror of the Blessed Life of Jesus Christ*, a work which opposes the Wycliffites directly. Here too, the corrected adjectives and adverbs (Table 8.4) convey not facts but the speaker's opinions, now orthodox ones. For example, when this scribe of Love's *Mirror* stops and writes over erasure in an attack on what 'þe [----]{fals} lollarde seyþe' (xvi), the quoted Lollard opinion is neutralized by ensuring that the adjective 'fals' is present. The proliferation of the words 'falsehed' and 'falseli' in the adjacent lines, the ensuing references to 'þe lewed lollardes' and the marginal note 'c*ontra* lollardos' make the matter clearer still.[71] Ironically, the emphatic assertion of falsehood in this copy is continued by an uncorrected error which still stands: while 'fals' is authoritative, the reference to a 'lollarde' is wrong; the standard textual tradition has the vaguer word 'heritik'.[72] Both the correction to supply 'fals' and the erroneous precision of 'lollarde' look like an emphatic opinion – a

[69] HEHL, MS HM 503, ff. 97^{r} (Hudson (ed.), '*Omnis plantacio*', 2373), 111^{v} (2694), 20^{v} (470), 125^{v} (3025). See also ff. 72^{v} (1704, adding 'wonder' or *wonderfully*), 120^{v} (2921, adding 'ful').

[70] CUL, MS Dd.14.30, ff. 2^{v} ('trewe'), 10^{r} ('meedful'), 21^{v} ('fleshli'), 97^{v} ('pore'), out of 36 marginal additions.

[71] HEHL, MS HM 1339, ff. 66^{v}–67^{r}. Other marginal notes identify nameless 'schrewes' as 'lollardos' (f. 9^{r}).

[72] *Mirror*, 152.1. E.g., the otherwise closely related CUL, MS Mm.5.15, f. 100^{v} lacks this slip of 'lollarde' and lacks the marginal note 'c*ontra* lollardos'. On its relationship to HEHL, MS HM 1339, see Chapter 5, n. 28 above.

Table 8.4 *Some corrections to doublets, adjectives and adverbs in* Mirror *in HEHL, MS HM 1339*

	text	*folio*	Mirror
i)	seynte Gregori [---]{*and* oþ*er*}e doctou*rs* seyne	3^r	11.2
ii)	not onli Martires; but also Confessours [*and*] vi*r*gynes *and* all þ*a*t lyuen riȝtwiseli	4^r	12.22
iii)	þ*o*u herest or þenkest of þe [----------]{t*r*inyte or of þ*e*}godhede or of gosteli creatures	8^v	23.31
iv)	touchynge þe gospell [->]{*and* þ^e p*ro*ces of þ^e i*n*carnaci*o*n of ih*es*u criste}	9^v	28.9–10
v)	þis day bigan þe hele [->]{*and* þ^e rede*m*pci*o*n of ma*n*kynde*and*þ*er*ereco*n*silyngtoþ^e fad*ur*} of heuene	9^v	28.27–8
vi)	o*ur* ^owen defaute	14^r	36.13
vii)	þise two //festes //g*re*te *and* solempnitees	17^r	42.14
viii)	is //nedefull //moste to vs	29^v	69.20
ix)	many ^grete wise men	40^v	94.37
x)	knowynge ^boþe good *and* yuell	44^v	104.35
xi)	^veyne worschipe	44^v	104.41
xii)	it is full p*er*ilous *and* full ^dredefull to be i*n* þe state of p*er*fecciou*n*	51^r	119.29
xiii)	seynt b*er*n*ard* *and* many oþ*er* [doctou*rs*] holi fadres *and* doctou*rs* comende	52^v	122.31–2
xiv)	his simple *and* pore disciples [a[-]{ll}] aboute hi*m* wit*h* his mod*ur* *and* oþ*er* deuoute wome*n* folwy*n*ge	61^v	140.38
xv)	[--]{his}^grete loue to he*m* *and* al mankynde	63^r	144.20
xvi)	onli i*n* figure as þe [----]{fals} lollarde seyþe	66^v	152.1
xvii)	take we heed wit*h* a deuoute mynde of [al] þis wonderfull deede	70^v	161.18
xviii)	schame to se hi*m* so standynge [-]^al naked	76^r	174.20
xix)	^notable wordes	77^v	177.6
xx)	his moste large merci is //schewed //openli	77^v	177.17–18
xxi)	he was verray god [*and* man]	83^v	191.10
xxii)	ih*esu* cam i*n* man*er* of a pilg*ri*me *and* felawschipid wit*h* he*m* ^askynge hem questiou*ns* *and* answeri*n*ge he*m* ^*and* tellyng swete wordes of edificaciou*n*	87^v	201.32
xxiii)	wher Thomas was //[p*re*sent] //þan p*re*sent wi*t*h hem	90^r	206.12
xxiv)	þe more open prof *and* ce*r*teynete of his ^verray Resurreccio*u*n	90^r	206.29
xxv)	þis hiȝ wonderfull sac*ra*mente of c*ri*stis [------]{p*re*ciouse flesch} *and* blood *And in the margin:* preci<-->	103^v	235.26
xxvi)	we haue //doctrine //her*e* *and* figure	64^r	147.2

Lollard panic – which matters to this scribe. Yet, as could be asked of the Wycliffite preacher's 'feyned' to describe the words of priests, who reading Love's *Mirror* needed to be told that heretics are false? What does this adjective really add? The pointlessness of such words is evident when the scribe corrects a reference to the resurrection by interlining 'verray': 'þe more open prof*and* cer*teynete* of his ^verray Resurreccio*un*' (xxiv). The line is emphatic already, with its doublet of proof and certainty, and the proof which is even 'more open' than it might have been; yet the scribe takes care to remind us that the Resurrection is *very*, in the sense of *true*. The proof referred to in this line is that which Christ gives to doubting Thomas, so 'verray' facts are the essential theme. But no fifteenth-century reader of this work doubted the veracity of the Resurrection, so the corrected word is not useful for being informative but for adding an emphatic tone.

One could explain these corrected words as specifications of important facts – Lollards are false, the Resurrection is true – made nervously in response to challenges to those facts. Love was writing within the Carthusian order which worried so much about textual transmission, and he was writing to oppose the Wycliffites. Half of the copies, including this one with 'fals' and 'verray' corrected, contain a *Memorandum* that the work has been shown to Archbishop Thomas Arundel for 'inspecting and examining as required' ('i*n*spicie*ndum*. *et* debite examinand*um*'), terms which evoke the common use of the verb *examino* for correcting.[73] Arundel issued Constitutions to control religious writing in English and, while their effect must not be overestimated, they might have prompted carefulness in textual production, just as they prompted 'chastisinge' and 'correctiuns' of ecclesiastical sorts.[74] The dissemination of Love's *Mirror* itself does show some degree of 'centralization' or even 'planning'.[75] And another important Carthusian manuscript in English, *The Boke of Margery Kempe*, contains corrections which have been argued to show somebody controlling its meaning by ensuring that Kempe's experiences are understood to be 'gostly' or *spiritual*, as is stated in an adjective added between the lines.[76] Might this correcting of diction in religious works, then, be considered defensive?

Perhaps not all textual engagements are so paranoid. After all, the Constitutions did not provoke systematic censorship.[77] So might the corrections

73 HEHL, MS HM 1339, f. 2r. On these terms, see Chapter 5, pp. 123–6 above.

74 *Mirror*, ed. Sargent, 29–37, 56–7, 147–50; Watson, 'A clerke schulde have it of kinde for to kepe counsell', 586–8. The influential account of this history is Watson, 'Censorship and Cultural Change'.

75 *Mirror*, ed. Sargent, 86–7.

76 Kerby-Fulton, Hilmo and Olson, *Opening Up Middle English Manuscripts*, 236.

77 *Mirror*, ed. Sargent, 74–81; Somerset, 'Censorship', 250–1, 248, 257–8.

to adjectives and adverbs be considered instead a positive strategy preserving a style? The mode of affective piety in a work such as Love's *Mirror* might encourage people to preserve the style. It is not only theological precision but also emotional expression which demands words otiose in logic but useful for inspiring, moving or energizing the reader. Many things in Love's *Mirror* are described in a hyperbolic tone thanks to the adjectives or adverbs which get corrected in this copy.[78] For example, the scribe restores *great* twice by interlining it and once by adding it too late and reordering the words with virgules (vii, ix, xv). Likewise, he preserves other adjectives with which Love expresses judgements and heightens the tone, such as, when Mary feels shame to see Christ 'so standynge [-]^al naked', the interlineated *all*, which expresses the absoluteness of Christ's abjection (xviii, and also xi, xix, viii). These words corrected fit the pattern of the other words copied in this book: for example, the '{p*re*ciouse flesch} *and* blood' (xxv) echoes the term 'p*re*cious sac*ra*ment' which occurs nearby.[79] The purpose of such writing is explained by Love in the prologue, where he repeatedly speaks of 'stirynge' the reader. That requires this stirring style, to which the corrected adjectives contribute.[80] Of course, affective piety was not a spontaneous overflow of powerful feeling but a phenomenon carefully controlled by ecclesiastical writers.[81] This copy of Love's *Mirror* illustrates such care too. The erasure used to insert *precious* is not hasty work but follows a prompt for it written in the margin, now rubbed off but just visible (xxv). Nor is the scribe excessive in correcting adjectives: all those he adds or restores are thought by the work's modern editor to be authorial. And the scribe even removes by subpuncting two uses of hyperbolic *all* which were not so authorized (xiv, xvii). In these erroneous adjectives it looks as though the scribe is himself stirred to add emphasis, as editors find that scribes often are, but then stops himself.[82] The few errors suggest his awareness of and investment in the features he usually corrects accurately. He is responsive to the emotion of Love's *Mirror* and the words which stir it; but this is a response born of correctly reading his exemplar.

Similarly, this copy of Love's *Mirror* has also a few corrections to its doublets, and none are susceptible of interpretation as signs of anti-Lollard

[78] Only (xii) in Table 8.4 seems necessary for grammar.

[79] HEHL, MS HM 1339, e.g., f. $104^{\mathrm{r-v}}$ (*Mirror*, 236.29, 237.34–5).

[80] HEHL, MS HM 1339, ff. 2^{v}–3^{r} (*Mirror*, 10.12, 10.35).

[81] Gayk, 'Images of Pity', 202–3, makes an analogous point which influences mine.

[82] Oddly in HEHL, MS HM 1339, f. 61^{v} (*Mirror*, 140.38), **ll** in 'all' is over erasure, so not entirely spontaneous; then the whole word is subpuncted. Possibly the scribe confused the two ascenders in **ll** and the hooked ascender in **b** in 'aboute'.

edginess. Some are difficult to comprehend, as they are written over thorough erasures (i, iii, iv, v) or involve reordering to keep paired nouns together (vii, xxvi).[83] Two other corrections to doublets might suggest the scribe's attentiveness to them beyond just a general accuracy. The first is again an error: the scribe writes and then deletes a doublet that is not part of the textual tradition: he describes Christ as 'verray god [*and* man]' whereas at this stage in the argument it is only Christ's divinity that is relevant.[84] The error suggests the scribe's expectation of doublets even when there are none. It also suggests one influence on that: the thinking in pairs that typifies Christianity: God and man here, but also maid and mother, justice and mercy, faith and works, sin and grace, heaven and hell. Did such thinking make scribes attentive to doublets? That would be only a nebulous influence and would be very difficult to prove. But another correction to a doublet is if not in cause then in effect a recognition of doublets: the scribe interlines, in paler ink, the otiose element *both* clarifying the syntax of a doublet which is already complete in substance (x). Adding *both* is like making a metalinguistic comment on the syntactical and conceptual doubleness.

A conscious response to the syntax of doublets emerges in some additions in other works of religious prose. In the Huntington Library's manuscripts, doublets are most often corrected by John Pery, the canon of Holy Trinity, Aldgate (whose dialectal changes are noted in Chapter 7), in a copy of Walter Hilton's *The Scale of Perfection* which Pery had copied by another scribe but also corrected for himself (Table 8.5). In five of his corrections to doublets the error was evidently ungrammatical or unidiomatic (ii, iii, x, xiii, xix). But in the other fourteen Pery and the original scribe correct doublets which already have both synonyms present, but about which Pery and the scribe are not satisfied. Fussily, they add between the lines or in the margins little words which ensure that the syntactic parallel between the two halves of the doublet is obvious: they repeat the 'understood' or elided elements of the second noun-phrase or co-ordinated verb-phrase; they add the same preposition, article or auxiliary verb before the main verb or noun; or they add *both* before the doublet (Figure 4). Such sentences made sense beforehand, but the corrections make their grammar more explicit.[85] One of these needless corrections might reflect deference

[83] He also erroneously adds the brevigraph for *and*, creating a doublet (HEHL, MS HM 1339, f. 4[r]; *Mirror*, 12.22), where the closely related CUL, MS Mm.5.15, f. 5[r], also has the abbreviation for *and*, left uncorrected.

[84] HEHL, MS HM 1339, f. 83[v] (*Mirror*, 191.10).

[85] Burnley, 'Curial Prose', 596–7, notes that writers themselves often sought this clarity.

Table 8.5 *Some corrections to doublets in HEHL, MS HM 112, compared with* Scale *and also Hilton,* The Scale of Perfection, *ed. Bestul*

	text	*folio*	Scale / *Bestul*	*person*
i)	a sikir trouth. and al articles of þe faith . and ^[of] sacramentes of holi chirche	16[r–v]	47 / 534 *	Pery
ii)	I sal pray be trauel ^ [*and*] bi desire of þe spirit *And in the margin: and*	24[v]	72 / 802	Pery ?
iii)	a meditacion of his manhode. also of his byrth ^[or] of his passion and of þe compassion of oure lady	26[v]	79 / 896	scribe
iv)	þy hert risis vp in to aloue and ^[a] gladnes of hym	27[r]	80 / 913 *	scribe
v)	¶ I schal di lyuer hym and ^[I schalle] make hym glorius in my blis	29[r]	85 / 974	Pery
vi)	and in flescheli sauo*ur* ^ in þe wytes as ^[in] glotony and ^[in] lechory *And in the margin:* ^ bothe	35[r]	101 / 1175–6 *	'in' = Pery
vii)	a litil of þe dignite and ^ þ*at* gosteli fairnes *And in the margin:* ^ of	37[r]	111 / 1308 *	Pery ?
viii)	be þat ocupacion þ*o*u sekest hy*m* ^ *and* best fyndest hym *And in the margin:* ^ best	38[r]	113 / 1337	Pery
ix)	breke þe loue of syn | [f. 41[v]] and ^[of] vanite	41[r–v]	121–2 / 1455	Pery
x)	ȝe wirche merakiles or casten out deuelles ^ or p*re*chen *And in the margin:* ^ or teche*n*	43[r]	124 / 1474	Pery
xi)	sotheli to Iues and ^[too] sarsonis wyche trow noght in crist	45[v]	135 * / 1601 *	Pery
xii)	comen to gode and to bad to chosen *and* ^[to] reproued	54[v]	157	Pery
xiii)	nor lykyng haue in þe holdying ^[ne] in þe kepyng	61[r]	173 / 2068 *	unclear
xiv)	it strangiles þe loue of god and ^[of] her euen cr*is*ten	62[r]	175 / 2088	Pery
xv)	lettes hym fro þe feruo*ur* of charite and also ^[fro] þe special mede	62[r]	175 / 2089	Pery
xvi)	þe lykyng þat comes vnder þe colo*ur* of þis nede and passis þis ^ is lesse syn *And in the margin:* nede	63[r]	178 / 2136	red crayon
xvii)	þ*o*u schalt ^ rysyn and smyten away þe vnskilful stirrynges *And in the margin:* boþe	65[r]	183 / 2189 *	Pery
xviii)	a man myght see wi*th* his gostely ee how foule pryde and couetyse aren in þe syght of god *and* ^ contrary to hym *And in the margin:* ^ how	65[r]	184 / 2196	Pery
xix)	a stirryng or lykyng outher of glotony . ^ lechery *And in the margin:* ^ or of	65[r]	184 / 2199 *	Pery

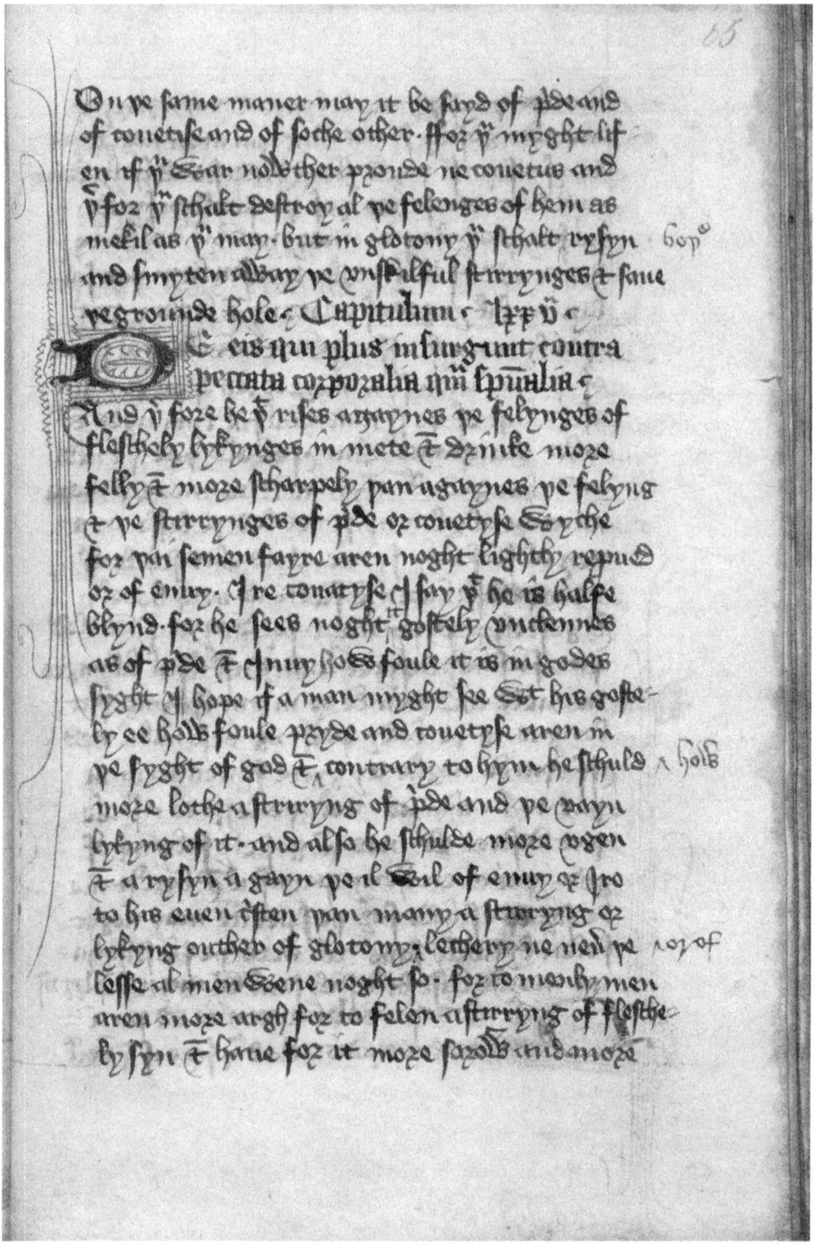

Figure 4 HEHL, MS HM 112, f. 65r: three additions in the margins in Walter Hilton's *The Scale of Perfection*

to scriptural language, as the clarified doublet echoes the patterning of a biblical quotation which the English work is loosely paraphrasing: the extra 'I schalle' (v) echoes the Latin future-tense endings which appear on both verbs in the Vulgate quoted nearby ('eripiam eu*m* *et* gl*orifi*cabo eum').[86] But precision in translation is not Hilton's point nor usually the point of the people correcting here; the people correcting seem instead attentive to the pattern of doublets in Hilton's style.

This could, of course, be mere meticulous checking of an exemplar: most of these additions are attested in the modern edition collated and in another edition checked for this detail. But it is possible, though not provable, that the scribe and reader registered this stylistic pattern in a conscious way. First, they intrude some clarifications of doublets where editions record that other scribes did not (marked with asterisks in Table 8.5). Such corrections make this copy's syntax here more explicit than other copies are, as though Pery is trying to untangle the layers of doublets, and doublets within doublets, in mystical prose. If what look like corrections to this feature are sometimes witting inventions, then might the other, centripetal corrections to it also reflect conscious interest, as well as adherence to the exemplar? Such alertness is suggested in another manuscript by the scribe, also corrected by Pery and probably once bound with the Huntington Library's one.[87] In the first part of this manuscript, Pery continues to repeat the prepositions, adjectives and other words which precede nouns or verbs (*all*, *at*, *by*, *from*, *of*, *on*, *thy*) so that he clarifies the symmetry of the doublets or phrases in apposition: 'of hys scurgynge at vndirne *and* ^of þe holygost comynge', 'onour—e— þy fader and ^þi moder', 'verry god and ^verai man'.[88] This correcting of doublets, then, persists beyond Hilton's *Scale*, so that it seems to reflect Pery's concern as much as any one author's. That is suggested too when others correct Hilton's *Scale* and do not attend to the doublets especially: for example, the other manuscript of it in the Huntington Library, copied by the Carthusian John Clerk, has only one clarification of a syntactic parallel.[89] The attention to doublets is

86 HEHL, MS HM 112, f. 29^{r} (*Scale*, 85, quoting Psalm 90.15). The necessary correction to (ii) also has a scriptural source: 'Orabo *et* sp*irito*. orabo *et* mente' (1 Corinthians 14.15).

87 As noted in Chapter 7, n. 41 above.

88 BL, MS Add. 10053, ff. 3^{v}, 12^{r}, 13^{v}, and, e.g., 3^{r}, 7^{v}, 14^{v}, 23^{r}, and among the more scattered corrections later in the MS, 41^{v} (3 times), 81^{r} and so on.

89 HEHL, MS HM 266, f. 18^{v} (*Scale*, 178): 'for as myche þ*a*t nede is ^þe grounde of þis synne. *and* ^þat nede is no synne'. There are also two more needful corrections to things missing in both halves of a doublet: ff. 4^{r} (*Scale*, 164), 8^{r} (387). This MS, though, already contains many of the words added to syntactic parallels in HEHL, MS HM 112, so correction was not needed.

distinctive to Pery and his scribe and so perhaps a conscious choice, beyond mere unthinking duplication.

This activity might tell us something about literary language in this period. First, it suggests that some elements of style might be, in Stanley Fish's terms, 'the product of certain ways of paying attention'.[90] It might be the scribe or reader who can see words worthy of precision in Lydgate's poetry or in recipes, say. We might find not literary language here but literary appreciation – the craft and intelligence of the scribes and others such as Pery. That intelligence seems likely to me – though, as the people are long gone, unprovable.

But that is not all this activity suggests. The fact that most of the corrections are centripetal, reproducing the text which editors think should be there, suggests that the scribes were not often wrong to attend to the features they do. Of course, these religious works, from a magical charm to *The Scale of Perfection*, are often artfully styled; many have a sense of their gravity which demands attention; so do many secular poems in the Chaucerian tradition. Such works might themselves have power to engage those who correct them. For instance, Pery and his scribe might have been influenced or schooled by reading Hilton's style to develop an acute sense of its rhythms and patterns which shaped their correcting of other works. This suggestion slightly modifies the argument of this chapter and of this book so far. The argument so far has been that the practical processes of craftsmanship encourage the intelligent understanding of the text by the people who correct it. But might the text also encourage this intelligence and the processes of craftsmanship? That is difficult to prove with style, but (as the next two chapters argue) other aspects of form and structure clearly shape the making of the material text by inviting correction.

90 Fish, *Is There a Text*, 11–12.

CHAPTER 9

Form

> of his fasnesse . hit dullith me to rime
> Euer whanne I speke . of his [falsnesse] falshede .
> for shame of hym my chekis wex rede
>
> Oxford, Trinity College, MS 49, f. 253v
> Geoffrey Chaucer, *The Canterbury Tales*, VIII.1093–5

Sometimes it is the scribes' general care in correcting which makes them attentive to finer points of style, but sometimes the works themselves also encourage close attention: doublets cause difficulties of parsing which require finicky attention to their repetitive structure, or the emphatic tone of poetry tempts scribes into adding an extra *so*. But it is difficult to be sure whether and which features of style might influence correcting; could the word *so* really attract attention? The influence of the text on correcting is more certain in another element of works: verse-form. For instance, a scribe can leave the inadequate spelling 'fasnesse' meaning *falseness* uncorrected midline (in the epigraph to this chapter) but he must distinguish between 'falsnesse' and 'falshede' at the end of the line because, although they are synonyms, one would disrupt the poem's rhyming form. The concern to 'rime' by the poet both requires and assists carefulness by the scribe. Here, it is not the process of craft that makes possible insights like those of the formalist literary critic; it is literary language and the poets' and scribes' expectations of it which influence their craftsmanship.

Indeed, the scribe or reader correcting to restore rhyme or stanzas is not only worrying over the craft of writing a material *book* – say, how to be accurate, how to spell clearly; rather, he is worrying over something immaterial, almost: the form of the *text* in general. While we often recognize that the history of the material text – the labour, time and pay of artisans and the supply of materials – underpins literary history, here literature moulds the making of material texts. In particular, ideas about literary form might shape the real activities of scribes in book production. As Maura Nolan has put it, as a general principle, 'form . . . shapes and molds history'.[1] The scribes think about their craftsmanship as they fit stanzas onto pages or copy more precisely by deducing how the poem rhymes. While *form* has been defined well as 'the written shape that unspools on any page in which that text could be said to appear',[2] in the work of scribes it informs the making of pages.

Of course, formal patterns and structures occur in other modes beyond poetry or self-consciously literary language. The notion of 'form' need not be 'a synecdoche for literature or aesthetic experience'.[3] The scribes of the books in the Huntington Library attend to the form of the least literary writing too, such as the structuring of practical texts into sections or by means of a certain page-design. For instance, the sample's only documentary work in a bound book is a set of financial accounts for the funeral of Henry VII in 1509, where the scribe follows a set order and layout for payment, payee and thing being paid for. He sometimes forgets to keep things in separate columns but he corrects himself by crossing out and starting again in the right place.[4] The visual form matters in accountancy just as it does in a concrete poem, whether for true utility or for its suggestion of trustworthiness and order. Similarly, another useful layout is fixed in two tables of contents, which the scribe had to go back and alter in order to leave room for the initials and alphabetical systems which make the tables navigable.[5] Even utilitarian things, then, have an intricate form which needs preserving correctly for them to function.

For these reasons, to limit a study of form to verse-form is not ideal, as theoretical accounts have warned.[6] The Huntington Library's sample suggests that scribes do correct verse more frequently than prose, but only moderately so: they correct 91 per cent of pages of verse but only 68 per cent of pages of prose.[7] This is not an extreme difference and might be a difference of genre more than mode: for example, *The Prick of Conscience* and *Piers Plowman* might elicit frequent correcting because

[1] Nolan, 'Historicism after Historicism', 63. [2] Cannon, *Grounds of English Literature*, 12.

[3] Rooney, 'Form and Contentment', 33–4, 42, 44. Levinson, 'What Is New Formalism?', 559, warns that few critics have studied form beyond the canon.

[4] HEHL, MS HM 745, pp. 25 ('xxv s' crossed out and moved from the column for items to that for costs), 42 ('gennuwye' or *Genoese* crossed out so that it does not stray from the column for people into that for costs). See also the duplication on pp. 72, 80, 91.

[5] HEHL, MS HM 127, f. 1^{v}; MS HM 28561, f. 326^{r}. More substantially, the table for Edward of York, *The Master of Game* in HEHL, MS El. 35.B.63, f. 1^{r}, is corrected for missing out a chapter (which occurs on ff. 14^{v}–15^{r}).

[6] Cannon, 'Form', 178; Smith, 'Medieval *Forma*', 71.

[7] On 5,009 pages of verse there were 4,533 corrections, whereas on 6,867 pages of prose there were 4,687 corrections. Table 6.1 in Chapter 6 gives figures for the whole sample. HEHL, MS El. 26.C.9, MS HM 114, MS HM 144 and the fragments of English included both verse and prose; their corrections have been divided accordingly.

they are religious rather than because they are in verse. Yet there are some special qualities or kinds of attention which verse-form demands from, and gives to, the scribes' craft. For that reason this chapter focuses on verse-form and focuses less on the diverse books of the Huntington Library and more on copies from diverse libraries of similar sorts of poems, especially Chaucer's *The Canterbury Tales* and John Lydgate's *The Fall of Princes*. It is often suggested that by attending to form we identify 'the mysterious, self-justifying nature of the literary itself'.[8] In these corrections, we might identify not necessarily general or even genuine literariness but at least the scribes' thinking about one specific feature of it: their understanding of verse-form.

It might seem anachronistic to claim a widespread understanding of English verse before the late sixteenth century, when such understanding was properly codified in treatises. It has been noted that English poems of this earlier period lack an 'explanatory context' of readers' comments on what they saw and thought.[9] It has been argued that 'metrical patternings and their physical appearance in lines' were 'not intrinsic to the text' before the sixteenth century, that 'rhyme (hence lexicon), stanzaic patterning, and lexical arrangement . . . were not in fact integral' to earlier works and that some scribes could alter their visual layout to fit 'the demands of space and even, perhaps, scribal whimsy'.[10] It is true that throughout the fifteenth century scribes alter layouts to suit the materials they have: insufficient space on the page, insufficient red ink for consistent rhyme 'braces' and insufficient effort all lead scribes to simplify, disrupt or abandon layouts. Yet others have found that the English scribes of the courtly verse of the late fourteenth and the fifteenth centuries could be 'assiduous in their attention to a poem's structure and form division', both explicitly, by labelling inset lyric modes, and implicitly, by marking stanza-divisions.[11] The corrections give further evidence of the awareness or expectations of verse-form by people who copied and read it. They tell us about literary thinking in a culture before literary criticism.

Rhyme's influence on craft

In the corrections to verse, the scribes' perception of special qualities is more surely astute. It is debatable (in Chapter 8) whether the nuances

8 Leighton, *On Form*, 19. 9 Cannon, 'Form', 178.

10 Machan, *Textual Criticism*, 155, 156, 157. This might be truer of the early fourteenth century, the period from which Machan takes his example.

11 Butterfield, '*Mise-en-page* in the *Troilus* Manuscripts', 62–3.

of wording corrected by the scribes were truly intended by the authors, or whether it is the scribes who '*produce* what can thereafter be said to be there'.[12] By contrast, the rhymes and stanzas which scribes correct were definitely intended by the authors. For example, when the person who corrects Lydgate's *The Fall of Princes* in the copy in the Huntington Library acts *as if* Lydgate's choice of words merits respect (as Chapter 8 argued), he might be wrong; his sense that the exact word matters is indisputable, though, when he corrects words which rhyme. When Lydgate says that the typical tyrant pursues 'vengeau*n*ce', that word cannot be right, although tyrants are vengeful, for this vice must rhyme with 'pilage', so somebody writes a prompt to emend 'vengeau*n*ce' to 'avauntage'.[13] Likewise, in another copy of the poem the line 'And moral Senec concludith i*n* sentence' made perfect sense but needed fixing to 'And moral Senec concludith i*n* [sentence] ^substau*n*ce' so that it would rhyme with the line 'In his t*ra*gedies makyng reme*m*brau*n*ce'.[14] Although in fifteenth-century English the *sentence* of a text is its moral *substance*, these words interchangeable in meaning are not interchangeable in form because they sound different. Lydgate's rhymes evidently were intended: only the mythical monkeys with typewriters would produce 36,000 lines of rime royal by chance, and Lydgate was a monk, not a monkey. Whoever checked very carefully the words in rhyming position, then, is not over-reading but is recognizing the poet's intentions.

Moreover, those literary aspirations of poets determine the actions of the scribes and others. First, the patterns of verse-form are in part responsible for eliciting error from scribes. Rhymes bring words which look alike into close proximity, and this invites eyeskip. In eyeskip, scribes glancing back at the exemplar for the next phrase look instead at a similar word nearby and thereby omit or repeat some intervening passage.[15] There are some interesting examples of this in a copy of *The Canterbury Tales* made by two scribes, the second of whom checks the work of the first.[16] Somebody also adds 'ex*aminatur*' next to the catchwords, checking the book quire by quire.[17] Eight times the scribes skipped whole lines, and the probable cause is the likeness of rhyme-words, for it is most often the second half of a couplet which is missing. It looks as though the scribe copies to the

[12] Fish, *Is There a Text*, 327. [13] HEHL, MS HM 268, f. 102^{r} (*Fall*, IV.3219).

[14] Warminster, Longleat House, MS 254, f. 13^{r} (*Fall*, I.2381–5).

[15] Vinaver, 'Principles of Textual Emendation', 355–60. Rhyme can also lead to 'contamination', where scribes reuse a similar but different word from nearby, creating accidental rime riche or autorhyme.

[16] *LMES*, entry for BL, MS Egerton 2726.

[17] BL, MS Egerton 2726, at the end of every quire from ff. 102^{v} to 262^{v}, except for 206^{v}, 238^{v}.

first rhyme-word but then glances back in his exemplar to the second rhyme-word and so skips what intervenes.[18] The ease of skipping between rhymes is especially evident because he often jumps between rhyming syllables which not only end the same way but start the same way: from the line ending 'recorde' to the next ending 'accorde', from 'in one' to 'anone', 'dane' to 'dyane' or the rime riche 'leef' meaning *willing* and 'leef' meaning *leaf*.[19] This scribe's collection of eyeskips from rhyme is typical: other scribes err at the same lines, for instance, often skipping lines or duplicating them when there is rime riche.[20] Rime riche offers an extreme instance of the repetition in rhyme which encourages error.

Yet while verse-form provokes error, it also provokes the scribes to recognize these sound-patterns and to correct the problems they induce. But is rhyme's help really needed in correcting? After all, in the (aforementioned) copy of *The Canterbury Tales* with lines skipped from 'recorde' to 'accorde' and so on, the missing line is added in the margin or at the foot of the page, so there was evidently some recourse to the same or another exemplar in order to find it: did the scribes just collate the text, without worrying about the rhyme? No. The usefulness of the rhyme emerges from other errors which are left uncorrected in this book. The scribe or a colleague restores these eight half-complete couplets and misses only two – a fair rate of success;[21] but nobody corrects or even marks up seventeen places where what is missing is one or more whole couplets.[22] Twice these missing whole couplets are next to half-couplets which have been completed, so the scribe is evidently checking the exemplar at some point.[23] But he has not noticed that the whole couplet is missing, and that

18 The exception is BL, MS Egerton 2726, f. 44^{v} (skipping *Tales*, i.3509).

19 BL, MS Egerton 2726, ff. 11^{r} (skipping *Tales*, i.830, and adding it in the margin), 23^{r} (i.1772), 26^{v} (i.2064), and 23^{v} (i.1838). Others are ff. 3^{v} (i.221), 163^{v} (vi.336), 212^{v} (vii.3084). The corrections on ff. 11^{v} and 26^{v} may be by a second person.

20 E.g., CUL, MS Mm.2.5, f. 36^{r} (*Tales*, i.3275–6, confused by 'queynte'); BL, MS Sloane 1686, ff. 29^{r-v} (*Tales*, i.1837–8, 'leef'), 199^{v} (v.1091–2, 'Armes'); OTC, MS 49, ff. 46^{r} (i.3275–6, 'queynte'), 193^{r} (ii.793–6, 'wise', an error for the word 'juyse' meaning *justice*), 193^{v} (ii.837–8), 224^{v} (vii.2266–8, 'wight').

21 Of the two incomplete couplets he missed, one is hidden by an adjacent longer omission leaving five rhymes on <ie> or <ye> (BL, MS Egerton 2726, f. 224^{v}; *Tales*, viii.580–3, 587); another was marked with two crosses in what looks like the scribe's usual ink (f. 133^{v}; *Tales*, iv.2020; Tokyo, Takamiya collection, MS 24, f. 125^{v}, copied from this MS, leaves a gap).

22 BL, MS Egerton 2726, ff. 4^{r} (*Tales*, i.252b–c), 40^{r} (i.3155–6), 47^{r} (i.3721–2), 68^{v} (ii.328–9), 95^{v} (iii.1307–8), 97^{r} (iii.1443–4), 103^{v} (iii.1953–4), 139^{v} (v.69–72, two couplets), 147^{r} (v.671–2), 152^{r} (v.1063–4), 157^{r} (v.1455–6), 157^{v} (v.1493–8, three couplets), 163^{r} (vi.297–8), 163^{v} (v.333–4, but they recur before v.347), 182^{r} (vii.893–4), 224^{v} (viii.584–5, but they recur after viii.593), 233^{r} (viii.1238–9). Also two spurious lines conceal omissions: ff. 107^{r} (for iii.2229, placed after 2230), 163^{v} (for vi.346, placed after 345).

23 BL, MS Egerton 2726, ff. 3^{v} (restoring *Tales*, i.221, still missing 219–20), 163^{v} (restoring vi.336, still missing 333–4).

suggests that although he checks his exemplar to find lost lines, he relies on the verse-form to show him where the losses are.[24] While the scribes do have a general zeal for accuracy and a readiness to check their exemplars (noted in Chapter 6), they use their knowledge of rhyme to meet that end. Rhyme was not their focus but it was their tool.

The effect of this use of rhyme might be gleaned from a manuscript of *The Canterbury Tales* owned in the early sixteenth century by one John Leche.[25] It is copied in handwriting modelled mostly on secretary script, but with a sigmoid word-final **s** more typical of anglicana; it is written extremely currently, with most letters joined up and many strokes perfunctorily made. Perhaps because it was hastily written, it has many errors. Yet while something encouraged the scribe to be hasty, something else encouraged him to pause to correct his work, usually by subpuncting or crossing out before he continued. In many cases, he relies on rhyme to guide him. This reliance emerges in one striking point where he leaves a gap for a missing word:

> the salte teres . and the waymantyng
> the firy strokis of the <gap> inge .
> that loues seruauntes . in this lif enduren[26]

He recognizes that his exemplar is missing a participle ending with *–ing* but not which one. It should be 'desirynge' – a nice irony for this unfulfilled line. This curious moment suggests the scribe's recognition that rhyme could guide his correcting. Indeed, there are sixty-seven of the corrections which seem to be necessitated only by the rhyme (Table 9.1).[27]

These errors either had spellings and inflexions attested elsewhere in English of the period or they made sense, in their specific context, as a fair paraphrase of the words which now replace them: a fair wife is also a fair 'wight' or person, and a character who 'saide' something might well have 'answerid'.[28] None of these words definitely needed to be corrected, except so that they could rhyme. This needlessness is most evident in the corrections to doublets: marriage might offer 'care and woo' or 'coste and

[24] Tokyo, Takamiya collection, MS 24, is copied from BL, MS Egerton 2726, and incorporates all its added lines silently on ff. 3ᵛ (misplacing the added *Tales*, I.222 before 221), 11ʳ, 22ʳ, 23ʳ, 25ᵛ, 43ʳ, 154ᵛ, 209ʳ.

[25] Traced by Bale, 'Late Medieval Book-Owners Named John Leche'.

[26] OTC, MS 49, f. 26ᵛ (*Tales*, I.1921–2).

[27] Table 9.1 excludes corrections not affecting the rhyming syllable (e.g., f. 170ᵛ; *Tales*, VII.421–2).

[28] Table 9.1, nos. i–ii, v–vi, ix–x, xv–xvi, xviii–xxi, xxiii–xv, xxix, xxxi–xxxiii, xxxv–xxxvii, xl, xlii–xlvi, xlviii, l–li, liii–liv, lvi–lviii, lx–lxi, lxiii–lxv, lxvii. Context is crucial: e.g., in (xlviii), 'man' and 'tre' are interchangeable only because the point is about the shadow of *any* tall object.

Table 9.1 *Corrections to rhyming words which already made sense in context in* Tales *in OTC, MS 49*

	folio	Tales	*first rhyme*	*second rhyme*	*third rhyme*
i)	9^{r}	I.617–18	A long surcote of pers . upon his [hond] hade	and by his side he bare a rusty blade .	
ii)	17^{v}	I.1343–4	In chaynes and in feteris for to [dwell] be dede	vpon his hede	
iii)	20^{v}	I.1540–2	withouten any more	I was [borne] bore	
iv)	21^{v}	I.1627–8	that [palamon and] Arcite and Palamon	vnto the toun	
v)	23^{r}	I.1707–8	vpe payne of lesyng of your [lif] hed	he schall anon be dede	
vi)	30^{v}	I.2171–2	he his . his lokis caste	his age I [gesse] kaste	
vii)	31^{v}	I.2249–50	in heuen [abouyn] aboue	my loue	
viii)	36^{v}	I.2577–8	Whenne sette was . theseus ful rich [a boue] and hie	Emelie	
ix)	46^{v}	I.3299–300	sette his [tyme] while .	begile .	
x)	46^{v}	I.3317–18	his eyen gray as [glasse] goos .	on his schois.	
xi)	48^{r}	I.3437–48	maistir [nycholas] . nycholay .	the longe day .	
xii)	49^{v}	I.3529–30	that was full [tre] true	rewe	
xiii)	50^{r}	I.3579–81	Maistir Nichola[s]{y}	gode morwe I se the wel for hit is day[1]	
xiv)	50^{v}	I.3607–8	go forth [anon] thi wey anon	echon	
xv)	51^{v}	I.3703–4	I swe^lte and [swynke] swete .	tete .	
xvi)	55^{r}	I.3971–2	a childe that was of half yere [olde] age	page	
xvii)	62^{r}	*Gam.* 89–90	thare	[there] thare .	
xviii)	65^{r}	*Gam.* 297–8	so broke I my [schyn] chyn	pynne .	
xix)	69^{v}	*Gam.* 625–6	they stode talkyn bothe [to gedir] in fere	were	
xx)	71^{v}	*Gam.* 785–6	both day and [nyght] othir	brothir	
xxi)	77^{r}	III.251–2	a grete tormen[tyng]^trie	malinkolye	
xxii)	86^{v}	III.937–8	no man p*re*ue vs of oure [vis] vice	nyce	
xxiii)	95^{v}	III.1523–4	that shalle nought be [falle] tide	wide	
xxiv)	97^{r}	III.1631–2	to repente me	for any thing that I haue hadde of [thine] the	
xxv)	99^{v}	III.1807–8	life	yit say I nought this day so faire a [wight] wfe[2]	
xxvi)	100^{r}	III.1851–2	I goo	within this wokes [tweyne] too	
xxvii)	107^{v}	IV.57–9	the weste side of [ytaile] ytalie	vitaile	

(*cont.*)

Table 9.1 *cont.*

	folio	Tales	*first rhyme*	*second rhyme*	*third rhyme*
xxviii)	107ᵛ	IV.65–8	his worthi elderes hym be [forne] fore	more	yore
xxix)	108ʳ	IV.110–11	if [it] you[r] [wille] liste[3]	reste .	
xxx)	109ʳ	IV.156–9	hir worthi elderes hym be forne	they ben engendrid and I [borne] bore	ther fore
xxxi)	128ʳ	IV.1519–20	herde	he [saide] to placebo [saide] answerid .	
xxxii)	128ʳ	V.1521–2	be pacient I [say] pray	herken what I say .	
xxxiii)	128ʳ	IV.1547–8	I fynde in hit but [care and woo] coste and care	and obseruaunce of al blissis bare	
xxxiv)	131ʳ	IV.1785–6	hewe	his bosome [vntruew] vntrewe	
xxxv)	135ᵛ	IV.2127–8	manere	Bi p*ri*amus and by Thebes [and] may men [see] lere	
xxxvi)	155ʳ	V.823–4	comfortid hir in al that eu*ere* they [myght] may .	day .	
xxxvii)	155ᵛ	V.861–2	than wolde hir herte quake | that on hir fete she myght not [stonde] sustene	grene	
xxxviii)	156ᵛ	V.937–8	venus	that clepid was [aurilius] Aurilius	
xxxix)	157ʳ	V.989–90	bi hie god aboue[n]	loue	
xl)	161ᵛ	V.1313–14	displese	I. fore. you haue suche [distresse] disese .	
xli)	162ᵛ	V.1391–2	hir armes too .	wolde she nott goo[n]	
xlii)	163ᵛ	V.1521–2	in eu*ery* [thinge] side	abide	
xliii)	165ʳ	V.1621–2	lordynges this question then wolde I axe [you] nowe	you	
xliv)	172ʳ	VII.530–2	he	ou*r* blisful lady [dere] free .	
xlv)	173ʳ	VII.594–7	mynde	Cristis modir meke and [mylde] kynde	fynde[4]
xlvi)	180ᵛ	VI.797–8	to bringe vs brede and drinke [of the beste] ful preuyly	subtilly .	
xlvii)	181ʳ	V.845–6	biee	his felowes twey[n][e]	
xlviii)	183ʳ	II.7–8	and sawe wel that the shadewe of eu*ery* [man] tre	was as in lengthe the same quantite	
xlix)	186ʳ	II.261–4	this woful day fatal is com[e]	al and som	ou*ere* come
l)	192ᵛ	II.751–4	creature	non so hardy was | that ony while durst ther in [a bide] endure .	auenture

Table 9.1 *cont.*

	folio	Tales	first rhyme	second rhyme	third rhyme
li)	196r	II.1002–4	senatour	Euerich of hem doth othir grete [reue*re*nce] honour*e*	
lii)	200v–201r	VII.915–18	well.	as did sir [p*e*rciual] . perciuelle	
liii)	223r	VII.2151–3	riall.	makid eche of hem to ben his [thralle] cherle .	
liv)	223v	VII.2196–8	oute of the Temple of Ier*usa*lem [brought] bi rafte	lafte	
lv)	227v	VII.2543	in to a gardyn fande he ^ [cherl*is*] ^ twey[ne] *in the margin:* ^cherlis	*see subsequent*	
lvi)	227v	VII.2545	*see previous*	to the Cherlis. twey he ganne to [sey] p*er*rey	
lvii)	229r	VII.2631–3	The scorne of Alisaundre is so [knowe] co*mm*vne	fortune	
lviii)	231r	VII.2807–8	tolde .	than spake oure hoste with reude speche and [boste] bolde	
lix)	232v	VII.2905–6	with glowyng eien twey[ne]	I sey	
lx)	236r	VII.3195–6	twenty degrees. and on and [more I wis] . somwhat more	lore.	
lxi)	238r	VII.3337–8	suyd .	that maiste nought be*n* [denyed] ^ eschewid	
lxii)	239r	VII.3429–30	flaterie	wynke with myn eie[n]	
lxiii)	240v	VIII.106–8	to sey	the sonne and the mone and st*er*res eu*ery* [where] . wey .	
lxiv)	253v	VIII.1094–5	Euer whanne I speke. of his [falsnesse] falshede .	rede	
lxv)	255v	VIII.1274–5	I prey for his [falsnesse] falshede .	dede	
lxvi)	255v	VIII.1280–1	welle muste [nede[s]] nede	spede	
lxvii)	261r	IX.289–90	a thousand [f] folke haue for rakil[nesse] ire	mire .	

[1] The scribe adds this line in the margin later.
[2] *Sic.*
[3] The preceding line ends 'yif hit your will be .' (*Tales*, IV.109).
[4] The second and third rhymes in (xlv) are switched in order to fit into this table.

care' (xxxiii), and the Host might speak 'with reude speche and boste', a hendiadys of two nouns, as much as 'with reude speche and bolde', one noun with two adjectives (lviii). One correction even swaps the interchangeable heroes 'palamon and Arcite' round into '[palamon and] Arcite and Palamon', in order to preserve the sound-pattern.[29] Given that there is already one half of the correct doublet present to convey the narrative sense, and given that even the stylistic fashion for doublets has been met, then the correction seems pointless. It is only the rhyme which demands that the scribe pay attention to Chaucer's exact wording.

This switching of doublets is not unique,[30] and all this care could just be part of the general tendency to seek centripetal accuracy: of the sixty-seven corrections to rhymes here, only four are not centripetal in restoring the text established by modern editors (i, xvii, liii, lvi).[31] Yet this scribe is not consistently attentive elsewhere; other errors of duplication or spelling are left uncorrected in the middle of lines where the rhyme is corrected (lxiv, lxv). The rhyme seems to wake him up at the line's end. An interesting analogy can be drawn here with a comment by the poet Susan Stewart: she notes from research into language acquisition that rhyme helps children to distinguish words from each other, and she suggests that 'In attending to rhyme in poems' as adults we likewise 'renew' our understanding of words and their various likenesses and differences of sound and sense.[32] I speculate that rhyme similarly invites scribes to pay renewed attention to the text and why one word is better than another. It is not that correcting inspired by rhyme is more important or more frequent than other correcting; verse in the Huntington Library's sample is only a little more frequently corrected (as was noted) and is not all rhymed, of course. But when rhyme *is* involved, then it might be helping to foster the scribes' intelligent attention.

In these ways rhyme might influence the pace of writing and the precision of the scribe's reading of his exemplar; his craftsmanship might be shaped by verse-form. Errors of eyeskip suggest that rhyme-words – spatially and aurally prominent – are used by scribes to orientate themselves on the

[29] This assumes in (iv) that the scribe writes the rhyme-word prematurely and so crosses it out and writes it again in rhyming position; it is possible that he duplicates it midline and so merely crosses out the first instance. There is no way to know for sure.

[30] E.g., BodL, MS Arch. Selden B.14, f. 44[r] (*Tales*, 1.2901–2), 'yghen [weete *and*] rede *and* wete', rhyming with 'strete'.

[31] Of the four, three are only slightly wrong: (i) has the correct word 'hade' but uses it as the noun *hood*; (xvii) is an explicable misreading of 'yare', given the likeness of **þ** to y; (lvi) is only an odd spelling of *pray* adding an abbreviation for *er*. Only (liii) disrupts the rhyme and the accuracy alike.

[32] Stewart, 'Rhyme and Freedom', 42.

page when they glance back at the exemplar. And corrections suggest that rhyme-words act as a check on the inaccuracy of that process. Thinking about verse makes the scribes move their eyes, hands and minds in new directions and speeds: it encourages them to slow down, instead of relentlessly hurrying through their exemplar; it encourages them to interrupt the flow of their work in order to look forward and backward to see whether one line rhymes with another; it encourages them to check the exemplar again. As Robert Kaufman puts it, in more abstract terms, 'material' – which might denote the physical processes of scribal labour – is shaped by 'an act of form'.[33] That is, while the physical, economic and dialectal pressures of writing might impinge on the transmission of the poem, conversely copying and correcting are themselves influenced by the form of the poem.

Rhyme and ordinary language

This influence emerges more starkly when we consider errors and corrections which challenge not only the pace of the scribe's writing, making him stop to correct himself, but even the ordinary language or dialect he uses. As has been repeatedly seen, many errors occur when scribes, writing quickly, paraphrase the author's words into conventional language and translate his dialect into one they prefer. So does the copyist of *The Canterbury Tales* owned by Leche: his errors are in simple and common English collocations such as *day and night* or *meek and mild* (xx, xlv, and also xvi, xlii, lxi, lxiii). For instance, when somebody should be threatened with losing his 'hed', it is unsurprising that the scribe instead assumes that he loses his 'lif' (v); the error is the familiar idiom *losing his life* which works in context. It even has a sound-pattern of its own; like many idioms, it alliterates.[34]

Yet the influence of verse-form then leads the scribe to distort this ordinary language and to preserve the particular poetic utterance. In his hurried copying he reaches for idioms which were becoming set phrases such as 'eu*ery* thinge' or 'eu*ery* where', but in his pause for correcting he restores Chaucer's less common wording such as 'eu*ery* side' or '*eu*ery wey' (xlii, lxiii).[35] In his copying, he omits some words which hindsight shows

[33] Kaufman, 'Everybody Hates Kant', 207.

[34] Sometimes, there are also visual prompts to error: in (li), the cue to 'reu*er*ence' instead of 'honour*e*' is likely the presence of 'Reu*er*ence' in rhyming position in the previous stanza (OTC, MS 49, f. 196r; *Tales*, II.1001).

[35] The spellings recorded in *OED*, *everywhere* (*adv.*), *MED*, *everiwhere* (*adv.*), *OED*, *everything* (*pron.*), and *MED*, *everi-thing* (*n.*), treat these phrases both as single compound-words and as two words; the collocations are well attested by the fifteenth century.

were obsolescent such as 'while' or 'in fere' in favour of ones which have come to replace them such as 'tyme' and 'to gedir', but then he restores the more archaic word (ix, xix).[36] It is possible that he simplifies and modernizes unwittingly in each case, as though the errors trip off the tongue or pen, when he dictates the line from his exemplar back to himself. But he halts this process and changes his mind – in a very literal sense, by reprogramming his linguistic repertoire. As Simon Horobin has brilliantly shown, scribes were often careful to preserve features of Chaucer's language which were obsolete but characteristic of the poet's voice.[37] Here the rhyming form helps: it does not quite 'renew' the scribe's knowledge of words, as Stewart put it, so much as remake it in old-fashioned style.

There is good precedent for altering one's linguistic preferences in order to rhyme. Poets exploit the changing and unstandardized nature of English to use variants interchangeably, preserving variety within their own usage. Chaucer himself oscillates between variant inflexions or spellings in order to rhyme, for example, using both 'liketh' and the elided 'list', or northern spellings in *–and* and southern ones in *–ond*.[38] By contrast, scribes tend to respond to the lack of standardization by translating their exemplars from one dialect into another, homogenizing what they find into their preferred usage. Yet it is well known that scribes do sometimes preserve the dialect of a particular text when it contributes to the poem's rhyme; they can eschew dialectal translation with 'sensitivity' in rhyme-words.[39] They very occasionally use the conscious process of correcting to counteract the automatic dialectal translation. For example, when a scribe of *The Fall of Princes* impulsively or instinctively spells the word *hand* with <a> as 'hand', somebody later notes that it needs correcting to 'hond', in order to rhyme with 'lond'.[40] These words tended to be spelt with <o> in southern England and, it seems, in Lydgate's own usage; but the vowel <a> used in the north came back into use further south during the fifteenth century.[41] Spelling with <a> clearly came easily to this scribe or the scribe of his exemplar, but the person correcting notes that this translation upsets the rhyme. In such cases, correction does not preserve the English language

36 Best traced in *OED*, *while* (*n.*), and *fere* (*n.*2); for the latter, most quotations after the early fifteenth century come from archaizing writers.

37 Horobin, *Language of the Chaucer Tradition*, 144–5.

38 Horobin, *Chaucer's Language*, 62–6, 73, 76–7, 81, 97, 109–10, 113, 117.

39 Benskin and Laing, 'Translations and *Mischsprachen*', 71; Horobin, *Language of the Chaucer Tradition*, 102, 105. But Horobin shows scribes insensitive to metre (102–11).

40 HEHL, MS HM 268, f. 25v (*Fall*, II.960–4). For a similar correction, see BL, MS Harley 4203, f. 172v, '[h<->]{ho}nd' partly over erasure, rhyming with 'lond' (*Fall*, IX.1182–3).

41 Rábade, *Handbook*, 158–61 (nos. 296–7); Lass, 'Phonology and Morphology', 46–7.

as the scribe evidently thinks it should be written; the rhyme requires an artificial, perhaps poetic language.

Examples are numerous among the other corrections to rhyming words in the copy of *The Canterbury Tales* owned by John Leche (Table 9.1); the scribe some twenty-three times corrects the spelling or morphology in order to assist the rhyme (iii, vii, xi–xiii, xvii, xxii, xxvi–xxviii, xxx, xxxiv, xxxviii–xxxix, xli, xlvii, xlix, lii, lv, lix, lxiv–lxvi and perhaps lxii).[42] This direction of influence is significant: it is not that the rules of the language require corrections of the poem, but that the poem's form requires corrections of the language. For example, two errors in writing 'falsnesse' in place of 'falshede' (lxiv, quoted in the epigraph to this chapter, and lxv; cf. lxvii) might reflect the declining productivity of the derivational morpheme –*hood* in the fifteenth century, as *–ness* began to be used instead; it is as though the scribe's first impulse was to prefer *–ness*.[43] But he corrects it back, less likely because he has a fogeyish or prescriptive preference for *–hood* and more likely because it had to rhyme with 'rede' and 'dede'.[44] Elsewhere, he shifts between inflexions with and without *–n* on irregular past participles and prepositions (iii, vii, xxviii, xxx, xxxix, xli), and between the variants 'too', 'twey' and 'tweyne' for the number *two* (xxvi, xlvii, lv, lix). In each case his first impulse is to slip into some dialect more comfortable, but further reflection leads him to realize the poetic constraints on his preferences, and he corrects the translation.[45] While both the scribe's and the poet's variants are acceptable English, only one is acceptable for the verse-form.

In a final few corrections this scribe had to correct his presumptions of what was normal English back to something rather abnormal, indeed, arguably wrong, as when he repeatedly gives the names of Chaucer's characters in more customary spellings (xi, xiii, lii) but then corrects them into something outlandish. He spells *Nicholas* in the Miller's Tale with <as>, but he realizes on two occasions it must end with <ay> to rhyme with 'day' (xi, xiii). This does not seem to be an otherwise attested diminutive of Nicholas, nor even a fair approximation of a French pronunciation with a silent <s>; the scribe elsewhere writes it as 'nicholas', where that

42 In (xiii) the scribe also skipped a line and added it in the margin.

43 The word 'fasnesse', a misspelling of *falseness*, might have prompted the error in (lxiv): OTC, MS 49, f. 253^{v} (*Tales*, VIII.1093). *OED*, *–hood* (*suffix*), and *–ness* (*suffix*) show that the morpheme *–hood* was less productive by the fifteenth century.

44 For another change of *–ness* to *–hood*, see PML, MS M.124, f. 21^{r}, correcting 'frendly‸^{hede}[nesse]' to rhyme with 'dreede' (*Fall*, 1.4003–4).

45 He also does this midline: e.g., OTC, MS 49, f. 10^{v} (*Tales*, 1.743, 'to for [yeuyn] yeue').

rhyme is needed.[46] Yet after the correction of this name, he manages to write 'Nicholay' on the first attempt in a later line, perhaps because he has become alert to the variant, or because this later use is in the second half of a couplet when the preceding rhyme, 'lay', would have warned him to use 'Nicholay'.[47] Similarly, in the Tale of Sir Thopas the name 'p*er*ciual' is crossed out and replaced with 'perciuelle'. In one respect it seems necessary to correct <al> to <elle> to rhyme with 'watir of the welle' (lii), yet in another respect it seems unnecessary. After the Tale of Sir Thopas Chaucer is told that his 'drasty rimyng is nought worth a torde', so it might have been acceptable to leave the rhyme of 'p*er*ciual' and 'welle' imprecise. Did the scribe change it to 'perciuelle' as a sincere attempt at rhyme? Or did he realize with sly humour that the poet was squeezing this word into a deliberately uncomfortable rhyme-scheme? It is not clear how ironic his thinking was, but it is clear that he recognized that Chaucer modified the spelling of names in order to rhyme them. Some other scribes share similar recognitions.[48] For example, in a copy of *The Canterbury Tales* by Geoffrey Spirleng (discussed in Chapter 3), in the part for which the exemplar survives there are eight corrections which modify the spelling or morphology in order to preserve the rhyme. Spirleng subpuncts 'Nicholas' and instead writes 'Nicholay', only on a second look seeing that his exemplar similarly has a final <y> in 'Nicolay'; and the scribe of the exemplar writes his <y> over an erasure, which one would guess was an erased <s>.[49] Spirleng also, like other scribes, corrects irregular past or passive participles with or without <n>.[50] Even in those odd cases such as names or grammatical inflexions, the scribes remake the everyday language they prefer at first attempt with a second attempt at poetic form.[51]

Some of these differences would require different pronunciations, but they would not always clearly do so. Many of the changed spellings suggest almost imperceptibly different allophones in sound but some notion of

46 E.g., in close proximity to spellings in <y> see spellings with <s> rhyming with 'Thomas' and 'cas': OTC, MS 49, ff. 48^{r} (*Tales*, I.3426–7), 49^{v} (I.3525–6). The spelling with <a> and the length make it unlikely to be a hypocorism.

47 OTC, MS 49, f. 53^{r} (*Tales*, I.3823–4).

48 E.g., correcting 'pandarus' to 'pandar[us]^{e}' in Durham, UL, MS Cosin V.ii.13, f. 51^{r} (*Troilus*, III.1105).

49 GUL, MS Hunter 197 (U.1.1), f. 18^{v} (*Tales*, I.3437–8), copying CUL, MS Mm.2.5, f. 37^{v}. Spirleng gets it right elsewhere, rhyming 'Nicholay' with 'leye' (f. 19^{v}; *Tales*, I.3647–8).

50 E.g., GUL, MS Hunter 197 (U.1.1), f. 3^{v} (*Tales*, I.795–6, 'by fallen' crossing out <n> and an otiose macron above it to give 'by falle[n]' rhyming with 'ale'), copying CUL, MS Mm.2.5, f. 9^{v} ('be falle', 'ale'); Chicago, Newberry Library, MS f33.7, ff. 21^{v} ('ben' corrected to 'be[n]'; *Regiment*, 1439), 69^{v} ('drawen' to 'dradde'; *Regiment*, 4782); BodL, MS Rawl. poet. 163, f. 94^{r} ('dyspose' to 'dyspo[se]^{ne}' rhyming with 'done'; *Troilus*, V.300–1).

51 In Table 9.1, there is one counter-example where the correction disrupts the rhyme (xxvii). But he elsewhere leaves 'ytaile' rhyming with 'faile' (OTC, MS 49, f. 226^{v}; *Tales*, VII.2460–2).

acceptable spelling. With 'p*er*ciual' and 'perciuelle' it is debatable how different the two final syllables would sound. If the vowel were in unstressed position, either <a> or <e> could be realized identically as schwa (/ə/, like the identical vowel sounds of the last two syllables in *syllable*). Elsewhere, fretting how to spell the diphthong in *true* and *untrue* or whether to have <c> or <s> in *vice* or a word-final <e> on *come* (Table 9.1, xii, xxii, xxxiv, xlix) probably did not much affect pronunciation.[52] So although the errors are caused by the habits of speech, as the scribe transfers the exemplar into his own dialect, the corrections, by contrast, look like care for the conventions for writing (like those in Chapter 7).[53] And even if the careful spelling were designed to fix our pronunciation as readers, it would still then be the mediation of the written page that was the concern. Or the concern might be to make the rhyming form visible on the page. This emerges when Spirleng, for example, corrects two rhymes in ways which seem to have little effect on pronunciation but do make them look more similar: he replaces 'hole' with 'hool' to rhyme with 'fool' and replaces 'ye' with 'eye' to rhyme with 'lye'. By contrast, his exemplar blithely rhymed 'fole' with 'hoole' and 'ee' with 'lie' with different vowels;[54] and both 'ee' and 'ye', for instance, are well-attested spellings of *eye*. But Spirleng seems to want the rhyme to be not only audible but visible in the repeated letters <ye>: truly an eye-rhyme.

A concern with eye-rhyme is not common but nor is it unique. Many scribes correct just one or two spellings in order to render a rhyme which was already audible more visible. There is often a fuss over long vowels and diphthongs (as in Chapter 7). For example, Thomas Hoccleve modifies the use of single and double <e> in 'appe^ere' so that its rhyme with 'cheere' and 'preyeere' is more visible.[55] Later scribes of *The Canterbury Tales* do likewise, for instance in modifying the spelling of word-final <e> as it shifted from a separate syllable to a marker of length in the preceding vowel or diphthong.[56] Arguably some such corrections make individual words difficult to recognize; but they do make the rhyming pattern visible. The priority of the pattern over the individual word is evident in some dubious rhymes in the poetry of Lydgate, and in the scribes' responses

[52] *MED*, *vice* (*n.*) records many spellings with <s> for the second consonant.

[53] The existence of such visual conventions is argued by McIntosh, 'Analysis of Written Middle English', 4–6.

[54] GUL, MS Hunter 197 (U.1.1), f. 16r (*Tales*, I.3005–6, 3015–16), copying CUL, MS Mm.2.5, f. 33r.

[55] MS HM 111, f. 29r (Hoccleve, *MP*, VII.18–21).

[56] E.g., BodL, MS Arch. Selden B.14, f. 44v ('popelere' corrected to 'popeler[e]' rhyming with 'laurer'; *Tales* I.2921–2); BL, MS Sloane 1685, f. 6r ('specialle' corrected to 'speciall[e]' rhyming with 'ryalle' corrected to 'ryall[e]'; *Tales*, I.1017–18).

to them. For example, one scribe runs into trouble with an envoy from Lydgate's *The Fall of Princes*:

> But touchyng that . he put hem in dyspence
> Caste hym nevyr . resortyn in ther da[y]{v}es
> List they wolde breke . the sentence of hys la[y]{v}es[57]

Lydgate has forced an uneasy rhyme between 'dawes' for *days* and 'lawes' for *laws* (as the modern edition spells them). This scribe, or that of an exemplar he follows, writes 'dayes', quite sensibly avoiding 'dawes', but then he needs 'layes' to rhyme. But that odd spelling is incomprehensible. Somebody then, whether the scribe or a reader, erases the descender of **y** to shorten it to **v** in the second line but also in 'dayes', too, to give 'daves', quite insufficient to render *days*, even if <v> were vocalic.[58] He leaves sense, sound and spelling in tatters, in order to preserve the visual symmetry on the page.

This trouble is most vivid in the work of the scribe who makes the most such corrections to eye-rhyme among copyists of *The Fall of Princes*. He has a fine handwriting modelled on bastard secretary with delicate calligraphic strokes and needless horns and spurs on his letters. His effortfulness and delicacy extend to spelling too, for he changes thirty-eight spellings which were already legible beforehand (Table 9.2). He also makes fifty more corrections which fix the rhyme, but in those other fifty the choice of word itself was wrong; the thirty-eight others change only the spelling.[59] Why? Three corrections were required to preserve the rhyme at all: the scribe on first thoughts wrote 'continue' and 'ytalye', but he shifted to the more archaic 'contune' and 'ytayle' which better rhymed (iii, vi, xxxiii) – words which vex other scribes.[60] Three more corrections seem based on etymology, as they restore letters found in the Latin or French roots of English words (xv, xix, xxvi); sometimes this disrupts the eye-rhyme.[61]

57 BL, MS Harley 4203, f. 75v (*Fall*, III.3225–7). Similarly, in this MS somebody corrects both or all three rhyming words elsewhere (f. 55v, III.1626–9: 'corrupcyon[-]', 'speccyon[-]' and 'dysposycyon[-]'; f. 78v, III.3842, 3850: 'dy[------]{spence}' autorhyming in a refrain.

58 *OED*, *day* (*n.*), and *MED*, *dai* (*n.*), record spellings with <u> and <w> used vocalically but not <v>, which in the middle of words would usually represent a consonant.

59 PML, MS M.124 also has corrections which affect not only the rhyming word but much of the rest of the line, written over erasure, in which it is impossible to be sure what prompted the correction. They are very numerous: a sample of just one quire checked exhaustively (ff. 73r–80v) has 86 corrections thus.

60 Cf., e.g., n. 51 above and GUL, MS Hunter 5 (S.1.5), f. 4r, correcting 'continue' to 'contune' to rhyme with 'Fortune' (*Fall*, I.692).

61 See the <e>, <a> and <b> respectively optional in fifteenth-century English but echoing medieval Latin *hebreus*, French *realm* or Latin *subtilis*, as noted in *OED*, *Hebrew* (*n.* and *adj.*), *realm* (*n.*) and *subtle* (*adj.*), and *MED*, *sotil* (*adj.*). In (xxvi) in Table 9.2, the change of the vowel does create an eye-rhyme, although the aim seems to be to restore the etymological <b>.

Table 9.2 *Corrections to the spelling of rhyme-words in* Fall *in PML, MS M.124*

	corrected word	*rhyme A*	*rhyme B*	*rhyme C*	*folio*	Fall
i)	*dead*	de^^{e}de	dreede		15^{v}	I.2869–70
ii)	*dread*	dede	hede	dre^^{e}de[1]	22^{r}	I.4162–3
iii)	*continue*	[continue] contune	fortune		23^{v}	I.4507–8
iv)	*sleep*	sle^^{e}pe	keepe		25^{r}	I.4787–8
v)	*counsel*	couns[e]^^{a}ile	tayle	disavaile	25^{r}	I.4811–14
vi)		Ita[l]y^^{l}e	assaile		28^{r}	I.5333–4
vii)	*chairs*	cheie^^{e}rs	yeeris		32^{v}	I.6264–5
viii)	*cheer*	cheere	cleere	Ryue^^{e}re	33^{v}	I.6400–3
ix)	*lead* (*v.*)	le^^{e}de	heede	dreede	33^{v}	I.6476–80
x)	*shed* (*v.*)	she^^{e}de	in deede		38^{r}	II.260–2
xi)	*head*	he^^{e}de	heede		38^{v}	II.365–7
xii)	*visibly*	[visibly] visibely	bodyly		39^{r}	II.447–8
xiii)	*again*	ag[e]^^{a}yn	slayne		39^{r}	II.477–9
xiv)	*manner*	mane^^{e}re	appeere		48^{v}	II.2239–40
xv)	*Hebrew*	vertu	hebr^^{e}u		49^{v}	II.2416–18
xvi)	*altar*	aute^^{e}re	*see subsequent*		51^{r}	II.2718–21
xvii)	*censer*	*see previous*	[censeure] censeere	cleere	51^{r}	II.2718–21
xviii)	*banners*	bane^^{e}rs	cheeris		53^{v}	II.3277
xix)	*realm*	Ierusalem	Re^^{a}m		55^{r}	II.3499–500
xx)	*tarrying*	comynge	tary^^{i}nge[2]		72^{r}	III.2318–20
xxi)	*bleed*	ble^^{e}d<e>	heede		79^{r}	III.3683–5
xxii)	*let*	le^^{e}te	seete	quieete	84^{r}	III.4622–5
xxiii)	*manner*	leere	man^^{e}^ere		86^{v}	III.5125–7
xxiv)	*transport*	rapoort	transpo^^{o}rte		90^{r}	IV.699–700
xxv)	*features*	fetur^^{i}s	vesturis		91^{r}	IV. 848–50
xxvi)	*subtle*	[sotell] subtyle	wyle		95^{v}	IV.1714–15
xxvii)	*lere* ('teach')	le^^{e}re	appeere		105^{v}	IV.3680–1
xxviii)	*maintain*	maynte^^{e}[y]ne	meene	greene	110^{r}	V.534–7
xxix)	*lead* (*v.*)	le^^{e}de	heede	feede	122^{r}	V.2867–70
xxx)	*consuler* ('consul')	yeere	[beggere] consule^^{e}re	cheere	125^{r}	VI.541–4
xxxi)	*matter*	mate^^{e}re	heere	entiere	126^{r}	VI.302–6[3]
xxxii)	*consuler* ('consul')	consule^^{e}re	neere		131^{v}	VI.1574–5
xxxiii)	*Italy*	yta[l]y^^{l}e	bataile		152^{r}	VIII.265–6
xxxiv)	*censer*	cense^^{e}re	speere		157^{r}	VIII.1268–70
xxxv)	*steel*	deele	[ste^^{e}lle] steele[4]		161^{r}	VIII.2064–5
xxxvi)	*contrary*	contra[r]y^^{r}e	Balisayre		167^{r}	VIII.3212–13
xxxvii)	*say* (3rd p. pl., pres.)	[seyn] seye	werreye		177^{v}	IX.1959–60
xxxviii)	*die*	d^^{e}ye	seye		179^{v}	IX.2273–5

[1] Subsequent couplet on f. 22^{r} rhymes 'bleede' and 'succeede' (*Fall*, I. 4164–5).

[2] In fact there are two minims and then an interlineated third one for the second minim of **n**, but the intention is to add **i** so I have transcribed it thus.

[3] PML, MS M.124, ff. 123^{r}–126^{v}, are bound in the wrong order (*Fall*, ed. Bergen, vol. IV, p. 84).

[4] The scribe first interlineated, then crossed out and started again.

But these are the exceptions; most of these corrections seem designed to create eye-rhyme.[62] In particular, some twenty-two times this scribe tinkers with <e> preferring a double <ee> (i–ii, iv, vii–xi, xiv, xvi–xviii, xxi–xxiii, xxvii, xxix–xxxii, xxxiv–xxv).[63] This is not an entirely happy process, because some of Lydgate's rhymes were strained: 'shede' for the past participle *shed* was Lydgate's poor rhyme for 'in deede' before this scribe turned it into the even poorer 'she^^{e}de' (x). Like this, some of the corrections seem likely to impede communication by blurring the phonological distinctions between different words, so that *head* and *heed* look alike, or so that *cheers* and *chairs* look alike to rhyme with *banners* and *years* (viii, xi, xviii). Other corrected spellings just seem counterintuitive, as the spelling makes the meaning or grammar difficult to parse. For example, six corrections put a double <ee> in the second syllable of *river*, *manner*, *altar*, *banner* or *censer*, which would seem to place the stress on the second syllable (viii, xiv, xvi, xviii, xxiii, xxxiv). The second syllables of these words have varied etymologies, morphemes and pronunciations; all that seems to unite them is the need to look as though they rhyme with words spelled with double <ee>. The concern is not so much with clear communication, nor even with sound; the concern instead seems to be that the rhyme should be as visible as possible on this scribe's elegant pages.

Forming the page

Some of these changes to rhyme, then, are urgently required, when they prevent the drift to paraphrase or dialectal translation; others are less needful, when they wrench the spelling to create visual patterns. But in each case, something similar occurs: the scribes let poetic form mould their working process. They reflect on their craft of copying and they change the visual artefact of the book, as a striking result of their thinking about poetic form. When a scribe recognizes and remedies an eye-rhyme, he thinks beyond the unspooling of the text line by line to think about the page as a whole. An eye-rhyme is important not as an accurate rendering of any word on its own (unlike the careful spellings in Chapter 7) but in relation to other spellings nearby. Such corrections betray a more 'oculocentric' or bird's-eye view of the poem's form and how it holds

62 Only the <n> in (xxxvii) would seriously mar the rhyme.

63 The scribe of PML, MS M.124, also tinkers with the problematic diphthong now spelled <ai> six times, if one includes 'yta[l]^^{y}le' and 'contra[r]y^^{r}e' (v, vi, xiii, xxviii, xxxiii, xxxvi).

together.[64] That oculocentric perspective is part of planning a book: pages are perceived as part of an arrangement of facing pages, one in contiguity with another, within quires.[65] Scribes exploit the opportunities for design, and the economies of effort, of such an overarching view of the codex. For instance, the corrected eye-rhymes in this manuscript of *The Fall of Princes* occur within an elaborate layout where each stanza is in a symmetrical position relative to others in the adjacent column and page, revealing the consistent pattern of Lydgate's verse.

That regular layout also regularizes the scribe's craft of copying. Copying verse from the outset – let alone correcting it – organizes the scribe's time, gestures and spatial arrangement of the page slightly differently from copying prose. The line-break requires a break in the flow of writing: a turn (Latin *versus*) of the eye about the exemplar and the hand about the page, sooner than there would have been one in prose. The arrangement of verse also helps the scribe to plan his layout more easily, for the text is in readily divided units. That is, the formal demands of verse guide the scribe's making of the page. Most of the time, the influence is imperceptible and the copying looks automatic or unthinking: the near-identical layouts in which several copies of some poems circulated often suggest the scribes' inert following of models rather than any reflection on verse-form. But the errors in such layouts do reveal the pressures a poem exerts on its copyist.[66] So do the corrections, and they sometimes reveal the understanding of verse-form latent in the practical and usually unreflective arrangement of layout. A vivid witness comes in a manuscript of William Langland's *Piers Plowman* copied in a monastic milieu around 1400 in a two-column layout like that of the large Latin prose works earlier in this manuscript.[67] The scribe often finds that Langland's long lines are too long for these narrow columns and some 125 times he must write the final word of the line in the space after a shorter line above or below, boxed in red; forty-five more times he does not realize that he needs to 'run on' thus until he has already started the final word, and so he subdivides it, half above or below. But twice he does not just divide the incomplete word but subpuncts it as an erroneous false start and recommences below:

64 For this term, see Gallagher, 'Formalism and Time', 306. 65 Mak, *How the Page Matters*, 14.

66 Partridge, 'Designing the Page', 79–80, and *passim*. Pearsall, 'Organization of the Latin Apparatus', offers the best case-study of such pressures.

67 CUL, MS Dd.1.17, ff. 1ʳ–31ʳ, described by Benson and Blanchfield, *Manuscripts of Piers Plowman*, 32–8.

And thanne wanhope to a wake hym so w*ith* no wille [ame]
For he leueth be lost . this is hir laste ende amende
And thay to haue and to holde . And hire he[u]{y}res after[68]

These amendments stop the poem straying out of the ruling. They also suggest – though he would not have used these terms – that the scribe fleetingly registers the tension between the poem's verse-form and the materials on which he tries to place it.

That attempt is registered sometimes when scribes endeavour not to break couplets over page-breaks, nor to disrupt stanzas there: the poem's verse patterning must not be upset by the book's alternative structure. One keen preserver of couplets is an early scribe of *The Canterbury Tales*. He is generally meticulous; he forms his handwriting with fussiness, separating the minims of **m** and **n** and putting little ticks on the bottom, and putting fiddly broken strokes into letters such as **d** and **w** under the influence of secretary script.[69] He rules the page for a regular layout of forty-two lines of text, and so could in theory end each page with a couplet closed, but the frequent headings and shifts of verse-form in *The Canterbury Tales* upset this tidiness. Nonetheless, he strives to end pages with the couplets tidily closed, as though to preserve the form of the poem despite the spatial limits of the book. When a couplet looks set to straddle a page-break, he modifies his layout to ensure that this does not happen. He has a variety of techniques for doing this. A few times he merely avoids using the final ruling;[70] twice he draws an extra line of ruling, visibly more roughly than the usual ones;[71] but most often he just writes an extra line of verse below the last ruling at the foot of the page.[72] He does not manage to keep all couplets from being split over pages: he leaves 60 pages out of 346 still with a couplet dangling.[73] But most such pages occur in the second half of the work where frequent shifts to prose or stanzas disrupt the layout too much. Otherwise, in twenty-nine places he corrects the layout in order to

68 CUL, MS Dd.I.17, f. 3^{r} (*Piers B*, II.100–2). See also f. 13^{r} (X.143), subpuncting 'gro' and starting 'grounde' below.

69 BL, MS Lansdowne 851: Seymour, *Catalogue*, vol. II, 134, suggests that the hand is modelled on anglicana formata, but **a**, **d**, **g**, **r** and word-final **s** all come from secretary.

70 BL, MS Lansdowne 851, ff. 5^{r}, 18^{v}, 22^{v}–23^{r}, 150^{v}, 223^{v}. Curiously, the cognate leaves of ff. 5^{r} and 18^{v} (6^{v}, 25^{r}) do not have an unused ruling; something more complex happened here.

71 BL, MS Lansdowne 851, ff. 12^{v}, 57^{v}.

72 BL, MS Lansdowne 851, ff. 16^{v}, 29^{r}, 39^{v}–40^{r}, 48^{r-v}, 53^{v}, 61^{r}, 83^{v}–84^{r}, 87^{r}, 102^{r}, 103^{r}, 110^{v}, 114^{r}, 131^{v}, 135^{v}, 144^{r}, 172^{v}, 174^{r}, 180^{r}.

73 Some 161 of 507 pages in BL, MS Lansdowne 851 end in stanzas or prose. Only once does the scribe add a line and therefore end with a couplet open (f. 162^{v}; *Tales*, VIII.942).

end the page with couplets closed.[74] Only a few other scribes correct the layout like him, in order to present couplets as coherent units: for example, one just once writes below the ruling and once ignores the last ruling to prevent couplets from crossing pages;[75] another begins at the Clerk's Tale with ruling for three stanzas of rime royal and blank lines between them (twenty-three lines), but after the next tale shifts to couplets he first writes below this ruling and then shifts to ruling for twenty-four lines in order to end most pages with the couplets closed.[76] These are rare modifications, but they show that scribes could be alert to the need to alter the book to accommodate the verse-form of the poem.

Such corrections which harmonize poetic and visual form are more frequent with rime royal stanzas of seven lines. In the fifteenth century it was common to present rime royal with a symmetrical disposition of the same number of stanzas on each page, unbroken at page-breaks. Chaucer's *Troilus and Criseyde* tends to be disposed in five stanzas per page, Thomas Hoccleve's *The Regiment of Princes* in four.[77] There is variety in all these textual traditions, but *The Fall of Princes* offers interesting evidence for the scribal handling of layout, because the copies vary a lot in the number of stanzas per column and the number of columns; in one instance, even the same scribe differs in his two copies.[78] The variation suggests that somewhere in the textual transmission choices were made, and correcting these layouts strengthens this sense that the scribes took a conscious interest in this method for displaying poetic form.

Roughly three-quarters of the copies of *The Fall of Princes* are disposed in two columns with five, six, seven or eight stanzas for each, usually with a line of ruling blank between each stanza. Each stanza is thus visually distinct; the regularity of the stanzas is visible; and the pages are individually and as

74 On five occasions the scribe also corrects the missing line that caused the page to end with a couplet incomplete: BL, MS Lansdowne 851, ff. 12^{v} (restoring *Tales*, I.906), 29^{r} (I.2306), 40^{r} (I.3240), 48^{r} (I.3896), 61^{r} (*Gamelyn*, 561). But on four occasions he remedies the page-break only and not the omission: ff. 16^{v} (skipping I.1250), 57^{v} (*Gamelyn*, 263–5), 84^{r} (*Tales*, V.414), 135^{v} (garbling IV.1817–19).

75 BL, MS Sloane 1685, ff. 49^{r}, 56^{v}, by scribe B of this MS, who copies ff. 46^{r}/10–62^{v}/36. Scribe A (ff. 1^{r}/1–46^{r}/9) positions his rubrics so that he ends every page with a couplet closed (except f. 3^{v} which ends with two blank lines at the end of a section); scribe C (ff. 63^{r}/1–222^{v}) does not seem to care.

76 Tokyo, Takamiya collection, MS 22: contrasting ff. 1^{r}–32^{v} (the Clerk's Tale ff. 2^{v}–29^{r}, followed by the start of the Wife of Bath's Prologue), with writing below the ruling on ff. 31^{v} (*Tales*, III.76) and 35^{r}, III.242), and 24 lines on ff. 33^{r}–77^{v} (from the start of quire V, including the rest of fragment III).

77 Edwards and Pearsall, 'Manuscripts of the Major English Poetic Texts', 264.

78 New York, Columbia UL, MS 255 (with a stray leaf in Tokyo, Takamiya collection, unnumbered fragment), has eight stanzas per column; Tokyo, Takamiya collection, MS 30, has seven. On this 'slanted hooked-g scribe', see Mooney and Mosser, 'Hooked-g Scribes', 180; and Horobin, 'The Hooked-g Scribe'.

two-page openings symmetrical. This allows economies of effort by ruling bifolia, the conjoined pairs of leaves, regularly in advance. Evidence that scribes of *The Fall of Princes* rule their leaves thus comes from mistakes in patterns of ruling, which tend to occur on pairs of joined or cognate pages.[79] The formal regularity might also allow scribes to calculate the materials required, duplicate their exemplar page-by-page in its layout, or even share the labour with colleagues by predicting where one stint will stop and another will begin.[80] Some such calculations are visible in one copy of *The Fall* in two columns of six stanzas each; in it, six quires and two further leaves are in different handwriting from the rest, but their similar appearance suggests that the division of labour was planned, and it is the poem's formal regularity which would allow this planning.[81] Moreover, there is evidence of similar organization being carried over to further copies, using this one as the exemplar, for somebody has entered numbers into this book dividing it up for recopying.[82] The numbers specify that the further copy will also have quires of eight leaves with two columns of six stanzas on each page. What is curious is that the person numbering the stanzas for recopying did not plan to duplicate exactly the layout of this physical *book*, following its page-breaks, but imposed instead his own page-breaks at different points, following the formal regularity of the *text* in its arrangement into stanzas. The future scribe's work, then, would be shaped not merely by the simplest economies of effort, perhaps by inertia, following a previous book as model; rather his work would be aided by thinking through verse-form.

Of course, some other scribes could have followed their exemplars unthinkingly and not reflected on verse-form as they made the layout

79 E.g., too many or too few rulings on BodL, MS Rawl. poet. C.448, ff. 41^{r}–56^{v} (excepting cognates 51^{v} and 54^{r}), with too few rulings throughout quires VI–VII; and BodL, MS Hatton 2 (*olim* Hatton 105), on cognate leaves ff. 21^{v}–22^{r}, 23^{v}–24^{r} (quire III^{6}), 29^{r}, 30^{v} (IV^{8}), 130^{v}, 131^{v}–132^{r}, 135^{v}–136^{r}, 137^{r} (XVII^{8}), 148^{r}, 149^{r}–151^{r}, 152^{v}–154^{v}, 155^{v} (XX^{8}), 156^{v}–158^{r}, 161^{v}–163^{r} (XXI^{8}). BodL, MS Hatton 2, is by the so-called 'upright hooked-*g* scribe' (Mooney and Mosser, 'Hooked-g Scribes', 182). Both scribes write below the ruling, add extra freehand ruling or leave ruling unused, as required, to correct the symmetrical layout.

80 Pearsall, 'Ellesmere Chaucer', 269–70; Edwards and Pearsall, 'Manuscripts of the Major English Poetic Texts', 264; Partridge, 'Designing the Page', 81.

81 PUL, MS Taylor 2, quires II–IV and XVI–XVIII are by hand B, and the outer bifolium of quire X is by a third scribe. Bergen, *Fall*, vol. IV, p. 82, suggests that they were 'supplied at a somewhat later date', but Hanna and Turville-Petre, *Wollaton Medieval Manuscripts*, 126, describe a 'main hand and two correctors'; the three contributions seem planned.

82 PUL, MS Taylor 2: 'Incipit q*uaternus*' or some variant on ff. 72^{r}/b22, 82^{r}/b29, 86^{r}/b29, 90^{r}/b29, 98^{v}/a29, 102^{v}/a29, 107^{v}/a8, 115^{v}/b22, 123^{v}/a22, 140^{v}/a1, dividing 32 lots of 6 stanzas, except twice where the counter overlooks some 'widowed' stanzas; then numbers 2 to 22 from ff. 90^{v}/a36–95^{r}/b22 (and evident erased ones from ff. 96^{r}/a22–98^{r}/b29); numbers 2 to 23 from ff. 98^{v}/b29–104^{r}/a22, where every fourth number has 'fol' after it; and letters B to S from ff. 123^{v}/b22–127^{v}/b30.

of books. Yet it proves difficult for scribes to reproduce the layout and contents of pages as though they are photocopying – at least throughout a whole book: they err and when they correct their errors in the page layout they have to think about the layout at least for the odd page. Even when they use symmetrical stanzas on each page, the ruling can go awry or omissions in the text can upset the number of lines required. When that occurs, scribes use a variety of tricks to impose the pattern of layout on the chaos of book production. They sometimes rule extra lines to fit a final stanza completely on the page; they sometimes write extra lines below the ruling; they sometimes squeeze the last three lines of a stanza onto two lines of ruling; or they do not use all the ruling if there is more ruling than they need. As a result, they preserve the presentation of a regular number of stanzas to a page and avoid breaking any stanzas over page-breaks. Some manuscripts use all these expedients in a long struggle to present verse tidily, as does one copy of Chaucer's *Troilus and Criseyde* with nine stanzas per page.[83] Such care to correct the layout suggests that verse-form is important not merely because it is an aid to the scribe's labour in dividing up his exemplar but because it is something desirable to see in its own right. Were the tidy layout only an aid to the task of copying, then correcting it would be less necessary, for as soon as pen were put to paper the division by stanzas would have done its job. Instead, corrections ensure that the symmetrical layout by stanzas is visible to readers, long after it has helped the scribes.

An aesthetic interest in the presentation of verse-form is evident when scribes correct it in what seem like needless ways. This attention is evident when they take trouble to leave a line of the ruling blank between the stanzas, separating them clearly. It was not standard in this period to use blank space to separate stanzas; more common was a paraph or other punctuation mark. A space between stanzas was 'reserved for the works of prestigious authors such as Chaucer and Lydgate', for it wasted expensive parchment or paper.[84] The scribes' deliberateness is clear when they waste effort, too, in correcting themselves. When they forget and start the next stanza without a blank space, they sometimes abandon the false start and recommence on a line below, leaving a mess in the space which should be empty;[85] sometimes, they erase the false start completely before they

[83] BL, MS Harley 1239, ff. 15^{r}, 18^{r}, 21^{v}, 23^{r}, 27^{v}, 29^{v}–30^{r}, 31^{r}–33^{r}, 35^{v}, 36^{v}–38^{r}, 40^{r}, 41^{r}, 44^{r}, 49^{v}, 52^{r}. The remaining oddities are ff. 22^{r-v}, 38^{v}–40^{r} and 59^{v}–62^{v}.

[84] Purdie, *Anglicising Romance*, 67; and briefly Parkes, *Pause and Effect*, 103.

[85] E.g., PUL, MS Garrett 139, p. 266 (*Fall*, v.2277–8). This scribe also rules extra lines to accommodate eight-line 'envoy' stanzas (p. 231, col. b; p. 232 col. a; p. 258, col. a; p. 261 col. a) and leaves gaps after such octets to ensure that the seven-line stanzas which follow do not cross a page-break (p. 323, col. a; p. 403, col. b).

recommence, leaving a clear white space.[86] Not all scribes take care all the time: the so-called 'upright hooked-g scribe', in his contributions to a copy of Lydgate's *The Fall of Princes*, sometimes cannot leave a space between stanzas as he has used up room on the page for a large initial; other times he perhaps just forgets.[87] But another lavish copy by the closely related 'slanted hooked-g scribe' shows the luxurious interest in the visual form of stanzas, and the need for correction to realize that vision. This book is in a remarkably delicate handwriting modelled on bastard secretary, with purple ruling and much gold decoration: appearances matter. So it is no surprise that the scribe corrects his layout in order to continue his orderly pattern of two columns of eight stanzas on every page. When he realizes that he or some assistant has ruled too few lines for the eight stanzas, then he adds one more ruling below; the extra ruling is identifiable because usually only the bottom two rulings extend into the margins, but on these pages a third ruling does too.[88] Sometimes, the scribe realizes that there are too few rulings before he finishes the column, and so he does not leave a gap before one of the earlier stanzas, in order to ensure that the final one will fit in the column.[89] By contrast, when he has ruled one line too many, he leaves two lines blank between some stanzas, so that the last line of text sits on the last line of ruling.[90] He conceptualizes the poem in blocks of seven and uses that idea about the poem's form as a guide to handling his materials.

The power of this thinking about verse-form leads the scribes to correct erroneously, as in one fascinating error in this copy of *The Fall of Princes*. At one point, the scribe spots that he has drawn one ruling too many on his page, and as he likes to end his columns neatly at the end of a rime royal stanza, he pre-emptively leaves two rulings blank before the last stanza, to ensure that he ends it exactly where the column ends. Unfortunately, he does not know or remember that not all the stanzas in *The Fall of Princes* have seven lines; Lydgate intermittently uses octets for envoys, and the final

86 E.g., PUL, MS Garrett 139, p. 130, with 'gaf' just visible under erasure in the gap (*Fall*, II.3752–3). For similar corrections, see Chicago, Newberry Library, MS f33.7, f. 28^{v} (*Regiment*, 1932–3); BL, MS Add. 21410, ff. 60^{r} (*Fall*, III.2135–6), 104^{r} (V.1656–7); PUL, MS Taylor 2, f. 98^{r} (*Fall*, III.4424–5).

87 BL, MS Add. 21410, e.g., ff. 101^{r} (*Fall*, V.1043–4), 102^{r} (V.1218–19), 102^{v} (V.1309–10), 103^{r} (V.1477–8), 108^{v} (V.2515–16), 161^{v} (IX.2244–5), 166^{r} (IX.3309–10), with space for initials, but no initials supplied, because the book is unfinished; and, e.g., ff. 30^{v} (II.980–1), 59^{r} (III.1883–4), simply forgetting to leave a gap. On this scribe, see Mooney and Mosser, 'Hooked-g Scribes', 182.

88 New York, Columbia UL, MS 255, ff. 3^{v}, 8^{r}, 14^{r} col. a. He also draws an extra ruling that he does not need and then spaces out the stanzas in order not to leave the last ruling blank (ff. 38^{v}, 41^{v}).

89 New York, Columbia UL, MS 255, ff. 17^{r} col. b, 18^{v} col. a, 18^{r} col. b, 20^{v}.

90 New York, Columbia UL, MS 255, ff. 14^{r} col. b, 15^{v}, 16^{r}, 32^{v}, 44^{v}, 45^{r}, 46^{v}, 50^{v}, 51^{r}, 53^{v} col. a. Also, he wrongly leaves two lines blank on f. 47^{v} col. a.

stanza in this column is the first of a set of such octets. Because the scribe has only left seven rulings now, he is forced to finish it with the eighth line of text 'widowed' at the top of the next column.[91] He corrects his layout, then, to achieve a tidy page in his book – and thereby upsets the stanza-form of the poem. This faulty correction suggests two things. In particular, it suggests that the prevalence of rime royal stanzas in courtly poetry after Chaucer misled scribes, so that they expected stanzas of seven lines more frequently than they occurred. There are also other occasions when scribes or illuminators mishandle octets, assuming that they are couplets or rime royal.[92] More generally, this fault suggests that scribes assume that verse-form will be orderly and consistent throughout a work. This is a false assumption, for English writing of this period is often 'unusual and unpredictable' in its actual form,[93] and many fourteenth- and fifteenth-century poets shift verse-form, as Lydgate does. But the scribes – perhaps because they seek regular habits of work – expect formal patterning to be regular. Interestingly, this mistaken scribe of *The Fall* does check whether his page has the correct number of ruled lines, as though he knows that ruling can be irregular, like other elements of book production. It is as though he thinks his idea about the poem's form is more trustworthy than his practical craft as a scribe.

His idea about the poem's form, of course, is wrong: an idea which the poet never had and which was not in his exemplar. Nor does this poetic thinking prevent him also treating his book, like so many copies of *The Fall of Princes*, as a material commodity, with its fine handwriting and decoration. Indeed, his concerns with the luxurious look of the page seem to drive his pursuit of the poem's form largely as a visual quality. This holds true of other scribes who put into practice their ideas about stanzas in disregard of reproducing the text accurately. Such corrections which disregard the actual text are rare: corrections are usually centripetal, of course; but there are a few. For instance, a scribe of Hoccleve's *The Regiment of Princes* twice makes a false start on a stanza, leaving no space before it; he does not erase and recommence but instead leaves a space half way through the stanza, after three lines; this corrects the symmetry of the page overall, for the subsequent stanzas can start in their due position, but

91 New York, Columbia UL, MS 255, f. 24^{v} (*Fall*, v.1590–7).

92 BL, MS Sloane 1685, f. 203^{v} (*Tales*, VII.2053–4), draws a paraph to divide an octet wrongly into a unit of seven lines, miscorrecting what he recognized as a previous paraph erroneously dividing them into six; BL, MS Add. 5140, f. 260^{r-v}, adds rhyme-braces to octets as though they are couplets and then, ff. 262^{r}–274^{r}, tries to fit four octets to a page, as his colleague had fitted four stanzas of rime royal (ff. 69^{r}–87^{v}, 129^{r}–149^{r}, 230^{v}–234^{r}, 285^{r}–294^{v}), but to do so has to stray below the ruling.

93 Cannon, 'Form', 178.

destroys the misplaced stanza itself.[94] Such people correcting thus seem more concerned with an idea about the look of the verse-form than with the actual text.

Similar priorities influence an odd and extensive miscorrection of rime royal in the Huntington Library's manuscripts. It is in an excerpt from Lydgate's *Life of Our Lady* in a miscellany copied in the last couple of decades of the fifteenth century, possibly by an Augustinian canon for his own use, in very current handwriting and on paper. The miscellany has only an excerpt of Lydgate's poem, about the Four Daughters of God and the Annunciation, which begins a series of excerpts from various works which together form a life of Christ. This scribe regularly compiles excerpts like this.[95] He does, though, preserve the integrity of Lydgate's rime royal.[96] Despite not ruling for the lines of text, he places the stanzas fairly symmetrically, four on each page. Unfortunately, at one point, in the middle of the sixth line of a stanza he or the scribe of his exemplar jumps, between recurrences of the word 'shal', from the penultimate line of one stanza to what should be the first line of the next. That he is able to jump and not notice suggests that he is copying an exemplar without clear divides between stanzas and that he is imposing the layout which highlights these divisions.[97] That he is imposing this layout is further suggested because, despite his eyeskip joining two stanzas, he still breaks his text and leaves a space after seven lines of writing, forming a false stanza with the rhyme-scheme *ababbde*, five rhymes from one stanza, two from the next; then the next block of seven lines has the rhymes *deeff* of one stanza followed by the first *gh* of the next, the one after that *ghhiijk* and so on.[98] Next, to worsen things, the text incorporates six lines from elsewhere in the poem;[99] and then the scribe makes another eyeskip between two

94 BL, MS Harley 116, ff. 2^{v} (*Regiment*, 106, 109), 3^{r} (134, 137). A sixteenth-century reader annotated where 'A nue Staff' should begin. *OED*, *staff* (*n.*) II.19b, records the use of *staff* for a stanza from 1533.

95 See Harris, 'Unnoticed Extracts', 179–80, 182–3; and Chapter 7, pp. 175–8 above.

96 HEHL, MS HM 144, ff. 11^{r}–20^{r}. Likewise, Harris, 'Unnoticed Extracts', 185, notes that metre restrains him from smaller adaptations in the Monk's Tale.

97 For such a 'continuous' layout of this poem, see, e.g., Champaign, Illinois UL, MS 85; but that MS does include the divisions into chapters (e.g., f. 16^{v}) which HEHL, MS HM 144, also ignores (e.g., f. 18^{v}).

98 HEHL, MS HM 144, f. 16^{r}/20 (skipping from *LOL*, II.300 to 302); the effect continues over ff. 16^{r}–17^{v}. None of the MSS which the editors of *LOL*, p. 14, identify as textually close to this one have this error: TCC, MS R.3.21, f. 99^{r}; CUL, MS Kk.1.3 (Part 10), f. 20^{r}; BL, MS Harley 2382, f. 10^{v}; BL, MS Harley 5272, f. 14^{v}; HEHL, MS HM 115, f. 25^{v}.

99 HEHL, MS HM 144, f. 17^{r}/9–16 (*LOL*, II.347, 615–20, 348). The addition looks deliberate, as it glosses a reference to a 'lyon' and a 'mayde' in the text here.

words ending <ste>.[100] After each error, the stanza-breaks get misplaced in a series of different ways, but the scribe continues breaking the poem into seven-line pseudo-stanzas with four disposed neatly on each page. He even ends eight of these pseudo-stanzas with a *punctus* and a virgule, giving them an air of finality. In disregard of the sense and the rhyme-scheme, and at the expense of mangling the rime royal, he has striven to preserve the visual form of four blocks of seven lines. Indeed, with ironically misplaced meticulousness, at one point he forgets to leave a line between two of the pseudo-stanzas, so copying eight lines without a break; but this upsets his preference for seven-line blocks, so he crosses out the erroneous eighth line, leaving a space and recommencing the eighth line as the start of the next false stanza instead (Figure 5).[101] He pursues visual regularity remorselessly yet is completely deaf to the sound-patterning. It might be that he is pursuing a visual model he has seen elsewhere: he knew other books set out in pages of four stanzas thus; for instance, he copies into this miscellany part of Caxton's printed quarto edition of another poem by Lydgate, *The Horse, the Sheep and the Goose*, which was set out by Caxton thus.[102] He also is touchingly unlike the poet Lydgate who, in the lines being bungled here, expresses 'drede of presumpciou*n*' in being able to 'wryte of any p*er*fytnes'.[103] Unlike Lydgate, the scribe is presumptuous about, and aspires to perfection in, the form of the poem.

Nor was he alone in this obsession with dividing Lydgate's verse into seven-line chunks regardless of actual stanza-divisions. Another scribe of Lydgate's *Life of Our Lady* also makes an eyeskip in the lines about presuming to be an excellent writer; as a result he fuses parts of two stanzas together into one new pseudo-stanza which he breaks after seven lines, regardless of rhyme and syntax. He, however, realizes quickly, in his very next pseudo-stanza, which he allows to run for nine lines until he can break it in the correct place for the rhyme-scheme.[104] Likewise, a scribe of Lydgate's *The Fall of Princes*, who does not otherwise set out stanzas symmetrically, skips a line in one stanza and so, in order to complete a

100 HEHL, MS HM 144, f. 17v/9 (*LOL*, II.369, skipping to 370); the effect continues over ff. 17v–20r.

101 HEHL, MS HM 144, f. 18v/14: after *LOL*, II.431, copying 432, crossing it out, leaving a space and then starting a new stanza with 432. He also corrects 'semphyne' to 'hevyn' in *LOL*, II.431, which editors think should be 'Seraphyne'.

102 John Lydgate, *The hors. the shepe* and *the ghoos* (Westminster: Caxton, 1476; *STC* 17019). Yet oddly, HEHL, MS HM 144, ff. 141v–145v, transfers that text into a layout with five stanzas per page.

103 HEHL, MS HM 144, f. 18r–v (*LOL*, II.403, 411, 413, 418, 419, 423–4).

104 CUL, MS Kk.1.3 (Part 10), f. 22r, skipping *LOL*, II.426–30, and breaking stanzas wrongly between 431–2. Intriguingly, this false stanza-break falls where the scribe of HEHL, MS HM 144, f. 18v, corrects his false break (n. 101 above). Although the MSS are textually close, this shared false stanza-break arises by coincidence from different errors.

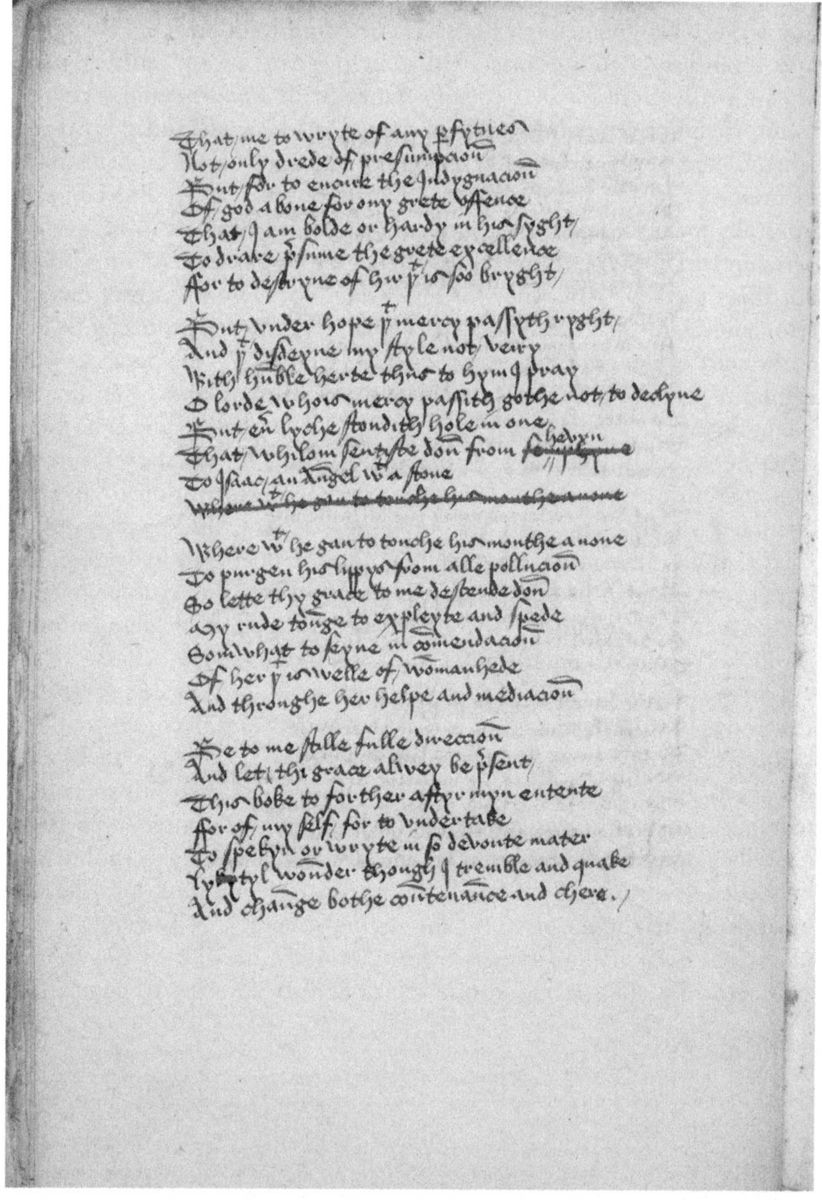

That me to wryte of any [illegible]
Not only drede of presumpcion
But for to eschue the indygnacion
Of god above for ony grete offence
That I am bolde or hardy in his syght
To drawe presume the grete excellence
For to descryve of hir that is so bryght

But under hope that mercy passyth ryght
And that dysdeyne my style not very
With humble herte thus to hym I pray
O lorde whos mercy passith gothe not to declyne
But ever lyche stondith hole in one
That whilom sentyde don from hevyn [illegible]
To Isaac an angel with a stone
[illegible]

Where with he gan to touche his mouthe anone
To purgen his lippys from alle pollucion
So lette thy grace to me descende don
My rude tonge to expleyte and spede
Somwhat to seyne in comendacion
Of her that is welle of womanhede
And throughe her helpe and mediacion

Be to me stille fulle direccion
And let thi grace alwey be present
This boke to forther after myn entente
For of my self for to undertake
To spekyn or wryte in so devoute mater
Lytyl wonder though I tremble and quake
And change bothe contenance and chere.

Figure 5 HEHL, MS HM 144, f. 18v: the correction of misdivided stanzas in John Lydgate's *Life of Our Lady*

set of seven lines, ends that false stanza with what should be the first *a* rhyme of the next; and he continues to the end of the chapter of the poem malformed thus, rhyming *babbccd*, *edeeffg* and so on for a few pages. The same error recurs later, causing fourteen more stanzas to rhyme like this for a spell.[105] These errors are extreme in their emphasis on visual order, but they exemplify how powerful the scribes' ideas about the verse-form are. As with a few mistaken attempts to conflate different recensions into one text or to supply adjectives where such hypercorrection was not required, so these wonderfully wrong corrections of stanza-breaks reveal the thinking behind the more common, more accurate corrections to rhyme and stanzaic layout. It has been well said, in one of the handiest definitions, that '*form is that which thought and things have in common*' and which reveals 'a bridge between the immaterial and the material'.[106] This is strikingly the case here. These corrections reflect not only the general carefulness of craftsmen but reflect too their recognition of verse-form and their desire to mark it on the page: some formalist thinking about literary works which shapes the practical craft of making and mending a layout.

[105] Philadelphia, Rosenbach Museum and Library, MS 439/16, ff. 53r–54r (*Fall*, II.1485–1666), after omitting II.1486, perhaps because of eyeskip with the next line; and again on ff. 69v–70v (II.4103–263), after omitting II.4107 and again omitting II.4212 on f. 70v.

[106] Cannon, *Grounds of English Literature*, 5 (his italics), and 'Form', 178.

CHAPTER 10

Completeness

[. . .] I goo nat vpright
but stoupe and halt / for [faute]^[lak] of eloquence

New York, Pierpont Morgan Library, MS M.124, f. 184v
John Lydgate, *The Fall of Princes*, IX.3387–8

The craftsmanship of scribes encourages them to pay close attention to the works they correct, but when scribes alter their spelling or the layout on the page, their practical activities are influenced by their thinking about verse-form. Ideas influence also another aspect of correcting: a concern for the completeness of texts. Identifying where a work is incomplete and how to complete it requires not only skill in craft but speculative, inventive thinking about texts. Those ideas are not only about the material text: while sometimes the scribes consult other exemplars to complete their copies, in order to spot that they need to do so they must deduce that something is absent. As when they correct centripetally by conflating different recensions or when they presume that verse-form will be more consistent than it actually is, so when they seek completeness they worry that a better text might survive elsewhere, in books other than those they possess: an immaterial text, so to speak. What influence them are their ideas about the text – how big it is, how it should be structured. Like the assumptions about the possibility of a single version of *The Prick of Conscience* or the precision of Lydgate's vocabulary, it sometimes seems that these ideas are more real to the scribe than the imperfect text he inherits or produces. These imaginings help the scribes to present and correct their copies.

Such ideas could seem a sort of idealism, like that for which modern editors are alleged to strive. But this is not quite or consistently so: rather (as Chapter 6 concluded), the scribes display not any idealization of the perfect text but the negative recognition, born from their practical experience as craftsmen, of the problems of the material texts they make and use. Their solutions to these problems with incomplete texts, as with variant ones, are often make-do-and-mend and so do not imply any idealization of a single, authoritative text. While at times they dutifully refuse to write what they do not know, at other times they simply hunt for a better rather than an ideal text; and occasionally they even invent something to fit the physical gap and what they think should be there. As when they mistakenly tinker with style and form, again a few mistaken completions uncover the thinking about literature behind the practical solution of the craftsman.

Of course, the craftsman's basic task includes finishing the job and so implies an interest in completeness. That concern for finishing one's task is evident in the way that, overall, correcting broadly adds more to manuscripts than it removes. This tendency emerges in the manuscripts in English in the Huntington Library, although it is not easy to see. A fifth of the corrections uses techniques which seem to delete things (22 per cent or 2,012 of 9,220), whereas nearly a third uses techniques which add things (31 per cent or 2,892 of 9,220). Moreover, what these techniques might be used for sharpens the difference: the techniques used for adding words cannot be used for removing things; by contrast, the techniques which seem to delete text can be used to add more as well. This occurs when the scribe commits eyeskip or anticipation, jumping forward in the text, but realizes immediately that he has omitted something; often then he crosses out or subpuncts the premature words and recommences with the missing words before reaching the previously premature ones in due course: here deletion is used not to cut but to complete. The process of adding text, then, is more frequent than the 31 per cent of corrections using techniques which involve adding to the page.

Furthermore, nearly half the corrections (45 per cent or 4,178 of 9,220) both remove something and add something in its place; some do so by combining techniques such as crossing out and interlining, but most do so by erasing and writing over the top (42 per cent or 3,894 of 9,220).[1] While these combined techniques might seem useful to replace or rephrase, they are often used to restore words which were missing. This is how earlier monastic scribes had used erasure, and this is how some scribes of these fifteenth-century books in English use it (as Chapter 5 observed). It is of course not always clear what went wrong under erasures, but in many it looks as though the scribe has omitted something which he is now reinstating. For example, in a copy of *Polychronicon* in English there are 104 erasures overwritten. Some surely sort out garbled spellings or names,

[1] More detailed figures for the frequency of use of these techniques appear in Chapter 5.

as where tiny erasures occur mid-word, but others might remedy eyeskip where the scribe has jumped forward and omitted things. In nine places the erasure follows words which recur only a little further on, so it is likely that the scribe jumped from the first use of the repeated word to the second, omitting everything in between. This passage was likely first copied as:

> ¶ þe iiij from crist to þe comyng of saxons ¶ þe v. from danes to þe normans

It should be, and is now over erasure, copied as:

> ¶ þe iiij from crist to þe comyng of saxons ¶ þe v. from [->]{saxons to þe danes ¶ þe vj fr}om danes to þe normans[2]

In all erasures of eyeskip like this, apart from one,[3] the grammar and rough sense would have been fine were the omission left uncorrected, but the scribes restore the fuller, repetitious passages, as found in other copies.[4] As it happens, some of the decoration of this book is not completed;[5] but the scribes do pursue completeness in the text, using erasure and overwriting.

Chronological sequence and completion

Among the methods for fixing omissions, interlinear and marginal additions reveal the time delay and retrospection involved in correcting. Marginal additions only occur in 8 per cent of corrections (693 of 9,220) and mostly in a circumscribed group of about a fifth of the books in the Huntington Library's sample, including practical works or some volumes of religious writing corrected by other people.[6] Interlining is present in nearly a quarter of corrections (24 per cent or 2,199 of 9,220), occurring in all bar three manuscripts.[7] These two techniques make visible the fact that correcting occurs later than copying, when it is too late to fit the new words on the usual line. There is also delay and retrospection, though, in crossing out or erasing – necessarily done to what has already

2 HEHL, MS HM 28561, f. 44v (*Polychronicon*, i.iii.29), and also ff. 52r (four words over erasure after 'Cedar', i.xiv.127), 60v–61r (61 from 'cleped', i.xv.245), 93r (one after 'of', ii.v.227), 94v (six after 'þritty', ii.vi.243), 153r (four from 'in', iii.xxxii.39), 172v (three after 'of', iv.i.277), 176v (ten after 'shewingis', iv.v.335), 201r (two after 'Agarenes', v.xiv.17).

3 HEHL, MS HM 28561, f. 172v (three after 'of', iv.i.277).

4 HEHL, MS HM 28561, ff. 153r and 176v: some supplied words are not in the modern edition of *Polychronicon* but are in other MSS given in the textual apparatus.

5 Driver and Orr, 'Decorating and Illustrating the Page', 111–12.

6 See Chapter 5, pp. 114–15 above.

7 HEHL, MS HM 26054, *arma Christi*, a short roll with one correction; MS El. 26.A.13 (Part II), the short and sparsely corrected *Joseph and Asenath*; MS El. 27.A.17, the superbly neat 'Stafford' copy of John Gower's *Confessio amantis*.

been written. How much delay is difficult to describe securely, as Anne Hudson has warned.[8] With some crossing out, for example, we could see the scribe jumping ahead through eyeskip, realizing almost immediately and crossing out the premature words before he continues; or we could see the scribe duplicating words and only realizing much later. But however late, the quest for completeness disrupts the usual sequence of copying. This is obvious but the effect on scribes' experience of the text is intriguing. Usually the scribe copies the words in the order in which they occur in the text; the order of the text determines the scribe's movements.[9] But the synchrony of the text's sequence of letters and the scribe's workflow breaks down, both in skipping something and in striving to complete it: he has to stop and go back, and perhaps to move elsewhere on the page such as the margins. Sometimes it is not even the same scribe but another person who intervenes. Also, by interrupting the flow of copying thus, the scribe copies the text's words out of their textual sequence. This is a simple point, but the implication is that he attends to the text as something which transcends the immediate moment of his physical labour. Indeed, his thinking about the text disrupts and reorders the processes of making of the book.

Marginal additions illustrate the delay in completing the text and the scribes' and readers' continued attention to the text beyond the initial moment of copying. For example, in an early fifteenth-century copy of *The Canterbury Tales*, the first and main scribe some seven times skips a line at the bottom of a verso, the back page of a leaf. These skips seem to result from the practicalities of book production: as the scribe finishes one leaf and reaches for the next, he forgets where he has got to in the exemplar. But at all seven points the scribe completes the text later by tacking an extra line onto the foot of the page where the omission occurs, or on the top of the next page:

> And eke therto he is aprisoner
> P*er*petuelly. *and* noȝt onli for aȝer ¬ // who so kouthe ryme i*n*
> e*n*glisch p*ro*p*er*<ly>¬
> [f. 2^{r}] His martirdom forsoth hit am nouȝt I
> Ther fore I passe as lightli as I may[10]

8 Hudson (ed.), *English Wycliffite Sermons*, 140–1.

9 There is little evidence that scribes wrote 'by imposition' out of textual sequence, but Smith, 'Imposition in Manuscripts', 151–2, reviews what there is.

10 BL, MS Add. 25718, ff. 1^{v}–2^{r} (skipping and restoring *Tales*, I.1459), 2^{v}–3^{r} (I.1524), 5^{v}–6^{r} (I.1890), 9^{v}–10^{r} (I.2192), 11^{v}–12^{r} (I.2311), 54^{v}–55^{r} (VI.440, and 441 on the top of the second page).

That these lines are added later is evident from the darker colour of ink and the problems fitting them on the page; they have often ended up trimmed off by a binder. The process of book production, then, left the text incomplete, as the scribe turned his leaves; completing the text required supplementing those processes later.

The completion of the text out of temporal sequence emerges also in a late fifteenth-century copy of *The Canterbury Tales* in handwriting modelled on a slanting French style of secretary script written elegantly but also quickly. As it happens, this scribe too has problems with page-breaks: in his case he duplicates lines at the bottom of one leaf and top of the next, some twenty-one times; these he crosses out.[11] He also, though, has problems completing the text: eighteen times, he spots that whole lines are missing in the middle of pages and then restores them further down the page (Table 10.1).[12] His techniques show that there are temporal delays of varying lengths in this restoring. Sometimes he realizes his omission quickly enough to write it just a line or two later, and to signal the correct ordering of the lines with the letters *a*, *b* and sometimes *c* in the margin (i, iii, vi–viii):

Nowe have I tolle you sothely. in a clause
.b. Why that assembled was this company
.a. The astat the arraye. / the nombre *and* eke the cause
In southwerke at this gentil hostelery[13]

The other twelve times he restores missing lines at a greater distance, and likely greater time-lag, from the omission, for he has to insert them at the foot of the page, below the final ruling on the page, or on some extra ruling added for the purpose.[14] Indeed, in some of the corrections the scribe has already filled the page and has, in fact, already made the different error of duplicating the last line or two of this page on the top of the next, and so has crossed out that duplication before adding the missing line below it

11 BL, MS Sloane 1686, ff. 8^{v}–9^{r}, 20^{v}–21^{r} (two lines), 29$^{r–v}$, 55^{v}–56^{r}, 123^{v}–124^{r}, 129^{v}–130^{r}, 136^{v}–137^{r}, 139^{v}–140^{r}, 164^{v}–165^{r} (two lines), 168^{v}–169^{r}, 184^{v}–185^{r}, 188^{v}–189^{r}, 199^{v}–200^{r}, 222^{v}–223^{r}, 223^{v}–224^{r}, 230^{v}–231^{r}, 231^{v}–232^{r}, 237^{v}–238^{r} (two lines), 242^{v}–243^{r}, 273^{v}–274^{r}, 284^{v}–285^{r}. By contrast, only eight lines are duplicated in the middle of the page and then crossed out in red: ff. 22^{v}, 34^{r}, 63^{v}, 127^{v}, 131^{v}, 209^{v}, 261^{r} (in prose), 288^{v}. It is not clear what happened on f. 63^{v}.

12 Also, lines are crossed out due to eyeskip near the foot of a page with the lines written more fully afresh on the next page: BL, MS Sloane 1686, ff. 103$^{r–v}$, 128$^{r–v}$, 235$^{r–v}$.

13 Table 10.1, no. (i): BL, MS Sloane 1686, f. 11^{r} (*Tales*, I.713–16).

14 Usually there is only one ruling through the margin, but where there is an extra ruling, two rulings run through the margin; such through-rulings are not present on the other half of the bifolium. Only (xi) and (xii) were written on the planned ruling and so were perhaps spotted earlier, before the scribe had finished the page.

Table 10.1 *Lines copied out of sequence in* Tales *in BL, MS Sloane 1686*

	folio	*labelled* a	*delayed line* b	*copied after*	*any line marked* c?	b *is how many lines late or early?*	*placed at the foot of the page?*	*on extra ruling or without ruling?*	*after a duplicated page-ending?*
i)	11^{r}	I.714	I.715	I.716	no	1 early	no	n/a	no
ii)	14^{r}	I.921	I.922	I.926	I.923	4 late	yes	extra ruling	no
iii)	20^{r}	I.1284	I.1285	I.1283	no	1 early	by chance, yes	n/a	no
iv)	23^{v}	I.1487	I.1486	I.1498	I.1489	10 late	yes	extra ruling	no
v)	26^{r}	I.1641	I.1642	I.1651	I.1643	9 late	yes	extra ruling	no
vi)	34^{r}	I.2135[1]	I.2136	I.2137	no	1 late	no	n/a	no
vii)	37^{v}	I.2357	I.2358	I.2359	no	1 late	no	n/a	no
viii)	41^{v}	I.2615	I.2616	I.2614[2]	no	1 early	no	n/a	no
ix)	57^{r}	I.3573	spurious version of I.3574	I.3593	no	19 late	yes	extra ruling	no
x)	69^{v}	I.4340	I.4339[3]	I.4344	no	4 late	yes	extra ruling	yes of I.4333
xi)	75^{v}	none	*Gam.*250–51[4]	*Gam.*252	*Gam.*252	3 late	yes	no	no
xii)	87^{v}	II.41	II.42	II.64	II.43	22 late	yes	no	no
xiii)	109^{v}	V.165	V.166	V.170	I.167	4 late	yes	extra ruling	no
xiv)	139^{v}	III.1331	III.1332	III.1339	no	7 late	yes	extra ruling	yes of I.1339
xv)	199^{v}	V.1091	V.1092	V.1099	V.1093	7 late	yes	below ruling	yes of V.1099
xvi)	230^{v}	VI.845	VI.846	VI.873	VI.847	27 late	yes	below ruling	yes of VI.873
xvii)	231^{r}	VI.883	VI.884	VI.904	no	20 late	yes	below ruling	no
xviii)	233^{v}	VII.81	VII.82	VII.80[5]	VII.83	11 late	yes	below ruling	no

1 Also, the scribe in eyeskip first wrote the rhyme-word of I.2136 ('strong') on both I.2135 and I.2136, then crossed it out in I.2135 and interlineated the rhyme-word of I.2136 ('long').

2 Also, the scribe in eyeskip first wrote the end of I.2615 ('w*ith* his tronchon') on the end of 2614, then crossed it out and wrote adjacent the proper end of 2614 ('as doth a. ball'). This midline jump likely caused the scribe to skip the next line.

3 The lettering *a* and *b* here is the wrong way round.

4 Two lines are delayed and marked together *a* and *b*.

5 Here the scribe first conflated VII.80 and 81 ('And how that he. encresed were or noon'), then corrected the end of 80 ('dispended had his good') and supplied 81 in full below.

(x, xiv–xvi). So he has finished copying one page and begun the next, at least, before he restores missing lines; he is going back later. This might be when he rubricates the book, for he decorates the construe-marks *a, b* and *c* with red. Indeed, he uses red ink to adorn over half his corrections of all sorts,[15] so even if some of his corrections are first made in the flow of copying he returns and decorates them later. The complete text emerges from looking back at a later moment.

In a poem the recognition that something is missing might result from the listening backwards and forwards, from one line to another, which rhyme requires (as Chapter 9 noted). Once more it is possible that the echo prompts the error in the first place: all bar two of the lost and found lines in this copy are the second halves of couplets, so could be easily skipped by the scribe jumping from one rhyme-word to the next; five involve Chaucer's rime riche or a rime riche generated by a slip of copying, and this repetition might be especially easy to confuse (v–vii, x, xv). But, again, rhyme has a vital role in prompting the scribe to notice the omission. Few of the omissions obviously disrupt the sense; many missing lines are vapid phrases which offer mere description or recap something but are inessential for the plot. For example, there is a description of an animal which sees a hunter coming:

> .a. And heryth hym russhyng. / in the leves
> .c. And thynketh here come. my mortall enmy

These lines are a hugely extended simile, adding ornamental detail about the animal's view of the hunter, in order to describe Palamon and Arcite. It adds nothing essential to the plot to expand the simile of the hunter with this line on extra ruling at the foot of the page:

> .b. And breketh. bothe bowys / and the leves. /[16]

Similarly useless, when Dorigen is told that she has her 'lusty husbonde. / in thyn Armes', she does not need to be told that he is 'The fressh knight. the worthy man of Armes' (xv). One of the restored lines is wholly phatic: 'This is a verry sothe. / without. glose', a narrator says, and the scribe who has left the line out then slots it at the foot of the page (xiii). Why bother restoring that unless to perfect the verse-form? But rhyme encourages an 'oculocentric' perception of the text as something in which the parts

[15] In BL, MS Sloane 1686, up to f. 250^{v} 133 corrections have red ink added and 108 do not. On ff. 250^{v}–295^{v}, water damage makes it difficult to discern corrections without red ink; there are perhaps 22 more with it.

[16] Table 10.1, no. (v). The first rhyming word should be 'greves'.

must cohere,[17] so it encourages the scribe to interrupt or supplement his sequence of copying – the movement of the hand down the page – in order to complete the text.

Gaps: imagining a future text

Other techniques convey people's sense of the text's existence outside the scribe's material resources and his initial campaign of work. These techniques are when the scribes leave gaps on the page for the missing text, and when they or others comment explicitly on gaps. Sometimes the gaps and comments accompany each other, sometimes one occurs without the other. The gaps for missing text look like those which scribes leave where the exemplar is difficult to understand. Those gaps for obscure text tend to last only a word or two, though, whereas gaps for missing text tend to be longer, most often a whole line of verse or more. (The shorter gaps where scribes simply did not understand the exemplar are a different phenomenon and not considered here.) The longer gaps are a familiar sight in copies of poetry in English, as scribes work out from the verse-form that there is something amiss. But not all scribes spot these omissions or leave room to fill them later; and some make up the omission with spurious lines.[18] So what makes some scribes leave gaps? The gaps evince an interesting literary nous alongside a practical understanding of copying.

Deducing where to leave a gap shows once more the scribe's recursive thinking, looking back to see what's missing in what he's already copied; and it shows him imagining proleptically the completion of the text in a future process. The role of retrospection is evident in the fact that the scribes do not always work out that something is missing at the exact point where it is; they often work it out, and so leave a gap, a few lines later. This often occurs when they use the rhyme as a guide, for rhyme reveals that part of a couplet or stanza is missing only when the couplet or stanza ends, or ends too soon, and not necessarily where the omission occurs, in the start or middle. This is visible when the scribe of *The Canterbury Tales*, who adds lines with the construe-marks *a*, *b* and *c*, also leaves nine gaps or notes where he thinks that he lacks a line (Table 10.2). His reliance on rhyme emerges from his muddles, where there is a rhyme-word absent, but where some mangling of the rhyme-words which are present misleads him into locating the absence in the wrong place (ii, iv–v, vii, ix). What seems to

[17] For this term, see Chapter 9, n. 64 above.

[18] E.g., Edwards, 'Manuscripts and Texts', 79–81, finds this range of responses in one poem.

Table 10.2 *Gaps left for missing lines in* Tales *in BL, MS Sloane 1686*

	folio	Tales	*gap right, early, late?*	*note right, early, late*
i)	104^{v}	II.1056	2 lines late	1 line late: 'caret'
ii)	196^{r}	V.880	no gap	3 lines late: 'caret *versus*'
iii)	208^{v}–9^{r}	VIII.77	right	no note
iv)	210^{v}	VIII.181–2	right	no note
v)	211^{v}	VIII.230	1 line late	no note
vi)	224^{r}	VI.466	right	no note
vii)	241^{v}	VII.580	1 line late	no note
viii)	268^{v}	VII.1957–9	half a line late	no note
ix)	269^{v}	VII.2007–15	right	right: 'Adam'
x)	292^{r}	IX.123–7	gap not needed	no note

be a rhyme-word hides the omission; only looking back later when another rhyme-word fails to appear does the scribe leave a gap.

Likewise, many stanzas only reveal that they are incomplete when the scribe reaches the end and finds them short; that occurs five times in this copy of *The Canterbury Tales*. So in (i) the scribe is missing the fifth line of a stanza but only leaves a gap for it after the seventh, as though he only notices then. He does write 'caret' (*it is lacking*) in the correct place, as though on reflection he can deduce where the error lies. The delayed reaction to incomplete stanzas is especially evident when rime royal stanzas are set out in symmetrical patterns on the page, as in many of the copies of *The Fall of Princes* (as the previous chapter showed). The layout of stanzas seems to guide the scribes in spotting omissions in two copies of *The Fall* which are textually close (Table 10.3).[19] The scribes of both copies leave gaps where they think that there is a line lost: sometimes they get it right but more often they leave a gap too late.[20] There are two instances where one of the scribes leaves a gap too early, guessing that the first half of a

19 Chicago, Newberry Library, MS +33.3, and PUL, MS Garrett 139, with similar layouts, handwriting and styles of decoration. In the file at the Newberry Library, a printed description comments that these MSS are textually related. Notably, both MSS leave room for 17 or 25 stanzas respectively where 144 are missing (Chicago, Newberry Library, MS +33.3, f. 96$^{r–v}$; PUL, MS Garrett 139, pp. 197–9; *Fall*, III.4873–IV.728). The number 144 suggests that an exemplar antecedent to both copies had lost six leaves with two columns of six stanzas on each page.

20 Sometimes the scribes do not leave gaps at all: e.g., PUL, MS Garrett 139, p. 241 (for *Fall*, IV.201); Chicago, Newberry Library, MS +33.3, ff. 113^{r} (IV.3473), 113^{r} (IV.3489–90), 127^{r} (V.1764), 127^{v} (V.1884). Some unspotted omissions occur in octets; it is possible that the scribes are expecting rime royal and so do not notice when an eighth line is missing.

Table 10.3 *Gaps left in the right and wrong places for lines missing in* Fall *in PUL, MS Garrett 139 and Chicago, Newberry Library, MS +33.3*

	PUL, MS Garrett 139				*Chicago, Newberry Library, MS +33.3*			
	page	*line missing*	*gap left after*	*right, early, late?*	*folio*	*line missing*	*gap left after*	*right, early, late?*
i)	105	II.1699	II.1698	right	–	–	–	–
ii)	124	II.3323	II.3322	right	57^{v}	II.3323	II.3325	late
iii)	–	–	–	–	62^{r}	II.3552–3	II.3556	late
iv)	128	II.3645	II.3644	right	–	–	–	–
v)	–	–	–	–	67^{r}	II.4431	II.4430	right
vi)	143	III.292	III.294	late	69^{r}	III.292	III.294	late
vii)	174	III.2858	III.2863	late	–	–	–	–
viii)	–	–	–	–	105^{v}	IV.2238	IV.2240	late
ix)	220	conflation of IV.2453–4	IV.2452	seemingly right	107^{r}	conflation of IV.2453–4	IV.2457	late
x)	220	IV.2483	IV.2485	late	107^{r}	IV.2483	IV.2485	late
xi)	–	–	–	–	110^{v}	IV.3064	IV.3066	late
xii)	–	–	–	–	117^{v}	V.184	V.183	right
xiii)	–	–	–	–	117^{v}	V.201	V.200	right
xiv)	–	–	–	–	120^{r}	V.609	V.607	early
xv)	–	–	–	–	123^{v}	V.1175	V.1176	late
xvi)	–	–	–	–	125^{r}	V.1425	V.1428	late
xvii)	267	V.2415	V.2414	right	–	–	–	–
xviii)	–	–	–	–	129^{v}	V.2219	V.2221	late
xix)	–	–	–	–	139^{v}	VI.777	VI.775	early
xx)	–	–	–	–	149^{r}	VI.1349	VI.1351	late
xxi)	–	–	–	–	153^{v}	VI.2454–5	VI.2453	right
xxii)	–	–	–	–	157^{v}	VI.3266	VI.3269	late
xxiii)	–	–	–	–	159^{r}	VI.3664–5	VI.3668	late
xxiv)	330	conflation of VII.863–64	VII.865	late	–	–	–	–

couplet is missing when it is the second half (xiv, xix).[21] But frequently the scribes register something missing only when they reach the end of a stanza. In particular, often a line is missing from the middle of a stanza, especially the fifth line, the uneasy shift from cross-rhyme to couplets, but a scribe only leaves a space at the end. Of course, it might not always be the current scribes who spot the omission; they might inherit the gaps from their exemplars: that looks possible where both manuscripts leave a gap

[21] Oxford, Corpus Christi College, MS 242, f. 24^{r} (*Fall*, I.2450), also has a gap left too early once, where a second person then added the missing line in the correct order.

too late (vi, x). But the other gaps look unlikely to come from previous exemplars, at least not from similar ones, for they mostly occur at different points in each copy (as Table 10.3 shows); indeed, twice the slightly more adept scribe of one copy puts a gap in what looks like the proper position whereas the other puts it too late (ii, ix).[22] Such divergences suggest that the scribes are spotting omissions independently by their own reflection on the stanzaic form.

This reflection about stanzas is likely not driven by an interest in poetics, for it is part of the practical processes of book production. The scribes are, presumably, just trying to finish the job. They leave gaps to help themselves, their colleagues or their readers to be wary of unfinished business and perhaps to finish it later with some other exemplar or other assistance. The gap reflects a realistic expectation that making a manuscript could involve different stages of work with different exemplars, tools and personnel. Leaving gaps is a normal part of a scribe's work; they leave gaps for adding material in red ink or for illuminations. These practicalities are evident in the Huntington Library's sample where gaps for whole missing lines appear mostly in the more lavish manuscripts which bear signs of several stages of writing, checking and decorating, or at least the expectation of such: notably, in four copies of prestigious works of English verse, two of them expensively made: copies of Hoccleve's *The Regiment of Princes*, where room is left for a missing stanza, and Lydgate's *The Fall of Princes*, with a few gaps for lines.[23] In the latter, the scribe might well have expected that somebody else would fill the gaps later, for his work was checked extremely carefully in a second stage by somebody who spotted miscopied words and wrote the right ones in the margins, as prompts for the scribe to come along and enter them in a third stage; somebody also wrote 'ex*aminatur*' at the end of quires to verify that it was checked.[24] Similarly, another copy of *The Fall of Princes*, outside the Huntington Library, has several notes explaining where 'lakketh a v*er*se', 'lakketh vij v*er*se' or 'here lakketh vj balades'. This book is also planned to be lavish: it is huge in size and copied by several scribes in impressive handwriting modelled on bastard secretary script. The person who notes what 'lakketh' seems to be checking the copy against the exemplar, for he is able to deduce not only

[22] In fact, in (ix) the problem is more complex, but the scribe could not know that.

[23] Respectively HEHL, MS El. 26.A.13 (Part I), f. 28^{v} (*Regiment*, 603–9), and MS HM 268, ff. 96^{v} (*Fall*, IV.2483–5), 128^{v} (VI.1320), 144^{v} (VII.561). See also gaps in MS HM 114 in Chapter 4, n. 86 above, and in MS HM 140, f. 39^{r}, missing Lydgate, *Saint Albon*, III.752, which the editor (p. 162) records is also missing in another MS and is replaced with a spurious line in a third MS.

[24] See Chapter 4, nn. 96–9, and Table 8.2 above. This is true also of the copy of *Regiment* in HEHL, MS El. 26.A.13 (Part I).

lines missing within stanzas, which rhyme would reveal, but also where one or more complete stanzas are lost, and exactly how many.[25] He could only spot these oversights if his exemplar reveals them, and perhaps because he himself makes the mistake, so he leaves gaps with a realistic expectation of fixing the problems later. This manuscript contains other prompts on errors, besides omissions, which give the text which must be inserted. One such prompt is marked with the abbreviation for 'M*emorandum*': this is a practical note of something to remember to do.[26] The notes on what was missing fitted into regular methods of book production which envisaged completing the book in stages.

Unfortunately, those stages were sometimes more imagined than achieved: many gaps remain visibly unfilled, although presumably filled gaps might now be invisible. For instance, the (aforementioned) copy of *The Fall of Princes* with notes on what 'lakketh' never had its correction nor indeed its decoration completed, for some reason.[27] In another copy, the missing lines were not supplied and the person who rubricated the book foolishly decorated the lines after the gaps as though they were the starts of new stanzas, with paraphs and coloured tracery.[28] Unfilled, the gaps end up less as aids to successful book production and more as unintended records of the scribes' thinking. They suggest both that copyists are aware of the vicissitudes of textual transmission or book production, of the limits of the material form of the text, and that they have in mind an idea about the text which is fuller than the books they can make. This thinking about the immaterial text is not always to the forefront of the history of the book; understandably, such study most often works 'against the abstraction of the text' to show that the literary work must 'depend on material considerations', as Roger Chartier puts it.[29] Of course, the gap reflects the scribe's hope that a fuller text exists in another exemplar somewhere. Yet in order to hope for another book, the scribes must also conceive of the 'abstraction' of the underlying text – its completeness, just as they envisaged its verse-form – as something which the text's material transmission has mangled. As Chartier also mentions, in a useful caveat, the 'variations' in material forms 'do not undermine the idea that the work retains a permanent

[25] BL, MS Add. 21410, ff. 71^{r} (*Fall*, I.4519), 113^{r} (VI.197–245, 252), 113^{v}–114^{r} (VI.344–92), 114^{v} (VI.503).

[26] BL, MS Add. 21410, ff. 63^{v} (*Fall*, III.2864), 67^{r} (III.3704). Also on f. 67^{r} a second person supplies III.3641 which the scribe has left out.

[27] BL, MS Add. 21410, e.g., spaces for illumination on ff. 54^{v}–55^{r} (after III.1148), 74^{v} (III.5152). Somebody did, though, apply a pale yellow wash to the first letter of most lines.

[28] HEHL, MS HM 268, ff. 128^{v}, 144^{v}.

[29] Quoting Chartier, *On the Edge of the Cliff*, 85, and *Inscription and Erasure*, ix, and also 31.

identity, which readers or listeners recognize immediately'.[30] In leaving a gap for more than they have, the text has some sort of 'permanent identity' in the mind of the scribe, if not actually on the pages of his exemplar or copy.

Deficit: describing what is not there

This paraphrase of the scribes' thinking is couched in terms which they do not use, but they, their colleagues and their readers do have words to refer to the immaterial text. While gaps only imply awareness of the text beyond the book, there are also written comments which state explicitly that the text itself has a wholeness that the book in hand does not. People write in the margins of incomplete texts, sometimes next to gaps and sometimes not, that something 'lakketh', as in the copy of *The Fall of Princes*. Outright comment by scribes on textual errors is rare and mostly limited to these comments on incompleteness. There is a practical reason why: when people know what the correction should be, they can write the words of the text itself, perhaps in a prompt (as noted in Chapter 4), and need not comment further; but when they spot something missing, but not what, then the only way to respond is by metatextual comment like this.

The comments suggest therefore – perhaps more vividly than was true – that concern for completeness was widespread. There were certainly consistent terms across Latin, English and perhaps French. People write the Latin word *caret* from the verb *careo*, which might be translated as *it is lacking*, in various manuscripts (some described above).[31] They also write *deficit* or other forms of the verb *deficio*, which might be translated similarly as *it is lacking* or *it is wanting*. These terms are common, for example, where scribes find passages from single lines to whole prologues missing in *The Canterbury Tales*: one reader of such an incomplete copy can write 'hic defic*it* pr*o*logus'.[32] The term *deficit* had long been used by scribes of

30 Chartier, *On the Edge of the Cliff*, ix. Eggert, 'Brought to Book', 28, 30, also emphasizes the importance of the 'work' as an animating concept in the history of the book.

31 E.g., GUL, MS Hunter 5 (S.1.5), ff. 47v (*Fall*, II.1194), 49v (II.1488), 66r (II.4212), 142v (V.523), and contrast lines left blank without *caret* on ff. 67v (II.4436), 78r (III.1881). For other marks of *caret*, see also, e.g., BL, MS Harley 7335, f. 99r (*Tales*, VIII.553); BL, MS Harley 3943, f. 23v (*Troilus*, II.509); BL, MS Sloane 1686, f. 104v (*Tales*, II.1055); BodL, MS Rawl. poet. C.448, f. 65r (by a reader spotting a jump from *Fall*, III.959–1044, where presumably the scribe skipped a page of an exemplar with two columns of six stanzas); Philadelphia, Rosenbach Museum and Library, MS 1084/1, f. 7v (*Gamelyn*, 281–3, on which lines see n. 67 below).

32 Lincoln, Cathedral Library, MS 110, f. 182r (where the scribe left a gap of 23 lines between the Pardoner's and the Shipman's Tale). See also BL, MS Harley 1758, ff. 71v, '¶ Defectus. no*ta*' (*Tales*,

languages other than English.[33] Scribes and readers apparently felt familiar enough with *deficit* to abbreviate it to 'def', 'de' with a superscript 't' or perhaps just 'd' on its own.[34] It is difficult to be sure of the significance of 'd' on its own the few times when it appears; it could conceivably abbreviate some part of the verb *deleo* and be an instruction *to delete*, as later in the proofreading symbols for printing.[35] But one scribe offers both '+d' and 'defect*us*' in full either side of the same line, which suggests that 'd' did often note something missing.[36] These Latin terms are neatly paralleled by the English ones which suggest the language in which scribes and readers might chat about these flaws. The verb *lack* is common, along with some vague note of what is lacking.[37] The terms *fail* and *fault* also occur, as when the person who spots missing prologues in *The Canterbury Tales* also writes that 'þe p*ro*log*e* failleth'.[38] These English verbs *to lack* and *to fail* could both have the same sense as Latin *careo*: *to be lacking in something*. Likewise, the English noun *fault* came from the French *faillir*, and *faute*, and meant not a general error but a deficiency or lack.[39] When people describe the text explicitly, what they almost always describe is its incompleteness in or absence from the book.

People are often able to deduce an absence from what remains. In one instance, a copyist of Thomas Hoccleve's *The Regiment of Princes* finds that the sense jumps and writes 'no*ta* saltu*m et* q*ue*re .' q*uia* no*n* valet' which means something like 'Note the jump and look for it, because it does not work'; he sounds confused, able to see that something is missing but not what or why.[40] Commoner and more precise are deductions of what is

v.346), 167ᵛ 'de*ficit*' thrice (VII.800, 814, 824), 168ʳ 'de*ficit*' (VII.888), 180ᵛ, 'defect*us*' (VII.1754); BL, MS Royal 18.C.ii, f. 107ᵛ (*Tales*, III.188–94); HEHL, MS HM 115, f. 26ʳ (*LOL*, II.337–43).

33 E.g., in an early fourteenth-century book in Anglo-Norman: HEHL, MS HM 903, ff. 140ʳ (written twice, both erased), 170ᵛ (by a slightly later hand).

34 E.g., Lincoln, Cathedral Library, MS 110, f. 1ᵛ (lacking *Tales*, I.440–3); BL, MS Harley 7335, f. 90ʳ (jumping between *Tales*, III.2294 and VIII.1); New York, Columbia UL, MS 256, f. 6ᵛ (where Harvey (ed.), *The Court of Sapience*, 374, lacks 'powere'); PUL, MS Taylor 2, f. 25ᵛ/a34, 'd' (where *Fall*, I.4024, lacks 'no'). In Chicago, UL, MS 565, 'd' alone resembles the **d** in 'hic defect*us*' on f. 266ᵛ (lacking *Fall*, III.3815) but recurs frequently where no lines are lacking: ff. 225ᵛ, 228ʳ, 228ᵛ, 254ʳ, 262ʳ.

35 Noted by Grafton, *Culture of Correction*, 28, as early as 1475.

36 BL, MS Harley 1758, ff. 167ᵛ (*Tales*, VII.814), 168ʳ (VII.888).

37 See n. 25 above, and BodL, MS Rawl. poet. C.448, f. 66ᵛ ('lakkith').

38 Lincoln, Cathedral Library, MS 110, f. 169ʳ. The scribe leaves a gap on ff. 169ʳ⁻ᵛ between the Canon's Yeoman's Tale and the Physician's Tale.

39 *MED*, *failen* (*v.*) 1, 5f, 9a; *faute* (*n.*) 1a; *OED*, *fail* (*v.*) I.1a, II.6a; *fault* (*n.*) 1a (obsolete). It is not always clear which language these terms are: e.g., 'v*er*sus faut +' (Philadelphia, Rosenbach Museum and Library, MS 1084/1, f. 102ᵛ; *Tales*, III.1894) might blend Latin and English or Latin and French.

40 CCCC, MS 496, f. 48ᵛ, which jumps from *Regiment*, 4179 to 4390. Because 30 stanzas are lost, this scribe's (William Wilflete's) exemplar was perhaps set out with five stanzas to a page, ten to a leaf,

lost based on form or structure. Many people realize that the versification is incomplete. For example, one late fifteenth-century reader of Walton's translation of Boethius' *De consolatione philosophiae* into octets and rime royal counts how many lines are missing with terms such as 'fault ij' where two lines are lost and so on. He is presumably not collating, as he cannot supply the omissions; he seems to be judging by the stanzaic form – no easy task, as the stanza-divisions are not visually marked in this copy, and as the poem shifts midway from octets to rime royal. Evidence of his reliance on verse and not on collation is that he writes 'faut iiij +' by what seems to be a stanza missing four lines of its seven but where in fact the scribe has skipped sixty lines – perhaps two pages in an exemplar with thirty lines per page; the reader sees only what looks like an unfinished stanza.[41] Other people describe what is missing in terms of the Latin *versus* or English *verse*, words which meant a single line ('defic*it* v*ersus*', 'caret v*ersus*', 'lackketh a v*er*se'), or more rarely in terms of a stanza called a *ballade* ('here lakketh vj balades').[42] Interestingly, these recurrent terms bear witness to a knowledge of versification long before it was formally codified in English by the Elizabethans. But the comments on gaps extend to other aspects of the form or structure: 'h*ic* deficit v*ersus*' can note a missing biblical passage in a prose Psalter, and people pick out missing Gospel readings ('Hic caret vno eu*a*ngelio').[43] In the patchy textual tradition of *The Canterbury Tales* the scribes and readers are able to see where they are missing links such as the words of the Host or a prologue ('Allocucio hospitis def'; 'hic deficit | cu*m* pr*o*logo').[44] Those comments can extend even to tiny elements, as

like lots of copies of *Regiment*, and had lost three leaves. Wilflete also untangles a passage copied out of sequence (f. 56r–v; *Regiment*, 5022–99). On Wilflete, see Wakelin, 'Instructing Readers', 450.

41 CUL, MS Add. 3573, ff. 9v, 15v, 41r, 42v, 44v, 48v, 50v (miscounting two lost lines as one: 'fault j.'), 68v, 69r, 73v, 75v ('faut iiij +'). A note on f. 76r of '+ ii' might be in different handwriting. Walton (trans.), *Boethius*, ed. Science, xx, confusingly once describes this MS as being closely related to CUL, MS Gg.4.18 and Oxford, New College, MS 319, but also as sharing no common errors with those MSS (xxxii). As it happens, CUL, MS Gg.4.18, ff. 47v, 84r, has only two of the losses remarked in CUL, MS Add. 3573, ff. 42v, 73v, and they go unremarked there.

42 Respectively, CUL, MS Dd.4.24, f. 204r (*Tales*, VIII.711); Philadelphia, Rosenbach Museum and Library, MS 1084/1, f. 7v (*Gamelyn*, 281–3); Table 10.3, no. (ii), above; BL, MS Add. 21410, in n. 25 above; BodL, MS Rawl. poet. C.448, f. 66v (where no stanza is lost between *Fall*, III.1330 and 1331). See *OED*, *verse* (*n.*) 1a; *MED*, *vers(e* (*n.*) 1a.

43 Respectively, BodL, MS Bodley 288, f. 101r (cf. *MED*, *vers(e* (*n.*) 2a); HEHL, MS HM 129, f. 196v (*NHC*, 59.1, numbered wrongly for 25 Trinity, after the previous sermon, f. 193r, is numbered as 23 Trinity).

44 See nn. 32–8 above, and also BL, MS Harley 7335, ff. 90r (*Tales*, at a jump between III.2294 and VIII.1, before the Second Nun's Tale), 99r (VIII.553, at the end of the Second Nun's Tale, either missing the fact that IV.1, a prologue, follows, or referring again to the lack of words of the Host before this Tale at VIII.1).

when somebody spots a missing heading ('deficit rubrica').[45] From their previous reading, people recognize patterns in the structure of texts which allow them to predict what is missing.

Not all the comments do, in fact, rightly identify things missing. One scribe of *The Canterbury Tales* writes 'wantyth' (*wanteth* meaning *lacks*) next to a passage where nothing is wanting.[46] A few scribes and readers comment that something is missing, where it is only misbinding which has led to jumps in sense in this copy or in its exemplar; the lost words do crop up elsewhere. For instance, one scribe and a reader write 'hic desidiu*n*t duo folia' (*here two folios are missing*) and 'hic deficit' in a copy of John Lydgate's *The Fall of Princes*, where the leaves are merely disordered.[47] Another was copying a common version of *The Fall* in which a set of stanzas was out of order and he writes '<d>efic*it*', where the text seems to jump.[48] A third scribe of the poem skips a few pages of his exemplar as he moves from one quire to another, and, confused, writes that 'her*e* lakkyth a balade' or just one stanza; he then realizes, crosses out his note and begins the new quire where he should.[49] Such erroneous identifications suggest that one of the first explanations that came to mind, when people found things unclear, was incompleteness. In these comments, as in the gaps, they assume that the work exists in a better form elsewhere.

Collating and deducing omissions

How do they recognize and rectify these omissions? To see something absent is difficult. It might involve inherited knowledge, when a scribe's exemplar or a reader's copy already marks an absence with a comment or a gap (like those surveyed). It might involve deduction, when the verse, grammar or content of what survives lets one deduce, structurally, that something is lost. Or it might involve collation, when the scribe or somebody else checks

45 PUL, MS Taylor 2, f. 106ᵛ (*Fall*, IV.512).

46 Tokyo, Takamiya collection, MS 32, f. 123ʳ (*Tales*, VII.2170–1).

47 BL, MS Harley 3486, quire XIII, which should be read in the order ff. 92, 95, 94, 93, 98, 97, 96, 99, with comments on ff. 96ᵛ, 97ʳ and 98ᵛ. Latin *desidero* can mean *to be lost*; 'desidiu*n*t' seems a misspelling of that.

48 Chicago, UL, MS 565, f. 92ᵛ (jumping from *Fall*, I.5565 to 5864), and also 'No*n* co*rrigitur*'.

49 PUL, MS Taylor 2, f. 79ᵛ, ends with *Fall*, III.1330, but had a catchword for 2339, then corrected to one for 2340. This jump of 144 stanzas suggests that he turned over three folios of an exemplar with two columns of six stanzas per page. This leaf (f. 79ᵛ) was the end of quire X, which was on an outer bifolium added to quire X by scribe C, which probably explains the confusion. When scribe B transfers back to scribe A at the foot of f. 24ᵛ, there is a similar mistake in the catchword (I.3914), later corrected (I.3907). On 'casting off' this MS for use of it as an exemplar, see Chapter 9, n. 82 above.

the copy against its exemplar or a second exemplar, or collates the exemplar in advance against another. Editors often call this collating 'conflation' or 'contamination', because it is problematic for certain forms of editing; but it would be fairer to recognize the impressive achievement of such collation.[50] Both deduction and collation help people to restore missing lines, and while collation might seem likelier than deduction to produce good or 'centripetal' corrections, the motive behind both techniques seems similar: a concern with the completeness of the work. The different processes and results of deduction and collation, but also their similar underlying motive, emerge from a comparison of several copies of Chaucer's *The Canterbury Tales*.

Full collation of a whole text, in every detail and in its entirety, is arduous and might only occur in particular milieux or under particular influences, such as the zeal for communal correcting in religious communities (noted in Chapter 4). There are only occasional comments on the search for fuller exemplars in English, and usually in terms which imply that the search has not yet been done or has proved futile: a scribe of the prose *Brut* warns that he 'wanted þe trewe copy' and simply leaves a gap so that the reader might add more 'whene he gett*es* þe trew copy'; John Shirley reports once that he 'kouþe fynde no more of þis copye'.[51] Although certain groups of religious and scholarly readers did pursue and discuss collation, direct reference to it by fifteenth-century users is rare in books in English, although there are some such as the warning 'hic libri | no*n* co*n*corda*nt*' ('here the books do not agree') in the margin of one copy of *Piers Plowman*.[52] Ralph Hanna has warned that the supply of vernacular exemplars was 'an unfocused, arbitrary, fitful process', and that this 'exemplar poverty' might militate against collation of multiple exemplars.[53] Yet the unplanned come-and-go of exemplars might also serendipitously have aided collation: it might have forced scribes to consult multiple exemplars when they lost access to one before they had finished with it, and so sought another to complete the text. As Hanna has also noted, copying English literature in the fifteenth century was 'something of a fanatic's occupation', and many people recopied works that they had already read.[54] The scriveners of London who copied books of

[50] Reynolds and Wilson, *Scribes and Scholars*, 214.

[51] Respectively, BL, MS Egerton 650, f. 111^{r}, discussed by Thompson, 'Middle English Prose *Brut*', 255; TCC, MS R.3.20, p. 356.

[52] BL, MS Add. 10574, f. 42^{r} (*Piers*, B, XI.35–6). In BodL, MS Bodley 814, f. 42^{r}, a cognate copy (discussed in Chapter 3 above), the passage thus marked is identical in every letter and punctuation mark, except that the cognate copy omits the definite article 'þe'.

[53] Hanna, *Pursuing History*, 8–9.

[54] Hanna, 'Problems of "Best Text" Editing', 88–9.

English literature alongside their work as bureaucrats are often speculated to have been part of a network with access to multiple exemplars.[55]

One mid-fifteenth-century scribe of *The Canterbury Tales* collated his copy fully when he encountered a second exemplar which supplemented his first. It has been suggested that a team of scribes produced and corrected this manuscript in a 'workshop', but on reflection there seems to be one hand in the copying and correcting alike.[56] His work is highly professional, with his writing modelled on a bastard anglicana, boxy in aspect, almost like textura; he signs his colophon as 'Cornhyll' in large red handwriting modelled on textura quadrata.[57] The layout is carefully rubricated and illuminated, with spaces for illustrations of the tale-tellers, although they were not filled. Cornhyll corrects his work more frequently than most people, over twice per page.[58] The aspiration to produce a book of high quality might suggest the sort of project in which it was feasible to collate the omissions fully; that would be a slow and therefore expensive process. His collation is evident from many of the 377 corrections he writes in the margins, with a *caret* mark in the line to show their position. The position of these additions suggests that Cornhyll makes them when he has already finished copying the rest of the adjacent passage. Moreover, many of these marginal additions restore details which could not be guessed, such as adjectives or adverbs (Table 8.3). Others restore passages omitted by eyeskip between repeated words in the Tale of Melibee, where the repetitious prose would make it difficult to guess that something was amiss without collating.[59] Finally, he adds ten whole lines of verse and six sections of a few lines which he had omitted somehow when copying (Table 10.4). To complete these elements would obviously require checking the copy against its exemplar or a second exemplar.[60]

There is some evidence that it was a second exemplar. Many of the longer corrections look less likely to be putting right Cornhyll's eyeskip than to be adding things which were not in his first exemplar, but which he finds in a second one. Only one omission definitely interrupts a rhyming

55 Mooney and Stubbs, *Scribes and the City*, e.g., 35–7, 58.

56 Mooney, 'New Scribe of Chaucer and Gower', and Mosser, *Digital Catalogue*, 'Ha^{2}', argue that this is just one scribe, correcting Manly and Rickert (eds.), *Text of the Canterbury Tales*, vol. I, 199, who suggest three scribes in a workshop.

57 BL, MS Harley 1758, f. 231^{r}. For other MSS ascribed to him, see *LMES*, under 'Cornhyll'.

58 Counted from a sample of BL, MS Harley 1758, ff. 1^{r}–23^{v} (*Tales*, i.1–2231), 76^{r}/1–102^{r}/20 (v.73–708, iv.1245–2418, iii.1–1264), and 169^{r}–182^{r} (vii.967–1889, in prose), with 283 corrections likely by the scribe (2.29 per page) and 38 unidentifiable or by later hands. Cf. the mean frequency in Table 6.1.

59 E.g., BL, MS Harley 1758, f. 172^{r}, skipping from 'Frende' (*Tales*, vii.1160), 177^{v}, from 'noght' (vii.1504), 178^{r}, from 'men' (vii.1557), 181^{v}, from 'iugeme*n*t' (vii.1869).

60 As noted by Owen, *Manuscripts*, 58–60.

Table 10.4 *Whole lines or longer passages added in the margins of* Tales *in BL, MS Harley 1758*

	folio	*preceding line or lines in the main text*	*addition after*	*marginal addition*	*added lines*
i)	57v	[---]{And} argumentis casten vp *and* doun . --- T[--]{hei|}speke of Magike *and* of Abusion . ---	II.212, 214	[¶] Manye a sotill reson forth þei leiden . [¶] But fynalli as in conclusioun .	II.213, 215
ii)	59r	Sche schall haue nede to wasche a wey the rede . ^o	II.356	^o Thogh sche a font full of watir *with* hir lede .	II.357
iii)	60r	¶ Ne ther was Surreyne non that was co*n*uertid @	II.435	[¶] That of þe|co^w^nceile of þe Sowdan woot .	II.436
iv)	88r	Gan pullen vp the smok *and* yn he throng . ^	IV.2353	^ ¶ A gret tente he þrest yn *and* a long . Sche seide it was þe meriest fit . That euyr in hir lyue sche was at yit . Mi lordis tente sche seide *ser*ueþ me not þus . He foldith twifolde bi swete Ihesus . He maie not swyue worth a leke . And yet he is full gentill *and* full meke . This is leuyr to me than Euensong .	spurious
v)	88r	Out help allas harrow he gan [to] crye . +	IV.2366	<+>{¶} For sorow almost he gan to|dye . That his wif was swyued in þe perye .	spurious
vi)	88r	Strogle q*uod* he ye algate yn it wente . ^	IV.2376	¶ Stif *and* rounde as ony belle . It was no wondir þouȝ hir beli swelle . The smok on his brest laie to seche . And eu*er* me thought he poynted on þe breche .	spurious
vii)	95r	I had the beste q*uonia*m that myght be . +	II.608	<[+]{¶}> For certis I am all fulli reu*er*yan . In felyng *and* myn herte all marcian . Venus me yaf my lust my liky*ng and* licorousnes . And Mars yaf me my sturdi hardynes .	III.609–12
viii)	95r	Mi chambre of Venus from a good felawe . ^	II.618	<[+]{¶}> Yet haue I a marke of Mars vp on my face . And also in another pryue place . For god so wisse be my saluacion . I louyd neuyr bi non discrescion . But euyr folewid myn appetite . All were he schort long blak or white . I toke no kepe so that he liked me . How pore he was ne eke of what degre .	III.619–26

Table 10.4 *cont.*

	folio	*preceding line or lines in the main text*	*addition after*	*marginal addition*	*added lines*
ix)	107v	A goddis kechill or a trip of chese . ^	iii.1747	^ Or ellis what ye list I maie not chese .	iii.1748
x)	140v	Sethyng thou wolt thyn ydolis despise . ^	viii.297	<[¶^]> Go w*ith* þi broþer now *and* þe baptise .	viii.298
xi)	167v	The cuntre of fairye . + For in that contre was ther non . Neither wif ne childe on . ^	vii.802, vii.804[1]	. de*ficit* . ⌐¶ So wilde for to drede .⌐	garbled vii.803
xii)	187v	Ne non Ermyn ne non Arabiene . ^	vii.2338	[¶] Ne Surreyn ne non Egipciene .[2]	vii.2339
xiii)	188r	And sche that helmyd was in starke schoures . ^	vii.2370	And wan bi fors townes strong *and* toures .	vii.2371
xiv)	189v	Rather than in ^[other] turmentise . ~	vii.2517	~ And thus hath Nero slayne his maister dere .	vii.2518
xv)	190r	Full pryuely sche stall fro eu*ery* wight .	vii.2573	And in to þe Cite sche is wente .	garbled vii.2574

[1] This passage still lacks vii.803 and 805; part of 803 recurs in the spurious addition.
[2] But the rhyme-words on vii.2338 and 2339 are switched in order.

couplet (ix) and so could be guessed from the verse; many occur in stanzas where there are some rhyming words nearby, so that the scribe would have to listen very carefully to deduce that the text was incomplete from its sound. The lines the scribe supplies in the Merchant's Tale (iv–vi) suggest that he was checking another text, for these lines occur in only four of the surviving manuscripts. The lines seem to be sly additions to the poem by somebody who stuck more rude detail, some of it graphic, into the bawdy passages.[61] It would be a flukish coincidence if this scribe had himself skipped over some lines which just happened to be rare, unauthorial additions; it is likelier that the scribe first uses an exemplar without these lines and then collates it against one with them.[62] Further traces of a second exemplar might be that he uses the letter **þ** frequently in these and other corrections, but hardly ever in his first copying: he might be working later, having forgotten his usual protocols for this job of copying,

[61] *Ibid.*, 58; Blake, 'Language and Style', 70–3; Field, 'Superfluous Ribaldry', 353–7.

[62] A third scenario is possible: that they were supplied in his exemplar on added sheets or in marginal positions, difficult to see at first; but this would still involve this scribe collating his copy to restore them.

or might be imitating the spelling of a different source.[63] The fact that these lines of saucy humour are inauthentic would be unknowable to him without modern editorial scholarship to guide him. His use of collation and of the techniques of correction – *caret* marks, marginal additions and perhaps some interlineations – suggest that Cornhyll thinks he is correcting his exemplar's oversights in order to restore the most complete copy possible.

Such full collation is unusual, especially for a secular work in the vernacular copied for money, as this smart book would seem to be. Indeed, in Cornhyll's copy of *The Canterbury Tales* about half these marginal additions were adorned with painted paraphs, before somebody erased them again: this might betray that the rubricator was unfamiliar with collations and mistook them for annotation.[64] Collation is seldom found and seldom as thorough; comparing two copies takes a lot of effort. At other times, scribes simply read the copy and think about it – simpler processes of deduction – rather than collate it whole; they turn to collation only when they spot for themselves that there is something wrong. Deduction like this might lie behind corrections of other sorts, from fixing grammar to spotting historical errors in chronicles; deduction is part of the close reading which develops alongside correcting. But its usefulness for fixing incompleteness is limited: while deduction can identify that something is lost, only collation can identify what. Deduction might lead merely to metatextual comment – in gaps and notes of what *deficit* – and not to the full text itself. Of course, if deduction does lead to completing the text, then its effects are difficult to distinguish from those of collation: while collating can produce corrections which deduction cannot, everything deduction produces can be just as well produced by collation.

Happily, the role of deduction is visible in a mid-fifteenth-century copy of *The Canterbury Tales* which later served as the exemplar for Geoffrey Spirleng's (discussed in Chapters 3 and 9). The scribe writes a current handwriting but has an orderly and spacious layout. In a balance of care and sloppiness, he spots lines missing and supplies them in the margin in a way which shows that he does so while hurrying through drawing 'braces' on the rhyme-scheme. For example, when he skips a line from a couplet in the Knight's Tale, he notices when rubricating the braces: he

63 BL, MS Harley 1758 does use þ very occasionally elsewhere (e.g., ff. 48^{v}/39, 201^{r}/19–20, 201^{v}/1) but mostly in the Tale of Melibee (ff. 169^{r}–182^{r}) and at the start of the Parson's Tale (16 times, ff. 205^{r}/31–206^{r}/6). That might suggest a different exemplar for the prose or might reflect different attitudes to reproducing the spelling of the exemplar in prose, as in corrections.

64 On 179 of 377 marginal corrections in BL, MS Harley 1758. Field, 'Superfluous Ribaldry', 357–8, illustrates some.

mistakenly draws a brace from the single remaining line to the first half of the following couplet, as though they might rhyme; then he continues to draw braces thus linking the second half of one couplet to the first half of the next, some fourteen times overall down the page. It is only after marking fourteen unrhyming pairs that he realizes that the braces are out of kilter and why; so he erases the incorrect braces and draws correct ones; and where the missing line has caused this muddle, he adds that line in the margin. It is clear that he spots the oversight while still rubricating because, after the fourteen false braces have been corrected, proper ones resume, without any erasure.[65] This is a recurrent process of recognition: thirteen more times in the book he adds missing lines in the margin and on all bar one of them he has misapplied red braces to several couplets, or once to a stanza, for a few subsequent lines before he realizes the omission which upsets the rhyme (Figure 6). The time it takes him to realize ranges from just two couplets of bracing to as many as fifteen. He sometimes realizes that the red braces are wrong only when he reaches the foot of the page where he would need to think about whether the couplet and brace would straddle the page-break.[66] The erased braces betray that he does not collate his copy in full; he spots problems almost by chance while rubricating; and these deductions send him back to check the exemplar only for the missing line. Although few manuscripts have visibly erased rubric like this to betray when and how the scribe deduces that there are omissions, it is likely that much collating is prompted initially thus by close reading.

Misfilling the gaps

But ingenious scribes and others not only spot where rechecking the exemplar might supply something missing; they also sometimes spot places where the exemplar too is lacking. That scribe of *The Canterbury Tales* twice finds lines missing from his exemplar and writes defensively 'hic deficit v*er*sus in copia' ('here a verse is lacking in my exemplar'); he can add nothing.[67] Spotting a lacuna does not always lead to finding the missing

65 CUL, MS Mm.2.5, f. 16^{v} (skipping *Tales*, I.1452, noticed at 1479). On this MS, see Mosser, *Digital Catalogue*, 'Mm'; Seymour, *Catalogue*, vol. II, 56–61; and Chapter 3 above.

66 CUL, MS Mm.2.5, ff. 22^{v} (skipping *Tales*, I.2034, noticed by 2038), 29^{v} (I.2654, noticed at 2697 at page-break), 32^{v} (I.2934, noticed at 2957), 36^{r} (I.3276, noticed at 3306 at page-break), 43^{v} (I.3968, noticed by 3972), 50^{r} (*Gamelyn*, 136, noticed by 150), 60^{r} (VII.113, noticed by 124, at page-break), 62^{v} (VII.340, noticed by 346), 89^{r} (II.1004–6, noticed at 1008 at the stanza-end and page-break), 91^{v} (V.18, noticed by 26), 100^{r} (IV.1264, noticed at 1299 at page-break), 110^{r} (IV.2126, noticed by 2130).

67 CUL, MS Mm.2.5, ff. 51^{v} (*Gamelyn*, 281–3, on which lines see n. 31 above), 52^{v} (*Gamelyn*, 375–7, without 'hic'). Both are obvious eyeskips, but of three lines. On f. 51^{v}, somebody later supplied the missing lines at the foot of the page, with construe-marks to show their position. This handwriting differs from the scribe's, as it is modelled more on secretary than anglicana.

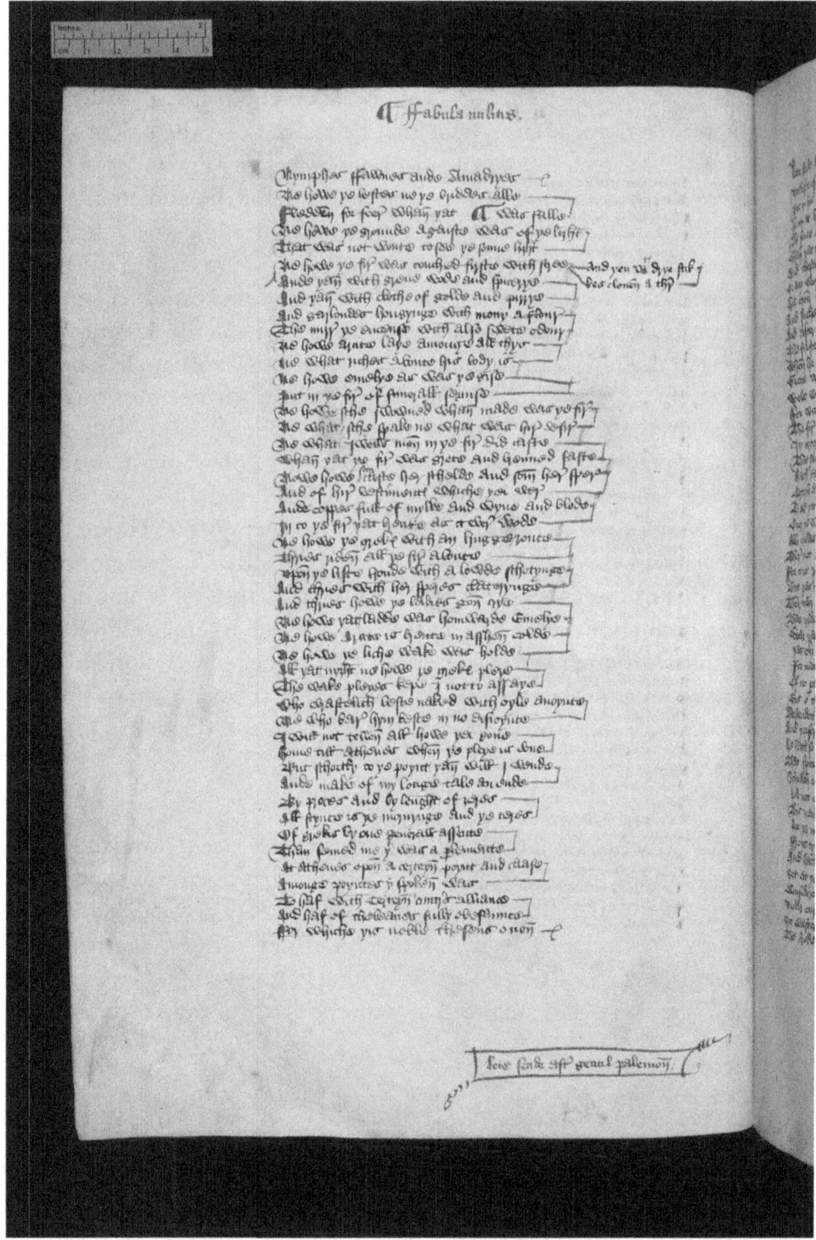

Figure 6 CUL, MS Mm.2.5, f. 32v: erased braces in Geoffrey Chaucer's *The Canterbury Tales*

pieces: sometimes it can lead only to cautious gaps or notes; and sometimes it leads others to over-ingenious rewriting to hide the hiatus. Such patching up suggests a preference for conjecture beyond fidelity to the evidence of the exemplar. The cleverness which happily enables scribes to spot errors also leads them to correct in ways that are erroneous. And there, in mistaken attempts to complete texts, emerges one – not all, just one – of the sources of the variance in English manuscripts: critical ingenuity without textual scholarship.

One radical but unusual solution occurs in a copy of *The Canterbury Tales* by scribes associated with the Leicester house of the Augustinians.[68] The solution here to the puzzle of incompleteness is to cut more, in order to lessen the disruption. Some thirteen times somebody using this book deduces that the copy has only one half of a rhyming couplet; but rather than seek in scholarly fashion what is absent, he crosses out what is present; he deletes the surviving half of the incomplete couplet and so removes the stray unrhyming line. Rubrication was again the occasion for the careful reading, for most of the time the crossing out is in red.[69] The person rubricating had made other corrections too.[70] The thirteen lines could be blithely deleted without damaging the sense in most cases, for they are syntactically complete and merely add subclauses needless for the plot, such as caveats or decorative details; it seems likely to be, once more, the incomplete sound of the couplet which upsets the person correcting. But in this book deduction either did not lead to collation at all or led to collation with an exemplar also incomplete, so that the scribes could not solve the problem accurately. This is characteristic of this book: at other points the Leicester canons indulge in variance rather than accuracy: they leave out some bawdy bits and some jokes at the expense of their fellow clergy. Their willingness to vary might reflect the fact that theirs is not a copy made for others for money but one made for 'recreational' enjoyment in a closed community.[71] At other times, however, these canons are not that different from Cornhyll, the accomplished scribe and collator, even when they delete. Though the solutions are poor, they are trying to solve

68 Kline, 'Scribal Agendas', 118–19; Mosser, *Digital Catalogue*, 'Ha^3'.

69 BL, MS Harley 7333, in red ff. 40^v (*Tales*, I.615, an unrhyming spurious line, 618), 41^r (I.683), 47^r (I.1843), 55^r (I.3372, after 3367–71 are missing), 56^v (I.3712), 66^r (a gap after V.105–6 are conflated), 66^r again (V.147), 66^v (V.255 before V.256 is missing), 69^r (IV.1358, after I.1355–7 are missing), and in black ff. 72^r (IV.2006, after 2004 is missing), 95^r (VI.466). Two (ff. 47^r, 56^v) are preceded by corrections of the rhyme in the previous couplet.

70 E.g., crossing out a line mangled by eyeskip: BL, MS Harley 7333, f. 64^v (*Tales*, II.1024–5).

71 Owen, *Manuscripts*, 69–70; Kline, 'Scribal Agendas', 116–18, 125–8, 130. None of the half-couplets missing nor the incomplete rhymes then deleted were rude or anticlerical.

the problems. Their attempt is visible elsewhere in the book, where people drew crosses where some other lines are missing, and the scribes then supply the missing lines in the margin; they do well there.[72] It is possible, then, that the other incomplete couplets also prompt these scribes to check the exemplar, but that they find the exemplar incomplete as well here and so cannot restore the losses and give up. They might be doing the best they can, just as Cornhyll is. After all, his collation is not to our standard: he adds lines which we know are spurious – albeit in good faith. Though with different sorts of error and maybe different degrees of care, Cornhyll and the Leicester canons are similar in kind: neither is undertaking an historical reconstruction of Chaucer's text, as a modern editor might; all are simply concerned to make sense of the resources they've got.

Their priority is (I speculate) having a coherent form of the text in its own right, regardless of its authorial form. It is such a priority which could lead both to Cornhyll's willingness to incorporate as much text as is possible and to the Leicester canons' tidying up of half-done couplets. But if one's concern is with the words on the page and not with their historical original, then the remedy for incompleteness could be not only careful scholarship but mere ingenuity. It could prompt cutting to conceal the gaps, though that is rare, or inventing new words to fill them. This invention has been observed frequently: for example, in the copies of Hardyng's *Chronicle*, some scribes left gaps when their exemplar was lacking but others devised new lines in these places.[73] Such inventions are frequent in copies of *The Canterbury Tales* too. Some seem to result from frustration that gaps left by the scribe have still not been filled. For example, one scribe of *The Tales* inherits from his exemplar three places where he rightly deduces that he should leave a gap for a missing line, but the gaps went unfilled until eventually the scribe wrote a spurious line in one of them. The scribe might not have been inventing these lines for himself; one recurs in another copy.[74] But these guesses are wholly wrong according to modern editors,

72 BL, MS Harley 7333, with red crosses on ff. 57v (*Tales*, I.3955, mangled), 58v (I.4136, mangled), 60v (II.117–20), 61v (II.324, later erased again), 62r (II.485), 63v (II.796, mangled), 66r (V.118, mangled), 69r (IV.1308, mangled), 69r again (to supply IV.1361–5, but with only one, different line), 69v (IV.1432), 69v again (to supply IV.1460, but wrongly), and in black alone on ff. 47v (I.1995, but wrongly), 56r (I.3616), 56v (I.3724) and 72r (to supply IV.1986 but wrongly). There are marginal additions in the other works in this manuscript too on ff. 33v twice, 36r, 36v, 121r, 209v.

73 Edwards, 'Manuscripts and Texts', 79–82.

74 BL, MS Add. 25718, ff. 23v (space left for *Tales*, I.3043, after 3044), 49r (space left for VI.69, after 70; spurious line added, like that in BodL, MS Hatton donat. 1, f. 154), 50v (no space left for VI.172; but a spurious line squeezed in), 53v (space left for VI.356). That these additions were made later is evident in slight differences in their handwriting, which has greyer ink, a smaller module, extra ticks on word-final **d** and **e** and one-compartment **a**.

and except in that they rhyme: there is little interest in the authorial origin; there is an interest in the formal completeness of the text, not in Chaucer's text.

Sometimes fabrications like these are inherited from earlier exemplars; sometimes there is evidence of scribes inventing such replacements for themselves. The scribe's inventions can be well studied in a copy of *The Canterbury Tales* which is the cognate of another copy still surviving, seemingly made from the same exemplar (as discussed in Chapter 3); the two texts are close, reproducing the same text word-for-word over 97 per cent of the time (Table 3.2).[75] There are eleven points in the poem at which the cognate copy (Mc) is missing a line or two but this copy (Ra^{I}) has a spurious line or more to replace the omission (Table 10.5). For example, where a missing line and a muddled line leave three successive lines with the matching rhymes 'plesaunce', 'vengeaunce' and 'Geneloun of fraunce', this copy turns the line about 'fraunce' into a second couplet by adding a spurious description of Ganelon 'Of whom ben made gestes *and* rymaunce' (x). It is tempting to wonder whether the scribe's poetic invention made him think of filling the gap with a line about such invention; it is also intriguing that he completes the rhyme with the unusual spelling 'rymaunce', with <rym> suggesting that rhyme is on his mind.[76] Was this scribe, though, inventing the lines for himself, or just copying them? As it happens, the cognate copy never has any gap or marking for those missing lines, so it looks likely that the shared exemplar did not mark them and that the scribe of this copy with spurious lines spotted the omissions by his own deduction. And while at most points he writes the spurious lines seamlessly without visible fuss, in two of the earlier (i, iv) some of the words or rhymes are written over erasure, as though the scribe is working out that there is something missing and is composing a replacement as he goes along. The most drastic erasure occurs in the first such invention, where he rewrites the rhymes of several adjacent lines as well, as though he were still working out that such omissions might occur and how to replace them.[77] One final line which fills an incomplete couplet looks like an afterthought slotted into a

[75] Chicago, UL, MS 564 (hereafter Mc), and BodL, MS Rawl. poet. 141 (hereafter Ra^{I}).

[76] Neither *MED*, *romaunce* (*n.*), nor *OED*, *romance* (*n.*), records spellings with <y> or <i>.

[77] Ra^{I} also has three spurious lines earlier than (i) in Table 10.5: ff. 2^{r} (missing *Tales*, I.2655, with a spurious line after 2656), 3^{v} (missing I.2741; spurious after 2742), 10^{r} (missing I.3147; spurious after 3148), with no visible disturbance on the page. Mc has lost the corresponding leaves, so it is impossible to guess whether these lines were invented by Ra^{I} or were in the shared exemplar. There are also four spurious lines added in Ra^{I}, ff. 6^{r} (after I.2909 and 2910), 14^{r} (after I.3411 and 3412) where nothing is missing; they are also inexplicable without Mc's equivalent leaves surviving. There are also muddles and omissions and spurious lines in the Tale of Sir Thopas in both Mc, ff. 73^{v}, 74^{v} (VII.731–2, 735, 805, 823), and Ra^{I}, ff. 88^{v}, 89^{r}, 89^{v}.

Table 10.5 *Missing lines in* Tales *in Mc, with invented and modified lines in the cognate copy, Ra*^{1}

lines missing in Mc	*folio in Mc*	*folio in Ra*^{1}	*line(s) invented in Ra*^{1}	*lines partly or wholly rewritten in Ra*^{1}	*the invented lines or rewritten line-endings in Ra*^{1} *in bold (and adjacent genuine text in ordinary type)*
i) II.425	17^{v}	35^{v}–36^{r}	after II.430 late	II.426 over erasure, II.428, II.431 over erasure, II.432	Upon thi glad day [->]{**thenk wel on thesse**} The vn war wo that cometh bihynde Shortly for to telle **ther may ye fynde .** ¶ The soudan *and* the cristen euerychon Ben alto hewen *and* styked at the bord [f. 36^{r}] **Of hem laft on lyue was ther not oon** But only dame Custaunce [->]{**at on wo**}rd . This olde soudanesse **of vengeaunce the sword .**
ii) II.595	20^{v}	38^{v}	after II.594 right		**There as these ladyes were *and* slepte**
iii) II.822–3	24^{r}	42^{r}	after II.821 right, after II.824 late		**That sheo shulde haue non other grace** But natheles sheo taketh in good entent . **And euer in hur mynde hath this talent .**
iv) II.949	26^{r}	44^{r}	after II.948 rightly, over erasure; II.950 also over erasure		[->]{**Now hiderward *and* thiderward bothe night *and* day .**} [->]{Till cristes moder blessed be sheo ay .}
v) V.94	31^{v}	49^{r}	after II.93 right		**And gentell lange *and* plesaunce**
vi) V.106	32^{r}	49^{r}	after II.105 right		**The mater*e* on this wyse shall I fyle .**
vii) V.509	38^{v}	55^{v}	after II.510 late		**Of al that he mente *and* wolde seyne .**
viii) IV.642–3	52^{r}	68^{r}	after II.644 late, the first over erasure		[->]{**Taketh hit feyre forth as shall I**} **Hit wol non other be dame sikerly**
ix) IV.1197	61^{r}	77^{r}	after IV.1196 right		**Caste al a syde *and* from you youre pacyence**
x) VII.192	64^{v}	80^{r}	after II.194 late	II.191	And to do you what **seruyse *and* plesaunce** And but I do god on me take vengeaunce . As foul as hedde Geneloun of fraunce **Of whom ben made gestes *and* rymaunce .**
xi) VII.1978	107^{r}	115^{v}	after VII.1977 right		**And cometh to nought fynally .**

gap at first left blank: the handwriting is either the scribe's at a different time or a good imitation of the scribe's, which suggests an interruption before finding or inventing this spurious line (xi).[78] Further evidence that he is finding or deducing omissions for himself is that he seems only to spot omissions and invent replacements where the loss upsets the rhyme. The only two points where he spots that a whole couplet is lost are in rime royal stanzas, where the omission would be noticeable from the stanzaic form (iii, ix). By contrast, he fails to supply extra lines in twelve places where whole couplets are missing, and the rhyme-scheme is unaffected.[79] Overall, it is likely that this scribe is inventing these replacements for himself.

The 'complete' text he produces is definitely not authorial, then; the corrections are not centripetal in outcome. But, as often, while the text remains erroneous, the process of correcting reveals the scribe's understanding and attention. He is attentive enough to spot so many of the gaps – all bar three of those observable from the disrupted rhyme-scheme – apparently without collating a second copy, and the fact that he invents things to complete the text suggests that he cares about what he copies, if not about the author. He was not alone in such invention: after all, the exemplar which his copy and the cognate copy reproduce already had seven points at which one of Chaucer's lines was lost but somebody had invented a new line to make up the loss, which both copies then reproduce.[80] Indeed, as that suggests, this scribe and that of the cognate copy otherwise reproduce their exemplar fairly closely, diverging from each other and so presumably from it only seldom (as Table 3.2 shows). Neither scribe seems to be careless; so the rewriting seems best explained as a perverse sort of carefulness. What might explain the co-existence of what seem like contradictory methods for dealing with incompleteness – dutiful collation; wild invention – and the co-existence of accurate copying and wilful invention? This 'seeming paradox', as George Kane called it, of mostly careful copying mixed with

78 Ra^{1}, f. 115^{v}/21 (*Tales*, VII.3168, 'And cometh to nought fynally'), where Mc, f. 107^{r}, has a line missing. The handwriting has more numerous broken strokes and a different treatments of strokes descending below the line in **g**, **y** and the limb of **h**.

79 McCormick, with Heseltine, *Manuscripts*, 327–33, 426–32: namely *Tales*, III.195–6, 575–84, 609–10, 619–20, 1493–4, 1873–4, VII.3093–4 [B^{2}, 4283–4]. The exceptions are VII.2205 [B^{2}, 3395] in the long stanzas of the Monk's Tale), III.671 and 1378. The loss of III.260 is compounded by the loss of another odd number of lines, III.255–7, just beforehand, to form a dysfunctional couplet from halves of two others, III.258–9.

80 McCormick, with Heseltine, *Manuscripts*, 327–33, 426–32: namely *Tales*, I.4355–6, II.1187–8, IV.535–7, VII.215–16 [B^{2}, 1405–6], III.1617–19, III.1731–2, III.2047–9. There are also three invented lines which do not fill gaps but add to the text after I.4394, I.4396 and VII.2172 [B^{2}, 3362], the latter partly corrected in Mc, f. 110^{r}, and two passages in the Tale of Sir Thopas where both cognate copies invent patches for complex muddles (VII.733, 800–5 [B^{2}, 1923, B^{2}, 1990–5]).

occasional deliberate variance, has many possible motives.[81] It is not an interest in what the author wrote, for the inventions ignore that; but nor is it a blithe acceptance of the accidents of the text's material transmission. What unite their different ways of handling incompleteness are the scribes' almost formalist ideas about the text's completeness and coherence, and their understanding of what its diction, verse-form and contents might be like. Even when part of the literary work is not present in their exemplars, the scribes are able to imagine and understand those absent words in ways which shape their craftsmanship in correcting.

[81] As noted by *Piers A*, ed. Kane, 127–8.

PART IV

Implications

CHAPTER 11

Authorship

eke als [auto] Auctores seyn

Henry Daniel, *The Dome of Urynes*, II.v
San Marino, Huntington Library, MS HM 505, f. 54^{v}

The invention of lines to fill gaps suggests that the interest of scribes and readers was not an historical one in the author but a formalist one in the text and its internal coherence and accomplishment. Yet how can they disregard the author? The works which scribes and readers corrected did have authors, and early poets, scribes and readers do often invoke or invent the power of the author in this period, whether cast as the scholastic *auctor* or as the courtly laureate.[1] While (as Chapter 2 showed) the poets requested others to correct their work, their requests betrayed some sense of the aspirations they themselves had for their work – their own aim to get it right. Unsurprisingly, then, there is evidence of authors pursuing correction for themselves. One of the poets who requests correction from scribes or readers also reports his own efforts – or, rather, their interruption. In Guillaume de Deguileville's *Pilgrimage of the Life of Man*, in John Lydgate's English translation, the author reports that he has not had time to correct the first draft, implying that such correction would be part of his customary practice. He wrote down his dream vision while it lingered 'freschly yn my mynde', hoping that he might 'after, by leyser, | Correcte hyt when the day wer*e* cler'. But his copy, his 'wrytyng', was circulated without his permission before he was able:

> To putte away, and eke to adde,
> What that me lyst, lyk as I wende.
> ffor ther was mychë thyng to mende,
> To ordeyne, & to correcte,
> And bet in order to directe;

[1] Lerer, *Chaucer and His Readers*, 9–12; in general Minnis, *Medieval Theory of Authorship*, esp. 160–7; and Meyer-Lee, *Poets and Power*, esp. 3–4.

ffor many a thyng, yt ys no nay,
Mot be prouyned, & kut a-way,
And yshape of newe entaylle,
In ordre dresse hyt, & yraylle.[2]

Although in this case it has not happened, composing should involve stages of adding, removing, ordering, reshaping, through the techniques of correcting.

Firstly, authors in English often compose works that are corrective in some loose metaphorical sense. They often purport to correct or 'amende' the sins of other people or to correct the mistakes of past writers. For instance, Thomas Hoccleve does both: while counselling his prince he sets out the need for fraternal correction and urges the prince to correct others in turn; in *Lerne to Dye* he seeks to correct the sinner, God's 'handwerk' in a nice metaphor of craftsmanship. Elsewhere, he himself seeks to 'amendes make' to women for translating *Lespistre de Cupide* which offends them; this is ironic for *Lespistre de Cupide* is translated from one of Christine de Pizan's works and is itself designed to correct the 'wrong wrytyng' about women by other authors.[3] It is typical for English writers to offer such metaphorical corrections. They also (as this chapter shows), undertook correcting in various literal, practical senses: mastering grammar and rhetoric, which were the arts of learning to speak correctly; finding the right orthography; composing rough drafts on wax tablets that could be scraped clean as one improved them; polishing presentation copies for patrons who would expect a job done well; revising their earlier work for new occasions or for style; checking others' copies of their work. Some of these activities of authorship are evident when authors copy out their own works in autograph, signed or unsigned; they of course correct these copies. Some are evident in the works which survive not necessarily in authors' copies but in revised and improved versions which reflect authors' efforts. The practical processes of correcting shape English literature directly.

Stages of correcting

Correcting occurs at various stages.[4] At the start of composition, authors incised in wax and then jotted in unbound loose quires, all of which allowed

[2] Lydgate, *Pilgrimage of the Life of Man*, 221, 223–4, 231–2, 238–46. He repeats the terms 'Adde, & putte a-way' for supplementing and deleting (261–2).

[3] Respectively, *Regiment*, 2488–92, 2782–97; Hoccleve, *MP*, xxiii.437, 563, and also 362, 366, 370, 413, 428, 878, xxi.786, xix.218–19, 281–7.

[4] Beadle, 'English Autograph Writings', disentangles the autograph MSS from different stages of composition. Richard Beadle's Lyell Lectures for 2013, 'Aspects of Medieval English Autographs', will, when published, supersede that study and the present chapter.

for processes of correcting. From antiquity until the sixteenth century at least, much ephemeral writing was done on wax tablets, which have a far longer history and 'a more intimate relationship with literary creation' than other media.[5] They survive from all over Europe; there is some text in fourteenth-century English recorded on wax tablets excavated at York.[6] Tablets were pieces of wood with a waxen surface that could be incised and then scraped clean with an implement sharp at one end for the inscription and blunt at the other for rubbing it off.[7] They were ubiquitous for writing which did not need to be kept, such as the initial stages of drafting. Composition thus used a technology which nurtured correcting, without wasting expensive parchment: it involved surfaces which could be erased because they were judged 'wrong' in some respect, or at least not as right as they should be. Indeed, the tool for writing and erasing was known by the fourteenth and fifteenth centuries as a *stylus*, which became a metaphor for polished composition – one's style.[8] A similar significance was registered in an etymology imagined for the Latin word *litera* (*letter*) from *litura*, the word for an erasure or a scraping out on a wax tablet, from the verb *lituro*.[9] Authors began their work on an instrument which allowed correcting, then, and that tool shaped their terms for language and authorship.

People did also use scraps of parchment for rough drafts and, from the late fourteenth century as imported paper became more readily available in England, they used sheets folded into small quires for jottings. An author would eventually need to transfer his or her compositions from wax tablets or loose quires to larger units of parchment or paper for a further stage of composition. While incisions in wax tablets and the fragile materials of rough drafts rarely survive, because they are so ephemeral, these second drafts in which the author writes out his work and then revises it do exist. In such 'working copies' the techniques of correcting – erasing, subpuncting, crossing out, interlining, adding leaves, reordering with 'construe-marks' – are frequent.[10] Indeed, it is often the copiousness of these techniques which is cited as evidence that a manuscript might be in the author's own handwriting.[11] There are some difficulties in making such identifications, not least because corrections are frequent in copies by other people too

5 Quoting Rouse and Rouse, 'Vocabulary of Wax Tablets', 220. See also Chartier, *Inscription and Erasure*, 3–4, 24.

6 O'Connor and Tweddle, 'Set of Waxed Tablets', 315.

7 For details, see Rouse and Rouse, 'Vocabulary of Wax Tablets', 220–1, 224–35; Teeuwen, *Vocabulary of Intellectual Life*, 175–6, 207–8; Gasnault, 'Supports et instruments de l'écriture', 22–4.

8 Rouse and Rouse, 'Vocabulary of Wax Tablets', 224–5.

9 E.g., by Priscian, quoted in Copeland and Sluiter (eds.), *Medieval Grammar and Rhetoric*, 173, and by Philippe de Harvengt, quoted in Stiennon, *L'Écriture*, 110.

10 Beadle, 'English Autograph Writings', 260–3.

11 E.g., Robinson, *Catalogue*, nos. 21, 67, 153, 281.

(as this book has shown). On the one hand, judging the content and effect of corrections to be authorial improvement rather than amendment of scribal error or scribal revision is a little subjective; on the other hand, circularly, recognizing or judging that the handwriting is the author's leads us to judge the effect of corrective techniques as authorial improvements. What is the correction of error, what the revision or rewriting by the author or another, is not always easy to say.

One manuscript whose corrections have caused it to be identified as a working copy is the English scientific work known as *The Equatorie of the Planetis*. This has attracted lots of interest because it has been claimed as a work by Chaucer in his autograph copy; certainly tables in other parts of the same manuscript refer to astronomical calculations by Chaucer's name ('Radix Chaucer').[12] In fact, recent discoveries suggest that this work is not by Chaucer, but by a Benedictine monk connected with Tynemouth Priory in Northumberland.[13] It does, however, seem to be an holograph by some author. The parchment, layout and handwriting all suggest that it is not a polished work for presentation but perhaps a working draft of the treatise, in an intermediate stage of development.[14] The techniques of correcting also suggest – in the usual circular way – that this is the author's own work in progress. The corrections are employed seldom to fix errors of copying; only a few could conceivably remove errors such as eyeskip.[15] Otherwise, there are changes to the content by somebody familiar with it, likeliest to be its author. Several additions to the content are left as prompts in Latin for future expansions and rewriting – as many of us leave 'notes to ourselves' in earlier drafts for details to complete later.[16] Most boldly, the person writing marks two long sections as misleading – 'this canon is fals' – and lightly crosses out one of them, as though he is rethinking.[17] Among the numerous words added between the lines, many could of course be the customary corrections of eyeskip, and of elements such as missing adjectives or incomplete doublets to which scribes often attend.[18] Yet the added words at some points follow patterns which suggest revision rather than the correction of haphazard error. In particular, there are additions

[12] Rand Schmidt, *Authorship*, 4–5, surveys the debate prior to 1993.

[13] This discovery is announced on the website of Kari Anne Rand Schmidt as the subject of a forthcoming study: www.hf.uio.no/ilos/english/people/aca/kschmidt.

[14] Rand Schmidt, *Authorship*, 18–20, and see the full description at 103–13.

[15] E.g., Cambridge, Peterhouse, MS 75.1, f. 72^{v}/33, jumping ahead to 'þ*at*'; f. 75^{r}/6, erased error conceivably involved eyeskip from 'plate' to 'pl*anete*'. There is a facsimile and helpful facing transcription in Rand Schmidt, *Authorship*, 116–43.

[16] Robinson, 'Geoffrey Chaucer and the *Equatorie*', 21; Rand Schmidt, *Authorship*, 21–2.

[17] Cambridge, Peterhouse, MS 75.1, ff. 76^{r}, 77^{r}.

[18] As argued by Edwards and Mooney, 'Is the *Equatorie of the Planets* a Chaucer Holograph?', 33.

of a few adjectives which offer more specificity: a date of measurement is not just 1392 but is '*com*plet' 1392; a line mentioned is the 'forseide' one and some signs are 'the same' signs; a line should not be drawn any old how but drawn 'ouerthwart'; the part required is the 'vpperest' part; the compass-point to be used is the 'moeuable' one; the thread to be used is 'white'.[19] Increasing the clarity might be considered loosely corrective for it would prevent misunderstanding by readers. Other changes look like improvements in style.[20] For example, there are several instructions which begin with an imperative verb such as *take* or *turn* modified by the adverb *then* or its synonym *tho*; as these instructions often have some element over erasure or interlined, it is possible that there was care in ordering them by picking the right verb or ensuring that the sequential adverb *then* or *tho* was present.[21] These changes might again heighten the clarity for readers; others might strengthen the rhetorical force: such would be another added adjective and an adverb, 'sothly' (*truly*) and 'verrey' (*true*).[22] The words which scribes troubled to preserve in practical prose, an author troubled to insert. On the whole the techniques of correcting are used in working copies such as this to improve the composition of the work in a further draft. Similar things could be said of those in autograph manuscripts of the romance *Sir Ferumbras* or William Worcester's *The Boke of Noblesse*.[23]

In later stages of preparation, though, there is often evidence not of revision but of correction. From working drafts, the author might transfer his text to 'fair copies', making them himself or getting another scribe – perhaps a professional, more adept one – to do so. These fair copies more often seem an attempt to issue the work in authoritative form, whether as an exemplar for future copies or as a gift for the earliest dedicatee or patron.[24] Yet even this first public version is a copy, relative to the working draft; and as is well known, authors are not necessarily accurate copyists of their own work, so even if the author makes the fair copy he is still susceptible to errors and to corrections much like those found in other manuscripts.[25] They have been traced magisterially by Peter Lucas, for

19 The following additions, arguably, clarify with further detail: Cambridge, Peterhouse, MS 75.1, ff. 72^{r}/24, 72^{v}/1, 72^{v}/7, 73^{r}/5, 73^{v}/2, 75^{r}/18, 75^{r}/20, 75^{r}/29, 76^{r}/17, 76^{r}/23, 76^{v}/23, 78^{r}/30. But, by contrast, on f. 71^{v}/11, the writer crosses out 'the forseide' as well.

20 Rand Schmidt, *Authorship*, 16–17.

21 Cambridge, Peterhouse, MS 75.1, ff. 71^{v}/17, 72^{r}/36, 73^{r}/10, 75^{r}/10, 78^{r}/32. See also the addition of a whole instructional clause (f. 76^{v}/23), of 'tak there' (f. 77^{v}/32) and of temporal adjectives in declarative clauses (ff. 77^{r}/12, 78^{r}/2).

22 Cambridge, Peterhouse, MS 75.1, ff. 75^{r}/28, 77^{r}/30.

23 See Hardman, 'MS Ashmole 33 *Sir Ferumbras*'; and Shepherd, 'The Ashmole "Sir Ferumbras"'.

24 Beadle, 'English Autograph Writings', 265–6, lists a range of qualities.

25 In general, see Reeve, *Manuscripts and Methods*, 3–23.

example, in the numerous copies of the works of John Capgrave, made in his own handwriting or made for him by scribes associated with him. (Lucas's detailed findings need not be repeated here.) One of Capgrave's autographs is a working copy, like that of *The Equatorie of the Planetis*;[26] others seem to be fair copies, some for presentation, but these too include the author's corrections. Sometimes, Capgrave has presentation copies made by other scribes but he then enters corrections into them, ensuring that his work is reproduced well.[27] Indeed, a copy of Capgrave's *The Solace of Pilgrimes* was abandoned in the middle of the third quire and destroyed – a quite extreme form of correction – perhaps because it was too inaccurate a reproduction.[28] At other times, though, Capgrave copies his works for himself and he too is quite able to err, albeit less frequently than do some other scribes of his work.[29] His correction of his own slips of the pen is seen in his autograph copy of *The Life of St Norbert* in verse, completed in 1440, which is in the Huntington Library's sample. Despite the fine quality and public purpose, there are 111 corrections, of which most (73) are definitely by him and many more (25) are likely to be.[30] About a quarter use the near-invisible technique of erasure with overwriting (29 of 111). Many address recognizable slips in copying: for example, a whole line over erasure at the start of a stanza seems to fix eyeskip back or forwards, for under the third and fourth letters of the line appears the tail of an erased long **s** which occurs at exactly this point in the lines before, after and at the start of the subsequent stanza.[31] Far more corrections (65 of 111) involve interlining something: the interlineations seem to be supplied in two stages; about half use a thinner nib, darker ink and smaller module and look like temporary prompts to alteration; a few are done in part in red, so are quite noticeable.[32] Most simply supply words or letters needed for good grammar or legible spelling. The poet is making and mending mistakes like any other scribe.

26 Lucas, *From Author to Audience*, 38–9. 27 *Ibid.*, 23–4.

28 *Ibid.*, 43–6, 94–7, 105. The abandoned parchment was used to bulk out some bindings. The copy diverges from its exemplar in 3.55 per cent of words, as Lucas reports; as Table 3.1 above reports, divergence usually affects about 2 per cent of words. However, there is a second, more accurate copy in the author's own handwriting, which is also abandoned; so the rejection might not be of errors but of the text in general.

29 *Ibid.*, 69–71, 78–9, 84.

30 HEHL, MS HM 55. The edition, Capgrave, *The Life of St Norbert*, ed. Smetana, misses many erasures. But I could not see the subpunction which the editor sees under the first <l> in 'noblel' (f. 12^{r}, 796) and thought that the blotting of the second <e> in 'grete' (f. 13^{r}, 841) was accidental.

31 HEHL, MS HM 55, f. 18^{v}/29 (Capgrave, *Life of St Norbert*, 1254). Cf. ff. 18^{v}/28, 18^{v}/30 and 19^{r}/1.

32 Perhaps 29 are in the usual handwriting, 22 in the later form and 11 difficult to apportion. Of them, one is in red: f. 25^{v} (Capgrave, *Life of St Norbert*, 1730); two have red *caret* marks: ff. 20^{r} (1356), 21^{r} (1408). Also, three might be by readers: ff. 2^{v} (130), 36^{r} (2453), 41^{r} (2833).

There is more care over accurate transmission in the manuscripts written by the poet Thomas Hoccleve (*c.* 1367–1426). Three autograph anthologies of his shorter poems have long been known, and Linne Mooney has argued that a copy of his longer poem *The Regiment of Princes* is in his handwriting.[33] She has also identified hundreds of documents copied by him as a clerk in the office of the Privy Seal, part of the royal bureaucracy, and described his contribution to a formulary for that office (discussed in Chapter 4).[34] As is well known, Hoccleve's work is shaped in all manner of subtle ways by his work as a clerk.[35] In *The Regiment of Princes* he comments on the craft of 'writynge', by which he means *copying*, 'withowten varyance'.[36] In the so-called 'Series' he describes himself composing the poems in hand and conjures the illusion that the poem we read is a physical object made by him.[37] And he does comment on the poet physically writing, in a way which requires textual correction, in a dedicatory poem to the Duke of York: he worries lest 'þ*a*t I in my wrytynge foleye', in which case the Duke must correct it. The problems of 'wrytynge' he lists sound like problems of composing: 'Meetrynge amis', choosing unfitting diction, forgetting to 'weye' his meaning, setting his rhetorical colours 'nat to the ordre of endytyng'. But when he requests the Duke to 'amende and correcte' them, he seems to refer to the manual craft of correcting a book, which would involve the poet 'wrytynge' in the sense of copying.[38] The intellectual process and the manual one combine.

As well as inviting readers to correct, Hoccleve like Capgrave both errs in and corrects his copies himself. Most corrections in his autograph

33 Mooney, 'Holograph Copy', 280–6, on BL, MS Royal 17.D.xviii. The identification of the handwriting as Hoccleve's is not entirely secure, but as the only case to have been argued fully in print (at time of writing) is Mooney's, this chapter treats it as such. It is important to note, however, that this could be a scribe trained by or close to Hoccleve, imitating some shibboleth graphs of his, such as the curious descender on **y**. Some graphs are unlike Hoccleve's, such as the curling tail on the last minim of word-final **m** or **n**; the broken strokes in the crossbar and tongue of **e**; the lotus-flower **w** with a pointed tapering bottom and flattened loops above. More importantly, occasionally the ductus has a more jagged movement, with points in letters such as **g** and even in the descender of **y** on occasion (e.g., f. 26^{v}/21, 'yong'). But the general aspect is similar, notably in the proportions. And if the poet is not the scribe, the scribe is close to the poet and records what often looks like a revision by the poet.

34 Mooney, 'Some New Light', esp. 298.

35 Knapp, *Bureaucratic Muse*, e.g., 90–2, traces this influence.

36 BL, MS Royal 17.D.xviii (hereafter = siglum Ry^{3}), ff. 19^{v}–20^{r} (*Regiment*, 985–1005, 1028), quoted in Chapter 4, pp. 89–90 above. Tolmie, 'The Professional', 342–3, tries to free him from that context but, 344–5, interprets *Regiment*, 993 and 995–1029, as an account of poetic composition, rather than copying.

37 As argued by Watt, "I this book shal make", esp. 144, 151.

38 HEHL, MS HM 111, f. 33^{v} (hereafter = siglum HM 111); Hoccleve, *MP*, IX.46–54. Tolmie, 'The Professional', 344–5, stresses the sense of *composition* (in n. 12).

Table 11.1 *Frequency and types of correction in definite or possible autograph manuscripts of Thomas Hoccleve's poetry*

	written pages	*total number of corrections*	*frequency: pages corrected*	*erasure overwritten*	*interlineation or insertion*	*other methods*
Durham, UL, MS Cosin V.iii.9[1]	165	45	27%	30	15	0
HEHL, MS HM 111	93	51	55%	40	10	1
HEHL, MS HM 744 (Part II)	88	51	58%	44[2]	8	2
BL, MS Royal 17.D.xviii	197	27	14%	17[3]	9	1
total	543	174	32%	131	42	4

1 Du, f. 13r/4, 13r/21 (Hoccleve, *MP*, XXI.256, 273), also contains three interlineations by a sixteenth-century hand and a supply of ff. 3r–12v, by the sixteenth-century antiquary John Stow; these later changes have been ignored.

2 In HM 744 (Part II), three corrections used both erasure overwritten and interlineation and so are counted twice.

3 This includes one erasure where the scribe forgot to write over the top: Ry3, f. 16r (*Regiment*, 797).

anthologies and copy of *The Regiment of Princes*, if the latter is by him, fix slips of the pen easily made. As Table 11.1 shows, the frequency of correction varies a lot, with one anthology far less often corrected, but two others close in their frequency.[39] Overall, Hoccleve does well: although he corrects less frequently than some scribes of English overall, according to the Huntington Library's sample, he also errs little in copying his own work.[40] Others have counted eight errors in 2,000 lines or eight in two sections of 672 lines each; but those sections also contain in total 68 corrections.[41] Whereas some scribes of direct and cognate copies only caught about a tenth of the errors they made (as Chapter 3 showed), Hoccleve puts right nearly four times as many things as he leaves wrong. The poet is a skilled corrector. One of his techniques suggests well a poet's care to transmit his work as he wishes. Hoccleve uses the more definite technique of erasure more

39 As noted by *Thomas Hoccleve: A Facsimile*, ed. Burrow and Doyle, xxx, with more detail on xxii, xxv. Of those mentioned in the 'Introduction' to the facsimile, I could not see one on HM 111, f. 43r (Hoccleve, *MP*, XVII.51), but others are visible in the MSS and not the facsimile.

40 Cf. his frequency of correcting on 32 per cent of pages (Table 11.1) with the mean of 78 per cent (Table 6.1). As the sample of Hoccleve's copying is smaller, the comparison of figures might be misleading.

41 Bowers, 'Hoccleve's Two Copies', 448–9; and Schulz, 'Thomas Hoccleve, Scribe', 75.

than scribes do overall in the Huntington Library's sample and he largely eschews crossing out and subpuncting.[42] Indeed, he even, distinctively, tends to use erasure to remove things when nothing is to replace them, when others might use crossing out. And when a replacement is shorter than the erasure, he then doodles a line over the erasure to fill the space, sometimes a little wavy, sometimes adding vertical 'hatching'; he does this ten times in his poetic manuscripts.[43] The technique might reflect his training in copying administrative documents, where blank spaces which allowed others to intrude words could cause legal problems; interestingly, Hoccleve uses these lines to fill spaces over erasure in his formulary for the Privy Seal office too.[44] It also suggests a concern not to leave room for others to intrude their words, a concern which would make sense for a poet being proprietorial of his work.

Presentable corrections

Yet a poet might be careful in correcting his work not only out of his own interest in it, but also if he is presenting it to a patron. In a presentation copy, though, it is not only accuracy which might matter; so might appearances, being neat and tidy; the working copies like those of *The Equatorie of the Planetis* would not look good for dedication. Some French authors took great care over fair copies, with firm ideas for their layout and illustration; that care could extend to correcting them.[45] Peter Lucas's study of Capgrave's autograph manuscripts found that in a presentation copy of one work Capgrave corrects less frequently by visible means such as interlining and prefers the discreet method of erasure.[46] That might explain Hoccleve's use of erasure instead of crossing out. But what about Hoccleve's use of interlineations, or indeed Capgrave's preference for interlineations in *The Life of St Norbert*? That latter is certainly a presentation copy, with decoration and an illustration of Capgrave giving the book to a patron.[47] How are the visible interlineations permissible in a presentation

[42] Cf. his use of erasure for 75 per cent of corrections (Table 11.1) with the mean use for 42 per cent (Table 6.1).

[43] Durham, UL, MS Cosin V.iii.9 (hereafter = siglum Du), ff. 18r (Hoccleve, *MP*, xxi.732), 33v (xxii.298), 61r (xxiii.352), 62r (xxiii.408), 63v (xxiii.457), 66v partial (xxiii.597); HM 111, ff. 2r (Hoccleve, *MP*, ii.71), 2v partial (Latin note accompanying ii.89 onwards), 26v partial (iv.16); HEHL, MS HM 744 (Part II) (hereafter = siglum HM 744), f. 65v (Hoccleve, *MP*, xxiii.527).

[44] BL, MS Add. 24062, ff. 17r, 21r, 44v. Hoccleve also there seems (on a non-exhaustive survey) to use more erasures than interlineations, and few other techniques.

[45] E.g., Michon, 'Une édition manuscrite d'Eustache Deschamps', 32–5, 41.

[46] Lucas, *From Author to Audience*, 89.

[47] HEHL, MS HM 55, f. 1r.

copy which needs to impress a dedicatee? Might correction make a good impression?

Most methods of correcting go unhidden and some were even highlighted by rubricating (as Chapter 5 noted). There is some evidence that visible correction might be acceptable, even desirable, in two luxurious copies of *The Regiment of Princes* which are not in Hoccleve's handwriting but which were likely made close to the poet, and which seem likely to have been given to the poet's patrons.[48] These copies are more frequently corrected than Hoccleve's autograph copies, although one more than the other.[49] Each scribe corrects some of his slips as he goes along, writing over erasure frequently, often likely for eyeskip, where the word before the erasure recurs in a line nearby.[50] There were also slower stages of checking and rectifying, for both copies have prompts for corrections in the margins.[51] The prompts are in baggy handwriting with anglicana graphs, like that used for such prompts in other manuscripts by what look like professional book producers. That conventional rough style of handwriting for prompts makes it difficult to tell whether the scribe himself is responsible or somebody else. Given the closeness to the poet, one might wonder whether Hoccleve himself had mastered this rough annotating hand for correcting others' work – though that is only speculation with no evidence to support it. What is certain is that care was taken in preparing these copies, probably for the poet to present to his patrons. The accuracy of the words mattered in these gifts as much as the decorations did.

That is evident especially in one correction which these two copies share and which is beautiful and witty. Both scribes omit the same stanza and

48 BL, MS Arundel 38 (hereafter = Ar); BL, MS Harley 4866 (hereafter = Ha^4). Perkins, *Hoccleve's Regiment of Princes*, 114–17, 155–7, 171–2, and Kerby-Fulton, Hilmo and Olson, *Opening Up Middle English Manuscripts*, 82, 87, 92–4, place both MSS close to the poet and his patrons. One problem for considering Ha^{4}as a presentation copy is that the text stops five lines short of the end of the poem itself (f. 95^v; *Regiment*, 5434) before the usual dedicatory envoy or envoys which would have followed on another leaf.

49 Ar, with 171 corrections in 196 pages (87 per cent of pages); Ha^4, with 114 corrections in 188 pages (61 per cent of pages, ignoring 16 corrections and 4 additions of punctuation by an early modern hand).

50 Ar: 66 erasures overwritten by the scribe, most of them very discreet and difficult to see, plus one left accidentally incomplete (f. 38^v; *Regiment*, 2093); Ha^4: 88 erasures overwritten, 12 of them with marginal prompts. For eyeskip as cause, see the erasures on or after syllables or words which recur on lines above or below: Ar, ff. 1^v, 'wel' / 'welfare' (*Regiment*, 52), 5^v, 'the' (278), 58^v, 'hem' (3217, which *Regiment* prints as 'him'), 63^r, 'ben' (3448) and 73^v, inflexional *–eth* (4038); and Ha^4, ff. 11^v, 'cause' (604), 28^v, 'sone' (1550–1), 39^r, 'it' (2239), 43^v, from 'ofte' with 'of' above and below (2533–4), 58^v, 'And' (3364), 72^r, 'And' (4127–9), 81^r, 'large{---}[sse]' with 'large' below (4622).

51 Ar has 42 prompts (and one more in red on f. 78^v, *Regiment*, 4306), of which 27 have been entered; Ha^4 has 12 prompts. In Ar, not only erasures but 5 of 51 interlineations have prompts visible, which is unusual.

have to add it in the right-hand margin. Then in each book a limner painted a man using a rope like a lasso to pull the misplaced stanza into position; the man leans back with the effort against a grassy plot in the bottom margin.[52] Such decoration is rare: no similar adornments occur in the Huntington Library's sample of English.[53] The effort and expense were distinctive: it might have been economically feasible to scrap the leaf, for in both copies it is the first leaf of a quire (quire IX), and wasting one bifolium might not have been too costly relative to the cost of the books overall; indeed, paying the limner for the picture might have cost more money and time. The cause for such expense might be the unthinking reproduction of a shared exemplar, for these copies descend from the same exemplar which they reproduce very closely, with identical quiring, layouts, illustrations and disposition of lines per page.[54] That duplication includes reproducing this error and its jokey correction.[55] But if this picture were in the exemplar too, that is even odder: why would three manuscripts leave a correction not only visible but highlighted in books made close to the poet and for his patrons? This picture highlights a mistake; but it also, of course, highlights the effort taken to remove it. It ensures that the patrons are conscious of the poet's and scribes' effort in their service, their meticulousness and their wit. Correcting seems to be something an author can be proud of.

Corrections and revisions

However, when he records his shorter poems in tidy anthologies, Hoccleve not only corrects errors but uses the techniques of correcting to aid the process of anthologizing his works retrospectively and recording their social origins more vividly, as though for posterity.[56] Hoccleve modifies the titles and introductory notes to poems with insertions and writing over erasure.[57]

[52] Ar, f. 65r (*Regiment*, 3578–84); Ha4, f. 62r. Kerby-Fulton, Hilmo and Olson, *Opening Up Middle English Manuscripts*, 92–4, reproduces and discusses it; Harris, 'Patron of British Library MS Arundel 38', identifies the patron.

[53] See Chapter 5, n. 91 above.

[54] Smith Marzec, 'Latin Marginalia', 271, 279. The two manuscripts are almost *literatim* copies: e.g., in 45 words and 5 punctuation marks around the problematic stanza, the only divergences between the MSS are 5 choices between the letters <y>/<i>, <i>/<e>, <c>/<s>, 4 abbreviations and 1 punctuation mark.

[55] However, Ar, f. 65r is slightly better in quality, as the Latin sidenote to the stanza is also included inside the lasso, and as the man's posture and knot are more convincingly painted. In Ha4, f. 62r the Latin annotation appears adjacent to a different nearby stanza (*Regiment*, 3657–60).

[56] As argued by Thompson, 'A Poet's Contacts', 82–3, 87–90.

[57] HM 111, f. 31r, adding 'ensuyante' or 'following' to the title (*MP*, VIII); HM 744, f. 52v, adding over erasure the second line of a couplet about the sequence of poems ('Heer folwith a lessoun of heuynesse'); HM 111, f. 38v, expanding a title's reference to the occasion (Hoccleve, *MP*, XIII, title). The latter two changes upset braces already drawn round this couplet and this title.

Techniques of correction help him to create a more orderly record.[58] Yet this is not just tinkering with the presentation: at one point he even goes so far to modify the dedicatee of one poem, writing the surname 'Carpenter' over erasure, upsetting the poem's metre of ten syllables thereby.[59] There is some sort of time-lag here, evident when he renames that addressee or expands the title of a poem to explain 'when' it was written ('qu*ant*'). This might be considered less a specimen of composing than of rewriting. Hoccleve uses correcting not only to preserve but to revise his work.

As tools for revising, techniques of correcting might, then, be important for English literary history of the fourteenth and fifteenth centuries. That history includes many works which exist in more than one version: William Langland's *Piers Plowman*, Chaucer's *Legend of Good Women*, with possible traces of earlier stages in *Troilus and Criseyde* and *The Canterbury Tales*, Gower's *Confessio amantis*, possibly Lydgate's *The Fall of Princes*, to name only the most famous, besides innumerable romances, works of devotional prose and minor poems. We often know of such revision in copies by scribes who silently reproduce only one of the versions. Likewise, in the more polished or presentation copies there is much less evidence of revision visibly done with techniques of correcting on the pages, for understandable reasons. Nonetheless, authorial autograph manuscripts can show signs of revision at later stages. Capgrave's *Life of St Norbert*, in the (aforementioned) autograph presentation copy, might offer a few. The interlineations in this book are fairly frequent and so might evoke 'working copies'; some could be improvements rather than corrections of actual errors. Capgrave interlines the adverbs and intensifiers which heighten the tone of much English poetry, *so*, *all* and *full*.[60] Some corrections add clarification, like the supply of epithets such as 'forseide' and 'the same' in *The Equatorie of the Planetis*: Capgrave interlines 'same' into 'þese $^{\wedge\text{same}}$ bestis too' which clarifies that he is referring to a 'wolf' and 'litil goot' mentioned on the previous page; and 'he seid' at one point which reminds us who is speaking, which is not always obvious given the lack of punctuation for speech.[61] Lots of these changes might not be revisions, for they are just the sort of little words which one might omit in error when copying one's work and so need to

58 Cf. similar attempts to organize his formulary with tables of contents (BL, MS Add. 24062, ff. 2^r^–4^v^, 198^r^–201^v^) and notes ordering the items (e.g., f. 14^r^, 'Ista l*itte*ra deberet inseri [. . .]'; f. 75^r^, '‡ A ceste signe ap*res* [. . .] q*ui* deussent auoir este escrites ycy').

59 HM 111, f. 41^r^ (*MP*, XVI.1), discussed by Thompson, 'A Poet's Contacts', 91–2; Mooney and Stubbs, *Scribes and the City*, 130.

60 HEHL, MS HM 55, ff. 21^r^ (Capgrave, *Life of St Norbert*, 1408), 39^r^ (2679), 51^v^ (3545). A mild narratorial surprise might also be conveyed by two interlineations of 'eke' at ff. 3^v^ (194), 24^r^ (1625).

61 HEHL, MS HM 55, ff. 37^r^ (Capgrave, *Life of St Norbert*, 2546, and cf. f. 36^v^), 16^r^ (1056–7).

correct. Without another copy of an earlier recension to compare, it is impossible to be sure whether Capgrave is remedying errors or revising.

Moreover, Capgrave's interlinings are few and unusual: revisions, even in authorial autographs, are not always achieved visibly on the page by the techniques of correcting. That is the case with a revision of Hoccleve's *The Regiment of Princes*, slightly different from that in the early presentation copies, even though it survives in what Linne Mooney has argued to be Hoccleve's handwriting.[62] In this copy the revision has left little sign of correcting on the page. (This manuscript, then, cannot be the focus of this chapter on processes of correcting, as it reveals only their outcome.) Yet even when revisions are not visibly entered as corrections in surviving copies, many of them were presumably made with the techniques of correcting – interlining, crossing out and so on – on some lost rough working exemplar, which the surviving copy silently includes. As Phillipa Hardman has argued, when later scribes are muddled about where to include words or passages, the confusion can often be explained by imagining interlinear or marginal additions, unclear deletions, added leaves and *signes de renvoie* in authorial exemplars.[63] For instance, the manuscripts of John Gower's works have detailed corrections which probably reflect scribes' encounters with Gower's revisions.[64] And the two lavish presentation copies of Hoccleve's *The Regiment of Princes* made by other scribes share just one correction which looks likely to reflect a correction on the page of their lost exemplar: the addition of the adverb 'rather' (*sooner*) which one copy has interlined and the other has over erasure; the shared oversight of this word, and corrections of it, could come from an authorial exemplar with the word as a revision between the lines, say.[65] Surviving variant versions might, then, attest to authors using techniques of correcting to revise.

Yet whether effected visibly on the page or inherited invisibly by later copies, authorial revisions might be corrective in spirit. When an author judges which word is better and then removes it, he is, if not judging one word to be in absolute error, then at least judging one as less good than another. If an author did not think anything was wrong, why would he rewrite? Revision implies that the author's first version was an imperfect realization of his intention. The author's willingness, therefore, to alter the

62 Ry^3, described by Mooney, 'Holograph Copy', 280–6; Smith Marzec, 'Latin Marginalia', 271, 279.

63 Hardman, 'MS Ashmole 33 *Sir Ferumbras*'. See, e.g., Hudson (ed.), *Two Revisions*, vol. 1, cxxvi; Hanna, *Pursuing History*, 214; Warner, *Lost History*, 37–40.

64 Parkes, 'Patterns of Scribal Activity', 95–6, argues that the scribes gathered these revisions by their own initiative, without Gower's prompting.

65 Ar, f. 33^r (*Regiment*, 1808); Ha^4, f. 33^r.

work is analogous to the scribes' willingness sometimes to rewrite when they correct, in fidelity not to the work's origin but to its ongoing internal coherence and accomplishment. There is no reverence for the first draft when a better draft is possible.

The corrective spirit of revisions might be seen in some of Hoccleve's autograph copies – although it is not always clear which direction revision goes in, which is judged wrong and which right. This emerges from two dedicatory envoys to *The Regiment of Princes* in the supposed autograph copy. These dedicatory envoys were both reproduced about a decade later in one of Hoccleve's autograph miscellanies, and their divergences can be compared (Table 11.2). The two copies of the dedications supposed to be in Hoccleve's handwriting have twenty-one words diverging in thirteen of their total fifty-three lines. This is quite a lot: between two autograph copies of another work by Hoccleve, *Lerne to Dye*, there are only twenty-six substantive variants in 672 lines, much less frequent divergence.[66] Was Hoccleve carefully revising the dedicatory poems? Is one version of each better than the other? It is difficult to say without obvious criteria for assessment; our preferences might not be the six-hundred-year-old poet's. Yet a few points of improvement can be identified. For example, other writers are interested in clarity of reference when they correct, as both the author of *The Equatorie of the Planetis* and Capgrave add terms which stress what was 'forseide'. And such clarity interests Hoccleve too in his formulary, where he adds the legalistic phrase *said*, 'p*re*d*ic*ti' or 'diz', as though to clarify the people named in documents.[67] There might, then, be a corrective clarification in the greater precision of reference in line (xii), where the earlier version repeats the name of Master Massy but the later calls him 'my said Maistir'. Other stylistic preferences emerge: for instance, two changes remove repetition, as Hoccleve, like other poets and scribes, seeks lexical variety: the later copy removes 'nakid' and 'hert', both of which recur in adjacent lines (i, iv).[68] But although these changes occur in a book made a decade later, they could be copied from an earlier recension of the text; this later text shares wording with both the main textual tradition of *The Regiment of Princes* (i, ii) and with the rare revision (iii, iv, v). Nor is it always clear whether one version is better; some changes seem deliberate or consistent but value-neutral: for instance, the later copy acquires two

[66] Bowers, 'Hoccleve's Two Copies', 443–4.

[67] See BL, MS Add. 24062, ff. 5^{r}, 21^{r}, with interlineations, or f. 28^{v} with part of 'de[---]{ssu}diz' over erasure. Cf. also his addition of *ensuing* to a French title of one of his poems: 'Ceste balade ^ensuyante feust faite tost apres' (HM 111, f. 31^{r}; Hoccleve, *MP*, VIII, title).

[68] Cf. (i) with Ry^{3}, f. 99^{v}, 'nakid' (*Regiment*, 5443), and (iv) with 'hertes' in (iii).

Table 11.2 *Variant lines in two copies of dedicatory poems from* Regiment

line		*Ry*[3]		*HM 111*	
	Regiment				
i)	5445	Al nakid / sauf thy kirtil bare also	99v	Vnclothid sauf thy kirtil bare also	39v
ii)	5446	I am ful seur / his humble pacience	99v	I am right seur his humble pacience	39v
iii)	5458	Of endytynge / and with hertes meeknesse	99v	Of endytynge / and with hertes humblesse	40r
iv)	5461	And þ*at* for thyn goode herte / he be nat fo	99v	And þ*at* for thy good wil / he be nat fo	40r
v)	5463	That knowith h<e /> whom nothynge is hid fro	99v	Þ*at* knowith god / whom no thyng is hid fro	40r
	MP				
vi)	XI.2	I humble Clerk / with hertes lowlynesse	100r	I humble Clerc / with al hertes humblesse	37v
vii)	XI.7	As þ*at* me oght / vnto your hy noblesse.'	100r	As þ*at* me oghte vn to your worthynesse	37v
viii)	XI.10	¶ I drede also. lest my Maister Massy	100r	I dreede lest þ*at* my maistir Massy	37v
ix)	XI.11	That fructuous is of intelligence	100r	Þ*at* is of fructuous [-------]{intellig}ence	37v
x)	XI.18	Secreetly / and what mis is rectifie	100r	Secreetly / *and* what is mis ~ rectifie	37v
xi)	XI.20	To the speke I / and thus I to thee seye	100r	To thee speke I / and this I to thee seye	37v
xii)	XI.22	Beforn my Maister Massy / and him preye	100r	Beforn my seid Maistir / *and* to him preye	37v
xiii)	XI.26	Of his <t>reso<r / > nat deyneth his nobleye	100r	Of his tresor / nat deyneth hir nobleye	38r

references to 'humblesse', as though this word had found new favour with the poet (iii, vi).[69] In one change the later manuscript has the less elegant phrase: in the earlier copy, Hoccleve hopes that the reader will 'what mis is rectifie' but in the later hopes that he will 'what is mis ~ rectifie' (x). This later copy is more syntactically regular, with the complement after the verb, but *mis* sounds metrically rougher in this position and risks being confused as a prefix to 'rectifie', a risk acknowledged in the heavy

69 The repetition of the added 'humblesse' would not matter in HM 111 as the two envoys are copied as separate poems some pages apart.

punctuation.[70] For comparison, in another possibly revised line Hoccleve moves 'mis' away from an adjacent verb.[71] Some of the divergences look like corrective improvements, then – greater clarity, less repetitious diction – but with others it is difficult to judge which is the first version, which the later, and then which is in content more correct.

Such judgements are easier, though, when the techniques of correcting are employed in the author's handwriting. The visibility, consciousness and retrospection of such techniques do suggest that changes were later and were deliberate. Interestingly, in the later copy of the two dedicatory envoys, one revised line (ix) includes a word written over erasure: the word itself occurs in the earlier version too but with a different word-order. It looks as though Hoccleve is modifying his line by correcting this later copy: he moves 'is of' from a place after 'fructuous' to one before it, as he begins the line, but forgets and so repeats 'is of' in their original position, before he realizes, erases 'is of' and writes 'intelligence' over the erasure. This one slight slip suggests that Hoccleve might be revising his poem as he copies it, or that he is working from an exemplar with his revisions entered with confusing deletions and interlinings. Likewise, in his two autograph copies of part of *Lerne to Dye*, other corrections occur where revisions do. For example, one autograph copy has the dying man cry out:

> O cruell deeth / thy comynge is sodeyn [. . .]
> Thy⌐n⌐[- - - y-g]{hour} was vn to me ful vncerteyn[72]

Yet in Hoccleve's other autograph, the dying man cries out in the second line, 'Thy comynge vn to me / was vncerteyn'.[73] Hoccleve had something like this in the corrected line too, for below the erasure there are still visible the curly descenders of **y** and **g**, likely from 'comyng'. This could be the same mistake made in two copies, writing 'comyng' by eyeskip from the line above, but corrected on only one copy. Textual criticism has shown the importance of such 'coincident variation'.[74] But it could equally be the case that the corrected copy contains a deliberate – visible, conscious,

[70] This is the sinuous mark which forms the top part of his *punctus elevatus*, which Hoccleve employs sometimes alone to signal rising intonation: *Thomas Hoccleve: A Facsimile*, ed. Burrow and Doyle, xxxix–xl, esp. n. 3.

[71] See the revision in Ry³, f. 25ʳ, 'al mis he dooth', of *Regiment*, 1298, 'al he misdooth'. For the prefix *mis–* separated, see Ry³, e.g., f. 25ʳ, 'mis kept' and 'mis dispendith' (*Regiment*, 1301, 1303).

[72] HM 744, f. 56ᵛ.

[73] Du, f. 55ʳ. Besides Hoccleve, *MP*, XXIII.117, see Hoccleve, *'My Compleinte' and Other Poems*, ed. Ellis, 199 (line 117). Bowers, 'Hoccleve's Two Copies', 453, notes the variant but not the correction.

[74] *Piers A*, ed. Kane, 62, explains it.

retrospective – revision. That revision removes a flaw of style: the repetition of ‘comynge’ within the stanza.[75] This visible correction makes the silent divergences (Table 11.2, nos. i, iv, discussed above) look like amendments to style, in this case removing repetition. Hoccleve also uses the techniques of correcting to amend the content, notably in two consistent sets of changes: four times he changes the gender of the soul from male to female, by erasing ‘his’ and writing ‘hir’, presumably echoing the gender of the Latin word *anima*;[76] eighteen times he alters the singular pronouns *I*, *me* or *my* to plural *we*, *us* or *our* over erasure, sometimes also altering a nearby verb to give it the plural inflexion <n>, to allow Cupid to speak with the ‘royal *we*’ as he does elsewhere in the poem.[77] The techniques of correcting, then, improve style, content and grammatical convention.

Metre too would be open to this conscious attention and this judgemental attitude. If Hoccleve adheres to rules of syllable counting, then a revision to such a count is a judgement of aesthetic impropriety. Some variants between copies of *Lerne to Dye* or his two dedicatory poems for *The Regiment* seem like repairs to faulty metre, for they create ten syllables or even, sometimes, create different rhythms in those syllables. In the two versions of his dedicatory envoys (Table 11.2), some lines feel metrically smoother than their equivalents (viii, ix). Moreover, three of Hoccleve’s visible corrections on the page improve the metre: he interlines the needless adverb ‘ofte’, or extra syllables into ‘aftir ˹þat˺’ and ‘Whan ^˹þat˺’, in constructions where *that* is optional.[78] They are only four lines among thousands,[79] but they suggest the possibility of witting revision of metre in other lines of Hoccleve’s verse.

More evidence of revisions to metre entered as corrections emerges in one final manuscript of supposedly autograph poetry. This is the collection of religious lyrics and carols or, as the colophon says, a ‘book of songs and hymns’ which the Franciscan friar James Ryman ‘composed’ in 1492 (‘liber

75 Shortening ‘comyng’ to ‘hour’ could also allow Hoccleve to increase intensity by supplying ‘ful’ without exceeding 10 syllables.

76 HM 111, f. 29^{v}.

77 HM 744, ff. 44^{v} (Hoccleve, *MP*, XIX.219, 221, 231 twice), 45^{r} (XIX.233, 234, 241, 242, 244), 47^{r} (XIX.316), 48^{r} (XIX.365 adding <n> too), 48^{v} (XIX.380, 383), 49^{r} (XIX.411 adding <n> too), 49^{v} (XIX.423, 428, 432, 434). Fenster and Erler (ed.), *Poems of Cupid*, 205, note Hoccleve’s preference for the ‘royal *we*’.

78 Du, ff. 13^{v} (Hoccleve, *MP*, XXI.289), 22^{v} (XXI.660); HM 111, f. 22^{v} (III.284).

79 Also, three corrections improve the rhyme by introducing eye-rhyme with similar spellings: HM 111, ff. 29^{r} (Hoccleve, *MP*, XLIV.18), 30^{v} (XLVI.82, 84). Somebody also erases the final word of one line, just about visible as ‘amen’ still, as though modifying its rhyme with ‘men’ (Du, f. 32^{r}; *MP*, XXII.245). Bowers, ‘Hoccleve’s Two Copies’, 448 and 283, lists this as an error of copying, but it might be an incomplete revision or correction aiming at an auto-rhyme of ‘men’.

ympnor*um* et canticor*um* quem composuit Frater Iacobus Ryman ordinis Minor*um*').[80] Ryman was a Franciscan friar from Canterbury, ordained acolyte in 1476, but otherwise little known.[81] This book is complex in construction and evidently grew over time, itself 'revised' in its physical structure. The colophon follows the middle nine quires which are copied in consistent handwriting and layout, presented as one coherent unit.[82] The main scribe jots a few more verses on a blank page after that. There has been some assumption that the composer of the poems, James Ryman, is the copyist of these original nine quires.[83] Some evidence for the assumption that this is an autograph copy comes, as often, from the use of techniques of correcting to make revisions.

The techniques of correcting are often used to sharpen the poetic form. Like Hoccleve, Ryman modifies the spelling of some rhyme-words, by interlining or by writing one letter over the top of another, to form eye-rhymes.[84] But he makes far more changes to improve the metre than Hoccleve does. Most noticeably, he makes twenty-seven interlineations to the original nine quires (Table 11.3, nos. x–xxxvi), of which twenty-three improve the syllable count by bringing the line to eight syllables.[85] Interlineation is most often, then, used to revise the metre. A few of these interlineations might amend errors in copying, for they supply words needful for grammar (xxviii, xxx) or sense (x, xx). Others, though, merely increase the tone of adoration, adding the intensifying words *all* and *so* which Capgrave interlines in *The Life of St Norbert* and which other scribes preserve carefully in devout works (xii, xxxv). Others supply needless details likely known to fifteenth-century readers such as the fact that the 'welthe' pursued by sinners is 'wordly' (*worldly*, xxxiii). There are also shifts between acceptable orthographic or grammatical variants such as 'Thorgh' and 'Thor^{u}gh' (xxvii), the hedging phrases 'certayne' and 'in certayne' (xviii) or 'to' and 'for to'

80 CUL, MS Ee.1.12 (hereafter Ee), f. 80^{r}. Ryman, 'Die Gedichte', ed. Zupitza, prints all apart from those on a later, added bifolium, ff. 1^{r}–2^{v}; Greene (ed.), *Carols*, 321, describes the MS.

81 For the few details, see Little, 'James Ryman'; and Scattergood, 'Two Unrecorded Poems', 48.

82 Ee, ff. 11^{r}–80^{v}.

83 The suggestion seems to come from Zupitza, in Ryman, 'Gedichte', 167, accepted by Edwards, 'Fifteenth-Century Middle English Verse Author Collections', 107.

84 Ee, respectively ff. 25^{v} (Ryman, 'Gedichte', 20.1.1: 'moist^{o}ure' with 'flour*e*', 'savyour*e*', 'dishonour*e*'; Greene (ed.), *Carols*, 203), 70^{v} (91.1.3: 'f[-]{a}ynte' with 'co*n*playnt'), 78^{r} (106.1.1: 's[e]{a}ide' with 'denayde' and 'mayde'; Greene (ed.), *Carols*, 160) and less successfully 61^{r} (74.6.3: 'co[o]{s}t' with 'lost' but also 'moost'; Greene (ed.), *Carols*, 288), and in the second stint, f. 82^{v} (113.2.1: 'm[-]{e}yde' with 'a freyde' and 'seyde'; Greene (ed.), *Carols*, 250). In the second stint he tolerates a spelling, even after correction, of *moisture* as 'm[-]{o}ystowre' (f. 86^{v}, 118.6.1; Greene (ed.), *Carols*, 56).

85 In Table 11.3, only (xiii) and (xxxi) ruin lines which already had eight syllables; (xiv) makes no change; (xxvii) is a line of six syllables.

Table 11.3 *Interlineations into Ee, with corresponding poem-stanza-line numbers from Ryman, 'Gedichte', ed. Zupitza*

	correction	folio	Zupitza	hand of the text and the correction, unless noted
s	*A bifolium (quire I) added by another hand in front of the book.*			
i)	Synge we now ^^{both} all and sum	1^{r}	not printed	hand B, Tudor
ii)	Born was thys chylde so ^^{fayer} $^{\textit{and}}$ fre	1^{r}	not printed	hand B, Tudor
iii)	That lorde *and* kyng shal ^^{ever} be	1^{r}	not printed	hand B, Tudor
iv)	lorde helpe vs yf thy wyl ^^{it} be	1^{r}	not printed	hand B, Tudor
	The first page of quire II, roughly filled in multiple stints.			
v)	Crist that lyght. and .^{day} so clere	3^{r}	$166b^{1}$.2.1	hand A, stint 2
vi)	And lete alle ^{care} $^{\textit{and}}$ sorowe goo	3^{r}	166.b^{2}.1	hand A, stint 2
vii)	And brought us owt of ^{payn} $^{\textit{and}}$ woo	3^{r}	166.b^{2}.2	hand A, stint 2
	Quire II added in front of quires III–XI in rougher handwriting and layout.			
viii)	Bo^{ug}[-]h‾t‾with thi bloode. thatte were most thralle	4^{r}	150.5.4	hand A, stint 2
ix)	Of the sowle thow. thatte ^^{art} defense	4^{v}	151.6.3	hand A, stint 2
	Quires III–XI copied by hand A in a consistent layout and dated 1492.			
x)	In her*e* ^{age} vj monethes agoo	12^{r}	2.8.2	hand A; corr. by another
xi)	As the sonne ^^{beame} as clere *and* bright	21^{v}	14.4.2	hand A
xii)	Haile vessell of ^^{all} purite	22^{r}	15.2.1	hand A
xiii)	Th[–]{at} is to sey god wi*th* vs ^^{to} dwell	23^{v}	17.5.3	hand A
xiv)	As aaron yerde wi*th*oute moist^{o}ure	25^{v}	20.1.1	hand A; corr. by A?
xv)	For ^^{he} the mekenes hath beholde	26^{r}	21.2.1	hand A
xvi)	To god and ^^{to} his sonne Ihesue	27^{v}	22.6.2	hand A
xvii)	And eu*ery* ^^{þing} that ther in is	30^{v}	27.5.3	hand A
xviii)	Magnifiyng god. ^^{in} certayne.	34^{v}	32.6.2	hand A
xix)	For ^^{thi} mercyes that so grete be	46^{v}	50.2.2	hand A
xx)	But thou shalt ^^{sei} man at a tyde	49^{v}	55.7.3	hand A
xxi)	Ete .^{ye} it so ye be not ded	49^{v}	56.1.4	hand A
xxii)	ete .^{ye} it so ye be not ded	50^{r}	56.2.4	hand A
xxiii)	ete .^{ye} it so ye be not dede	50^{r}	56.3.4	hand A
xxiv)	ete .^{ye} it so ye *et cetera*	50^{r}	56.4.4	hand A
xxv)	Brought king*is* .^{iij} oute of the eest	53^{r}	61.1.2	hand A
xxvi)	King herode fayne wolde .^{them} haue slayne	53^{v}	61.7.1	hand A
xxvii)	Thor^^{u}gh thyne hert shall goo	56^{v}	65.5.2	hand A
xxviii)	To me it .^{shold} be grete doulour*e*	57^{v}	67.2.3	hand A
xxix)	Fare wele fro vs .^{both} alle and su*m*me	58^{v}	70.burden.2	hand A

(*cont.*)

Table 11.3 *cont.*

	correction	*folio*	*Zupitza*	*hand of the text and the correction, unless noted*
xxx)	That ^.^{was} sent fro the Trinite	62^{v}	80.5.4	hand A
xxxi)	Elizabeth.^^{tho} thus seid also	62^{v}	80.6.1	hand A
xxxii)	To save mankyende that he ^{hath} wrought	63^{v}	82.2.4	hand A
xxxiii)	That aftur ^.^{wordly} welthe will goo	64^{v}	84.1.8	hand A
xxxiv)	And to blisse it ^^{for} to restore	68^{r}	86.8.4	hand A
xxxv)	*With* a sharpe spere wounded ^^{so} wyde	70^{r}	90.1.7	hand A
xxxvi)	They that wake tyme^^{ly} shall me fyende	73^{v}	97.8.2	hand A
	Quires XII–XIV added at the end of quires III–XI in rougher handwriting and layout.			
xxxvii)	The glasse is more pure and ^^{itte} wasse	86^{v}	118.5.1	hand A, stint 2
xxxviii)	Laudeth ^^{þe} lorde thatt hast no pere	92^{r}	129.7.2	hand A, stint 2
xxxix)	Moder he seyde take thou ^^{no} nought	103^{v}	146.13.1	hand A, stint 2

(xxxiv).[86] These are needless changes except for their metrical effect. Most strikingly, four times Ryman adds the pronoun 'ye' to the refrain of a carol about the Eucharist: 'Ete .^{ye} it so ye be not ded' (xxi–xxiv). By the fifth stanza, the refrain has 'ye' in it anyway ('ete ye it so ye be *et cetera*'), so it might be that Ryman realizes at this point that there is something wrong, returns to fix the lines already written and writes the final two refrains with 'ye'. This correction too was needless: whether 'Ete it' is an imperative, in which 'ye' would be unusually emphatic, or a concessive subjunctive, in which it would be optional, the line is grammatical both before and after the correction.[87] Indeed, Ryman leaves it unemended in the second line of the burden, where the extra 'And' makes the number of syllables correct: 'And ete it so ye be not dede'.[88] It is not the grammar but the metre which the scribe corrects by supplying 'ye'. The rationale for such meticulous metre is suggested by the addition of 'both' quite needlessly to the doublet 'alle and su*m*me' (xxix). A jolly incorporation of *both all and some* is typical of carols, including one copied and corrected by somebody

[86] Cf. variation recorded by *MED*, *thurgh* (*prep.*), *certain* (*adj.*) 10b, *certain* (*adv.*) 2a; Mustanoja, *Middle English Syntax*, 514 (*for to*).

[87] Mustanoja, *Middle English Syntax*, 143, 475, and 123, 141, 469, describes these constructions.

[88] Ee, f. 49^{v} (Ryman, 'Gedichte', 56; Greene (ed.), *Carols*, 318).

on a flyleaf of this very book.[89] Ryman's added 'both' might be echoing one of those sung carols or, more likely and more generally, might be creating the rhythm and syllable count traditional for carols. That would be useful if these carols were to be sung or recited – say by a Franciscan in preaching. Ryman's lyrics have been described as suitable to serve as hymns, borrowing the eight syllables and four stresses typical of much Latin hymnody.[90] The numerical rules of music or the syllable count of metre can provide a clear standard against which to correct the poems, so that in these contexts revision distinguishes right and wrong.

Authorial variance

Not all authorial correcting is as tidy as this, though. Not all of it obviously emends errors, nor is it always clear which of the different states of the text is to be considered authorized. Authors' texts were often rewritten in other ways, not only by scribes in their customary variance, but by the authors themselves. As a result, many authors' texts survive in more than one version which seems to be authorial and the relative authority of which is not entirely clear. The puzzles which result are widespread in English writing of the fourteenth and fifteenth centuries: it is difficult to think of an important poet in English – pre-eminently Langland, but also Chaucer, Gower, Lydgate, Bokenham, perhaps (in the details explored above) Hoccleve – some part of whose work does not survive in competing versions. The revisions could sometimes be interpreted as corrective, in a looser, metaphorical sense, but it is not always as obvious which version is right, which wrong, as it might be in metre. And when autograph copies survive, the techniques of correcting play their part not in fixing the text but in varying it in these ways. Whereas in a fair copy corrections can finalize the text, they can also be used instead to change it. As Matthew Fisher has noted, authorial autograph manuscripts do not offer a more stable text than any other sort of manuscript.[91] For instance, Ranulph Higden's Latin *Polychronicon* survives in the author's autograph in what began as a fair copy but became a working copy, as Higden revised the text over years with further insertions and erasures; it 'preserves the text in multiple forms, serving several roles for different generations of subsequent audiences.'[92] Besides the simple correction of copying errors, and besides rewriting

89 Cf. (xxix) with the same correction in (i) and also Greene (ed.), *Carols*, 29, which shares the rhyme with 'cu*m*'.

90 Jeffrey, 'James Ryman', 306–7.

91 Fisher, 'When Variants Aren't', 208.

92 *Ibid.*, 216, 221.

things such as metre susceptible to judgement of right and wrong, then, correcting is used for authorial revisions which look more like variance. We now recognize that various genres displayed an 'openness to scribal emendation' and consider scribes' variance as a kind of authorship.[93] By extension, we can also recognize that authors could create variance in the destabilizing manner of scribes.

This can be seen in Ryman's autograph manuscript. After the neat quires of his poems were complete and corrected, the booklet was expanded with three more quires at the end and one quire in front, visibly imitating the layout of the main quires but much more scruffily; in the same stint, the person responsible adds corrections into Ryman's original quires. It should be noted that the handwriting differs from that of the main quires in its more current execution and in a few graphs.[94] Some features make this added handwriting look slightly later: notably the way that the stem of **t** protrudes so far above the crossbar and curls to the right, and some more pronounced horns on the top of **e**. These tendencies could conceivably be two scribes trained in a similar script but slightly different in age and calligraphic skill. But on balance the likenesses suggest that the second scribe is Ryman himself, adding four more quires more roughly to a book he earlier made more neatly. Many graphs are similar in structure. The increased splay on that **t** and other letters could all be caused by writing more quickly and on a larger module in the added quires than in the neat main quires, or they could conceivably reflect developments over time in Ryman's handwriting. While the possibility cannot be ruled out that somebody else added more poems to Ryman's book, what looks likeliest is that Ryman himself returned to his book, expanded the number of quires and poems and rewrote some of the poems, at a later date. Authorship, like scribal variance, is open-ended and subject to rewriting.

Correction contributes to that. In one stanza in the original quires, Ryman himself erases and writes over erasure the last line of a stanza:

Moder and mayde in one persone
Was neuir none but thou alone O mater ora *et cetera*
Wher fore goode lady here our*e* mone
For thy meke chaste virginite
vacat As we rede in diuinitee O mater ora filiu*m*
[->]{In the restyd the trinite}

[93] Stamatakis, *Sir Thomas Wyatt*, 5–6, 9; and most powerfully Fisher, *Scribal Authorship*, *passim*.

[94] One crucial difference is **h**, which in the added quires has a less elaborate limb, but on the first pages in the added quires (Ee, ff. 3^{v}–4^{r}), **h** is more like that of the main quires.

Then (as shown) in his later, more current handwriting he marks the whole stanza 'vacat' for deletion and adds an extra stanza below, at the foot of the page:

⌜Sith thou hast born in virginite
The secunde person in trinite   O. mater ora filium
The sonne of god in diuinite⌝[95]

The first revision, after the short erasure and overwriting, wrongly says that the Trinity rested inside Mary. The second revision in the added stanza rightly says that only 'The secunde person in trinite' resided in her womb; the second revision then glosses that person as 'The sonne of god' and, perhaps to ensure that we understand the significance of this, notes that the son also exists 'in diuinite'. The need for precision is intriguing: the wording is not based closely on the votive antiphon *Mater ora filium* to which the refrain alludes; and for the purposes of a carol, any old praise for Mary would suffice, and making her the mother of the whole Trinity might be emotionally fitting. But it would be untrue and the revision removes theological error. The change is one of a handful of clarifications of facts by correction, such as a change to the numbers in an account of the Trinity in another carol and an addition of the fact that there were three kings in a couple of corrections.[96] It might also be a sort of creative game, for the revision manages to use the same rhymes, with an ingenuity evocative of the rhetorical trope of *traductio*, and alters the general drift of the carol – praise for Mary – barely at all. And the earlier version remains visible, merely marked with 'vacat', so that his modification can be read as a response, not a replacement. A comparison might be the poems of response and revision at the Tudor court in the circle of Thomas Wyatt.[97] There is a playful engagement in rewriting in ways which, even if this is Ryman's handwriting, is akin to variance.

That openness continues when Ryman, in his latter, scruffier handwriting, adds four more quires of poems in similar genres, forms and layout to those in the original quires. Having created one rather delicate record of his work, he then merrily upsets it not only with revision but with less polished pages of his ongoing composition. Indeed, on a leaf formerly

[95] Ee, f. 17^{r} (Ryman, 'Gedichte', 8.2.1–8.3b.4; Greene (ed.), *Carols*, 195).

[96] Ee, respectively ff. 45^{r}, deleting 'i' from '[i]ij' (Ryman, 'Gedichte', 47.4.3; Greene (ed.), *Carols*, 283), 52^{r}, 't[–]{hre}' partly over erasure (Ryman, 'Gedichte', 59.5.1; Greene (ed.), *Carols*, 127), and (xxv) in Table 11.3.

[97] Stamatakis, *Sir Thomas Wyatt*, 14–18.

blank at the front of the added quires, he jots what look like working drafts, in overlapping space, multiple different inks and handwriting of varying appearance. Corrections on this page of jottings suggest composition underway: he completes his syllable counts and elaborates his style, for example, by expanding single words into doublets twice (Table 11.3, vi–vii). The openness of the polished authorial book to variance is most strikingly shown when he tries out on this rough leaf two versions of the stanza on the Trinity which he emended in the neater quires. The trials look like this:

As we rede in diuinite
Thou hast born in virginite O. m*ate*r ora filium
The secunde p*er*son in trinite

And this:

Sith thou hast born in virginite
The secunde person in trinite O. mat*er* ora fi*liu*m.
The sone of god in diuinite[98]

It takes him two attempts to find the version he will insert into the neater heart of the book. Nor are all the jottings on this page first attempts; some are revisions of poems earlier copied in what looked like finished form. The authorial text invites not only correction to ensure its accurate copying but also authorial variance, such as one imagines existed in the working papers of prolific rewriters such as Langland and Chaucer.

That makes sense within genres such as carols which were designed for use and for the flexibility of performance. Ryman's book reveals more such adaptation, finally by a somebody who is not the author: another person adds to this book an extra bifolium, or folded sheet, with just two carols, one of them a garbled version of a poem which survives from a different, much earlier manuscript.[99] This person also supplies music for one of Ryman's carols, roughly at the foot of one of Ryman's pages; he labels one of Ryman's poems as 'anthonys songe', perhaps naming it for its singer rather than its poet; and he recopies snippets from Ryman's poems onto the blank leaves at the back, perhaps so that he can remember them or find them more readily for performing.[100] Ryman's book was, then, open

[98] Ee, f. 3[r] (Ryman, 'Gedichte', 166a[2].1.1–166a[2].2.4). Zupitza prints the jottings on this page as separate poems.

[99] Ee, ff. 1[r]–2[v] (Greene (ed.), *Carols*, 21.D); cf. TCC, MS O.3.58, recto (Greene (ed.), *Carols*, 21.C), a roll from the first half of the fifteenth century.

[100] Ee, respectively ff. 46[v] (Ryman 'Die Gedichte', 50.burden.1; Greene (ed.), *Carols*, 276), 24[v] (19.burden.1–2; Greene (ed.), *Carols*, 174), and extracting from 40[r] (40.burden.1–1 and 40.1.1;

for expansion and reuse by somebody other than the author. Yet even this user and adapter of the book shares some concerns with Ryman and some methods for polishing his work through correcting. On his extra carols on the rough bifolium, he too worries about getting his metre right: like Ryman, he adds 'both' to form a conventional burden ('Synge we now ^both all and sum'); like Ryman in his second stint, he expands a single word into a doublet (Table 11.3, i, ii); one of these changes rectifies the syllable count too.[101] In the work of this user of the book, as in the poet's own, correcting helps to create, refine and recreate a sequence of poems. In their corrections, authorial composition and scribal revision look alike, for they share the qualities of responsible attention and critical judgement which this practice nurtures.

Greene (ed.), *Carols*, 84) onto 114^r and from 41^v (42.1.1; Greene (ed.), *Carols*, 71), marked with a star, onto 114^v. In addition, some carols in CUL, MS Add. 7350, f. 1^r–v, have been ascribed to Ryman.

101 His music on Ee, f. 1^r, might offer guidance on his metrical thinking: below that stave he repeats the line 'Synge we now all *and* sum', without the added 'both'.

CHAPTER 12

Conclusion: varying, correcting and critical thinking

Þus [ended] hadde þese wretches to her endyngges
Þus ended ben / these homycides twoo

Glasgow, University Library, MS Hunter 197 (U.1.1), f. 62r
Geoffrey Chaucer, *The Canterbury Tales*, VI.890–3

Sometimes the people who correct English books – predominantly their copyists, the scribes – produce new errors. While correcting often seems to be a quest for accurate reproduction of the text (as Chapters 3 and 6 showed), not infrequently it results in divergence. A majority of corrections is centripetal, but a fair minority of one in six is not (16 per cent in Table 6.4). Some corrections muddle the textual tradition despite the scribes' best efforts, because the tradition is too knotty to untangle; sometimes the scribes choose to intervene. The retrospection and visibility of correcting make it more conscious than some elements of scribes' work, and so the scribes do make conscious changes which start to approach new acts of authorship. Some of those interventions – adding prepositions to doublets, inventing lost lines – lack the 'centripetal' quality espied in other corrections for they neither involve reproducing more closely what was in the exemplar nor collating another exemplar; they recall the 'appropriation' which fuels the 'essential variance' in the making of manuscripts.[1]

Varying and correcting

Distinguishing correction from variance is not easy. While they differ in *origin*, imaginative, invented corrections might not differ in *outcome* too much from the more common centripetal ones, which restore a text found in exemplars or even restore the author's own words. Corrections which end up being centripetal might well start with invention: a scribe or

[1] Cerquiglini, *In Praise*, 21, *Éloge*, 42.

reader might just guess sensibly some small details easily determined from grammar, rhyme or context. For instance, independent judgement or wilful invention might motivate the interlining of the word *not* to tidy up some seeming heresy (in Chapter 7). Most such interlineations might happen to end up being centripetal, but the fact that in two cases the supply of *not* is misplaced suggests that much of the good judgement in correcting was just that: judgement, which is fallible, and not scholarly fact-checking. A small number of even such guessable corrections as improvements to grammar turn out wrong. So do a few corrections which seem only to improve the style, adding an unauthorial *full*, or to adorn the verse, marking seven lines of rime royal where the stanzas are octets. Might it be that the likeliness and length of shorter omissions is what makes them tend to be good guesses? And might it be only the practical problems of guessing longer additions which make them likelier to be exposed as guesswork? Even accurate correcting might often have involved invention akin to variance – just adept variance for the most part and overly audacious variance only under duress.

Conversely, correction by the meticulous collating of exemplars can result in error. For instance, when Cornhyll finds a second exemplar of *The Canterbury Tales* with spurious lines of bawdy, he incorporates them into his own copy quite wrongly (as noted in Chapter 10). The most striking instances of misplaced meticulousness occur when people conflate different versions of texts, as notably with William Langland's *Piers Plowman*. For example, the text copied by the scribe Richard Osbarn in the Huntington Library's sample is more 'complete' than any by Langland himself as it conflates three versions.[2] This is said to have become more common as scribes became better informed about English poems and their variants from the late 1300s on: the best connected scribes, such as Osbarn, were 'certainly capable of accessing multiple archetypes'.[3] In particular, scribes of *Piers Plowman*, became 'jealous for the completeness of their copies' and had desires for '"complete" texts'.[4] The scribes draw on the exemplars they receive but do not put their faith in the manuscript evidence they have; they seem motivated instead by their ideas of what the text should be like, even without material evidence for it.

[2] HEHL, MS HM 114, discussed by Russell and Nathan, '*Piers Plowman* Manuscript', 119; Hanna, *Pursuing History*, 204–13; Bowers, 'Two Professional Readers', 140.

[3] Hanna, *Pursuing History*, 212, and *London Literature*, 244. Mooney and Stubbs, *Scribes and the City*, 30–1, 35–7, debate Osbarn's exemplars.

[4] *Piers A*, ed. Kane, 38 (and in general 29–39), cited and extended by Warner, *Lost History*, xi (and see also xv, 15–16, 20), whose distinctions between text and document are useful here.

But it is difficult to call such drastic inaccuracy 'correcting'. Such dramatic changes only occasionally involve the practical techniques of correcting – erasing, interlining, crossing out, adding in the margins – visible on the pages (and which are the focus of this book). Those techniques which suggest the witting engagement of scribes, their colleagues or readers with the words on the page are only seldom visible when variant texts emerge. Richard Osbarn's compilation of the complete *Piers Plowman* is not visibly produced by the technical processes of 'correcting': the pages have little sign of cobbling together but are copied regularly without disturbance at points where versions are spliced. Only twice is correcting required: one passage had been woven into this compilation twice, and a reader – not Osbarn – notices and marks the recurrence of these lines as wrong by writing 'vacat'.[5] But otherwise even this radically varying text of *Piers Plowman* does not visibly emerge from correcting. This is typical of other variance which was most often simply copied rather than corrected into existence on the pages of surviving books. There is even very little visible use of the techniques of correcting in the process of inventing spurious lines to fill omissions; only two of the thirteen lines invented in one cognate copy of *The Canterbury Tales* (in Table 10.5) were emended on the page. The rewritten texts which are found in manuscripts likely were the product of correction, in a technical sense of that word, in earlier exemplars, emended by interlining, deleting, extra leaves and so on.[6] But those exemplars with corrections seldom survive, and when we do have surviving evidence of people using those techniques, they most often use them to pursue not variance but correctness – though they seldom achieve it fully and they sometimes pass on variance unwittingly. We might exonerate many of the people copying and correcting from the charge of rewriting.

Therefore, variance can seldom be properly called *scribal* and considered part of *copying*, for it is seldom visibly the work of scribes. We might then define a *scribe* purely by his activity as a *copyist*, as pseudo-Bonaventure does in a famous passage.[7] This copying includes whatever scholarship or imagination is required to correct the copy, sometimes guessing things which are not there, but it is not the same as rewriting a lot. It is true that the roles of authors and scribes can seem as though they 'sometimes merge in provocative ways',[8] but it might be helpful to observe their differences

[5] HEHL, MS HM 114, ff. 81^r–82^v, discussed by Russell and Nathan, '*Piers Plowman* Manuscript', 123.

[6] A point made by Hardman, 'MS Ashmole 33 *Sir Ferumbras*'.

[7] Translated in Minnis and Scott, with Wallace (eds.), *Medieval Literary Theory and Criticism*, 229 ('iste mere dicitur scriptor'). Bryan, *Collaborative Meaning*, 19, stresses the word 'purely' ('mere').

[8] Machan, 'Editorial Certainty', 295.

carefully. We might ask whether the term *scribe* is adequate for somebody who rewrites heavily; we might want to credit more of the people who rewrite texts with the title, instead, of *author*, as Matthew Fisher urges us to – people translating, adapting, excerpting, quoting and reworking and indeed correcting their sources, as was all part of authorship in the fourteenth and fifteenth centuries.[9]

Then, even when this author-like rewriting does occur, its spirit is often corrective, as for the people conflating *Piers Plowman* or supplying missing lines in *The Canterbury Tales*; it is often rather different from the wilful creativity that is often described in commentary on variance; it is more dutiful in its service if not of the author's prerogative then of the text's. The most striking examples of such corrective varying in English are attempts to make the missing links in *The Canterbury Tales*. As is well known, Chaucer left the work incomplete and, in response, the manuscripts contain many spurious additions, extending even to extra tales or prologues woven seamlessly into Chaucer's work.[10] It is possible to describe these continuations and additions, as does Andrew Higl, as the product of 'interactive readers' who 'participated in the ongoing creation and production of the work'.[11] Yet it is also possible to describe them as simply an attempt to get the work right from 'dedication' and 'a commitment to accuracy'.[12] These inventions are similar in kind, though larger in size, to the lines which scribes invent to fill small gaps in *The Tales* or to the guesses where *not* is required. It might be speculated (although this brief Conclusion has no room to prove it) that this dramatic variance was prompted by attitudes similar to those which underpin efforts to collate exemplars or fix smaller omissions: a recognition of the limitation of the exemplars and a commitment to preserving or creating the better text they have in mind from the poor one they have in hand. People's understanding of the form of the text – its parts, its shape – drives but then exceeds their practical capabilities in correcting. It is true that in some copies of *The Tales* there are striking inventions, such as a new ending for the Cook's Tale, the interpolation of one of Hoccleve's poems or *The Tale of Beryn*; but these are something else again: wilful, knowing, creative acts of new authorship rather than kinds of scribal copying.[13] Tellingly, these three outlandish additions occur only

9 Fisher, *Scribal Authorship*, 11–12.

10 These attempts have been brilliantly described by Partridge, 'Minding the Gaps'.

11 Higl, *Playing the Canterbury Tales*, 3.

12 Horobin, 'Compiling the *Canterbury Tales*', 385.

13 Printed by Bowers (ed.), *Canterbury Tales: Fifteenth-Century Continuations and Additions*, 23–40, 55–164; and some are discussed in Bowers, *Chaucer and Langland*, 66–72.

in single manuscripts. There are also many shorter spurious links which fit seamlessly into the narrative and diction of poem; and many scribes reproduce those passages with unblinking accuracy. Even such bolder appropriations as *The Tale of Gamelyn* or John Lydgate's *The Siege of Thebes* are inserted once into the textual tradition and then replicated umpteen times faithfully. The majority of scribes, then, reproduced *The Canterbury Tales* as they found it or could best reconstruct it. While one fascinating activity of fifteenth-century men of letters was 'a kind of rewriting',[14] another activity was simply writing out the text – and correcting it, as part of that.

That dutiful activity is no less fascinating than independent recreation. In manuscript studies it has long been customary to praise variance, or at least to find it intriguing – especially in comparison with textual practices of the twentieth century, when printed works seemed fixed, locked in libraries, catalogued by a named author, subject to laws of intellectual property. But in comparison with our new textual culture of fluid digital forms and social media, it might be worth praising invariance now, or at least noting how intriguing it is. The attempt to get the text right – to think about the text in a way faithful to it and to somebody else's intentions for it – is worthy of curiosity and comment. First, because, it must be stressed, variance of extreme sorts was an option for vernacular scribes, therefore the quest for correctness must not be taken for granted.[15] It is striking that many scribes used correcting to recuse themselves from the very real opportunity they had to rewrite. Moreover and more interestingly, regardless of its proportions in the activity of scribes, attending to something closely, trying to preserve it, to understand it on its own terms, involved a process of intellection that is impressive. Postmodernist artworks which experiment with imitation and reproduction – Andy Warhol's screen-prints, found objects, photorealism – and technologies and media which incorporate reproduction rather than invention – file-sharing, Tumblr, even word-processors' cutting and pasting – suggest ways in which exact reproduction might tell us something about the craft, the intelligence, the quality of attention and above all the agency of the person reproducing. As has been observed of some recent experimental 'artworks' in which artists merely copy out other people's texts verbatim, there can nonetheless be self-expression in duplication, but 'obliquely . . . as a result of the writing process rather than by authorial intention'; such works can express senses of

[14] Lerer, *Chaucer and His Readers*, 12.

[15] Of course, the fact that there was a choice of procedure might have made variance more striking to contemporaries as well.

celebration, beauty and possibility merely in copying.[16] Something similar might be said of scribes. Bibliography, since the work of D.F. McKenzie, has focused on 'the human presence' in changes in the text or its presentation: the 'history of misreadings'.[17] Yet artisans also invest their agency in reading things accurately, in not changing things or in correcting them. There is no less of a human presence in reproduction than in divergence, although the presence is difficult to hear when the surface of the text is unruffled. Difficult but not impossible: between the static of misreading and the silent reading of reproduction (as it were), correcting is an audible effort by the artisan to muffle his own mediation, when it had intermittently created noise in the textual transmission.

Correcting and critical thinking

In their correcting, then, we can hear people thinking. And what are they thinking about? For as well as allowing us to eavesdrop on the attitudes to copying and variance, the corrections speak too of the scribes' and readers' attitudes to textuality, to the English language and to its literature (in ways which this book has tried to trace). The first thing we can readily espy is an interest in their own craftsmanship. The pride of professionals, the devotion of the professed religious and the passion of amateurs all emerge from correcting, as these people seek simply to do a good job – to get things right and to get better at them. The job involved the reproduction of linguistic artefacts in particular, and people took great care over language: they sought to convey it lucidly, consistently, legibly. There was, implicit in that, an attitude to the English language: while the people correcting did not, as is well known, have a standardized English, they did sometimes regularize locally, within the individual book. The dialectal diversity of fifteenth-century English was very occasionally restrained, as scribes, their colleagues and readers corrected transcription, spelling and 'working in'.

That close attention to the detail of their copying process – its accuracy, its linguistic forms – then extended to close attention to the texts they copied. They transmitted those works with care for more than just basic communicative efficiency: with care for verbal nuances of the tiniest sorts, in ways which suggest an awareness – like that of a poet or a critic – of the power of verbal form as well as intellectual content. In particular, they preserved details which would contribute to style and tone, for whatever

[16] Goldsmith, *Uncreative Writing*, 247. See generally Boon, *In Praise of Copying*, esp. 246–7.

[17] McKenzie, *Bibliography*, 25, 29.

persuasive or emotive purposes on the authors' part. Were scribes aware of the value of these words they preserved? Sometimes this was likely just a blanket effort at accuracy; but some of their misguided efforts at preservation suggest their consciousness of value. I speculate that the scribes' own work as craftsmen in words made them attentive to the textual surface thus. After all, they were alert to verse-form too, and their practical task of setting out verse on the page contributed to their awareness of it. They recognized the size and shape of stanzas and they recognized the requirements in rhyme, even down to eye-rhyme in a few cases. The scribes' interest in the style and form of works fed, also, their interest in those works' completeness or integrity. As there are few other comments on diction or verse-form or textual structure in English before the Elizabethan period, these insights are illuminating.

This interest in works' integral qualities suggests two interesting elements of the thinking behind correcting. The first is that the scribes and readers had a curious disregard for the author's proprietary interest in the work: they sometimes even seem interested in the work at the expense of the author. This attitude is continuous with that which lies behind the quite different habits of revision and variance, where an author's words can be cited, compiled in *florilegia*, translated or commented on. As Seth Lerer describes this culture: 'The idea of authority rests with texts, rather than individuals.'[18] They seldom focus on the historical or biographical reconstruction of a text as an author actually wrote it – and in this respect their corrections, even their collations, differ from the textual critical emendations of editors from the sixteenth century and later.[19] As craftsmen of texts and not historians, they are not as interested in the author as later scholars have been but treat the work as a self-standing focus of attention.

Nor are they – not quite – in pursuit of the ideal text, for they are happy to fabricate and make do and mend, when the text is broken; whether they conflate two versions of *The Prick of Conscience* or leave gaps to write missing lines later, they try out practical solutions. Yet what drives those practical solutions is, ironically, a keen awareness of the limits of the material forms of texts which they use and produce. They often trust their ideas about the text more than its material manifestations. They are, if not idealists, formalists of sorts, thinkers about 'the words on the page', as we say, whether they appear on the pages they have to hand or not. Correcting, by definition, involves seeking a not-yet-material text. This is slightly chastening for

18 Lerer, *Chaucer and His Readers*, 12.

19 Contrast the figures described by Grafton, *Culture of Correction*, 57–8, 111, 135, 161.

those who study that material text. It is easier (as a palaeographer) to focus on the material, practical, physical and economic aspects of book production, for they can be more safely deduced from the surviving books; it is important, though, not to overlook the thinking which underpins book production. The thinking which underpins correcting includes a set of ideas about scribal craft – its accuracy, its legibility – and a set of ideas about English texts – their diction, their verse, their structure. What influences the correcting of books is, if not ideals, then ideas.

It is nothing new to note the effect of scribes' ideas about texts on their copies: some decades ago, Barry Windeatt brilliantly called the scribes of *Troilus and Criseyde* Chaucer's 'early critics', using the term slightly ironically, perhaps, as their response was often incomprehension, error and variance.[20] This book also calls them critical readers, for the corrections continue to show the scribes' responses – but this book finds those responses more conscious and more accomplished. The quality of their attention is similar in quality to the 'professional' reading described by Kathryn Kerby-Fulton, wherein scribes use page layouts and annotations to interpret and articulate texts,[21] but the field of interest traced here is more like Windeatt's. Their close reading, formalist reading, reverent reading, discernment, judgement, distinction between bad and good writing are all, by loose but suggestive analogy, like early literary criticism.

Could the scribes' reading even be part of the ancestry of modern literary criticism? This book has neither room nor evidence to argue for that genealogy across the intervening centuries; but the hypothesis to test might look like this. The scribes, by bothering to treat English works with the close attention evident in correcting, helped those works on their way to becoming objects of prestige and scholarship in later centuries. First, those corrections did very practically help – along with the rest of the scribes' less eventful moments of copying – to preserve that literature. Secondly, might the attitudes evident in such care be passed on to people who then handled these books later? That might occur directly when later people saw the corrections in them, although in the long run this would apply only to a few of the earliest printers and then antiquaries. It might occur, more likely, indirectly: did the close attention of the scribes either express or influence a wider interest in reading these works attentively? And could this more nebulous set of attitudes be passed on to future ages and finally to our own practices of criticism? After all, people in the sixteenth and seventeenth

20 Windeatt, 'Scribes as Chaucer's Early Critics'.

21 Kerby-Fulton, Hilmo and Olson, *Opening Up Middle English Manuscripts*, 207–44.

centuries continued to correct these manuscripts; printers continued to correct these works at the press; and early modern commentators often discuss these works as objects deserving of correction or emendation. And through that sixteenth- and seventeenth-century interest in English literature develops, circuitously and with innumerable other influences of course, our own interest in it. So that could be one argument to test: that the corrections are not only analogous to our own disciplines of literary study but might be ancestral to them.

But that hypothesis about the origins of our own literary life is not needed to make the scribes' and readers' literary life in the late fourteenth and fifteenth centuries fascinating in its own right. Whatever its influence, the correcting in English books of those years often displays impressive craftsmanship and often betrays careful thinking about English language and literature in an age when such thinking goes otherwise little recorded. In these fleeting moments when they choose what to write, even if they choose *merely* to write rightly, the scribes and readers, and scribes as readers, express their interest in this literature.

Bibliography

PRINTED AND DIGITAL PRIMARY TEXTS

Arntz, Sister Mary Luke (ed.), *Richard Rolle and Þe Holy Boke Gratia Dei: An Edition with Commentary*, Salzburg Studies in English Literature, Elizabethan and Renaissance Studies 92 (Salzburg: Institut für Anglistik und Amerikanistik, 1981)

Ashby, George, *Poems*, ed. Mary Bateson, EETS es 76 (London: Kegan Paul, Trench, Trübner, 1899)

St Augustine, *De doctrina Christiana*, ed. and trans. R.P.H. Green (Oxford: Clarendon Press, 1995)

Bowers, John M. (ed.), *The Canterbury Tales: Fifteenth-Century Continuations and Additions* (Kalamazoo, MI: Medieval Institute Publications, 1992)

Brie, Friedrich W.D. (ed.), *The Brut or The Chronicles of England*, EETS os 131, 136, 2 vols. (London: Kegan Paul, Trench, Trübner, 1906–8)

Brodin, Gösta (ed.), *Agnus Castus: A Middle English Herbal* (Uppsala: Almqvist and Wiksell, 1950)

Brown, Carleton (ed.), *Religious Lyrics of the XVth Century* (Oxford: Clarendon Press, 1939)

Burgh, Benedict (trans.), *Paruus Catho* (Westminster: Caxton, 1476; *STC* 4851)

Burgh, Benet (trans.), *Paruus Cato Magnus Cato*, ed. Fumio Kuriyagawa, Seijo English Monographs 13 (Tokyo: Seijo University, 1974)

Calabrese, Michael, Hoyt N. Duggan and Thorlac Turville-Petre (eds.), *The Piers Plowman Electronic Archive: 6. San Marino, Huntington Library Hm 128 (Hm, Hm2)* (Woodbridge: Boydell and Brewer, 2008)

Capgrave, John, *The Life of St Norbert*, ed. Cyril Smetana (Toronto: Pontifical Institute of Mediaeval Studies, 1977)

Cassiodorus, *Institutiones*, ed. R.A.B. Mynors (Oxford: Clarendon Press, 1937)

Institutions of Divine and Secular Learning and On the Soul, trans. James W. Halporn, intro. Mark Vessey, Translated Texts for Historians 42 (Liverpool University Press, 2004)

Cawley, A.C. and Martin Stevens (eds.), *The Towneley Cycle: A Facsimile of Huntington MS HM 1*, Leeds Texts and Monographs: Medieval Drama Facsimiles 2 (University of Leeds School of English, 1976)

Chaucer, Geoffrey, *The Canterbury Tales*, in *The Riverside Chaucer*, ed. Larry D. Benson (Oxford University Press, 1988), 1–327

'Chaucers wordes unto Adam, his owne scriveyn', in *The Riverside Chaucer*, ed. Larry D. Benson (Oxford University Press, 1988), 650

'The Complaint of Venus', in *The Riverside Chaucer*, ed. Larry D. Benson (Oxford University Press, 1988), 648–9

The Legend of Good Women, ed. Janet Cowen and George Kane (East Lansing, MI: Colleagues Press, 1995)

Troilus and Criseyde, ed. B.A. Windeatt (London: Longman, 1984)

Copeland, Rita, and Ineke Sluiter (eds.), *Medieval Grammar and Rhetoric: Language Arts and Literary Theory, AD 300–1475* (Oxford University Press, 2009)

Corda, Oswald de, *Opus pacis*, ed. Belinda A. Egan, Corpus Christianorum: Continuatio Mediaeualis 179 (Turnhout: Brepols, 2001)

Daniel, Henry, 'Henry Daniel's *Liber Uricrisiarum* (Excerpt)', ed. Ralph Hanna III, in Lister M. Matheson (ed.), *Popular and Practical Science of Medieval England*, Medieval Texts and Studies 11 (East Lansing, MI: Colleagues Press, 1994), 185–218

Dean, James M. (ed.), *Richard the Redeless and Mum and the Sothsegger* (Kalamazoo, MI: Medieval Institute Publications, 2000)

Denifle, Heinrich, OP (ed.), 'Die Handschriften der Bibel-Correctorien des 13. Jahrhunderts', *Archiv für Litteratur- und Kirchen Geschichte des Mittelalters*, 4 (1888), 263–311, 471–601

Dobson, E.J. (ed.), *The English Text of the Ancrene Riwle*, EETS os 267 (London: Oxford University Press, 1972)

Dyboski, Roman (ed.), *Songs and Carols and Other Miscellaneous Poems*, EETS es 101 (London: Kegan Paul, Trench, Trübner, 1907)

Dyboski, R. and Z.M. Arend (eds.), *Knyghthode and Bataile*, EETS os 201 (London: Oxford University Press, 1935)

Fenster, Thelma S. and Mary Carpenter Erler (eds.), *Poems of Cupid, God of Love* (Leiden: Brill 1990)

Forshall, Josiah and Frederic Madden (eds.), *The Holy Bible, Containing the Old and New Testaments, with the Apocryphal Books, in the Earliest English Versions Made from the Latin Vulgate by John Wycliffe and His Followers*, 4 vols. (Oxford University Press, 1850)

Francis, W. Nelson (ed.), *The Book of Vices and Virtues*, EETS os 217 (London: Oxford University Press, 1942)

Gerson, Jean, *De laude scriptorum*, in his *Oeuvres complètes*, ed. Palémon Glorieux, 10 vols. (Paris: Desclée, 1960–73), vol. IX, 423–44

Gloucester, Robert of, *Metrical Chronicle*, ed. William Aldis Wright, RS 86 (London: HMSO, 1887)

Greene, Richard Leighton (ed.), *The Early English Carols*, 2nd edn (Oxford: Clarendon Press, 1977)

Gribbin, Joseph A. (ed.), *Liturgical and Miscellaneous Questions, Dubia and Supplications to La Grande Chartreuse from the English Carthusian Province in the*

Later Middle Ages, Analecta Cartusiana 100:32 (Salzburg: Institut für Anglistik und Amerikanistik, 1999)
Hamer, Richard, with Vida Russell (eds.), *Gilte Legende*, 3 vols., EETS os 327–8, 339 (Oxford University Press, 2006–12)
Hanna, Ralph and Sarah Wood (eds.), *Richard Morris's 'Prick of Conscience': A Corrected Edition*, EETS os 342 (Oxford University Press, 2013)
Harvey, E. Ruth (ed.), *The Court of Sapience* (University of Toronto Press, 1984)
Higden, Ranulph, *Polychronicon*, trans. John Trevisa, ed. Churchill Babington and J. Rawson Lumby, RS 41, 9 vols. (London: HMSO, 1865–86)
Prolicionycion [*sic*] (Westminster: Caxton, 1482; *STC* 13438)
[Hilton, Walter], *The Scale of Perfection*, ed. Thomas H. Bestul (Kalamazoo, MI: TEAMS, 2000)
The Scale of Perfection, ed. Evelyn Underhill (London: Watkins, 1923)
Hoccleve, Thomas, *Minor Poems*, ed. Frederick J. Furnivall, EETS es 61 (London: Kegan Paul, Trench, Trübner, 1892)
'My Compleinte' and Other Poems, ed. Roger Ellis (University of Exeter Press, 2001)
The Regiment of Princes, ed. Charles R. Blyth (Kalamazoo, MI: Medieval Institute Publications, 1999)
Thomas Hoccleve: A Facsimile of the Autograph Verse Manuscripts, ed. J.A. Burrow and A.I. Doyle, EETS ss 19 (Oxford University Press, 2002)
Hogg, James (ed.), *The Evolution of the Carthusian Statutes*, 4 vols., Analecta Cartusiana 99 (Salzburg: Institut für Anglistik und Amerikanistik, 1989)
Horstmann, C. (ed.), *Yorkshire Writers: Richard Rolle of Hampole, an English Father of the Church, and His Followers*, 2 vols. (London: Sonnenschein, 1895–6)
Hudson, Anne (ed.), *English Wycliffite Sermons: Volume I* (Oxford: Clarendon Press, 1983)
(ed.), *Selections from English Wycliffite Writings* (Cambridge University Press, 1978)
(ed.), *Two Revisions of Rolle's English Psalter Commentary and the Related Canticles*, 2 vols., EETS os 340 (Oxford University Press, 2012)
(ed.), *The Works of a Lollard Preacher*, EETS os 317 (London: Oxford University Press, 2001)
Jefferies Collins, A. (ed.), *Manuale ad vsum percelebris ecclesie Sarisburiensis*, Henry Bradshaw Society 91 (Chichester: Moore and Tillyer, 1960)
Kuhn, Sherman M. (ed.), 'The Preface to a Fifteenth-Century Concordance', *Speculum*, 43 (1968), 258–73
Langland, William, *Piers Plowman: The A Version: Will's Visions of Piers Plowman and Do-Well*, ed. George Kane, rev. edn (1960; London: Athlone, 1988)
Piers Plowman: The B Version: Will's Visions of Piers Plowman, Do-Well, Do-Better and Do-Best, ed. George Kane and E. Talbot Donaldson, rev. edn (1975; London: Athlone, 1988)
Piers Plowman: The C Version: Will's Visions of Piers Plowman, Do-Well, Do-Better, and Do-Best, ed. George Russell and George Kane (London: Athlone, 1997)

Liddell, Mark (ed.), *The Middle English Translation of Palladius De Re Rustica* (Berlin: Ebering, 1896)

Love, Nicholas, *The Mirror of the Blessed Life of Jesus Christ*, ed. Michael G. Sargent (University of Exeter Press, 2005)

Lydgate, John, *The chorle and the birde* (Westminster: W. Caxton, 1477?; *STC* 17008)

Fall of Princes, ed. Henry Bergen, EETS es 121–4, 4 vols. (London: Oxford University Press, 1924–7)

The hors. the shepe and the ghoos (Westminster: Caxton, 1476; *STC* 17019)

Life of Our Lady, ed. Joseph A. Lauritis, Ralph A. Klinefelter and Vernon F. Gallagher, Duquesne Studies: Philological Series 2 (Pittsburgh, PA: Duquesne University Press, 1961)

Lives of Ss Edmund and Fremund and the Extra Miracles of St Edmund, ed. Anthony Bale and A.S.G. Edwards (Heidelberg: Winter, 2009)

Minor Poems, ed. Henry Noble MacCracken, EETS es 107 (London: Oxford University Press, 1911)

Minor Poems, ed. Henry Noble MacCracken, EETS os 192 (London: Oxford University Press, 1934)

The Pilgrimage of the Life of Man, ed. F.J. Furnivall, EETS es 77, 88, 92, 3 vols. (London: Kegan Paul, Trench, Trübner, 1899–1904)

Saint Albon and Saint Amphibalus, ed. George F. Reinecke, Garland Medieval Texts 11 (New York: Garland, 1985)

Troy Book, ed. Henry Bergen, EETS es 97, 103, 106, 126, 4 vols. (London: Kegan Paul, Trench, Trübner, 1906–35)

Lydgate, John and Benedict Burgh, *Secrees of Old Philisoffres*, ed. Robert Steele, EETS es 66 (London: Kegan Paul, Trench, Trübner, 1894)

Maidstone, Richard, *Penitential Psalms*, ed. Valerie Edden, Middle English Texts 22 (Heidelberg: Winter, 1990)

Matheson, Lister M. (ed.), *Death and Dissent: Two Fifteenth-Century Chronicles* (Woodbridge: Boydell, 1999)

Metham, John, *Amoryus and Cleopes*, ed. Stephen F. Page (Kalamazoo, MI: Medieval Institute Publications, 1999)

Minnis, A.J. and A.B. Scott, with the assistance of David Wallace (eds.), *Medieval Literary Theory and Criticism c.1100–c.1375: The Commentary Tradition* (Oxford: Clarendon Press, 1988)

Moon, H.M. (ed.), *Þe Lyfe of Soule: An Edition with Commentary*, Salzburg Studies in English Literature: Elizabethan and Renaissance Studies 75 (Salzburg: Institut für Englische Sprache und Literatur, 1978)

Morris, Richard (ed.), *The Pricke of Conscience (Stimulus conscientiae)* (Berlin: Asher, 1863)

Muir, Kenneth (ed.), *Unpublished Poems Edited from the Blage Manuscript* (Liverpool University Press, 1961)

O'Mara, V.M. (ed.), *A Study and Edition of Selected Middle English Sermons*, Leeds Texts and Monographs, ns 13 (University of Leeds, School of English, 1994)

Paston Letters and Papers of the Fifteenth Century, ed. Norman Davis, Richard Beadle and Colin Richmond, 3 vols., EETS ss 20–2 (Oxford University Press, 2004–5)

Richard de Bury, *Philobiblon*, ed. and trans. E.C. Thomas, rev. Michael Maclagan (Oxford: Shakespeare Head Press, 1960)

Robbins, Rossell Hope (ed.), *Secular Lyrics of the XIVth and XVth Century* (Oxford: Clarendon Press, 1952), with poem and line numbers

Rolle, Richard, *The Psalter or Psalms of David and Certain Canticles*, ed. H.R. Bramley (Oxford: Clarendon Press, 1884)

Ryman, Jakob, 'Die Gedichte des Franziskaners Jakob Ryman', ed. J. Zupitza, *Archiv für das Studium der neueren Sprachen und Literaturen*, 46 (1892), 167–338

Sands, Donald B. (ed.), *Gamelyn*, in Sands (ed.), *Middle English Verse Romances* (1966; University of Exeter Press, 1986), 154–81

Sieper, Ernst (ed.), *Lydgate's Reson and Sensuallyte*, EETS es 84, 89, 2 vols. (London: Kegan Paul, Trench, Trübner, 1901–3)

Somerset, Fiona (ed.), *Four Wycliffite Dialogues*, EETS os 333 (Oxford University Press 2009)

Steer, Francis W. (ed.), *Scriveners' Company Common Paper 1357–1628 with a Continuation to 1678* (London: London Record Society, 1968)

Stevens, Martin and A.C. Cawley (eds.), *The Towneley Plays*, 2 vols., EETS ss 13–14 (Oxford University Press, 1994)

Thompson, Anne B. (ed.), *The Northern Homily Cycle* (Kalamazoo, MI: Medieval Institute Publications, 2008)

Trithemius, Johannes, *De laude scriptorum / Zum Lobe der Schreiber*, ed. Klaus Arnold, Mainfränkische Hefte 60 (Würzburg: Freunde Mainfränkischer Kunst und Geschichte, 1973)

Usk, Thomas, *The Testament of Love*, ed. R. Allen Shoaf (Kalamazoo, MI: Medieval Institute, 1998)

Vinsauf, Geoffrey of, *Poetria Nova*, trans. Margaret F. Nims (Toronto: Pontifical Institute of Mediaeval Studies, 1967)

Walton, John (trans.), *Boethius: De consolatione philosophiae*, ed. Mark Science, EETS os 170 (London: Oxford University Press, 1927)

Whitehead, Christiania, Denis Renevey and Anne Mouron (eds.), *The Doctrine of the Hert* (University of Exeter Press, 2010)

Wyclif, John, 'Þe Pater Noster', in Thomas Arnold (ed.), *Select English Works of John Wyclif*, 3 vols. (Oxford: Clarendon Press, 1869–71), vol. III, 98–110

SECONDARY WORKS

Alcorn Baron, Sabrina, 'Red Ink and Black Letter: Reading Early Modern Authority', in Sabrina Alcorn Baron, Elizabeth Walsh and Susan Scola (eds.), *The Reader Revealed* (Washington, DC: Folger Shakespeare Library, 2001), 19–30

[Alcorn Baron, Sabrina, Eric N. Lindquist and Eleanor F. Shevlin], 'A Conversation with Elizabeth L. Eisenstein', in Sabrina Alcorn Baron, Eric N. Lindquist and Eleanor F. Shevlin (eds.), *Agent of Change: Print Culture Studies after Elizabeth L. Eisenstein* (Amherst: University of Massachusetts Press, 2007), 409–19

Allen, Rosamund, 'Some Sceptical Observations on the Editing of *The Awntyrs off Arthure*', in Pearsall (ed.), *Manuscripts and Texts*, 5–25

Bahr, Arthur and Alexandra Gillespie, 'Medieval English Manuscripts: Form, Aesthetics and the Literary Text', *ChRev.*, 47 (2013), 346–60

Bale, Anthony, 'Late Medieval Book-Owners Named John Leche', *Bodleian Library Record*, 25 (2012), 105–12

Beadle, Richard, 'English Autograph Writings of the Later Middle Ages: Some Preliminaries', in Paolo Chiesa and Lucia Pinelli (eds.), *Gli Autografi medievali: Problemi paleografici e filologici* (Spoleto: Centro Italiano di Studi Sull'Alto Medioevo, 1994), 249–68

'Geoffrey Spirleng (c. 1426–c. 1494): A Scribe of the *Canterbury Tales* in His Time', in P.R. Robinson and Rivkah Zim (eds.), *Of the Making of Books: Medieval Manuscripts, Their Scribes and Readers: Essays presented to M.B. Parkes* (Aldershot: Scolar, 1997), 116–46

'Middle English Texts and their Transmission, 1350–1500: Some Geographical Criteria', in Margaret Laing and Keith Williamson (eds.), *Speaking in our Tongues: Proceedings of a Colloquium on Medieval Dialectology and Related Disciplines* (Cambridge: Brewer, 1994), 69–91

'Some Measures of Scribal Accuracy in Late Medieval English Manuscripts', in Gillespie and Hudson (eds.), *Probable Truth*, 223–40

Les Bénédictins du Bouveret, *Colophons de manuscrits occidentaux des origines au XVIe siècle*, 6 vols. (Fribourg: Éditions Universitaires, 1965–82)

Benskin, Michael and Margaret Laing, 'Translations and *Mischsprachen* in Middle English manuscripts', in Michael Benskin and M.L. Samuels (eds.), *So Meny People, Longages and Tonges: Philological Essays in Scots and Mediaeval English Presented to Angus McIntosh* (Edinburgh: privately printed, 1981), 55–106

Benson, C. David and Lynne S. Blanchfield, *The Manuscripts of Piers Plowman: The B-Version* (Cambridge: Brewer, 1997)

Blair, Ann, 'Errata Lists and the Reader as Corrector', in Sabrina Alcorn Baron, Eric N. Lindquist and Eleanor F. Shevlin (eds.), *Agent of Change: Print Culture Studies after Elizabeth L. Eisenstein* (Amherst: University of Massachusetts Press, 2007), 21–41

Blake, N.F., '"Astromye" in "The Miller's Tale"', *N&Q*, 224 (1979), 110–11

'Language and Style in Additions to *The Canterbury Tales*', in Jacek Fisiak (ed.), *Studies in Middle English Linguistics*, Trends in Linguistics, Studies and Monographs 103 (Berlin: Mouton de Gruyter, 1997), 59–78

'Manuscript to Print,' in Griffiths and Pearsall (eds.), *Book Production*, 403–32

Boffey, Julia, *Manuscript and Print in London, c. 1475–1530* (London: British Library, 2012)

Boivin, Nicole, *Material Cultures, Material Minds: The Impacts of Things on Human Thought, Society and Evolution* (Cambridge University Press, 2008)

Boon, Daniel, *In Praise of Copying* (Cambridge, MA: Harvard University Press, 2010)

Bowers, John M., *Chaucer and Langland: The Antagonistic Tradition* (University of Notre Dame Press, 2007)

'Hoccleve's Two Copies of *Lerne to Dye*: Implications for Textual Critics', *Papers of the Bibliographical Society of America*, 83 (1989), 437–72

'Two Professional Readers of Chaucer and Langland: Scribe D and the HM 114 Scribe', *SAC*, 26 (2004), 113–46

Boyle, Leonard E., OP, 'The Friars and Reading in Public', in Maria Cândida Pacheco (ed.), *Le vocabulaire des écoles des Mendiants au moyen âge*, Études sur le vocabulaire intellectuel du moyen âge 9 (Turnhout: Brepols, 1999), 8–15

Bozzolo, Carla and Ezio Ornato, *Pour une histoire du livre manuscrit au moyen âge: Trois essais de codicologie quantitative* (Paris: CNRS, 1980)

Brantley, Jessica, 'The Prehistory of the Book', *PMLA*, 124 (2009), 632–9

Breen, Katharine, *Imagining an English Reading Public, 1150–1400* (Cambridge University Press, 2010)

Brewer, Charlotte, *Editing Piers Plowman: The Evolution of the Text* (Cambridge University Press, 1996)

Briggs, Charles F., 'MS Digby 233 and the Patronage of John Trevisa's *De regimine principum*', *EMS*, 7 (1998), 249–63

Brown, Bill, 'Objects, Others, and Us (The Refabrication of Things)', *Critical Inquiry*, 36 (2010), 183–217

Bryan, Elizabeth J., *Collaborative Meaning in Medieval Scribal Culture: The Otho Laȝamon* (Ann Arbor: University of Michigan Press, 1999)

Bucci, Richard, 'Mind and Textual Matter', *SB*, 58 (2007–8), 1–47

Budny, Mildred, 'Assembly Marks in the Vivian Bible and Scribal, Editorial, and Organizational Marks in Medieval Books', in Linda L. Brownrigg (ed.), *Making the Medieval Book: Techniques of Production* (Los Altos Hills, CA: Anderson-Lovelace, 1995), 199–239

Burnley, J.D., 'Curial Prose in England', *Speculum*, 61 (1986), 593–614

Burrow, J.A., 'Scribal Mismetring', in A.J. Minnis (ed.), *Middle English Poetry: Texts and Traditions. Essays in Honour of Derek Pearsall* (York Medieval Press, 2001), 169–79

Butler, Pierce, *Legenda Aurea – Légende dorée – Golden Legend* (Baltimore, MD: Murphy, 1899)

Butterfield, Ardis, '*Mise-en-page* in the *Troilus* Manuscripts: Chaucer and French Manuscript Culture', in Seth Lerer (ed.), *Reading from the Margins: Textual Studies, Chaucer, and Medieval Literature*, a special issue of *HLQ*, 58 (1995), 49–80

Campbell, Gordon, *Bible: The Story of the King James Version 1611–2011* (Oxford University Press, 2010)

Cannon, Christopher, 'Form', in Paul Strohm (ed.), *Middle English* (Oxford University Press, 2007), 177–90

The Grounds of English Literature (Oxford University Press, 2004)

The Making of Chaucer's English: A Study of Words (Cambridge University Press, 1998)

Carlson, John Ivor, ' Scribal Intentions in Medieval Romance: A Case Study of Robert Thornton', *SB*, 58 (2007–8), 49–71

Carroll, Ruth, 'Middle English Recipes: Vernacularisation of a Text-Type', in Irma Taavitsainen and Päivi Pahta (eds.), *Medical and Scientific Writing in Late Medieval English* (Cambridge University Press, 2004), 174–91

Cerquiglini, Bernard, *Éloge de la variante: Histoire critique de la philologie* (Paris: Seuils, 1989)

In Praise of the Variant: A Critical History of Philology, trans. Betsy Wing (Baltimore, MD: Johns Hopkins University Press, 1999)

'La paraphrase essentielle de la culture scribale', *Cahiers de linguistique hispanique médiévale*, 14–15 (1990), 9–16

Chaplais, Pierre, *English Royal Documents: King John–Henry VI, 1199–1461* (Oxford: Clarendon Press, 1971)

Chartier, Roger, *Inscription and Erasure: Literature and Written Culture from the Eleventh to the Eighteenth Century*, trans. Arthur Goldhammer (Philadelphia: University of Pennsylvania Press, 2007)

On the Edge of the Cliff: History, Language and Practices, trans. Lydia G. Cochrane (Baltimore, MD: Johns Hopkins University Press, 1997)

Chaudhuri, Sukanta, *The Metaphysics of Text* (Cambridge University Press, 2010)

Christianson, C. Paul, *A Directory of London Stationers and Book Artisans 1300–1500* (New York: Bibliographical Society of America, 1989)

Clark, James G., *A Monastic Renaissance at St Albans: Thomas Walsingham and His Circle, c.1350–1440* (Oxford: Clarendon Press, 2004)

Clemens, Raymond and Timothy Graham, *Introduction to Manuscript Studies* (Ithaca, NY: Cornell University Press, 2007)

Coates, Alan, *English Medieval Books: The Reading Abbey Collections from Foundation to Dispersal* (Oxford: Clarendon Press, 1999)

Cohen-Mushlin, Aliza, 'The Division of Labour in the Production of a Twelfth-Century Manuscript', in Rück and Boghardt (eds.), *Rationalisierung der Buchherstellung*, 51–67

A Medieval Scriptorium: Sancta Maria Magdalena de Frankendal, Wolfenbüttler Mittelalter-Studien 3, 2 vols. (Wiesbaden: Harrassowitz, 1990)

'The Twelfth-Century Scriptorium at Frankenthal', in Linda L. Brownrigg (ed.), *Medieval Book Production: Assessing the Evidence* (Los Altos Hills, CA: Anderson-Lovelace, 1990), 85–101

Connolly, Margaret, *John Shirley: Book Production and the Noble Household in Fifteenth-Century England* (Aldershot: Ashgate, 1998)

The Index of Middle English Prose: Handlist XIX: Manuscripts in the University Library, Cambridge (Dd–Oo) (Cambridge: Brewer, 2009)

Connolly, Margaret and Linne R. Mooney (eds.), *Design and Distribution of Late Medieval Manuscripts in England* (York Medieval Press, 2008)

Corradini, Erika, 'The Composite Nature of Eleventh-Century Homiliaries: Cambridge, Corpus Christi College 421', in Orietta Da Rold and Elaine Treharne (eds.), *Textual Cultures: Cultural Texts* (Cambridge: Brewer, 2010), 5–19

Craun, Edwin D., *Ethics and Power in Medieval English Reformist Writing* (Cambridge University Press, 2010)

Crow, Martin Michael, 'Corrections in the Paris Manuscript of Chaucer's *Canterbury Tales*: A Study in Scribal Collaboration', *Studies in English*, 15 (1935), 5–18

D'Evelyn, Charlotte, 'An East Midland Recension of *The Pricke of Conscience*', *PMLA*, 45 (1930), 180–200

Da Rold, Orietta, 'Materials', in Gillespie and Wakelin (eds.), *Production of Books in England 1350–1500*, 12–33

'The Significance of Scribal Corrections in Cambridge, University Library MS Dd.4.24 of Chaucer's *Canterbury Tales*', *ChRev.*, 41 (2007), 393–438

Dahan, Gilbert, 'La critique textuelle dans les correctoires de la Bible du XIIIe siècle', in A. Galonnier, A. Elamrani-Jamal and A. de Libera (eds.), *Langages et philosophie: Hommage à Jean Jolivet*, Études de philosophie médiévale 74 (Paris: Vrin, 1997), 365–92

Dain, A., *Les manuscrits*, 3rd edn (1949; Paris: Les Belles-Lettres, 1975)

Dane, Joseph A., *Abstractions of Evidence in the Study of Manuscripts and Early Printed Books* (Farnham: Ashgate, 2009)

Davis, Rowenna and Alison Flood, 'Jonathan Franzen's Book Freedom Suffers UK Recall', *Guardian*, Friday 1 October 2010, www.guardian.co.uk/books/2010/oct/01/jonathan-franzen-freedom-uk-recall

de Hamel, Christopher, *Scribes and Illuminators* (London: British Library, 1992)

The Book: A History of the Bible (London: Phaidon, 2001)

de la Mare, A.C., 'Duke Humfrey's English Palladius (MS. Duke Humfrey d.2)', *Bodleian Library Record*, 12 (1985), 39–51

Derolez, Albert, 'The Codicology of Italian Renaissance Manuscripts: Twenty Years After', *Manuscripta*, 50 (2006), 223–40

The Palaeography of Gothic Manuscript Books From the Twelfth to the Early Sixteenth Century (Cambridge University Press, 2003)

'Pourquoi les copistes signaient-ils leurs manuscrits?', in Emma Condello and Giuseppe de Gregorio (eds.), *Scribi e colofoni: Le sottoscrizioni di copisti dalle origini all'avvento della stampa* (Spoleto: Centro Italiano di Studi sull'Alto Medioevo, 1995), 37–56

Dodd, Gwilym, 'Writing Wrongs: The Drafting of Supplications to the Crown in Later Fourteenth-Century England', *MÆ*, 80 (2011), 217–46

Dove, Mary, *The First English Bible: The Text and Context of the Wycliffite Versions* (Cambridge University Press, 2007)

Doyle, A.I., 'Book Production by the Monastic Orders in England (c.1375–1530): Assessing the Evidence', in Linda L. Brownrigg (ed.), *Medieval Book Production: Assessing the Evidence* (Los Altos Hills, CA: Anderson-Lovelace, 1990), 1–19

'English Carthusian Books Not Yet Linked with a Charterhouse', in Toby Barnard, Dáibhí Ó Cróinín and Katharine Simms (eds.), *'A Miracle of Learning': Studies in Manuscripts and Irish Learning. Essays in Honour of William O'Sullivan* (Aldershot: Ashgate, 1998), 122–36

'Reflections on Some Manuscripts of Nicholas Love's *Myrrour of the Blessed Lyf of Jesu Christ*', *Leeds Studies in English*, 14 (1983), 82–93

'William Darker: The Work of an English Carthusian Scribe', *Viator* (special issue 2011), 199–211

Doyle, A.I. and M.B. Parkes, 'The Production of Copies of the *Canterbury Tales* and the *Confessio amantis* in the early fifteenth century', in M.B. Parkes and Andrew G. Watson (eds.), *Medieval Scribes, Manuscripts and Libraries: Essays presented to N.R. Ker* (London: Scolar Press, 1978), 163–210

Driver, Martha W., '"Me fault faire": French Makers of Manuscripts for English Patrons', in Jocelyn Wogan-Browne and others (eds.), *Language and Culture in Medieval Britain: The French of England c.1100-c.1500* (York Medieval Press, 2009), 420–43

Driver, Martha and Michael Orr, 'Decorating and Illustrating the Page', in Gillespie and Wakelin (eds.), *Production of Books in England*, 104–28

Duggan, Hoyt N., 'Scribal Self-Correction and Editorial Theory', *NM*, 91 (1990), 215–27

Duncan, Thomas G., 'A Middle English Linguistic Reviser', *NM*, 82 (1981), 162–74

Dutschke, C.W., *Guide to Medieval and Renaissance Manuscripts in the Huntington Library*, 2 vols. (San Marino, CA: Huntington Library, 1989); available online at http://sunsite.berkeley.edu/hehweb/toc.html

Dwyer, R.A., 'The Newberry's Unknown Revision of Walton's Boethius', *Manuscripta*, 17 (1973), 27–30

Edwards, A.S.G., 'Chaucer and "Adam Scriveyn"', *MÆ*, 81 (2012), 135–8

'Fifteenth-Century Middle English Verse Author Collections', in A.S.G. Edwards, Vincent Gillespie and Ralph Hanna (eds.), *The Medieval English Book: Studies in Memory of Jeremy Griffiths* (London: British Library, 2000), 101–12

'The Huntington *Fall of Princes* and Sloane 2452', *Manuscripta*, 16 (1972), 37–40

'The Influence of Lydgate's *Fall of Princes* c.1440–1559: A Survey', *Mediaeval Studies*, 39 (1977), 424–39

'The Manuscripts and Texts of the Second Version of John Hardyng's Chronicle', in Daniel Williams (ed.), *England in the Fifteenth Century: Proceedings of the 1986 Harlaxton Symposium* (Woodbridge: Boydell, 1987), 75–84

Edwards, A.S.G., and Linne R. Mooney, 'Is the *Equatorie of the Planets* a Chaucer Holograph?', *ChRev.*, 26 (1991), 31–47

Edwards, A.S.G., and Derek Pearsall, 'The Manuscripts of the Major English Poetic Texts', in Griffiths and Pearsall (eds.), *Book Production*, 257–78

Eggert, Paul, 'Brought to Book: Bibliography, Book History and the Study of Literature', *Library*, 7th ser., 13 (2012), 3–32

Embree, Dan and Elizabeth Urquhart, 'The Simonie: The Case for a Parallel-Text Edition', in Pearsall (ed.), *Manuscripts and Texts*, 49–59

Field, Rosalind, '"Superfluous Ribaldry": Spurious Lines in the *Merchant's Tale*', *ChRev.*, 28 (1994), 353–67

Figuet, Jean, 'Corrections, par languettes collées sur des grattages, dans la «Bible de Saint-Jacques» (BNF lat. 17719–16722)', *Scriptorium*, 53 (1999), 334–9

Fish, Stanley, *Is There a Text in This Class? The Authority of Interpretive Communities* (Cambridge, MA: Harvard University Press, 1980)

Fisher, Matthew, *Scribal Authorship and the Writing of History in Medieval England* (Columbus: Ohio State University Press, 2012)

'When Variants Aren't: Authors as Scribes in Some English Manuscripts', in Gillespie and Hudson (eds.), *Probable Truth*, 208–22

Furnish, Shearle, 'The *Ordinatio* of Huntington Library, MS Hm 149: An East Anglian Manuscript of Nicholas Love's *Mirrour*', *Manuscripta*, 34 (1990) 50–65

Gallagher, Catherine, 'Formalism and Time', in Wolfson and Brown (eds.), *Reading for Form*, 305–27

Gasnault, Pierre, 'Supports et instruments de l'écriture', in Weijers (ed.), *Vocabulaire du livre*, 20–33

Gayk, Shannon, 'Images of Pity: The Regulatory Aesthetics of John Lydgate's Religious Lyrics', *SAC*, 28 (2006), 175–203

Gehin, Paul, *Lire le manuscrit médiévale: observer et décrire* (Paris: IRHT, 2005)

Gilissen, Léon, *Prolégomènes à la codicologie*, Les Publications de Scriptorium 7 (Ghent: Éditions Scientifiques Story-Scientia, 1977)

Gillespie, Alexandra, 'Reading Chaucer's Words to Adam', *ChRev.*, 42 (2008), 269–83

Gillespie, Alexandra and Daniel Wakelin (eds.), *The Production of Books in England 1350–1500* (Cambridge University Press, 2011)

Gillespie, Vincent and Anne Hudson (eds.), *Probable Truth: Editing Texts from Medieval Britain* (Turnhout: Brepols, 2013)

Goldsmith, Kenneth, *Uncreative Writing: Managing Language in the Digital Age* (New York: Columbia University Press, 2011)

Gould, Karen, 'Terms for Book Production in a Fifteenth-Century Latin-English Nominale (Harvard Law School Library MS. 43)', *Papers of the Bibliographical Society of America*, 79 (1985), 75–99

Grafton, Anthony, *The Culture of Correction in Renaissance Europe* (London: British Library, 2011)

Greenblatt, Stephen, 'What is the History of Literature?', *Critical Inquiry*, 23 (1997), 460–81

Greetham, D.C., 'Challenges of Theory and Practice in the Editing of Hoccleve's Regement of Princes', in Pearsall (ed.), *Manuscripts and Texts*, 60–86

Gribbin, Joseph A., *Aspects of Carthusian Liturgical Practice in Later Medieval England*, Analecta Cartusiana 99:33 (Salzburg: Institut für Anglistik und Amerikanistik, 1995)

Griffiths, Jeremy, 'Book Production Terms in Nicholas Munshull's Nominale', in Carol Garrett Fisher and Kathleen L. Scott (eds.), *Art Into Life: Collected*

Papers from the Kresge Art Museum Medieval Symposia (East Lansing: Michigan State University Press, 1995), 49–71

Griffiths, Jeremy and Derek Pearsall (eds.), *Book Production and Publishing in Britain 1375–1475* (Cambridge University Press, 1989)

Grindley, Carl, 'The A-Version Ancestor of BmBoCot', *YLS*, 24 (2010), 63–88

Gullick, Michael, 'Professional Scribes in Eleventh- and Twelfth-Century England', *EMS*, 7 (1998), 1–24

Guyotjeannin, Olivier, 'Le vocabulaire de la diplomatique', in Weijers (ed.), *Vocabulaire du livre*, 120–34

Hamel, Mary, 'Scribal Self-Corrections in the Thornton *Morte Arthure*', *SB*, 36 (1983), 119–37

Hamer, Richard, 'Spellings of the Fifteenth-Century Scribe Ricardus Franciscus', in E.G. Stanley and Douglas Gray (eds.), *Five Hundred Years of Words and Sounds: A Festschrift for Eric Dobson* (Cambridge: Brewer, 1983), 63–73

Hanna, Ralph, *The English Manuscripts of Richard Rolle: A Descriptive Catalogue* (University of Exeter Press, 2010)

'George Kane and the Invention of Textual Thought: Retrospect and Prospect', *YLS*, 24 (2010), 1–20

The Index of Middle English Prose: Handlist I: A Handlist of Manuscripts Containing Middle English Prose in the Henry E. Huntingdon Library [*sic*] (Cambridge: Brewer, 1984)

Introducing English Medieval Book History: Manuscripts, Their Producers and Their Readers (Liverpool University Press, 2013)

'John Dygon, Fifth Recluse of Sheen: His Career, Books, and Acquaintance', in Stephen Kelly and John J. Thompson (eds.), *Imagining the Book* (Turnhout: Brepols, 2005), 127–41

London Literature, 1300–1380 (Cambridge University Press, 2005)

'Middle English Books and Middle English Literary History', *Modern Philology*, 102 (2004), 157–78

'Problems of "Best Text" Editing and the Hengwrt Manuscript of *The Canterbury Tales*', in Pearsall (ed.), *Manuscripts and Texts*, 87–94

Pursuing History: Middle English Manuscripts and Their Texts (Stanford University Press, 1996)

'The Scribe of Huntington HM 114', *SB*, 42 (1989), 120–33

'Two British Library Biblical MSS: Some Observations', *JEBS*, 8 (2005), 189–96

Hanna, Ralph and Thorlac Turville-Petre, *The Wollaton Medieval Manuscripts: Texts, Owners and Readers* (York Medieval Press, 2010)

Hardman, Philippa, 'MS Ashmole 33 *Sir Ferumbras*: Thoughts on Reading a Work in Progress', a paper given at the conference of the Early Book Society, York, July 2011

Harris, Kate, 'The Patron of British Library MS Arundel 38', *N&Q*, 229 (1984), 462–63

'Unnoticed Extracts from Chaucer and Hoccleve: Huntington MS HM 144, Trinity College, Oxford MS D 29 and *The Canterbury Tales*', *SAC*, 20 (1998), 167–99

Hector, L.C., *The Handwriting of English Documents*, 2nd edn (London: Arnold, 1966)
Higl, Andrew, *Playing the Canterbury Tales: The Continuations and Additions* (Farnham: Ashgate, 2012)
Hobbins, Daniel, *Authorship and Publicity before Print : Jean Gerson and the Transformation of Late Medieval Learning* (Philadelphia: University of Pennsylvania Press, 2009)
Holm, Sigurd, *Corrections and Additions in the Ormulum Manuscript* (Uppsala: Almqvist and Wiksells, 1922)
Horobin, Simon, 'Adam Pinkhurst and the Copying of British Library, MS Additional 35287 of the B Version of *Piers Plowman*', *YLS*, 23 (2009), 61–83
Chaucer's Language (Basingstoke: Palgrave Macmillan, 2007)
'Compiling the *Canterbury Tales* in Fifteenth-Century Manuscripts', *ChRev.*, 47 (2013), 372–89
Does Spelling Matter? (Oxford University Press, 2013)
'The Hooked-g Scribe and his Work on Three Manuscripts of *The Canterbury Tales*', *NM*, 99 (1998), 411–17
The Language of the Chaucer Tradition (Cambridge: Brewer, 2003)
Housman, A.E., 'The Application of Thought to Textual Criticism' (first published in 1921), in Ronald Gottesman and Scott Bennett (eds.), *Art and Error: Modern Textual Editing* (London: Methuen, 1970), 1–16
Hudson, Anne, 'Five Problems in Wycliffite Texts and a Suggestion', *MÆ*, 80 (2011), 301–24
The Premature Reformation: Wycliffite Texts and Lollard History (Oxford: Clarendon Press, 1988)
'Tradition and Innovation in Some Middle English Manuscripts', *Review of English Studies*, 17 (1966), 359–72
Hunt, Tony, *Plant Names of Medieval England* (Cambridge: Brewer, 1989)
Jacobs, Nicholas, 'Regression to the Commonplace in Some Vernacular Textual Traditions', in Charlotte Brewer and A.J. Minnis (eds.), *Crux and Controversy in Middle English Textual Criticism* (Cambridge: Brewer, 1992), 61–70
Jeffrey, David L., 'James Ryman and the Fifteenth-Century Carol', in Robert F. Yeager (ed.), *Fifteenth-Century Studies: Recent Essays* (Hamden, CN: Archon, 1984), 303–20
Johnson, Charles and Hilary Jenkinson, *English Court Hands A.D. 1066 to 1500*, 2 vols. (Oxford: Clarendon Press, 1915)
Jones, Claire, 'Discourse Communities and Medical Texts', in Irma Taavitsainen and Päivi Pahta (eds.), *Medical and Scientific Writing in Late Medieval English* (Cambridge University Press, 2004), 23–36
Jones, Edward, 'Jesus College Oxford, MS 39: Signs of a Medieval Compiler at Work', *EMS*, 7 (1998), 236–48
Kane, George, *Chaucer and Langland: Historical and Textual Approaches* (Berkeley: University of California Press, 1989)
Kato, Takako, 'Corrected Mistakes in Cambridge University Library MS Gg.4.27', in Connolly and Mooney (eds.), *Design and Distribution*, 61–87

'Corrected Mistakes in the Winchester Manuscript', in K.S. Whetter and Raluca L. Radulescu (eds.), *Re-Viewing Le Morte Darthur* (Cambridge: Brewer, 2005), 9–25

Kaufman, Robert, 'Everybody Hates Kant: Blakean Formalism and the Symmetries of Laura Moriarty', in Wolfson and Brown (eds.), *Reading for Form*, 203–30

Keiser, George R., 'Vernacular Herbals: A Growth Industry in Late Medieval England', in Connolly and Mooney (eds.), *Design and Distribution*, 292–307

Ker, N.R., *Books, Collectors and Libraries: Studies in the Medieval Heritage*, ed. Andrew G. Watson (London: Hambledon, 1985)

Catalogue of Manuscripts Containing Anglo-Saxon (Oxford: Clarendon Press, 1957)

'The Correction of Mistakes in Twelfth-Century Manuscripts, Illustrated from Winchcombe Books', in A.C. de la Mare and B.C. Barker-Benfield (eds.), *Manuscripts at Oxford: An Exhibition in Memory of Richard William Hunt (1908–1979)* (Oxford: Bodleian Library, 1980), 30–2

English Manuscripts in the Century after the Norman Conquest (Oxford: Clarendon Press, 1960)

Ker, N.R. and A.J. Piper, *Medieval Manuscripts in British Libraries*, 5 vols. (Oxford: Clarendon Press, 1969–2002)

Kerby-Fulton, Kathryn, 'Professional Readers of Langland at Home and Abroad: New Directions in the Political and Bureaucratic Codicology of Piers Plowman', in Derek Pearsall (ed.), *New Directions in Later Medieval Manuscript Studies* (York Medieval Press, 2000), 103–29

Kerby-Fulton, Kathryn, Maidie Hilmo and Linda Olson, *Opening Up Middle English Manuscripts: Literary and Visual Approaches* (Ithaca, NY: Cornell University Press, 2012)

Kidd, Peter, 'Supplement to the *Guide to Medieval and Renaissance Manuscripts in the Huntington Library*', *HLQ*, 72 (2009), 1–92

Kline, Barbara, 'Scribal Agendas and the Text of Chaucer's Tales in British Library MS Harley 7333', in Thomas A. Prendergast and Barbara Kline (eds.), *Rewriting Chaucer: Culture, Authority, and the Idea of the Authentic Text, 1400–1602* (Columbus: Ohio State University Press, 1999), 116–44

Knapp, Ethan, *The Bureaucratic Muse: Thomas Hoccleve and the Literature of Late Medieval England* (University Park: Pennsylvania State University Press, 2001)

Kurath, Hans and others (eds.), *The Middle English Dictionary* (Ann Arbor: University of Michigan Press, 1952–2001); http://ets.umdl.umich.edu/m/med

Lapidge, Michael, 'Textual Criticism and the Literature of Anglo-Saxon England', in Donald Scragg (ed.), *Textual and Material Culture in Anglo-Saxon England* (Cambridge: Brewer, 2003), 107–36

Lass, Roger, 'Phonology and Morphology', in Norman Blake (ed.), *The Cambridge History of the English Language*, vol. II: 1066–1476 (Cambridge University Press, 1992), 23–155

Latham, R.E., *Revised Medieval Latin Word-List from British and Irish Sources* (London: British Academy, 1965)

Lawton, David, 'Dullness and the Fifteenth Century', *English Literary History*, 54 (1987), 761–99

Leclercq, Jean, 'Pour l'histoire du canif et de la lime', *Scriptorium*, 26 (1972), 294–300

Leighton, Angela, *On Form: Poetry, Aestheticism, and the Legacy of a Word* (Oxford University Press, 2007)

Lemaire, Jacques, *Introduction à la codicologie* (Louvain-la-Neuve: Institut d'Études Médiévales, 1989)

Lerer, Seth, *Chaucer and His Readers: Imagining the Author in Late-Medieval England* (Princeton University Press, 1993)

Error and the Academic Self: The Scholarly Imagination, Medieval to Modern (New York: Columbia University Press, 2002)

Levinson, Marjorie, 'What Is New Formalism?', *PMLA*, 122 (2007), 558–69

Lewis, Charlton T. [with Charles Short], *A Latin Dictionary* (Oxford: Clarendon Press, 1879)

Lewis, Robert E. and Angus McIntosh, *A Descriptive Guide to the Manuscripts of the Prick of Conscience* (Oxford: Society for the Study of Mediaeval Languages and Literatures, 1982)

Linde, Cornelia, *How to Correct the Sacra Scriptura? Textual Criticism of the Latin Bible between the Twelfth and Fifteenth Century* (Oxford: Society for the Study of Mediaeval Languages and Literatures, 2012)

Little, A.G., 'James Ryman – A Forgotten Kentish Poet', *Archaeologia Cantiana*, 54 (1941), 1–4

Liuzza, Roy Michael, 'Scribal Habit: The Evidence of the Old English Gospels', in Mary Swan and Elaine M. Treharne (eds.), *Rewriting Old English in the Twelfth Century* (Cambridge University Press, 2000), 143–65

Lowe, E.A., 'The Omission Signs in Latin Manuscripts: Their Origin and Significance', in his *Palaeographical Papers 1907–1965*, ed. Ludwig Bieler, 2 vols. (Oxford: Clarendon Press, 1972)

Lucas, Peter J., *From Author to Audience: John Capgrave and Medieval Publication* (University College Dublin Press, 1997)

Lutz, Angelika, 'Vocalisation of "post-vocalic r" – an Early Modern English sound change?', in Dieter Kastovsky (ed.), *Studies in Early Modern English*, Topics in English Linguistics 13 (Berlin: Mouton de Gruyter, 1994), 167–85

Machan, Tim William, 'Editorial Certainty and the Editor's Choice', in Matthew T. Hussey and John D. Niles (eds.), *The Genesis of Books: Studies in the Scribal Culture of Medieval England in Honour of A.N. Doane* (Turnhout: Brepols, 2012), 285–303

English in the Middle Ages (Oxford University Press, 2003)

Textual Criticism and Middle English Texts (Charlottesville: University Press of Virginia, 1994)

Mak, Bonnie, *How the Page Matters* (University of Toronto Press, 2011)

Manly, John M., Edith Rickert and others (eds.), *The Text of the Canterbury Tales, Studied on the Basis of All Known Manuscripts*, 8 vols. (University of Chicago Press, 1940)

Mann, Jill, 'Chaucer's Meter and the Myth of the Ellesmere Editor of *The Canterbury Tales*', *SAC*, 23 (2001), 71–108

Matheson, Lister M., 'The Arthurian Stories of Lambeth Palace Library MS 84', *Arthurian Literature*, 5 (1985), 70–91

'Printer and Scribe: Caxton, the *Polychronicon*, and the *Brut*', *Speculum*, 60 (1985), 593–614

The Prose Brut: The Development of a Middle English Chronicle, Medieval and Renaissance Texts and Studies 180 (Tempe, AZ: Medieval and Renaissance Texts and Studies, 1998)

McCormick, Sir William, with Janet E. Heseltine, *The Manuscripts of Chaucer's Canterbury Tales: A Critical Description of their Contents* (Oxford: Clarendon Press, 1933)

McDonald, Peter D. and Michael F. Suarez, SJ, 'Introduction' to D.F. McKenzie, *Making Meaning: Printers of the Mind and Other Essays*, ed. Peter D. McDonald and Michael F. Suarez, SJ (Amherst: University of Massachusetts Press, 2002), 3–10

McIntosh, Angus, 'The Analysis of Written Middle English', in McIntosh, Samuels and Laing (eds.), *Middle English Dialectology*, 1–21

'A New Approach to Middle English Dialectology', in McIntosh, Samuels and Laing (eds.), *Middle English Dialectology*, 22–31

'Towards an Inventory of Middle English Scribes', in McIntosh, Samuels and Laing (eds.), *Middle English Dialectology*, 46–63

'Two Unnoticed Interpolations in Four Manuscripts of the *Prick of Conscience*', *NM*, 77 (1976), 63–78

'Word Geography in the Lexicography of Mediaeval English', in McIntosh, Samuels and Laing (eds.), *Middle English Dialectology*, 86–97

McIntosh, Angus, M.L. Samuels and Michael Benskin, with the assistance of Margaret Laing and Keith Williamson, *A Linguistic Atlas of Late Mediaeval English*, 4 vols. (Aberdeen University Press, 1986)

McIntosh, Angus, M.L. Samuels and Margaret Laing (eds.), *Middle English Dialectology: Essays on Some Principles and Problems* (Aberdeen University Press, 1989)

McKenzie, D.F., *Bibliography and the Sociology of Texts* (Cambridge University Press, 1999)

McKitterick, David, *Print, Manuscript and the Search for Order 1450–1830* (Cambridge University Press, 2003)

Meyer-Lee, Robert J., 'Conception is a Blessing: Marian Devotion, Heresy, and the Literary in Skelton's A Replycacion', in Shannon Gayk and Kathleen Tonry (eds.), *Form and Reform: Reading Across the Fifteenth Century* (Columbus: Ohio State University Press, 2011), 133–58

'The Emergence of the Literary in John Lydgate's *Life of Our Lady*', *Journal of English and Germanic Philology*, 109 (2010), 322–48

'Manuscript Studies, Literary Value, and the Object of Chaucer Studies', *SAC*, 30 (2008), 1–37

Poets and Power from Chaucer to Wyatt (Cambridge University Press, 2007)

Michon, Patricia, 'Une édition manuscrite d'Eustache Deschamps: le Double Lay de la Fragilité Humaine', in François Bessire (ed.), *L'Écrivain éditeur, 1: Du Moyen Âge à la fin du XVIIIe siècle*, Travaux de littérature 14 (Geneva: Droz, 2001), 27–41

Millett, Bella, '*Mouvance* and the Medieval Author: Re-Editing *Ancrene Wisse*', in A.J. Minnis (ed.), *Late-Medieval Religious Texts and their Transmission: Essays in Honour of A.I. Doyle* (Cambridge: Brewer, 1994), 9–20

Milroy, James, 'Middle English Dialectology', in Norman Blake (ed.), *The Cambridge History of the English Language*, vol. II: *1066–1476* (Cambridge University Press, 1992), 156–206

Minkova, Donka, 'The Forms of Verse', in Peter Brown (ed.), *A Companion to Middle English Literature and Culture* (Oxford: Blackwell, 2007), 176–95

Minnis, A.J., *Medieval Theory of Authorship: Scholastic Literary Attitudes in the Later Middle Ages* (London: Scolar, 1984)

Mooney, Linne R., 'A Holograph Copy of Thomas Hoccleve's *Regiment of Princes*', *SAC*, 33 (2011), 263–96

'Locating Scribal Activity in Late-Medieval London', in Connolly and Mooney (eds.), *Design and Distribution*, 183–204

'A New Scribe of Chaucer and Gower', *JEBS*, 7 (2004), 131–40

'Some New Light on Thomas Hoccleve', *SAC*, 29 (2007), 293–340

'Vernacular Literary Manuscripts and their Scribes', in Gillespie and Wakelin (eds.), *Production of Books in England*, 192–211

Mooney, Linne R. and Daniel W. Mosser, 'Hooked-g Scribes and Takamiya Manuscripts', in Takami Matsuda, Richard A. Linenthal and John Scahill (eds.), *The Medieval Book and a Modern Collector: Essays in Honour of Toshiyuki Takamiya* (Cambridge: Brewer, 2004), 179–96

Mooney, Linne R., Simon Horobin and Estelle Stubbs, *Late Medieval English Scribes*, www.medievalscribes.com, ISBN 978-0-9557876-6-9

Mooney, Linne R. and Estelle Stubbs, *Scribes and the City: London Guildhall Clerks and the Dissemination of Middle English Literature, 1375–1425* (York Medieval Press, 2013)

Moore, J.K., *Primary Materials Relating to Copy and Print in English Books of the Sixteenth and Seventeenth Centuries*, Oxford Bibliographical Society Occasional Publications 24 (Oxford Bibliographical Society, 1992)

Moretti, Franco, 'Critical Response II. "Relatively Blunt"', *Critical Inquiry*, 36 (2009), 172–4

Graphs, Maps, Trees: Abstract Models for a Literary History (London: Verso, 2005)

'The Slaughterhouse of Literature', in Wolfson and Brown (eds.), *Reading for Form*, 283–304

'Style, Inc. Reflections on Seven Thousand Titles (British Novels, 1740–1850)', *Critical Inquiry*, 36 (2009), 134–58

Mortimer, Nigel, *John Lydgate's Fall of Princes: Narrative Tragedy in its Literary and Political Contexts* (Oxford: Clarendon Press, 2005)

Mosser, Daniel W., *A Digital Catalogue of the Pre-1500 Manuscripts and Incunables of the Canterbury Tales* (Cambridge: Brewer, 2010)

'The Two Scribes of the Cardigan Manuscript and the "Evidence" of Scribal Supervision and Shop Production', *SB*, 39 (1986), 112–25

Munk Olsen, Birger, *La réception de la littérature classique au Moyen Age (IXe–XIIe siècle)* (Copenhagen: Museum Tuscularium Press, 1995)

Mustanoja, Tauno F., *A Middle English Syntax: (Part I). Parts of Speech* (Helsinki: Société Néophilologique, 1960)

Muzerelle, Denis, *Vocabulaire codicologique*, http://vocabulaire.irht.cnrs.fr/pages/vocab1.htm

Nolan, Maura, 'Historicism after Historicism', in Elizabeth Scala and Sylvia Federico (eds.), *The Post-Historical Middle Ages* (Basingstoke: Palgrave Macmillan, 2009), 63–85

O'Connor, Sonia, and Dominic T. Tweddle, 'A Set of Waxed Tablets from Swinegate, York', in Élisabeth Lalou (ed.), *Les tablettes à écrire de l'antiquité à l'époque moderne* (Turnhout: Brepols, 1992), 307–22

Olson, Glending, 'Author, Scribe and Curse: The Genre of *Adam Scriveyn*', *ChRev.*, 42 (2008), 284–97

O'Neill, Patrick P., 'Further Old English Glosses and Corrections in the Lambeth Psalter', *Anglia*, 111 (1993), 82–93

Ornato, Ezio, 'Exigences fonctionelles, constraintes matérielles et pratiques traditionelles dans le livre médiéval: quelques réflexions', in Rück and Boghardt (eds.), *Rationalisierung der Buchherstellung*, 7–31

Ouy, Gilbert, 'Le *Valdebonum* perdu et retrouvé', *Scriptorium*, 42 (1988), 198–205

Owen, Charles A., Jr, *The Manuscripts of The Canterbury Tales*, Chaucer Studies 17 (Cambridge: Brewer, 1991)

The Oxford English Dictionary, ed. John A. Simpson and E.S.C. Weiner, 2nd edn, 20 vols. (Oxford: Clarendon Press, 1989); www.oed.com

Pappano, Margaret A. and Nicole R. Rice, 'Medieval and Early Modern Artisan Culture', *Journal of Medieval and Early Modern Studies*, 43 (2013), 473–85

Parkes, M.B., 'Patterns of Scribal Activity and Revisions of the Text in Early Copies of Works by John Gower', in Richard Beadle and A.J. Piper (eds.), *New Science Out of Old Books: Studies in Manuscripts and Early Printed Books in Honour of A.I. Doyle* (Aldershot: Scolar Press, 1994), 81–121

Pause and Effect: An Introduction to the History of Punctuation in the West (Aldershot: Scolar, 1992)

'The Provision of Books', in J.I. Catto and Ralph Evans (eds.), *The History of the University of Oxford*, vol. II: *Late Medieval Oxford* (Oxford: Clarendon Press, 1992), 407–83

Their Hands Before Our Eyes: A Closer Look at Scribes (Aldershot: Ashgate, 2008)

Partridge, Stephen, 'Designing the Page', in Gillespie and Wakelin (eds.), *Production of Books in England*, 79–103

'Minding the Gaps: Interpreting the Manuscript Evidence of the Cook's Tale and the Squire's Tale', in A.S.G. Edwards, Vincent Gillespie and Ralph Hanna (eds.), *The English Medieval Book: Studies in Memory of Jeremy Griffiths* (London: British Library, 2000), 51–85

Patterson, Lee, *Negotiating the Past: The Historical Understanding of Medieval Literature* (Madison: University of Wisconsin Press, 1987)

Patwell, Niamh, 'Canons and Catechisms: The Austin Canons of South-East England and Sacerdos parochialis', in Vincent Gillespie and Kantik Ghosh (eds.), *After Arundel: Religious Writing in Fifteenth-Century England* (Turnhout: Brepols, 2011), 381–93

Pearsall, Derek, 'Editing Medieval Texts: Some Developments and Some Problems', in Jerome J. McGann (ed.), *Textual Criticism and Literary Interpretation* (University of Chicago Press, 1985), 92–106

'The Ellesmere Chaucer and Contemporary English Literary Manuscripts', in Martin Stevens and Daniel Woodward (eds.), *The Ellesmere Chaucer: Essays in Interpretation* (San Marino, CA: Huntington Library, 1995), 263–80

'The Organization of the Latin Apparatus in Gower's *Confessio amantis*: The Scribes and their Problems', in Takami Matsuda, Richard A. Linenthal and John Scahill (eds.), *The Medieval Book and a Modern Collector: Essays in Honour of Toshiyuki Takamiya* (Cambridge: Brewer, 2004), 99–112

'Variants vs. Variance', in Gillespie and Hudson (eds.), *Probable Truth*, 197–205

(ed.), *Manuscripts and Texts: Editorial Problems in Later Middle English Literature* (Cambridge: Brewer, 1987)

Peri, Vittorio, '"Correctores immo corruptores". Un saggio di critica testuale nella Roma del XII secolo', *Italia medioevale e umanistica*, 20 (1977), 19–125

Perkins, Nicholas, *Hoccleve's Regiment of Princes: Counsel and Constraint* (Cambridge: Brewer, 2001)

Petti, Anthony G., *English Literary Hands from Chaucer to Dryden* (London: Arnold, 1977)

Phillips, Noelle, 'Seeing Red: Reading Rubrication in Oxford, Corpus Christi College, MS 201's *Piers Plowman*', 47 (2013), 439–64

Pollard, A.W. and G.R. Redgrave, *A Short Title Catalogue of Books Printed in England, Scotland, and Ireland, and of English Books Printed Abroad, 1475–1640*, ed. W.A. Jackson, F.S. Ferguson and Katherine F. Pantzer, 2nd edn, 3 vols. (London: Bibliographical Society, 1976–91)

Pollard, Graham, 'The Pecia System in the Medieval Universities', in M.B. Parkes and Andrew G. Watson (eds.), *Medieval Scribes, Manuscripts and Libraries: Essays presented to N.R. Ker* (London: Scolar Press, 1978), 145–61

Pouzet, Jean-Pascal, 'Book Production Outside Commercial Contexts', in Gillespie and Wakelin (eds.), *Production of Books in England*, 212–38

'Southwark Gower: Augustinian Agencies in Gower's Manuscripts and Texts – Some Prolegomena', in Elisabeth M. Dutton, with John Hines and Robert F. Yeager (eds.), *John Gower, Trilingual Poet: Language, Translation, and Tradition* (Cambridge: Brewer, 2010), 11–25

Price, Leah, 'From *The History of a Book* to a "History of the Book"', *Representations*, 108 (2009), 120–38

Purdie, Rhiannon, *Anglicising Romance: Tail-Rhyme and Genre in Medieval English Literature* (Cambridge: Brewer, 2008)

Pye, David, *The Nature and Art of Workmanship*, rev. James Pye and Elizabeth Balaam (1968; London: Herbert Press, 1995)

Rábade, Luis Iglesias, *Handbook of Middle English: Grammar and Texts* (Munich: LINCOM, 2003), 158–61

Rand Schmidt, Kari Anne, *The Authorship of The Equatorie of the Planetis* (Cambridge: Brewer, 1993)

Reeve, M.D., *Manuscripts and Methods: Essays on Editing and Transmission* (Rome: Storia e Letteratura, 2011)

Reiter, Eric. H., 'The Reader as Author of the User-Produced Manuscript: Reading and Rewriting Popular Latin Theology in the Late Middle Ages', *Viator*, 27 (1996), 151–69

Reynhout, Lucien, *Formules latines de colophons*, Bibliologia: Elementa ad librorum studia pertinentia 25, 2 vols. (Turnhout: Brepols, 2006)

Reynolds, L.D. and N.G. Wilson, *Scribes and Scholars: A Guide to the Transmission of Greek and Latin Literature*, 3rd edn (1968; Oxford: Clarendon Press, 1991)

Reynolds, Suzanne, *Medieval Reading: Grammar, Rhetoric and the Classical Text* (Cambridge University Press, 1996)

Richardson, Malcolm, *Middle-Class Writing in Late Medieval London* (London: Pickering & Chatto, 2011)

Roberts, Jane, 'On Giving Scribe B a Name and a Clutch of London Manuscripts from *c.*1400', *MÆ*, 80 (2011), 247–70

Robinson, P.R., *Catalogue of Dated and Datable Manuscripts c.737–1600 in Cambridge Libraries*, 2 vols. (Cambridge: Brewer, 1988)

Robinson, Pamela, 'Geoffrey Chaucer and the *Equatorie of the Planetis*: The State of the Problem', *ChRev.*, 26 (1991), 17–30

Rooney, Ellen, 'Form and Contentment', in Wolfson and Brown (eds.), *Reading for Form*, 25–48

Rothwell, William, 'Synonymity and Semantic Variability in Medieval French and Middle English', *Modern Language Review*, 102 (2007), 363–80

Rouse, Mary A. and Richard H. Rouse, 'Correction and Emendation of Texts in the Fifteenth Century and the Autograph of the *Opus Pacis* by Oswaldus Anglicus', in Sigrid Krämer and Michael Bernhard (eds.), *Scire litteras: Forschungen zum mittelalterlichen Geistesleben* (Munich: Bayerische Akademie der Wissenschaften, 1988), 333–46

'The Dissemination of Texts in Pecia at Bologna and Paris', in Rück and Boghardt (eds.), *Rationalisierung der Buchherstellung*, 69–77

Manuscripts and their Makers: Commercial Book Producers in Medieval Paris, 1200–1500, 2 vols. (Turnhout: Miller, 2000)

'The Vocabulary of Wax Tablets', in Weijers (ed.), *Vocabulaire du livre*, 220–30

Rück, Peter and Martin Boghardt (eds.), *Rationalisierung der Buchherstellung im Mittelalter und in der frühen Neuzeit* (Marburg an der Lahn: Institut für Historische Hilfswissenschaften, 1994)

Russell, G.H. and Venetia Nathan, 'A *Piers Plowman* Manuscript in the Huntington Library', *HLQ*, 26 (1963), 119–30

Samuels, M.L., 'Spelling and Dialect in the Late and Post-Middle English Periods', in J.J. Smith (ed.), *The English of Chaucer and His Contemporaries* (Aberdeeen University Press, 1988), 86–95

Sánchez-Martí, Jordi, 'Pynkhurst's "Necglygence and Rape" Reassessed', *English Studies*, 92 (2011), 360–74

Sargent, Michael G., *James Grenehalgh as Textual Critic*, Analecta Cartusiana 85, 2 vols. (Salzburg: Institut für Anglistik und Amerikanistik, 1984)

Scattergood, John, 'Two Unrecorded Poems from Trinity College, Dublin MS 490', *Review of English Studies*, 38 (1987), 46–9

Schulz, H.C., 'Thomas Hoccleve, Scribe', *Speculum*, 12 (1937), 71–81

Scott, Kathleen L., 'Limning and Book-Producing Terms and Signs In Situ in Late-Medieval English Manuscripts: A First Listing', in Richard Beadle and A.J. Piper (eds.), *New Science Out of Old Books: Studies in Manuscripts and Early Printed Books in Honour of A.I. Doyle* (Aldershot: Scolar Press, 1994), 142–88

'Representations of Scribal Activity in English Manuscripts c. 1400–c. 1490: A Mirror of the Craft?', in Michael Gullick (ed.), *Pen in Hand: Medieval Scribal Portraits, Colophons and Tools* (Walkern: Red Gull Press, 2006), 115–49

Scragg, D.G., *A History of English Spelling* (Manchester University Press, 1974)

Sennett, Richard, *The Corrosion of Character: The Personal Consequences of Work in the New Capitalism* (New York: Norton, 1998)

The Craftsman (2008; London: Penguin, 2009)

Seymour, M.C., *A Catalogue of Chaucer Manuscripts*, 2 vols. (Aldershot: Scolar, 1995–8)

Shepherd, Stephen H.A., 'The Ashmole "Sir Ferumbras": Translation in Holograph', in Roger Ellis (ed.), *The Medieval Translator* (Cambridge: Brewer, 1989), 103–21

Sherman, William, *Used Books: Marking Readers in Renaissance England* (Philadelphia: University of Pennsylvania Press, 2008)

Simpson, Percy, *Proof-Reading in the Sixteenth, Seventeenth and Eighteenth Centuries*, rev. edn (1935; Oxford University Press, 1970)

Skemer, Don C., *Binding Words: Textual Amulets in the Middle Ages* (University Park: Pennsylvania State University Press, 2006)

Smalley, Beryl, *The Study of the Bible in the Middle Ages*, 3rd edn (1941; Oxford: Blackwell, 1983)

Smith, D. Vance, 'Afterword: Lydgate's Refrain: The Open When', in Lisa H. Cooper and Andrea Denny-Brown (eds.), *Lydgate Matters: Poetry and Material Culture in the Fifteenth Century* (New York: Palgrave Macmillan, 2008), 185–95

'Medieval *Forma*: The Logic of the Work', in Wolfson and Brown (eds.), *Reading for Form*, 66–79

Smith, Jeremy, *An Historical Study of English: Function, Form and Change* (London: Routledge, 1996)

'Standard Language in Early Middle English?', in Irma Taavitsainen, Terrtu Nevalainen, Päivi Pahta and Matti Rissanen (eds.), *Placing Middle English in Context* (Berlin: Mouton de Gruyter, 2000), 125–39

Smith, Margaret M., 'Imposition in Manuscripts: Evidence for the Use of Sense-Sequence Copying in a New Fragment', in Brownrigg (ed.), *Making the Medieval Book: Techniques of Production* (Los Altos Hills, CA: Anderson-Lovelace, 1995), 145–56

Smith Marzec, Marcia, 'The Latin Marginalia of the *Regiment of Princes* as an Aid to Stemmatic Analysis', *Text*, 3 (1987), 269–84

Somerset, Fiona, 'Censorship', in Gillespie and Wakelin (eds.), *Production of Books in England*, 239–58

St Clair, William, *The Reading Nation in the Romantic Period* (Cambridge University Press, 2004)

Stamatakis, Chris, *Sir Thomas Wyatt and the Rhetoric of Rewriting: 'Turning the Word'* (Oxford University Press, 2012)

Stercal, Claudio, *Stephen Harding: A Biographical Sketch and Texts*, trans. Martha F. Krieg, Cistercian Studies 226 (Collegeville, MN: Liturgical Press, 2008)

Stewart, Susan, 'Rhyme and Freedom', in Marjorie Perloff and Craig Dworkin (eds.), *The Sound of Poetry and the Poetry of Sound* (University of Chicago Press, 2009), 29–48

Stiennon, Jacques, *L'Écriture*, Typologie des Sources du Moyen Âge Occidental 72 (Turnhout: Brepols, 1995)

Tanselle, G. Thomas, *Bibliographical Analysis: An Introduction* (Cambridge University Press, 2009)

Tatlock, John S.P., 'The Epilog of Chaucer's "Troilus"', *Modern Philology*, 18 (1921), 113–47

Tatlock, John S.P. and Arthur G. Kennedy, *A Concordance to the Complete Works of Geoffrey Chaucer and to the Romaunt of the Rose* (Washington, DC: Carnegie Institute, 1927)

Teeuwen, Mariken, *The Vocabulary of Intellectual Life in the Middle Ages*, Études sur le vocabulaire intellectuel du moyen âge 10 (Turnhout: Brepols, 2003)

Thompson, John J., 'The Middle English Prose *Brut* and the Possibilities of Cultural Mapping', in Connolly and Mooney (eds.), *Design and Distribution*, 245–60

'A Poet's Contacts with the Great and the Good: Further Consideration of Thomas Hoccleve's Texts and Manuscripts', in Felicity Riddy (ed.), *Prestige, Authority and Power in Late Medieval Manuscripts and Texts* (Cambridge: Brewer, 2000), 77–101

Timpanaro, Sebastiano, *The Freudian Slip*, trans. Kate Soper (London: NLB, 1976)

Il lapsus freudiano: Psicanalisi e critica testuale (Florence: La Nuova Italia, 1974)

Tolmie, Sarah, 'The Professional: Thomas Hoccleve', *SAC*, 29 (2007), 341–73

Troncarelli, Fabio, '*Litteras pulcherrimas*. Correzioni di Cassiodoro nei codici di Vivarium', *Scrittura e civiltà*, 20 (1996), 89–109

Trumpener, Katie, 'Critical Response I. Paratext and Genre System: A Response to Franco Moretti', *Critical Inquiry*, 36 (2009), 159–71

Turville-Petre, Thorlac, 'Putting It Right: The Corrections of Huntington Library MS Hm 128 and BL Additional MS. 35287', *YLS*, 16 (2002), 41–65

Vinaver, Eugène, 'Principles of Textual Emendation', in *Studies in French Language and Mediæval Literature Presented to Professor Mildred K. Pope* (Manchester University Press, 1939), 351–69

Wakelin, Daniel, 'The Exemplar for Caxton's *The Chronicles of England*?', *JEBS*, 14 (2011), 55–83

'Editing and Correcting', in Gillespie and Hudson (eds.), *Probable Truth*, 242–59

Humanism, Reading and English Literature 1430–1530 (Oxford University Press, 2007)

'Instructing Readers in Fifteenth-Century Poetic Manuscripts', *HLQ*, 73 (2010), 433–52

'Scholarly Scribes and the Creation of *Knyghthode and Bataile*', *EMS*, 12 (2005), 26–45

'When Scribes Won't Write: Gaps in Middle English Books,' *SAC*, 36 (2014)

'Writing the Words', in Gillespie and Wakelin (eds.), *Production of Books in England*, 34–58

Warner, Lawrence, *The Lost History of Piers Plowman: The Earliest Transmission of Langland's Work* (Philadelphia: University of Pennsylvania Press, 2011)

Watson, Andrew G., *Catalogue of Dated and Datable Manuscripts c.700–1600 in the Department of Manuscripts, British Library*, 2 vols. (London: British Library, 1979)

Watson, Nicholas, 'Censorship and Cultural Change in Late-Medieval England: Vernacular Theology, the Oxford Translation Debate, and Arundel's Constitutions of 1409', *Speculum*, 70 (1995), 822–64

'A clerke schulde have it of kinde for to kepe counsell', in Vincent Gillespie and Kantik Ghosh (eds.), *After Arundel: Religious Writing in Fifteenth-Century England* (Turnhout: Brepols, 2011), 563–89

Watt, David, '"I this book shal make": Thomas Hoccleve's Self-Publication and Book Production', *Leeds Studies in English*, 34 (2003), 133–60

Webber, Teresa, *Scribes and Scholars at Salisbury Cathedral c.1075–c.1125* (Oxford: Clarendon Press, 1992)

Weijers, Olga (ed.), *Vocabulaire du livre et de l'écriture au moyen âge*, Études sur le vocabulaire intellectuel du moyen âge 2 (Turnhout: Brepols, 1989)

Whalley, Joyce Irene, *Writing Implements and Accessories from the Roman Stylus to the Typewriter* (Newton Abbot: David and Charles, 1975)

Windeatt, B.A., 'The Scribes as Chaucer's Early Critics', *SAC*, 1 (1979), 119–41

Windross, Michael, 'Loss of Postvocalic *r*: Were the Orthoepists Really Tone-Deaf?', in Dieter Kastovsky (ed.), *Studies in Early Modern English*, Topics in English Linguistics 13 (Berlin: Mouton de Gruyter, 1994), 429–48

Wolfson, Susan J. and Marshall Brown (eds.), *Reading for Form* (Seattle: University of Washington Press, 2006)

Wright, Laura, 'More on the History of *Shit* and *Shut*', *Studia Anglica Posnaniensia*, 32 (1997), 3–16

Załuska, Yolanta, *L'Enluminure et le scriptorium de Cîteaux au XIIe siècle*, Cîteaux, Commentarii Cistercienses, Studia et Documenta 4 (Nuits-Saint-Georges: Cîteaux, 1989)

Zettersten, Arne, 'A Manuscript of "Agnus castus" in the Huntington Library', *N&Q*, 216 (1971) 130–1

Index of manuscripts

General index

The index alphabetizes works under their authors, translations under their translators; however, it alphabetizes works or translations of which the author or translator is anonymous or uncertain under the title. It alphabetizes writers known by a Christian name and a toponym by the toponym. It indexes some fifteenth-century English and Latin metatextual terms; English ones follow the spelling of the headword in *MED*.

CAMBRIDGE STUDIES IN MEDIEVAL LITERATURE

1 Robin Kirkpatrick *Dante's Inferno: Difficulty and Dead Poetry*
2 Jeremy Tambling *Dante and Difference: Writing in the 'Commedia'*
3 Simon Gaunt *Troubadours and Irony*
4 Wendy Scase *'Piers Plowman' and the New Anticlericalism*
5 Joseph Duggan *The 'Cantar De Mio Cid': Poetic Creation in its Economic and Social Contexts*
6 Roderick Beaton *The Medieval Greek Romance*
7 Kathryn Kerby-Fulton *Reformist Apocalypticism and 'Piers Plowman'*
8 Alison Morgan *Dante and the Medieval Other World*
9 Eckehard Simon (ed.) *The Theatre of Medieval Europe: New Research in Early Drama*
10 Mary Carruthers *The Book of Memory: A Study of Memory in Medieval Culture*
11 Rita Copeland *Rhetoric, Hermeneutics and Translation in the Middle Ages: Academic Traditions and Vernacular Texts*
12 Donald Maddox *The Arthurian Romances of Chrétien de Troyes: Once and Future Fictions*
13 Nicholas Watson *Richard Rolle and the Invention of Authority*
14 Steven F. Kruger *Dreaming in the Middle Ages*
15 Barbara Nolan *Chaucer and the Tradition of the 'Roman Antique'*
16 Sylvia Huot *The 'Romance of the Rose' and its Medieval Readers: Interpretations, Reception, Manuscript Transmission*
17 Carol M. Meale (ed.) *Women and Literature in Britain, 1150–1500*
18 Henry Ansgar Kelly *Ideas and Forms of Tragedy from Aristotle to the Middle Ages*
19 Martin Irvine *The Making of Textual Culture: Grammatica and Literary Theory, 350–1100*
20 Larry Scanlon *Narrative, Authority and Power: The Medieval Exemplum and the Chaucerian Tradition*
21 Erik Kooper *Medieval Dutch Literature in its European Context*
22 Steven Botterill *Dante and the Mystical Tradition: Bernard of Clairvaux in the 'Commedia'*
23 Peter Biller and Anne Hudson (eds.) *Heresy and Literacy, 1000–1530*
24 Christopher Baswell *Virgil in Medieval England: Figuring the 'Aeneid' from the Twelfth Century to Chaucer*
25 James Simpson *Sciences and Self in Medieval Poetry: Alan of Lille's 'Anticlaudianus' and John Gower's 'Confessio Amantis'*
26 Joyce Coleman *Public Reading and the Reading Public in Late Medieval England and France*
27 Suzanne Reynolds *Medieval Reading: Grammar, Rhetoric and the Classical Text*
28 Charlotte Brewer *Editing 'Piers Plowman': the Evolution of the Text*

29 Walter Haug *Vernacular Literary Theory in the Middle Ages: The German Tradition in its European Context*
30 Sarah Spence *Texts and the Self in the Twelfth Century*
31 Edwin Craun *Lies, Slander and Obscenity in Medieval English Literature: Pastoral Rhetoric and the Deviant Speaker*
32 Patricia E. Grieve *'Floire and Blancheflor' and the European Romance*
33 Huw Pryce (ed.) *Literacy in Medieval Celtic Societies*
34 Mary Carruthers *The Craft of Thought: Meditation, Rhetoric, and the Making of Images, 400–1200*
35 Beate Schmolke-Hasselman *The Evolution of Arthurian Romance: The Verse Tradition from Chrétien to Froissart*
36 Siân Echard *Arthurian Narrative in the Latin Tradition*
37 Fiona Somerset *Clerical Discourse and Lay Audience in Late Medieval England*
38 Florence Percival *Chaucer's Legendary Good Women*
39 Christopher Cannon *The Making of Chaucer's English: A Study of Words*
40 Rosalind Brown-Grant *Christine de Pizan and the Moral Defence of Women: Reading Beyond Gender*
41 Richard Newhauser *The Early History of Greed: the Sin of Avarice in Early Medieval Thought and Literature*
42 Margaret Clunies Ross *Old Icelandic Literature and Society*
43 Donald Maddox *Fictions of Identity in Medieval France*
44 Rita Copeland *Pedagogy, Intellectuals, and Dissent in the Later Middle Ages: Lollardy and Ideas of Learning*
45 Kantik Ghosh *The Wycliffite Heresy: Authority and the Interpretation of Texts*
46 Mary C. Erler *Women, Reading, and Piety in Late Medieval England*
47 D. H. Green *The Beginnings of Medieval Romance: Fact and Fiction 1150–1220*
48 J. A. Burrow *Gestures and Looks in Medieval Narrative*
49 Ardis Butterfield *Poetry and Music in Medieval France: From Jean Renart to Guillaume de Machaut*
50 Emily Steiner *Documentary Culture and the Making of Medieval English Literature*
51 William E. Burgwinkle *Sodomy, Masculinity, and Law in Medieval Literature*
52 Nick Havely *Dante and the Franciscans: Poverty and the Papacy in the 'Commedia'*
53 Siegfried Wenzel *Latin Sermon Collections from Later Medieval England*
54 Ananya Jahanara Kabir and Deanne Williams (eds.) *Postcolonial Approaches to the European Middle Ages: Translating Cultures*
55 Mark Miller *Philosophical Chaucer: Love, Sex, and Agency in the 'Canterbury Tales'*
56 Simon Gilson *Dante and Renaissance Florence*
57 Ralph Hanna *London Literature, 1300–1380*
58 Maura Nolan *John Lydgate and the Making of Public Culture*
59 Nicolette Zeeman *Piers Plowman and the Medieval Discourse of Desire*
60 Anthony Bale *The Jew in the Medieval Book: English Antisemitisms 1350–1500*
61 Robert J. Meyer-Lee *Poets and Power from Chaucer to Wyatt*

62 Isabel Davis *Writing Masculinity in the Later Middle Ages*
63 John M. Fyler *Language and the Declining World in Chaucer, Dante and Jean de Meun*
64 Matthew Giancarlo *Parliament and Literature in Late Medieval England*
65 D. H. Green *Women Readers in the Middle Ages*
66 Mary Dove *The First English Bible: The Text and Context of the Wycliffite Versions*
67 Jenni Nuttall *The Creation of Lancastrian Kingship: Literature, Language and Politics in Late Medieval England*
68 Laura Ashe *Fiction and History in England, 1066–1200*
69 J. A. Burrow *The Poetry of Praise*
70 Mary Carruthers *The Book of Memory: A Study of Memory in Medieval Culture* (Second Edition)
71 Andrew Cole *Literature and Heresy in the Age of Chaucer*
72 Suzanne M. Yeager *Jerusalem in Medieval Narrative*
73 Nicole R. Rice *Lay Piety and Religious Discipline in Middle English Literature*
74 D. H. Green *Women and Marriage in German Medieval Romance*
75 Peter Godman *Paradoxes of Conscience in the High Middle Ages: Abelard, Heloise and the Archpoet*
76 Edwin D. Craun *Ethics and Power in Medieval English Reformist Writing*
77 David Matthews *Writing to the King: Nation, Kingship, and Literature in England, 1250–1350*
78 Mary Carruthers (ed.) *Rhetoric Beyond Words: Delight and Persuasion in the Arts of the Middle Ages*
79 Katharine Breen *Imagining an English Reading Public, 1150–1400*
80 Antony J. Hasler *Court Poetry in Late Medieval England and Scotland: Allegories of Authority*
81 Shannon Gayk *Image, Text, and Religious Reform in Fifteenth-Century England*
82 Lisa H. Cooper *Artisans and Narrative Craft in Late-Medieval England*
83 Alison Cornish *Vernacular Translation in Dante's Italy: Illiterate Literature*
84 Jane Gilbert *Living Death in Medieval French and English Literature*
85 Jessica Rosenfeld *Ethics and Enjoyment in Late Medieval Poetry: Love After Aristotle*
86 Michael Van Dussen *From England to Bohemia: Heresy and Communication in the Later Middle Ages*
87 Martin Eisner *Boccaccio and the Invention of Italian Literature: Dante, Petrarch, Cavalcanti, and the Authority of the Vernacular*
88 Emily V. Thornbury *Becoming a Poet in Anglo-Saxon England*
89 Lawrence Warner *The Myth of 'Piers Plowman'*
90 Lee Manion *Narrating the Crusades: Loss and Recovery in Medieval and Early Modern English Literature*
91 Daniel Wakelin *Scribal Correction and Literary Craft: English Manuscripts 1375–1510*

31224988R00205

Made in the USA
Middletown, DE
29 December 2018